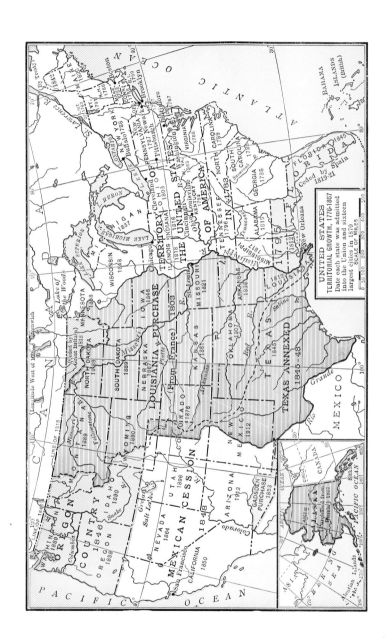

WESTERN AMERICA

THE EXPLORATION, SETTLEMENT, AND DEVELOPMENT OF THE REGION BEYOND THE MISSISSIPPI

BY

LeROY R. HAFEN

HISTORIAN, STATE HISTORICAL SOCIETY OF COLORADO
PROFESSOR OF HISTORY, UNIVERSITY OF DENVER

AND

CARL COKE RISTER

RESEARCH PROFESSOR OF HISTORY
UNIVERSITY OF OKLAHOMA

SECOND EDITION

PRENTICE-HALL, INC.
Englewood Cliffs, N. J.

PRENTICE-HALL HISTORY SERIES

First Printing .... May, 1950
Second Printing .... May, 1951
Third Printing ...... October, 1953
Fourth Printing ... November, 1954
Fifth Printing ...... January, 1957
Sixth Printing .... September, 1957
Seventh Printing .... August, 1959
Eighth Printing .... February, 1961
Ninth Printing .... April, 1962
Tenth Printing .... June, 1964

PRINTED IN THE UNITED STATES OF AMERICA
95064—C

To
HERBERT EUGENE BOLTON
Scholar, Teacher, Friend

INTRODUCTION

This VOLUME is devoted primarily to the exploration, settlement, and development of the trans-Mississippi West. As closely as possible, the authors have followed a chronological sequence. Thus, chapters two to five are concerned with the achievements of the Spaniards and the French in establishing themselves in the Southwest, on the Pacific Coast, and in the Mississippi Valley. The Spaniards had been in the region beyond the Mississippi for more than two centuries, and the French for half as long, before Englishmen in considerable numbers began to come into this land. But once arrived, the Anglo-Americans quickly assumed leadership.

To explain that primacy and achievement, a brief survey of the Anglo-American background is given in the next four chapters. In the preceding decades, English colonials had been transformed into Americans through contact with the wilderness and by mixtures with non-English stocks. Although these hardy and aggressive pioneers were to dominate the vast new region, relations with the earlier Spanish and French inhabitants and the potent influence of physical environment were to have a large effect upon their culture as evidenced by their economic, political, and social growth.

The remaining chapters are concerned with the gradual emergence of the new Westerner, his problems, his institutions, his interests, and his culture. Consequently, such subjects as early explorations, colonization, Indian wars, territorial conquests, border traders and trappers, border posts, transportation, railroad building, mining, the livestock industry, the making of new states, the disappearance of the frontier, reclamation, agrarianism, and the rise of a regional culture are each considered and evaluated. We shall see how presently within the trans-Mississippi West the manners and customs of the incoming settlers were modified and new techniques suitable to a new environment were employed; and how, with these changes, a Westerner evolved who was a regionalist, not superior perhaps to any other of the nation, but certainly distinctive.

The Indian deserves space in any history of Western America. The authors have confined their attention largely to a presentation of his relations with the white man. They leave to the anthropologist and the archaeologist the study of the prehistoric inhabitants of America and to the ethnologist the detailed study of Indian customs, religion, inter-tribal relationships, and similar subjects. Wars between the white man and the red, and other problems arising from the contact of the races, are considered in several chapters of this book.

Necessarily, the authors have devoted much space in this narrative to pioneering achievement. Generally, when the country was won and settled, when free land disappeared, the pioneering period ended. Thereafter, the pattern of Western America's development blended interestingly with those of contiguous areas. Still, there were certain problems and developments, e.g. the reclamation of arid lands, conservation, the agrarian revolt, city building, and the rise of the petroleum industry, that are peculiarly western and that have been followed well into our present era to give students a better understanding of this area's role in present-day national life.

L. R. H.
C. C. R.

ACKNOWLEDGMENTS

I N THE PREPARATION of this work, help has come from numerous sources. The following persons have been kind enough to read portions of the manuscript and give us the benefit of their suggestions: Herbert E. Bolton, University of California; Edward Everett Dale, University of Oklahoma; Chauncey Thomas, State Historical Society of Colorado; Wendell H. Stephenson, Tulane University; Lansing B. Bloom, University of New Mexico; Rupert N. Richardson, Hardin-Simmons University; A. B. Sears, University of Oklahoma; Louis Pelzer, University of Iowa; A. P. Nasatir, San Diego State College; Paul C. Phillips, University of Montana; Leland H. Creer, University of Utah; Lawrence K. Fox, South Dakota State Historical Society; Arthur J. Larsen, Minnesota Historical Society; and Cornelius J. Brosnan, University of Idaho.

Mrs. Mattie May Rister and Mrs. Ann Woodbury Hafen have given valued assistance by correcting manuscript, typing, and proofreading.

THE AUTHORS

CONTENTS

MAPS AND ILLUSTRATIONS

MAPS

ILLUSTRATIONS

WESTERN AMERICA

The Exploration, Settlement, and Development of the Region beyond the Mississippi

I

THE NATURAL SETTING

"Hɪsᴛᴏʀʏ ɪs but geography in motion."
The two are so interrelated that history cannot be comprehended unless one visualizes the physical stage upon which the action took place.
In studying the pioneer development of a region—its exploration, the
routes of travel, the areas of settlement—reference should constantly
be made to a map of the territory.

Lying in the temperate zone, the United States has the climate, temperature, and other physical features generally favorable to human
habitation. But the great variations in altitude, rainfall, soil, and
topography cause corresponding variations in the ability of areas to
support human life.

The historical development of a region is not only affected, but in
large part predetermined, by its geography. Good farming land invites
agriculture; a timber stand brings lumbering; minerals induce mining.
Travel is diverted by mountain barriers, while river valleys provide
gradual ascents to mountain passes and thus determine the routes for
trails and roads.

Of the 3,026,789 square miles of territory embraced in continental
United States, more than two-thirds of the area lies west of the Mississippi River. It is this western region that exhibits the nation's greatest
variations in topography, climate, and resources. This diversity in
environmental factors has required great versatility and adaptability
on the part of settlers who have undertaken to make homes and win a
livelihood in this western land.

Persons going into the first tier of states west of the Mississippi, extending from Minnesota to Louisiana, found a land similar to that immediately east of the river. It was timbered country for the most part,
one with deep and rich soil. Much of the eastern part of the next tier
of states, from North Dakota to Texas, was of like character. Farmers
moving to this land encountered problems similar to those which their
fathers had faced in areas farther east.

1

But as westward-moving pioneers approached the ninety-eighth meridian, conditions began to show a marked change. Rainfall diminished, and the stretches of timber gave way to treeless plains. This new country, extending to the Rocky Mountains and known as the Great Plains, was the first distinctly different geographic unit of Western America encountered by Anglo-Americans. The eastern portion was generally carpeted with tall grass; the western section was shortgrass country.

For much of the year the Great Plains, when first seen by white explorers, were unattractive. The monotonous stretches, waterless and treeless, resembled a desert and were so designated by Pike and Long. In summer the region was visited by drought, hot winds, clouds of grasshoppers, and occasional sandstorms; and in winter by northers or "black blizzards." But the spring and early summer seasons stood out in pleasant relief. Dry gulches and creeks now became brooks visited by wild fowl and game. Buttercups, daisies, gaillardias, primroses, larkspur, and other wild flowers splotched the carpet of green grass with patches of color.

Beyond the Great Plains, the west-moving emigrant encountered the Rocky Mountains, a barrier to easy travel. This area was a hunting ground for the early trappers and fur gatherers but was uninviting to pioneer farmers. However, the mineral wealth hidden in the hills was, in time, to lure prospectors and induce permanent settlement.

The Arid Plateau Region beyond the Rocky Mountains was barren and forbidding. But with irrigated agriculture the settler was able to achieve a notable adaptation to his environment and develop green garden lands in the desert.

Across the high Sierra and Cascade ranges the pioneer came into a verdant land of ample rainfall and rich resources. To this favored Coastal Area he was attracted long before he moved back to conquer the last American frontier—the high plains and the Rocky Mountain empire.

TOPOGRAPHY OF WESTERN AMERICA

Six major physiographic regions are found in the United States: the Coastal and Gulf Plains; the Appalachian Highlands; the Interior Plains; the Rocky Mountain System; the Intermontane Plateaux; and the Pacific Coastal Area. All of these except the Appalachian Highlands are represented in the Trans-Mississippi West.

The physical features of these regions produce variations in temperature and rainfall, and these account for the types of plant and animal life that existed in the respective areas. The flora and fauna in turn definitely affected human entry and settlement.

The Gulf Plain, with an elevation below 500 feet, includes Louisiana, southern Texas, and the flood plain of the Mississippi. This is an area of deep, rich soil, abundant rainfall, and was originally covered with verdant forests.

The *Interior Plains* embrace the Central Lowlands south and southwest of the Great Lakes, and the Great Plains farther west. The two areas are similar topographically, both being generally level. Their differences are primarily in altitude and rainfall, and the resultant variance in vegetation. Most of the eastern section is below 1,500 feet in elevation and is a well-watered prairie country. The Great Plains to the west is a semi-arid plateau that rises from about 2,000 feet along the 100th meridian to an elevation of 5,000 to 6,000 feet at the base of the Rockies. It was the short-grass country that was once the range of the buffalo and the nomad Indian.

The *Rocky Mountain System* is the eastern flank of the great Cordillera that stretches from New Mexico to Alaska. It is divided into three regions: the Northern Rocky Mountains, the Wyoming Basin, and the Southern Rocky Mountains. The Northern section extends from Canada into Montana as a series of parallel ranges such as the Lewis, Flathead, and Selkirk mountains. Then the system spreads into such irregular groups as the Bridger, Big Belt, Absaroka, Wind River, and Big Horn ranges. In southern Wyoming the mountains fade into a high plateau region known as "the Wyoming Basin." Here lie South Pass and Bridger Pass, the low and easy routes for emigrant crossings of the continental divide. The Southern Rockies are mainly in Colorado, where the mountains assume grand proportions, with fifty-one peaks reaching elevations in excess of 14,000 feet. The Front, Park, Sawatch and Sangre de Cristo ranges are the principal mountain chains. The lowest crossing of the continental divide in Colorado is at Cochetopa Pass, with an elevation over 10,000 feet.

The *Intermontane Plateaux* comprise numerous small mountain ranges, separated by desert plains. There are three principal areas: the Columbia Plateaux, the Colorado Plateaux, and the Basin and Range Region. Much of the Columbia Plateaux, which embrace most of the drainage areas of the Columbia and Snake rivers, has been covered with comparatively recent lava flows. In places the rivers have cut canyons hundreds of feet deep. The Colorado Plateaux have also been deeply dissected by such gorges as the Grand Canyon of the Colorado, Black Canyon of the Gunnison, and the canyons of the Green and Yampa rivers. The northern portion of the Basin and Range Region comprises the Great Basin of Nevada and Utah, that vast interior desert with no outlet to the sea. The southern portion is the elevated desert area of Arizona and New Mexico, which is an extension of the highland of northern Mexico.

The *Pacific Coast Region* comprises the high Sierra-Cascade range on the east, the lower Coast ranges abutting the Pacific, and the valleys that lie between. The principal river valleys, running north and south, are the Willamette of Oregon and the Sacramento and San Joaquin of California. The high Sierra and Cascade ranges are a wall that precipitates most of the moisture before it crosses to the east. The heavy rainfall in most of this region has produced large forests, grasslands, and farming areas.

Climate and Rainfall

In Western America there are three major climatic regions: the Plains, the Plateaux, and the Pacific Coast Area. Each of these may be divided into a northern and a southern district.

The *Plains* region has more sunshine, a greater range of temperature, and more wind than does the eastern United States. There is a gradual decrease in rainfall as one goes westward from the Atlantic and the Gulf of Mexico. The eastern portion of the Plains generally receives more than 25 inches of rainfall; west of the 100th meridian the precipitation is usually less than 20 inches, which is considered insufficient for the production of crops without irrigation. Scientific dryfarming, however, succeeds in favored areas of the high plains, especially in the northern region where evaporation is less than in the greater heat of the south. The rain is heaviest in summer, but no month is entirely devoid of precipitation.

The *Plateau* region, with its mountains, valleys, and desert tablelands, exhibits corresponding variations in temperature that are reflections of the altitude. The summers are hot, especially in the southern area, but the low humidity makes the heat less oppressive. The winters in the south are generally mild; in the north they are frequently severe. The region is noted for its clear blue sky, persistent sunshine, and brilliant stars. The high altitude and dry air cause wide variations in temperature from day to night and between sunshine and shade. The entire plateau region is semi-arid, the southern portion being the driest part of the United States. There is usually more precipitation in winter than in summer. The snowfall on the mountain ranges varies almost directly with the altitude; five times as much snow piles on the 14,000-foot peaks as falls on the 5,000-foot plains. The snowfall on the Rocky Mountains is lighter than on the Sierra Nevadas.

The *Pacific Coast* area is dominated by the ocean. The region may be divided into two parts. The northern portion, especially in winter,

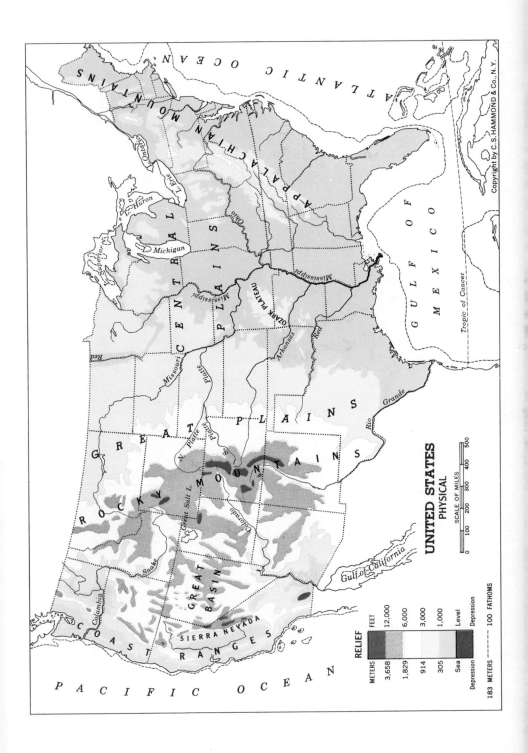

UNITED STATES
PHYSICAL

SCALE OF MILES

0 100 200 300 400 500

RELIEF

METERS		FEET
3,658		12,000
1,829		6,000
914		3,000
305		1,000
Sea		Level
Depression		Depression

183 METERS - - - - - - - 100 FATHOMS

ATLANTIC OCEAN

APPALACHIAN MOUNTAINS

L. Ontario

L. Erie

Ohio

L. Huron

L. Michigan

L. Superior

CENTRAL PLAINS

Mississippi

OZARK PLATEAU

Mississippi

Arkansas

Red

GULF OF MEXICO

Tropic of Cancer

Copyright by C. S. HAMMOND & Co., N.Y.

Missouri

Platte

N. Platte

S. Platte

Rio Grande

GREAT PLAINS

ROCKY MOUNTAINS

Great Salt L.

Colorado

Snake

Columbia

COAST RANGES

GREAT BASIN

SIERRA NEVADA

Gulf of California

PACIFIC OCEAN

resembles the British Isles, with its wet and chilly weather. The southern portion has a Mediterranean type of climate, with slight seasonal variation of temperature. There are two principal seasons—the wet season of winter and the dry season of summer. The rainfall increases from south to north, varying from 10 inches in parts of southern California to 100 inches in portions of Washington.

RIVER SYSTEMS

The principal drainage basins of Western America are the Missouri, the Arkansas and Red River branches of the Mississippi, the Rio Grande and Texas Coast rivers, the Colorado River, the Columbia River, the Great Basin (with no outlet to the sea), and the Sacramento and San Joaquin river basins.

Rivers have been great agencies of transportation throughout history. Many of the streams of eastern United States, being navigable, have been highways of commerce. But most of the rivers of western United States are too shallow or too broken with cataracts to permit navigation. However, their graded valleys offer the most practical routes for land travel.

The Mississippi and Missouri rivers became great arteries of commerce, with hundreds of ships plying their courses. Portions of their Arkansas, Red, and Des Moines affluents were also to carry much water-borne traffic. On the other hand, the Platte, Arkansas, and Smoky Hill served man's transportation needs only by providing a gradual grade along the banks for land travel. They also afforded a water supply for man and his draft animals. Some far-western rivers, such as the Humboldt of Nevada, the Gila of Arizona, and the Mohave of California shaped the pattern of early transportation in the far West. Travel across arid deserts was made possible by the life-sustaining waters of these streams.

In most of Western America the rivers are more important for irrigation than as aids to transportation. Not only is the direct flow of the streams diverted through canals to fructify the soil, but dams control the floods, and reservoirs impound the precious water to irrigate additional and otherwise-barren acres. There is also the utilization of the water for production of hydro-electric power. These phases of water use are treated subsequently in Chapter 35.

FLORA AND FAUNA

Plant Life. The vegetation of a region, sustaining as it does animal and human life, is a determining feature of human geography. Grass and shrubs capable of being grazed by animals constitute an important natural resource. The central lowlands of the Mississippi Valley and the Great Plains to the west were rich in such production. The tall grass of the prairies and the short grass of the high plains fed the vast herds of buffaloes, and these sustained the Indian tribes and the white pioneers. After the slaughter of the buffaloes, the grazing area supported herds of domestic cattle.

The Intermontane Plateau is a region of scant vegetation. The short-lived grass and repellent sagebrush were incapable of sustaining large game animals. The cactus, creosote, and yucca, so widespread over the area, offered spiked resistance to animal life. But sheep are able to sustain themselves in the less arid sections of this wasteland.

Primeval forests originally covered virtually all of eastern United States and extended into the second tier of states west of the Mississippi. Most of the trees were deciduous, the common ones being oak, walnut, hickory, ash, chestnut, maple, and beech. Beyond this forest area treeless plains extended westward to the Rocky Mountains. In these mountains grew forests of fir, spruce, and pine. West of the Rocky Mountains and the almost treeless plateau and Great Basin rise the Sierra Nevada and Cascade ranges. These Pacific Coast mountains were and still are heavily timbered, the great forest extending to the coastline in Washington, Oregon, and northern California. This is the largest natural forest area remaining in the United States. The timber resources here have made lumbering an important industry of the Pacific Northwest.

In addition to the grass and trees, Nature provided other gifts. Wild fruits and berries, such as cherries, plums, raspberries, and service berries, were gathered by Indians and whites. Native edible roots, such as potatoes, yams, yampa, and kamas, were used to vary human diet.

Animal Life. In relation to human history, perhaps the most important native animal was the buffalo. Vast herds of these shaggy, lumbering creatures grazed the prairies and plains of the West and roamed beyond the Rocky Mountains. The plains Indians were especially dependent upon the buffalo. They used its flesh for food—taking the fresh meat for immediate use and drying the surplus for future needs. They used its skin (with hair retained) for clothing and bedding; its hide (with hair removed) for tepees and parfleches (box-like containers). From the bones the Indians fashioned tools; sinews became bowstrings; the stomach and intestines served as water and food containers; the chips (dried dung) served as fuel.

Other game animals—deer, antelope, elk, bear—supplied the Indian and the white pioneer with food and clothing. Buckskin and elk skins especially found wide use. Wild fowl—geese, ducks, and turkeys—were used as food, while eagles and turkeys provided feathers for Indian adornment. Rabbits and hares (jack rabbits) were frequently found where other game was scarce. The Indians used the rabbit skins to make clothing and the meat for food. Fish, especially the salmon of the northwest coast, constituted the principal food of a number of native tribes.

Fur-bearing animals were historically significant. The beaver was especially important in bringing white trappers into the West and thus promoting exploration of the region. Fox and mink also were hunted for their pelts. Hunters, trappers, and fur traders were to be the vanguard of white penetration into the wilderness and to blaze the trails for subsequent homeseeking settlers.

Certain animals were of doubtful help or an outright hindrance to human occupancy of the land. The coyote was to match its wits and endurance with man's and survive through changing conditions. The prairie dog ate much grass that might have supported game animals or cattle. The grizzly bear, cougar, and wolf were unwelcome denizens of the wilderness. Snakes, lizards, grasshoppers and ants, although used as food by the destitute Digger Indians of the deserts, were generally enemies of man and a hindrance to settlement. Mosquitoes and gnats were great annoyances to early explorers and settlers.

ABORIGINAL INHABITANTS

The full description and study of the culture of the Indians who inhabited Western America when the white man came must be left to the ethnologist and anthropologist. But a few generalizations may be useful to the historical student who wishes to understand the environment that the white man encountered in different areas.

On the interior lowlands adjoining the Mississippi River and the Gulf Coast lived Indians who depended upon both agriculture and hunting for their subsistence. Their principal crops were corn and squashes; their meat was from deer and other large game of the forest and from squirrels, rabbits, and fowl. They lived in permanent villages and had willow-frame houses covered by bark, reeds, or skins, or had earth-covered houses such as those of the Pawnees and Mandans.

The principal inhabitants of the high plains were the Sioux, Blackfeet, Crows, Cheyennes, Arapahoes, Kiowas, and Comanches. They were nomads who depended on hunting for subsistence. Buffalo, deer, and antelope were their principal game animals. These Indians lived in villages that were movable communities that shifted location as food supply and grass became scarce. The shelter of the plains Indians was the cone-shaped tepee, made of skins stretched about a frame of lodgepoles. After obtaining the horse from the white man, these Indians rapidly modified their life and habits. They became more mobile and wandered farther on their hunting and raiding ventures.

The chief mountain Indians were the Utes, Snakes, and other branches of the Shoshonean Family. They too were hunters and despised agriculture. Some of these Indians had skin tepees, others used wickiups and brush shelters made of tree branches, willows, or sagebrush.

Piutes, Goshutes, and other poor relations of the Shoshones inhabited the desert areas of Utah and Nevada. They had crude wickiups and lived on rabbits, lizards, insects, grass seeds, pinon nuts, and berries.

In New Mexico and Arizona were sedentary Indians who dwelt in stone or adobe communal houses and raised corn, beans, squashes, and melons on their little irrigated farms. They were principally Pueblos, Hopis, Zunis, and Navajos. These tribes were noted for their excellent pottery. After obtaining sheep from the early Spaniards, some of these tribes, especially the Navajos, became proficient in weaving fine blankets.

Most of the Indians of the California coast were backward in development. Acorns, grass seeds, small game, and fish provided their subsistence. Farther north, in the Columbia River basin and around Puget Sound the natives depended principally upon fish for food.

The Indian served both as a help and hindrance to the white conquest of the West. He guided the explorers to the mountain passes, habitable valleys, and to life-saving springs in the deserts. He taught the pale newcomer methods of hunting, fishing, agriculture, and how to adjust to a new and frequently hostile environment. He gave new foods—potatoes, corn, turkeys. He made contributions in art, handicrafts, music, dancing, literature, and folklore.

But when whites invaded his homeland, fenced his hunting grounds, and drove him from the graves of his forefathers, he put on his war bonnet, beat the drum, mounted his favorite horse, and rode to war. The story of the resulting conflicts will be related in subsequent chapters.

BIBLIOGRAPHY

For general discussions of geographic conditions and their effects in western America consult the following: N. M. Fenneman, *Physiography of Western United States* (New York, 1931); E. W. Gilbert, *The Exploration of Western America, 1800–1850; an Historical Geography* (Cambridge, 1933); R. H. Brown, *Historical Geography of the United States* (New York, 1948); R. de C. Ward, *The Climates of the United States* (Boston, 1925); A. J. Henry, *Climatology of the United States* (Washington, 1906); I. C. Russell, *River Development* (London, 1907); B. E. Livingston and F.

Shreve, *The Distribution of Vegetation in the United States as Related to Climatic Conditions* (Washington, 1921); and U. S. Geological Survey, *Water-Supply Papers,* Nos. 241–252.

General information on American Indians may be found in Clark Wissler, *The Indians of the United States* (New York, 1940); F. W. Hodge (Ed.), *Handbook of American Indians North of Mexico* (2 vols., Washington, 1912); and A. L. Kroeber, *Cultural and Natural Areas of Native North America* (Berkeley, 1939).

For data on individual tribes and particular areas the following are useful: G. B. Grinnell, *The Cheyenne Indians* (2 vols., New Haven, 1923); R. H. Lowie, *The Crow Indians* (New York, 1935); G. E. Hyde, *Red Cloud's Folk, a History of the Oglala Sioux Indians* (Norman, 1937); Dane and M. R. Collidge, *The Navajo Indians* (Boston, 1930); R. N. Richardson, *The Comanche Barrier to South Plains Settlement* (Glendale, 1933); P. E. Goddard, *Indians of the Northwest Coast* (New York, 1934); A. L. Kroeber, *Handbook of the Indians of California* (Washington, 1925); W. C. Macleod, *The American Indian Frontier* (New York, 1928); and E. E. Dale, *The Indians of the Southwest* (Norman, 1949).

2

THE COMING OF WHITE MEN

$\mathbb{T}$HE DISCOVERY of America inaugurated a new epoch in world history. It opened a virgin field for exploitation and colonization. Most of the European nations were slow to recognize the opportunities offered or were unprepared to take advantage of them. Spain, however, had achieved a territorial, religious, and political unification by 1492 that fitted her for colonial expansion. Portugal also was active and alert. These Hispanic countries began at once to plant overseas settlements. England and France made some abortive attempts at colonization during the sixteenth century, but in general they were content to prey upon Spanish treasure ships and towns, endeavor to break down the monopoly of Spain and Portugal, and win a share in the trade of America and the Far East.

The seventeenth century was to present a very different picture, with various nations—England, France, Holland, Sweden, and Denmark—planting colonies in the New World. And when once rooted in American soil, some of these countries, especially England and France, were to give vigorous competition to established empires. Indeed, England and her independent offspring were ultimately to win predominance in North America.

Colonial empires in the New World were not founded on altruism. Colonies were established, protected, and maintained for the benefit of the homeland. To insure commercial advantages to the mother country, each nation evolved and enforced laws and regulations that confined trade to her own nationals. Under the monopolistic restrictions of this "mercantile system," colonists were subordinated and their true interests frequently ignored or sacrificed.

Each of the imperial nations developed its own agencies of colonial government, but the likenesses were more striking than the differences. Legislative and administrative councils and special ministers in Europe devoted themselves to colonial affairs. Viceroys, governors and intendants, provincial councils and audiencias governed in America. Authority centered in Europe, with officials in the colonies exercising only the powers delegated to them. Marked distinctions separated the various social classes. "Nearly every mother country revived in America some vestige of feudalism," writes Herbert E. Bolton. "Spain tried the encomienda, Portugal the *capitanía*, Holland the patroon system, England the proprietary grant, France the seigniory." [1] But none of these was to thrive in the new soil. Institutions shaped to American conditions and needs were evolved.

Spain was not only first among the nations to come to the Western Hemisphere as a whole, but she was also first to explore and to colonize that area which primarily concerns us here, the western portion of the present United States. Her approach was from the south, from bases in Mexico and the West Indies. Before she had won mastery of the region, her hold was challenged by other nations, now grown vigorous. England developed a powerful westward movement from the Atlantic seaboard; France pushed southward from the Great Lakes and westward from bases on the Mississippi. Finally, Russia threatened from the far Northwest. Keen international rivalry was to develop for possession of the trans-Mississippi West. The contest became an important phase of the region's early history. As we proceed, the story will unfold, but let us start with the beginning, with the pioneering of Spain.

The Spanish Approach

Accompanying Columbus on his second voyage, in 1493, came about 1,500 colonists, eager to find fortune and adventure in the mysterious new country. For decades thereafter, from 1,000 to 2,000 immigrants came regularly each year to settle the land. Often the demand for passage was so insistent that the small sailing vessels were overburdened with passengers and closely packed cargoes. The immigrants brought horses and cattle, sheep and swine, to stock farms and ranches, and familiar seeds of grain, cotton, cane, and vegetables to test unfamiliar soil.

The area of earliest colonization was the West Indies, with Española, or Haiti, as the center. From this base the other islands were quickly conquered and occupied. The considerable amount of gold found was soon exhausted, but agriculture and stock raising flourished for a time. The natives were subjugated, despite efforts of the Spanish Crown in their behalf. *Encomenderos* (protectors), who were directed to civilize and Christianize the Indians under their jurisdiction, came soon to be concerned primarily with the exploitation of the natives. Under this

---

[1] "The Epic of America," in the *American Historical Review*, XXXVIII (April, 1933), 452.

harsh *encomienda* system, the Indians of the West Indies were soon wiped out, and Negro slaves were brought in to take their places.

From the island bases, exploration went rapidly forward. Gold and pearls on the northern coast of South America lured Columbus and his successors. In 1513 Balboa, having learned from his Indian brother-in-law of a great ocean to the westward, forced a way through the forty-five miles of tangled forest across the Isthmus of Panamá and gazed upon the mighty Pacific. In the same year, Ponce de León sailed from Puerto Rico in search of new land, wealth, and perhaps a Fountain of Youth. He reached a peninsula to which, because it was covered with flowers and was discovered at Easter time, he gave the name of *Florida*. In 1517 Yucatán was explored; and two years thereafter Pineda, sailing from Florida to Vera Cruz, completed the mapping of the Gulf Coast. On the voyage, he discovered the Mississippi River and named it the *Río del Espíritu Santo*.

The expedition to Yucatán having learned of gold and cities in the interior, a party was organized by Velásquez, governor of Cuba, to seek them. Hernando Cortés headed the expedition. With audacious leadership he moved into the heart of Mexico. Horses and firearms helped overawe the natives. A knowledge he acquired of their customs and superstitions gave him advantages. Learning of the widespread discontent among the people subject to the Aztec overlords, he assumed the role of deliverer; and in 1519, with the help of Indian allies, he marched into lake-encircled Mexico City, the largest and most powerful native city in North America. The Aztecs, tiring of their unwelcome guests, and incensed at their arbitrary measures, rose up and drove out the intruders. Half of the Spaniards were slain along the causeways leading from the city during the terrible *Noche Triste* (Sorrowful Night) of the bloody retreat. But the stubborn white men and their indomitable leader were not permanently defeated. Cortés reorganized and reinforced his army, built boats and launched them on the lake, and at the end of two years had conquered the Aztec capital.

Mexico City now became the base of Spanish expansion on the mainland. From this center, lieutenants of Cortés carried forward the conquest in all directions. Mexico City was made the capital of New Spain, which came to include, from the Spanish point of view, the whole of western North America. The Spaniards pushed their frontier rapidly northward from Mexico City, opening rich mining areas and enslaving the Indians to work the mines. They developed cattle ranches and farms to provide food for the mining camps.

In the meantime stories were being told of wonders farther north. From the West Indies expeditions moved into Florida, seeking new lands, pearls, and gold. Futile attempts at conquest and colonization

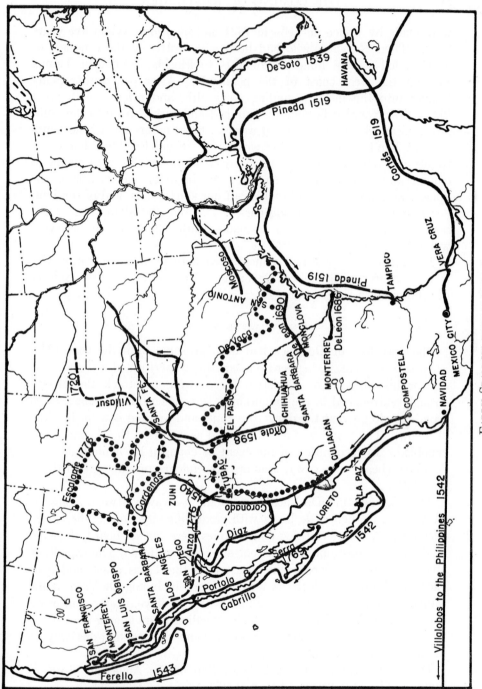

EARLY SPANISH EXPLORATIONS

13

were made by Ponce de León in 1521 and by Judge Ayllón five years later. Then Narváez, who had been with Cortés in the conquest of Mexico, led several hundred colonists to Florida, landing at Tampa Bay on the west coast of the peninsula. After penetrating many leagues into the interior, finding no wealth, and meeting with great difficulties, Narváez became discouraged and turned back to the Gulf. Not finding his ships, he set to work to build others out of the materials at hand. In six weeks, writes the chronicler, "five barges of twenty-two elbow lengths each were ready, caulked with palmetto oakum and tarred with pitch. . . . Of the tails and manes of the horses, we made ropes and tackles, of our shirts, sails, and of the juniper that grew there we made oars, ... We flayed the legs of the horses and tanned the skin to make leather pouches for carrying water."

The Narváez expedition is mentioned here primarily because with it, as treasurer, went Cabeza de Vaca, destined to be the first explorer of southwestern United States.

De Vaca and Stephen

The ancestors of De Vaca had been peasants until the year 1212, when one of them, a shepherd named Alhaja, performed a signal service for his king. The Christian forces were to attack the Moors, strongly entrenched in the mountain passes, when this peasant showed a path to circumvent the dangerous route and marked it with the skull of a cow. The result was a victory, and as a reward the shepherd was ennobled. In recognition of the event he changed his name to *Cabeza de Vaca* (head of a cow), and his descendents proudly retained the appellation.

The Narváez and De Vaca party made its way westward along the Gulf Coast in their little boats with great difficulty, for, as the chronicler reports, "after clothing and supplies were put on board, the sides of the barges rose only half a foot above the water." The expedition finally suffered shipwreck and disaster on the Texas coast, and Narváez, the leader, was lost. A few survivors, including De Vaca, found refuge among the Indians. Serving in turn as slave, trader, and medicine man, De Vaca lived through six gruelling years among the various tribes of the vicinity, always hoping some day to find his way to Mexico and white men.

De Vaca gives us our first description of the American bison, or buffalo. Of these "cows," he says: "They appear to me of the size of those in Spain. Their horns are small, like those of the Moorish cattle; the hair is very long, like fine wool and like a peajacket; some are

brownish and others black, ... These cows come from the north, . . . and are found all over the land for over four hundred leagues." Of the country, he writes: "All over the land are vast and handsome pastures, with good grass for cattle, and it strikes me the soil would be very fertile were the country inhabited and improved by reasonable people."

He describes the numerous tribes encountered in his wanderings, but some of the features he mentions and the incidents he details are rather too fantastic for credibility. However, the ethnologist can doubtless glean from this earliest account of a large area of our Southwest much valuable data regarding the Indians and their life at the time of first European contact.

With three companions—Andrés Dorantes, Alonzo del Castillo, and Dorantes's Negro slave, Estevanico (or Stephen)—De Vaca made his way westward, hoping to reach Mexico. Assuming the roles of medicine men, their success was so marked as to be embarrassing. At one village, writes De Vaca, "So great was their excitement and eagerness to touch us that, everyone wanting to be first, they nearly squeezed us to death, and, without suffering our feet to touch the ground, carried us to their abodes." People of one village followed them to the next. "Often," he says, "we had with us three to four thousand persons. And it was very tiresome to have to breathe on and make the sign of the cross over every morsel they ate or drank."

The route of De Vaca and his companions cannot be determined with certainty, but their course was evidently through western Texas and across southern New Mexico and Arizona. For ten months after escaping from slavery in the Texas country, they traveled a generally westward course. Early in 1536, they reached Culiacán, then the northernmost Spanish outpost on the west coast of Mexico, where they were received by Melchor Díaz, chief Alcalde and captain of the settlement.

During the years of De Vaca's sojourn among the tribes in Texas, some of his more fortunate countrymen had been winning wealth in South America. Pizarro and De Soto had conquered the great Inca empire of Peru in 1532–1533, and had wrested from the emperor, as ransom, a roomful of gold in the form of vases, plates, jewelry, and other varieties of native handiwork.

News of this rich treasure inflamed the imaginations and whetted the desires of Spaniards in Mexico. So when De Vaca and his companions came out of the mysterious North telling that they had heard of cities with high houses and of a land where copper, emeralds, and turquoises were obtained, everyone listened eagerly. The native wealth that Cortés had conquered in Mexico City was now recalled, and noble and peasant alike began to talk of "another Mexico" and "another Peru" awaiting conquest in the North.

While Dorantes, companion of De Vaca, was at Vera Cruz during the winter of 1536–1537, awaiting passage to Spain, he received a request from Viceroy Mendoza to remain in Mexico and lead an expedition which the Viceroy promised to equip and send to explore the northern country. But the undertaking did not materialize. Instead, the Viceroy purchased from Dorantes his slave, Stephen, and decided to use this Negro as guide for a preliminary expedition. To lead the reconnoitering party he chose Friar Marcos de Niza, who had been with Pizarro in Peru and was familiar with exploration and with successful Spanish methods of acquiring gold.

Friar Marcos and Stephen, with many native companions, set out from Culiacán in March, 1539. After moving northward to southern Sonora, the friar sent some Indians westward to the coast to gain information about reputed pearl islands, and dispatched Stephen northward to explore. The Negro was instructed, in case he had good news, to send "a white cross the size of the palm of his hand." If the news were very promising, the size of the cross should be correspondingly large. Presently a cross the size of a man was sent back and the messengers told of "seven very large cities" called Cíbola, with houses three and four stories high, and whose doorways were studded with turquoises. As the friar proceeded, he found other high crosses planted by Stephen.

The Negro had pushed on ahead. His experience as a successful medicine man with De Vaca no doubt encouraged him to assume the role again. Writes Castañeda, the chronicler: "Stephen reached Cíbola loaded with the large quantity of turquoises they had given him and some beautiful women whom the Indians who followed him and carried his things were taking with them and had given him.

"But as the people in this country were more intelligent than those who followed Stephen, they lodged him in a little hut" while they considered what to do with him. The Negro told of "two white men who were following him, sent by a great lord, who knew about things in the sky." But the people of Cíbola thought "he must be a spy or a guide from some nations who wished to come and conquer them, because it seemed to them unreasonable to say that the people were white in the country from which he came and that he was sent by them, he being black. Besides these other reasons, they thought it was hard of him to ask them for turquoises and women, and so they decided to kill him. They did this."

Companions of Stephen fled from the village and carried a report back to Friar Marcos. Though fearing now to enter Cíbola, the friar tells us that he did continue his journey to a point from which he saw it at a distance. He writes:

It has a very fine appearance for a village, the best that I have seen in these parts. The houses, as the Indians told me, are all of stone, built in stories, and with flat roofs. Judging by what I could see from the height where I placed myself to observe it, the settlement is larger than the city of Mexico. . . . It appears to me that this land is the best and largest of all those that have been discovered.

CORONADO

When the friar returned to Mexico with such a report, it is little wonder that eagerness to conquer the rich land was almost unbounded. Keen rivalry arose among various *conquistadores* for the privilege of conquering the new country. Cortés, Alvarado, and Guzmán vigorously presented their claims, and a representative insisted that De Soto's license covered the region of the Seven Cities. The prospect, however, was so promising that the Crown and Viceroy Mendoza refused all bids of those asking to undertake the expedition at their own expense and, instead, decided to finance and direct the conquest as a royal venture.

Francisco Vásquez Coronado, who had come to New Spain in the retinue of Viceroy Mendoza in 1535, was chosen as leader of the expedition. His company consisted of some 200 horsemen, many of whom were gentlemen adventurers of rank and influence, 70 foot soldiers, and nearly 1,000 Indian allies and servants. Equipment and supplies were furnished in abundance. Weapons and munitions fresh from the royal arsenals of Spain were distributed; 1,000 extra horses were provided; pack mules were laden with elaborate equipment; pieces of light artillery were supplied; and droves of cattle, sheep, goats, and swine were driven along for food.

Viceroy Mendoza traveled the 110 leagues from the capital to Compostela on the northwestern frontier of Mexico to review the splendid company, the grandest perhaps that ever invaded the American West. Young cavaliers were astride picked horses from the largest stock ranches of New Spain, the spirited mounts resplendent with colorful blankets flowing to the ground. Some riders were arrayed in polished coats of mail, others in vizored headpieces of tough bullhide. All had swords at their sides and lances held erect. The foot soldiers were armed with swords and shields or crossbows and arquebuses. The Indian allies, their bodies splashed with black and vermilion, carried bows and clubs. At the head of the impressive cavalcade, in rich gilded armor, rode the Viceroy's trusted leader—Captain-General Coronado.

To support the land expedition and carry additional supplies went

three vessels in charge of Alarcón. He moved along the west coast to
the head of the Gulf of California, in a course explored for Cortés by
Ulloa the year before (1539), and then ascended the Colorado River
some 200 miles. But he failed to make contact with the land company. Melchor Díaz was later sent by Coronado to communicate with
Alarcón. He reached the Colorado River, and found there, at the foot
of a tree, a letter from Alarcón. But the captain had tired of waiting
and had sailed back down the Gulf. Díaz crossed the river near the
site of Yuma and traveled for four days before returning, being thus
the first to penetrate the southeastern tip of present California.

Late in February, 1540, Coronado set out from Compostela. The
early stages of his northward march along the west coast of Mexico
need not detain us here. At Culiacán, Coronado divided his force.
Leaving the main army behind, he selected about 75 horsemen and 25
foot soldiers, and with these pushed ahead. Early in July he reached
the first of the Seven Cities, one of the Zuñi towns (Háwikuh) at the
middle of the western border of present New Mexico. The natives
made a defense of their stone and mud communal village, sending
arrows and stones against the invaders. But the trained Europeans
soon overcame the resistance, captured badly needed food supplies,
and occupied the village.

Visions of wealth were shattered, however. The disappointment of
the Spaniards is reflected in the account of Castañeda, principal historian of the expedition: "When they saw the first village which was
Cíbola, such were the curses that some hurled at Friar Marcos that I
pray God may protect him from them." The friar soon found occasion to return to Mexico.

While the main army was being brought up to Zuñi, exploration was
carried on from this base. Cárdenas and 12 men took a northwest
course toward a large river the Indians had reported. They were to
be the first white men to view the stupendous Grand Canyon of the
Colorado. Writes Castañeda:

After they had gone twenty days, they came to the banks of the river,
which seemed to be more than 3 or 4 leagues above the stream which
flowed between them. . . . [They spent three days on this bank, looking for a passage down to the river, which looked from above as if the
water was 6 feet across, although the Indians said it was half a league
wide. Finally] the three lightest and most agile men [succeeded in descending one-third of the way down the canyon.] Those who stayed above had
estimated that some huge rocks on the sides of the cliffs seemed to be about
as tall as a man, but those who went down swore that when they reached
these rocks they were bigger than the great tower of Seville.

Another party, under Alvarado, was sent eastward from Zuñi. It came first to the village of Ácoma, perched on a high fortress rock. The inhabitants, whose descendants through four hundred years have continued to occupy the picturesque location, gave the Spaniards "a large number of [turkey-] cocks with very big wattles, much bread, tanned deerskins, pine nuts, flour [corn meal], and corn."

Continuing eastward, Alvarado reached the Rio Grande, a little north of present Albuquerque. Here he found Indian pueblos with supplies of food, so he sent word back to Coronado, advising him to winter in this new region. The rear detachment and the General moved on to the Rio Grande. The Indians of one village had been induced to abandon it, that the Spaniards might have lodgings. Demands on the various villages for clothing and supplies were so peremptorily made and so harshly executed that the natives were presently in revolt. Some individuals who were captured and some who had submitted on promise of pardon were burned at the stake. So the word spread among the natives that the Spaniards did not respect peace and were without honor. Friction and hostilities continued throughout the winter.

An Indian slave whom the Spaniards called "Turk," "because he looked like one," told of the rich land of Quivira, off to the east. He described

    . . . a river in the level country which was two leagues wide, in which there were fishes as big as horses, . . . He said also that the lord of that country took his afternoon nap under a great tree on which were hung a great number of little gold bells, which put him to sleep as they swung in the air. He said that everyone had their ordinary dishes made of wrought plate, and the jugs and bowls were of gold.

At least, such was his description as interpreted by the hopeful Spaniards. Some doubted the veracity of the Indian slave, and the Spaniard who had him in charge "solemnly swore that he had seen the Turk talking with the devil in a pitcher of water." But Coronado and others were pleased to believe the fantastic stories, and so with the coming of spring the General set out for the golden land of Quivira.

Taking a generally eastward course, Coronado and his little army were soon upon the high plains and among the great buffalo herds. The chronicler records that for many leagues they "had seen nothing but cows and the sky." On the level plains, game hunters and stragglers from camp frequently became lost. Guides of the expedition made piles of buffalo chips to direct the course of the army.

Following the buffalo herds and living upon them were nomad Indians. Of these Coronado writes in a letter to his king:

I came to a settlement of these Indians who are called Querechos [herdsmen], who travel around with these cows, who do not plant, and who eat the cow flesh and drink the blood of the cows they kill, and they tan the skins of the cows, with which all the people of this country dress themselves. . . . They have dogs which they load, which carry their tents and poles and belongings.

These Indians of the Plains had no wealth, not even permanent houses or towns, but from them Coronado learned of permanent settlements to the north. By now it was apparent that the Turk's statements were untrue, so he was displaced as guide. Coronado decided to divide his force and with selected horsemen to seek Quivira in the north. The remainder of the army butchered some 500 buffalo, jerked the meat, and, thus assured of food, returned to the Rio Grande.

After 42 days' march north by the compass, Coronado and his horsemen reached Indian settlements, probably in south central Kansas, although some students think it was farther south. The Indians here lived in straw huts and raised a little corn. The chief wore a copper plate on his neck, but of gold and silver there was no evidence. A sojourn of several weeks among the different villages revealed no wealth. The Turk, now entirely repudiated, confessed that he had been induced by the New Mexico Indians to deceive the Spaniards and to lead them far eastward and lose them on the endless plains. The angry white men now strangled him to death.

Coronado had reached the end of his eastward journey. In the midsummer heat, the northern mystery had exploded, the visions of wealth had evaporated. Disheartened and disillusioned, he turned back by a more direct course to the Rio Grande, and, after spending the winter of 1541–1542 in New Mexico, he led the bedraggled remnant of his once splendid caravan back to Mexico.

While it is true that the expedition did not realize the golden dream of its members and promoters, it cannot be called a failure. And though Coronado did not gain wealth, he won enduring fame. His contribution to history and to geographical knowledge was notable. Through his great exploring expedition, a large area of the American West was first made known to white men. All subsequent development is predicated on that initial discovery.

CABRILLO

Comparable to the Coronado expedition in the field of discovery was the contemporary ocean voyage of Cabrillo and Ferrelo. This, too, was launched under the direction of Viceroy Mendoza. The Viceroy, through a partnership arrangement with Alvarado (chief lieutenant of Cortés in the conquest of Mexico), had succeeded to his partner's vessels upon Alvarado's death in 1541. He thereupon divided the fleet, sent part of it across the Pacific under Villalobos to conquer the Philippines, and dispatched two vessels up the Pacific Coast in charge of Juan Rodríguez Cabrillo. The latter division, it was hoped, would discover a strait through North America.

The equipment and iron work for these small craft had been transported across Honduras on the backs of natives. Cabrillo's two vessels were poorly built, badly outfitted, and manned by conscripts and natives. When we add to these unpropitious conditions the inclement season and the fierce and continual storms endured, the voyage takes on heroic proportions.

Cabrillo and his crew set sail from Navidad, a port due west of Mexico City, on June 27, 1542. They coasted the outer edge of the peninsula of Lower California and were soon in unknown waters. Late in September they discovered beautiful and important San Diego Bay. Upon landing, they found natives, writes the journalist of the expedition, who informed them by signs that:

. . . in the interior men like us were traveling about, bearded, clothed and armed like those of the ships. They made signs that they carried crossbows and swords; and they made gestures with the right arm as if they were throwing lances, and ran around as if they were on horseback. They made signs that they were killing many native Indians, and for this reason they were afraid. These people are comely and large. They go about covered with skins of animals.

Apparently news of Coronado and his men had traveled fast and far.

Continuing up the California coast, Cabrillo's party landed frequently, found the country good, and encountered many natives. The first of these were friendly fishermen, who dressed in skins and owned many canoes. They told of maize-growing Indians in the interior. A little above the site of present Los Angeles, Cabrillo saw a pueblo with large houses. He landed and took possession of the country with due ceremony. After sailing through the Santa Barbara channel he reached Point Conception, where his real difficulties began. Buffeted by the wind and storm, his tiny sailing vessels crept up the coast. Having missed Monterey Bay and San Francisco Bay, and finding no shelter, he turned back in November to the Santa Barbara region, where he spent the two following months. Here Cabrillo died, and Ferrelo assumed command.

The new captain decided to make another attempt at northern exploration. Going well out to sea and then turning north, he sailed beyond sight of land until he reached Point Arena, about 100 miles above San Francisco Bay. Pushing on, he rounded Cape Mendocino, and on March 1 reached his farthest point north, probably near the Rogue

River of Southern Oregon. The return voyage was made safely, and the vessels reached Navidad on April 14, 1543.

The general features of much of the Pacific Coast and the character of the numerous Indian inhabitants were thus early made known. This voyage of discovery greatly extended the boundaries of New Spain. Three centuries later, the United States, having succeeded to Spanish territorial rights north of California, used the Cabrillo-Ferrelo voyage of discovery as the first basis for claiming the vast Oregon country.

De Soto

While Cabrillo was making his notable voyage up the Pacific Coast and Coronado was penetrating overland far into the interior of the West, a third great contemporary expedition, under De Soto and Moscoso, was pursuing its tragic course in unknown lands. As the first extensive exploring expedition into the southeastern part of present United States, the venture is of primary interest to that region. But De Soto crossed the Mississippi and penetrated the plains beyond; hence, the latter reaches of his journeying brought him into the trans-Mississippi West, the region that primarily concerns us here.

Hernando De Soto, with wealth and fame won in the land of the Incas, returned to Spain and obtained authorization for new exploits. Designated by the king of Spain as Governor of Cuba and *Adelantado* of Florida, he organized and equipped a grand expedition for further discovery and conquest. In Florida—and the term then embraced all southeastern United States—he hoped to find "another Peru," and to win glory and wealth. Ponce de León and Narváez had previously ventured into Florida, only to reap disaster, but the resolute De Soto, experienced chief lieutenant of the great Pizarro, could not fail.

In May, 1539, De Soto sailed from Havana and landed at Tampa Bay, on the west coast of the peninsula. With 600 men, 200 horses, and extensive equipment and supplies, he plunged into the wilderness. His fortune during the ensuing two years need not be followed here. Traveling from one inhabited region to reputedly rich lands beyond, he pursued the ever-retreating land of gold. Natives were enslaved as beasts of burden, cornfields pillaged, supplies requisitioned, and whole villages wiped out when they resisted his arbitrary demands. De Soto made his way through northern Florida, went northeast through Georgia, turned northwest into Tennessee, southwest to Alabama, and north and west to the banks of the Mississippi. In South Carolina he had found a chieftainess with a pearl necklace, and from her people and from the graves of their ancestors he obtained over three hundred pounds of pearls. But of gold he found none. Even the pearls were lost during a native uprising, when a village was burned. His force was weakened and reduced by Indian battles, hardships, and disease.

In May, 1541, De Soto stood on the east bank of the Mississippi. From across the mighty river, writes the journalist of the expedition, came an Arkansas chief "with two hundred canoes filled with men, having weapons. They were painted with ochre, wearing great bunches of white and other plumes of many colors, having feathered shields in their hands, with which they sheltered the oarsmen on either side, the warriors standing erect from bow to stern, holding bows and arrows." They brought presents of fish and dried fruits for the white chief. But friction developed, and hostilities ensued.

After devoting a month to building barges, the Spaniards crossed the river and moved northward into present Arkansas. The country was rather densely populated, was rich with fruits, fish, and corn, and had an abundance of furs and skins for clothing. Learning from the Indians of a land where "there was a foundry of gold and copper," De Soto sent 80 men to seek it, but they "returned in great extremity," and without success.

The Spaniards moved westward through a land "yielding maize in such profusion that the old was thrown out of store to make room for the new grain. Beans and pumpkins were likewise in great plenty: both were larger and better than those of Spain." Continuing to western Arkansas or to eastern Oklahoma, De Soto remained for a month to fatten his horses in the ample cornfields. From the Indians of the region he obtained many "cow-skins" (buffalo robes) that "were very soft and the wool like that of sheep." Learning that to the west were many cows but few people, De Soto turned back to the southeast and went into winter quarters (1541–1542), apparently on the Ouachita River, in present Louisiana. Here, in a tall palisade, he spent three months enjoying the greatest plenty of maize, beans, walnuts, and dried plums; also rabbits, which the Indians taught his men to trap.

In the spring he returned to the Mississippi. Having lost nearly half of his men and over three-fourths of his animals, he now planned to go down the Mississippi to the seacoast, build two vessels, and dispatch them to Cuba and Spain for more men and horses. A party sent to learn the distance to the Gulf found among the Indians no knowledge of the sea.

Circled by hostile Indians, his party weakened and discouraged, and with no hope of early succor, De Soto "sank into a deep despondency at sight of the difficulties that presented themselves." Broken in spirit and sickened in body, he died of fever. He had boasted to the natives that he was a "Child of the Sun" and his followers feared an uprising if they reported his death and thus revealed his mortality. So under cover of night they buried him in the Mississippi River.

Luís de Moscoso, who succeeded to the command, decided to try to reach Mexico by land. Taking a westward course, he penetrated Texas beyond the Trinity River, and there, finding supplies growing scarce and fearing to face another winter in unknown land, turned back to the Mississippi. Here his men spent the winter. Marshaling their remaining resources, they set about building boats. They constructed a crude furnace, and from the slave chains and iron shot made spikes to fasten together the hewn timbers. Anchors were made from melted stirrups, and ropes from the bark of mulberry trees.

By June the seven brigantines were finished. Twenty-two horses were taken on board, the remainder being killed and the meat jerked. The last of the hogs were butchered to obtain pork for the voyage. Of the 600 remaining Indian slaves, 100 were placed on the boats and the others were liberated.

The little fleet sailed down the Mississippi, reaching its mouth at the end of 17 days. It experienced storms and privations at sea, but finally, on September 10, 1543, reached the mouth of the Pánuco River, some distance above Vera Cruz. Says the chronicler: "Many, leaping on shore, kissed the ground; and all on bended knees, with hands raised above them and their eyes to heaven, remained untiring in giving thanks to God."

We have now seen that, during the first 50 years after the discovery of America, four great expeditions—those of De Vaca, Coronado, Cabrillo, and De Soto—had made known large areas of the West. These were the high marks of sixteenth-century Spanish exploration in North America. The journeys had exploded the northern mysteries, dispelled such mythical chimeras as the Seven Cities of Cíbola, Quivira, the Amazon Island, and the Fountain of Youth. "Another Mexico" and "another Peru" had not been found in the North American wilderness, and disappointed Spaniards now settled back to develop regions nearer their bases in the West Indies and Mexico.

THE FOUNDING OF NEW MEXICO

But as decades passed, interest revived in the northern lands, especially in the pueblo towns of the New Mexico-Arizona country. Zealous churchmen saw in the sedentary tribes there a missionary vineyard ripe for the harvest. From a new northern outpost at the head of the Conchos River (which flows northward into the Rio Grande), a new and shorter trail was opened to New Mexico. Over this route in 1581 went Rodríguez and two companion missionaries to establish Christianity among the Pueblos. The next year Espejo led a party to the upper Rio Grande to trade, explore, and perhaps rescue the endangered friars. Though the missionaries had already been put to death, the other objects of the expedition were achieved. At the Moqui towns of Arizona, the traders obtained four thousand native cotton blankets; and in the vicinity of present Prescott, they discovered mines. Enthusiasm flared for conquest and settlement of the region.

Another factor promoting the same project resulted from the great voyage of Sir Francis Drake. This famous Elizabethan seadog rounded South America in 1579, raided Spanish ships on the Pacific Coast, landed at Drake's Bay (just north of the Bay of San Francisco), and took formal possession of the region for England. Spanish rumor said that Drake had found a strait through North America and that the English were planning to occupy and control it. To forestall such a move, Spain must push her frontier northward. After the destruction of his great Armada in 1588, King Philip of Spain, with renewed zeal, turned to check England's advance in the New World. He ordered the colonization of California and New Mexico. Although the Pacific Coast project was not effected at this time, the settlement of the upper Rio Grande region was accomplished.

From a number of applicants for the New Mexico commission, Juan de Oñate was chosen. He was to become the founder of the first white colony in the trans-Mississippi West. Oñate, a wealthy citizen of northern Mexico, was of a military family which had helped conquer New Spain. His wife was a granddaughter of Cortés and a great-granddaughter of Montezuma. With Oñate as recruiting officer came his two nephews, Juan and Vicente Zaldívar. Spiritual charge of the conquest was assigned to the Franciscans.

In February, 1598, Oñate set forth with his colonists from the outpost of Santa Bárbara, in northern Mexico. Of the 400 men in his party, 130 were soldier-settlers (most of whom took their families), while the remainder, excepting the eight missionaries, were Indian and Negro slaves. Eighty-three wagons and carts carried women, children, baggage, and supplies, while 7,000 head of stock accompanied the train. Upon reaching the Rio Grande, just below present El Paso, he took formal possession of the country in the name of King Philip.

Going ahead with 60 men, Oñate traversed the Pueblo region, and at Santo Domingo, New Mexico, in early July "received the submission of the chiefs of seven provinces." He established headquarters at San Juan, which point was reached by the rear division of his caravan on August 18. During that month and with the aid of numerous natives, an irrigation ditch and a church were begun. After completion of the church on September 8, representatives of the surrounding tribes were assembled, their chiefs were given "rods of office," and the eight Franciscan missionaries were assigned fields among the various pueblos.

With the foundations of settlement laid, Oñate turned to exploration. A party led by Juan de Zaldívar went northeastward to the plains and returned with a large supply of buffalo hides, tallow, and meat. The governor himself went west to Moqui and to the reputed goldfields of Arizona. On this journey he found abundant salines. "Salt," he reports, "is the universal article of traffic of all these barbarians and their regular food, for they even eat or suck it alone as we do sugar." Later he went west to California. In 1601 he traveled east and north with 70 picked men, taking eight carts, four cannons, and 700 horses and mules. He reached the Quivira visited 60 years before by Coronado, but covered little new ground and found no wealth. After ten years of service, Oñate was dismissed from the New Mexico post, and various other governors followed. The struggling colony grew slowly. No workable mines were found; irrigated agriculture yielded small returns. But the missionary harvest was great—at least apparently so. By 1630 there were 25 missions with 60,000 converts in 90 pueblos. Fifty friars were busy teaching the Indians Christianity and reading, writing, music, and useful crafts. While the natives were instructed, they were also exploited. Contributions of labor and produce were demanded. Under these exactions and the discipline imposed, resentment and enmity developed. The malcontents occasionally fled from the missions to the wild tribes on the plains.

The discontent culminated in the Pueblo Revolt of 1680. In this tragic uprising, led by Popé the medicine man, over 400 Spanish settlers—about one-sixth of the white population of New Mexico at the time—were slaughtered. The survivors fled down the river to El Paso. In their frenzy, the Indians tried to blot out all vestiges of Christianity and of the superimposed white civilization.

Twelve years after the uprising, Governor Diego de Vargas began the reconquest of New Mexico. But it took six years and considerable fighting to re-establish complete Spanish authority in the province. Thereafter, for more than a century, New Mexico continued as a Spanish colony, but remained sparsely populated and poor in material wealth, while the admixture of Indian blood gradually absorbed the original Spanish strain.

BIBLIOGRAPHY

For general accounts of Spanish exploration and settlement in North America, see H. E. Bolton and T. M. Marshall, *Colonization of North America, 1492–1783* (New York, 1920); E. G. Bourne, *Spain in America* (New York, 1904); H. I. Priestley, *The Coming of the White Men* (New York, 1930); and the excellent and readable account in H. E. Bolton, *Spanish*

Borderlands (New Haven, 1921). Another popular account is C. F. Lummis, *The Spanish Pioneers* (Chicago, 1893). Useful books are: Woodbury Lowery, *The Spanish Settlements within the Present Limits of the United States, 1513–1561* (New York, 1901); Cleve Hallenbeck, *Alvar Nuñez Cabeza de Vaca* (Glendale, Calif., 1940); C. E. Chapman, *History of California: The Spanish Period* (New York, 1921); Carl Sauer, *The Road to Cíbola* (Berkeley, 1932); the volumes of H. H. Bancroft's *Works* relating to California, New Mexico, and Arizona; and R. E. Twitchell, *The Leading Facts of New Mexican History* (2 vols., Cedar Rapids, 1911). The fullest account of the founding of New Mexico is G. P. Hammond, *Don Juan de Oñate and the Founding of New Mexico* (Santa Fe, 1927).

Original contemporary journals and accounts of early Spanish expeditions are assembled in *Spanish Explorers in the Southern United States, 1528–1543,* edited by F. W. Hodge and I. H. Lewis (New York, 1907), and in *Spanish Exploration in the Southwest, 1542–1706,* edited by H. E. Bolton (New York, 1916). Original narratives are also available in the *Trail Maker Series* as follows: A. F. and Fanny Bandelier (eds.), *The Journey of Alvar Nuñez Cabeza de Vaca* (New York, 1905); E. G. Bourne, *Narratives of the Career of Hernando de Soto* (2 vols., New York, 1904); and G. P. Winship, *The Coronado Expedition* (New York, 1904). A more elaborate edition of the documents relating to the Coronado expedition was edited by Dr. Winship and published in Spanish and in English in the *Fourteenth Annual Report of the Bureau of American Ethnology* (Washington, 1894). New Coronado documents are: "Coronado's Muster Roll," by A. S. Aiton, in the *American Historical Review,* XLIV, 556–570; and "Coronado's Testimony in the Viceroy Mendoza *Residencia,*" by A. S. Aiton and Agapito Rey, in the *New Mexico Historical Review,* XII, 288–329. In David Donahue, "The Route of the Coronado Expedition," *Southwestern Historical Quarterly,* XXXII, 181–193, is presented the view that Coronado did not penetrate beyond the confines of present Texas. R. E. Twitchell, *The Spanish Archives of New Mexico* (2 vols., Cedar Rapids, 1914), is a calendar of original Spanish documents relating to New Mexico. The rare Villagrá, *Historia de la Nueva Mexico* (1610), a history of New Mexico written in verse, appears in English translation as *Quivira Society Publications,* Vol. IV (Los Angeles, 1933). Other original accounts are *Obregón's History of 16th Century Explorations in Western America,* translated and edited by G. P. Hammond and Agapito Rey (Los Angeles, 1928); and *The Gallegos Relation of the Rodríguez Expedition to New Mexico,* translated and edited by G. P. Hammond and Agapito Rey (Santa Fe, 1927). See also G. W. Hackett (ed.), *Historical Documents Relating to New Mexico, Nueva Vizcaya, and Approaches Thereto, to 1773* (Washington, 1923); and *Final Report of the United States De Soto Expedition Commission,* in *House Document 71,* 76th Congress, 1st Session (Washington, 1939). See, too, the volumes by G. P. Hammond and A. Rey, *Narratives of the Coronado Expedition, 1540–1542* (Albuquerque, 1940), and Herbert E. Bolton, *Coronado, Knight of Pueblos and Plains* (New York, 1949).

3

FRENCH EXPLORATION
AND SETTLEMENT

Fance was to play a lead part in
the drama of the West, though her entry on the stage was late and her
role was brief. Not until the latter half of the seventeenth century did
she reach the trans-Mississippi country, while her chief work in the
region was done in the eighteenth century.

The Italian Wars and the religious conflicts at home largely absorbed
French attention during the sixteenth century, the period of Spain's
foundations in the New World. France did, however, carry on some
exploration and make two attempts at settlement in North America
during that period. The Florentine navigator, Verrazano, sailing in
1524 for Francis I of France, appears to have explored the North
American coast from Cape Fear to Newfoundland. In 1534 Jacques
Cartier entered the Gulf of St. Lawrence and, returning the next year,
ascended the St. Lawrence River to Lachine Rapids and the site of
Montreal. As Captain-General for Roberval, the newly-appointed
French viceroy, Cartier came again in 1541 to the St. Lawrence region
to establish a colony. He built a post at Quebec and spent an unhappy
winter there before returning to France. Roberval arrived with reinforcements the next spring and reoccupied Quebec. But after spending a long, cold winter with insufficient supplies and enduring a severe
siege of scurvy, he, too, was ready to return to France and forsake his
colonization venture.

Another French attempt at settlement in North America was made
in the sixteenth century. Persecuted French Protestants sought a religious haven in the new land. One band settled in Brazil, but was
driven out by the Portuguese. Other Huguenots, led by Ribaut and
Laudonnière, attempted in 1562–1565 to establish themselves on the
northern border of Florida. Discontent, sickness, and desertions weakened the colony. Then the Spaniards under Menéndez came and
cruelly but effectively expelled the French Protestants. No further

attempts at colonization were made for some years, and the sixteenth century ended with no French settlement in America.

But the seventeenth century witnessed a strikingly different performance. In the year 1600 a partnership, formed by Pontgravé, De Monts and Chauvin, was given by the king of France a monopoly of the fur trade in the New World. Successful trading and the establishment of forts were begun at once in the St. Lawrence and the Bay of Fundy regions. In 1603 there came with the fur traders to these northern waters a man destined for a great career in New France—Samuel de Champlain. He, perhaps more than any other man, pushed the design to establish French dominion here. Not only was fur trade to be pursued, but permanent settlements were to be established. In accord with this plan, he founded Quebec in 1608. Of the 28 original colonists, only eight withstood the first winter, but the survivors did not desert. Reinforcements came in the spring, and the rock-ribbed settlement developed into the capital of New France.

To the Great Lakes and the Mississippi

Next year Champlain began his movement into the interior. Having formed an alliance with the Algonquin Indians, he accompanied one of their war parties up the St. Lawrence and its Richelieu branch to the lake that bears his name. Here he routed the Iroquois, almost singlehanded, with his mysterious thunder stick, and thus accentuated an Iroquois hostility to the French that, reinforced by other factors, persisted throughout most of the period of French dominion in America. In 1613 Champlain explored some distance up the Ottawa River and two years later continued farther up this stream and crossed to Georgian Bay, the large arm of Lake Huron. He thus opened to the upper Great Lakes a direct route that became the great fur traders' highway into the interior, a route beyond the reach of hostile Iroquois.

Farther west went one of Champlain's agents, Jean Nicolet. In 1634 this adventurer took the Ottawa route to Lake Huron, crossed to Lake Michigan, and explored the Green Bay region of present Wisconsin. Here, from the Indians, he heard of a "great water" to the south, but did not continue to the Mississippi.

With the death the next year of Champlain, "Founder of New France," the moving force was lacking, at least for the time being, to push further exploration. But the profits of the fur trade kept adventurous Frenchmen in the wilderness. Also, an important new agency and interest had entered the field—missionaries and a passion to win the Indians to Christianity. In 1615 some Recollect Franciscans had been introduced to New France, but it was the Jesuits, brought in 1625, who became the great French missionaries of the far interior. Not only were they zealously to teach the Christian religion and many of them win the coveted crown of martyrdom, but the numerous reports of their labors, published as the *Jesuit Relations,* in 73 volumes and carrying detailed accounts of lands and natives, were to become the great sourcebook of the history of France in North America.

Missionary zeal, the fur trade, and desire for dominion were the compelling motives that brought France into the heart of the continent and kept her there for more than a century. During that period she was to explore the great interior region and throughout its vast stretches scatter trading posts and missions.

In the development of the fur trade, the French adopted the policy of granting exclusive control of designated areas to individuals or companies. Indeed, monopoly and regulation characterized official French activity in the New World. In trade and in dealings with Indians France had marked success, but her efforts to induce sufficient immigration to hold the great domain she claimed fell short of the mark. "The French have never been fond of colonizing," says R. G. Thwaites, historian of the French in America. "Bounties to immigrants, importation of unmarried women to wed the superabundant bachelors, ostracism for the unmarried of either sex, official rewards for large families —all these measures were freely and persistently adopted by the French colonial officials." [1] Despite such measures, colonists were slow to respond and the French population in America was never large.

France adopted a paternalistic policy that, with undue solicitude and excessive regulations, defeated its own purposes. An autocratic government was planted in America, and colonists were given no experience in self-government. Under the Old Regime, New France was dominated by three officials: the Governor, in control of civil and military administration; the Intendant, a legal and financial officer; and the Bishop, concerned with ecclesiastical affairs. Local government was unknown to the peasants. They turned to the priests for guidance, not only in spiritual affairs, but in temporal matters as well.

In an effort to promote colonization, France attempted to establish a form of feudalism in America. Certain military officers were given a rank of nobility and were assigned tracts of land along the rivers and lakes as seigniories. The frontage of these varied from half a league to six leagues, and the tracts generally extended a league or two back from the water's edge. In these areas *habitants,* or tenants, were given narrow strips (usually less than 800 feet wide) to till. The *habitant* was obliged to work a few days each year for his *seigneur,* patronize the latter's grist-mill and bakery, and give him a portion of the fish caught. In many cases seignior and peasant were equally poor, and the social

---

[1] Thwaites, R. G., *France in America,* New York, Harper and Brothers, 1905, 128.

distinctions attempted were artificial. On this narrow strip of land the peasant built his log house close to that of his neighbor. The string of these whitewashed dwellings along the river bank formed the settlement, with the parish church as the nucleus of village life.

Into the wilderness region went singly and in brigades the *coureurs de bois* (rangers of the wood). To ply their trade in furs, they pushed out among the Indians instead of waiting for the natives to bring in their peltries to the forts. Some of these traders complied with the royal decrees and respected the privileges granted favored persons, while the more common type not only ignored all such restrictions but broke with civilization as well. They joined the Indian bands, married Indian wives, became adopted sons of the tribes, and took on the Indian dress and manner of life. They sold their peltries to whomever they pleased, often to Dutch and later to English traders. The far wanderings of such renegades were not and cannot be recorded, though theirs were the first visits by Europeans to many sections of the interior. Descendants of these venturers were to accompany most of the trapping parties and exploring expeditions to the Rocky Mountains and to the Pacific Coast when those regions were opened in the early nineteenth century.

Among the most famous French fur traders of the mid-seventeenth century were the brothers-in-law, Radisson and Groseilliers. They visited the region south of Lake Superior and traded with the Sioux in eastern Minnesota. It is possible that they reached the Mississippi, but, if so, the significance of the discovery was not made known at the time. Following them into this region came Nicolas Perrot in 1665. After spending the five succeeding years among the Indians, he was well equipped to act as interpreter and agent at the French Council of 1671 with the interior Indians. This impressive spectacle was staged at Sault Ste. Marie, on the passageway between Lakes Superior and Huron. Here, with pageantry and ceremony, Simon Francois Daumont, Sieur de St. Lusson, took formal possession of the interior of North America in the name of King Louis XIV of France.

Perrot had assembled representatives of 14 tribes to be impressed by the splendor. St. Lusson in his colorful uniform, the missionaries in priestly vestments, and the soldiers fully armed marched to the top of the hill overlooking the Jesuit post and the village of the Sauteurs. Here a large wooden cross, after having been solemnly blessed by one of the Fathers, was planted on the hilltop, while the Frenchmen, uncovered, sang the *Vexilla Regis*. Then a cedar post, bearing a metal plate engraved with the royal arms, was placed beside the cross. Thereupon St. Lusson, in high-sounding phrase, proclaimed possession of "Sainte Marie du Saut, as also of Lakes Huron and Superior, the Island of

Manatoulin, and all countries, rivers, lakes, and streams contiguous and adjacent thereunto: both those which have been discovered and those which may be discovered hereafter, in all their length and breadth, bounded on the one side by the seas of the North and of the West, and on the other by the South Sea." As a symbol of possession, a piece of earth was raised three times, the Frenchmen greeting each raising with a shout of *Vive le Roi*. As the white men fired their muskets and cheered, the assembled Indians joined in with native whoops and yells. They liked ceremony and were certain the Frenchmen had powerful medicine.

But the canny Frenchmen were wise enough to know that a proclamation could not insure possession of so vast a territory. They would follow up with further discoveries, with trading posts and settlements. Talon, Intendant of New France, was anxious that the great western river, of which the Indians spoke, should be explored and its course determined. To pursue this project he commissioned Louis Joliet, an energetic young American-born Frenchman. Jacques Marquette, 35-year-old Jesuit, who spoke six Indian languages and liked exploratory work, was chosen to accompany him.

They set out from St. Ignace, at the northeast end of Lake Michigan, on May 17, 1673. In their birch canoes were five companions and supplies of smoked meat and Indian corn. After reaching Green Bay and making their way to the head of this arm of Lake Michigan, they ascended Fox River. Innumerable birds, frightened by the canoes, flew in flocks from the far-stretching swamp fields of wild rice. In carrying their canoes across the mile-and-a-half portage, at the site of the modern city of Portage, they left the drainage basin of the St. Lawrence and embarked on the Wisconsin River. Paddling their way down this stream, they reached, on June 17, the looked-for great river. Whither did it lead—to the Gulf of Mexico, the Gulf of California, or the South Sea? That was their quest.

Cautiously they moved down the Mississippi, anchoring the boats in the stream at night and keeping a man on watch. After a fortnight without meeting anyone, they saw Indian tracks in the mud, and a well-trodden path on the west bank. Landing and following the trail some miles into present Iowa, they came upon an Indian village. Here they were well received and honored at a four-course dinner of porridge, fish, dog, and buffalo.

After more days of floating and paddling, the little party was suddenly terrified by a great muddy torrent surging into the blue drift of the Mississippi. They had reached the mighty Missouri. On the swell of the combined rivers the voyageurs floated southward. Past the mouth of the Iroquois-named Ohio, or Beautiful River, they con-

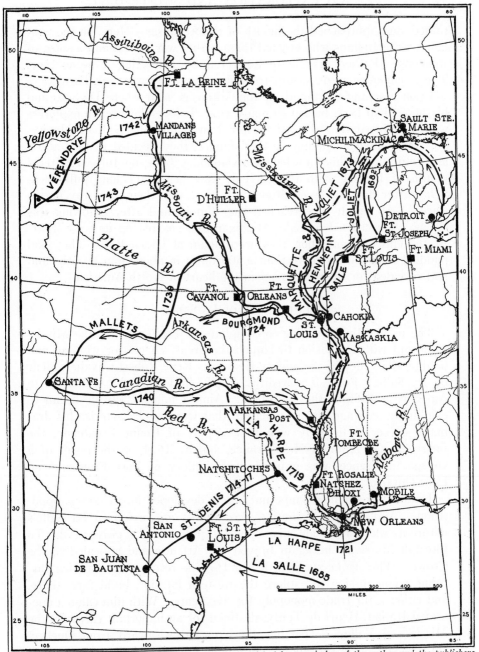

Base map from Hall, "Outline Maps and Graphs." Published by permission of the author and the publishers, John Wiley & Sons. Inc.

EARLY FRENCH EXPLORATIONS

33

tinued, and approached the mouth of the Arkansas. Here, on the west bank, were Indians who greeted them with a war whoop and a show of weapons. Father Marquette answered by exhibiting a peace pipe. The Frenchmen went ashore trembling, but they were not harmed.

Upon reaching the mouth of the Arkansas, near where De Soto and his hopes had been buried so many years before, the French explorers were convinced that the Mississippi flowed into the Gulf of Mexico. So, rather than encounter further danger, they decided to face about and return with this knowledge to Canada. Thus, on July 17, after a month of floating with the current, they began the long pull back. "Day after day and week after week, they won their slow way northward." At length they reached the Illinois, and after following this stream they crossed to Lake Michigan and coasted up its west shore. At the end of September, they were again at Green Bay. They had paddled their canoes more than 2,500 miles in about four months and had revealed for their countrymen the heart of North America.

The Vision of La Salle

The man with the daring to complete the exploration of the Mississippi and with the vision to launch the great scheme for winning and holding the valley of the mighty river, was René Robert Cavalier, Sieur de La Salle. Born of a wealthy family in France, he had come to America in 1666 at the age of 23. Almost immediately he began to exhibit the courage and imagination that were to characterize his dramatic career. He early won the support of Count Frontenac, the far-seeing Governor of New France, and by 1674, as the result of a voyage to France, was granted the seigniory of Fort Frontenac on Lake Ontario.

Jealousy of fur merchants and others developed into vigorous opposition. And, since conciliation was almost as foreign to La Salle's nature as was submission, his hopes and plans were in grave peril. To forestall his rivals he again braved the Atlantic and appealed to the Crown. The stroke succeeded. In 1678 he returned to America carrying a commission to explore the western interior, build forts there, and enjoy a fur trade monopoly for five years. With him came a one-armed Italian, Henri de Tonty, destined for an important career in the Mississippi Valley. Together they pushed westward from Quebec. On the Niagara River, above the famous falls, they built and launched the *Griffin* for carrying trade goods and furs. La Salle proceeded to the head of Lake Michigan, and thence to the Illinois River, where he established Fort Crèvecoeur and began building a boat with which to descend the Mississippi.

In the meantime the *Griffin,* which had sailed from Green Bay with a rich cargo of peltry, had not been heard from. The marketing of those furs, worth 10,000 crowns, was important to La Salle, so he set out to investigate. A strenuous overland journey in the early spring of 1680 brought him to Niagara, where crushing news greeted him. The *Griffin* had been lost, and his supply ship from France had been wrecked. Undismayed, he pushed on to Montreal, procured new supplies, and again moved westward. Soon came bearers of another report of disaster. His fort on the Illinois had been destroyed by Indians and most of his men had deserted.

Such accumulated reverses would have crushed most men. Writes Francis Parkman,[2] "The shattered fabric of his enterprise was prostrate in the dust. His friends desponded; his foes were blatant and exultant. Did he bend before the storm? No human eye could pierce the depths of his reserved and haughty nature; but the surface was calm, and no sign betrayed a shaken resolve or an altered purpose."

La Salle hurried westward with aid for faithful Tonty. Finding the Illinois country ravaged by the Iroquois, he was forced to return to Montreal for reinforcements. Placating his creditors and obtaining fresh supplies, he once more faced the West. He was determined to explore the Mississippi.

At Fort Miami, on the southeastern extremity of Lake Michigan, he completed preparations in the late fall of 1681. The exploring party he organized included 23 Frenchmen and 18 Indian braves with their wives and three children. The party crossed the tip of Lake Michigan to Chicago River. Winter had now closed the streams, so they made sleds, placed their canoes and baggage upon them, and pulled these over the ice. Crossing to the Illinois River and descending this stream, they reached the Mississippi on February 6, 1682. After they had waited a week, the river was sufficiently clear of floating ice to permit navigation, so the little canoes were pushed into the current and the voyage to the Gulf began.

Without incident worthy of mention here, the voyagers floated and paddled their way southward day after day. Presently shimmering spring, with warm breath, moved noiselessly up the valley to greet them, bearing the perfume of new flowers. They were soon in the land of swamp and canebrake.

Near the mouth of the Arkansas they were cordially entertained by the Indians whom Joliet and Marquette had visited. La Salle raised a cross and took formal possession of their country. Two Arkansas Indians were secured as guides. Some 300 miles farther down the river,

---

[2] In *La Salle and the Discovery of the Great West,* Boston, 1880, 188.

these guides pointed out the pathway to the great town of Taensas, in present Tensas Parish, Louisiana. The Frenchmen visited the place and were amazed at the houses they saw. They were large, square, adobe structures covered with dome-shaped cane roofs. In a room 40 feet square they found the chief, "three of his wives at his side, while sixty old men, wrapped in white cloaks woven of mulberry-bark, formed his divan. . . . He received the visitors graciously, and joyfully accepted the gifts which Tonty laid before him." The Indians worshiped the Sun and had the custom of offering enemies as sacrifices to their deity. La Salle visited the Natchez Indians and found a similar culture.

In early April, the Frenchmen reached the delta of the Mississippi and explored the three principal outlets to the Gulf. Then they reassembled on dry ground a short distance above the river's mouth.

Here was enacted the ceremony of taking formal possession. After raising a standard bearing the arms of France, La Salle proclaimed: [3]

In the name of the most high, mighty, invincible, and victorious Prince, Louis the Great, by the grace of God, King of France and of Navarre, Fourteenth of that name, I, this ninth day of April, one thousand six hundred and eighty-two, in virtue of the commission of his Majesty which I hold in my hand, and which may be seen by all whom it may concern, have taken, and do now take, in the name of his Majesty and of his successor to the crown, possession of this country of Louisiana, the seas, harbors, ports, bays, adjacent straits, and all the nations, people, provinces, cities, towns, villages, mines, minerals, fisheries, streams, and rivers within the extent of the said Louisiana, . . . along the river Colbert, or Mississippi, and the rivers which discharge themselves thereinto, . . . hereby protesting against all who may hereafter undertake to invade any or all of these aforesaid countries, peoples, or lands, . . .

Volleys of musketry and shouts of *Vive le Roi* greeted his words. A cross was planted beside the standard and an inscribed lead plate buried at its foot. The patriots then joined in singing the hymn of the *Vexilla Regis:*

> The banners of Heaven's King advance,
> The mystery of the Cross shines forth.

Claim to the vast drainage basin of the Mississippi was thus set forth. There remained only the making good of that claim.

The long voyage back, against the current of the river, was slow and difficult. And, to add to the burden, the intrepid leader fell sick and for 40 days was seriously ill. But a great vision buoyed him up. He

---

[3] Parkman, Francis, *La Salle and the Discovery of the Great West,* Boston, 1880, 286–287.

would abandon the St. Lawrence approach to the Mississippi Valley and establish a French outpost on the Gulf of Mexico, where furs could be sent directly to France. In the meantime, he would establish a colony in the Illinois country as a storage place for the furs gathered in the interior and from which these skins could be floated down the Mississippi to the sea. With Tonty's help, he built such a station at the picturesque citadel of "Starved Rock" on the Illinois River and named it Fort St. Louis.

His staunch supporter, Count Frontenac, having been recalled from Canada, La Salle now faced the active opposition of a new and jealous governor. But this did not thwart him. Ignoring officialdom at Quebec, he sailed for the homeland and presented his plan to the king himself. Louis XIV was very much interested. He had previously become irritated by Spanish conduct in excluding Frenchmen from American ports and forbidding them to enter the Gulf of Mexico. War had just broken out between France and Spain, and the time now was especially opportune to demonstrate French authority in the Gulf of Mexico, perhaps even to capture Spanish mines in northern Mexico by a combined French and Indian attack, as La Salle suggested. The king was also warned that, if the project were delayed, England might anticipate him, occupy the mouth of the Mississippi, and hem in New France.

The result was that La Salle was given more than he asked; instead of two vessels, four were provided. A hundred soldiers were enlisted; missionaries, gentlemen, and laborers volunteered, and several families joined the enterprise Altogether, there were nearly 400 persons on board when the little fleet set sail from La Rochelle in July, 1684. Others, from the French West Indies, joined on the way.

Misfortune and dissension marked the expedition from the first. Captain Beaujeu, of the royal navy, in command of the vessels, and La Salle quarreled bitterly; sickness attacked the colonists; and Spanish buccaneers captured one of the ships. At Santo Domingo, La Salle was taken seriously ill, and men deserted while the expedition was leaderless. Finally, when he did continue the voyage, he missed the mouth of the Mississippi and landed at Matagorda Bay on the Texas coast in January, 1685. A fort, named St. Louis, was erected as a temporary protection while they sought the mouth of the Father of Waters. Misfortune continued to dog the enterprise. One ship was lost on a sand bar, Captain Beaujeu sailed away with the second, and the third was finally wrecked on the shore. During the winter of 1685–1686, La Salle conducted an unsuccessful search for the elusive Mississippi. A second effort was made the following spring. But, after spending some months, and crossing to the east border of present

Texas, he again gave up and returned, having lost 12 of his 20 men. Among the Cenis (Asinai) Indians of east Texas, he found loot obtained from the Spaniards and acquired five Spanish horses.

With little likelihood of a vessel coming for the colonists, their only hope of rescue was in the long journey to Canada. Their numbers had been reduced by disease, Indian attacks, and accidents to less than 40. Early in 1687 La Salle set out with nearly half of these in an effort to reach the Illinois country and Canada. On the way, near the Brazos River, in the vicinity of Navasota, he was murdered by some of his own men. The remnant pushed on to the Mississippi and, at the mouth of the Arkansas, found two of Tonty's followers. The faithful Italian had descended the Mississippi to its mouth and searched diligently but in vain for his chief. The surviving comrades of La Salle finally reached Canada. But the little band left in Texas, receiving no relief from France, was attacked by the Indians, and those not killed were taken prisoners. When Spanish expeditions, seeking La Salle's colony, shortly afterward found Fort St. Louis, it was already deserted and in ruins.

Thus ended the first great project to plant a French colony on the Gulf Coast. And thus also ended in tragedy the career of one of America's greatest explorers. Despite his haughtiness, arbitrariness, and such minor faults, La Salle looms through the years as France's most distinguished son in the West. Parkman, the historian of France in America, picture him thus: "He was a tower adamant, against whose impregnable front hardship and danger, the rage of man and of the elements, the southern sun, the northern blast, fatigue, famine, and disease, delay, disappointment, and deferred hope emptied their quivers in vain."

Occupancy of the Mississippi Valley

La Salle's great plan did not die with its projector. But, before we discuss its revival and fruition, let us turn again to the Great Lakes region and note the westward expansion that had taken place in that area.

Duluth, a cousin of Tonty, had gone to the Lake Superior region in 1678, and for several years thereafter traded among the Indians of the Minnesota country. From the Sioux in 1680, he rescued Accau and Hennepin, whom La Salle had sent from the Illinois River to explore the upper Mississippi. They had reached the site of present Minneapolis.

Perrot, previously mentioned, continued in the fur trade west of the lakes. In 1686, he built Fort St. Antoine on the Mississippi, in western Wisconsin, and established other posts in the vicinity. He discovered and worked the Galena lead mines of present Iowa. Le Sueur, another prominent trader, was in Minnesota in the 1680's. He built a post on the Mississippi, near the mouth of the St. Croix, in 1693, and, four years later, obtained permission to work the Lake Superior copper mines. Coming from France with Iberville's colony (to be discussed shortly), and ascending the Mississippi from the Gulf, Le Sueur again reached the Lake Superior region. In 1700, he built Fort L'Huiller on a west branch of the Mississippi in southern Minnesota.

How far into the West unlicensed *coureurs de bois* penetrated during this period none can say. Adventuresome Frenchmen were known to be trading in present Missouri and Iowa in the early 1690's. But most of their journeys were never reported and their work of exploration goes unrecorded.

In 1699 a mission was founded on the east bank of the Mississippi, at Cahokia, Illinois. The next year, some French Jesuits and traders joined the Kaskaskia Indians in planting a village at the site of modern St. Louis, Missouri. Although it was abandoned in 1703, it ranks as the first French mission and settlement in present Missouri.

Returning now to the La Salle project for making a base at the mouth of the Mississippi, we find the enterprise finally placed in the hands of Pierre Le Moyne, better known as Iberville. With 200 soldiers and colonists aboard four vessels, he set sail from Brest in October, 1698. After touching at Santo Domingo for additional supplies, he sailed to the Gulf Coast. The Spaniards kept him out of Pensacola Bay, so he established himself, in February, 1699, at Biloxi, a little east of the mouth of the Mississippi. From here, he rediscovered the mouth of the great river and explored it as far north as the Red River branch. But the marshy character of the delta region precluded settlement there, and Iberville feared that an inland site might be at the mercy of the Indians. So the principal base was established east of the river, first at Biloxi and later (1710) at Mobile. Tonty came down from the Illinois country and assisted in promoting friendly relations with the Choctaws and Chickasaws. Thus, the original Louisiana was the Alabama Basin.

But the colony had its difficulties—sickness, shortage of supplies, desertions. The royal government soon tired of the project and, in 1712, turned it over to Antoine Crozat, a wealthy merchant. In return for a monopoly of trade, mining, land grants, and the slave traffic, he agreed to bring in two shiploads of settlers annually. Lamothe Cadillac, who had founded Detroit in 1701, was brought in as the first governor. Louisiana witnessed some development. Trade with the

Indians was expanded, forts were established on the Alabama River and at the site of Natchez, and lead mines were opened in Missouri.

An effort was made to open trade relations with the Spaniards of northern Mexico, for the wealth and glamor of Spanish mines had an irresistible appeal. The post of Natchitoches on the Red River was established with this in mind. From here Louis Juchereau de St. Denis, guided by two survivors of the La Salle expedition, journeyed across the breadth of Texas in 1714. At the Rio Grande, he was arrested by the Spaniards. The garrison became so alarmed at this French intrusion that they launched a counter thrust and at once began the settlement of Texas (to be treated in the following chapter). Personally, St. Denis was treated well and was allowed to marry a Spanish girl; but, when he came again to the north Mexico frontier in 1717, with articles for trade, his goods were seized by order of the Mexican viceroy, and the French trader fled in the night.

In the meantime Frenchmen had been pushing westward from the Illinois country, with eyes fixed on New Mexico. In 1702, 17 adventurers set out from Cahokia with the object, as Iberville reported, "to explore New Mexico, trade in piasters [dollars] and see what are the mines of which the Indians spoke to them." They ascended the Missouri River some distance, but were turned back by Indians. "This," says G. J. Garraghan, prominent Jesuit historian, "would appear to be the first regularly organized expedition of white men known to have gone up the Missouri."[4] About four years later, Derbanne ascended the Missouri nearly 400 leagues and among the Indians found Spanish articles obtained from New Mexico.

Crozat, finding that his Louisiana colony was a constant expense rather than an asset, surrendered his patent in 1717. The Louisiana country was now turned over to the speculator John Law and the Company of the West, or the Mississippi Company. The great promoter, with his grand financial scheme based on credit, played up the Louisiana country and its imaginary gold mines as the center of the glamorous project.

Extensive tracts of land along the Mississippi, the Red River, and the Yazoo were granted to *concessionaires* who agreed to bring out settlers. Inasmuch as but few colonists would volunteer, their numbers were supplemented by groups taken from the jails and hospitals. One shipment included 80 girls from the Parisian House of Correction. Negro slaves were introduced, and with their labor agriculture was developed. Soldiers were brought in and garrisons were established at Natchitoches and other posts.

Bienville, the "Father of Louisiana," a younger brother of Iberville,

---

[4] *Chapters in Frontier History,* Milwaukee, Bruce Publishing Company, 1933, 62.

was made Governor. In 1718 he founded New Orleans. With its strategic location on the great river, it was in a position to control the interior commerce and become the capital of the region.

The "Mississippi Bubble" burst, as all such airy inflations must, in 1720, and John Law, the boasted savior of France, fled for his life. But the Mississippi Company, though humbled and reduced, continued for more than a decade in control of the Louisiana country. Colonization had finally taken root. The company brought in more than 7,000 whites and some 600 Negro slaves. The Negroes increased so rapidly that there was fear that they would dominate the colony, and a "Black Code" was promulgated in 1724 to insure their subordination.

The Illinois country, which was annexed to Louisiana in 1717, had experienced marked growth. Settlements were founded on both sides of the Mississippi, in the present states of Illinois and Missouri. This region came to be called the "Garden of New France," and shipments of grain were sent north to Detroit and down the Mississippi to New Orleans, to Mobile, and even to France. Slaves were introduced; tobacco culture was begun. As the lead mines and the salines of Missouri were worked, settlements grew about them.

Far Western Exploration

However, trade with the Indians for furs continued as the primary object in the Mississippi Valley. As Frenchmen pushed farther into the West, they found Indians under Spanish influence who were carrying on trade with the Spaniards of New Mexico. Such Indians must be won for France if the trade of the great Mississippi Valley was to flow to its natural market at New Orleans. In carrying out such a program, Frenchmen became the first explorers of vast stretches of the West.

In 1719 Du Tisné ascended the Missouri River some distance and was turned back by Indians. Then he journeyed on horseback to the Osages and moved westward to the Pawnees (probably in present Kansas), where he traded with Indians for Spanish horses. He had meant to continue farther westward to the Padoucas (usually identified as Comanches), but was prevented by the Pawnees. So he contented himself with raising a French flag in the Pawnee village and returned to the Mississippi.

In 1719, also, Benard de la Harpe went up the Red River some distance above Natchitoches and crossed over to the Canadian and the Arkansas. He found the Indians here supplied with Spanish horses. Two years later, La Harpe made an expedition by water along the Texas coast to Galveston Bay, but was expelled by the Indians. Later that year he conducted an expedition up the Arkansas to the vicinity of Little Rock, with a view of developing trade with the Indians and opening a path of commerce to Santa Fe. But he fell far short of the latter objective.

The threat of Spanish expansion into the Mississippi Valley was given visible proof when the Villasur expedition from New Mexico (see the following chapter) penetrated to the Platte River in present Nebraska in 1720. The alarmed Frenchmen resolved to stop further Spanish incursion and to win the intervening Indians. The effecting of such a program was entrusted to Étienne Veniard de Bourgmond, one-time commander of Detroit. In 1712 he had gone to Missouri, where he became a *coureur de bois,* married an Indian woman, adopted the Indian manner of life, and became an idol of the natives of the region. In 1714 he had ascended the Missouri to the mouth of the Platte, and later appears to have continued to the Dakotas. His relations with the Indians made him an especially suitable person to be entrusted with the French project. He was now directed to establish a fort on the Missouri and to make peace with the Padoucas, who were located farther west. They were known to trade with the Spaniards, and to be at war with Indians allied to the French.

In November, 1723, Bourgmond led a party of 40 Frenchmen up the Missouri River and founded Fort Orleans. It was located on the north bank of the river, in present Carroll County, Missouri. From here, in July, 1724, he set out on his western mission, going up the river to the vicinity of present Kansas City. From the Kansas Indians he purchased several Padouca slaves and sent them ahead to their people as a peace offering. After recovering from a sickness that caused his return to Fort Orleans, Bourgmond again moved westward in late September. With him he took delegations of Missouris, Osages, Otoes, and others. In central Kansas, probably in the vicinity of present Ellsworth, he reached the Padouca camp. A welcome awaited him which was made more enthusiastic when the Indians beheld a great array of presents.

The Frenchmen had brought guns, sabers, axes, knives, combs, awls, kettles, bells, beads, cloth, rings, boxes of vermilion, and so forth. As Bourgmond stood among the piles of glittering merchandise, holding the French flag in his hands, he harangued the assembled Padoucas. He wanted them to make peace with the Indians he had brought, to visit and trade with them, and to trade with the French and allow them to pass through the country to the Spaniards. The goods, he said, were from the great French king, who gave them freely to the Padoucas.

Thereupon the chief took the flag and responded: "When the French will come to see us, we will receive them well and in case they want to go to the Spaniards to trade, we will guide them there. They [the Spaniards] are only at a distance of twelve marching days from our village; every spring they come to see us, they bring us horses and bring us a few knives and a few awls and a few axes, but they are not like you, who give us here a quantity of merchandise, such as we have never seen and we cannot return such presents."

The Padoucas, in return for the gifts, presented seven horses to Bourgmond. By the fifth of November, the Frenchmen were back at Fort Orleans.

The following summer (1725) Bourgmond escorted a delegation of Missouri, Osage, and Oto Indians to France. Among these was the "Princess of Missouri," who was married in Notre Dame to one of Bourgmond's lieutenants. The Indians were lionized in Paris and were presented to the king. They danced at the Opera and hunted in the Bois de Boulogne. Their speeches were translated into poetry. One of their comments was that the perfumed French court ladies "smelled like alligators." Bourgmond, having fulfilled his mission, received a patent of nobility from Louis XV. The court heraldic expert designed his special coat of arms, which on a blue background represented an Indian sitting on a mountain of silver.

But the project for opening trade with New Mexico, though grandly begun, was not immediately consummated. The French suffered reverses. The great Fox chief, Kiala, organized a widespread conspiracy to expel the French intruders. It embraced most of the tribes on the southern and western sides of the Great Lakes and extended to the Missouris and Otoes. The Natchez also were giving trouble on the lower Mississippi. In the face of these difficulties, Fort Orleans was abandoned in 1728 and the penetration of New Mexico was postponed.

French traders, however, gradually worked their way into the western regions. From Natchitoches and other posts farther up the Red River, they carried trade to the tribes of eastern and northern Texas. From Arkansas Post they bartered with the Indians of present Arkansas and eastern Oklahoma. Beyond the bend of the Missouri, they traded with the Kansas and Pawnees, and gradually pushed up the muddy river to the Aricaras and Mandans in the present Dakotas. Finally an expedition penetrated the country of hostile Apaches and Comanches and reached New Mexico in the summer of 1739.

This, the first recorded French expedition to reach Santa Fe, was led by the Mallet brothers, Peter and Paul. With six companions, they made their way some distance up the Platte River, then turned southwest, across Kansas and southeastern Colorado over "barren prairies where the only fuel for lighting a fire was buffalo chips." They ascended the Arkansas River some distance and encountered Laitanes (probably Comanches), among whom they found an Aricara Indian who "had been a slave among the Spaniards and had even been baptized there." They engaged him as guide, and were led to the Spanish settlements, reaching Santa Fe on July 22.

They were well received and remained in New Mexico through the winter, awaiting a reply to their petition to the viceroy of Mexico, presumably asking for the privilege to open trade. Word finally came, and the Frenchmen were asked to stay in New Mexico and explore the region to the westward. But they preferred to return home. On May 1, 1740, they set out on a new and eastward course which brought them to the Canadian River. Here the party divided, part turning northeast to Illinois and four continuing eastward. The latter group built boats and floated down the Arkansas and the Mississippi to New Orleans.

The report of their adventures caused considerable excitement in the French capital, and Governor Bienville resolved to follow it with further exploration. Fabry de la Bruyère was sent in 1741 on such a mission, guided by the Mallet brothers. They ascended the Canadian River some distance, but failed to reach New Mexico.

With the establishment of peace between the Comanches and their enemy neighbors to the east in the late 1740's, the Arkansas River route to New Mexico was made safe. A number of French expeditions now followed this course to trade with the Spaniards. It was the beginning of traffic on what was later to be known as the Santa Fe Trail. In 1740 Pierre Satren led a party to Santa Fe, and the next year another group reached the New Mexico capital by the same route. In 1751 Jean Chapuis led an expedition from Illinois with a commission from the commander of Fort Chartres. "Arriving at Santa Fe in 1752," says Bolton, "he proposed a regular caravan trade with military escort. The intruders were arrested and sent to Mexico, where they languished in prison for many months and were finally sent to Spain." [5] That kingdom was still jealously guarding her empire against foreign intrusion. And France was just now engaging with England in the final contest for empire in North America.

In the meantime, and before the opening of that far-reaching French and Indian War, the French were making known the northern section of our American prairies. There had long been a desire to find a route from the Great Lakes region to the Pacific. But during the first decade of the eighteenth century, hostility of the Fox Indians had retarded or prevented the necessary exploration. Then there came into the field a man with a passionate zeal for discovery—Pierre Gaultier de Va-

---

[5] Bolton and Marshall, *Colonization of North America*, New York, The Macmillan Company, 1920, 286.

rennes de la Vérendrye. He offered to search for the Western Sea, and the French government gave him a monopoly of the fur trade of the region as an aid to the enterprise. With remarkable persistence in the face of great difficulties, Vérendrye pursued his project, and within ten years he had established a string of six forts extending from Lake Superior northwestward by way of Lake Winnipeg to the forks of the Saskatchewan.

The Assiniboin Indians told him of a tribe on the upper Missouri who knew the way to the Western Sea, so he turned in that direction. Late in 1738, he crossed from Fort La Reine on the Assiniboin River to the Missouri River, reaching a Mandan village near present Bismarck, North Dakota. This village, the smallest of six in the vicinity, comprised 130 lodges, each housing a number of families. The structures looked like hillocks, the round, earth-covered roofs being supported by sturdy interior posts. Having lost his interpreter and his presents, Vérendrye did not remain long at the village, but he left two of his men behind to learn the native language.

When these two returned to Fort La Reine the following September, they gave an interesting report. To the Mandan village had come from the western plains, as was their annual summer custom, a number of tribes well supplied with horses and bringing buffalo robes and furs to trade to the Mandans for corn and beans. One of these visiting tribes was said to have come from a far country where there were bearded white men who lived in houses built of brick and stone and who prayed by repeating *Jesus Marie* while holding books that had leaves like the husks of corn. This and other evidence they gave of contact with the Spaniards.

Vérendrye immediately sent his son Pierre back to the Mandans, directing him to seek the Western Sea. Unable to obtain Mandan guides, he returned; but in 1742 he went again to the Missouri, accompanied by his younger brother, Chevalier. The Mandans had never seen the ocean, but they said that the Horse Indians (probably the Cheyennes) to the west knew the way. So, on July 23, 1742, the Vérendrye brothers set out on horseback to find these Indians.

The long and interesting journey cannot be traced in detail here. After traveling 20 days in a west-southwest direction, they found the Beaux Hommes (Handsome Men), probably Crows. After remaining with this tribe for three weeks, the explorers moved on, taking a generally southwest course. After visiting several other tribes, they reached, in middle November, the Horse Indians, who were just then in great distress because the Snake Indians to the west had been destroying their villages. The Frenchmen next encountered the Bow Indians. "All the people of this country," writes Vérendrye, "have great numbers of horses, donkeys, and mules. They use them to carry their luggage and for riding, as much for the hunt as for their travels." Thus far afield had the Spanish horses found their way. The chief of the Bows could even speak a few words of the Spanish language. The Frenchmen understood from these Indians that the ocean was just beyond some western mountains, so the younger Vérendrye accompanied the Bows on a war expedition against the enemy Snake Indians who inhabited the mountain country. On January 12, 1743, the war party reached the mountains, which "were for the most part well wooded with all kinds of timber, and appeared very high." Upon finding a deserted Snake village, the Bow Indians became frightened and beat a hasty retreat. So Vérendrye did not reach the "shining summits," from whence he had expected to see the western ocean. The identity of the mountains reached has not been definitely established; but they were probably the Big Horn Mountains of Wyoming.

The return journey was in a generally eastward course which brought them to a village of the "Little Cherry Indians" (probably Aricaras) on the Missouri River, considerably south of the Mandans. On a hill overlooking the village, the Vérendryes buried, on March 30, 1743, an inscribed lead plate as a sign of French possession. The fortunate discovery, by some school children, of this plate 170 years later, on February 16, 1913, gives us the definite location. It is the hill that overlooks the town of Fort Pierre, South Dakota. From this point, the Frenchmen traveled northward to the Mandan villages and then back to Fort La Reine.

After the death of the elder Vérendrye, his successor, St. Pierre, continued up the Saskatchewan River to the Rockies, and there built Fort La Jonquière in 1752. Thus, by the middle of the eighteenth century, Frenchmen had reached the Rocky Mountains by practically every stream from the Red River to the Saskatchewan. They had reinforced La Salle's claim to the drainage basin of the Mississippi River by far-reaching journeys of discovery.

In the meantime, and during the last years of French dominion in the Mississippi Valley, their settlements had witnessed some growth. In Louisiana, rice, cotton, indigo, and tobacco were produced; fig and orange trees were introduced. The population of this lower country increased to 5,000 whites and 2,000 Negroes. But the agricultural production of the Illinois country had diminished, and the settlements there had been reduced to missions and to stations for the fur trade.

BIBLIOGRAPHY

The best general, comprehensive account of French achievements in America is by Francis Parkman, in numerous editions and generally in 12 volumes.   Briefer accounts are R. G. Thwaites, *France in America* (New York, 1905); W. B. Munro, *Crusaders of New France* (New Haven, 1918); G. M. Wrong, *The Conquest of New France* (New Haven, 1918).

The western phases of French activity are treated in: L. P. Kellogg, *The French Regime in Wisconsin and the Northwest* (Madison, 1925); W. F. Raney, *Wisconsin, a Story of Progress* (Chapter II) (New York, 1940); Justin Winsor, *The Mississippi Basin* (Boston, 1895); F. A. Ogg, *The Opening of the Mississippi* (New York, 1904); L. J. Burpee, *The Search for the Western Sea* (Toronto, 1908) and *Pathfinders of the Great Plains: a Chronicle of La Vérendrye and his Sons* (Glasgow, 1914); J. G. Shea, *Discovery and Exploration of the Mississippi Valley* (Albany, 1903); *South Dakota Historical Collections*, Vol. VII (Vérendrye Journal); A. C. Laut, *Pathfinders of the West* (New York, 1904); G. J. Garraghan, *Chapters in Frontier History* (Milwaukee, 1933); J. C. Parish, *The Man with the Iron Hand* (Boston, 1913); Marc de Villiers du Terrage, *Les Dernières Années de la Louisiane Française*, and *La Découverte du Missouri* (Paris, 1925); G. L. Nute, *The Voyageur* (New York, 1931); Jean Delanglez, *Some La Salle Journeys* (Chicago, 1938); H. E. Bolton, "French Intrusions into New Mexico, 1749–1752," in *The Pacific Ocean in History* (New York, 1917); Henri Folmer, "French Expansion toward New Mexico in the Eighteenth Century" (Ms., University of Denver, 1939).

The principal documentary source books dealing with the French in America are: Pierre Margry, *Découvertes et Etablissements des Français* (6 vols., Paris, 1879–1888); R. G. Thwaites (ed.), *The Jesuit Relations and Allied Documents* (73 vols., Cleveland, 1896–1903); and L. P. Kellogg, *Early Narratives of the Northwest, 1634–1699* (New York, 1917). See also I. J. Cox, *Journeys of René Robert Cavelier Sieur de La Salle* (2 vols., New York, 1905); and the journals of the Vérendryes in *South Dakota Historical Collections*, Vol. VII (1914).

4

SPANISH TEXAS AND THE FRENCH CHALLENGE

Spain HAD been in America many years before her frontier of settlement reached Texas. During that earlier period, she had developed a fairly elaborate system of administrative machinery. The colonies were considered personal possessions of the crown. Aiding the king in Spain were two important agencies: the Council of the Indies, the supreme legislative and administrative body; and the House of Trade, which controlled shipping and enforced the trade monopoly. In America viceroyalties were established (in Mexico, Peru, and so forth), at the head of which, as the representative of the king, stood the viceroy. An aid to this official, and a check upon him, was the *audiencia,* an administrative court. Subordinate to this was the governor, the head of the province. *Alcaldes* and *cabildos* governed the towns. Separate from this regular hierarchy of officialdom were certain independent fiscal officers and inspectors.

Much graft and corruption existed in the Spanish administrative system. Offices were regularly bought, and officials reimbursed themselves by appropriating a part of the taxes and by accepting payment for favors and exemptions. Trade and manufacturing were stultified by numerous restrictions. The labor supply, largely Indian and Negro, was forced and inefficient. Education was on a class basis, and society was organized on an elaborate caste system. Progress, economic and cultural, was retarded by numerous handicaps.

But despite shortcomings of policy and administration, Spanish dominion spread over a great part of the Americas. As the frontier of settlement advanced, certain agencies of expansion were evolved. And inasmuch as those parts of present United States which Spain once ruled were on the outer fringe of the Spanish colonial empire, Spanish frontier institutions have particular interest and importance for these "Spanish Borderlands."

Among the most effective of Spain's frontier institutions was the *mission*. Church and state were not separate in Spain, and ecclesiastical and civil objectives in the colonies were closely correlated. Gold, glory, and gospel have been listed by some as the triumvirate of forces motivating the early conquistadores. A passion to convert the heathen and a desire to conquer lands and peoples merged to bring about the conquest of new territories.

From the standpoint of the church, the duty of the mission was to spread the Faith; from the viewpoint of the Government, the purpose was to extend, hold, and civilize the frontiers. Because of this dual function, the missions were largely supported by the state; and, where political ends were paramount, the governmental support was correspondingly large. Through journeys to remote tribes, missionaries became important explorers. Their influence over the neophytes counteracted foreign influence and won valuable aid in holding back distant hostiles. "If the Indian were to become either a worthy Christian or a desirable subject, he must be disciplined in the rudiments of civilized life," writes Bolton. "Hence the missions were designed not only as Christian seminaries, but also as so many industrial and agricultural schools."

Closely associated with the Spanish mission were two other frontier institutions—the Indian *pueblo*, or village, and the *presidio*, or garrison. If wild Indians were to be successfully instructed, they must be kept in a definite location where discipline could be imposed. Sedentary tribes, like the Pueblos of New Mexico, could be taught in their native villages, but nomad tribes must be gathered and settled in a given locality before the civilizing process could make headway. Thus, the missionaries undertook to assemble the Indians into pueblos and there impart Christianity and church ritual along with instruction in farming, grazing, and the crafts that would make the natives self-supporting. These mission villages were usually provided with a limited self-government, but were rather closely supervised by the Spaniards.

To protect the missions and the accompanying Indian pueblos, garrisons, called *presidios*, were frequently provided. These were symbols of the authority of the state, and they helped to keep the Indians submissive to discipline. When some of the natives occasionally ran away from the missions, the soldiers of the presidio were employed to recover them.

In the occupancy of Texas, the mission, presidio, and pueblo were dominant agencies, as we shall presently see. In fact, in the founding of New Mexico, already effected, and in the settlement of Arizona and

California, accomplished subsequently, they were outstanding and significant institutions of Spanish expansion.

FIRST EXPEDITIONS INTO TEXAS

Spaniards entered the region of present Texas at an early date. Following the Cabeza de Vaca journey, already recounted, the next contact that came was incidental to expeditions headed for the New Mexico country. The Rodríguez party had descended the Conchos River and ascended the Rio Grande into New Mexico in 1581, and other parties soon followed the same route. Then Oñate, breaking a new trail due north through Chihuahua, reached the Rio Grande at the site of El Paso, and thence led his colonists northward to found New Mexico.

From the New Mexico base, trading and missionary expeditions early penetrated the plains east of the Rio Grande. One of these, led by Father Salas in 1632, visited the Jumano Indians on the upper Colorado River of Texas, some 500 miles southeast of Santa Fe. In 1650, a party of soldiers led by Captains Martín and Castillo reached the same locality, discovered pearls (so they claimed), and then continued eastward more than a hundred miles to visit the Tejas Indians. Thereafter, small parties went regularly to trade with these Indians of north central Texas.

In 1659 the mission of Guadalupe was founded at El Paso (on the west side of the Rio Grande, at present Ciudad Juarez), and soon a few settlers came into the district. Then the meager population was suddenly increased in 1680, when the Spanish settlers of New Mexico fled down the Rio Grande to El Paso to escape the fury of the native uprising under Popé. The El Paso region was now attached to New Mexico, and a presidio was established there in 1683 to defend it. In the same year, missions were founded farther south, in the La Junta district of Chihuahua, at the junction of the Conchos River and the Rio Grande. Within a year, seven churches had been built for the tribes living on both sides of the Rio Grande.

An expedition led by Captain Mendoza and Father López journeyed from this La Junta district to the Colorado River of Texas in 1684. The party reported the killing of 4,000 buffaloes and the baptizing of numerous Indians during its six weeks' stay in the region east of present San Angelo. Mendoza and López were so impressed with the country and its inhabitants that, after returning to La Junta, they went to Mexico City and prepared memorials asking for the establishment of missions and presidios in this Jumano country. The project would probably have been carried out had it not been for the distraction caused by French intrusion on the Gulf coast of Texas just at this time.

In the meantime, a Spanish advance toward Texas was being made up the eastern part of Mexico from Monterrey in the province of Nuevo Leon. This colony had been established in the latter half of the sixteenth century, and its capital, Monterrey, had become a frontier outpost. Indian hostility, however, had been so persistent that development was slow in this area. One expedition against the Indians, led by Azcué in 1655, crossed the Rio Grande from the Monterrey base and entered present Texas. One hundred Indians were killed and 70 taken prisoners. This was the first recorded entry into Texas from the south.

In 1670 Father Lários began work on this frontier. Soon missions and the town of Monclova were founded. From this area, in 1675, the Bosque-Lários expedition crossed the Rio Grande near Eagle Pass and penetrated as far as present Edwards County, Texas. At each stopping place, Lieutenant Bosque took formal possession of the country; and Father Lários, the Franciscan missionary, set up his portable altar, said mass, and preached to the Indians. Soon four missions were founded in Coahuila to serve the Indians of that region and also those north of the Rio Grande in present Texas.

Thus, we see that, from the bases of New Mexico, El Paso, Chihuahua, and Coahuila, Spanish expeditions had penetrated present Texas. But by 1685 no missions or settlements had been established in this country. This year, however, brought an important event, one that was to stimulate vigorous Spanish action in the region. La Salle landed his colony on the Texas coast.

First Missions Established

The La Salle project was a grave threat to Spanish dominion. Establishment of a French base on the Gulf Coast would separate Spanish Florida from Mexico and might be an entering wedge to win the middle area of North America for the French crown. The very development that was to occur under the French banner was seen in embryo by Spain at the outset. Little wonder, then, that alarm spread among Spanish colonial officials, and that steps were taken immediately to thwart the French design.

Several Spanish expeditions—four by sea and five by land—were sent out to discover the La Salle colony. One of the coastwise searchers found the wrecks of the French vessels and concluded that the colonists had been lost. Alonso de León, soon to be made Governor of Coahuila (in 1687), led all the searching expeditions by land. In 1686 he traveled east from Monterrey to the Rio Grande and followed the stream to its mouth. He conducted expeditions into Texas in 1687 and 1688, on the latter of which he captured a Frenchman among the

Indians. The next year he and the Franciscan, Father Massanet, led a party farther inland and reached the site of La Salle's colony. Scattered about the wooden fort were corpses, dead pigs, torn-up books, shattered weapons, and general debris—the result of an Indian raid. A fenced plot where corn had been raised and an asparagus bed were noted. Among the natives, León found two French captives.

The Spanish expedition found the Texas area large, fertile, and with a good climate. The Franciscan friar saw in the region a promising missionary field. Thus, under the triple urges of conquest of land, conversion of the Indians, and expulsion of the French, a plan was made for the occupation of Texas.

In 1690 Governor León, with 110 soldiers, escorted Massanet and three other missionaries across Texas. En route they passed the site of the La Salle establishment and paused while Massanet set fire to the remnant of the French fort. Late in May, they reached villages of the Asinai, or Texas, Indians—those called Cenis by the French—near the Neches River, on the east border of present Texas. The region was thickly settled, and about the towns were fields of corn, beans, pumpkins, and watermelons. The Spaniards learned that Frenchmen had visited these Indians and had chosen a site for a French settlement. To make a favorable impression, the Spaniards gave the Indians clothing and other presents, and were careful to exhibit every evidence of friendship.

Before the assembled Indians, on May 25, writes Governor León, "the feast of the Most Holy Sacrament was celebrated with all solemnity and a procession, all the officers and soldiers, the Indian governor and many of his people accompanying the procession and witnessing the high mass. Mass having been completed, the ceremony was enacted of raising the flag in the name of his Majesty (whom God protect), . . . I delivered to the governor [of the Indians] a staff with a cross, giving him the title of governor of all his people, . . . He accepted the staff with much pleasure, promising to do all that was desired of him, and the company fired three salutes." Trees were felled and, in three days, a church was completed. Here mass was said, and the royal standard raised; the mission of San Francisco was thus established. A second mission also was soon founded.

Governor León had planned to leave 50 soldiers here, but Father Massanet objected to the presence of so many, fearing their influence on the Indians. So when the main party, under León and Massanet, set out on the return to Coahuila, only three soldiers and three missionaries remained behind to hold Spanish dominion in Texas. For the soldiers, León left nine horses, guns, and ammunition; for the priests, "twenty-six loads of flour, twenty cows, two yoke of oxen, ploughs with ploughshares, axes, spades, and other little necessaries." A small, though short-lived, colony had been founded.

The east Texas region was now designated a *Province,* and Domingo Terán was appointed the first governor. In 1691 the new governor, accompanied by Father Massanet, journeyed to the new province and continued to the Red River. But they accomplished little. The priests objected to the establishment of presidios, so but nine soldiers were left with Massanet and the other missionaries. Before long, hostility developed among the Asinai. Crop failures and disease increased difficulties. Thereupon the Indians ordered the Spaniards to leave. With a military force so small, no effective defense could be presented, so in October, 1693, the priests burned the church and fled beyond the Rio Grande to Coahuila. For more than two decades thereafter, Texas was abandoned by the Spaniards.

But the Coahuila frontier of settlement was soon pushed eastward to the bank of the Rio Grande. Between 1699 and 1703, three missions and the presidio of San Juan Bautista were founded on the west side of the Rio Grande, some 30 miles below Eagle Pass. Settlers moved into the district, and it became an important trade center for the Indians on both sides of the river. Missionary and trading expeditions were conducted into Texas from this San Juan base.

SPANISH REOCCUPATION OF TEXAS

In the meantime came the fruition of La Salle's project, the planting of French colonies, under Iberville, in Louisiana (discussed in the preceding chapter). These French establishments on the Gulf Coast were made possible, in part, by a change in dynasties on the Spanish throne. The last of the Hapsburg line, favorable to Austria, died in 1700, and the powerful Louis XIV of France was able to place his grandson on the Spanish throne as Philip V. The new monarch was naturally favorable to France and offered little or no resistance to French colonization of Louisiana. But frontier Spanish officials and higher administrative officers were not so favorably inclined toward France. So rivalry continued and at times blazed into war.

It was fear of French expansion westward from the Mississippi that brought about the permanent occupancy of Texas by Spain. We noted previously the trading venture of St. Denis from Louisiana across Texas to Coahuila in 1714. On arriving at San Juan Bautista, he was arrested and news of his arrival was sent to Mexico City. Officials were alarmed at the French intrusion; and in a council of war, in August, 1715, they decided to reoccupy Texas. Domingo Ramón was placed in charge of the military and civil phases of the project, and the Franciscan Fathers Espinosa and Margil were given charge of the ecclesiastical branch. St. Denis, who, during his detention beyond the Rio Grande, had expressed a desire to become a Spanish subject and had married Manuela Sánchez, a niece of Captain Ramón, now, strangely enough, was employed to guide the Spanish expedition to east Texas.

In April, 1716, the colonists began their trek. There were 65 persons in the party, including nine missionaries and six women. Arms and ammunition for a presidio, agricultural implements for farms, and paraphernalia for the missions were carried by the colonists, while a thousand head of cattle, sheep, and goats were driven along in the train. Upon reaching east Texas, and with the help of the Indians, four Franciscan missions were founded immediately and a presidio with 25 soldiers was established. The next year, two more missions were founded. Through the influence of St. Denis and the presence of Spanish women among the settlers, the Indians were generally friendly.

But the maintenance of these outposts so far from the permanent bases of supplies was a difficult problem. In addition, the nearness of the French post of Natchitoches on the Red River and the possibility that Indian hostility might be engendered by the French made the Spaniards on this far-flung frontier very uneasy. Through numerous gifts of attractive merchandise, native loyalty was being won and held by the Frenchmen. To compete successfully, the Spaniards must have presents to offer. Also, they needed a halfway base on the long route across Texas. Proposals incorporating these needs gained the approval of the viceroy of Mexico, and he ordered establishment of the way station on the San Antonio River.

In the meantime St. Denis, after accompanying the Spaniards to east Texas, continued to Mobile, the French capital of Louisiana. He obtained trade goods, returned to Texas, and continued toward the Rio Grande. At his arrival in Coahuila in April, 1717, his goods were seized and he was sent to Mexico City. After release, he returned to the Rio Grande, disposed of his merchandise, and went again to the Mexican capital. Having sought in vain a government position there, he threatened to influence the Indians against the Spanish frontier settlements. Then, fearing imprisonment, he fled Mexico and made his way to the French outpost of Natchitoches.

In early April, 1718, a Spanish expedition, led by Governor Martin de Alarcón of Coahuila, crossed the Rio Grande into Texas. In this party, going to found the midway station in Texas, were 72 persons, including seven families. Over 500 horses, six droves of mules laden with clothing and supplies, herds of sheep and goats, and a flock of chickens were taken along. The colonists followed the regular trail to the San Antonio River, and there, on May 1, 1718, founded the mission of San Antonio de Valero, later known as the Alamo. About two miles upstream, they started the Villa of San Antonio de Béjar four days later. This was the beginning of the city of San Antonio, famous in Texas history. The missionary work in this field was placed in the hands of the Franciscan Father Olivares.

In the same year (1718) the French Governor Bienville founded New Orleans. The contemporary origins of San Antonio and New Orleans, the important centers, respectively, of Spanish and of French culture and institutions on the Gulf Coast, emphasize the development and the rivalry of Spain and France in the region. And presently the rivalry assumed a militant aspect.

In January, 1719, France declared war on Spain. Although the conflict originated in Europe, it spread immediately to the colonies. In June, the French at Natchitoches moved against the enemy outposts in east Texas; and the Spaniards, without making a defense, retreated to San Antonio. The French planned to conquer Coahuila and New Mexico, and to establish themselves on the Texas coast, but these designs were never consummated, although two unsuccessful expeditions were sent to Matagorda Bay in 1720 and 1721.

The reconquest of Texas for Spain was undertaken by the Marquis of Aguayo, now Governor of Coahuila. Largely at his own expense, he raised eight companies of cavalry (over 500 men) and 5,000 horses. These he led in November, 1720, from Monclova, whence he reached and strengthened San Antonio. He sent a force to Matagorda Bay, where his garrison anticipated La Harpe and the French expedition which later that year attempted to occupy the same place on the coast.

Before Aguayo could reach east Texas with his military force, peace had been declared. So at the Neches River St. Denis met him, announced the establishment of peace, and consented to the Spanish reoccupation of their abandoned locations. The presidio and six missions were re-established accordingly, and Aguayo, for good measure, added a presidio still farther east, at Los Adaes. This outpost was within 15 miles of French Natchitoches and well within the boundaries of present Louisiana (at Robeline). Aguayo fixed the hold of Spain on Texas. Four centers of settlement were established—Los Adaes, the Neches River, Matagorda Bay, and San Antonio. In these four districts were ten missions and four presidios. Texas was now set up as a Spanish province, with Los Adaes as capital. The little Arroyo Hondo came to be recognized as the Franco-Spanish boundary. Nearly a hundred years later (in 1819), the international boundary was moved west to the Sabine River, which to this day is the line between Louisiana and Texas.

FRANCO-SPANISH RIVALRY ON THE GREAT PLAINS

While Franco-Spanish interests were clashing in east Texas, a contest was being waged in the more northern interior. New Mexico, founded by Oñate at the end of the sixteenth century, had been undisturbed by foreign incursions during its first century. But, by 1700, rumors of the French approach from the east were causing alarm in Santa Fe. And not only was there fear of Frenchmen themselves, but more dreaded was French hostile influence among the Indian tribes of the plains.

Control of the Indians had always been a primary concern of the New Mexico settlers. Their very lives depended on it. Not only must the numerous villages be held in subjugation through the work of missionary, soldier, and diplomat, but the wild tribes of the plains must be properly met. These nomads might be won by trade, defied by defense, or disciplined by punitive expeditions.

In times of peace, these wanderers of the plains came to New Mexico with buffalo robes and dried meat to trade for knives, horses, and numerous trinkets and gewgaws. Annual fairs at Taos and Santa Fe developed into great trading institutions to which Indians from far afield came regularly. On other occasions, these Indians found it easier to steal than to buy their horses. So raids were frequent, and the Spanish settlements were in constant danger from marauders. As a result of trade and raid, the Indians of the plains were soon mounted, horses and Spanish goods passing from one tribe to another. So it was that when the first Frenchmen reached the Dakota and Montana country (after 1700), they encountered Indians already mounted on Spanish horses.

Occasionally some of the sedentary Pueblo Indians of New Mexico tired of the discipline and tribute to which they were subjected, and fled to the wild tribes of the plains. One such group ran away from Taos shortly after 1664 and was enslaved by Apaches in present eastern Colorado. Juan de Archuleta, with soldiers and Indian allies, brought them back. On the journey he heard that the Pawnees, farther to the northeast, were trading with Frenchmen. Frequently thereafter news came, through the Indians, of the presence of French traders among the tribes to the eastward. In 1699, a Navajo war party returned from a raid on the Pawnees and brought back to New Mexico French carbines, powder flasks, clothing, and the like.

In 1706, Juan de Ulíbarri, with 40 soldiers and 100 Indian allies, was sent to the eastern plains to recover some runaway Pueblo Indians. As interpreter he took a survivor of La Salle's Texas expedition, L'Archevêque, who had made his way to New Mexico. Ulíbarri took a generally northward course to the Napestle, or Arkansas, River at present Pueblo, Colorado, and then moved eastward to El Cuartelejo. This location, according to Dr. A. B. Thomas, translator of the Ulíbarri diary, was near the eastern border of present Colorado. Here, in the village of the El Cuartelejo Apaches, the fugitive Pueblos were found. Before returning with them, Ulíbarri took "possession" of this Apache country. After religious ceremonies performed by Father Aranz, Ulíbarri reports that

the royal Ensign Don Francisco de Valdés drew his sword, and I, after making a note of the events of the day and the hour on which we arrived, said in a clear, intelligible voice: "Knights, Companions and Friends: Let the broad new province of San Luis and the great settlement of Santo Domingo of El Cuartelejo be pacified by the arms of us who are the vassals of our monarch, king and natural lord, Don Philip V—may he live forever." The royal ensign said: "Is there anyone to contradict?" All responded, "No." Then he said, "Long live the king! Long live the king! Long live the king!" and cutting the air in all four directions with his sword, the ensign signaled for the discharge of the guns. After throwing up our hats and making other signs of rejoicing, the ceremony came to an end.

The Apaches said that they had recently been attacked by Pawnees and Frenchmen, and had killed a white man and his wife and captured a French gun. They asked the Spaniards to join in a campaign against the French and Pawnees who were distant "only a seven days' journey across level land," but Ulíbarri declined. Instead, he gathered up the Pueblo Indians and returned with them to New Mexico. The Ulíbarri diary gives the earliest description of a large area of frontier country and sheds important light on the Franco-Spanish contest for Indian allies and for control of the plains region east of the Rocky Mountains.

Despite evidence of French penetration, the New Mexico officials took no immediate steps to combat it. Instead, Indian hostility nearer home gave them concern. Some of the punitive campaigns against marauders became important exploring expeditions. One led by Hurtado in 1715, and directed against the Faraón Apaches, went east of Santa Fe 150 miles to the Canadian River. It encountered no Frenchmen. The Utes and Comanches were giving trouble on the northern frontier. News of their raids was carried to Viceroy Valero at Mexico City. At the same time a message from Captain Ramón reported French incursions into Texas. So the Viceroy, late in 1718, ordered countermoves against the French on both the Texas and New Mexico frontiers.

Governor Valverde of New Mexico was directed to lead an expedition against the Utes and Comanches, and to reconnoiter the French position on the northern plains. In the fall of 1719 the governor, with a force of 100 whites and over 650 Indian allies, set out from New Mexico. He entered southern Colorado, followed the foothills of the Rockies north to the Arkansas River, and then turned eastward. Apparently he was not anxious to meet the enemy and was more interested in hunting and camping pleasures than in fighting. But he did get news of the French. A delegation of Cuartelejo Apaches visited him and told of French establishments among the Pawnees and Jumanos, and of French guns being supplied those French allies.

After the outbreak of war between France and Spain in 1719, Viceroy Valero ordered Governor Valverde to establish a presidio and missions at El Cuartelejo on the northeastern plains, as an outpost against the French, and to reconnoiter beyond for enemy locations. The order for the presidio and missions was presently rescinded, but the reconnaissance was made. So far as we know, this expedition was the farthest penetration—into present Nebraska—made by the Spaniards of New Mexico into disputed territory. It was the climax of Spanish offensive moves from Santa Fe in the Franco-Spanish contest for the plains and prairies.

The expedition was led by Pedro de Villasur and embraced 45 white soldiers, 60 Indian allies, a priest (Father Mínguez), and the Frenchman L'Archevêque as interpreter. Taking a generally northeastward course from Santa Fe, they crossed the Arkansas River, reached El Cuartelejo, and continued to the South Platte River, which they called the Río Jesús María. Having found no signs of the French, they continued eastward. Upon reaching a Pawnee camp, they attempted to open a parley but were coldly received. Thereupon Villasur fell back. Foolishly, he encamped in an indefensible position in tall grass beside the river. (The location is usually identified as the vicinity of present North Platte, Nebraska, although some students believe it was farther east and near the junction of the Loup Fork with the Platte.) Unheedful of the signs that a hostile party was stalking his camp, Villasur took no adequate precautions for safety. At daybreak, August 13, 1720, his party was suddenly attacked by the Pawnees, possibly under the leadership of Frenchmen, as the surviving Spaniards reported. The surprise was so complete that the Spanish leader was killed before he could reach his weapons. The Pawnees circled the camp and poured into it a deadly hail of arrows. Only 13 Spaniards escaped the slaughter. These, together with their surviving Indian allies, made a bedraggled flight back to Santa Fe.

The defeat was a serious blow to the New Mexican settlements and to Spanish prestige on the northeastern frontier. A third of the meager garrison of Santa Fe was thus lost. And, although the Spaniards continued to talk a great deal about repelling the French, adequate troops were not available and no further military demonstration on the north-eastern plains was attempted. In fact, the New Mexico settlements were hard pressed to defend themselves against Ute and Comanche incursions; while farther out on the plains French influence was winning its way westward among the tribes.

As told in the preceding chapter, Bourgmond visited the Padoucas in 1724, and these Indians, who had previously traded with the Spaniards, offered to guide the Frenchmen to New Mexico. Other traders pushed westward from the Illinois country and by 1739 had reached Santa Fe. Officially, they were not welcomed by the Spaniards, who were still maintaining their exclusive and monopolistic trade policy. But there was insufficient military power in New Mexico to enforce exclusion, and, in addition, officials could usually be bribed by canny traders. Hence, as previously recounted, a number of French trading parties entered New Mexico during the middle eighteenth century and before the final expulsion of France from America.

TEXAS IN THE MIDDLE EIGHTEENTH CENTURY

Let us turn again to the Texas region, where Aguayo had established the Spanish hold on Texas. Rivalry continued between the Spanish and French colonials on the east Texas frontier, but no open war developed. The relationship of the two kings in Europe accounts for that. But the far-flung outposts on the northern frontiers of New Spain were constantly threatened by Indians and were maintained at considerable expense and effort. With a view to economy, Pedro de Rivera made a general inspection of frontier defenses during the years 1724–1728. He advocated certain reforms and advised retrenchment. As a result, the presidio on the Angelina River in eastern Texas was abandoned in 1729 and the garrisons at other places were reduced. Thereupon the friars moved three of their missions from east Texas and re-established them near San Antonio.

In the same locality the village of San Fernando de Béxar was founded in 1731, primarily by immigrants from the Canary Islands. With the increase in population and the corresponding safety from Indian attacks, farming areas expanded and cattle ranches developed in the San Antonio area. But the settlements were not yet self-supporting. From below the Rio Grande came pack-trains loaded with supplies for missions, presidios, and villages. The easternmost Spanish outposts, on the Louisiana border, obtained some supplies from their near neighbors, the French, at Natchitoches, and some food from the surrounding agricultural Indians.

During the 15 years following 1731, no new Spanish missions were founded in Texas, and the province was on trial as a buffer against the

French.   But the established outposts expanded their activities.   More Indians were gathered about the missions and were taught not only religion, but arts and crafts as well.   Some of the neophytes, smarting under restraint, occasionally ran away, but they were usually induced to return, sometimes by the help of the soldiers.   By 1745 the missions at San Antonio, with Indian labor, were raising corn, beans, sweet potatoes, cotton, and so forth.   The four Querétaran missions there raised 8,000 bushels of corn in 1745 and pastured over 9,000 head of horses, sheep, and goats on their ranches.   At one of the missions, shops were built for spinning and weaving cotton and woolen cloth. The Plains Apaches and other Indians to the west and north of San Antonio were a constant danger.   Campaigns were occasionally directed against them, the soldiers frequently being reinforced by mission Indians.

In east Texas, the missions were not so successful as those about San Antonio, for the Indians on the eastern border were more independent.   There they produced regularly their own food supplies and enjoyed the favor and trade of the French.   Hence, they were unwilling to submit to the restrictions and discipline that the Spanish mission system involved.

The period from 1745 until the transfer of Louisiana to Spain in 1762 witnessed marked expansion in Texas.   Three missions and a presidio were founded on the San Gabriel branch of the Brazos in the years 1745–1751.   The long-hostile Plains Apaches, now pressed southward by the enemy Comanches, asked for missions.   A presidio and a mission were founded far to the north, on the San Sabá River, in 1757. But the mission was sacked and two Franciscan missionaries were killed by the Comanches the next year, whereupon the mission was moved south to the upper Nueces River.

In the southwestern extremity of Texas, settlements were established during this period.   These were part of the movement to occupy the new province of Nuevo Santander, located principally south of the Rio Grande.   José de Escandón brought to the province over 3,000 settlers in 1749, and established them in some 20 settlements.   Some of these, notably Laredo and Dolores, were located north of the Rio Grande, in present Texas.

Frenchmen were operating among the Indians on the Gulf coast of eastern Texas in the middle of the eighteenth century.   Some of these traders, on the lower Trinity River, were arrested in 1754 and sent to Mexico.   To counteract the French influence and to safeguard the region, Spain established the presidio of San Augustín and a mission near the lower Trinity in the vicinity of present Houston in 1756–1757.   The French governor of Louisiana protested against the establishments and claimed the region.   The area remained in dispute until France's cession of Louisiana to Spain in 1762.

During the 15 years preceding that cession, which so changed the course of historical events, Texas had experienced considerable growth. Four new Spanish missionary fields had been opened, fresh trails broken, and virgin areas explored.   Four new presidios and eight missions had been established.

The French and Indian War began in the Ohio country in 1754 as a contest between England and France for colonial empire.   The border aspects of the struggle between the colonials of these nations will be treated in Chapter 7.   Here we call attention merely to relations between France and Spain.   From the beginning of the conflict, France attempted to win the aid of Spain.   But until the accession of Charles III to the Spanish throne in 1759, she made no headway.   The new and vigorous Spanish king early looked toward the acquisition of Louisiana, and French diplomats presently began to offer it to him in return for a cash loan and an early entry into the war on the side of France.   An alliance, known as the Family Compact, was made in August, 1761, but the territory was not yet ceded to Spain.   Because of Spanish aid to France, England declared war on Spain January 2, 1762.

England now sent a powerful fleet to the West Indies, and in August, 1762, Havana, looked upon by Spain as impregnable, was captured, together with twelve ships, stores, and specie valued at $15,000,000. Spain, stung by this loss, wanted to fight on; but France was anxious for peace.   She now offered Louisiana to Spain to reimburse her for any losses Spain might sustain through the war and also to win her to an immediate peace.   The move succeeded, and on November 3, 1762, the preliminaries of peace were signed.   On the same day Louis XV ceded to Spain the Louisiana country west of the Mississippi.   The French diplomats played it up as a generous gift, and Charles III dramatically and gallantly responded: "I say, no, no, my cousin [Louis XV] is losing altogether too much.   I do not want him to lose anything in addition for my sake, and would to heaven I could do yet more for him."   But the Spanish king accepted the territory nevertheless. Its eastern boundary was to run along the Mississippi River and through what was termed its eastern mouth—by way of the Iberville River and lakes Pontchartrain and Maurepas to the Gulf—thus placing New Orleans on the Spanish side.   Under the final terms of peace in 1763, Spain had to give up Florida to England, but she regained Havana.   France retained a few islands in the West Indies, but was forced to relinquish Canada and all French and Spanish territory east of the Mississippi to England.

France was thus eliminated from North America.   In the long and bitter contest with England, she had been defeated. Even her more friendly rivalry with Spain for possession of the trans-Mississippi country, a contest that had been carried on for more than half a century, brought her no permanent dominion. Her holdings west of the Mississippi were lost along with her other American possessions, more or less as an incidental result of the English victory. In the final peace of 1763, the Mississippi River was thus established as an international boundary, and England and Spain now faced each other across the Father of Waters.

BIBLIOGRAPHY

For accounts of the early explorations and first missionary efforts in Texas, see: Herbert E. Bolton, *Spanish Exploration in the Southwest, 1542–1706* (New York, 1916). Original accounts of the expeditions are therein reproduced in translation, together with introductions and explanatory notes.

Accounts of the settlement of Texas are found in the following: R. C. Clark, *The Beginnings of Texas, 1684–1718* (Austin, 1907); H. H. Bancroft, *History of the North Mexican States and Texas* (San Francisco, 1884); C. W. Hackett, *Pichardo's Treatise on the Limits of Louisiana and Texas* (Austin, 1931); W. E. Dunn, *Spanish and French Rivalry in the Gulf Region of the United States, 1678–1702* (Austin, 1917); Fray F. Céliz, *Diary of the Alarcón Expedition into Texas, 1718–1719,* translated and annotated by F. L. Hoffman (Los Angeles, 1935); L. F. Hill, *José de Escandón and the Founding of Nuevo Santander* (Columbus, Ohio, 1926); H. E. Bolton, *Texas in the Middle Eighteenth Century* (Berkeley, 1915); C. E. Castaneda, *The Mission Era; The Finding of Texas, 1519–1693,* and *The Mission Era; The Winning of Texas, 1693–1731* (Austin, 1936).

Among important articles in historical magazines, the following may be noted: H. E. Bolton, "The Spanish Occupation of Texas, 1519–1690," in the *Southwestern Historical Quarterly,* XVI, 1–26; and "The Location of La Salle's Colony on the Gulf of Mexico," in the *Mississippi Valley Historical Review,* II, 165–182; C. C. Shelby, "St. Denis's Second Expedition to the Rio Grande, 1716–1719," in the *Southwestern Historical Quarterly,* XXVII, 190–216; E. H. West, "De Leon's Expedition of 1689," in the *Quarterly of the Texas State Historical Association,* VIII, 199–224; E. C. Buckley, "The Aguayo Expedition into Texas and Louisiana, 1719–1722," *ibid.,* XV, 1–65; M. A. Hatcher, "The Expedition of Don Domingo Terán de los Ríos into Texas," in *Preliminary Studies of the Texas Catholic Historical Society,* II; P. P. Forrestal, "The Venerable Padre Fray Antonio Margil de Jesus," *ibid.;* A. S. Aiton, "The Diplomacy of the Louisiana Cession," in the *American Historical Review,* XXXVI, 701–720.

The outstanding work on the northward expansion of New Mexico is A. B. Thomas, *After Coronado* (Norman, Okla., 1935). The original accounts of the expeditions are presented in translation and accompanied by introductions and notes. Other general works on New Mexico are R. E. Twitchell, *The Leading Facts of New Mexican History* (2 vols., Cedar Rapids, Iowa, 1911); R. E. Twitchell (ed.), *The Spanish Archives of New Mexico* (2 vols., Cedar Rapids, Iowa, 1914); H. H. Bancroft, *History of Arizona and New Mexico* (San Francisco, 1889). See also A. B. Thomas, "Massacre of the

Villasur Expedition," in *Nebraska History*, VII, 68–81; C. C. Shelby, "Projected Attacks upon the Northeastern Frontier of New Spain, 1719–1721," in *Hispanic American Historical Review*, XIII, 457–472; A. B. Thomas, "Spanish Expeditions into Colorado," in the *Colorado Magazine*, I, 289–300; H. E. Bolton, "French Intrusions into New Mexico, 1749–1752," in *The Pacific Ocean in History* (New York, 1917); C. W. Hackett, "Policy of the Spanish Crown Regarding French Encroachments from Louisiana, 1721–1762," in *New Spain and the Anglo-American West, Historical Contributions Presented to Herbert Eugene Bolton* (privately printed, 1932).

5

BEGINNINGS OF ARIZONA AND CALIFORNIA

Having traced to 1763 the general story of Spain's expanding frontier in the Texas and New Mexico regions, we turn now to the Pacific Slope area and note the comparable advance that resulted in the initial settlement of present Arizona and California.

Exploration of the California Coast

The great expeditions of Coronado and Cabrillo in the first half of the sixteenth century had made known the Pacific Slope area up to the mouth of the Colorado River and had revealed the outline of the Pacific Coast as far north as southern Oregon. Failure of those expeditions to realize their golden hopes discouraged for some decades further ventures in that direction. But in the meantime there were developments across the Pacific and in the Philippines that affected California.

After Magellan's historic crossing of the Pacific (1519–1521), Cortés had built the shipyard of Zacatula on the west coast of Mexico and in 1527 had sent Saavedra across the Pacific to engage in the spice trade of the far East. Viceroy Mendoza, as mentioned previously, divided Alvarado's fleet and in 1542 dispatched Cabrillo up the California coast and Villalobos across the Pacific. The latter reached the Philippines, but was expelled by native hostility. Then Legazpi sailed from Mexico in 1565 and began the Spanish conquest of the Philippines. He was directed to discover a return route to Mexico, for heretofore the voyages had all been from America across the Pacific. The westward journey was easy, but it was difficult to get back. This undertaking was placed in the hands of Andrés de Urdaneta, who, by sailing northeast into the course of the Japan Current and the westerly winds, succeeded in reaching the North American coast and in following it down to Mexico.

This practicable return route, that appears so roundabout on a flat map but in reality is as short as the latitudinal course, was thereafter continuously used and served to tie the Philippines to Mexico. Those islands were presently made a part of the viceroyalty of New Spain, and a lucrative trade in silks, spices, and chinaware developed between these far-flung sections of Spain's colonial empire. For some 200 years Manila galleons regularly crossed the Pacific, carrying their precious cargoes to Mexico. And during that long period these vessels, sailing down the Pacific Coast of North America, were the principal contact with California.

But the Pacific was not exclusively a Spanish sea in those early colonial years. Elizabethan seadogs and Dutch freebooters ventured through the Straits of Magellan or around the Horn to attack Spanish treasure ships on the South American coast. The most famous of such voyages, and one having an interesting connection with California history, was that of Francis Drake, the colorful English seaman who has already been mentioned. After entering the Pacific, in his *Golden Hinde,* he began his series of remarkable raids upon the unsuspecting Spaniards. At Valparaiso he captured a vessel from which he took 1,770 jars of wine, and gold worth $24,000. At other points he made comparable seizures, and climaxed all on March 1, 1579, with the capture of the Peruvian treasure ship bound for Panama. From this he took, says the chronicler,

certaine quantities of jewels and precious stones, 13. chests of ryals of plate, 80. pound waight in gold; 26. tunne of vncoyned siluer; two very faire siluer drinking boules, and the like trifles, valued in all at about 360,000. pezoes. We gaue the master a little linnen and the like, for these commodities.

After raiding the Nicaraguan and Mexican coasts, and obtaining Spanish charts and instructions for sailing the Pacific, the ruddy buccaneer steered northward to seek a haven and await the favorable season for his voyage to the Moluccas. Thus, he came into the North Pacific, and after touching at several points, cast anchor in a "fit harborough" that is now generally identified as Drake's Bay, some 30 miles north of the Golden Gate. He landed on June 17, Old Style (June 27, new calendar), 1579, and was to remain here for five weeks. He built a stone fortification to protect his men from the Indians of the region. But if we can believe the chaplain of the *Golden Hinde,* there was little need of defense, for the natives believed the armored and bearded Englishmen to be gods and lavished gifts upon them. The local chieftain, the "Great Hyóh," came with a large retinue to pay homage to his visitors, bearing a feathered headdress and bone necklace for the white god. In knitted headgear and fur coat, the chief led his naked but gaily painted followers in a ceremonial dance, the maneuvers accented by appropriate chanting. Then followed an exhibition of native eloquence which the Englishmen interpreted as "supplications that hee [Drake] would take the Prouince and kingdome into his hand, and become their king and patron." And, "that they might make vs indeed beleeue that it was their true meaning and intent; the king himselfe, with all the rest, with one consent and with great reuerence, ioyfully singing a song, set the crowne vpon his head; inriched his necke with all their chaines; and . . . honoured him by the name Hyóh."

The gallant Captain was willing to accommodate the natives. With gold and silver his ship was already overburdened, but native goodwill and title to new lands he could safely carry. "Wherefore, in the name and to the vse of her most excellent maiesty [Queen Elizabeth], he tooke the scepter, crowne, and the dignity of the sayd countrie into his hand."

Drake called the new land New Albion, "and that for two causes," says the chaplain, "the one in respect of the white bancks and cliffes [reminiscent of old England], which lie toward the sea: the other, that it might have some affinitie, euen in name also, with our owne country, which was sometime so called" [by the Romans]. Thus was the first New England located on the Pacific Coast, and it antedated the landing at Plymouth Rock by 41 years. As a token of possession, the newly crowned Hyóh of New Albion nailed to a "faire great poste" a brass plate proclaiming English dominion.

In the summer of 1936, near the north shore of San Francisco Bay, was found an old brass plate, covered with what at first appeared to be unintelligible scratches. It came into the hands of Professor Herbert E. Bolton, who cleaned and deciphered it, and after thorough study declared it "California's choicest archeological treasure." The inscription reads:

BEE IT KNOWNE VNTO ALL MEN BY THESE PRESENTS
IVNE 17 1579

BY THE GRACE OF GOD AND IN THE NAME OF HERR MAIESTY QVEEN ELIZABETH OF ENGLAND AND HERR SVCESSORS FOREVER I TAKE POSSESSION OF THIS KINGDOME WHOSE KING AND PEOPLE FREELY RESIGNE THEIR RIGHT AND TITLE IN THE WHOLE LAND VNTO HERR MAIESTIES KEEPEING NOW NAMED BY ME AN TO BEE KNOWNE VNTO ALL MEN AS NOVA ALBION.

FRANCIS DRAKE.

The authenticity of this brass plate has been fully established by metallurgical and other tests by Professor Colin Fink of Columbia University.

Leaving the California coast, Drake crossed the Pacific to the East Indies, took on some spices, sailed around the Cape of Good Hope, and eventually reached England. Here, as the first Englishman to circumnavigate the globe, and a bearer of rich treasures, he was acclaimed by the populace and knighted by "good Queen Bess."

Although other freebooters followed Drake into Pacific waters and some of them conducted profitable raids, none seriously attempted to establish territorial dominion on those distant shores. But the piratical raids caused alarm among Spanish officials, who proceeded to arm the galleons and increase naval forces at their Pacific ports. The danger threatening the Manila galleons suggested the desirability of establishing on the California coast a port of call, where warnings could be given of pirate danger. Also, a California station could serve as a supply and repair depot. In those early years, when scurvy was the scourge of the sea, and when it was not uncommon on a long voyage for half the crew to die of that dread disease because of lack of raw foods, a way station on the coast of California could offer succor to vessels in distress.

Accordingly, orders were given that exploration of the California coast be conducted by Manila galleons bound for Mexico. The most important of such early reconnaissances was that of Sebastián Rodríguez Cermeño, who sailed from Manila in the 200-ton *San Augustín* on June 4, 1595. On board he carried a knocked-down launch to be assembled for use in exploration work. Cermeño reached the California coast in the vicinity of Cape Mendocino and landed first at Drake's Bay, just north of the harbor of San Francisco. The launch was assembled, the shore explored, and contact with the Indians effected. On November 30, a storm arose that wrecked the *San Augustín* and sent its cargo of beeswax and fine porcelain to the bottom of the sea. Cermeño was left with only his launch, but with this open boat he continued his project. Following the shore closely and landing occasionally to obtain food from the Indians, he continued his hazardous course. He made a surprisingly accurate survey of the coast from 41° to 30°, but thereafter, because of the distress of his 70 men, he was induced to forego further exploration and continue an uninterrupted voyage to Mexico.

The loss of the *San Augustín* induced a decision to conduct future explorations of the California coast with smaller, unladen vessels sent from the Mexico base, rather than risk the galleons from the Philippines in such dangerous work. The first such undertaking of importance was led by Sebastián Vizcaíno, a merchant interested in the pearl fisheries of Lower California.

With three ships, about 200 men—including an expert map maker

and three friars—and provisions for 11 months, he set sail from Aca-
pulco on May 5, 1602. After fighting the usual head winds and experiencing numerous other difficulties, he reached, on November 10,
what the diarist recorded as "a port which must be the best to be found
in all the South Sea [Pacific Ocean]." Two days later, on the day of
Saint Didicus (San Diego), he celebrated mass and christened the bay
with the name it still bears—San Diego. Continuing up the California
coast, he rechristened with their present names Santa Catalina Island,
Santa Barbara Channel, Point Conception, Carmel, and Monterey Bay,
the last named being given the name of the Viceroy of Mexico. Vizcaíno pronounced Monterey "the best port that could be desired," an-
swering all requirements of a suitable port for the Manila galleons.

This description and appraisal are not justified by the facts, but "it
was precisely this departure from strict accuracy," writes Chapman,
"that had the most effect; the legend of the port of Monterey became
one of the moving factors for a century and a half in Spanish expansion
to the northwest." From this point one of the ships was sent back to
Mexico, carrying the sick and bearing reports of the voyage. It eventually made port, after having lost 25 of the 34 men on board.

On January 3, 1603, Vizcaíno continued the voyage northward.
After missing San Francisco Bay and visiting Drake's Bay, he reached
Cape Mendocino. Not far beyond this point he turned the prow
of his ship toward home, and in due time his scurvy-infested crew
reached port.

Royal orders were issued that Vizcaíno establish a settlement at
Monterey, but a new viceroy, who was opposed to the plan, now came
to office in Mexico. Contending that such a colony was not needed
and that it might serve the purposes of foreign freebooters, he induced
the Council of the Indies to abandon the project. A century and a
half elapsed before Spain planted her first colony in present California
(1769). Throughout that intervening period, interest continued in the
peninsula of Lower California, and many expeditions went thither to
seek pearls, but Upper California (the region of the present state) was
largely neglected throughout those many decades.

The Beginnings of Arizona

In the meantime, the frontier settlement had gradually moved northward by land along the Pacific Coast of Mexico. Much of this advance
was led by missionaries. The settlement of Sinaloa was begun at
Culiacán in 1531. Sixty years later, the Jesuits entered the province
and began their earnest labors among the Indians. Slowly they moved
northward, winning tribe after tribe and founding missions in one valley after another. With kindness, gifts, and ceremonies they gathered

the natives about the missions, instructed them in Christianity, and taught them simple arts and crafts and the cultivation of the soil. Settlers followed the missionaries, establishing ranches and towns and developing the grazing, agricultural, and mineral resources of the region. By the middle of the seventeenth century, the mission frontier had reached the upper Sonora Valley, where bases were established for further advances.

Into this region came a great missionary, one destined to be the outstanding pioneer in the region that would become Arizona. This intrepid leader was Eusebio Francisco Kino, Italian by birth, Bavarian by education, Spanish missionary by consecration. He arrived in Mexico in 1681, and six years later, after a year or more in Lower California, came to the northwestern frontier of Mexico, to Pimería Alta, land of the upper Pimas, the region comprising northern Sonora and southern Arizona of today. On the San Miguel River of northern Sonora, Father Kino built the mission of Dolores. It was the base for his extensive labors and his home station for nearly a quarter of a century.

Kino began his exploration of present Arizona in 1691 by visiting a Pima village on the Santa Cruz River. The next year he entered the valley of the San Pedro to the eastward. In 1694 he descended the Santa Cruz to the Gila River, and there examined the Casa Grande, an impressive prehistoric ruin. During the years 1697–1699 he made three journeys by different routes to the Gila. These exploratory tours were also missionary journeys on which he taught and baptized at every opportunity. While in Pimería Alta, Father Kino alone baptized 4,000 Indians.

Despite his ardor for ecclesiastical conquests, Kino did not neglect material things. He developed large farms and extensive stock ranches, from which he was able to send supplies to new and struggling missions. At one time he sent 700 head of cattle across the Gulf of California by boat to the hard-pressed missions of Lower California. In 1696 he prepared for the founding of missions in Arizona by establishing cattle ranches in the valleys of the Santa Cruz and the San Pedro. Then in 1700, with the aid of the local Indians, he built the adobe mission of San Xavier del Bac, a few miles south of present Tucson. The mission still stands, an honored shrine of Arizona history. Within the next two years, he founded two more missions in the Santa Cruz Valley of present Arizona and reinforced them with farms and stock ranches.

Altogether, this missionary explorer, during his 24 years in Pimería Alta, made over 50 journeys, ranging from 100 to 1,000 miles in length. He produced good maps of the regions traversed. In 1702 he reached the mouth of the Colorado River and made known the fact, lost during the preceding century, that Lower California was a peninsula instead of an island. Although committed to kindness, he could employ force when necessary. More than once he marshalled his Pima neophytes and sent them to war against hostile Apaches. And on the return of his emissaries he helped count the scalps, that his warriors might receive in full the bounties offered by the government.

When Kino died, in 1711, a fellow missionary said of him: "He died as he had lived, with extreme humility and poverty. . . . No one ever saw in him any vice whatsoever, for the discovery of lands and the conversion of souls had purified him. . . . He was merciful to others but cruel to himself."

For two decades after the passing of Kino, there was little Spanish activity in Arizona. Then Apache depredations brought a military inspection and a missionary revival. A new band of Jesuits, mostly Germans, came to this frontier in 1732, and reoccupied some of the abandoned missions.

With the finding of silver nuggets at Arizonac—in the Altar Valley of northern Sonora, just south of the present Arizona line—a mining "rush" occurred in 1736. It is from this silver camp and mining boom that Arizona derives its name. Within five years, the Arizonac mines had played out and the camp was abandoned, but the mining rush had given rise to plans to advance the frontier northward. The Jesuits were assigned the Moqui country north of the Gila, but they had difficulty in reaching it because the way was blocked by Apaches. Father Keller, who crossed the Gila in 1743, was driven back by these hostiles. The next year Father Sedelmayr, another German missionary, ascended the Colorado River to Bill Williams Fork. These Jesuits urged the occupation of these areas as bases for advance to the Moqui country of northern Arizona and to California. But Indian wars and needs in the Texas country caused postponement.

In 1751 the Pimas revolted. Several missionaries and over a hundred settlers were killed on the Arizona border. Governor Parrilla suppressed the uprising the following year and established two new presidios—at Altar in northern Sonora and at Tubac in southern Arizona. Quarrels between the Governor and the Jesuits ensued, and Indian troubles continued. A number of villages were destroyed by the Indians, but several small Spanish settlements grew up about the presidios. By 1763 there were about 1,500 persons in these presidios and settlements of Pimería Alta, and eight missions were functioning in the area. Most of these settlements still exist.

In 1767 the Jesuits were expelled from all Spanish dominions by the king of Spain. Their place in Pimería Alta was taken by the Franciscan order, with Francisco Garcés in charge of the mission of San Xavier del Bac and the surrounding area. Under his able administration, the territory that had been lost during the Indian uprisings was regained. The site of Tucson was occupied by a Spanish settlement, and in 1776 the presidio of Tubac was moved northward and established at Tucson. In addition to his work in Arizona, Garcés explored a route to California (as we shall presently see), and southern Arizona became the outfitting base for the colony that was to found San Francisco, California.

THE FOUNDING OF CALIFORNIA

The planting of the first missions and settlements in present California—the Alta (Upper) California of that day—was undertaken from bases in the peninsula of Baja (Lower) California. Spanish interest in Lower California dates back to the days of Cortés, and many were the attempts to found settlements on the peninsula. But not until the end of the seventeenth century did any such efforts succeed. In 1687 Baja California was placed in the hands of the Jesuits, who were given military and civil authority. Salvatierra, in charge of the work here, faced unusual difficulties, especially because of the sterility of the country. But with persistence and through aid from other regions, especially Sonora, foundations were laid; and by the time of Salvatierra's death in 1717, there were five missions in the middle area of Lower California, of which Loreto was the capital. His successors occupied the southern end of the peninsula. Explorations were made northward, with a view to opening a supply route by land around the head of the Gulf of California. Between 1752 and 1767 three missions were established in the northern section of the peninsula. When the Jesuits were expelled (1767), their places in Lower California were taken by Franciscans, with Junípero Serra as president. Thus were bases founded in Baja California from which could proceed the important advance into Alta California.

Ever since the days of Vizcaíno, there had been some thought of occupying the port of Monterey. But throughout the long years, the declining resources of Spain had been absorbed elsewhere. Now, however, Spain saw foreign threats to her dominion in the Pacific, and the project for outposts in California was revived. Russian activity in the north Pacific was the important stimulating force.

During the seventeenth century, Russia had pushed across Siberia; and in the early years of the next century, her fur traders continued their eastward thrust. Vitus Bering, a Dane in charge of Russian exploratory work, made expeditions (1725–1741) into north Pacific waters, discovering Bering Strait and coasting the American mainland.

His report of fur resources brought Russian fur men along the 1,000-mile string of Aleutian Islands toward Alaska. Rumors of this Russian advance caused concern in Spain, and orders were sent the Viceroy of Mexico to investigate the matter. The danger, however, was rather remote and might well have produced no tangible results had it not been for the presence on the Spanish frontier of a man of action—José de Gálvez. He embraced the occasion not merely to investigate the Russian danger, but actually to launch an important countermove and effect the colonization of Alta California.

The project was to be carried out in typical Spanish fashion, soldier and friar going side by side to found the twin outposts of presidio and mission. While on his visit to Lower California in the summer of 1768, Gálvez organized and directed the colonizing expeditions. Don Gaspar de Portolá, Governor of California, was placed in charge of the military and civil phases of the venture, while Father Serra was given control of the ecclesiastical branch. Expeditions were to be sent by both land and sea.

The *San Carlos* and the *San Antonio,* which had been built to carry soldiers and supplies for prosecution of the Indian war in Sonora, were diverted to the new enterprise. The vessels were repaired in Lower California and were there loaded with men and supplies for the farther voyage. The *San Carlos,* of but 200 tons burden, set sail on January 9, 1769, under command of Vicente Vila. There were 62 men on board, including soldiers, two blacksmiths, and a baker for the new settlements. Agricultural implements, seeds for planting, tools, provisions, and church paraphernalia were taken along. The second ship, with Juan Pérez as captain, set forth on February 15. The number of passengers is not definitely known.

The land contingent was formed in two parties. The first of these, under the leadership of Captain Rivera, veteran commander at Loreto, comprised 25 soldiers, three muleteers, 42 Christian Indians, and Father Crespi. As they moved northward along the peninsula, they gathered some 400 domestic animals from the various missions and also obtained supplies for the journey. From Velicatá, the northernmost outpost, they set forth, March 24, on their 1,000-mile journey over an unexplored route. The men were provided with axes, picks, shovels, and crowbars to open a trail, while the soldiers were equipped with leather jackets and bull-hide shields for protection against Indians. With rugged mountains to climb and waterless desert stretches to traverse, they encountered many difficulties, even though no fighting with hostile natives occurred. Rivera reached San Diego Bay on May 14 and found the two ships lying at anchor. He had covered his first 400 miles. Francisco Ortega, chief scout, by going ahead every day to select a camp site and returning to camp with the caravan, had covered most of the route three times.

The voyagers by sea had endured the greater hardships. The *San Antonio*, the second ship to sail, had been at sea for 55 days; and when it reached port on April 11, most of the men were sick or disabled, though no lives had been lost. But the *San Carlos*, which took twice as long as its sister ship to make the voyage, arrived on April 29 in a terrible plight. Twenty-four of the crew had died of scurvy, and everyone else was afflicted with the disease. Even after they landed, scurvy continued to take a heavy toll.

Portolá and Serra, with the second land party, did not leave Velicatá until May 15. Following the Rivera trail and traveling in a favorable season, they made the journey with comparative ease and reached San Diego on July 1. With the arrival of the leaders and the reuniting of the four parties, formal possession was taken of the region. Father Serra said mass, the *Te Deum* was sung, and salutes were fired.

The condition of these California pioneers was not heartening. Ninety-three men had died on the *San Carlos* or since landing. Only a score of the Christian Indians remained, the others having died or deserted. Of the nearly 300 persons who set out from Lower California by land and sea, only 126 were now alive at San Diego, and many of these were sick. But Governor Portolá had been ordered to occupy Monterey, so with determination he proceeded to comply with instructions. Captain Pérez and a meager crew of eight men were sent back to San Blas in the *San Antonio* to obtain men and supplies. On July 14 Portolá, with 62 men, set out by land for Monterey, while Serra and a few companions remained behind to care for the invalids. On July 16, 1769, Father Serra formally founded the mission of San Diego, the first in Alta California.

Of Portolá's northward march, the doughty Captain writes:

The sick being placed under a hut of poles which I had had erected, I gathered the small portion of food which had not been spoiled in the ships, and went by land to Monterey with that small company of persons, or rather say skeletons, who had been spared by scurvy, hunger and thirst. We reached Monterey after struggling thirty-eight days against the greatest hardships and difficulties.

Portolá's route northward was chiefly along the coast. Pasture and water were plentiful most of the way, and the Indians were friendly. At Los Angeles River an earthquake was felt that "lasted about half as long as an Ave María." Beyond San Simeon, they crossed the Lucía Mountains with difficulty and reached the Salinas Valley, which they followed for six days before again reaching the coast, at Monterey Bay.

Portolá recognized the landmarks of Monterey Bay, but failed to find here anything like the fine harbor that was expected, so he concluded that it must be farther on.

He resumed his journey and presently discovered a forest of the giant redwoods. At Half Moon Bay he was able to see Point Reyes and to recognize Drake's Bay. Apparently he had passed the harbor of Monterey, if any such existed, but he decided to explore a little farther. Ortega, the scout, and some hunters seeking game in the hills to the eastward came almost simultaneously upon a great inland body of water. They had stumbled upon San Francisco Bay! For centuries ships had coasted the California shore line, but it remained for a land party to discover the region's greatest port. The diarist, Father Crespi, records: "It is a very large and fine harbor, such that not only all the navy of our most Catholic Majesty but those of all Europe could take shelter in." On the return trip supplies ran low. Writes Portolá:

I ordered that at the end of each day's march, one of the weak old mules which carried our baggage and ourselves should be killed . . . . we shut our eyes and fell to on that scaly mule like hungry lions. We ate twelve in as many days, ... At last we entered San Diego, smelling frightfully of mules.

They found conditions there deplorable. Numbers of the sick had died; hostile natives had pillaged the camp and even stripped the invalids of clothing; provisions were scarce. There was some talk of abandoning California. But instead, Rivera was sent by land to Loreto for stock and supplies, and the brave remnant stayed on. From the Indians some food was obtained by the barter of clothing. Months passed. Said the valiant Serra: "If I see that along with the food hope vanishes, I shall remain alone with Father Crespi and hold out to the last breath."

Finally relief came, the *San Antonio* returned. To the faithful friars it seemed that this supply ship had arrived in answer to their *novena*— a nine-day vigil of prayer. California was saved.

Portolá returned to Monterey by land while Serra went by water, and in June, 1770, they established the presidio of Monterey and the mission of San Carlos. The "royal fortress" was built of logs and earth, equipped with small cannon, and manned with 20 men. Thus was the faraway Russian threat defied and Spain's frontier on the Pacific Coast advanced 900 miles.

After the outposts were established, Portolá sailed back to Mexico. The news he carried was joyfully received in the capital of New Spain. The Viceroy "ordered a general ringing of the bells of the cathedral and all the other churches, in order that all might realize the importance of the Port of Monterey to the Crown of our monarch, and also to give thanks for the happy success of the expeditions." A mass of thanksgiving was celebrated in the cathedral, with the whole viceregal court in attendance.

But the Spanish foundations in California were yet far from secure. During the first years, the military stations were weak; the missionary efforts, almost fruitless. In 1770 there were 43 soldiers in California, and these were rough half-breeds who frequently did more harm than good. They mistreated the Indian women, and their conduct caused several Indian outbreaks. The Indians were slow to respond to the teachings of the missionaries. There was not a single baptism during the first year at San Diego, and none at Monterey for six months. But the Franciscans were not easily discouraged. They founded two more missions—San Antonio and San Gabriel—in 1771 and established San Luis Obispo the next year. By 1773 there were five missions and two presidios in California, though the Spanish population comprised but 61 soldiers and 11 friars. The urgent needs were for provisions and supplies, domestic animals, and settlers—especially women.

It is hard for us now to understand how, in a land of such bountiful natural resources, there was then such poverty and such utter dependence on the importation of food and supplies from the outside. But crops were not raised successfully during the first years, and it took time for domestic animals to increase. Lower California had been practically stripped for the initial foundings farther up the coast, and so could contribute little more. Supply ships from Mexico were, therefore, the chief reliance, but these were too small and the hazards of the sea too great for the carriage of families of settlers or herds of livestock. Land routes must be discovered, over which colonists might trek and cattle be driven, if the California outposts were to be made permanent.

The pioneers in achieving this goal were Francisco Garcés and Juan Bautista de Anza, leaders in Sonora and Arizona. Father Garcés, from his mission of San Xavier del Bac, journeyed northward to the Gila and the Colorado rivers, and in 1771 crossed the Yuma and the California deserts to the foot of the Sierras. Captain Anza and 20 soldiers, with Garcés as guide, carried the project farther and opened a land route from Tubac (near Tucson) to Monterey in 1774. After returning to Arizona and going to Mexico City, he was directed to lead a soldier colony to San Francisco Bay. In Sinaloa and Sonora he recruited some 250 persons—soldiers, friars, and 30 families. Like most pioneers in America, these settlers of California were poor people. Most of them were destitute and, before they could set out, had to be given their pay in advance in the form of clothing and supplies. Two hundred cattle were driven along to stock their settlement.

Anza and his settlers left Tubac, Arizona, in late October, 1775. Descending the Santa Cruz and the Gila, they reached the Colorado River. Here, at the site of modern Yuma, they erected a cabin, and Father Garcés and a companion remained to found a mission among the Yumas. Anza now followed his former trail and arrived at Monterey in March, 1776, having successfully guided his colonists on their 1,000-mile trek. After exploring the San Francisco Bay region, they selected sites for their establishments. All lived for the first few weeks at the mission, while the presidio was being built. The presidio was formally dedicated in September, and the mission of San Francisco de Asís (later called Dolores) in October. It was 1776, a year destined for fame through the daring and achievements of other pioneers. Eastward across the continent, Anglo-American patriots were laying the foundations of a nation.

Some Spanish officials believed that New Mexico would be a better supply base than Sonora and Pimería Alta for the California missions. So an effort was made to open such a route. Garcés, the trail-blazing padre, set out from the mouth of the Gila, ascended the Colorado to the Needles, and turned west across the Mohave Desert. He reached San Gabriel Mission, near Los Angeles, went north into the San Joaquin Valley, and then recrossed the desert to the Colorado River. He now journeyed east to the Moquis; but, being accorded an unfriendly reception here, he returned to his mission at San Xavier del Bac.

At the same time, an effort was being made from the New Mexico base to open a route to the California missions. In that historic July, 1776, Fathers Domínguez and Escalante and 12 companions set out from Santa Fe to seek a trail to Monterey. They traveled through western Colorado and over the Wasatch Mountains to Utah Lake. They then turned southwest toward the Virgin River; and at Black Rock Springs, on account of snow and the lateness of the season (October 5), they decided to abandon their objective and return to New Mexico. They turned eastward, crossed the Colorado at the "Crossing of the Fathers" (30 miles above the Navajo Bridge of today), and returned to Santa Fe. Although they failed in their purpose to open a new route to California, they had visited new tribes of Indians and had made the first exploration of a large inland area.

In 1777 Monterey was made the capital of California, and the Governor was instructed to found pueblos, or Spanish villages, in the province. Accordingly, the Pueblo of San José was founded with families from Monterey and San Francisco. Near it, in the same year (1777), the Mission of Santa Clara was established. The second pueblo was founded near Mission San Gabriel. Families were recruited in Sinaloa and Sonora, and with these colonists Los Angeles was begun in 1781. The next year, the presidio of Santa Bárbara was established, and the planting of missions in the vicinity followed. The strategic areas of California were now occupied, the foundations of the province firmly laid.

Subsequent developments cannot be followed in detail here. The growth was slow but substantial. The missions increased until they numbered 21. To these the wild Indians were gathered, and here were taught not only religion but arts and crafts as well. Flocks and herds increased until the animals owned by the missions and tended by the neophytes were numbered by many thousands. Vineyards, olive groves, and orchards were planted about the missions and were cared for by Indian labor. Mission grain fields increased, the surplus wheat becoming an article of commerce.

The missions became rude manufactories, with Indians weaving blankets and coarse fabrics, tanning hides, making shoes and saddles, fashioning pottery, and operating flour mills. When foreign traders came to the California coast, the missions were able to supply the largest quantities and best quality of hides, tallow, and grain, which the traders sought. The missionaries, says Chapman,[1] "were something more than teachers of religion. The wide power of their administration made them virtual owners and managers of a vast economic plant. They were farmers, cattlemen, manufacturers, traders, and, in a sense, bankers and inn-keepers, as well as preachers."

Less romantic than the missions, yet "the backbone of the province," were the presidios. They checked the thousands of Indians and helped the friars maintain discipline among their wards. No mission was without its military guard, usually a corporal and five or six soldiers. The presidios helped prevent invasion by foreign nations. These posts were not only the military stations, but the political and social centers as well. With officers' and soldiers' families about the presidios, towns sprang up, and these were in time given town government. The only regular Spanish pueblos, or civilian towns, of any consequence before 1800 were Los Angeles and San José. The inhabitants of these were, for the most part, ignorant, poor, and lazy persons of mixed breeds. These colonists, like many other groups of pioneer settlers in America, were recruited from prison and gutter. California was as yet sparsely settled. Exclusive of Indians, the total population of the province in 1800 has been estimated at but 1,200 persons. In view of the small

[1] Chapman, C. E., *A History of California: The Spanish Period*, New York, The Macmillan Company, 1921, 387.

number of colonists, the achievements of these Spanish pioneers during the first 30 years of settlement in California are noteworthy indeed.

While the foundations of mission, presidio, and pueblo were being laid in California, Spanish officials did not lose sight of the original incentive for founding these outposts. A watchful eye was kept upon the activity of foreign nations in Pacific waters. Added to the Russian danger came rumors in 1773 of renewed English attempts to reach the Pacific by rounding the northern coast of North America. To offset such a move, the Viceroy sent Juan Pérez to take formal possession of the coast as far north as 60°. He sailed from San Blas in 1774 and reached 55°. The next year, Heceta and Bodega were sent northward. The former reached 49°, the present northern boundary of the United States, discovering the mouth of the Columbia River en route; the latter reached 58° and on the way discovered Bodega Bay. They found no Russians or Englishmen. But Captain James Cook set sail from England for the Pacific Northwest in 1776, and with his entry on the scene we begin a new era. His story, however, pertains primarily to the Oregon country, and will therefore be reserved for later treatment (Chapter 14).

BIBLIOGRAPHY

General accounts of Spanish beginnings on the Pacific Coast area of present United States may be found in Herbert E. Bolton, *The Spanish Borderlands* (New Haven, 1921); J. W. Caughey, *History of the Pacific Coast of North America* (New York, 1938); H. E. Bolton and T. M. Marshall, *The Colonization of North America, 1492–1783* (New York, 1920).

For the sea explorers, the best account is H. R. Wagner, *Spanish Voyages to the Northwest Coast* (San Francisco, 1929). See also his *Sir Francis Drake's Voyage Around the World, Its Aims and Achievements* (San Francisco, 1926). Regarding Drake's brass plate and its discovery, see the special publication of the California Historical Society, *Drake's Plate of Brass, Evidence of His Visit to California in 1579* (San Francisco, 1937), and subsequent articles in the *California Historical Society Quarterly*.

The standard general account of California for this period is: Charles E. Chapman, *The Founding of Spanish California, 1687–1783* (New York, 1916). See also Herbert I. Priestley, *José de Gálvez, Visitor-General of New Spain* (Berkeley, 1916); H. E. Bolton, *Fray Juan Crespi, Missionary Explorer on the Pacific Coast, 1769–1774* (Berkeley, 1927); Bolton, *Outpost of Empire* (New York, 1931); the same author's edition of Francisco Palóu, *Noticias de la Nueva California* (4 vols., Berkeley, 1926), and his *Anza's California Expeditions* (5 vols., Berkeley, 1930); Elliott Coues, *On the Trail of a Spanish Pioneer, the Diary and Itinerary of Francisco Garcés* (2 vols., New York, 1900); Z. S. Eldredge, *The Beginnings of San Francisco* (2 vols., San Francisco, 1912); and H. H. Bancroft, *History of California* (7 vols., San Francisco, 1884–1890).

The original and the best biography of Father Serra is Francisco Palóu, *Junípero Serra* (Mexico, 1787; translation by C. S. Williams, Pasadena, 1913).

For accounts of the beginnings of Arizona, consult: H. H. Bancroft, *History of Arizona and New Mexico, 1530–1888* (San Francisco, 1889); F. C. Lockwood, *Story of the Spanish Missions of the Middle Southwest* (Santa Ana, 1934); and, by the same author, *Pioneer Days in Arizona from the Spanish Occupation to Statehood* (New York, 1932); F. C. Lockwood and D. W. Page, *Tucson—the Old Pueblo* (Phoenix, n. d.).

The career of Father Kino has received considerable attention during recent decades. Among the resulting volumes are: H. E. Bolton, *Kino's Historical Memoir of Pimería Alta* (2 vols., Cleveland, 1919); the same author's *The Padre on Horseback* (San Francisco, 1932), and his *Rim of Christendom* (New York, 1936); R. K. Wyllys, *Pioneer Padre, the Life and Times of Eusebio Francisco Kino* (Dallas, 1935).

6

THE ENGLISH WESTWARD
MOVEMENT

IN THE preceding four chapters, we
have traced the beginnings of white exploration and settlement in the
West. There was little occasion to refer to Anglo-Americans, for these
people who were destined to play the outstanding role in the trans-
Mississippi region had scarcely entered it before the beginning of the
nineteenth century. They had, however, been in the New World for
about two centuries, having begun permanent colonization in the first
years of the seventeenth century. The founding of Jamestown in 1607
and of Quebec in 1608 exemplifies the contemporary character of
English and French colonial beginnings in America.

But France, with her emphasis on the fur trade, had been more expansive than England during the early years. By means of the Great
Lakes and the interior rivers, she was first in the heart of the continent
and first to challenge Spanish dominion in the Far West. England, on
the other hand, had confined her acitvities during the first century
rather closely to the Atlantic seaboard. Not until the latter half of
the eighteenth century did she seriously invade the trans-Appalachian
country and reach the Mississippi. But during those important years
she was planting English roots deep in fertile American soil. When
duly matured and properly acclimated, these could be confidently
transplanted and re-transplanted in successive fields farther and farther
from the Atlantic Coast.

When the English-speaking pioneer crossed the Mississippi, he was
no longer an Englishman. Sprung from a new soil, transformed by
contact with forest and Indian, an admixture of non-English blood in
his veins, he was a newly molded type—an American. Inasmuch as
his character and institutions were fashioned during the preceding,
formative years, and since these factors were of transcendent importance in shaping the history of the West, we turn now in the next

four chapters to a brief survey of that all-important American background upon which the achievements in the trans-Mississippi West were built.

EMERGENCE OF AN ANGLO-AMERICAN CULTURE

At the end of the reign of James II (1688) the English colonists along the Atlantic seaboard numbered slightly above 200,000. The settled area was a narrow strip from about 10 to 50 miles wide, except here and there where it extended inland along the rivers emptying into the Atlantic. In New England, settlements reached from the Pemaquid to the New York border; in the middle colonies, they included almost all of Long Island, up the Hudson to a point a few miles north of Albany, and eastern parts of Delaware and Pennsylvania; and in the south, they reached the Potomac as far west as the great bend and the shores of the Chesapeake, and scattered settlements were found in North Carolina about Albemarle Sound and as far south as the Chowan River. By 1760, however, the Tidewater region was fairly well occupied, and ambitious settlers were penetrating the Piedmont country. Almost the whole of Massachusetts, Rhode Island, and Connecticut had been occupied. One arm of settlement reached up the New Hampshire and Maine coast as far as the Penobscot and about 50 miles up the Kennebec; another extended up the Merrimac into central New Hampshire; and a third followed the Connecticut Valley for 50 miles above the northern Massachusetts line. In New York, settlers had invaded the lower Mohawk Valley. New Jersey, eastern Pennsylvania, the lower Susquehanna Valley, and the western shore of Delaware Bay were occupied. Maryland and Virginia had overflowed into the valleys beyond the Blue Ridge; and the population of North and South Carolina and Georgia was crowding down the eastern slopes of the Appalachians.

In general, the seaboard colonies expanded westward in three segments. The New England type, based on an industrial and commercial economy, was democratic, theocratic, and corporate; while the Southern, premised on the plantation system, was aristocratic and individualistic, with a flair for expansion. Here the use of slaves and indentured servants, plus the rise of a landholding class, tended to stratify society, although hereditary castes were not recognized by law. Then between these two types was still a third segment, hardly as distinguishable, which acted as a buffer and which tended to merge along its borders with its neighbors. Since it was farther removed from English institutions, it tended to conform to the American way of life.

Both New England and Southern colonists were accustomed to

certain usages of a traditional nature which were observed both in England and America. For example, Biblical theocracy and Calvinistic severity strongly influenced government and religion in New England, as it had in England during the Interregnum. Good Englishmen everywhere recognized the supremacy of the law; a statute was binding equally on the King, Parliament, a colonial assembly, and the subject. As a consequence, the colonists were accustomed to orderly government and sought to improve its forms; and they held common law to be binding alike on prince and subject. Also, there was a belief in a higher law above King, Parliament, or colonial assembly. The King could not of himself initiate a constitutional change, nor could an arbitrary governor annul or modify a charter right. This belief was to have a significant part in the development of colonial government.

Since border customs stemmed largely from English traditional institutions as set up in the South and in New England, it is necessary here to give them brief consideration. For this purpose, the Virginia colony offers a fair example of Southern rural life. Here prior to 1619 general government was first in the hands of the London stockholders, then the governor and colonial council; but in 1619 Governor George Yeardley asked the free inhabitants of each plantation to meet with him and the council at Jamestown in passing ordinances for the colony.

The King had transmitted grants to the Virginia Company; but when its charter was revoked in 1624, all lands not already granted reverted to the Crown. Soon the head-right system arose, whereby a head of a household, each member of his family, and each slave was allowed a grant of 50 acres. Thus, one family might acquire title to a large estate and become prosperous. The first grants were made along the river valleys in order to give the planter a means of transportation for his products, and here and there were erected plantation houses with appurtenant barns, slave huts, and wharves along the river bank. To manage and work these extensive acreages, indentured slaves were imported from England (until Negroes finally supplanted them); but when they had finished their periods of servitude, they, too, became landholders and occasionally rose to positions of wealth and leadership. As brief as was the master's ownership, his needs were fairly well supplied by additional importations of indentured slaves—the unfortunate poor who sold their services for a period of years for transportation to America, political prisoners, children, and occasionally criminals recruited from the English jails.

The first settlers cleared their fields by girdling them; and, until the dead timber was removed, they used hoe and spade to prepare the ground for planting. Their needs were simple and were easily met. From their small fields they were supplied with grain and vegetables, and from the forests they obtained game in abundance. Their cattle and hogs were allowed to roam the forests and pasturelands, fattening on nature's storehouse. Tobacco soon became the most important crop and was produced in such quantities as to furnish large surpluses for the European market. Even the King's annual quitrent was paid in this commodity, and it was commonly used as a medium of exchange. From the beginning the Virginia farmer was bountifully rewarded. Hence, he was not greatly burdened by the Crown's requirement to clear for farm purposes a part of each head right and erect thereon a dwelling, a precaution which gave considerable emphasis to the expansion of the agricultural region.

The Virginians introduced English institutions to which they had been accustomed. Their county government, administered by justices of the peace, levied taxes and attended to various kinds of business, and the sheriff executed the law, much as was done in England. Likewise, the justices of the peace were selected from the principal families of the county. Military matters were intrusted to a county lieutenant, corresponding to the English lord lieutenant. The English parish system was also employed, although on an enlarged scale. Parishioners were authorized by law to elect members of the governing body (vestry) to sit with the parson; but in time vacancies were generally filled by members in office. And since the Virginians were members of the Anglican Church, they supported the clergy by taxes and loyally upheld its observances. But the county was more important as a political unit than the parish; consequently, the Church hardly influenced the life of the colony as it did in New England. About the county courthouse centered not only the business interests of the community, but also political and social activities.

In New England, conditions were strikingly different, as exemplified by Massachusetts' "Bible Commonwealth." For a short time general government was administered by Governor John Winthrop and his assistants, but after 1634 freemen from the towns acted with the assistants. As in Virginia, land ownership was vested in the King, but settlers also recognized Indian claims and often acquired them by purchase. Ownership passed from the King to the General Court through the Council of New England. Actual settlement of a given area, however, began with a grant from the General Court to a group of proprietors, who in turn would allot lands to individuals and lay out a town. As a result, landowners were given absolute title, and in later years paid no quitrents and performed no feudal services.

The Massachusetts Puritans were intensely loyal to their religious tenets, and rigorously conformed to Old Testament idealism. Simplicity in attire and sobriety in daily conduct were enforced. Winthrop and his assistants had sought to maintain an affinity between the magistrate and the minister, and to banish those of dissenting faiths. Although after a short period of turbulence this was abandoned, yet in their brief period of control they succeeded to a large extent in establishing fundamental Puritan institutions in New England. Since the pastor and his congregation were the unit of town-building, this was not difficult, for not only in church matters but also in local government was community life governed by religious leaders. Church membership was a prerequisite for voting; and as need arose, in their town meetings, the Puritans constituted themselves into a body politic and enacted laws to safeguard their every interest.

The New England Puritan was as frugal and resourceful as he was circumspect in his church loyalty. Like the Virginian, he had early turned to agriculture as a means of livelihood, but the poor New England soil offered him meager returns for his labors. Yet environment was kind. From the forest he derived furs and lumber, and from the Banks of Newfoundland he supplied the market with fish. These industries also stimulated shipbuilding and trade; and by the end of the seventeenth century large numbers of seamen were employed. Moreover, the farmer also supplemented his income by domestic manufactures. During the long winter evenings, he and his sons could find employment about the forge and anvil in making nails, tools, and farm implements, or in providing meal and flour from an improvised hollow-block mill, while his wife and daughters were engaged in carding wool, sewing, or in operating the spinning wheel and loom. From these small beginnings, as in England, there presently arose important manufacturing industries. In 1631 a windmill was erected at Boston, in the next year a watermill at Dedham, and soon thereafter other thriving industries of a similar sort. By thrift, hard labor, and resourcefulness the New England Puritan evidenced as much foresight as he had lofty idealism in spiritual affairs. Many master-workmen were quite skilled in wood-carving, cabinet-making, gun-smithing, metal-engraving, and other crafts, and trained their sons and other apprentices to follow in their chosen trades.

Aside from religion, the Puritan's emphasis on education is best remembered. Some 40 or 50 of the early leaders of Massachusetts were well trained in English universities, especially at Cambridge. In the New World they could not rely on English institutions; consequently, in 1636 the Massachusetts General Court established a college for the training of young ministers. This institution was presently named Harvard, in honor of John Harvard, a young minister who died and left a considerable legacy for the college. The Puritans also stressed the home training of children, and more than one town supported elementary schools by land grants and otherwise. In 1649 the General Court enacted a law requiring every town of 50 householders to maintain an elementary school, and towns of 100 householders were expected in addition to establish a grammar school for the training of boys who wished to enter college. Reading, writing, arithmetic, and the catechism were required in the elementary school, and in the grammar school emphasis was placed on the Latin classics and advanced writing and mathematics. For several decades New Englanders had not yet adapted their schools to their local needs, and it was not until 1690 that the *New England Primer,* their first textbook, appeared. But it is to their credit that a basis was laid for a sound system of education, while Southerners were showing less interest. In Virginia, a family tutor, the parish parson, or a favored member of the family instructed the child. Young men seeking advanced training were sent to England.

It is not difficult to find Southern and New England concepts and practices along the frontier in subsequent decades. Yet environment and infiltrating alien patterns had made them less distinctive. By the time the frontier had approached the foot of the Alleghenies, tens of thousands of European immigrants, fleeing from religious and political oppression, had arrived.

English exploitation and religious persecution of the Irish led thousands to seek lands elsewhere. And many found homes along the Atlantic seaboard, while others sought the free lands of the border. Then, after the revocation of the Edict of Nantes (1685), persecution of French Huguenots drove large numbers of these to America. By 1750 they had settled in New York and along the frontiers of Virginia and the Carolinas (particularly South Carolina). Along the border, they met many thousands of Germans who had fled Old World exactions, as will be noted later. Moreover, Scandinavians and Jews also helped to swell still more this foreign immigrant tide and to make more diversified the American amalgam.

The border infiltration of these immigrants had interesting results. None of the non-English groups had filial devotion to England, nor were they bound by English traditional concepts. Consequently, the life of the Tidewater belt, which strongly reflected English influence, affected them little. Also, they represented many religious faiths. German Mennonites, Dunkers, Moravians, and Lutherans; French Huguenots; Irish Catholics; and Scotch Presbyterians were only a few of the groups present that needed to work out a practical program of religious freedom. And social castes were as foreign to border life as sectarian persecution. Here former indentured servants, political exiles, poor home-builders, and others had to live on terms of political and social equality.

Yet new and separate experiences were to bring significant changes. From a common stem of the Stuart period were to grow side by side two new cultures, one (English) dominated by European influences, and the other (Colonial) by American concepts. With the passing of decades, each became markedly unlike the other, but both still reflected their common origin. Separatism was to become a disturbing factor during the American revolutionary era, to be evidenced by colonial protests against purported tyrannies of King and Parliament and, conversely, by punitive measures initiated by the latter. Undoubtedly frontier innovations and adaptations were to a large extent the cause of the new colonial concepts. With every advance into a well-defined topographical area, modifications and new techniques must be employed. This is well observed toward the middle of the eighteenth century, for, while English customs yet dominated the Tidewater belt, new practices were transforming border life in the Piedmont. Perhaps a lack of adequate communication between the two sections in part brought about this change, but necessary adaptations were also contributing factors. It was in this respect that the West was to become a proving ground of American nationalism during the eighteenth and nineteenth centuries. By the end of the French and Indian War (1763), a positive American cultural pattern was discernible.

A New Colonial Amalgam

From 1689 to 1754 the white population of the 13 colonies increased from about 200,000 to more than 1,000,000, of which approximately 200,000 settled along the frontier. By the beginning of the American Revolution, the back-country development was even more significant. This tremendous increase was in large part due to natural colonial growth and immigration from England. Large families, from five to ten members, were common. The coming of other national elements was also a contributing factor. In fact, by 1750 a large part of the population of the middle colonies consisted of Dutch, German, Scotch-Irish, Irish, Scotch, Swedes, and French; and within the Piedmont region of the South was a large element of Scotch-Irish, Germans, and French Huguenots.

The arrival of these non-English people during this period was a result of adverse European conditions—economic, political, religious, and social. Wars and political upheavals had impoverished the nations, piling up huge war debts, which in turn necessitated heavy taxes, deepening religious prejudices and increasing persecution. To provide for their future security, military exactions were heavy, particularly in the German states.

And the fact that Europeans regarded America as a haven of refuge was important. Colonial officials and agents for American land speculators were quick to capitalize on Old World conditions. For example, Benjamin Furley and John Peter Purry, representing colonial proprietors, distributed in Europe much advertising matter (books and pamphlets) which portrayed the lands of their employers as ideal for future Utopias and Gardens of Eden. Some colonial governments offered not only lands to the landless, but also direct aid in moving and initial expenses entailed in beginning their new venture.

Up until the end of the first decade of the eighteenth century, German immigration to the Colonies was small, but thereafter it was considerable. In the earlier years it was largely the persecuted sects that migrated. In 1683 Francis Daniel Pastorius arrived in Pennsylvania as the advance agent of Frankfort-on-the-Main Pietists, and shortly his followers established Germantown. In the next year German Labadists settled on the Bohemian River in Delaware; and in 1694 forty German Rosicrucians under John Kelpius came to the Wissahickon River. By 1707 German immigrants had arrived in Morris County, New Jersey, and still later they had also settled in Bergen, Essex, and Somerset counties.

European response to American advertising was rather prompt. In 1709 approximately 13,000 Germans left the Palatine (southwestern Germany) for England. Queen Anne temporarily provided living quarters and an allowance of ninepence per day. Later they moved on to southern Ireland or to America. Six hundred and fifty of these settled at Newbern, North Carolina, near the mouth of the Neuse River; and 3,000 others went to New York, where Governor Hunter hoped to use them to produce tar and pitch. They were settled on the Livingston Manor. But they believed that their opportunities were limited here, so they subsequently moved westward to the Schoharie and Mohawk valleys. Again they were disappointed. Albany landowners soon appeared to claim their lands. Some now moved to the Mohawk Valley between Fort Hunter and Frankfort; and others, under Conrad Weiser, crossed over into Pennsylvania. Within the next decade other arrivals helped them to occupy Berks, Lancaster, and Montgomery counties. Indeed, by 1756 more than 75,000 Germans had gone to Pennsylvania. A part of these settled along the Lehigh and Susquehanna valleys. Others followed the slopes of the mountains into the back country of Maryland and Virginia, ascending the Shenandoah Valley and settling in the region from Harpers Ferry (founded by Robert Harper, 1734) to Lexington, Virginia. A. B. Faust is authority for the statement that by this southern approach, "they settled in North Carolina and Virginia, and later in Kentucky and Tennessee. Pennsylvania, therefore, was the distribution center for the German immigration, whence German settlers spread over all the neighboring provinces." [1]

Meanwhile other racial elements were coming. Moving westward from the seaport towns of Boston, New York, and Philadelphia, and often preceding the Germans, the Scotch-Irish were another large element to occupy the border. More than 3,000 under Henry McCulloch settled in Dauphin County, North Carolina. But it was as frontiersmen that they were to play a conspicuous role. They began to arrive in America about 1715, and by 1775 it is probable that they numbered more than 400,000. They had little regard for Indian claims to lands, contending that such pretensions were against the laws of God and nature, particularly while "so many Christians wanted to work and raise their bread."

New England also profited by the Scotch-Irish and German immigration. During the summer of 1718 over 500 Scotch-Irish arrived in Boston, and the colony was so alarmed that it adopted a policy of sending the new arrivals to the frontier. In 1731 Pelham was established 30 miles west of Worcester; and two years later, Colerain, 20 miles farther within the wilderness, was formed. From these border settlements new arrivals followed up the Connecticut Valley and settled in Windsor, Orange, and Caledonia counties in Vermont and in Grafton County in New Hampshire. German immigrants, attracted by Massachusetts' colonial policy, presently joined them. A district near Fort Massachusetts in modern Franklin County and extending beyond into present Vermont was first settled by them. Indeed, so great was the German influx that 1,500 entered New England in 1752–1753. Then on the eve of the American Revolution, pioneers from Connecticut, Massachusetts, and New Hampshire entered the Green Mountains to swell Vermont's population and to establish its claim to statehood when once constitutional government had been launched in the United States.

INDIAN AFFAIRS AND THE BORDER

From the establishment of Jamestown until the disappearance of the last American frontier, the white intruders generally dealt ruthlessly with the Indians. The policy of Peter Minuit in buying Manhattan from the Indians as a colonial site, and of William Penn in acquiring by treaty a Quaker domain, although he had received his land by royal grant, did not constitute precedents that were followed by others.

---

[1] Faust, A. B., *The German Element in the United States,* Boston, Houghton Mifflin Company, 1909, Vol. I, 129.

Generally, relations between the two races tended to fall within a vicious circle. First border squatters would venture within the Indian country and establish their cabins here and there. These would be raided by the angry Indians; and, in turn, the settlers would retaliate. Then an Indian war would follow in which the whites would be successful and force the red men to relinquish the squatter-occupied area. Settlers would now rush into the ceded district, and once again the squatters, seeking "elbow room," would encroach on Indian lands, and the process would be repeated.

Yet outwardly, the colonial governments sought to remain on friendly terms with the Indians, some maintaining one or more agents on the border. Moreover, the English home government sought to integrate all local efforts. The invasion of the Ohio country and the Mississippi Valley by the French caused the Board of Trade in 1696 to seek to counteract their influence by playing off one tribe against another, by expending large sums for Indian presents, and by encouraging Iroquois trade. The Iroquois confederacy could put in the field a force of 4,500 warriors; and so long as England could hold them as allies, she could maintain an effective buffer along the New York and Pennsylvania frontiers. The French were aware of the importance of Iroquois friendship, and made more than one effort to wean them away from their English friends, but only during the governorship of Frontenac were they in part successful.

In colonial-Iroquois relations, Albany was the scene of almost yearly conferences. Here traders came with goods and liquor to exchange for furs. In 1749 a Swedish traveler was led to remark: "There is not a place in all the British colonies, the Hudson Bay Settlements excepted, where such quantities of furs and skins are bought of the Indians as at Albany." Even this was not the ultimate reach of British trader influence; a lively barter was carried on with the Indians at Oswego and within the Ohio Valley.

The British government quickly sensed the importance of trade. So long as the Iroquois and other affiliated tribes could be bound to the colonies by this definite material tie, an effective Indian buffer could be maintained between the French and English occupied areas. In 1675 a board of commissioners for Indian affairs was set up, and tribal relations were put on a sounder footing. Later Sir William Johnson, a resident of the Mohawk Valley who was to play a prominent part in border relations, became an influential member of this board, and three years later was sole commissioner. Often during the period of these subsequent relations, the commissioners were also traders, and used their official positions to exploit the natives. They sold liquor to the Iroquois although the sachems of the tribes protested bitterly. But profits were considerable, and the sales continued.

In spite of all efforts of the home and colonial governments to maintain friendly relations, occasional devastating wars occurred which to some extent nullified them. King Philip's War (1675–1676) is an example. Efforts of the Plymouth colonists to force King Philip of the Wampanoags to submit to colonial authority and the encroachment of settlers on Indian lands were two important causes of the war. Plymouth authorities, believing that a general Indian war was imminent, formed a confederacy with Connecticut and Massachusetts, and put a large force in the field. When the Wampanoags saw that these two colonies were joining forces with Plymouth, they attacked the settlements in Rhode Island; and an associated tribe, the Nipmucks, spread terror throughout the Connecticut Valley by attacking Deerfield, Springfield, Northfield, and Hatfield. The colonists then fell upon the Narragansetts, who were about to join the Wampanoags and Nipmucks, in a fort near Kingston, Rhode Island (although this colony was not a member of the confederacy) and effectively crushed their military power. On April 3, 1676, Canonchet and 43 Narragansett warriors were captured and slain in cold blood; and in a subsequent engagement on May 18 one of their villages on the Connecticut River was destroyed and 120 old men, women, and children were slain. Then in August following, resistance was finally overcome when King Philip himself was taken and executed.

The results of the war were appalling. Six hundred of the colonial troops were killed, in addition to a large number of women and children. Homes were destroyed and crops were in ruin, and military expenses for war purposes had approximated $100,000. One-half an Indian population of 12,000 had perished in battle. Hundreds of others were sold as slaves and the proceeds therefrom were given to the common war debt. One authority estimates that Plymouth alone shipped 500 Indian slaves to the West Indies and elsewhere. Thus the Indian power in New England was broken, and the conquered lands were occupied by the whites.

About the same time, Virginia also was having her Indian troubles. In 1674 Maryland forced the Rappahannocks to move from the border to the headwaters of the Potomac. The Indians had hardly become settled in their new home before they observed that Virginia settlers were advancing westward. Trouble came in the summer of 1675, when one of these border settlers was killed either by the Doegs occupying the southern shores of the Potomac or by a roving band of Iroquois. At the order of Governor Berkeley, the militia under Colonel John Washington marched out to the Rappahannock country. Here they were joined by 250 Maryland troops. Washington asked the Indians to surrender six sachems as hostages; and when this was done, he later slew them. In accordance with tribal custom, the Indians then killed 36 settlers (six for each sachem), and thus the war began. The border settlers now abandoned their homes and called on the governor for protection. This was promised; but before a punitive force could reach the Indian country, it was recalled. The Virginia assembly took the side of the settlers and demanded that the Indians be punished, and when the governor refused, a civil war broke forth, led by a planter, Nathaniel Bacon. Bacon not only put in the field a force to oppose the governor, but he led another against the fortified camp of the Pamunkeys on an island in the Roanoke River, killed 150 of its inhabitants, and brought others back as prisoners. In still another expedition the warring tribes were driven back within the interior. The rebellion against the governor collapsed a short time later when Bacon died.

Moreover, the Carolina settlers were to have their Indian troubles. In 1711 the Tuscaroras attacked the North Carolina settlements and killed about 200 settlers. But Virginia and South Carolina sent aid, and the Indians were subdued. The tribal remnant then moved northward and was incorporated as the sixth tribe of the Iroquois Nation. Four years later, the Yamassee Indians, urged on by the Spaniards of St. Augustine, struck the southern border of South Carolina; and the Creeks and Cherokees, under French influence, joined them. Governor Craven quickly raised a strong force, marched it out to the disturbed area, defeated the confederates in several bloody engagements, and drove the Yamassees beyond the Edisto River.

During the period of colonial wars (1689–1763), both England and France sought to win the western Indians as allies. The Iroquois particularly held a strong position. So long as they could control New York and much of the Ohio Valley, they, as allies of the English, could prevent the French from occupying the Hudson Valley and from dividing the seaboard colonies. Furthermore, the French would be compelled to establish border forts along an irregular line of approximately 2,000 miles to be secure from English invasion through the Iroquois country. The French tried to win the Five Nations by favorable trade treaties, but the English could undersell them. Then they gave liquor to the warriors and sought by inebriation to reduce their man power; and when this failed, they next sought to destroy them by war. Still the Iroquois maintained both their integrity and their fighting efficiency. On the eve of the last war (1754), the English asked the Iroquois to join forces with them against the French, but the nation as a whole remained neutral. However, Sir William Johnson succeeded in gaining the adherence of the Mohawks and a part of the warriors from the other tribes.

The English were not so successful elsewhere with their Indian relations. Their final victory over the French caused the Great Lakes tribes to realize their impending doom. Chief Pontiac of the Ottawas formed a strong alliance of the disgruntled tribes, and in May, 1763, captured ten English posts from Bedford, Pennsylvania, to Michilimackinac at the entrance of Lake Michigan. All the border forts but Detroit, Fort Pitt, and Niagara fell without a blow being struck by the defenders. The garrisons at Presque Isle, Le Boeuf, Venango, Mackinac, Sandusky, St. Josephs, and Ouiatanon were massacred, and that at Green Bay fled before the advance of the Indians. Subsequently, a relief expedition under Major Loftus was sent up the Mississippi River, but it was defeated and turned back by the Tunicia Indians at Rocher de Davion. When promised French aid was not forthcoming, and when it was learned that Louisiana had been transferred to the Spaniards, Pontiac negotiated peace with Sir William Johnson, at Oswego, New York, on July 25, 1766.

In October, 1763, King George III sought to allay western Indian unrest by his now well-known proclamation which established the Alleghenies as the western limit of colonization. The Spanish- and French-inhabited areas along the Gulf of Mexico were set up as the Provinces of East and West Florida, and the St. Lawrence Valley settlement as the Province of Quebec. Between these southern and northern jurisdictions was a vast region, reaching from the Alleghenies to the Mississippi, which was reserved for the Indians; and all grants made therein by the colonies to speculators were null and void. Later Johnson became superintendent of the "Northern District" and Captain John Stuart superintendent of the "Southern District." Each officer was to be assisted by subordinates, who were to enforce all regulations for the protection of Indians against the machinations of avaricious traders and land-grabbing speculators.

BORDER LIFE

By 1763 sharp regional contrasts were evident in the Tidewater and Piedmont belts. In New England and the middle colonies, order was beginning to emerge from early colonial beginnings. Neatly built cottages in prosperous villages, sentineled conspicuously by tall-spired churches standing along well-shaded streets, bespoke progress. In the South, the broad-verandahed country homes and the well-tilled rice and tobacco fields likewise indicated cultural growth. And all seaboard settlements were fairly well supplied with a variety of goods and comforts by ships which plied regularly between England and such colonial ports as Boston, New York, and Charleston.

But the Piedmont settlers had no such advantages. In their isolated communities they found conditions much the same as at Jamestown and Plymouth a century earlier. The frontiersman's cabin, made of roughly hewn logs, usually stood lonely and detached in a small, stump-dotted patch; and all about was the wild, untamed wilderness. Stockaded forts stood here and there—grim reminders of lurking Indian foes. There were no roads or canals, and but few navigable streams providing the settlers with means of transportation and communication; therefore, the border occupants must travel on foot through virgin wastes or along deer and Indian trails.

These general conditions forced the settler to rely on his own resources and the wilderness to supply his needs; and in adapting himself to the country, in culture he became half Indian and half white man. To clear away enough of the forest for a small corn patch, to prepare with an ax enough logs for his cabin, to construct a clay-and-stick chimney, to provide necessary furnishings for his cabin from the trees, to supply his larder with venison and other wild game and his family with deerskin garments, and to exchange peltries he might acquire in trapping or bartering with the Indians for shot, powder, salt, and other necessities—all required individual effort. The exercise of this self-reliance developed within him a strong love for freedom and democracy. Without legal restrictions, except as indifferently imposed by distant royal agents, he must be ingenious and opportunistic. These characteristics were reflected in border social customs, Indian relations, and political and religious practices.

The raw and virgin wilderness was a leveler of classes. Prince and pauper worked side by side in its conquest, and social and political distinctions were few and impractical. At best, life was exacting and hazardous; social isolation, deprivation, grim want, and danger drew border settlers together. More than one traveler of the mid-eighteenth century was impressed with Piedmont poverty and isolation. A German missionary who traveled from the borders of New Hampshire to South Carolina had to use a hatchet here and there to carve a trail through the wilderness. At one place he found Irish settlers clothed in deerskins, with no food but deer and bear meat and Johnny-cakes. About the same time George Washington, while surveying the Virginia border estate of Lord Fairfax, wrote a friend that on many a cold night he sought refuge in the log cabin of a settler, and that he slept on straw, fodder, or a bearskin with man, wife, and children about the fire on the hearth. And happy was he who got the place nearest the fire!

BIBLIOGRAPHY

The best general accounts of the advancing frontier and the emergence of the American cultural pattern are F. J. Turner, *Significance of the Frontier in American History* (Chicago, 1899); and F. L. Paxson, *History of the American Frontier, 1763–1893* (Boston, 1924). Other studies of importance are as follows: Clarence W. Alvord and Lee Bidgood, *The First Explorations of the Trans-Alleghany Region by the Virginians, 1650–1774* (Cleveland, 1912); Clarence W. Alvord, *The Illinois Country, 1673–1818* (Springfield, 1920), I; William Bartram, *Travels Through North and South Carolina, Georgia, East and West Florida* (London, 1792); Verner W. Crane, "The Southern Frontier in Queen Anne's War," in *American Historical Review*, XXIV (1919), 379–395; J. T. Adams, *Provincial Society* (New York, 1927); R. G. Thwaites, *Daniel Boone* (New York, 1902); Charles J. Stillé, *The Life and Times of John Dickinson* (Philadelphia, 1891); L. Dodson, *Alexander Spotswood* (Philadelphia, 1932); A. T. Volwiler, *George Croghan and the Westward Movement* (Cleveland, 1920); L. K. Koontz, *The Virginia Frontier* (Baltimore, 1905); Verner W. Crane, *The Southern Frontier, 1670–1732* (Durham, 1928); and H. E. Bolton and Mary Ross, *The Debatable Land, a Sketch of the Anglo-Spanish Contest for the Georgia Country* (Berkeley, 1925).

Studies related to the European migration movement to America and religious and social amalgams are A. B. Faust, *The German Element in the United States* (New York, 1909); C. K. Bolton, *The Scotch-Irish in America* (Boston, 1910); C. A. Hanna, *The Scotch-Irish* (New York, 1902); H. J. Ford, *The Scotch-Irish in America* (Princeton, 1915); L. F. Bittinger, *The Germans in Colonial Times* (Philadelphia, 1907); C. H. Smith, *The Mennonites* (Scottsdale, 1909); P. A. Strobel, *Salzburghers of Georgia* (Baltimore, 1855); A. L. Fries, *Moravians in Georgia* (Raleigh, 1905); J. Fiske, *The Dutch and Quaker Colonies in America* (2 vols., Boston, 1899); J. W. Wayland, *History of the Shenandoah Valley* (Strasburg, 1927); S. G. Fisher, *The Quaker Colonies* (New Haven, 1919); A. H. Hirsh, *Huguenots of Colonial South Carolina* (Durham, 1928); S. B. Weeks, *Religious Development in the Province of North Carolina* (2 vols., Baltimore, 1902); and Carl Wittke, *We Who Built America—The Saga of the Immigrant* (New York, 1939).

Since the Iroquois played a prominent role in early western colonial Indian relations, such studies as W. T. Morgan, "The Five Nations and Queen Anne," in *Mississippi Valley Historical Review*, XIII (1926) 169–189, should be read in connection with this chapter. For other Indian studies, and for Colonial-French relations also, see Arthur H. Buffington, "The Policy of Albany and English Westward Expansion," *ibid.*, VIII (1922), 327–366; Helen Broshar, "The First Push Westward of the Albany Traders," *ibid.*, VII (1920), 228–241; C. W. Alvord, *Mississippi Valley in British Politics* (2 vols., Cleveland, 1907); Francis Parkman, *A Half Century of Conflict* (2 vols., Boston, 1897); Justin Winson, *The Mississippi Basin. The Struggle in America between England and France, 1697–1763* (Boston, 1895); ———, ed., *Narrative and Critical History of America* (Boston, [circa, 1884]–1889); A. B. Hulbert, *Braddock's Road* (Cleveland, 1903); R. G. Thwaites, *France in America* (New York, 1905); G. M. Wrong, *Rise and Fall of New France* (2 vols., New York, 1928); ———, *Conquest of New*

France (New Haven, 1918); and John Fiske, *New France and New England* (Cambridge, 1904).

Other works of a general nature should be examined, such as Evarts B. Greene, "The Anglican Outlook on the American Colonies in the Early Eighteenth Century," in *American Historical Review*, XX (1914), 64–85; J. A. Doyle, *The English Colonies in America* (6 vols., New York, 1882–1907); Charles M. Andrews, *Colonial Self-Government, 1652–1689* (New York, 1904); H. E. Bolton and T. M. Marshall, *The Colonization of North America, 1492–1783* (New York, 1920); Herbert L. Osgood, *The American Colonies in the Eighteenth Century* (New York, 1924); J. C. Fitzpatrick (ed.), *Diaries of George Washington* (Boston, 1925); E. B. Greene, *Provincial America, 1690–1740* (New York, 1905); Mary Johnson, *Pioneers of the Old South* (New Haven, 1918); H. C. Lodge, *George Washington* (Boston, 1898); W. R. Smith, *South Carolina as a Royal Province* (New York, 1903); C. L. Raper, *North Carolina: A Study in British Colonial Government* (Chapel Hill, 1901); J. R. McCain, *Georgia as a Proprietary Province* (Boston, 1917); H. McCall, *History of Georgia* (2 vols., Savannah, 1811–1816); Wayland Fuller Dunaway, *A History of Pennsylvania* (New York, 1935); and William B. Hesseltine, *A History of the South, 1607–1936* (New York, 1936).

7

CREATING A PUBLIC DOMAIN

I MPRACTICAL WESTERN boundaries of the Atlantic seaboard colonies as provided by early charters led to many quarrels and rivalries. For example, the second Virginia charter of May 23, 1609, allowed the colony control over all land 200 miles north and south of "Cape Comfort," and "the land throughout from Sea to Sea, West and Northwest." The Massachusetts charter 20 years later was just as indefinite in providing for control of the region from the "Atlantick and Western Sea and Ocean on the Easte Parte, to the South Sea on the West Parte." And in 1661 the Connecticut charter advanced a claim to the area from "Narrogancett Bay on the East to the South Sea on the West Parte." Indeed, by the time James Oglethorpe had established his Georgia settlement (1734) 7 of the 13 colonies had claims to land beyond the mountains. Connecticut, Massachusetts, Virginia, North Carolina, South Carolina, and Georgia rested their claims on charter grants. New York's pretensions were based on its sovereignty over the Iroquois.

LAND SPECULATION

Although the Proclamation of 1763 (see Chapter 6) provided a temporary western limit to colonial expansion and for the expulsion of transmontane squatters, King George III had no intention of fixing a permanent western barrier. Later the ministry decided on a definite policy of gradual western expansion under the control of imperial agents, who should negotiate cession treaties with the Indians. Johnson and Stuart had already taken the initial steps in this direction. From 1765 to 1768 the Iroquois surrendered their claims to lands between the Ohio and Tennessee rivers in western Tennessee and Kentucky. By other understandings Superintendent Stuart secured a line from the southern boundary of Virginia to the St. Mary's River, Florida, and thence along the fall line to the Apalachicola River. Governor William Tryon and Stuart helped to establish a new

Cherokee line from Reedy River to Tryon Mountain, thence straight to Chiswell's Mine, and thence to the mouth of the Great Kanawha. Then by the treaty of Lochaber, October 18, 1770, the southern line was modified still more by running it west along the southern boundary of Virginia to the Holston River, and thence direct to the mouth of the Kanawha.

Colonies with charter claims to western lands took umbrage because of the King's transmontane policy, which tended to deny them their charter rights. They were even more chagrined to learn of the terms of the Quebec Act (1774), which extended the boundary of Quebec in a southwesterly direction to include the French Ohio Valley settlements. They saw in this an attempt on the King's part to attach the Ohio Valley to French-occupied Canada. Colonial leaders thought that the King and Parliament had made a deliberate attempt to reestablish the French in their rear. But there was little basis for this belief. The extension of a French administration over these (French) outposts was perhaps the most equitable solution of the problem. The act confirmed the Catholic clergy in its rights and privileges enjoyed under French regime and the church in its western properties. It substituted the French system of laws for representative government as implied in the Proclamation of 1763; it established French civil procedure, but the English criminal system was enforced; it continued tithes from the Catholic subjects to the clergy; and it provided for a council to apportion taxes. Thus the ministry seemingly sought not only to meet the demands of the French settlers, but to sever permanently the West from the Atlantic shore colonies. The settlers believed that future colonies planted in the Ohio country would be tied up in interests with the St. Lawrence Valley, with French-Canadian control. At the outlet of the Upper Lakes was Mackinaw, a trading post; on the Wabash was Vincennes; and on the east bank of the Mississippi were Cahokia and Kaskaskia—all settled by the French. These, it was argued, were only the vanguards of more extended Canadian plantations.

Meanwhile speculators in those colonies not having western lands were rivals of those in the more favored states. For more than two decades land speculation had been a bonanza, participated in by important colonial leaders. In 1757, Secretary John Blair reported to the Virginia executive council that the quantity of land then entered to companies and individuals amounted to 3,000,000 acres, a large portion of which had been granted prior to 1754. In subsequent years land speculation increased rapidly. The treaty of Fort Stanwix (1768) had much to do with the craze for land speculation. Companies were formed, and petitions praying for grants hardly less in area than those given under early colonial charters were sent to the King. Among these was the Mississippi Company (which had absorbed the interests of the Ohio Company of 1749), having such charter members as Francis Lightfoot Lee, Richard Henry Lee, George Washington, and Arthur Lee. Its directors sent Arthur Lee to London to lay a petition before the ministers to grant no less than 2,500,000 acres. Although the grant was not made, Washington and his principal surveyor, Major William Crawford, were in the west locating former grants and military warrants when Indian hostilities halted their endeavors.

About the same time a rival group was in the field. In 1768 Samuel Wharton and William Trent, Philadelphia merchants, who were sponsoring the interests of certain disgruntled traders to whom they had advanced considerable credit, concluded a treaty with the Six Nations whereby they and the traders were ceded approximately the same area. Knowing that Virginia would not recognize the cession, the two speculators then sought royal approval. But when they arrived in London, Lord Chancellor Camden was not willing to commit himself, although he conceded that the Six Nations were sovereign in making land grants. Nevertheless, such influential stockholders as Thomas Walpole and Benjamin Franklin lent weight to the enterprise.

When Wharton and Trent could not secure official confirmation of their Six Nations' grant, they became identified with the Vandalia Company's more extensive one. The proposed colony was to be established southwest of Pennsylvania, with the Ohio as its northern boundary, with an irregular line of mountains between the Fairfax Stone and Cumberland Gap on the south, and with the Kentucky River on the west. Franklin also supported the new proposal, as did Sir William Johnson. On October 28, 1773, an order was issued by the Privy Council granting the promoters a vast area including more than present West Virginia, and shortly thereafter the governor of Virginia was advised to grant to other promoters no additional lands within it. But the American Revolution soon halted the proposed venture.

Still another group of outside speculators was to make common cause with Wharton and Trent. In 1773 William Murray and associates organized the Illinois Company and secured a grant north of the Ohio River. Two years later the grant was enlarged, and the speculators formed what was known as the Wabash Company. Thus by 1775 three powerful groups of speculators were in the field to contest with those of the charter-claim colonies for a share in western lands.

Now began a lively controversy! Yet so long as some of the colonies held charter claims, their sons had a distinct advantage. And this was all the more reason why outsiders (for example, Governor Thomas Johnson, Charles Carroll, and Samuel Chase of Maryland; and Benjamin Franklin, James Wilson, and Robert Morris of Pennsylvania) sought to create a vast national domain during the revolutionary years. To accomplish their purpose, they proposed, first, to persuade the claimant states to surrender their western lands to the national government; and, second, then to carve new commonwealths from the ceded domain.

THE BORDER DURING THE COLONIAL WARS

As may readily be seen, the long period of colonial wars (1690–1763) had a direct bearing on the western land problem, for first the French and then the English were eliminated as competitors of the American claimants. The border phase of these wars, therefore, must now be considered.

During each struggle between England and France, since major army movements were of prime importance, frontier settlers were largely left to their own devices. Yet neither belligerent entirely ignored the settlements, for, with the opening of King William's War (1690–1697), Governor Frontenac of Canada sought to break the traditional Iroquois friendship for the English. To impress the Indians with French might, he sent three expeditions against the English frontier. On February 9, 1690, a strong force of French and Indians surprised Schenectady, New York, massacred 60 whites, and led away as captives 27 others. The second expedition resulted in the destruction of Salmon Falls, New Hampshire, and the third captured Fort Loyal, Maine (near the site of Portland). The colonists then planned a counterstroke against Quebec and Montreal; but the approach of winter, unnecessary delay, and the ravages of disease among the troops prevented its success. Thus, unpunished, the Indians continued their forays. In 1697 they captured Haverhill and led away Hannah Dustin, who later escaped by slaying her captors. During these trying days, the Iroquois remained steadfastly allied with the English, mainly through the influence of Peter Schuyler.

During Queen Anne's War (1701–1713), Iroquois friendship largely saved the New York frontier, but New England was less fortunate. In February, 1704, a force of 250 French and Indians scaled the stockade at Deerfield, Massachusetts, and slew 53 whites and took away 111 prisoners through the frozen forests. Seventeen of these were killed because they could not keep up with their captors, and others died of cold and hunger.

Likewise, the final struggle between England and France for control of Canada and the Ohio country had its counterpart on the frontier. The border had not suffered so much during King George's War (1745–1748) as during the two preceding conflicts; but hardly was the treaty of Aix-la-Chapelle signed (1748), before the French had taken steps to acquire control of the Ohio Valley. In 1749 the Governor of Canada sent Céleron de Bienville with 214 men to possess this region and to warn English traders and settlers to leave. Then four years later a second French force of 1,000 men appeared to claim the same region and to construct a road from Presque Isle (now Erie) to the Rivière aux Boeufs, a tributary of the Allegheny, where they built Fort Le Boeuf. And 40 miles farther south, on the Allegheny, they also erected Fort Machault.

Governor Robert Dinwiddie of Virginia became alarmed at these hostile demonstrations, and dispatched young George Washington to warn the French that they were intruding on Virginia soil. But the French ignored Virginia's claim. Presently, too, Dinwiddie sent another small party to build a trading post at the confluence of the Allegheny and Monongahela rivers, a short distance beyond the farthest advance of the French. This the French promptly captured, strengthened, and enlarged. It was now named Fort Duquesne in honor of the Governor of Canada. Actual fighting began on May 28, when Washington, with a force of 300 Virginians, surprised and defeated a French reconnoitering detachment under Jumonville at Great Meadows, 50 miles from Will's Creek. Then he built Fort Necessity to buttress the colonial frontier. On July 4, 1754, however, a superior French-Indian command forced his capitulation, but allowed his garrison to march away with the honors of war. A year later, the English suffered an even greater reverse when General Edward Braddock allowed his force to be trapped seven miles from Fort Duquesne. The regular troops were thrown into confusion because of the deadly fire of their hidden foe, and would have been annihilated had not Washington's Colonials saved the day. Braddock tried bravely to rally his men until he was mortally wounded. Of his 1,200 men in the fight, 877 were killed or wounded.

While during the early stages of the war the French were generally successful, in 1757 the tide turned in favor of England. William Pitt was given full control of war policies, and soon fresh troops and supplies were hurried to America. One strong French post after another was captured, including Fort Duquesne. General John Forbes, with 1,200 Highlanders and 5,000 militia from Pennsylvania, Maryland, Virginia, and North Carolina, captured this post on November 25, 1758, and renamed it Fort Pitt. Two years later both Quebec and Montreal were captured from the French, and presently the war was at an end. Spain entered the conflict in 1761, too late to render France, her ally, effective aid, but her trade ties with the Choctaws, Chickasaws, and Creeks caused England much concern. The Chero-

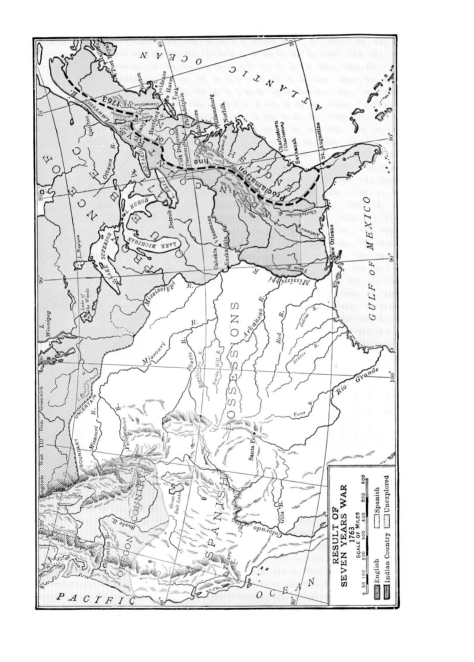

RESULT OF
SEVEN YEARS WAR
1763

SCALE OF MILES
0 50 100   200   300   400   500   600

English
Indian Country
Spanish
Unexplored

kees remained loyal to the English cause, however, and Spain's influence was in large part nullified.

By the time of the American Revolution, the border people were quite adapted to Indian fighting. While from Maine to Georgia the seaboard colonists were resisting the British invaders, the frontier settlers were also involved. They rendered conspicuous service to the colonial cause. Hardly had hostilities begun before English "Redcoats and Redskins" were following, toward New York, the Lake Champlain and Lake Ontario war trails formerly used by the French during their last conflict with the English. With the outbreak of hostilities both the British and colonists had made bids for Indian aid. The former were to some extent successful; consequently, once again border settlers were subjected to the scalping knife and tomahawk.

In November, 1775, a colonial force led by Richard Montgomery marched on Montreal by way of the Lake Champlain route and captured it; then Montgomery united his force with another under Benedict Arnold, who had advanced by way of Maine. The combined troops made an unsuccessful attack on Quebec in which Montgomery was killed (December 31). Justin H. Smith believes that Quebec might have become the *Fourteenth Colony*, had this enterprise been successful. But, as it was, it only paved the way for a counterstroke. Two years later the British made plans to sever New England from the Middle Colonies by launching a three-pronged invasion. One column was to ascend the Hudson from New York to Albany, another was to march on Albany *via* the Mohawk Valley, and a third was to move southward and unite with the other two. But unexpected border reverses set the English back on their heels. On August 6, 1777, General St. Leger's troops coming down the Mohawk were checked by Nicholas Herkimer's border troops at Oriskany. Ten days later Colonel John Stark's "Green Mountain Boys" destroyed General John Burgoyne's foraging column at Bennington. Meanwhile Sir William Howe set sail from New York with his troops for Philadelphia *via* the Chesapeake instead of ascending the Hudson as he was expected to do. So while Arnold's rear-guard actions were wrecking Burgoyne's army, Howe's men were finding comfortable winter quarters in Philadelphia. Defeated twice in severely fought actions, Burgoyne surrendered his army to the Americans on October 17, 1777.

Within two months after Cornwallis's troops had overwhelmed Horatio Gates' Colonials at Camden (August 16, 1780), the British met their first check in the South at King's Mountain (October 7). After Gates' defeat, Cornwallis had moved into North Carolina, living off the country. He halted at Charlotte and dispatched Major Ferguson with 1,000 men to scour the neighboring country for recruits and supplies.

News of Ferguson's approach flew along the border, and from South Carolina, Virginia, and Tennessee came frontiersmen, armed with long-barreled muskets, to join the hard-pressed North Carolinians. Isaac Shelby, John Sevier, and other notable borderers were among the backwoodsmen who stormed the strongly held British position on King's Mountain. On alternate sides the frontiersmen charged up the slopes. Early in the fight Ferguson and 200 of his troops were killed, and presently the 700 survivors surrendered. This severe loss forced Cornwallis to withdraw to South Carolina and caused sufficient Colonials to flock to General Nathaniel Green's standard to make up a formidable army. In the following year Cornwallis withdrew to the Yorktown peninsula, where Washington forced his surrender on October 19, 1781.

The French settlements of the Northwest composed the third field of action. In 1774 George Rogers Clark, a young Virginian from the Albemarle country, had crossed the mountains to make Kentucky his home. Here he found the border in turmoil and confusion because of speculator activities and, more particularly, Indian depredations. Shortly a convention was held at Harrodsburg, and Clark and another were sent eastward as delegates to present a petition to the Virginia Assembly asking for relief from Indian forays and for the organization of Kentucky as a county of Virginia. Although the Assembly had adjourned by the time the two delegates arrived, the mission was not entirely without success. Clark called on Governor Patrick Henry, explained the desperate plight of the frontier, and obtained 500 pounds of powder to supply the border settlers. As a result of his visit, too, Kentucky was subsequently set up as a county.

Clark's account of Indian atrocities was not overdrawn. Since the beginning of the war, British officials, agents, traders, and half-breeds had aroused the Indians to scalp and plunder on promise of helping them to drive the white men from their country. Moreover, they agreed to pay a liberal reward for scalps, offering as much for female hair as for that of a man. Even Lieutenant-Governor Henry Hamilton in June, 1778, was to congratulate assembled Chippewas, Hurons, Mohawks, and Potawatomies on the banks of the Detroit because of their murderous work, and to urge them to bring in more scalps and plunder.

Clark's work was not yet done. Later he conceived the plan of driving the British from the Northwest. Traders informed him that the French *habitants* would welcome an expedition to liberate them, and that all British posts were poorly manned and could be easily captured. Once more Clark crossed the mountains. He asked Governor Henry to furnish him with supplies for an expedition to capture the

"British post at Kaskasky." The request came opportunely. Gates had just received the surrender of Burgoyne's army, and the colonial cause was never brighter. After consultation with others—Thomas Jefferson, George Mason, and George Wythe—Henry approved of the plan, and on January 2, 1778, sent Clark on his way to accomplish one of the most spectacular feats of the war. To meet the costs of the campaign only £1,200 in depreciated continental currency was available. But this was enough. At Fort Pitt and Wheeling, Clark organized 175 men, and on June 24, in *bateaux*, they began the descent of the Ohio.

The expedition met with surprising success. Nine miles below the mouth of the Tennessee, Clark disembarked his men and began a hasty march overland in a northwesterly direction, across the virgin wilds of southern Illinois. Kaskaskia and Cahokia were taken without trouble before the British at Detroit knew that the Americans were in the country. And a French priest, Father Pierre Gibault, subsequently secured the surrender of Vincennes. Thus, without firing a shot, Clark won the vast Illinois and Wabash country.

When the astonishing news of Clark's expedition was brought to Governor Hamilton, he was soon in the field with 500 men, ready for a reconquest. In December he was again in possession of Vincennes. He also planned on a speedy recapture of Cahokia and Kaskaskia (where Clark was stationed with little more than 100 men), but cold weather necessitated postponement of the plan until the following spring. Most of the Detroit troops were allowed to return home, and the Indian allies scattered to their distant villages, all expecting to reassemble a few months later to complete a campaign so well begun.

But Hamilton was given another surprise! Clark saw that immediate action was imperative if he were to hold the country. A Spanish trader, Francois Vigo, brought him word that Vincennes was held with but few troops and could be taken easily, and that the French *habitants* would again welcome his coming. Within a short time, therefore, Clark was at the head of 230 men on the march for Vincennes. The campaign was not launched without misgivings. Heavy rains were falling, and the Little Wabash and other streams were raging torrents, inundating their valleys. At times Clark and his men waded through water up to their waists and for hours carried their powder horns above their heads to keep them dry. Becoming cold, hungry, and discouraged, some talked of abandoning the enterprise, but Clark buoyed them up by his unfailing good humor and untiring zeal. On February 23, they finally reached the high ground two miles below Vincennes. Hamilton, greatly overawed by this show of courage, offered little resistance. He finally surrendered when he learned that the French had gone over to the colonial cause, and he and 25 of his men were sent as prisoners of war to Governor Henry.

Virginians were much pleased with Clark's success, and were now ready to press their claim to ownership before the Continental Congress. But outsiders insisted that it did not give Virginia exclusive rights. The campaign had been a success only because British troops were so hard pressed elsewhere by the Continental Army that they could not march to the relief of Hamilton; and thus victory had been won by common effort. Since this was true, why should not all share the common fruits of victory? For more than three years Virginia would not recede from her position. Maryland was equally firm, however, and refused to ratify the Articles of Confederation until the western lands were made a part of the public domain. More than once Franklin and delegates from other landless states sought to show landholding states the necessity for surrendering their claims. Such acts of generosity would give needed strength to the central government and provide for the creation of new states and for the rapid occupation of western lands by homeseekers.

In spite of these arguments, Virginians were not convinced. To them it was significant that the champions of a public domain were largely identified with land speculation. Still, an effective common government was of pressing necessity, and ratification of the Articles of Confederation would meet this need. At last, on January 2, 1781, the Virginia assembly voted to surrender its claims. But, in doing so, it dealt a stunning blow to the outside speculators by providing that "all purchases and deeds from any Indian or Indians, or from any Indian nation or nations, for any lands within any part of the said territory . . . shall be deemed and declared absolutely void and of no effect." The outsiders were undoubtedly nonplussed by this surrender-reservation. And while they were yet engaged in formulating a counter-proposal, Maryland ratified the Articles on March 1, and they were immediately put into effect.

THE LAND ORDINANCE OF 1785

Members of the Continental Congress were not only interested in laying the basis for new states by placing the western lands under the jurisdiction of their common government, but they also hoped that their sale would provide a sufficient revenue to meet current government expenses and to absorb the public debt. Before unquestioned ownership of the Northwest could be established, however, Indian claimants must be satisfied. So in 1784, Oliver Walcott, Richard Butler, and Arthur Lee, representing Congress, concluded a treaty with the Six Nations whereby these Indians ceded to the United States almost all their claims on the Northwest. On January 21, 1785, other commissioners met sachems and warriors of the Wyandot, Delaware, Chippewa, and Ottawa nations at Fort McIntosh and persuaded them to accept a boundary approximating the watershed between Lake Erie and the Ohio and west of the Cuyahoga. Neither treaty met with the approval of tribes living within the abandoned area. In fact, the Six Nations had only slight claim on the country, and those tribes represented at Fort McIntosh lived principally along the lake shores.

As was previously noted, colonial pioneers, joined by ambitious, newly arrived Huguenots, Scotch-Irish, and Germans, had pushed across the mountains and were invading the Indian country set up by George III. In order to capitalize on this movement, therefore, Congress enacted the ordinances of 1784 and 1785. The first was largely the work of Thomas Jefferson. Under its terms the country between the mountains and the Mississippi was divided into tracts, each of which was to be admitted to the Union by a two-thirds vote of Congress, when each had a population equal to the smallest state already in the Union. Previous to statehood, settlers in each were to have restricted rights of self-government. A provision excluding slavery from any state thus created was stricken out before the ordinance was enacted. This enactment, as will be shown later, became the basis for a more comprehensive one three years later, and will be referred to again.

The Ordinance of 1785, resulting from a second report of the committee on western lands, was of equal importance. It laid the basis for both the survey and sale of all public lands. Its practical origin is obscure. Certain features of it resemble somewhat survey regulations in New England. But other colonies, for example, Virginia and the Carolinas, had used "indiscriminate locations" which had led to endless litigation. It was not uncommon for streams, hills, and even trees to be the basis for property lines.

The Land Ordinance provided for a rectangular system of survey. A base line was to be run, east and west, and intersecting it at right angles every six miles were to be "meridian lines" (running north and south). The area between two meridians was known as a "range." Then parallel with the base line, six miles apart, were other lines, cutting each "range" into square townships (or 36 sections of 640 acres each). In turn, each section could be divided into halves and quarters. Section 16 in each township was to be reserved for schools; and in addition, bounty lands for the use of the Continental Army were to be withdrawn by the Secretary of War.

The unit of sale was the section, and the minimum price was one dollar (in cash) per acre, although competitive bidding was supposed to bring the average to a higher level. Since $640 was the amount required to purchase the smallest unit of land sold, poor homeseekers had little chance of acquiring properties. It was hoped that group purchases would be made, thus making possible the sale of large bodies of land and at the same time caring for the needs of the individual homeseeker.

The Ordinance also provided a corps of surveyors, one from each state, to assist Captain Thomas Hutchins, the Geographer, in making the surveys. This corps began its first line where the Ohio River crosses the western boundary of Pennsylvania and ran it westward for 42 miles. Along it were set up seven ranges, each north of the Ohio. Indians who had formerly camped and hunted within the region were now greatly alarmed, and sought to interfere with the survey. To them, land was much like water and game—the common property of all. To allot it to individuals was unthinkable. Moreover, squatters had intruded west of the Ohio. Consequently, United States troops were used to protect the surveyors from Indian attack and to expel the unlawful homesteaders.

The Ordinance of 1787

During the period of the westward movement, pioneers regarded lightly the legal barriers about undeveloped wildernesses. So in spite of King George's proclamation of 1763 and dangers of Indian attack, they steadily pushed through every available pass of the mountains to build homes in a new land. By 1769 Virginians had filtered into the Watauga and Holston country of eastern Tennessee, while others followed Boone along the Wilderness Trail to Kentucky. Undoubtedly land speculation stimulated this movement, but the decrease of available farm lands east of the mountains and the steady increase of the European immigrant tide were more important factors. Although there was some settler activity south of the Ohio during the revolutionary years, it was not until after 1782 that there was any appreciable movement for the occupation of the Northwest. Discharged soldiers who were given bounty lands or who had been paid depreciated continental currency for their services (which they now wished to exchange for western lands) were ready to swell the immigrant tide. They banded together in a secret order, the Cincinnati, and were assertive and clamorous for their rights. As early as June, 1783, 285 officers, with the endorsement of Washington, petitioned Congress to set up a soldier colony west of Pennsylvania. According to one authority, this petition was the foundation of the Ohio Company Associates, organized at the "Bunch of Grapes" tavern in Boston, March 3, 1786. On this occasion General Rufus Putnam, Benjamin Tupper, and others organized a land company of 1,000 shares, at $1,000 each, payable in continental currency. And since the Land Ordinance of 1785 provided that a township was the largest unit of sale, the directors sent a representative to Congress to ask for the enactment of a more liberal purchase law and for the setting up of a territorial government for the Northwest.

When General S. H. Parsons, of Middletown, Connecticut, presented the Associates' memorial to Congress on May 9, 1787, he found that body of an indifferent quality. Few of its members were well known in political circles. There were now present no Franklins, Hancocks, or Jeffersons. Important leaders were members of their state legislatures, or they were delegates to the forthcoming Philadelphia constitutional convention. But credit for the enactment of a far-reaching ordinance was reserved for these lesser members of Congress. Parsons was an excellent lobbyist who urged his proposal in season and out of season, but he was not to witness Congressional endorsement. After he had presented his petition, he returned home and was succeeded by Dr. Manasseh Cutler, of Ipswich, Massachusetts. Fortunately Cutler was also an able man. He argued with the Congressional committee that the proposed enactment would meet every need better than one then up for its third reading. His reasoning was convincing, and Congress enacted his proposal in the form of an ordinance on July 13, 1787.

Thus, under the Articles of Confederation, Congress had enacted two ordinances of great importance. It has already been seen how the first provided for an accurate survey system and for the sale of land carved from the public domain. The second was to go a step further. According to the late Professor F. L. Paxson, it "included a partition scheme, a plan of government, and a bill of rights," [1] each of which will now be considered.

Article V of the Ordinance provided for the future formation of not less than three nor more than five states. If three, the common boundaries were to be the Wabash River and the Wabash-Vincennes meridian, and a line drawn due north through the mouth of the Great Miami River, approximately the common boundaries of Ohio, Indiana, and Illinois of today. If five states should be admitted, then a line drawn east and west through the southern extreme of Lake Michigan would provide two others, Michigan and Wisconsin.

Settler needs of government were wisely cared for under the ordinance. For the present, Congress was to appoint a governor for a term of three years, a secretary for a term of four years, and three judges for good behavior. The governor was to have sweeping powers.

[1] Paxson, F. L., *History of the American Frontier,* Boston, Houghton Mifflin Company, 1924, 67.

He was to be commander-in-chief of the militia, and was to "appoint and commission" officers below the rank of general officers, and such magistrates and civil officers in each county and township as were necessary. Moreover, he and the judges were to publish for use in the territory such civil and criminal laws of the original States as they deemed necessary, but subject to the approval of Congress. Any two of the three judges could form a court having common-law jurisdiction. A property qualification was required of all officers. The governor must own a freehold of 1,000 acres of land; the secretary and judges, 500 acres; and, when a legislature should be elected, each representative must hold 200 acres in his own right.

Then as the country to be administered under the ordinance was settled, two other steps were to be taken. As soon as 5,000 free white male adults had removed to the territory, it should be entitled to an elected legislature and a representative in Congress. But still Congress was to appoint its governor and select its council (upper house) from a list of persons nominated by the territorial representatives. When any one of the divisions set off as a proposed state had a population of 60,000 free inhabitants, it was then empowered to take the third step. Article V provided that it could be admitted "by its delegates into the Congress of the United States, on an equal footing with the original States in all respects whatever, . . ." and that it should be at liberty to form a permanent constitution and state government.

The usual guarantees of favored institutions and personal rights as are today found in the federal and state constitutions were couched in certain provisions of the ordinance, such as freedom of worship, encouragement of schools, trial by jury, and safeguards for property rights. But perhaps the best-known provision, in Article VI, reads: "There shall be neither slavery nor involuntary servitude in the said territory, otherwise than in the punishment of crimes, whereof the party shall have been duly convicted." Subsequently, since slavery was outlawed from those states north of the Mason and Dixon line, this provision was to have profound importance. It was to extend the line of cleavage between the slave states and antislave states from the western boundary of Pennsylvania to the Mississippi. Moreover, federal fugitive slave laws were anticipated, for any person escaping into the Northwest, "from whom labor or service is lawfully claimed in any one of the original States, such fugitive may be lawfully reclaimed. . . ." The last paragraph of this article declared null and void the Ordinance of 1784.

The way was now cleared for the occupation of the Northwest. Two weeks after the passage of the ordinance, Congress passed a special act authorizing the sale of more than 6,000,000 acres of land: 1,781,760 acres to the Ohio Associates and 4,901,480 to another speculative group, the Scioto Company. The price was one dollar an acre, payable in continental money, with a discount of one-third to take care of swampy or undesirable land within the grants. The Associates paid $500,000 in cash and pledged to pay the balance when the land was surveyed. The Scioto Company merely took an option on its proposed purchase and agreed to pay for it in six installments. Members of Congress were more than generally interested in western lands. Indeed, General Arthur St. Clair, president of Congress, was a stockholder of the Associates, and later became governor of the first territory. Winthrop Sargent, secretary of Congress, was also secretary of the Associates; two of the three judges chosen for the new territory were Representatives Parsons and J. M. Varnum; and the most active members of the Scioto group were no less active in Congress.

Thus, as may be seen, the sale of western lands became identified with national expansion, and the consequent national policy the subject of a heated sectional controversy. For the most part, Easterners advocated the disposal of the public domain in such a way as to obtain the maximum amount of revenue. But this point of view was sharply challenged by Westerners, who maintained that the national policy should point toward homes for the homeless and the advance of the western frontier. Although Alexander Hamilton was in sympathy with the Eastern point of view, in 1790 he recommended to Congress that homeseekers be allowed to acquire by purchase 100-acre tracts, and that a General Land Office be established. Congress was not disposed to enact into law his first proposal, and it was 20 years before the General Land Office was created. Six years later, however, a new enactment authorized the sale of single sections (640 acres) at a minimum price of $2 per acre. Buyers were allowed to pay one-twentieth of the purchase price down, nine-twentieths at the end of six months, and the remaining half within a year. Moreover, two western land offices were opened (at Pittsburgh and at Cincinnati). But the minimum tract was still too large, and the purchase price was yet beyond the reach of the average buyer, for there were few settlers who could pay $640 within a six-month period.

For these reasons Congress was willing to listen to William Henry Harrison's proposal for a more liberal policy and in 1800 to enact a law providing for four local land offices instead of two, for the sale of tracts as small as 320 acres, and for more lenient terms. All purchasers, under the new law, could pay one-fourth of the purchase price down and one-fourth with interest each succeeding year for a period of four years. The law also provided, as a concession to Easterners, that auctions should be held for a period of three weeks whenever a new tract was offered for sale, after which period all unsold land was to be offered at the minimum price of $2 per acre.

There is little doubt that the law of 1800 definitely stimulated the occupation of the Northwest Territory and turned the eyes of many immigrants toward the fertile lands of Mississippi and Alabama once they were made federal domain by the Georgia compact of 1802. By the law of 1800 Congress manifested its interest in the frontier in still another way. By its Ohio "enabling act," it laid the basis for active federal participation in public education and in road-building. One section out of every township was to be set aside for educational purposes; and five per cent of the proceeds of the sales of public lands within Ohio should be "applied to laying out and making public roads." These two wise provisions were to have great influence on the future development of the Ohio Valley.

But Western needs were not fully realized in the Land Law of 1800. Thousands of buyers soon found that the deferred payment plan was burdensome. Expectations were high, and many a prospective home-owner borrowed recklessly. Often the purchaser borrowed at high interest a sufficient sum to make the first payment and to clear away his land, to buy supplies, and to build his home, only to be disappointed in his hopes. Roads to market were poor or nonexistent, prices of farm products were low, and average crop returns were below expectations. Year by year, arrears due the government were accumulating. The government, however, was hesitant to evict homesteaders who could not meet their payments, and Western politicians were quick to seize upon this situation to propose deferred payment plans. The panic of 1819 added ruin and demoralization to an already difficult problem, and Congress now decided to bring to an end the unworkable credit system. In 1820 a law was passed which permitted an individual to purchase as little as 80 acres of land, and fixed the price per acre at $1.25 in cash. Thus, for $100, plus incidental fees, a settler might become the owner of a home. The law, however, only whetted the appetites of home seekers. They continued in subsequent years to bombard Congress with requests for the recognition of "squatter rights" and for free homesteads. Finally, as a consequence, the Distribution-Pre-emption Law (1841) and, still later, the Homestead Bill (1862) were the rewards of their efforts.

BIBLIOGRAPHY

Important general works dealing with the Northwest during the period of this chapter are Justin Winsor, *The Westward Movement: the Colonies and the Republic West of the Alleghanies, 1763–1798* (Cambridge, 1897); Clarence W. Alvord, *The Mississippi Valley in British Politics* (2 vols., Cleveland, 1917); ———, *The Illinois Country, 1673–1818* (in Centen-

nial History of Illinois, Springfield, 1918–1920); John W. Monette, *History of the Discovery and Settlement of the Valley of the Mississippi, by the Three Great European Powers, Spain, France, and Great Britain, and the Subsequent Occupation, Settlement, and Extension of Civil Government by the United States, Until the Year 1846* (2 vols., New York, 1846); Berthold Fernow, *The Ohio Valley in Colonial Days* (Albany, 1890); F. L. Paxson, *History of the American Frontier, 1763–1893* (Boston, 1924); Frederick Austin Ogg, *The Old Northwest* (in *Chronicles of America*, XIX, New Haven, 1919); and B. A. Hinsdale, *The Old Northwest* (Boston, 1899).

Studies on Indian land cessions, speculator activities, and settlements are as follows: H. B. Adams, "Maryland's Influence upon the Land Cessions to the United States," in *Johns Hopkins University Studies* (Baltimore, 1882–), Series III, I (1885); A. T. Volwiler, *George Croghan and the Westward Movement* (Cleveland, 1926); H. T. Leyland, "The Ohio Company," in *Quarterly Publications*, Historical and Philosophical Society of Ohio (Cincinnati, 1906–), XVI; F. J. Turner, "Western State Making in the Revolutionary Era," in *American Historical Review* (New York, 1895–), I; G. H. Alden, "New Governments West of the Alleghanies Before 1780," in University of Wisconsin *Bulletin* (Historical Series, II); Charles A. Hanna, *The Wilderness Trail* (2 vols., New York, 1911); Merril Jensen, "The Cession of the Old Northwest," in *Mississippi Valley Historical Review*, XXIII (June, 1936), 27–48; W. Neil Franklin, "Pennsylvania-Virginia Rivalry for the Indian Trade of the Ohio Valley," *ibid.*, XX (March, 1934), 463–480; James A. James, *The Life of George Rogers Clark* (Chicago, 1928); William Hayden English, *Conquest of the Country North of the Ohio River, 1778–1783, and Life of General George Rogers Clark* (2 vols., Indianapolis, 1896); Clarence Edwin Carter, *Great Britain and the Illinois Country, 1763–1774* (Washington, 1910); ————, *The Critical Period, 1763–1775* (Springfield, 1915); ————, *The New Regime, 1765–1769* (Springfield, 1916); and ————, *Trade and Politics, 1767–1769* (Springfield, 1921).

Source books containing important documents pertaining to the Northwest are Charles C. Tansil, *Documents Illustrative of the Formation of the Union of the American States* (selected, arranged, and indexed) (Washington, 1927); Clarence E. Carter (ed.), *The Correspondence of General Thomas Gage with the Secretaries of State, 1763–1775* (New Haven, 1931–), I; A. T. Volwiler, "William T. Trent's Journal at Fort Pitt, 1763," in *Mississippi Valley Historical Review*, XI (December, 1924), 390–413; Lewis J. Carey (ed.), "Franklin is Informed of Clark's Activities in the Old Northwest," *ibid.*, XXI (December, 1934), 375–378; A. H. Smyth (ed.), *The Writings of Benjamin Franklin* (New York, 1905–1907), III; *American State Papers* (Washington, 1834), *Public Lands*, II; Thomas Donaldson, *The Public Domain* (Washington, 1884); and Clarence Edwin Carter, *The Territorial Papers of the United States* (Washington, 1934), and *The Territory Northwest of the River Ohio, 1787–1803*, II, Part I.

8

THE OLD SOUTHWEST

As was noted in Chapter 6, the Pied-
mont frontiers of Virginia and the Carolinas were fairly well occupied
by the middle of the eighteenth century. During the period 1717–
1732, the population of North Carolina quadrupled, and the increases
of South Carolina and Virginia were also marked. In addition to the
usual English colonial westward movement, the immigration of the
German, Scotch, Scotch-Irish, Welsh, and French homeseekers was
considerable. And along with the landless and poverty-stricken newcomers were those in better economic circumstances or who represented
caste and aristocracy. The latter had left Europe because of civil,
economic, or religious oppression. Of this group were George Boone
of East Devonshire, Edward Morgan of Wales, Morgan Bryan of Denmark, Michael Finley (or Findlay) of Ireland, and Mordecai Lincoln
of England—all well-known names in subsequent border history.

In a log cabin on the east side of the Yadkin, beside the Great Trading Path leading from Virginia to the Catawba trading towns and to
those of other southern Indians, in a sylvan hunter's paradise, grew up
an adventurous border lad, Daniel Boone, "a Pennsylvania youth of
English stock, Quaker persuasion, and Baptist proclivities." Boone
was typical of many other border hunters—restless, daring, and adept
at woodcraft. Before his connection with the Transylvania Company,
discussed further along in this chapter, he had hunted and thoroughly
explored the back country of the Carolinas and Virginia, and had
crossed the mountains to hunt in the virgin wilderness of Kentucky
and Tennessee. Others from the seaboard colonies, such as John Findlay in 1752 and Elisha Walden in 1761, were also crossing the mountains and engaging in trade with the Indians, carrying by pack-horse
caravan such articles as guns, powder, shot, hatchets, and other things,
and bringing back valuable furs and deerskins. The caravans of William Byrd were among those traveling the Great Trading Path across

the mountains to the Catawba villages and the back-country tribes of the Carolinas.

THE SOUTHERN BORDER

More than one border leader saw service in the Indian country during the French and Indian War—Boone, Findlay, Bryan, and Waddell. Boone was a waggoner in Braddock's supply train, and barely escaped the massacre at Turtle Creek by cutting the traces of his team and fleeing on one of his horses. It was in the same affair that colonial troops were to prove their mettle. Under the leadership of Washington, they saved Braddock's regulars from annihilation by their defensive tactics.

During the war, the back-country settlements of Virginia, the Carolinas, and Georgia were exposed to Indian raids, north and south. As previously stated, the French officials and traders were not slow to take advantage of this situation, traveling as far south as the villages of the Cherokees to arouse the Indians. Aware of their peril, Virginia and North Carolina sent commissioners to hold a powwow with leaders of the southern tribes. A treaty was signed with the Catawbas at their principal village on February 21, 1756, and with the Cherokees on Broad River, North Carolina, on March 17. The colonial commissioners promised both groups of Indians protection against their enemies by building forts in their countries, and gave them certain supplies. In turn, the Indians agreed to furnish Forbes' army upward of 450 warriors. But the border settlements were given only temporary respite. Harrowing raids, plunder, and death were soon to be visited on the hapless settlers.

Blunders of white men precipitated a Cherokee war. In May, 1758, while a small band of warriors was returning from the Fort Duquesne campaign to their homes, they seized some stray horses, not seeming to realize that it was a serious offense against their white allies. Had they not seen white men do the same? But the owners of the animals quickly formed a posse and overtook and killed 12 or 14 of the Indians. This led the kinsmen of the dead to retaliate. Also, only a short time previously, Virginia hunters had attacked and wantonly murdered a small band of Cherokees. Moreover, General Forbes had offended Chief Atta-kulla-kulla and nine other head men. The Indians abandoned the English and started for their homes, but they were apprehended, disarmed, and forced to submit to other indignities. The Cherokees then resorted to war.

The lack of co-ordinated effort materially hampered the colonial cause. In January, 1760, Colonel Hugh Waddell marched to the relief of the South Carolina frontier with 500 North Carolinians; but before he reached the Indian country, Governor William Henry Lyttleton of South Carolina informed him that he had come to terms with the Cherokees. No sooner were his troops withdrawn than the Indians again engaged in depredations. In February, 1760, 100 mounted Cherokees massacred 50 settlers (men, women, and children) fleeing from the Long Cane settlement. Then raids and counter-raids followed, keeping the border in constant turmoil. On April 1, Colonel Archibald Montgomerie arrived at Charleston with better than 1,200 men, with instructions to march to the relief of Fort Loudon. There he was joined by more than 300 South Carolinians and, with his augmented force, started for the frontier. He met with minor success in the initial stages of this expedition; but before reaching his objective, he was ambushed by Si-lou-ee and a large force of hostiles, and compelled to withdraw, leaving Fort Loudon to its fate. Captain Raymond Demere surrendered the post on August 8, and on the following morning, as he and his men were marching toward Fort Prince George, they were attacked and he and 29 others were killed.

Finally, however, the three sorely stricken colonies learned to co-operate. One force of 2,600 men under the command of Colonel James Grant marched from Fort Prince George and defeated the Cherokees near the site of Montgomerie's defeat, and then laid waste their middle towns. Colonels Hugh Waddell and Adam Stephen led another force of North Carolina and Virginia troops to the Long Island of the Holston River, and there erected Fort Robinson. The Indians, beset on every hand by the whites, sued for peace; and on November 19, 1761, the war came to an end. A new era was now ushered in. Hundreds of men who had campaigned within the Indian country returned to the settlements resolved to return west and locate homes there in the near future.

Advancing the Frontier

Soon after King George's proclamation of 1763, North Carolina and Virginia settlers were advancing along the Holston and Clinch rivers and down Powell's River, east of the Cumberland Mountains and beyond the established boundary. Within a few years they had reached the Youghiogheny and Monongahela below the Red Stone Old Fort and westward to the Ohio. By 1766 the Virginia counties of Rockbridge, Augusta, Greenbrier, and Frederick, lying west of the Blue Ridge, were on the border; and the towns of Staunton, Lexington, and Winchester were remote trading-posts, inhabited by a few pioneers interested in trade with the Indians. Less than ten years before, Winchester had been an extreme frontier stockade post occupied by a few families who lived in apprehension of Indian massacre. Staunton, still farther westward, was laid off as a town in 1761; and Cumberland, Maryland, was

also a border military post more than 60 miles in advance of the settlements near Hagerstown, and 50 miles in the rear of those advancing
upon the sources of the Youghiogheny and Cheat rivers.

But by 1770 the advance was down the Youghiogheny and the Cheat,
and upon the Monongahela itself. This region soon became the focus
of immigration from Maryland, Pennsylvania, and northern Virginia;
and the fine valleys and rolling high grounds between, with their
sparkling, limpid streams, leaping along over rocky bottoms, were
extolled by surveyors and hunters alike who returned to visit eastern friends and relatives, until all were filled with bright visions of
establishing great landed estates in this hunter's paradise. The prospects were particularly alluring to the adventurous and youthful.

Based on Goode's Base Map No. 209E, by permission of University of Chicago Press

THE TRANS-ALLEGHENY FRONTIER, 1782–1800

The parent colonies were not slow to capitalize on this tendency. In 1770 the Virginia assembly enacted a law for the encouragement of western emigration. It allowed every actual settler, having a log cabin erected and any portion of the contiguous soil in cultivation, the right to 400 acres of land so located as to include his improvements. And a subsequent enactment extended the privilege further, allowing the owner of each 400 acres the preference of purchasing at a nominal cost 1,000 acres adjoining him. Other southern colonies enacted similar laws.

At this time surveying parties were at work upon the upper branches of the Great Kanawha, the Greenbrier, and the New rivers, and also upon the Little Kanawha and the Gauley. And the same emigrant tide was flowing westward from the southern parts of Virginia and North Carolina, beyond the sources of the Yadkin and Catawba, and upon the tributaries of the Clinch, beyond the limits assigned the whites by the treaty of Hard Labor (1768). The settlements on Powell's River and western branches of the Clinch were within the Indian country, and the Cherokees began to remonstrate against white intrusion. The treaty of Lochaber, however, set a new boundary to include within colonial jurisdiction the Clinch settlements.

The homeseekers moving to the upper Ohio and the Youghiogheny advanced across the mountains through Pennsylvania by way of Forts Bedford, Ligonier, and Loyal Hanna, while those from Virginia and Maryland traveled by way of Fort Cumberland and Red Stone Old Fort. The greater parts of these routes lay within an uninhabited wilderness of more than 200 miles. A wagon road was unknown west of the eastern settlements, and beyond was only a solitary horse-path meandering through rough defiles and over almost inaccessible mountains.

Because of the lack of roads, western emigrants were compelled to travel on horseback, in single file, carrying their small belongings upon the backs of pack-horses, driven likewise in single file. Most of those who traveled thus were fortunately encumbered with but a scanty share of this world's goods, "unless it were the poor man's 'boon,' a thriving family." In most cases, one or two pack-horses could bear the necessary impedimenta, commonly little more than a frying-pan or iron pot, a wheel, a hoe, an auger, and a saw, besides a few blankets and bedding. The indispensable part of each man's personal equipment was his long-barreled musket; his shot pouch and powder horn were a part of his buckskin apparel. If the emigrant must transport a family, an extra horse carried the wife with her personal effects, and another pack-horse, bestrode by two large hampers, bore the children.

Thus, traveling over dim border trails and on horseback, the earliest

Virginia and North Carolina homeseekers came to Watauga (1768).
Generally they were of a freedom-loving, hardy, and adventurous type,
of whom Acting-Governor William Nelson had complained as having
paid "very little if any Quit Rents . . . for his Majesty's use. . . ."
And there was an excellent reason why some of them were so disinclined! They had fled the North Carolina border to escape these
exactions. Thrilling accounts of the border country told by returning
hunters and surveyors—Boone, Findlay, and others—and disseminated
along the frontier by Judge Richard Henderson, the Harts, and John
Williams caused many a harassed back-country settler to seek the
western Utopia. During the years 1768–1769 Andrew Greer and
Julius Caesar Dugger were among the early arrivals within the
Watauga and Holston country. In the spring of 1770, James Robertson and other immigrants of Orange County, North Carolina, appeared.
Robertson was an able, conservative, and democratic leader of Scotch-
Irish ancestry. Here in the wilderness he was soon to command the
respect of settlers because of his untiring zeal in their behalf. And
not less endowed with the necessary qualities of leadership was another
with whom Robertson was to be associated—John Sevier, a young man
of Huguenot descent, from the Virginia Shenandoah town of Newmar-
ket. Both men had been trained in the rough-and-tumble life of the
border, where political idealism, social democracy, and a love for personal rights were in evidence. Not many years had passed before
isolated "stations" dotted the valleys of the Holston and Watauga.
Many settlers had come from North Carolina, where Governor William Tryon was attempting to suppress the Regulators who would dare
resist the collection of quit-rents and arbitrary exactions. And as
proof that these newcomers were not lawless, in 1772 they drew up a
written compact of government, the first of its kind west of the mountains. It continued in force until North Carolina incorporated the
area as a county in 1776. By 1773 the settlements extended down the
north branch of the Holston, upon the Nolichucky, French Broad, and
Clinch rivers; and within the year they spread along the western base
of the Allegheny range in a southwesterly direction for nearly 120
miles, and as far west as Long Island in the south fork of the Holston.

   Meanwhile Henderson, Robertson, and Boone were maturing their
plans for the Transylvania Company, to plant a large colony in what
is now Kentucky. But before Boone could blaze his Wilderness Trail
across the Cumberland Gap to Kentucky, more than 200 settlers
had already entered the country, most of whom had come down the
Ohio. Eighty of these, under James Harrod (from the Monongahela),
had established "Harrod's Station" on the Kentucky River. Others
had distributed themselves at other points. Even Boone had become

tired of waiting for the Transylvania colony to materialize. In September, 1773, he left the Yadkin with six families, including his own, and started toward Cumberland Gap. He was joined in Powell's Valley by 40 hunters, and the combined party moved on westward. But as it neared Cumberland Gap, on October 10, it was ambushed by a party of hostile Indians, and six of the men were killed and seven wounded. Among those slain was the 19-year-old son of Boone. All thought of going forward was now abandoned, and the homeseekers returned to the settlements.

But before the emigrant movement could meet with large results, Lord Dunmore's War had broken out. "Indian haters" had more than once embarrassed settlers in their border relations. Their behavior along the Ohio was much at fault during this period. Two peaceful Indian families on the Ohio below Wheeling were slain by them in the spring of 1774. Then, fearing reprisals from a peaceful neighboring tribe, Captain Michael Cresap, stationed at Fort Fincastle, led a mixed force of his troops and of local ne'er-do-wells in the massacre of some of its members. Then a few days later Daniel Greathouse and other traders murdered some Indians at Baker's Bottom, after pretending friendship and making them drunk on cheap liquor. Among those slain at this time were the brother and sister of Chief Logan of the Mingos. Then there was the long-standing Indian grievance—white settler encroachment on Indian lands. Only recently Governor John Murray Dunmore of Virginia had sent Thomas Bullitt, Hancock Taylor, James Harrod, and the three McAfee brothers (James, George, and Robert) to survey 200,000 acres of land promised officers and soldiers who had fought in the Seven Years' War. So, fearing final annihilation, the Shawnees, Mingos, and Ottawas, under Chiefs Cornstalk and Logan, now went to war.

When Governor Dunmore saw that an Indian war had come, he raised two bodies of troops and sent them hurrying out to the Ohio. One of these, comprising three regiments of volunteers and militia under Major Andrew Lewis, was assembled at Camp Union and marched to the mouth of the Great Kanawha; and another, under Governor Dunmore himself, moved to Fort Pitt. Fortunately the war was not of long duration, and many of the horrors of other border wars were avoided. Traders and colonial agents had seen the threatening war clouds and had warned the settlers at exposed stations to leave the Indian country. On October 10, 1774, Cornstalk and Logan with their warriors attacked Major Lewis' force at Point Pleasant, near the mouth of the Great Kanawha, and from early morning until after four o'clock in the afternoon the field was hotly contested. Indeed, the engagement was one of the most fiercely fought of all Indian battles. Colonel William

Preston of the Fincastle region wrote to Patrick Henry that the warriors behaved in battle with "inconceivable bravery." But a part of Lewis' force successfully carried out a flanking movement, and the Indians in despair fled from the field; and soon thereafter they sued for peace.

Many border men who were to rise to prominence in the approaching American Revolution served in this campaign. Marching in the ranks of Lewis' army were Isaac Shelby and William Campbell, leaders of the colonists at King's Mountain, and James Robertson, Valentine Sevier, Daniel Morgan, Major Arthur Campbell, Benjamin Logan, Anthony Bledsoe, and Simon Kenton. And with Dunmore were Adam Stephens, George Rogers Clark, and John Stuart. Most of these had seen service in previous border wars or had met the Indians in trade relations.

Although Henderson and his associates had planned a Kentucky colony, it was not until 1775 that active steps in this direction were taken. Boone now urged Henderson to negotiate a treaty with the Cherokees to relinquish their claims on the proposed site. And perhaps an additional incentive for haste was a report that a rival company, including such notable men as William Byrd, John Page, Patrick Henry, and William Christian, were planning a similar project. Henderson accepted Boone's suggestion, and early in 1775 reorganized his company by including such prominent men as the Harts (David, Nathaniel, and Thomas), John Williams, James Hogg, Leonard H. Bullock, John Luttrell, and William Johnston. Then at Sycamore Shoals, on the Watauga River, on March 17, 1775, he and his associates negotiated a treaty with the Cherokees whereby for a consideration of £10,000 in money and goods the Indians were to surrender some 20,000,000 acres, now embraced in Kentucky and a part of Tennessee. The council of the red and white men was well attended. In addition to 1,200 Indians present, there were also several hundred buckskin-clad frontiersmen, among whom were James Robertson, John Sevier, Isaac Shelby, and, at least for a part of the time, Boone.

But Boone had been given another important assignment. Before the "Great Grant" was signed, Henderson commissioned him to mark a route from the Watauga settlements to Kentucky. The doughty pioneer acted promptly. With a party of about 20 hunters and woodsmen, in March he began his arduous task of blazing a trail across Cumberland Gap to the Kentucky River, north of the present town of Richmond, Madison County, Kentucky. Indians watched with jealous interest the progress of the survey, and on two occasions they attacked Boone's camp, killing four men and wounding five others. But a few days later, in spite of perils and difficulties, Boone reached the banks of the Kentucky and immediately started the construction of a "station," subsequently known as Boonesborough.

Meanwhile Henderson, at the head of 40 armed men and a pack-horse caravan, started for Kentucky by way of Powell's Valley. Many adventurers joined him on the way or at Boonesborough a short time later. After the arrival of Henderson at his Kentucky colony, Boone returned to Virginia to conduct several families across the mountains, including his own wife and daughter. For the next two years the colony prospered. A popular assembly was created to govern the people and to set up offices and agents for the sale and survey of land. And, in order to provide for a greater measure of security, another station was established near the present site of Stanford, in Lincoln County, under the command of Colonel Benjamin Logan. Moreover, Harrodsburg, as previously noted, and Lexington had also become nuclei settlements. Yet Henderson and his associates were soon to meet with insurmountable difficulties. Virginia would not recognize the Sycamore Shoals treaty with the Cherokees, particularly when it was known that so much of her western domain was involved and that Henderson had boasted of an independent course if he could only receive 500 colonists. Thus supported, he would not care what position Virginia took in the matter. But, much to the chagrin of the colonizer, the Kentucky settlers, obviously to establish more certain claims to their homesteads, now began to rally to the support of Virginia. Nor would Congress support Henderson. Finally, after Transylvania agents had lobbied much, both in the halls of Congress and in the Virginia assembly, the associates were given 200,000 acres between the Ohio and the Green rivers for their Kentucky lands.

On December 7, 1776, the Virginia legislature erected that part of the Transylvania grant lying within her charter limits as the County of Kentucky. Similarly North Carolina created, in November, 1777, the County of Washington, including not only the settlements of the Watauga and Holston regions, but the whole of the present state of Tennessee. A short time later Henderson and Robertson made plans to colonize their new grant. Early in 1780 Robertson led the vanguard of settlers to the site picked for the colony, Nashborough (present Nashville). Some colonists came by boat down the Tennessee and up the Cumberland; some followed other routes. Thus middle Tennessee became a new land of promise. When Henderson arrived, he proceeded to draw up a plan of government, the "Cumberland Compact," which the settlers signed on May 13, thereby putting into operation another pure democracy within the western wilderness. Moreover, a land office was opened and claims were registered for the nominal sum of $10 per 1,000 acres. But, like Virginia in this respect, too, the

North Carolina legislature in 1783 voided Henderson's rights to the area, and gave him in exchange 190,000 acres in Powell's Valley.

As was seen in Chapter 7, the years of the American Revolution were characterized by Indian raids and massacres, British intrigues, and colonial retaliation along the border. The British agents, Stuart and Alexander Cameron, in 1776 conspired with southern chieftains to pillage the border settlements, and the usual raids followed. The frontiers of Rowan and Catawba were ravaged, and Old Abraham led his band of warriors in an attack on a border fort near Sycamore Shoals. But the colonists were quick to retaliate. They had learned a costly lesson during the previous Cherokee War. The Carolinas, Virginia, and Georgia conducted a joint campaign against the Indians. More than 3,000 troops, led by General Griffith Rutherford and Colonels Andrew Williamson, Samuel Jack, and William Christian, marched in separate columns into the Indian country, administered the warriors a series of costly defeats, laid waste their villages, and forced them to agree to peace terms. The crestfallen Indians now recognized that the white men were in the trans-Allegheny country to stay, although they continued their sporadic attacks.

The dawn of peace brought hundreds of eager homeseekers to the Kentucky and Tennessee areas. North Carolina extended her jurisdiction over the Nashborough area in 1783 by the creation of Davidson County; and Washington, Sullivan, and Greene counties were spread over the mountain regions. Yet the Watauga and Holston pioneers wished to maintain local control, for they had long since developed an antipathy for the tidewater overlords. Consequently, in 1784 when North Carolina ceded her western lands to the federal government, the Tennessee Valley settlements, under the leadership of Sevier, organized the State of Franklin. But its provisional government came to an inglorious end. North Carolina reasserted its control over the rebellious area in 1786, and Sevier was outlawed as a traitor (but finally pardoned and honored as a hero).

The phenomenal growth of Kentucky and Tennessee during the first seven years after the general treaty of peace was signed is revealed by the incomplete Census returns of 1790. Kentucky had a population of 73,677, while that of Tennessee was about half as much. When Congress accepted the North Carolina cession on April 2, 1790, the act of acceptance stipulated that the United States should "assume the government of the said ceded territory, which they shall execute in a manner similar to that which they support in the territory west of the Ohio . . . provided always that no regulations made or to be made by Congress shall tend to emancipate slaves." Then Congress enacted in the following month a law setting up a temporary government for all the territory south of the Ohio similar to that provided for the Northwest Territory three years previously, with William Blount as governor. Statehood soon followed. On June 1, 1792, Kentucky became a state, and her representatives presented themselves before Congress meeting in Philadelphia; and exactly four years later Tennessee followed, with Sevier as governor, Blount as one of its senators, and a rising young lawyer, Andrew Jackson, as one of its representatives.

SETTLEMENTS ALONG THE GULF AND THE MISSISSIPPI

At the end of the French and Indian War (1763), England acquired the Spanish Floridas in exchange for Havana, which an English fleet had occupied during the war. West Florida, with which we are more concerned in this book, was east of the Mississippi River, between the mouth of the Yazoo River and the Bayou Manchac, and extending eastward to the Chattahoochee River. East of Lake Maurepas, it comprised all the coast and ports of the Gulf of Mexico to Apalachicola Bay. This entire area was to be under an English governor (after the Proclamation of 1763), whose headquarters was at Pensacola. Early in February, 1764, Captain George Johnston arrived at Pensacola with a regiment of troops, which were distributed in garrisons at Conde, near Mobile, now renamed Fort Charlotte; at Fort Bute, erected in 1765 on the north bank of the Iberville; at Baton Rouge; and at Fort Rosalie, later called Fort Panmure. Presently measures were taken to put in operation a civil government under English commandants and magistrates, and to create superior courts under English judges.

Although a large portion of the French *habitants* migrated from West Florida before the beginning of British control, yet others remained when they were assured that their institutions and property would be secure under the English regime. Immigrants coming from various other lands tended to make the population quite diverse. This was encouraging to the English authorities, who sought to stimulate immigration by offering trade monopolies, by importing slaves to aid in cotton culture, and by promising large land grants. General Thaddeus Lyman, of Connecticut, was one of the first newcomers to capitalize on these promises. He was given 20,000 acres on the upper waters of Bayou Pierre, upon which he established a colony. And Amos Ogden, Dr. John Lorimer, William Grant, William Garnier, and Augustin Provost were others who received large grants ranging in size from 4,000 acres to 25,000 acres. Considerable effort was also put forth to encourage English, Irish, and West Indian colonists to come, and not without success. Scotch homeseekers were also attracted. In the early years of English occupation, a colony of Scotch Highlanders from North Carolina arrived in West Florida and located about 30 miles east of Natchez; and in subsequent years it received many accessions from Scotland.

Within a few years after Governor Johnston established his government in West Florida, large numbers of homeseekers came by way of the Ohio and the Mississippi from the Atlantic seaboard colonies. About 1767 a group from the Roanoke Valley of North Carolina planted the first Anglo-American colony on the banks of the Mississippi. During the next three years numerous others came from Georgia, the Carolinas, and New Jersey, and settled in the upland region from Baton Rouge to Grand Gulf Hills. Colonists from New England and the Middle Atlantic area made their way overland to the Monongahela, and thence on flatboats drifted down that stream, the Ohio, and the Mississippi to the Natchez country; while others from the Southern colonies joined them on the broad bosom of the Ohio by crossing Cumberland Gap and the Watauga and Holston region to the Tennessee, and thence down this river to the Ohio. Still others sailed around from the Atlantic seaboard across the Gulf to Pensacola and Mobile.

Thus, by the outbreak of the American Revolution, hundreds of immigrants from New England, the Middle Atlantic colonies, and the South, and from England, Scotland, Ireland, and the British West Indies, had found homes in the country from Natchez to Pensacola. Few of these were vitally interested in the controversy between England and her colonies along the Atlantic seaboard. Problems incident to the building of homes in this new land claimed their undivided attention. But with the outbreak of war, Whig and Tory sympathizers appeared: the latter, before the end of the war, receiving considerable strength from new arrivals who had been persecuted by the revolutionists because of supporting the English cause. Yet, on the whole, West Florida maintained a fair degree of neutrality, so much so that the King's sympathizers allowed more than one boat, loaded with guns, ammunition, and other supplies, to go up the Mississippi from New Orleans to the American forts on the Ohio.

The watchful Governor Bernardo de Galvez of Louisiana viewed with ill-concealed satisfaction the early successes of the Americans. He foresaw the time when France and Spain would support the colonial cause, at which time he proposed to overrun West Florida. He had been greatly incensed because of English efforts to monopolize the Southwestern Indian trade. Nor did he have long to wait. On May 8, 1779, Spain entered the war against England, and presently Galvez sent 1,400 troops against Fort Bute, which they carried by assault on September 7. English troops fought courageously to save West Florida, but the Spaniards outnumbered them and were better

supplied. By March 14, 1780, Galvez's troops succeeded in taking
Pensacola, and Spanish conquest was thereby complete. Spain was now
prepared to negotiate peace on the basis of *uti possidetis* (conquest).

But the American peace commissioners in Paris frustrated Spanish
designs on the Southwest. John Jay, John Adams, and Benjamin
Franklin were alarmed by Spanish intrigue; and although the French
Alliance pact had stipulated a joint agreement with England, they
concluded separate articles of agreement with England in 1782. The
western boundary of the United States was to be the Mississippi from
its source to the thirty-first parallel, in the event England lost West
Florida. From this point, the southern line was to run along the
thirty-first parallel until the Chattahoochee was reached, thence down
this river to the mouth of the Flint, thence in a line directly to the
source of the St. Mary's, and along its course to the sea. That part of
the southern boundary between the Mississippi and the Chattahoochee
would thereby become the northern boundary of West Florida. But a
secret clause of the understanding provided that if for any reason
England should be allowed to retain West Florida, she would reserve
the right to claim a northern boundary line from the mouth of the
Yazoo due eastward to the Chattahoochee (32° 28'), and thence along
that river as under the other condition. The Spanish ambassador in
Paris, realizing that he had been outmaneuvered, sought to influence
the French minister of foreign affairs, Vergennes, to renounce the
American-English agreement, but in this he was unsuccessful. By the
general treaty of September 3, 1783, England not only abandoned all
claim to the trans-Allegheny country, but she handed the two Floridas
over to Spain, thereby allowing the United States the thirty-first parallel as a southwestern boundary. And later, as will be explained
shortly, Spain reluctantly accepted the new line.

MISSISSIPPI AND ALABAMA

For twelve years following the general treaty, Spanish diplomats in
Washington and Madrid, and governors in New Orleans, made every
effort to nullify the American claim to the thirty-first parallel as a
southwestern boundary. Furthermore, Spain had ambitions on the
entire Southwest, and sought to alienate the Ohio Valley settlements
from that part of the new nation east of the Alleghenies. Agents went
among the Creeks and aroused them to hostility, even though Alexander McGillivray, one of their leaders, had been liberally compensated by the United States for losses which he had sustained as a Tory
during the Revolution (and peace had been concluded with other
chiefs). But "Mad" Anthony Wayne's victory over the Northwestern
Indians in 1794 abruptly halted a threatened war and taught the

Creeks to respect the power of their white neighbors. Other emissaries visited the disaffected areas of the Ohio Valley and sought to buy the support of important leaders who had grievances against the Spanish officials of Louisiana because of their restricting the American use of the Mississippi. Indeed, the era was one of plots and intrigues in which the ubiquitous Governors Estevan Miró and Carondelet sought to buy the services of the equally designing James Wilkinson and Judge Sebastian. Westerners were not only incensed because of Spanish denial of their right of Mississippi navigation, but also because of the venality of Louisiana officials. One Ohio Valley settler who had sought to transport his commodities down the river would return, sometimes after months, to report that his goods had been confiscated and he had been imprisoned; another, who had bribed the governor or collectors, would report that every consideration had been shown him. This was an ever-present source of annoyance to Kentucky settlers which increasingly endangered Spanish control of Louisiana. On the general practice of Spanish bribe-receiving, Daniel Clark, an American consul at New Orleans, wrote in 1803: ". . . all the officers will plunder when the opportunity offers; they are all venal. A bargain can be made with the governor, the intendant, a judge, or a collector, and all others down to a constable."

John Jay's tentative promise to the Spanish Ambassador in 1785 not to press the American demand for the free navigation of the Mississippi had greatly angered Westerners, and had caused some to desire other allegiance. And for a time Wilkinson and others could receive Spanish silver and be given favorable trade considerations at New Orleans without offense. But by 1795 western settlers lent no support to Spanish efforts to win them over. All the while the federal government did not desert them, and this they finally learned. Kentucky was admitted as a State in 1792, and Wayne's victory over the Northwestern Indians followed two years later. Now the Ohio Valley settlers could have more confidence in the strength of the national government. Moreover, Spanish diplomats had received a considerable scare when Citizen Genet in 1794 proposed to raise a western army to capture New Orleans. Then on October 20, 1795, at San Lorenzo, Thomas Pinckney concluded a treaty with Manuel Godoy, the Spanish minister, which gave the United States the right of free navigation of the Mississippi, recognized the thirty-first parallel as a southwestern boundary, and allowed the Mississippi traders the right of deposit at New Orleans with only the normal cost of storing their goods in warehouses until they could be reshipped.

But this did not solve the West Florida problem. Spanish officials at New Orleans still had hopes that Spain could retain control of all the West Florida country. At this time Natchez, Mobile, Pensacola, Baton Rouge, and Feliciana had a combined population of about 6,000, and Spain did not propose to surrender so easily such a thriving center of culture. The Spanish government refused to appoint surveyors to aid in establishing the boundary until 1798, and armed conflict within the Natchez district was narrowly averted. However, with the work of survey in this year and the arrival of General Wilkinson at Natchez with United States troops, Spain at last gave up her dilatory tactics.

In the same year of Spanish withdrawal from the northern part of West Florida (1798), Congress approved an act on April 7 to erect in the ceded area the Mississippi Territory. Its boundaries were the Mississippi on the west, the thirty-first parallel on the south, the line of 32° 28′ on the north, and the Chattahoochee-Apalachicola on the east. A few years later a supplemental act of Congress enlarged the territory by adding the Georgia cession south of Tennessee. By a second act on May 10, the new district was given a territorial government of the "first grade," as was done when the Northwest Territory was set up. The first governor was Winthrop Sargent, formerly secretary of the Northwest Territory. The territorial judges arrived at Natchez on August 6, 1798, and 20 days later General Wilkinson established his military headquarters there.

There was still another complication of the problem of the Southwest. Georgia also claimed the region in dispute between the United States and Spain because of her early charter grant, which she believed was strengthened by the general treaty of 1783. The rich alluvial lands between Natchez and the Georgia frontier were an ever-present attraction for speculators, not only in Georgia but in other Southern states also. Furthermore, the Georgia legislature sought to occupy the Yazoo country to encourage these unduly ambitious investors. Wild schemes of speculation pervaded the State's legislative halls; the "County of Bourbon" was set up to incorporate that part of the Natchez district contiguous to the Mississippi, and the legislature sold some 35,000,000 acres of land to four companies for the sum of $500,000. The Mississippi Company, with a grant of more than 3,000,000 acres, was one of these. The collusive interest of the legislature in the enterprise is shown by the fact that company stockholders included 19 legislators. And George Walker, Zachariah Coxe, William Longstreet, and Wade Hampton were important company leaders, whose family names were to be well known in subsequent Southern history. The Mississippi Company was not slow to take advantage of such liberal terms. Its promoters immediately set to work to dispose of the new grant by offering cheap land to homesteaders and by initiating an elaborate advertising campaign. But the outraged citizens of

Georgia turned out the old legislature and elected a new one which cancelled the grant made to the Mississippi Company. This led to much confusion, for already some of the company's lands had been sold. A court action growing out of these voided sales eventually came before the Supreme Court in the well-remembered Fletcher *vs.* Peck case (1810), wherein it was held that the original Act of 1795, conveying the Yazoo grants, was a contract within the meaning of the Constitution which might not be impaired by later legislation. But, in the end, Congress in 1814 compensated the luckless and defrauded claimants to the amount of $8,000,000.

After the invention of the cotton gin (1793), the increasing demand of European factories for lint stimulated the rapid expansion of cotton culture. The Southern crop in 1810 was worth $13,000,000; and 25 years later it had leaped to more than $75,000,000. Along with this production increase, large plantations were established throughout the South, and hundreds of thousands of slaves were imported to work the fields. Soon the best cotton lands were incorporated into the holdings of these "cotton kings," and many smaller landholders sold their properties and sought other frontiers. The inrush of cotton growers brought about a rapid growth in the population of Mississippi Territory. After the State of Georgia ceded her western lands to the federal government in 1802, the Territory was enlarged to include the whole of the present States of Alabama and Mississippi, north of the thirty-first parallel. The immigrant tide overflowed into West Florida during the summer of 1810, when Anglo-American settlers occupied the West Feliciana district; and on October 27, 1810, President James Madison authorized Governor W. C. C. Claiborne of Louisiana to take possession of West Florida to the Perdido River in the name of the United States. Congress subsequently joined a part of it to the State of Louisiana, and the rest to the Territory of Mississippi. Newly arrived settlers had come to Mississippi by every known approach—the Natchez Trace (across the western corner of Mississippi); the Ohio-Mississippi river route; across the Gulf of Mexico; and the Federal Road (from Fort Hawkins in western Georgia westward to the Chattahoochee, to Hickory Grove on the Alabama, thence to the Tombigbee, and then on to Natchez *via* the thirty-first parallel).

By 1810 the Territory of Mississippi had a population of 40,352, and seven years later Congress cut off its western part as the State of Mississippi. In the same year the eastern half was set up as the Territory of Alabama. But it was to remain under a territorial government for only two years before it, too, entered the Union as a State.

The development of the Southwest from 1784 to 1819 had far exceeded the dreams of Thomas Jefferson and his colleagues who had devised the first western ordinance. At the end of this period its well-established communities, its thriving plantation system, its millions of acres of well-cultivated cotton lands, and its rapidly developing trade and commerce constituted a living memorial to the courage and intrepidity of the buckskin-clad pioneer who had braved the horrors of Indian massacre and the hardships of border life in order to build a home in the western wilderness. But having succeeded in this monumental achievement, he had now reached the broad Mississippi and was ready to begin the conquest of the vast region beyond.

BIBLIOGRAPHY

In addition to the general accounts of Winsor, Alvord, Monette, and Paxson, as cited at the end of Chapter 7, which are also helpful in following the principal narrative of this chapter, there are others of particular value. Two of these generally cited in bibliographies because of their acknowledged merit are A. Henderson, *The Conquest of the Old Southwest* (New York, 1920); and C. L. Skinner, *Pioneers of the Old Southwest* (*Chronicles of America*, New Haven, 1919, Vol. XVIII).   Others are as follows: Thomas Marshall Green, *The Spanish Conspiracy: A Review of Early Spanish Movements in the Southwest* (Cincinnati, 1891); Theodore Roosevelt, *Winning of the West* (4 vols., New York, 1889–1896); William B. Hesseltine, *A History of the South, 1607–1936* (New York, 1936); G. W. Ranck, *History of Lexington, Kentucky* (Cincinnati, 1872); Edward S. Corwin, *French Policy and the American Alliance of 1778* (Princeton, 1916); F. J. Turner, *Significance of the Frontier in American History* (Chicago, 1899); L. K. Koontz, *The Virginia Frontier* (Baltimore, 1925); J. W. Pratt, *The Expansionists of 1812* (New York, 1925); I. J. Cox, *The West Florida Controversy* (Baltimore, 1918); A. B. Meek, *Romantic Passages in Southwestern History* (New York, 1857); H. Gannett, *Boundaries of the United States, and of the Several States and Territories* (Washington, 1885); and William Christie Macleod, *The American Indian Frontier* (New York, 1928).

Biographical studies of particular merit are as follows: J. S. Bassett (ed.), *Life of Andrew Jackson* (2 vols., New York, 1911); R. G. Thwaites, *Daniel Boone* (New York, 1902); John P. Hale, *Daniel Boone, Some Facts and Incidents not Hitherto Published* (Wheeling, n.d.); F. M. Turner, *The Life of General John Sevier* (New York, 1910); C. S. Driver, *John Sevier* (Chapel Hill, 1932); Royal Ornan Shreve, *The Finished Scoundrel* (Indianapolis, 1933); A. W. Putnam, *History of Middle Tennessee, or Life and Times of General James Robinson* (Nashville, 1859); Marquis James, *Andrew Jackson, the Border Captain* (Indianapolis, 1933); ————, *The Raven, A Biography of Sam Houston* (Indianapolis, 1929); James Parton, *Life of Andrew Jackson* (3 vols., Boston, 1870); and William Graham Sumner, *Andrew Jackson as a Public Man* (*American Statesmen*, Boston, 1882).

Documentary sourcebooks should be examined for territorial and state documents and for contemporary thought. The three divisions of *American State Papers* (Washington, 1834) listed as *Public Lands*, I, II, *Foreign Affairs*, I, and *Indian Affairs*, I, II, are indispensable. Others of interest are

J. S. Bassett (ed.), *The Writings of Colonel William Byrd of Westover* (New York, 1901); Clarence Edwin Carter (ed.), *Territorial Papers of the United States* (Washington, 1936), *Southwest Territory*, IV; Henry Steele Commager (ed.), *Documents of American History*, (*Crofts American History Series*, New York, 1934); and *Niles Register* (76 vols., Baltimore, 1811–1849), edited by Hezekiah Niles. The volumes of the last-named source have much material of value on the Southwest.

9

THE OLD NORTHWEST

ALTHOUGH NUCLEI settlements had
been planted in Kentucky, Tennessee, and West Florida by the end of
the American Revolution, the vast region between the Ohio and the
Great Lakes and west of Pennsylvania was uninhabited except for
some 2,000 French *habitants* living at Cahokia, Kaskaskia, Vincennes,
and other isolated posts. After 1783 immigrant trains moved west
over the Braddock Road (cut through the Upper Potomac region in
1755) and the Forbes Road of 1758, both of which ran to the Ohio
country from the tidewater towns of Alexandria and Philadelphia, respectively. But the back country of Pennsylvania and northwestern
Virginia remained relatively unchanged for some time to come. Even
as late as 1790 one authority noticed only a few islands of settlement
in and beyond the mountains. One, containing 63,218 people, was in
southwestern Pennsylvania; two others, containing together 55,873,
were clustered about Wheeling and near the mouth of the Kanawha;
and still another, containing 73,677, was in Kentucky below Licking
River. Yet these had been nonexistent, or very small, at the close of
the war. Western Virginia had only a few habitations on the Kanawha,
Greenbrier, Elk, and Cheat rivers; while the country near the Ohio,
from Fishing Creek to the Licking, a distance of 300 miles, was too
exposed to harrowing Indian raids to afford a safe residence. That
part of western Pennsylvania south of the Allegheny River was a
frontier. Clarksburg was a border village, and the region between the
Ohio and the west branch of the Monongahela, from 30 to 50 miles in
width, had only recently been subject to continual Indian incursions.

The slow advance here and the failure of settlers to occupy the
Northwest were in part owing to the fierce opposition of the Shawnee,
Delaware, Wyandot, and other resident Indian tribes under their
rallying cry, "White men shall not plant corn north of the Ohio." The
closing years of the American Revolution were accompanied by numerous Indian battles and massacres along the Ohio and the Virginia and
Pennsylvania borders in which the atrocities committed by the Indians

130

were hardly more inhuman than those perpetrated by pioneers. In 1782 a settler force under the command of Colonel David Williamson massacred 96 peaceful, Christian Indians at Gnadenhütten on the Muskingum, about halfway between the settlements and the hostile Indian country, on the pretense that they were furnishing encouragement to the Shawnee and other hostile bands who frequently raided the borders of Pennsylvania and Virginia. But this brutal act only stimulated the war bands to renewed barbarities, and shortly thereafter a second invading force under Colonel William Crawford afforded them a chance for revenge. Crawford's men were defeated, and when a retreat was ordered, the exultant savages picked off band after band of the stragglers and took prisoners, among them the commander, who was subsequently burned at the stake after being subjected to horrible tortures. Captain Caldwell suffered another severe defeat in the battle of Blue Licks, while operating in the Ohio country, and lost 71 men. As a result, George Rogers Clark again took the field at the head of a retaliatory expedition, and marched against the Indians' Miami towns. The warriors fled in terror before him; and, although no important battle was fought, Indian villages were burned and crops were laid waste. Consequently, the Kentucky settlements were to be free from Indian depredations for many years.

EARLY OHIO

Even before the close of the Indian war, the white man's westward march was resumed. Over Braddock's Road, Forbes Road, and the Wilderness Road, pack-horse and ox-drawn caravans were pushing toward the Ohio, carrying families, household goods, and supplies. Merchandise from Philadelphia and Baltimore was transported across the mountains by way of Ligonier and Cumberland to Pittsburgh and Brownsville, and, when the Ohio was reached, down that river by keelboat and scow to Limestone and the Kentucky settlements. As early as the summer of 1784 Daniel Broadhead opened the first dry-goods store in Louisville; and in the next year, "Colonel" James Wilkinson, who was later to gain an unenviable reputation as a Spanish agent in the West, set up another at Lexington. A few years later substantial residences were substituted for primitive lean-tos and log cabins, and stone chimneys displaced those of mud and sticks.

Meanwhile the Ohio Associates had matured their plans for colonization after they had once received their Muskingum grant. Already Benjamin Tupper and Samuel Holden Parsons had visited the Ohio and returned to New England to tell of the wonders of their promised land. Yet in 1788 the only evidences of the white man's hold on this country were two military posts—Fort McIntosh, at the mouth of the

Big Beaver, and Fort Harmar, at the confluence of the Muskingum and the Ohio. Still there was no lack of homeseekers ready for the journey. By the fall of 1787 General Rufus Putnam, with the vanguard of 47 persons, reached the Youghiogheny, bound for the "Northwestern Territory." For several weeks they had toiled over a rough, primitive road from Philadelphia through Pennsylvania before they reached "Sumrill's Ferry" on the Youghiogheny. Here they stopped for the winter, but they were not idle. Under the direction of a skilled builder, they constructed several small boats and a large barge, covered in such a way as to be bullet-proof and to protect the emigrants from Indian attack when once they started through the Indian country down the Ohio. In remembrance of their Pilgrim ancestors, they called it the *Mayflower*.

Toward the last of March, 1788, while a hint of winter was yet in the air, the *Mayflower* began its trip. Early in April the emigrants arrived at the mouth of the Muskingum. Putnam and others chose a site for the colony upon the east bank of the river where it joins the Ohio, opposite Fort Harmar. The colonists disembarked immediately and began their toils to establish the first important English settlement west of the Ohio. On July 2 they were joined by the families of General Edward Tupper and Majors Asa Coburn, Nathan Goodale, Nathaniel Cushing, and Ichabod Nye, all of whom had traveled overland to Wheeling, and thence by boat to the mouth of the Muskingum. On July 4 the combined party crossed the Muskingum and celebrated the Declaration of Independence fittingly with the soldiers at Fort Harmar.

Shortly after the coming of the second body of emigrants, the territorial officials arrived, and forthwith Governor Arthur St. Clair published his commission and those of his executive council, as well as the ordinance of Congress under which the territorial government was set up. Then in a public meeting he explained to the settlers the provisions of the Northwest Ordinance and asked their cordial co-operation, which was given. Later three militia companies with their complements of officers were organized; three justices of the peace were appointed; a probate court (and clerk) and a court of quarter sessions (with three associate justices, having jurisdiction over common pleas) were provided; and a sheriff was appointed.

The building of a formidable "station," much like that of Boonesborough, was one of the first accomplishments of the settlers. It was described by a mid-nineteenth-century historian as follows:

The walls of the main buildings formed a regular parallelogram of one hundred and eighty feet on each side. Each corner was protected subsequently, in 1791, by a strong projecting block-house, twenty feet square in the lower story, and twenty-four feet in the upper. Each block-house was surmounted by a tower, or sentry-box, bullet-proof; and the curtains, or sides of the parallelogram, were protected by a range of sharpened pickets, inclining outward. The whole was surrounded by a strong palisade ten feet high, and securely planted in the ground beyond which was a range of abattis.

The buildings were constructed of whip-sawed timbers four inches thick, and neatly dove-tailed at the corners, two stories high, and covered with good shingle roofs. The rooms were large and commodious, provided with good fireplaces and brick chimneys.

A guarded gateway on the west and south front gave admission and exit to the inmates; and over the gateway, facing the Muskingum on the south, was a large room, surmounted with a belfry, in which was suspended the churchgoing bell. The whole range of buildings was amply supplied with portholes for defensive firing. Such is the outline of the first regular station northwest of the Ohio, known as the "Campus Martius."

But "Campus Martius" was only the beginning of construction work. Shortly the plat of a town was laid off on the bank of the Ohio, above the mouth of the Muskingum, to which was given the name of Marietta, in honor of Queen Marie Antoinette of France. These first settlers were augmented by a second group which arrived in December, and by the following spring the colony had passed beyond its experimental stage.

Others followed quickly. Judge John Cleves Symmes, of the North-western Territory, backed by Elias Boudinot and Jonathan Dayton, acquired a land purchase of upward of 1,000,000 acres between the two Miami rivers, upon which three settlements were made. One of these, Columbia, near the mouth of the Little Miami, was founded by Benjamin Stites on November 18, 1788. The following January another was established by Mathias Denham, Robert Patterson, and John Filson opposite the mouth of the Licking, and called L-os-anti-ville. On a third site, 15 miles below L-os-anti-ville, on February 2, Judge Symmes with a small party founded North Bend. Most of these settlers of the Miami area were from New Jersey and the Middle Atlantic States, and made more heterogeneous the Northwestern population. For six months after L-os-anti-ville was established, it had only 11 families and 24 single men, because, perhaps, it was on an old Indian warpath. But good fortune favored it. Shortly Major Doughty, with 140 troops, arrived from Fort Harmar to establish a new post (Fort Washington) near by, and thereafter its growth was assured. The community was now rechristened Cincinnati, in honor of an ex-soldier society, of which many of the settlers were members. Then in 1790 Governor St. Clair transferred the capital thither from Marietta, and subsequently, too, the first territorial legislature sat in the same town. Thus, in later years Cincinnati grew in wealth and population, while Columbia and North Bend were to be less active.

The extensive region of the Virginia Military District next attracted settlers. Substantial Virginians, who later influenced the political life of the new commonwealth and who contributed another social element to that of the New Englanders and Middle Atlantic folk already in the country, claimed grants in this remote country. In 1796 General Nathaniel Massie and Duncan McArthur established the town of Chillicothe on the west bank of the Scioto. Massie had been one of a surveying party directed by Surveyor-general Richard C. Anderson, who in the autumn of 1787 had run the boundaries of the area between the Little Miami and the Scioto rivers. Near the close of 1790 he had also led the first group of colonists to a site 12 miles above Limestone, which was later named Manchester. Five years later, he had accompanied surveyors to the Paint Creek country, south and west of Chillicothe, with the object of establishing the site of a new colony; but they had met hostile Indians, and turned back to Manchester. In March following he returned with another party, traveling up the Scioto to the mouth of Paint Creek. Here he established a "station." From this center, settlements spread; while three miles above the "station," Chillicothe became a thriving village.

Connecticut's Western Reserve was also an early center of a large settlement within the present State of Ohio. Oliver Phelps and 55 other New Englanders had formed the Connecticut Land Company to colonize the Reserve. On September 16, 1796, Moses Cleaveland and other agents of the company visited Lake Erie and laid off the town of Cleveland upon a dry, wooded plain comprising a peninsula between the Cuyahoga River and the lake. From the arrival of this advance party for several years to come, New England settlers moved up the Mohawk-Genesee route across central New York to Lake Erie, bound for the new land. By 1800 twenty or thirty thriving settlements had sprung up in the vicinity of the first, with a total population of 1,302. At this time the area passed from the control of Connecticut to the Northwest Territory, and was organized as Trumbull County. Still Cleveland gained little in population until after it became the county seat of Geauga (later Cuyahoga) County in 1806, after which it grew rapidly. Meanwhile, about 120 miles away, on the upper Ohio around Fort Steuben, was still another settlement, later called Steubenville, founded by settlers from Pennsylvania and Virginia.

Thus by 1800 several of the Atlantic seaboard states were represented in the population of the Northwestern Territory, as well as in the settlements south of the Ohio. Many emigrants traveled the Mohawk route from New England to Ohio; many others from Pennsylvania, Maryland, New Jersey, and Virginia journeyed to Brownsville and Wheeling, and thence descended the Ohio by keel-boat to

Limestone and other points in Kentucky. However, some who reached Wheeling crossed the Ohio and traveled overland to one of the several Ohio colonies. By 1796 the white population of the Northwestern Territory had increased to about 5,000, distributed chiefly in the valleys of the Muskingum, Scioto, and Miami rivers. Cincinnati was now a thriving town of more than 100 log cabins, besides some 10 or 12 frame structures, and with a population of nearly 600. And within the Virginia Military District were several new settlements. Massie had surveyed most of the fertile lands between the Scioto and Little Miami as far north as Todd's Fork and Paint Creek, and settlers had quickly followed to claim home-sites.

"MAD" ANTHONY WAYNE'S INDIAN CAMPAIGN

During the period in which the Northwestern Territory was being occupied by the first settlers, three western problems sorely challenged the power of the new federal government. One of these arose when Spain, incensed because she was not allowed the 32° 28' boundary of West Florida, denied western settlers the rights of navigation of the Mississippi and deposit at New Orleans. We have already seen how this was solved by the Pinckney treaty of 1795, whereby these concessions were obtained. A contemporary, writing shortly after the treaty was made, thus explained the importance of Spain's concessions to the back-country settlers:

The superfluous provisions are sold to emigrants, who are continually passing through those settlements, in their route to the different districts of country, and which I have enumerated. Some considerable quantities of spirits distilled from rye, and likewise cider, are sent down the river to a market, in those infant settlements where the inhabitants have not had time to bring orchards to any perfection, or have not a superfluity of grain to distil into spirits. The beef, pork, and flour are disposed of in the same way. The flax and hemp are packed on horses, and sent across the mountain to the inland towns of Pennsylvania and Maryland, and (as I hinted in a former letter) in a few years, when grazing forms the principal object of those settlers, they will always find a market for their cattle at Philadelphia, Baltimore, and Alexandria.

The second problem came when federal officers sought to collect a whiskey tax from the farmers in the southwestern counties of Pennsylvania under the terms of the excise law of 1791. This act bore heavily on the border settlers in this region, as implied in the foregoing quotation, because it was easier to convert their grain into whiskey and transport it to eastern markets than it was to haul it in bulk over uneven roads or dim trails. But when they rose in rebellion against the law, the President acted quickly. By proclamation of August 7, 1794, a force of 13,000 men was sent to the trouble zone, and the farmers were quieted, thus enabling Washington to demonstrate in a practical way the newly acquired federal power of coercion.

The third problem was even more knotty to solve, and demands fuller treatment, since it relates more directly to the Northwest. From the time that the federal Geographer and his assistants began their survey of the Seven Ranges until the first Ohio colonies were established, the Northwestern tribes had resisted stubbornly the white men's intrusion. It would be hardly correct to say, therefore, that an Indian war began after the planting of Marietta. Undoubtedly British influence had much to do with Indian unrest during this period. England still retained eight or ten posts within American territory and refused to withdraw her troops therefrom, on the excuse that the United States had not observed certain provisions of the treaty of 1783, by which British debts and Tory rights were to be guaranteed. One of the posts thus held was Detroit, long a trouble spot on the American frontier. Here British agents and traders lent encouragement and gave war supplies to the Northwestern Indians, promising that soon England would regain control of the region and restore to the red man full possession of the country. English officials, of course, realized that they had lost control of this area, but they wanted to retain their Indian fur-trade supremacy. Gilbert Imlay, an American army officer, writing shortly after St. Clair's campaign, said: ". . . the moment they [the British posts] are possessed by the Americans, that instant the English fur trade of Canada will be reduced more than one-half of what it is at present." When United States authorities protested the gifts of guns and ammunition to the Indians, the British insisted that they were made in keeping with a long-established custom. Yet it was commonly known that the Indians used them in making war on the Northwestern border settlements.

By 1790 an impending war along the border greatly alarmed Governor St. Clair, and he reported his misgivings to the President. Already Washington had heard western complaints that the federal government had done and could do little for the settlements beyond the mountains. Indeed, Spanish officials at New Orleans had sought to use western unrest as a basis for their intrigues to attach Kentucky and Tennessee to Louisiana. Washington was well aware of the danger of a separatist movement, and resolved to act with vigor. He asked Kentucky and Pennsylvania to furnish a force of 1,500 men for the campaign, and to rendezvous them at Fort Washington, near Cincinnati, under the command of General Josiah Harmar. But Harmar was little fitted for his task. His men were poorly trained and indifferently disciplined to meet the difficult days ahead. When once he deemed all was in readiness, he moved his force out toward the Maumee, taking little precaution to guard against surprise and to keep on the alert. Consequently, he was defeated in a series of skirmishes near the confluence of the St. Mary's and St. Joseph rivers, and was forced to retreat to Fort Washington.

News of Harmar's defeat greatly aroused the President, and he asked St. Clair to take the field. Congress, no less concerned, voted him 2,000 troops for six months, besides two regiments of cavalry. St. Clair was little better fitted to organize freedom-conscious pioneers and train them for an Indian campaign than his predecessor, although he did show some military judgment by building Forts Hamilton and Jefferson on the border before winter set in. He was 57 years of age, afflicted with the gout, and knew little about Indian warfare. The poor quality of the enlistments made his task all the more difficult, but it is doubtful that he could have succeeded with better men. He underestimated the fighting ability of the Indians, was lax in discipline, and finally arrived in the Indian country with but little more than half the force he started with. While camped, on November 3, 1791, in a poorly chosen place on a branch of the Wabash, about 100 miles north of Cincinnati, his troops were encircled by an overwhelming force of determined Indians under Little Turtle. Hidden behind trees and other places of vantage, the savages poured in a deadly fire on the troops who stood exposed in rank. When St. Clair observed his peril, he gave orders for his men to break through the cordon of red warriors and save themselves as best they could. The battle ended in a riot, and undoubtedly the invaders would have been annihilated had the pursuing warriors not turned aside to plunder St. Clair's abandoned camp. So what the President and Congress had hoped would be a demonstration of the government's power to care for border interests had terminated in a severe disaster. Not since Braddock's defeat at Turtle Creek had a military campaign been attended with such momentous consequence, and the news of failure with such dismay.

The angry President reprimanded St. Clair, who obligingly surrendered command of the army. Washington then called into service "Mad" Anthony Wayne, the hero of more than one revolutionary battlefield—Ticonderoga, Brandywine, Germantown, and Stony Point. Washington seemed to have misgivings about his leadership, for he had previously characterized him as "brave and nothing else"; but he knew that he was audacious and severe in discipline. These last two qualities the preceding commanders had lacked, and Wayne might save the Northwest at this time.

English officials in the West were as pleased with the Indian victory as were the warriors. Promptly a British force was sent out from

Detroit to occupy a point near the present site of Toledo (Fort Miami). Washington was disturbed by this intrusion, and ordered Wayne to reduce the post if it hindered his operations against the Indians. Furthermore, Indian raiders supplied with English muskets now swarmed along the border. But Wayne was equal to the emergency. He did not rush into the war zone with a poorly trained force. On the contrary, he put the recruits who came to him at Pittsburgh under severe discipline and training; and after two years of preparation, so states one authority, his men were able to fire and reload their flintlocks while on the run. In the spring of 1794 he left Fort Washington for the Indian country 80 miles to the north with a force of 2,600 men; and at a point six miles north of Fort Jefferson he erected Fort Greenville. Then in July he advanced north to the site of St. Clair's defeat, where he built Ft. Defiance, thence down the Maumee, at the rapids of which Lieutenant-Governor John Graves Simcoe had built the post previously mentioned. At a place known as Fallen Timbers, a few miles southwest of the rapids, on August 18, he engaged the waiting Indians in battle. Although the warriors fought well, hidden among the trees, Wayne employed his cavalry and recently trained marksmen to good effect. The redskins were driven from cover and pursued for a considerable distance with great slaughter. The British commander of the nearby post asked Wayne to explain his near approach, but the American's reply was little less than a challenge for battle, which the Englishman was not prepared to accept. Wayne then withdrew westward to a point near the source of the Maumee and erected Fort Wayne.

The Indians now realized that British promises of aid were empty. Chief Little Turtle, of the Miami, was one of several influential Indians who therefore sought peace. Moreover, news was brought that John Jay had just concluded a treaty with the English whereby British troops were to be withdrawn from American territory. (Later, on July 11, 1796, some of Wayne's soldiers had the satisfaction of raising the Stars and Stripes over Detroit.) Wayne next assumed the role of a diplomat; he had been successful with the sword, now he was prepared to extend the olive branch. And the Indians were eager to accept it. Delegation after delegation of warriors soon appeared at Fort Greenville, until more than 1,000 chiefs and their braves were in attendance. The Treaty of Greenville, August 3, 1795, established a new boundary line starting on the Ohio opposite the mouth of the Kentucky River; thence it ran east of north to Fort Recovery, at which point it turned sharply to the east, running to the head of the Cuyahoga, and thence down this stream to Lake Erie. The area surrendered by the Indians embraced more than half of the present state of Ohio, a strip of southeastern Indiana, and also lands within the Indian country around military posts such as Fort Wayne, Detroit, and Michilimackinac. But, what was more important, the treaty brought a decade and a half of peace to the settlers. When Wayne returned to Philadelphia after the successful accomplishment of his mission, he was hailed as a national hero. Congress voted its thanks, and Washington added his congratulations.

NEW TERRITORIES AND STATES

Soon after the terms of the Jay treaty were made known, British troops evacuated the Northwestern posts west and south of Lake Erie. The settlements near the Detroit River and upon the Maumee were then joined to the Northwestern Territory and subsequently set up as Wayne County, which included present southeastern Michigan and northwestern Ohio eastward to the Cuyahoga River and the "portage path" to the Tuscaroras country, with Detroit as the county seat. Most of the troops that had been stationed at Fort Washington were now distributed at the more remote Forts Wayne, Miami, and Detroit; and a new road was opened from Cincinnati through the wilderness by way of Forts Wayne and Miami to Detroit, over which not only military supplies but incoming settlers made their way to the Detroit country.

For many years Detroit had been the principal town of the old French settlements. It had been occupied as early as 1700; and since the end of the French and Indian War, it had been an important British post and center of the western fur trade. Its citizens, as at Cahokia, Vincennes, and Kaskaskia, yet retained their quaint customs, speaking a broken dialect and living up to their French Creole traditions. Generally they were illiterate, superstitious, and devout Catholics, content to eke out a miserable existence by trade with the Indians and by cultivating indifferently fields contiguous to their town. Their general areas of settlement were on the Raisin, Detroit, and Maumee rivers and in the Illinois country. After the treaty of Fort Greenville, and the opening of the Cincinnati-Detroit road, incoming English-speaking settlers finally gave to the region a new cultural pattern.

In fact, for three years following, thousands of homeseekers arrived in the Northwest; and on October 29, 1798, when it was observed that the Territory was ready for a government of the "second grade," Governor St. Clair called an election in the then organized nine counties to choose 22 representatives to form a lower house of the new legislature. When the representatives met in their first session at Cincinnati, they presented Congress with a list of ten persons, from which a council (upper house) of five members was chosen: Henry Vanderburgh of

Vincennes, Robert Oliver of Marietta, James Findlay and Jacob Burnet of Cincinnati, and David Vance of Vanceville. That the upper house was to have a fair regional distribution of outstanding men is thus revealed. A young ex-Virginian and Republican, W. H. Harrison (24 years of age), who had served under Wayne at Fallen Timbers and who was later to gain much prominence in western affairs, was sent to Congress as a territorial representative. In 1800 he proposed a new land law, which was enacted by Congress, as previously mentioned. Land in tracts of 320 acres was to be sold at public auction to the highest bidder; and that not sold, after a three weeks' period of auction, was to be disposed of at private sale for $2 per acre, on a four-year-credit plan.

During the territorial days of the Ohio country, Governor St. Clair was often at odds with local political leaders. Many of the settlers had been reared in regions remote from the Atlantic seaboard colonies, and had set up their own local government. Under such circumstances they had again and again invoked the "Mayflower" concept and had instituted popular democracies. Others had fled from arbitrary tidewater control, or they had migrated from Europe, seeking political havens in the New World. Obviously, therefore, they could hardly tolerate the scolding, lordly attitude of St. Clair, who had little faith in their ability to share with him the responsibilities of local government. Yet the territorial governor's attitude was that of the average American politician. Indeed, more than one delegate to the Philadelphia Constitutional Convention in 1787 was willing to join with Edmund Randolph in restraining "if possible, the fury of democracy."

The Northwesterners were annoyed when St. Clair called the first territorial legislature to meet in session in Cincinnati without consulting other leaders, and likewise when he designed a territorial seal on his own authority. And during the legislative session quarreling and strife between the Republicans and the governor's friends were common. St. Clair added fuel to the popular flame when he vetoed all the important legislative measures, particularly those creating new counties and for the taking of a census. But his foes won a decided victory in choosing Harrison as their representative in Congress, a position which St. Clair had sought for his son; and later, by petition, they prevailed on Congress to call a constitutional convention to meet at Chillicothe, over the objections of the governor. Here St. Clair appeared before the convention and criticized both President Jefferson and Congress for aiding his foes. Jefferson promptly removed him from office because of insubordination. On February 19 following (1803), Ohio was admitted as a State of the Union, with Edward Tiffin as its first governor.

Having discussed the establishment of the settlements at Marietta, Cincinnati, Chillicothe, Cleveland, and elsewhere, and the final emergence of the State of Ohio, it is not necessary to dwell at great length on other state developments in the Old Northwest. In addition to Ohio, the Northwestern Territory contained the basic parts of three other states. From Knox County upon the Wabash came Indiana; from St. Clair County upon the Illinois, Illinois; and from Wayne County upon the Detroit and the Upper Mississippi, Michigan.

The Indiana territorial bill, which was also written by Harrison, on May 7, 1800, set apart that area west of the Greenville treaty line to Fort Recovery and thence due north to the Canadian boundary as a territory of the first grade. Soon afterward Harrison became its first governor. Indiana Territory embraced all the white settlements (a population of 5,640) upon the Illinois and the Upper Mississippi, as well as those in the vicinity of Detroit, in addition to many Indians. Other white homeseekers presently arrived, and on February 3, 1809, Congress authorized a territorial legislature under the terms of the Ordinance of 1787. Indiana Territory was now bounded on the west by a line running up the middle of the Wabash to Vincennes and thence by a meridian due north to the southern extremity of Lake Michigan, and between this line and the Mississippi the Illinois Territory of the first grade was created.

Michigan Territory, with a government also of the first grade, set up by Congress on January 11, 1805, occupied the peninsula north of a line running due east from the most southern part of Lake Michigan to Maumee Bay on Lake Erie. Detroit became the seat of government, to which came the newly appointed governor, William Hull, following A. B. Woodward, the presiding federal judge. Only a territory of the first grade was provided, since the population was scarcely 3,000 souls. A fire at Detroit on June 11, prior to the coming of the territorial officials, had destroyed the old town and made rebuilding a government seat necessary.

One other impediment to orderly development, however, should be reviewed briefly before we follow the settlers beyond the Mississippi. From 1795 to 1809 the Northwestern Indians were compelled by a series of ten treaties to surrender approximately 60,000,000 acres of land. The Indian's resentment of the white man's occupation of the last part of his hunting grounds precipitated a formidable Indian war which halted the westward march of the homeseekers during the War of 1812.

We have noticed that the Fort Greenville treaty had resulted in the surrender of only that part of the Indian domain embraced in southern Ohio, southeastern Indiana, and a few smaller areas elsewhere. There yet remained a considerable Indian country to the northward and westward, to the Lakes and the Mississippi. After 1800 the incoming settlers respected no barriers. By 1810 Indiana alone had a white population of 25,000; and recently arrived immigrants from New England, the Middle Atlantic States, and the South swarmed over the Indian frontier, slew the Indians' deer, bear, and buffalo, and offended the red men in many other ways. Rapidly the sturdy, warlike red men who had allied themselves with the French and later the British to keep the "Long Knives" from the country north of the Ohio, were supplanted by poor, dependent, and often drunken wretches. In 1801 Governor Harrison of Indiana wrote that the Northwestern Indian was "half-naked, filthy, and enfeebled by intoxication," and that although there were only 600 warriors on the Wabash, their annual consumption of whiskey was 6,000 gallons! The industrious and aggressive whites generally regarded them as vagabonds and thieves, and often slew them on slight pretext.

Yet there remained a spark of resistance. Two Creek-Shawnee half-breeds, Tecumseh and the Prophet, conceived the idea of building up a great western Indian confederacy to resist the white man's further advance. Cessions by browbeaten chiefs of valuable lands during the early years of the new century aroused hundreds of angry warriors to enlist in their movement. In the period 1803–1805 Governor Harrison made treaties with the Miami, Eel River, Piankeshaw, and Delaware tribes. The Indians ceded a strip of land 50 miles wide south of the White River, and in 1809 still another valuable tract for almost 100 miles within the Indian country up both banks of the Wabash. This was within the very heart of the already greatly diminished hunting range of the Indians, and a country which Tecumseh and his followers did not propose to surrender without a struggle. Tecumseh's plan brought a drastic change in Indian government. Individual chieftains were not allowed to surrender lands as in the past. All important decisions were to be made by the warriors in council. In the beginning, many Indians, particularly the chiefs, refused to enlist in such an enterprise; but continued encroachments by their white foes and the perpetration of other wrongs caused the idea to increase in popularity.

At this time the United States and England were on the eve of a two-year conflict, and British agents in the West sought the Indians as allies. But Harrison opposed them. Moreover, he was ambitious to emulate the deeds of Wayne. In 1811, while Tecumseh was away on a trip to arouse the Creeks, Choctaws, and Cherokees in favor of his movement, he marched northward with a force of 900 Kentucky and regular troops to destroy the Prophet's town near the mouth of Tippecanoe Creek, for there the Indians felt themselves secure behind the white man's treaty line and under the Prophet's magic power. As the invaders penetrated their country, the warriors offered no resistance. Finally, Harrison's force reached a point near the confluence of the Tippecanoe and Wabash, where, about four o'clock in the morning of November 7, it was fiercely assailed from every side. Yet after several hours of fighting, the Indians withdrew from the field with heavy losses, and Harrison occupied and burned their village. The success of the invaders was soon heralded throughout the nation as a great victory, and Harrison was regarded as a Western hero. But more thoughtful settlers knew that Tecumseh's power was yet to be reckoned with, for soon they heard that he had returned from the South with thousands of new adherents and had rebuilt the Prophet's town. The Northwestern tribes were effective allies of the British during the War of 1812, and raided the border with disastrous effect, but the formidable confederacy finally crumbled. Tecumseh was slain in the battle of the Thames, and General Brock was defeated. There was no other leader to hold together the various tribes.

Indian wars constituted a strong deterrent to settler occupation. At the beginning of the War of 1812, the Territories of Michigan, Illinois, and Indiana contained scarcely 40,000 inhabitants, including the French Creoles on the Detroit, Wabash, and Illinois rivers. The northern half of Michigan still belonged to the Indians and was in their sole possession. Two-thirds of northern Indiana was likewise under Indian control, and a still greater portion of Illinois. But the end of the conflict ushered in a new era. New Indian cessions were made, and hundreds of soldiers who had traversed the fertile plains and valleys in months past now came in peaceful garb with their families; and the older settlements of Kentucky, Tennessee, and Ohio also sent many of their sons. Immigration swelled the population of Indiana to 70,000 by 1816, and it was admitted to the Union. Jonathan Jennings was elected governor of the new state. Also, two years later, on December 3, Indiana's state constitution was approved. The growth of Ohio had also been considerable; it reached a population of 581,295 two years later.

By 1835 the Territory of Michigan had attracted 90,000 immigrants, distributed over 38 counties in the southern half of the peninsula and the attached Huron or Wisconsin district west of Lake Michigan. The new Detroit, built after the great fire of 1805, was a thriving town of 2,500 inhabitants, and the fertile Raisin River region was dotted with hamlets and towns. On January 26, 1837, Congress admitted Michigan as a State to the Union.

Meanwhile, the Huron district was erected into a separate territory under the name of Wisconsin, comprising the whole region from Lake

Michigan to Lake Superior, extending westward to the Missouri River, and including all the sources of the Upper Mississippi. Its southern limits were the northern boundaries of Illinois and Missouri, and its extent from north to south was 580 miles and from east to west 650 miles. Its first governor was Henry Dodge (1836–1841), and John S. Horner was territorial secretary. The first assembly consisted of a legislative council of 13 members appointed for two years, and a legislative assembly of 26 members, elected for one year. The settled portions of the territory were chiefly near the western shore of Lake Michigan, and the organized counties extended westward and northwestward to the banks of Fox River and Green Bay, as far as Winnebago, and thence down the Wisconsin River, on the southeastern side, for 30 miles below the portage. Immigrants came, by way of Milwaukee and Racine, to the upper tributaries of Rock River and as far west as Fort Madison. A few settlements extended westward to the banks of the Mississippi, north of Galena and the Illinois state line.

The last vestige of Sauk and Fox claims east of the Mississippi was wiped out by the Black Hawk War of 1832. These Indians held as tenants at will the east bank of the Mississippi between the Wisconsin and Illinois rivers after the treaty of 1804. During the summers of 1830 and 1831 white squatters appeared, and they refused to leave when the Indians protested the intrusion. Presently officials of the federal government demanded that Black Hawk and his followers withdraw to the west bank of the Mississippi, but this he refused to do until troops arrived to force compliance. Then he fled. Nevertheless, in April, 1832, he recrossed the river with more than 500 warriors and sought to drive out the whites. Regular troops supported by Illinois militia under Generals Henry Atkinson and James D. Henry, however, defeated the Indians. General Winfield Scott, who arrived at Fort Crawford on August 7, then forced the Indians to cede a strip along the right bank of the Mississippi, north of Missouri, some 50 miles wide, to prevent any future Indian invasion. This ceded territory, known as Scott's Purchase, became the nucleus of the present State of Iowa.

Black Hawk's defeat, and the treaty that followed in 1832, opened the area along the Mississippi for settlement; and in the next spring, squatters from Illinois crossed the river, built their cabins, and established farms. Settlements at Burlington, Sandusky, and Fort Madison were made; and presently hundreds of homeseekers were moving in. In 1834, Congress attached this territory (with Iowa County) to Michigan for temporary jurisdiction, and it was then organized as Dubuque and Des Moines counties. In 1836 their aggregate population was 10,531, and in the same year Congress organized Wisconsin as a separate territory with jurisdiction over the "Iowa District," since Michigan had applied for statehood. Two years later the Wisconsin territorial legislature was moved from the village of Madison to Burlington, west of the Mississippi. But shortly territorial officials learned of the organization of the Territory of Iowa (July 4, 1838). The legislature, finding itself outside its territorial boundaries, adjourned. Robert Lucas, a former governor of Ohio, was appointed governor and superintendent of Indian affairs of the new territory.

When the Anglo-American homeseeker at last arrived at the Mississippi River and gazed across its placid waters at the inviting region beyond, he was quite unlike the early colonists of Jamestown or Plymouth. One hundred years of environmental experience, plus the tradition-pattern of colonial groups from many sections and nations, were his heritage. The New England Puritan, the Hudson Valley or Pennsylvania trader, the Southern planter, the German, the Scotch-Irish, the Swede, the Spaniard, and the Frenchman—all had been welded into one people. A visitor in Kentucky about the time of statehood said of its people:

They are, in general, polite, humane, hospitable, and very complaisant. Being collected from different parts of the continent, they have a diversity of manners, customs, and religions, which may, in time, perhaps, be modified to one uniform. As yet united to the state of Virginia, they are governed by her wholesome laws, which are virtuously executed, and with excellent decorum. Schools for education are formed, and a college is appointed by act of assembly of Virginia, to be founded under the conduct of trustees in Kentucky, and endowed with lands for its use. An excellent library is likewise bestowed upon this seminary by the rev. John Todd, of Virginia.

The anabaptists were the first that promoted public worship in Kentucky; and the presbyterians have formed 3 large congregations near Harrod's station, and have engaged the rev. David Rice, of Virginia, to be their pastor. At Lexington, 35 miles from these, they have formed another large congregation, and invited the rev. Mr. Rankin, of Virginia, to undertake that charge among them. At present there are no other religious societies formed, although several other sects have numerous adherents. But from these early movements it is hoped that Kentucky will eminently shine in learning and piety, which will fulfil the wish of every virtuous citizen.

Yet there was still much turbulence and violence, much clashing of customs and religious tenets, and of racial, political, and social prejudices. But finally all classes and creeds were tolerated and, indeed, in part fused. Truly, a distinctive America had come from the border crucible, refined by frontier hardship, fierce wars, toil, and forced adaptations. Moreover, along with superficial changes, such as new customs, new techniques, and the conquest of physical environment, had come a complete mental and spiritual transformation. Nature's stern laws were at times harsh, but they taught the settler who came to the frontier the necessity of co-operation, change, toil, hospitality, tolerance, and justice.

In a timbered wilderness the settler had built his hut of trees, near a spring or running stream, and his meager home furnishings and fences of the same material. He had clothed himself and his family largely from the skins of animals, and had provided comfortable pineneedle and bearskin beds for winter. He did not know the delights of imported foods, spices, coffee, and tea; he was quite content to subsist on venison, hominy, "journey-cakes" (corn-pones), and occasionally sassafras tea. Perhaps deerskin clothing was not so pleasing to the eye as woolens, linens, cottons, and silks, but it was far more serviceable in a western wilderness. The buckskin hunting shirt, leggings, and moccasins were little known by Europeans; but attired in them, the American pioneer could journey through the forest's underbrush and briars more readily, and could match the savage foe in stealth and endurance. Many of these earlier customs, instruments, and usages must now be abandoned for others, for the Great Plains and mountains of the West constituted a new environment. Here the flintlock must be laid aside for a rifle of longer range (the Springfield or the "Big Fifty"); the tomahawk for the Colt's revolver; moccasins for boots; buckskin leggings for chaps; fence rails for barbed wire; bearskin rugs for buffalo robes; the Georgia stock for the "gang plow"; roughly hewn logs for cabin walls, for adobe, sod, or dugout; later, the "old oaken bucket" for the valve-controlled cylinder or windmill to draw water from great depths. Moreover, in the semi-arid West, the immigrant must adapt himself to such phenomena as the sandstorm, the "black blizzard," and the grasshopper swarm. Yet courage and resourcefulness, sired by tradition and nurtured by previous experience in the trans-Allegheny country, was able to solve many of these difficult and unusual problems. For example, as will be observed later, the desert and the mountain were spanned by rails of steel, "dry farming" methods claimed for the settlers a large part of the Great Plains, irrigation conquered much of the desert, and engineering feats made possible the exploitation of the mineral wealth of the Rockies and Sierra Nevadas.

BIBLIOGRAPHY

Early accounts of travelers in the West add immeasurably to our knowledge of the Northwestern border. Some of these have been republished in recent years and are found in the average library. But others yet carry early appearance dates and are found only in important collections and libraries. Among those who visited the border during colonial days was Rev. Joseph Doddridge, who left his valuable *Notes on the Settlement and Indian Wars, of the Western Parts of Virginia and Pennsylvania* . . . (Wellsburg, 1824). Doddridge's comments on border manners and customs are exceedingly interesting and reliable. Equally good as a source on the soil, climate, and resources of the trans-Allegheny country is James Hall's *Notes on the Western States* . . . (Philadelphia, 1838); and Gilbert Imlay, *A Topographical Description of the Western Territory of North America* (London, 1797, 3rd ed.). The latter also contains a set of interesting maps of the West. To this list of contemporary accounts should also be added Timothy Flint, *Recollections of the Last Ten Years* (Boston, 1826); *The Journal of Andrew Ellicott* . . . (Philadelphia, 1803); Thomas Ashe, *Travels in America* . . . (London, 1809); John Bradbury, *Travels in Interior of America in the Years 1809, 1810, 1811* (re-edited, Cleveland, 1904); Robert B. McAfee, *History of the Late War in the Western Country* (Lexington, 1824); Morris Birbeck, *Notes on a Journey in America* (London, 1818); Moses Dawson, *A Historical Narrative of the Civil and Military Services of Major General William H. Harrison* . . . (Cincinnati, 1824); and Jacob Burnet, *Notes on the Early Settlement of the North Western Territory* (Cincinnati, 1847).

Much incidental information as to population and industrial data may be found in guidebooks and census reports. In this class of materials should be listed Margaret Cross Norton (ed.), *Illinois Census Returns* (*Collections of the Illinois State Historical Library*, XXIV, 1810, 1818, and XXVI, 1820); George G. Steele, *Western Guidebook and Emigrant's Directory* . . . (Buffalo, 1836); and J. H. Colton, *Traveler and Tourist's Guide-Book through the Western States and Territories* (New York, 1856).

There is no lack of dependable present-day accounts, some of which are found listed in the bibliography at the end of Chapter 7. The following list is not exhaustive but representative, as were the studies of Hinsdale, Hosmer, and Winsor previously mentioned. Volumes IV and V of John Bach McMaster's *History of the People of the United States* (8 vols., New York, 1883–1913) are excellent for a general survey. In the same way, Archer B. Hulbert's *Historic Highways of America* (16 vols., Cleveland, 1902–1905), particularly Volumes VIII to XII, are indispensable for study of routes of travel across the mountains, emigration, and types of homeseekers. Others of merit are Beverly W. Bond, Jr., *The Civilization of the Old Northwest* (New York, 1934); Arthur C. Boggess, *The Settlement of Illinois, 1778–1830* (Chicago Historical *Collections*, Chicago, 1882–), I; Randolph Chandler Downes, *Frontier Ohio, 1788–1803* (*Ohio Historical Collections*, Columbus, 1935), III; Alexander C. Flick (ed.), *Conquering the Wilderness* (*History of the State of New York*, New York, 1933–1934), V; C. M. Bomberger, *Twelfth Colony Plus* . . . (Jeanette, 1934); Harvey Rice, *Pioneers of the Western Reserve* (Boston, 1890); ————, *Sketches of Western Life* (Boston, 1888); George C. Wing, *Early Years of the Western Reserve* (Cleveland, 1916); A. E. Jones, *The Early Settlers of Cincinnati* (Cincinnati, 1888); William H. Smith (ed.), *St. Clair, Life and Public Services* (Cincinnati, 1882); Thomas Boyd, *Mad Anthony Wayne* (New York, 1929); D. B. Goebel, *William Henry Harrison* (Indianapolis, 1926); David M. Massie, *Nathaniel Massie, A Pioneer of Ohio* . . . (Cincinnati, 1896); Col. William E. Gilmore, *Life of Edward Tiffin, First Governor of Ohio* (Chillicothe, 1897); Clarence W. Alvord, *The Illinois Country, 1673–1818* (Springfield, 1920); Julius W. Pratt, *Expansionists of 1812* (New York, 1925); Theodore Roosevelt, *Winning of the West* (4 vols., New York, 1888–1896); and Frederick Jackson Turner, *The Significance of Sections in American History* (New York, 1932); Eugene H. Roseboom and Francis P. Weisenburger, *A History of Ohio* (New York, 1934).

IO

LOUISIANA UNDER SPAIN

THE LOUISIANA country, officially ceded by France to Spain in 1762, embraced roughly that portion of the drainage area of the Mississippi west of the river, with the island of Orleans added. Citizens of New Orleans, unaware of the cession for nearly two years, received the news with consternation and chagrin. Why should their king give up hard-won dominion and transfer loyal subjects to another monarch? They assembled, voiced their vigorous objections, and sent a delegate—Jean Milhet—with a protest to France. But their plea went unheeded; in fact, it was not even given a hearing.

SPAIN ASSUMES CONTROL

It was not until 1766 that Spain first moved to assume control of the province. She sent Don Antonio de Ulloa, distinguished Spanish scholar, to be the first governor. The intention was to effect the transfer quietly and with as little change as possible, by inducing the French militia to accept service under the Spanish banner. This the French soldiers refused to do; and, inasmuch as Ulloa had brought a military force of but 90 men, he could not enforce his authority. So he left Aubry, the French governor, in immediate command and attempted to govern through him. "Ulloa held the purse, Aubry the sword." It was an anomalous situation that could not endure.

Governor Ulloa, more scholarly than diplomatic, did not hide his contempt for the simple people of the province. His haughtiness and his Peruvian wife gave offense to the *habitants*, who were soon blocking Spanish authority at every turn and making no effort to conceal their dissatisfaction. The prohibiting of trade with France, in October, 1768, brought opposition to a head and culminated in an insurrection. Ulloa was expelled from the province.

Spain, stirred by the insult to her authority, decided to put an end to all opposition. The undertaking was entrusted to Alexandro O'Reilly, Irishman by blood, Spanish soldier by adoption. He had fought under the flags of Austria, France, and Spain, and his long military career had imbued him with a passion for duty and discipline. After making extensive preparations and assembling a strong military force at Havana, he turned his fleet of 21 ships toward Louisiana. On August 17, 1769, they anchored at New Orleans. The French inhabitants, having learned of the strength of the expedition, had previously dispatched a delegation composed of prominent leaders to compliment O'Reilly and plead for leniency.

Preparations were made for the ceremony of Spanish assumption of authority. In the late afternoon of August 18, the discharge of a gun announced the landing of the Spanish troops. The French militia under Governor Aubry was drawn up on the plaza. The Spanish soldiers filed ashore in impressive form and took up their position on the same public square. A thunder of guns from the fleet, answered by a salute from the soldiers on land, announced the disembarking of General O'Reilly. Accompanied by officers in full regalia, he marched to the flagpole in the plaza and handed his credentials to Governor Aubry. After publicly reading the message, Aubry handed the keys of the city to the Spanish general. Then the *fleur-de-lis* was slowly lowered from the flagstaff and the Spanish banner was unfurled to the setting sun. Formal possession was thus taken peaceably, for the strength of the Spanish expedition had overawed the people. But the insult of insurrection must be avenged.

O'Reilly immediately gathered information regarding the instigators of the revolt against Ulloa, and presently had the leaders under arrest. A general pardon for all other citizens was then published, but these must take the oath of allegiance to Spain or else return to France. The arrested men—some of the most prominent in the colony—were then placed on trial for treason. Despite the strong sympathy among the populace for the defendants, the prosecution was pushed with stern vigor to its tragic end. O'Reilly pronounced sentence. The six principal leaders were condemned to death; six others were sentenced to prison; and the property of all was confiscated. Twenty-one other persons involved were exiled from Louisiana. All seditious literature was ordered burned in the public square. The sentence was executed forthwith.

To the inhabitants of Louisiana, the punishment seemed unduly severe. It won for the Spanish general the sobriquet "Bloody O'Reilly." But Professor Bjork, student of the O'Reilly episode, contends that, inasmuch as the general was following explicit instructions from the Spanish government, he had no choice in the matter and "was a true soldier, wedded to duty."

Having punished opposition and established unquestioned authority,

O'Reilly assumed a conciliatory role and appointed numerous French-men to important positions. Spanish law and administration were installed, except that the French Black Code was retained. New Orleans was given a *cabildo,* with direct appeal to the Council of the Indies in Spain. With order established, O'Reilly placed Luis de Unzaga in control as governor.

The new executive proved to be a popular official, for under him commerce flourished. The trade regulations that Ulloa had proclaimed in 1766 provided a monopoly for Spanish ships and had set forth other restrictions that curtailed trade. Unzaga winked at violations, and thus encouraged an enlargement of the carrying trade. English ships participated extensively in this illicit but profitable traffic, carrying goods not only to the white inhabitants of Louisiana, but to the Indians of the interior as well. And in addition to the commerce by water, there developed considerable trade across the Mississippi with the various English colonies, Spanish horses finding markets as far east as Virginia.

The region of present Missouri, in Upper Louisiana, developed into an important trade area, with the new post of St. Louis as the central station. Pierre Laclède, a merchant of New Orleans, and some asso-ciates had been given by the French government exclusive trade privi-leges for eight years in the region about the mouth of the Missouri River. Before the plan could materialize, the land nominally passed to Spain, but the change of ownership did not stop the project. The traders chose the site of their "interior capital," and their agent, Auguste Chouteau, effected the formal founding of St. Louis on Feb-ruary 14, 1764. The post remained under French control until 1770, when Spanish officials finally took over administration.

Following the close of the French and Indian War and agreement on the Mississippi as the boundary between British and Spanish territory, a number of the French inhabitants of the Illinois country moved across the river, preferring to live in Spanish rather than British terri-tory. These removals increased the population on the Spanish side of the river and made St. Louis predominantly French throughout its early years. With its strategic location, St. Louis became the capital of Upper Louisiana, and was destined to become the great fur em-porium of the West.

In carrying on their traffic with the Indians, the St. Louis traders were soon in competition with British traders, who, after 1763, re-placed the Frenchmen of the Great Lakes and Illinois regions. Neither group confined itself to its own side of the international boundary. Indians from Lake Michigan and the Ohio country brought furs for barter to St. Louis, and British traders were soon carrying attractive trade goods into the Spanish territory of present Iowa and Minnesota. Nationals of both countries made protests and threats, but the forbidden traffic continued to flourish.

Spain's traditional system of governing colonies underwent considerable modification in Louisiana. This was the first province she had acquired from another nation, the first in which a non-Spanish system of control of the Indians had been established. It is interesting to note that Spain here took over the French methods and institutions instead of supplanting them with her own. The typical mission, presidio, and pueblo were not installed; instead, the French institutions of trading post, licensed trader, and distribution of presents were employed. The plan worked very well, especially since French traders and officials were retained and their established influence was utilized to control the Indians. The fur trade continued as a primary industry in Louisiana. Natchitoches, the Arkansas Post, and St. Louis, as well as many lesser outposts, became important trading centers. To these the various tribes gathered, bringing in peltries for barter and receiving in exchange trade goods of attractive design and utility.

Some of these frontier officials were in difficult positions. Athanase de Mézières provides an example. He was a Frenchman who had been in charge of Natchitoches under the French regime. As a devoted agent of France, he had won the friendship of the Red River tribes and had doubtless promoted some hostility toward the rival Spaniards of Texas. Now, as a Spanish official, his was the delicate task of retaining Indian confidence and winning the allegiance and the trade of the tribes for the Spaniards. His marked success bespeaks his tact and diplomacy.

Spain's acquisition of Louisiana altered the character and functions of the establishments in east Texas. For half a century, the Spanish missions and settlements on the Texas-Louisiana border had been maintained as outposts against the French. Now, with France eliminated and the international boundary shifted to the Mississippi, there was no further need for defenses in this quarter. And inasmuch as the sustaining of these establishments had entailed considerable expense, Spain ordered their withdrawal. The order was not welcomed by the 500 settlers, soldiers, and missionaries who called the east Texas region their home. But the decree was explicit, and Governor Ripperdá had the unpleasant task of evicting the colonists.

On the appointed day, June 25, 1773, the journey toward San Antonio began. Homes, ripening crops, and even some of the stock were abandoned. Some of the settlers fled to the woods or to Natchitoches, and others dropped behind, pleading illness. But most of the colonists were moved to San Antonio. Gil Ybarbo, outstanding leader among the exiles, carried a petition to the Viceroy asking permission for the colonists to return to east Texas. The next year, they were permitted to return as far east as the Trinity River, where they established a settlement. But Indian troubles and floods finally brought about its abandonment, and the colonists moved eastward to the region of their former homes. In 1779 they settled at Nacogdoches, which developed into an important settlement and a strategic center for trade with the surrounding Indians. Here Ybarbo became the Indian agent.

The eviction of the colonists from east Texas in 1773 had been but part of a general plan to contract and make more defensible the northern frontier of New Spain. Persistent Indian raids made this advisable. In 1766 the Marqués de Rubí had made an extensive and thorough investigation of northern outposts, and had found the whole frontier from Arizona to Texas infested with the warlike Apaches and Comanches. He recommended rearranging the defenses into a cordon of 15 presidios and the inauguration of a war of extermination against the hostiles. In conformity with his suggestions, "New Regulations of Presidios" were issued in 1772, and Hugo O'Connor was ordered to rearrange the line of forts.

For efficiency in frontier administration, the northern provinces, from California to Texas, were erected in 1776 into an independent "Commandancy General of the Interior Provinces," with Chihuahua the capital. The first *comandante general*, Teodoro de Croix, at once began the task of checking the hostile tribes. He planned to unite the eastern Texas and the Red River Indians with the soldiers in a general attack upon the eastern Apaches. A war council at San Antonio early in 1778, and subsequent tours among the Indians by De Mézières, were parts of the plan. But Spain's entry into the American Revolution in 1779 diverted energy into other channels.

During the American Revolution

The American Revolution, which had begun in 1775, soon developed international complications. Almost from the beginning, France and Spain gave secret aid to the revolting colonists, but neither was yet ready to come out openly in war against England. In 1776 an agreement was made between France and Spain whereby Louisiana was permitted to trade with the French West Indies. With this trade avenue open, Bernardo de Gálvez, new governor of Louisiana, turned upon the English smugglers in his province and seized 11 of their vessels. Thereupon, most of the commerce of Louisiana passed into French hands. In 1778 produce from the province was admitted to any part of France or of the United States.

The Spanish officials at New Orleans gave aid to the Americans, selling them powder and other needed supplies for Fort Pitt and such frontier posts.   Oliver Pollock, official agent at New Orleans, who represented Virginia and later the Continental Congress, organized expeditions that captured English vessels on the Mississippi. Also, he furnished ammunition and supplies that enabled George Rogers Clark to retain his important conquests in the Illinois country.

France formed an alliance with the American colonies in 1778, and the next year Spain, being promised aid in recovering Gibraltar and Florida, declared war on England. Upon joining the contest, Spain ordered the seizure of British stations on the lower Mississippi. Governor Gálvez, with 1,500 men, ascended the river to Natchez and captured the English posts.

In the meantime England planned the capture of Spanish strongholds on the Mississippi. An expedition descending from Canada was to capture St. Louis, reconquer the Illinois country, and meet General Campbell coming up the river to Natchez from the Gulf. The campaign from the north was directed by Lieutenant-Governor Sinclair, commander of Mackinac. Captain Emmanuel Hesse, a trader and ex-soldier, assembled Indians and led the campaign against St. Louis. Spanish officials there learned of the intended attack, and made ready to repel it. Captain Fernando de Leyba, in command at St. Louis, brought the five cannon from abandoned Fort Carlos III (at the mouth of the Missouri) to St. Louis and mounted them in a tower which he had built. He ordered the 60 militiamen from Ste. Geneviève to St. Louis, and gathered in the traders from the surrounding country. He threw up intrenchments at the north and the south sides of the town.   When the British force of about 1,000 men, mostly Indians, made an attack in the afternoon of May 26, 1780, it met unexpected opposition. The preparations and the vigorous fighting of the 300 defenders of the town discouraged the attackers, especially the Indians, who soon retired to pillage farms of the countryside and then withdrew. An almost simultaneous attack on Cahokia, east of the Mississippi, was unsuccessful. A separate expedition, sent from Detroit to raid Kentucky, also failed, and was soon in retreat before George Rogers Clark. Campbell was prevented by Gálvez from ascending the river, and thus the whole British plan on the Mississippi failed.

Learning that England planned a second expedition from Canada, the commander of St. Louis launched some countermoves. He sent detachments up the Mississippi and ordered 65 men to cross over to Fort St. Joseph, in present Michigan, to destroy supplies known to be housed there. The midwinter venture to St. Joseph succeeded. In a surprise attack, the post was taken on February 12, 1781, and the stores were destroyed.

In the meantime Gálvez had captured Mobile from the British in March, 1780, and the next year he took Pensacola and received the surrender of General Campbell. The Spanish troops of Louisiana thus rendered invaluable service to the American colonies during the latter part of the Revolution. They frustrated the English plan to tie Canada to the Gulf of Mexico by way of the Mississippi and indirectly made possible the retention, by the Americans, of Clark's conquest of the old Northwest. At the end of the war, Spain regained possession of the Floridas, East and West.

ON THE UPPER MISSOURI

By the treaty at the end of the American Revolution, the united colonies obtained title to the territory extending west to the Mississippi. But for some years the possession of the western country was more nominal than real. British traders retained their posts south of the Great Lakes and continued to carry on their former trade with the Indians. Not only did they control the trade in the United States territory, but they crossed the Mississippi into Spanish Louisiana as well. They were especially active in present Minnesota and Iowa and were soon following old French paths to the Mandan villages on the upper bend of the Missouri. Spain began to fear that they would penetrate even to Santa Fe and threaten Spanish dominion in New Mexico. Thus, in the two decades following the close of the American Revolution, the British traders' inroads west and southwest from the Great Lakes spurred the Spaniards to renewed activity. Spanish traders from St. Louis also pushed farther and farther up the Missouri, seeking trade and influence with more and more tribes.

In 1789 Juan Munier obtained exclusive trade priviliges with the Poncas on the Niobrara River of northern Nebraska. The next year Jacques d'Eglise ascended the Missouri to the Mandans of present North Dakota and opened a trade with them. On a subsequent journey he was turned back by hostile Sioux and Aricaras. The British traders, bringing attractive goods and underselling the Spaniards, were becoming a grave threat to Spanish authority in the upper Louisiana territory. Spanish officials became thoroughly alarmed, and now planned a more vigorous trade program. In the spring of 1794, Jacques Clamorgan and other merchants and traders of St. Louis incorporated the "Company of Explorers of the Upper Missouri," usually referred to as the Missouri Company. Lieutenant-Governor Zenon Trudeau approved the organization, and when the papers were sent to Governor-General Carondelet at New Orleans, he was so elated over the project that he offered a prize of $2,000, later raised to $3,000, to the first Spanish subject who should reach the Pacific by way of the Missouri River.

The first expedition of the Missouri Company was led by Jean Baptiste Truteau, who set out from St. Louis with eight men in a pirogue on June 7, 1794. He was a schoolteacher by profession, and did not prove to be a good trader, but he did obtain from the Indians much valuable geographical information regarding the upper Missouri region and the country extending to the Rocky Mountains. He failed to reach the Mandans, but conducted trade with the Aricaras of the South Dakota region. The Missouri Company's second expedition, in the spring of 1795, was pillaged by the Poncas and soon went to pieces. Clamorgan and his associates now employed an experienced trader, James Mackay, a Scotsman by birth, to lead their third expedition. Mackay, as a British trader, had reached the Mandan villages from Canada in 1787. He had subsequently moved to the Missouri region and had become a naturalized Spanish subject.

With a party of 33 men, four pirogues, and 50,000 pesos worth of merchandise, Mackay set out from St. Louis in August, 1795. His object was, as he himself reports, "to open a commerce with those distant and Unknown Nations in the upper parts of the Missouri and to discover all the unknown parts of his Catholic Majesty's Dominions through that continent as far as the Pacific Ocean." It was thought that the expedition might require six years. Mackay was instructed to establish forts at the points necessary to protect Spanish trade from the British.

Among the Omaha Indians, some little distance above the mouth of the Platte River, he erected a fort and prepared to spend the winter. With him as a trusted lieutenant had come a Welshman, John Evans, recently arrived in America to seek a reported tribe of Welsh Indians. In the winter of 1795–1796 Mackay sent Evans farther up the Missouri, giving him instructions for his journey across the continent. "You will take care," directed Mackay, "to mark down your route and distance each day, whether by land or water; in case you will be short of ink, use the powder and for want of powder, in the summer you will surely find some fruit whose juice can replace both." Evans was provided with a supply of merchandise to win the friendship and help of the Indians encountered. He was told to take possession, in the name of King Charles IV of Spain, of the country traversed, and upon reaching the Pacific was to guard against giving offense to the Russians established there.

Evans reached the Mandan villages in September, 1796, and took possession of the British fort there. Throughout the ensuing winter he had considerable contact with British traders who brought goods over to the upper Missouri, principally from their post near the junction of the Mouse and Assiniboin rivers in Canada. Evans reports that these foreign traders intended "to open a trade by the Missouri with the Nations who inhabit the Rocky Mountains." He gave them Mackay's proclamation "forbidding all strangers whatever to enter on any part of his Catholic Majesty's Dominions in this Quarter under any pretext whatever." It is rather interesting to see these citizens and former citizens of the British Isles representing rival nations in a contest for trade and dominion in this northwest interior.

Evans fell far short of reaching his goal on the shores of the Pacific. In fact, he appears to have gone little if any distance beyond the Mandan country of North Dakota. And Mackay did not even reach the Mandans. Although other Spanish traders continued activity on the upper Missouri during the remaining years of the Spanish regime in Louisiana, they appear not to have gone beyond present North Dakota.

The various Spanish proclamations and warnings against the British traders were ineffective. Instead, agents of the English companies gradually strengthened their position among the western tribes. A. P. Nasatir, authority on the Anglo-Spanish rivalry on the upper Missouri, writes: [1] "With equal persistence but with more aggressiveness and success, the British traders with headquarters at Prairie du Chien were spreading westward, virtually monopolizing the trade of the Iowa-Minnesota country. They now began to capture the Ponca and Omaha trade, having established posts not only in the Iowa country but on the Platte River as well." Farther up the Missouri they were no less active. In 1802 Canadians reached the Rockies by way of the Yellowstone and the Big Horn rivers. When Lewis and Clark made their famous journey, they encountered both Spanish and British traders on the upper Missouri.

EXPLORATIONS FROM TEXAS AND NEW MEXICO

During the later years of the eighteenth century, Spain was carrying forward notable exploratory work not only from St. Louis into the upper Missouri country, but from the Texas and New Mexico bases as well. Now that Spain was in possession of the entire territory west of the Mississippi, after the French and Indian War, she needed lines of communication among the widely separated outposts of this portion of her empire. The outstanding leader who was to open these routes and blaze new trails was Pedro (Pierre) Vial, a Frenchman, now a

[1] Nasatir, A. P., "Anglo-Spanish Rivalry on the Upper Missouri," *Mississippi Valley Historical Review*, XVI, 525.

Spanish subject, who was well acquainted with the land and the Indians of the north Texas frontier. In 1786 Vial was commissioned by the Governor of Texas to explore a direct route from San Antonio to Santa Fe. Despite the age and relative propinquity of these important provincial capitals, the meager contacts between them had heretofore been conducted by a roundabout route through Coahuila, in part, at least, because of the persistent hostility of the Apaches and Comanches. But with better relations established with these tribes, the long-contemplated project of opening a direct route could be attempted.

In early October, 1786, Vial set out from San Antonio. He went northeast to the Colorado River of Texas, then east to the Brazos, and followed the latter nearly to its source before crossing to the Taovayas villages on the Red River in present Jefferson County, Oklahoma. He followed the Red River and then the Canadian in a generally westward course, passed several Comanche villages, and, in May, 1787, reached Santa Fe. He had made the journey, but his route was far from direct. Therefore, the Governor of New Mexico dispatched José Mares with a small party to find a shorter course. Mares followed the general route of Vial, omitting some of the latter's detours, and reached San Antonio in October, 1787. On his return journey he took an improved route, going directly north to the Red River and thence to Santa Fe. In the summer of 1788 Vial was sent from New Mexico to open a route to Natchitoches. He went to Pecos and thence in a direct line to the Taovayas villages. From here he traveled southeastward, struck the headwaters of the Sabine, followed the stream some distance, and then went directly to Natchitoches. From here he went westward along the well-established *Camino Real* to San Antonio. After a detention of several months here on account of illness, Vial returned to Sante Fe by a route approximating the northward course of Mares.

Vial's exploratory work between Texas and New Mexico suggested his employment for opening a route from Sante Fe to St. Louis. In May, 1792, he set out upon this journey. An eastward trail brought him to the Canadian River, which he followed to the eastern border of present New Mexico. He then turned northeastward and reached the Arkansas River a little east of present Dodge City. After following this stream to the Great Bend, he traveled eastward, reached the Missouri River near present Kansas City, and followed the stream to St. Louis. On his return journey to New Mexico the next year, he approximated the route later famous as the Santa Fe Trail.

AMERICANS ENTER LOUISIANA

While Spain was tying together the various outposts of her empire west of the Mississippi and endeavoring to ward off the British fur traders on the upper waters of that river and of the Missouri, she was having to deal with the activity of her new and aggressive American neighbors on the eastern side of the Father of Waters. During the years when Spain was in possession of the Louisiana country, the Anglo-Americans from beyond the Alleghenies crossed the mountains and rapidly pushed their way to the Mississippi. (This epic westward movement and the struggle for the all-important navigation of the Mississippi are briefly presented in Chapters 6–9.)

Spanish officials watched this westward-moving flood with grave misgivings, but pursued a varying course in their efforts to stem, control, or divert it. At times they bargained with Indians and white men to hold back the tide. At other times they intrigued with Americans to induce secession of the trans-Appalachian country from the American union and to effect annexation with Spanish Louisiana. Then, at still other times, the Louisiana officials prepared to defend their province against invasion of western Americans who were intent on conquering this Spanish territory and winning free navigation of the Mississippi.

Some far-seeing Spanish official observed that "the only way to check the Americans is with a proportionate population." So Spain undertook to promote immigration to Louisiana. She brought over several shiploads of colonists from the Canary Islands. She set aside an annual sum of $40,000 "to facilitate the establishment of the new colonists who may come to Louisiana." She invited British Loyalists and French and German Catholics to settle here. The revolution in Santo Domingo in 1791 sent new settlers to Louisiana, and the French Revolution drove a number of royalists to the same region. The Marquis de Maison Rouge, Baron de Bastrop and De Luzieres were among the Frenchmen who received large land grants in Louisiana.

But despite the various efforts to promote settlement by non-Americans, the immigration of such persons was comparatively small. Finally, the Spanish officials tried the doubtful expedient of admitting Americans, with the hope of converting them into loyal Spanish subjects and of using them to hold back the tide of their former countrymen. Even before she openly invited Americans to come, English-speaking pioneers had made their way into Louisiana. During the first years of the American Revolution, some refugees from West Florida sought protection in Spanish territory, and founded Galveztown on the Iberville, which Professor Lawrence Kinnaird designates "the first Anglo-American village in Louisiana." After the close of the Revolutionary War, Spain began to make concessions. In 1786 a royal order permitted Americans who would take the oath of allegiance to Spain to remain in Louisiana. Irish priests were to be sent to serve them. Some provision was made for the conditional admission of foreigners, and Diego de Gardoqui, the first Spanish minister to Washington, became active in promoting American immigration and issuing passports. One of the first colonizers to arrive at New Orleans was Bryan Bruin, who obtained liberal grants of land for himself and other Americans in West Florida. Colonists came by sea and down the Mississippi to the New Orleans region.

In 1787 Spain went a step further. She appointed Pierre d'Argés as immigration agent for Spain in the Kentucky region, and relaxed somewhat her religious regulations pertaining to settlers. George Rogers Clark, George Morgan, Baron Von Steuben, and others now planned to secure large land grants and to plant semi-independent American colonies on Spanish soil. Land could be acquired in Louisiana on more favorable terms than in the United States. American immigration was temporarily checked by the Clark-Genêt conspiracy in Kentucky and by other filibustering activity. However, the signing of the Pinckney Treaty in 1795, with its provisions for settling the West Florida boundary and for opening the Mississippi to American commerce, removed the principal causes of friction; and in 1796 a large American immigration into Spanish territory began. The settlers came primarily to three districts—West Florida, Lower Louisiana, and Missouri.

West Florida, with its large English population dating back to the close of the French and Indian War, received many new colonists. They remained primarily American, despite their oath of loyalty to Spain, and later were to declare their independence from Spanish authority.

Americans came into Lower Louisiana, west of the Mississippi. They moved up the valleys of the Red River and the Ouachita. The colonization projects of the Frenchmen Baron de Bastrop and the Marquis de Maison Rouge brought more colonists to the Ouachita from the United States than from Europe. Americans pushed westward and crossed the Sabine into Texas. In 1791 Edward Murphy received a grant of land on the Arroyo Hondo. Seven years later the estate was purchased by an American company that developed it into an outstanding ranching and trading enterprise. Along the Red River, Americans penetrated into the region of present Arkansas. Though Americans were still in the minority in Lower Louisiana, New Orleans, through the heavy commerce on the Mississippi, was becoming a great American port.

In the Missouri region of Upper Louisiana, the American influx was comparatively large, especially in the years following the close of the American Revolution. The Northwest Ordinance of 1787, with its prohibition of slavery north of the Ohio River, drove certain slave-holders across the Mississippi and into Louisiana. One of the largest colonization schemes attempted in Missouri was that of General George Morgan. Supported by Gardoqui in Washington, who assured him a grant of some 15,000,000 acres in southeastern Missouri, Morgan journeyed west and floated down the Ohio in 1789, gathering a party of interested persons en route. He made elaborate plans for an extensive settlement, and the Spanish officials supplied a small garrison. But the project did not receive the necessary official approval and did not fully materialize. However, some of Morgan's men remained and helped to settle New Madrid. Other Americans came; settlers moved in from Vincennes, and some Frenchmen, disappointed at the failure of Gallipolis and the Scioto land scheme in Ohio, moved to this section of present Missouri. By the end of Spanish control (1804), there were about 1,500 settlers, over half of whom were Americans, in the New Madrid district.

To the Cape Girardeau area, a little farther north, Americans began to come in 1795. They came principally from North Carolina and Tennessee, and comprised some 150 families by 1803. The Ste. Geneviève district, with its lead mines and farming lands, attracted Americans during the last years of the Spanish regime. Among the more famous of these was Moses Austin, who received a land grant in 1796. In the five years preceding 1804, the population of the district practically doubled, reaching 2,870. Americans coming into the St. Louis district after 1796 settled mostly on farms, while the town of St. Louis remained predominantly French. The St. Charles district, north of the Missouri River, was invaded by Americans, especially traders. Here a son of Daniel Boone founded Femme Osage. This settlement was for a time the home of Daniel Boone and the seat of his authority as a lesser official under the Spanish government. Later the famous Kentuckian moved to La Charette, where he died. By turns he had been a citizen of the British Empire, of the United States, and of Spain.

Professor Jonas Viles says that "the total population of Upper Louisiana at the time of the transfer [to the United States] was between nine and ten thousand, of which a majority was American and over fifteen per cent slave." [2] In general, the Americans were in small groups or on detached farms, while the French element was predominant in the villages and controlled the commerce, industry, and politics of the region. The Spaniards, who managed the government, were a small minority.

The products of Upper Louisiana included farm crops, furs, and lead. The exports from this district to New Orleans for the year 1799

[2] *Missouri Historical Review,* V, 212–213.

are listed as follows: "1,754 bundles of deerskins, $70,160; 8 bundles of bearskins, $256; 18 bundles of buffalo robes, $540; 360 quintals (a quintal equals 101.43 pounds) of lead, $2,160; 20 quintals of flour, $60. Of lead, 1,340 quintals were exported to the United States by way of the Ohio, Cumberland, and Tennessee rivers."

A few years of experience convinced the Spanish officials that the Americans would not make loyal Spanish subjects. They were imbued with ideas of liberty, and showed little respect for Spanish concepts of government and religion. Therefore, efforts were made to check the coming of Protestant Americans.

The Bishop of Louisiana wrote: "The emigration from the western part of the United States and the toleration of our government have introduced into this colony a gang of adventurers, who have no religion and acknowledge no God, and they have made much worse the morals of our people." Regulations were made more stringent, and in 1802 the King of Spain forbade the granting of any more land to citizens of the United States. But the change of policy had come late. Spain was now unable to stop the advance. Americans, evading regulations and officials, continued to enter the Louisiana country and even Texas.

LOWER LOUISIANA AND THE RETROCESSION

In the lower portion of the Louisiana territory there were some important developments during the later years of Spanish control. The first successful manufacture of sugar on an extensive scale in Louisiana was effected by Étienne de Boré in 1795. It is reported that a large crowd gathered to watch the experiment, and that when they saw the sugar granulate, they gave a great shout and almost overwhelmed Boré with their congratulations. By 1800 there were 60 sugar plantations in Louisiana, and their annual product amounted to 4,000,000 pounds of sugar.

Agricultural production in Lower Louisiana was dependent largely on slave labor. In 1795 a Negro insurrection occurred, but was promptly suppressed and 23 leaders were hanged. Importation of Negroes from Africa had been prohibited, but the rapid increase in sugar production following Boré's success created a need for more slave labor. So the cabildo, in 1799, asked and obtained the king's consent to suspend the prohibition against importation of slaves.

The annual production and trade of Louisiana was given in 1801 as follows:

4,000,000 pounds of sugar, at eight dollars a hundredweight, $320,000; 4,000 barrels of syrup, at fifteen dollars, $60,000; 100,000 pounds of indigo, $100,000; 200,000 pounds of tobacco, $16,000; sundry peltries, $100,000; Louisiana may furnish Santo Domingo, in time of peace only, lumber, specie, etc., for $50,000; 200,000 boxes are sent every year to Havana, and bring in return $225,000; 10,000 barrels of rice are exported every year to Santo Domingo, the ports of Cuba and Campeche, at the current price of five dollars, $50,000; the King of Spain pays every year in this province to his employes, $537,000; the extraordinary expenses of the government absorb the amount of the custom-house duties, which are not more than $100,000; the value of the merchandise that the ships from Louisiana introduce by smuggling into the Spanish ports of Havana and on the Gulf of Mexico amounts to $500,000; the total is $1,958,000.

A table of exports for 1801 lists 375,137 pounds of cotton and 80,-380 pounds of carrots. Among imports were 314,867 pounds of coffee and 322,500 pounds of soap.

New Orleans suffered great losses from fires in 1788 and in 1794. In the conflagration of the latter year, one-third of the houses, including most of the stores, were burned. But the capital was rebuilt and improvements were added. In 1796 a drainage and sanitary canal for the city was completed, 80 street lamps were installed, and a police force of 13 *serenos* was provided. The Negro insurrection of 1791 in Santo Domingo induced a number of whites to escape from that island. Among these was a troupe of comedians, who came to New Orleans and were the first actors in Louisiana. In 1794 appeared the first newspaper in Louisiana, the *Moniteur de la Louisiane*. It was a four-page octavo paper, with two columns on each page.

Educational facilities were provided in New Orleans. A school for girls had been founded by the Ursuline nuns in 1727. In 1772 the authorities established a Spanish school in New Orleans, but it experienced some difficulty in obtaining students, since most of the inhabitants preferred the French to the Spanish language. Eight schools were reported in 1788, with an attendance of about 400 boys and girls. In 1803 several specialized private schools were added to the older established institutions.

New Orleans showed considerable growth during the Spanish period. In 1769 the population was given as 3,190. By 1803 it had reached 8,056. The whole province of Louisiana had shown a comparable increase during the period, from approximately 10,000 to about 50,000. But even this increase left the province very sparsely settled, considering the vast extent of the Louisiana territory.

The French Revolution and consequent international complications during the last decade of the eighteenth century kept the officials of Louisiana in almost continual difficulties. Early in 1793 a petition signed by 300 Frenchmen in Louisiana asked France to take over her former province. Citizen Edmond Genêt, upon coming to the United States as French minister, declared, "The moment has arrived when despotism must disappear from the earth." He sent a ringing appeal from the "Freemen of France to their brothers in Louisiana," urging the latter to rise in revolt against "the tyrants by whom you have been so long oppressed." A Jacobin club was organized in New Orleans, incendiary placards were posted, and martial songs became popular. The Governor-General of Louisiana, Baron de Carondelet, with a military reinforcement of 300 men from Natchez (mostly Anglo-Americans), was able to maintain Spanish control in New Orleans. Early in 1795 the revolutionary movement broke out anew. Soon it was discovered that a Negro uprising, instigated by rabid Jacobins, was planned. The leaders were captured and hanged. An insurrection which occurred at Natchitoches later the same year was not quieted until 1796.

Citizen Genêt had attempted to launch an expedition in the Kentucky country against Spanish Louisiana, but his recall frustrated the scheme. The Westerners of the United States were presently appeased by the Pinckney Treaty of 1795, which gave Americans free navigation of the Mississippi and for three years the right to deposit their goods at New Orleans for reshipment.

Napoleon Bonaparte, upon coming to power in France, planned a revival of the French colonial empire. He induced King Charles IV of Spain and his Prime Minister, Manuel Godoy, to consent to a retrocession of Louisiana to France, in return for which the son-in-law of the Spanish king was to receive a duchy in Italy. The treaty was negotiated at San Ildefonso on October 1, 1800, but for some time was kept secret.

Napoleon now planned to take possession of Louisiana, and, as a first step, to conquer Santo Domingo. He dispatched his brother-in-law, General Leclerc, with an army to the West Indies to effect this purpose. France, England, and Spain made peace on March 25, 1802, and Napoleon thereupon began preparations for assuming control of Louisiana. He appointed General C. P. Victor as Captain-General, and Pierre Clément Laussat as Colonial Prefect for the province. A complete system of government was drafted, and 270 silver medals were struck for presentation to Indian chiefs in Louisiana. Delayed in getting supplies for the expedition, General Victor found his four vessels caught in the Holland ice, where they remained for nearly six months.

But Colonial Prefect Laussat, who was to administer the civil affairs of Louisiana, had set sail for the province. Upon arriving at New Orleans on March 26, 1803, he was received by Governor Salcedo amid the firing of salutes. On the following days he received visits of the officials and principal citizens and issued a proclamation to the inhabitants. The formal transfer to France awaited the arrival of

General Victor. On April 9 the principal French inhabitants of New Orleans presented an address to Laussat, which said in part: "Thirty-four years of a foreign domination have not weakened in our hearts the sacred love of country, and we return today under her banner with as much joy as we had grief when we had to part from it." The planters of Louisiana presented an address of similar tone.

On May 7 the Marquis de Casa Calvo arrived to act with Salcedo in ceding the province to General Victor. But still the French general and army did not arrive. Finally a rumor came that France had sold Louisiana to the United States. Laussat denounced it as "an impudent and incredible falsehood." But the rumor was well founded, as Laussat was soon to learn.

The preceding months had greatly changed the face of affairs, and with them Napoleon's prospects regarding overseas empire. In Santo Domingo the Negroes had exhibited unexpected resistance, sickness had decimated the French army, Leclerc had died, and the attempt to conquer the island had failed. England and France were again at war; and with England in control of the sea, Napoleon saw that his prospects for holding Louisiana were poor indeed. So he decided to sell the province to the United States before he lost it to the British fleet. The sale, to be discussed in the next chapter, was accordingly made.

Laussat was commissioned to receive Louisiana from Spain and to deliver it to the United States. The formal transfer to France took place with appropriate ceremonies on November 30, 1803. Twenty days later, control passed to the United States.

BIBLIOGRAPHY

Among the general books containing data relating to the subject matter of this chapter may be mentioned the following: Alcée Fortier, *A History of Louisiana* (4 vols., New York, 1904); Charles E. Gayarré, *History of Louisiana* (4 vols., New Orleans, 1903); H. Yoakum, *History of Texas*, etc. (2 vols., Edition of 1935); Louis Houck, *A History of Missouri*, etc. (3 vols., Chicago, 1908); H. E. Bolton and T. M. Marshall, *The Colonization of North America, 1492–1783* (New York, 1920); H. E. Bolton, *The Spanish Borderlands* (New Haven, 1921). Other useful volumes are: Amos Stoddard, *Sketches, Historical and Descriptive, of Louisiana* (Philadelphia, 1812); M. A. Hatcher, *The Opening of Texas to Foreign Settlement, 1801–1821* (Austin, 1927); H. E. Bolton, *Texas in the Middle Eighteenth Century* (Berkeley, 1915); Arthur P. Whitaker, *The Spanish-American Frontier, 1783–1795* (Boston, 1927), and his *The Mississippi Question, a Study in Trade, Politics, and Diplomacy* (New York, 1934); James A. James, *Oliver Pollock; the Life and Times of an Unknown Patriot* (New York, 1937); J. A. James, *The Life of George Rogers Clark* (Chicago, 1928); J. T. Scharf, *History of St. Louis City and County* (2 vols., Philadelphia, 1883).

Important original documents are found in the following: Louis Houck, *The Spanish Regime in Missouri* (2 vols., Chicago, 1909); J. A. Robertson (ed.), *Louisiana Under the Rule of Spain, France and the United States, 1785–1807* (2 vols., Cleveland, 1911); H. E. Bolton, *Athanase de Mézières and the Louisiana-Texas Frontier* (2 vols., Cleveland, 1914); Laura L. Porteous, "Index to the Spanish Judicial Records of Louisiana," in the *Louisiana Historical Quarterly*, XIX, 241–272, 510–546, 778–827.

In *New Spain and the Anglo-American West; Historical Contributions Presented to Herbert Eugene Bolton* (1932) are the following important contributions relating to Louisiana under Spain: David K. Bjork, "Alexander O'Reilly, and the Spanish Occupation of Louisiana, 1769–1770"; Lawrence Kinnaird, "American Penetration into Spanish Louisiana"; and A. P. Nasatir, "St. Louis During the British Attack of 1780."

Among pertinent artices in historical magazines, the following should be listed: Isaac J. Cox, "The Louisiana-Texas Frontier," in the *Quarterly of the Texas State Historical Association*, X, 1–75; E. R. Liljegren, "Jacobinism in Spanish Louisiana, 1792–1797," in the *Louisiana Historical Quarterly*, XXII, 3–53; Jane M. Berry, "Indian Policy of Spain in the Southwest, 1783–1795," in the *Mississippi Valley Historical Review*, III, 462–477; John C. Parish, "The Intrigues of Doctor James O'Fallon," *ibid.*, XVII, 238–256; D. C. Corbitt, "James Colbert and the Spanish Claims to the East Bank of the Mississippi," *ibid.*, XXIV, 457–472; Jonas Viles, "Population and Extent of Settlement in Missouri Before 1804," in the *Missouri Historical Review*, V, 189–213; Eugene M. Violette, "Early Settlements in Missouri," *ibid.*, I, 46–47; F. J. Teggart, "Capture of St. Joseph, Michigan, by the Spaniards in 1781," *ibid.*, V, 214–228; Joab Spencer, "John Clark, Preacher and Founder of Methodism in Missouri," *ibid.*, V, 174–178.

For excellent discussions of development in the Upper Louisiana country, see the following articles by Dr. A. P. Nasatir: "Anglo-Spanish Rivalry on the Upper Missouri," in the *Mississippi Valley Historical Review*, XVI, 359–382, 507–528; "The Anglo-Spanish Frontier in the Illinois Country During the American Revolution, 1779–1783," in the *Journal of the Illinois State Historical Society*, XXI, 291–358; "John Evans, Explorer and Surveyor," in the *Missouri Historical Review*, XXV, 219–239, 432–460, 585–608; "The Formation of the Missouri Company," *ibid.*, 10–22. See also A. H. Abel (ed.), *Tabeau's Narrative of Loisel's Expedition to the Upper Missouri* (Norman, 1939).

II

THE PURCHASE AND EXPLORATION
OF LOUISIANA

T HE SAN ILDEFONSO TREATY of October 1, 1800, had provided for the retrocession of Louisiana Territory to France. But Napoleon was not then ready to carry the arrangement into effect, so it was kept a secret. Nearly eight months elapsed before President Thomas Jefferson heard of the treaty, and then the report came as a rumor rather than as an official announcement. But when General Leclerc sailed with his French army to Santo Domingo in November, 1801, and began the subjugation of the island, credence was given to the report. Americans feared that Santo Domingo would be but a stepping-stone to Louisiana.

THE PURCHASE

President Jefferson watched French movements with grave anxiety, and at their early successes in the island became greatly alarmed. On April 18, 1802, he wrote Robert R. Livingston, our minister to France, a letter intended for reading by the French leaders. He expressed the great concern of the American people, and threatened an alliance with Great Britain. "The day that France takes possession of New Orleans," he warned, "we must marry ourselves to the British fleet and nation." On May 1 Secretary of State Madison wrote Livingston, instructing him to inquire into the extent of the cession, "particularly whether it includes the Floridas as well as New Orleans," and directing that he "endeavor to ascertain the price at which these, if included in the cession, would be yielded to the United States." A short time before, the United States had attempted to purchase Spain's holdings on the east side of the Mississippi, but our offer was refused (April 7, 1802), and not even a hint was given to our minister (Charles Pinckney) that the retrocession of Louisiana had occurred. Talleyrand, the wily French minister, denied the existence of such a treaty, and Living-

166

ston was unable to verify it in Paris. Thus, from neither France nor Spain could we obtain dependable information as to facts or their intentions regarding the Louisiana Territory.

In November, 1802, news reached Washington that Don Juan Ventura Morales, the Spanish Intendant at New Orleans, had closed the Mississippi to American commerce. This was immediately interpreted as being prompted by France and as indicative of French policy. The people of Kentucky and Tennessee began to talk of war, and excitement spread throughout the entire country. Secretary Madison directed Minister Pinckney at Madrid to protest Morales's order. Of our Westerners, Madison wrote: "The Mississippi to them is everything. It is the Hudson, the Delaware, Potomac, and all the navigable rivers of the Atlantic States formed into one stream." Federalists demanded war and loudly condemned France, to whom Jefferson, their political enemy, had heretofore been ardently attached. But by this time the President had recovered somewhat his wonted calm. "Never in all his long and varied career," writes Edward Channing, "did Jefferson's foxlike discretion stand him in better stead." He formulated a policy to meet the situation. He would quiet the public clamor for war, regain by diplomacy our previous commercial rights on the Mississippi, and carefully watch for a "break" in international relations that would make possible the acquisition of the New Orleans area.

When Congress convened in December, 1802, members were perturbed at the outlook. President Jefferson, in his Annual Message to that body, said: "The cession of the Spanish Province of Louisiana to France, which took place in the course of the late war, will, if carried into effect, make a change in the aspect of our foreign relations which will doubtless have just weight in any deliberations of the Legislature connected with that subject." But the actual transfer of Louisiana had not yet taken place, so the culmination that was feared might still be forestalled. On January 11, 1803, the President addressed the Senate and nominated his close and trusted friend, James Monroe, as minister extraordinary with authority to act in conjunction with our resident ministers in France or in Spain to make a treaty with either nation "for the purpose of enlarging and more effectually securing our rights and interests in the river Mississippi and in the Territories eastward thereof." The nomination was confirmed, and the House of Representatives in secret session voted two million dollars "to defray any expenses in relation to the intercourse between the United States and foreign nations."

Animated discussions regarding Louisiana resounded in the halls of Congress. Senator James Ross, of Pennsylvania, proclaimed our right by treaty and by nature to the free navigation of the Mississippi.

Why not seize then, what is so essential to us as a nation? Why not expel the wrong-doers?—wrong-doers by their own confession, to whom by seizure we are doing no injury. Paper contracts, or treaties, have proved too feeble. Plant yourselves on the river, fortify the banks, invite those who have an interest at stake to defend it; do justice to yourselves when your adversaries deny it; and leave the event to Him who controls the fate of nations.

Senator Ross offered resolutions on February 16 authorizing the President to take immediate possession of New Orleans and adjacent territory, and to call out state militias to achieve that end. Certain of his colleagues supported the resolutions, others opposed them. James Jackson, of Georgia, advised against the immediate precipitation of a war, though he was not overawed with fear of Napoleon:

We have been told much of Bonaparte, that he is the hero of France, the conqueror of Italy, the tyrant of Germany, and that his legions are invincible. We have been told that we must hasten to take possession of New Orleans whilst in the hands of the sluggish Spaniards, and not wait until it is in the iron grasp of the Caesar of modern times. . . . Bonaparte, sir, in our Southern country, would be lost, with all his martial talents; his hollow squares and horse artillery would be of little service to him in the midst of our morasses and woods. . . . With a body of only ten thousand of our expert riflemen around him, his laurels would be torn from his brow, and he would heartily wish himself once more on the plains of Italy.

Senator Clinton, of New York, spoke against the Ross resolutions:

Of all characters, I think that of a conquering nation least becomes the American people. What, Sir! shall America go forth, like another Don Quixote, to relieve distressed nations, and to rescue from the fangs of tyranny the powerful states of Britain, Spain, Austria, Italy, the Netherlands? Shall she, like another Phaeton, madly ascend the chariot of Empire, and spread desolation and horror over the world? Let us, Sir, never carry our arms into the territory of other nations, unless we are compelled to take them up in self-defense.

The Ross resolutions were rejected on February 25 and milder ones were adopted.

It was now France's and Spain's turn to guess what the United States was going to do. The representatives of these nations bestirred themselves in Washington to discover the plans of the administration. Jefferson began openly to court the British representative, and Pichon, the French *chargé*, became thoroughly alarmed. He wrote Talleyrand, telling of the bitter feeling in the United States and of the danger that Jefferson, normally friendly to France, would be forced "to yield to necessity his scruples against a British alliance."

On March 8 Monroe sailed from New York on his special mission. Jefferson had not hurried matters. He foresaw the early resumption of war between France and England, and understood the influence this event would have on Napoleon and upon the destiny of the Louisiana Territory. In April Secretary of State Madison wrote to Monroe and Livingston, instructing them to make an alliance with England should France "meditate hostilities or force a war with the United States, by closing the Mississippi to commerce."

The measures taken by the United States began to bear fruit. The Spanish Minister in Washington called on Madison with assurance that the right of Americans to deposit goods at New Orleans had been restored. The Intendant's order, it appeared, had been issued on his own responsibility, and the king had refused to ratify it.

In the meantime affairs had taken on a very different aspect for Napoleon. In Santo Domingo the resistance of the Negroes had been supplemented by the onslaughts of "Yellow Jack." In September, 1802, Leclerc wrote his brother-in-law and master that only one-seventh of his 28,000 men were fit for service, and that he needed 17,000 more soldiers. Within a month Leclerc himself was dead of the devastating fever. The Santo Domingo campaign had failed. And Napoleon never shot a second arrow to recover one already lost. War with England again was imminent, and Bonaparte realized how insecure was his title to Louisiana while Britannia ruled the waves.

On Easter Sunday (April 10, 1803) Napoleon held a conference with two of his counselors who had resided in the United States— Barbé-Marbois and Decrès—and spoke to them with great feeling:

I know all the value of Louisiana, and I have wished to repair the error of the French negotiator who abandoned it in 1763. A few lines of a treaty have given it back to me, and hardly have I recovered it when I must expect to lose it. But if I lose it, it will be dearer one day to those who compel me to abandon it than to those to whom I wish to deliver it. The English have successively taken away from France—Canada, Cape Breton, Newfoundland, Acadia, the richest parts of Asia. They are agitating Santo Domingo. They shall not have the Mississippi, which they covet. . . . They have twenty vessels in the Gulf of Mexico, they sail over those seas as sovereigns, while our affairs at Santo Domingo have grown worse every day since the death of Leclerc. The conquest of Louisiana would be easy if they merely took the trouble to land there. I have not a moment to lose if I wish to place it out of their reach. . . . I am thinking of ceding it to the United States. Hardly shall I be able even to say that I am ceding it to them, for it is not yet in our possession. If I leave any time to our enemies, I shall transmit only a vain title to those republicans whose friendship I seek.

Early the next morning Bonaparte spoke to his minister again.

It is not only New Orleans that I wish to cede, it is the whole colony, without reserving anything of it. I know the value of what I abandon, and . . . I renounce it, therefore, with great regret. To insist upon its preservation would be madness. I direct you to negotiate this affair with the envoys of Congress. Do not even wait for the arrival of Mr. Monroe; have an interview this very day with Mr. Livingston. But I have need of a great deal of money for this war, . . . If I were to regulate my terms on what these vast territories will be worth to the United States, the indemnities would have no limits. I shall be moderate, in consideration of the necessity to sell in which I am. But remember this well: I want fifty millions [francs], and for less than this amount I shall not treat.

Livingston was, of course, unaware of Napoleon's decision. For weeks the American minister had been approaching Talleyrand, seeking to buy New Orleans and West Florida, but apparently he was making no headway. Then on April 11, Talleyrand suddenly asked Livingston if the United States "wished to have the whole of Louisiana." Livingston replied that he sought only New Orleans and the Floridas, and that anything beyond that would have to await the arrival of Monroe. Talleyrand hastened to add that he was not speaking with authority—and very properly should he so explain—for that very day Napoleon had placed negotiations in the trustworthy hands of Barbé-Marbois.

When Monroe arrived in Paris the next day (April 12), Livingston was still doubtful of success for their negotiations. "Only force can give us New Orleans," he said at his first meeting with Monroe. "We must employ force. Let us first get possession of the country and negotiate afterwards." But a conference the next day with Barbé-Marbois quickly changed the outlook. The Frenchman showed his credentials and revealed Napoleon's willingness to cede all of Louisiana to the United States. The two lines of self-interest had converged— France was anxious to sell, the United States eager to buy. There remained only the question of price.

The three negotiators—Barbé-Marbois, Livingston, and Monroe— were old friends, having been well acquainted and associated during the American Revolution when the Frenchman held a diplomatic post in America. So there was unusual harmony pertaining to the negotiation. But, like lawyers, they were friends at dinner, enemies at the bar. Each side proposed terms beyond all hope of acceptance. In typical diplomatic fashion, the French minister said that the First Consul demanded 100,000,000 francs plus the settlement of the claims of American citizens against France. "Seeing by my looks," writes Livingston, "that I was surprised at so extravagant a demand, he added that he considered the demand as exorbitant, and had told the First Consul that the thing was impossible; that we had not the means of raising that." (A diplomat has been defined as a man who is willing to lie for his country.) Livingston had suggested to Talleyrand 20,000,000 francs as a possible figure. Now ensued several days of haggling, and then a final compromise at 60,000,000 francs for France, plus 20,000,000 to settle claims of American citizens against France—$15,000,000 in all.

Three weeks elapsed before the various matters were adjusted and the papers drawn. The French copy of the principal treaty was completed April 30 and the signatures were affixed to the documents early in May, but all were antedated to April 30, 1803. After signing the treaty, Livingston rose, shook hands with the other negotiators, and said prophetically: "We have lived long, but this is the noblest work of our lives."

Various phases of the Louisiana Purchase will hardly stand scrutiny as to law or ethics. Napoleon was selling territory he did not actually possess and that he had promised Spain not to alienate. Not having fulfilled his part of the bargain entered into at San Ildefonso in 1800, he did not have a legal title to Louisiana; and, were it French soil, the constitution of the French Republic forbade the executive to dispose of it. Livingston and Monroe, on their part, had not been authorized to purchase the Louisiana Territory, and there was some doubt as to authority under the Constitution to purchase any land. But the stakes were great, and there was no time to await further authorization from home. So the two Americans assumed responsibility and signed the documents. The importance of the Louisiana Purchase in the making of America can scarcely be overrated, so the acts of Livingston and Monroe not only heightened the stature of their statesmanship, but placed the citizenry of the new American nation eternally in their debt.

Fortuitous circumstances made the whole deal possible. The French chef drew from Europe's English-fueled oven the Spanish cake, and with burnt fingers dropped it into the lap of Uncle Sam.

Napoleon ratified the treaty of cession on May 22, 1803, no doubt prompted to expedite the matter by the outbreak of hostilities with England on that very day. On July 14 the treaty reached the United States, where it was received by Jefferson with mixed feelings of pleasure and misgivings. His fears for the safety and future of the nation had induced him to authorize the purchase of territory at the mouth of the Mississippi. Now that it was done, and on a grander scale than he had hoped for or authorized, his strict-constructionist scruples rose to mock him. He began to rationalize. To Senator Breckenridge he explained that he was in the position of a guardian who had invested the money of his ward in a promising estate. "I did this for your good," he said. "I thought it my duty to risk myself for you." To ease his conscience, he drafted amendments to the Constitution, authorizing and justifying the purchase, and promised himself that these would be advocated and adopted.

Livingston and Monroe had sent from France an explanation of

their actions, together with a marshalling of strong arguments in justification. Jefferson and Madison gave the paper sympathetic study,
and on July 29, the Secretary of State wrote the American negotiators:
"In concurring with the disposition of the French government to treat
for the whole of Louisiana, although the western part of it was not
embraced by your powers, you were justified by the solid reasons
which you give for it; and I am charged by the President to express to
you his entire approbation of your so doing."

Upon learning of the sale, Spain protested to both France and the
United States. The Spanish minister warned our government to "suspend the ratification and execution of the treaties of cession of Louisiana, as the French government in securing the province had contracted
an engagement with Spain not to retrocede it to any other power. . . .
France not having executed that engagement, the treaty cession was
void." Jefferson referred the Spanish authorities to France for explanations and satisfactions, and Napoleon was in a position to force
acquiescence.

In mid-August letters came from Livingston urging speedy ratification, as Napoleon might change his mind at any moment. Jefferson
thereupon advised his intimates that the less said about the constitutional aspects of the question, the better for the cause. Congress met
in extra session on October 17, 1803. After a few days of vigorous
debate, in which the Federalists switched position and argued for strict
construction of the Constitution and against the purchase, the treaty
was ratified. The purchase met with instant and general approval,
and all thought of constitutional amendment was soon lost in the
popular acclaim.

By one fortunate stroke the United States had practically doubled
its area. The all-important Mississippi was now free, and its unrestricted navigation was no longer contingent on the whims of a foreign nation. The conditions that had invited foreign intrigue among
our western frontiersmen and that had fed the fires of disunion were
removed. Not only a larger nation, but a united one, faced the future.
And from a governmental standpoint, the new constitution in this important test exhibited an elasticity that augured well for the future.

There was little immediate concern as to the exact boundaries of the
ceded province. The treaty copied the phrasing from the San Ildefonso Treaty of 1800, the cession being of "the colony or province of
Louisiana, with the same extent that it now has in the hands of Spain
and that it had when France possessed it, and such as it should be
after the treaties subsequently entered into between Spain and other
States." Our ministers tried to obtain from the French authorities
some statement as to the extent of Louisiana. When someone ex-

pressed regret at the obscurity relative to boundaries, Napoleon remarked: "If an obscurity did not already exist, it would, perhaps, be
good policy to put one there." And the wily Talleyrand parried all
efforts to draw from him a statement as to territorial limits. "You
have made a noble bargain for yourselves," he commented, "and I
suppose you will make the most of it." The veteran diplomat was
right. We immediately insisted that West Florida was a part of the
purchase; soon we claimed Texas; and ultimately we contended that
the Oregon country was included.

THE LEWIS AND CLARK EXPEDITION

Although the boundaries of the Louisiana Territory were undefined
and the region of its probable outer limits was unexplored, Americans
were not entirely ignorant of this land when it came into their hands.
In fact, as related in the preceding chapter, Anglo-Americans had for
years been making their way into the country beyond the Mississippi.
Many of these pioneers had established homes on soil of the present
states of Louisiana and Missouri. But the farther bounds of Louisiana
Territory—the Rocky Mountains and the headwaters of the Missouri
—were still unknown when the region was purchased in 1803. The
vague rumors afloat as to mountains of salt and other incredible features were soon to be dispelled by notable explorations. The first and
most important of these was the one now known to every schoolboy—
the Lewis and Clark Expedition.

This important venture, launched by Thomas Jefferson, was not the
first evidence of that great President's interest in the western country.
A desire to extend the bounds of knowledge in any direction had long
been a passion with the many-sided sage of Monticello. And regarding the unknown West, his curiosity was particularly keen and
persistent. He was anxious to learn of the source and course of the
Missouri, of the flora, fauna, and Indians indigenous to the Rocky
Mountain region. And there is some doubt as to whether his interest
in that quarter was purely and solely scientific. For instance, read a
letter of his written to George Rogers Clark in 1783. This communication may have been prompted in part by other events of that year—
the organization of the Northwest Fur Company at Montreal and the
publication of John Ledyard's account of Captain Cook's third voyage
into the Pacific. But, in any event, Jefferson wrote to the hero of
Vincennes on December 4, 1783:

I find they have subscribed a very large sum of money in England for
exploring the country from the Mississippi to California. . . . They pretend
it is only to promote knowledge. I am afraid they have thoughts of colonis-
ing into that quarter. . . . Some of us have been talking here in a feeble way

of making the attempt to search that country, but I doubt whether we have enough of that kind of spirit to raise the money. How would you like to lead such a party?

Nothing, however, appears to have resulted from this proposal. While Jefferson was minister to France in 1786, he became acquainted with John Ledyard, a picturesque and restless Connecticut Yankee who was in Europe endeavoring to finance a fur-trading voyage to the northwest coast of America. Writes Jefferson: "I suggested to him the enterprise of exploring the Western part of our continent by passing thro St. Petersburg to Kamschatka, and procuring a passage thence in some of the Russian vessels to Nootka Sound, whence he might make his way across the continent to America." The proposal appealed to Ledyard, and he set out upon the journey. But Empress Catherine objected to the project, and the American was turned back in Siberia.

Jefferson's next connection with western exploration was in relation to the plan of André Michaux. This famous French botanist proposed to the American Philosophical Society a scientific expedition to the northwest coast. The learned Philadelphia society endorsed the project and solicited funds to further it. Among the subscriptions were one by Washington for $25 and those of Jefferson and Hamilton for $12.50 each. Jefferson was especially interested in the plan and, in behalf of the sponsoring Society, drafted instructions for Michaux. The botanist was to ascend the Missouri River and thence by "a river called Oregon, interlocked with the Missouri," reach the Pacific. He was to take note of the country, "its general face, soil, rivers, mountains, its productions—animal, vegetable, and mineral." Michaux set out from Philadelphia in July, 1793. But he had become involved with the schemes of Citizen Genêt for launching an expedition in Kentucky against Spanish Louisiana, and his scientific expedition came to naught.

After his election to the Presidency, Jefferson turned again to his pet idea of an overland expedition to the Pacific. The lapse of an "Act for establishing trading houses with the Indian tribes" gave him the opportunity needed. In a secret message to Congress on January 18, 1803, he urged enactments to promote trade with our Indian tribes, and suggested, further, the desirability of reaching out to cultivate trade with the Indians of the Missouri River region. This could be accomplished by sending a party of American soldiers to visit the remote tribes. Such an expedition, he suggested to Congress, "might explore the whole line, even to the Western Ocean, having conferences with the natives on the subject of commercial intercourse, get admission among them for our traders as others are admitted." Congress acceded to the request and voted $2,500 "for the purpose of extending

the external commerce of the United States." Neither the executive
nor the legislative branch of our government appears to have had
scruples against sending a military expedition into foreign territory
(Spanish Louisiana).

Jefferson chose his private secretary and fellow Virginian, Meriwether Lewis, to lead the expedition, and sent him to Philadelphia
for several weeks to study botany and astronomy in preparation for his
duties. With the President's consent, Lewis invited William Clark
(brother of George Rogers Clark), to be co-leader of the enterprise.
The young men—Lewis was 28 and Clark 32—had been boyhood
friends in Virginia, both were experienced frontiersmen, and each had
seen military service on the western border. Their compatibility was
ideal, and three years of trying experiences were only to prove and to
deepen their friendship.

Instructions for the expedition were prepared by Jefferson. The
party was to ascend the Missouri, cross the mountains, and descend
by the most practicable river, "whether the Columbia, Oregon, or
Colorado, or any other river" to the Pacific. The explorers were to
observe and make a record of soils, minerals, plant and animal life,
climate, and all noteworthy features and resources. Facts regarding
the courses and sources of rivers were to be gathered, and the latitude
and longitude of important points determined. The routes of Canadian traders in traffic with the western Indians were to be ascertained.
The Americans were to learn whether the furs of the distant region
might not be advantageously collected at the head of the Missouri and
transported by that stream to the United States. Should they find
traders in coast vessels, letters of credit from the United States Government could be used to replenish supplies for the homeward journey.
Friendship and trade with the native tribes were to be cultivated,
and, if possible, a delegation of Indians was to be brought back to the
national capital.

In early July, 1803, Lewis said farewell to the President at Washington. It was the end of August before the boat was ready at Pittsburgh,
and the descent of the Ohio, now at low stage, was difficult. Clark,
with his Negro servant York, came from his home in Kentucky to join
the expedition on its way down the river. A call for young, robust,
unmarried volunteers had gone forward, and from those who offered
their services, 14 soldiers and 9 Kentucky hunters were selected. The
civilians were enlisted as privates, for the venture was to be a military expedition.

Before the party reached the Mississippi, winter was at hand. West
of the river, Spanish officials were still in control, for although the purchase of Louisiana Territory had been consummated, the actual trans-

fer of the Missouri region had not yet taken place. To avoid offense to the Spanish authorities and in order to draw rations from the War Department, the company made camp on the Dubois River, nearly opposite the mouth of the Missouri. Throughout the winter the men were engaged here, chiefly under Clark's direction, in drilling, building boats, and making general preparations for the trip. Lewis spent considerable time in St. Louis, gathering information from fur traders who were experienced in the navigation of the Missouri River and familiar with the Indians to be encountered in the upper country. On March 9 he was an official witness to the transfer of Upper Louisiana from Spain to France and from France to the United States.

On May 14, 1804, the expedition set out from its winter camp "in the presence of many of the neighboring inhabitants, and proceeded on under a jentle brease up the Missourie." There were three craft: a 55-foot keelboat with 22 oars, one open pirogue with seven oars, and another with six. All three boats were equipped with sails, push poles, and *cordelles* (tow lines) for use as occasion afforded. Arms and ammunition, scientific instruments, attractive articles for Indian presents, extra clothing, food, and general supplies were packed in the boats. Extra men were employed to aid in the voyage as far as the Mandan villages.

The first part of the journey was through well-known country, but the strong current, the numerous sandbars, and the treacherous snags made difficulties great and labor no less exacting. To make headway up the great river, the navigators were compelled to avoid the main current and to seek the eddies near the bank. And here the sawyers (concealed timbers) were thickest and danger from caving banks greatest. Less dangerous, but more annoying, were the numerous "ticks, musquiters and knats" that pestered the men in the daytime and kept them awake at night. Hunters, supplied with horses, were kept on shore to bring in meat to the night camps.

The last white settlement (La Charette), home of famous Daniel Boone, was passed on May 25. A little beyond the mouth of the Platte, in late July, the party contacted some Oto and Missouri Indians, told them that they were now the children of the Great White Father at Washington, and sweetened the tidings with presents of trinkets, medals, and flags. In August the one and only death of the expedition occurred. Sergeant Floyd, sick only a day, died of a "bilious colic" and was buried on a bluff with a cedar post to mark his grave. Floyd's River was named in his memory. Councils were held with the Omahas and later with various bands of Sioux. The Teton Sioux, encountered near present Pierre, South Dakota, on September 25, were the most troublesome and threatening. Young warriors, with drawn bows and arrows, threatened to hold members of the exploring party; but by a show of force, followed later by tactful conciliation, the expedition extricated itself. The Indians asked for "the Great Father's milk"—whiskey. Through the Sioux country game was found in abundance—buffalo, elk, deer, antelope, and turkeys.

On October 8 the expedition reached the country of the Arikara Indians and encamped near the principal village. Some French traders who were located here acted as interpreters and gave valuable information to the exploring party regarding the country and the Indians. The Arikaras were very friendly, giving the visitors corn, beans, and dried squashes.

At a general council Lewis and Clark "acknowledged three chiefs, one for each of the three villages, giving to each a flag, a medal, a red coat, a cocked hat and feather, also some goods, paint and tobacco." One of the chiefs volunteered to accompany the expedition to the country of the Mandans, where the explorers planned to winter. Under his guidance they reached the principal Mandan village, a little above present Bismarck, North Dakota, in late October. They had now crept up the great Missouri for 1,600 long miles, and on the journey had averaged about nine miles per day.

Three miles below the Indian village, in a grove of large cotton-woods, the explorers selected a winter camp site. Here they erected log houses and a stockade, and named the establishment Fort Mandan. Special features of the post were a blacksmith shop and a smoke house for curing meat. During the five months spent at this post, the Americans were visited frequently by Indians and occasionally by British and independent traders. With all they carefully nurtured friendly relations, though the length and frequency of Indian visits were often annoying and the influence of British traders upon the Indians was sometimes inimical to American interests. Lewis informed the Indians that the region was now United States soil, and that they must no longer accept flags and medals from the British. The Great Father at Washington would soon send them traders who would bring better goods and fairer prices than had previously come to the region.

One of the visiting traders was Toussaint Charbonneau, who had purchased and married Sacajawea, a Shoshone Indian girl. Inasmuch as the explorers planned to traverse the Shoshone country, Lewis and Clark engaged Charbonneau and his wife as interpreters and guides. The Indian woman was to prove a valuable aid to the party when her home country was reached. During the winter at Fort Mandan, on February 11, 1805, Sacajawea gave birth to a baby boy who was to be carried the entire journey to the Pacific and back. This half-breed lad later was to be educated by William Clark, be taken to Europe for seven years by a German prince, and finally to become an important guide and interpreter of the West.

Hunting game for food, bartering with the Indians, gathering specimens, and making preparations for resuming the journey occupied the winter months. Clark, the more practical of the two leaders, was generally in charge of the fort and of physical arrangements. Lewis attended to diplomatic affairs with the Indians and the traders. Once when the Mandan village was threatened with a Sioux attack, the American soldiers hurried to the defense and thus won the esteem and gratitude of the villagers. Routine tasks were on occasion put aside for relaxation or celebration. On New Year's Day, records Sergeant Ordway:

we fired a Swivel & drank a Glass. about 9 o.C. 15 of the party went up to the 1st village of Mandans to dance as it had been their request. carried with us a fiddle & a Tambereen & a Sounden horn. as we arrived at the entrence of the vi we fired one round then the music played. loaded again. then marched to the center of the village [and] fired again. then commenced dancing. a frenchman danced on his head and all danced around him for a Short time then went in to a lodge & danced a while, which pleased them verry much they then brought victules from different lodges & of different kinds of diet, they brought also a quantity of corn & Some buffalow Robes which they made us a present off.

Clark's Negro, York, was a source of constant interest and amusement. He amazed the Indians with his feats of strength and his skill in dancing.

With the coming of spring, preparations for the journey were quickened. Two cottonwood logs were hollowed out into pirogues, these to replace the keelboat for the upper river. Thirteen men were to return to St. Louis in the keelboat; 31 men and Sacajawea and her baby were to continue up the stream. On April 7, 1805, writes Ordway:

About 5 oClock we all went on board fired the Swivel and Set off on our journey. at the Same time the barge Set off for St. Louis 2 frenchmen in a perogue in company with them. they took down the letters and all the writings which was necessary to go back to the States also Some curious animals such as Goat Skins & horns, a barking Squerrell Some Mountain Rams horns a prairie hen & badgers Some birls cauled magpies & a number of other curious things too tedious to mention &. C.

Indian weapons, utensils, and articles of dress, dried plants, and rock specimens were among the articles sent back in the keel-boat. Numbers of these items, after reaching their destination, were to be exhibited for years at Monticello or at Peale's Museum in Philadelphia.

On that early April morning, as they set out in their two pirogues and six canoes, the Lewis and Clark party was in high spirits. "I could not but esteem this moment of my departure as among the most happy of my life," Clark records in his journal. The party reached the mouth of the Yellowstone on April 26. Here, wrote Lewis, was an excellent site for a trading post. No unusual difficulties were being met with, though sand blew in clouds from the bars and strong winds nearly filled the canoes with water. Game was plentiful—elk, deer, antelope, and buffalo, not to mention beaver, geese, and fish. Bears gave them much concern. These, writes Lewis, "being so hard to die reather intimeadates us all; I must confess that I do not like the gentlemen and had reather fight two Indians than one bear."

Clark generally acted as captain of transportation, while Lewis, accompanied by the big Newfoundland dog which he had brought from home, walked on shore, exploring the country, hunting, and gathering specimens. On June 3 they reached a place where "the river split in two" and it was difficult to determine which was the main stream. They finally chose the left-hand fork. Lewis named the other stream the Marias River, in honor of his cousin, Maria Wood. At this junction they cached the larger pirogue, some ammunition, provisions, specimens, and so forth, to await their return from the overland journey. They traveled on till they were halted by the Great Falls of the Missouri. Here they made carts, using cross sections of tree trunks for wheels, and hauled their canoes around the falls and the series of cascades above. A month was consumed in this 18-mile portage.

On July 25 they reached the place where three forks join to form the Missouri River. To these streams the explorers gave the names of the triumvirate of statesmen—Jefferson, Madison, and Gallatin—who were then managing affairs at the national capital. While they made their way up the Jefferson Fork, difficulties increased as the size of the stream lessened. Lewis now went ahead on foot, hoping to find Shoshone Indians who might supply horses and guide the party over the Continental Divide. On August 12 he reached the source of the mighty Missouri, a spring "issuing from the base of a low mountain." He crossed over the divide and came upon a west-flowing creek—the Lemhi, a tributary of the Columbia. In one day the explorers drank from Pacific and Atlantic waters. Following down the stream next day, Lewis reached an Indian encampment, surrounded by many horses. He induced a party of young men to return with him to the head of navigation on the Jefferson, where his party waited.

When Lewis and his friends reached Clark and the main party, Sacajawea at once recognized the Indians as her own people, the Shoshones. And, as good fortune would have it, the leader of the band proved to be her own brother, from whom she had been stolen five years before. The Shoshone girl now served as interpreter and used her influence for the procurement of horses and supplies. The Lemhi being unnavigable, the explorers must continue land transportation. From the Shoshones they were able to obtain some 30 horses, and, especially important, the Indians were able to lead them northwestward over the mountain trail which connected the head of the Jefferson with the navigable Clearwater Fork of the Columbia. The trail was steep, crooked, and dangerous. Food was scarce, and for days the men lived on "portable soup" or on horse and dog meat. Upon reaching a village of the Flathead Indians, more horses were obtained. Continuing, the men finally reached the forks of the Clearwater. The difficult journey of more than 300 miles on horseback over mountain trails had been accomplished through the aid of friendly Indians.

Five canoes were now made by hollowing out tree trunks. Then, caching their pack saddles and some supplies and branding their horses and leaving them in charge of a friendly chief, the explorers climbed into their canoes on October 7 and set forth for the Pacific. On the descent they encountered numerous Indians, from whom they procured fish, roots, and dog meat for food. As trade goods and presents diminished, the travelers resorted to novel means of impressing the natives and getting food. Cruzatte, the Frenchman, played his violin, the soldiers sang and danced, York performed, and Lewis shot his air gun, exhibited his watch, telescope, and compass.

On November 7, 1805, Clark exultantly wrote: "Great joy in camp, we are in view of the Ocian." The long westward journey had achieved its great objective; the continent had been spanned by Americans.

Winter quarters were established on Young's Bay. The post, similar in structure to Fort Mandan, they named Fort Clatsop, in honor of the Indians of the vicinity. The constant rains, the fleas, and the too-frequent visits of Indians were the principal annoyances through the winter. Men were sent to the ocean with kettles to boil out salt. From a whale washed on shore, meat and oil were obtained. Records one soldier, "We mix it with our poor elk meat and find it eats very well." Hunters were constantly out for game, and the skins were dressed and made into clothing. About 150 elk and 28 deer were killed during the winter, and 338 pairs of elkskin moccasins were made for the long trek homeward.

Having failed to find any white traders at the mouth of the Columbia, they left some papers and letters with the Indians for delivery to the first trading vessel. On March 23, 1806, the party set their faces toward home. In ascending the Columbia, they were able to obtain food only with difficulty. Their trade goods were almost exhausted, so Lewis and Clark assumed the role of doctors, receiving for their services dogs and other food supplies. Writes Lewis of their medical practice: "In our present situation I think it pardonable to continue this deception for they will not give us any provision without compensation in merchandize and our stock is now reduced to a mere handfull. we take care to give them no article which can possibly injure them."

On the Clearwater they recovered their horses from the Indians, and after some delay in waiting for the snow to melt, set out across the mountains. The party divided on Bitter Root River to explore possible new routes. Lewis took a short-cut course to the east and reached the Great Falls of the Missouri six days after crossing the Continental Divide. He then explored the Marias River. Unfortunately he was shot in the leg by his nearsighted French hunter who mistook him for a bear. For a month the explorer was disabled.

Clark followed in part the old route to Three Forks, and continued eastward. Reaching the Yellowstone River some distance north of Yellowstone Park, he followed this stream to the Missouri. The reunited parties reached the Mandans on August 14, and after being joined by Chief Big White and a small delegation, continued down the Missouri. They descended the river swiftly, making from 40 to 75 miles per day, and reached St. Louis on September 23, 1806. "We were met by all the village," writes Clark, "and received a hearty welcom from its inhabitants." Many were surprised at their return, thinking they had been lost in the unknown country.

The Expeditions of Freeman, Pike, and Long

Following the purchase of Louisiana, Jefferson's interest in the territory naturally increased. Through correspondence with well-informed persons in the West, he gathered available information; and, to augment this and to supplement the work of Lewis and Clark, he planned scientific expeditions up the Red and Arkansas rivers. Congress approved the idea and voted an appropriation of $3,000 on April 15, 1804.

Sir William Dunbar, who Doctor Isaac J. Cox says "was in his day the most noted scientist of the Mississippi Valley," was chosen by the President to direct these explorations. Doctor George Hunter, a chemist of Philadelphia, was to be one of the leaders. Late in May, Doctor Hunter journeyed to Pittsburgh, and thence, in a flat-bottomed boat, floated with supplies down the Ohio and Mississippi, reaching Natchez on July 24. Delays in getting men and more supplies from New Orleans, defection of some of the Osage Indians, and Spanish orders from Chihuahua against American entry into debatable territory caused a postponement of the major expedition. During the winter of 1804–1805, however, Dunbar and Hunter conducted a four-months scientific expedition up the Ouachita River, wholly within the present state of Louisiana. As the region was already known and in part settled, the contribution was to scientific knowledge only. The information gathered was supplemented by reports sent to Washington by Doctor John Sibley, Indian Agent at Natchitoches.

Jefferson obtained an additional $5,000 from Congress, and now directed an exploration to the source of the Red River. Again there were delays, and it was May, 1806, before the expedition got under way. Thomas Freeman was placed in charge of the party, which consisted of 24 men, 17 of whom were soldiers.

Spanish officials had been watching these developments with growing suspicion. They viewed such expeditions purely as attempts to gain military knowledge and to tamper with the allegiance of Indians. It must be remembered that Spain by no means acknowledged the Louisiana Territory as comprising the entire western drainage basin of the Mississippi. And inasmuch as the boundary line between the United States and the possessions of Spain had not been determined, this debatable area was very large. Early in 1806 had occurred a clash between Spanish and American troops on the Louisiana-Texas boundary. This, added to the general resentment which Spain felt toward the United States for our having acquired Louisiana, boded ill for the American expedition.

Don Nimecio Salcedo, Captain-General of the Internal Provinces of New Spain, ordered the Governor of Texas to send troops to watch the Red and Arkansas rivers and to turn back any American parties ascending those streams. Similar orders were sent to the Governor of New Mexico. But despite the prospect of Spanish opposition, the Freeman expedition set forth. In two flat-bottomed barges and a pirogue, it made its way up the Red River. At Natchitoches it took on additional trade goods and 13 more men. Shortly the "Great Raft," an extensive and formidable accumulation of logs, brush and mud, was encountered. But a long and arduous detour through bayous, creeks, and swamps finally brought the party again to the undivided channel. This they followed to a point 635 miles above the mouth of the river. Here they encountered Don Francisco Viana with a force of Spanish troops from Texas, who ordered them to turn back. Inasmuch as the Spaniards outnumbered Freeman's party five to one, and since Jefferson had given orders that hostilities be avoided at all hazards, the Americans agreed to return. They had gathered considerable information regarding the region and had held councils with the Indians, but in view of their failure to reach the source of the river and of the unfavorable impression which their forced retreat had on the Indians, the expedition can hardly be called a success. For a time Jefferson planned to send Freeman up the Arkansas in 1807, but the project was abandoned.

In the meantime an expedition under the leadership of Zebulon M.

Pike had been sent up the Mississippi. Lieutenant Pike, son of a veteran of the Revolutionary War, had entered his father's company at the age of 15 and was now, at 26, placed in charge of a small military party and directed to reach the source of the Mississippi. His orders, from General James Wilkinson at St. Louis, directed him to explore the region, visit and conciliate the Indians, and select sites for military and trading posts. Pike's diary of the journey begins thus: "Sailed from my encampment, near St. Louis, at 4 p.m., on Friday, the 9th of August, 1805, with one sergeant, two corporals, and seventeen privates, in a keel-boat 70 feet long, provisioned for four months."

Under sail, he made satisfactory progress up the river. Near the mouth of the Des Moines he held a council with Sac Indians on August 21. He reached the lead mines (site of Dubuque, Iowa) on September 1, and on the fourth passed the village of Prairie du Chien, then the extreme frontier post of the region. At the Falls of St. Anthony (St. Paul, Minnesota), on September 23, Pike held a council with the Sioux, apprising them of the new sovereignty over the region and advising them to make peace with the Chippewas.

He asked the Sioux for a tract of land at the falls and another at the mouth of the St. Croix, as locations for military posts. Writes Pike: "They gave me the land required, about 100,000 acres, equal to $200,000, . . . I gave them presents to the amount of about $200, and as soon as the council was over, I allowed the traders to present them with some liquor, which, with what I myself gave, was equal to 60 gallons." This was the first United States real estate deal in present Minnesota.

Near Little Falls, on October 16, a heavy snow presaged the approach of winter. Pike now constructed log houses as a winter base and laid in a supply of game. Leaving part of his men here, he set out with the others on December 10, supplied with sleds (for use on the ice) and a pirogue. Traveling northward for nearly a month, they reached a British trading post on Red Cedar Lake, and "observed the flag of Great Britain flying." At Sandy Lake, on January 8, 1806, they came to another British post, owned by the Northwest Fur Company. It had been in operation for 12 years and was well provisioned with game, locally grown potatoes, and wild rice and maple sugar purchased from the Indians.

After enjoying the hospitality of the Northwesters for some days, Pike continued his journey, and on February 1 reached Leech Lake, which he considered to be the main source of the Mississippi. Here he was entertained at another British post. But despite the hospitality accorded him, Pike could not view the foreign fur trade activity in the region as harmonizing with the dignity or laws of the nation he represented. Accordingly, he addressed a letter to the Britishers, protesting their activity and directing them to pay the usual customs duties and otherwise comply with the laws of the United States. Hugh McGillis, the factor, promised compliance, and the Union Jack over the fort was replaced by the Stars and Stripes. But the acquiescence was to be short-lived. With the departure of the Americans, the former trade was to be resumed and the English were to remain in complete control of the region until after the close of the War of 1812. Pike held a council at Leech Lake with the Chippewas, at which they agreed to give up their British flags and medals and to abandon the use of liquor.

On February 18 the Americans began their return journey, arriving at their post near Little Falls on March 5. After waiting a month for the river to open, they embarked and, following an uneventful voyage, reached St. Louis on April 30.

The success of the Mississippi expedition doubtless resulted in the choice of Pike as leader for a similar venture into the Southwest. This party was organized and instructed by General Wilkinson. Just what the General's motives and objectives were, it is difficult—if, indeed, possible—to determine. His duplicity in dealing with both Spain and the United States is well known, as is his connection with the Burr-Wilkinson scheme for dominion in the Southwest. Whether or not the expedition sent under Pike toward New Mexico had a definite relation to the Burr-Wilkinson project cannot be determined with certainty. In the mind of the wily Wilkinson, the Pike venture may have been conceived as a preliminary or a co-ordinating phase of the larger, questionable scheme. Or it may have been launched as a purely exploring tour, the findings from which would be of value either to the United States government or to the designing partners in their international intrigue. In any event, proof has not been found that Pike was partisan to the scheme. His conduct throughout the journey is easily explained on patriotic grounds.

On July 15, 1806, Lieutenant Pike, with his party of 22 men, set out from St. Louis. His first duty was to escort 51 Osages and Pawnees back to their own country and to arrange a peace between the two tribes. Thereafter he was to push westward and explore the headwaters of the Arkansas and Red rivers, and to conclude a treaty with the Comanches.

After proceeding up the Missouri and Osage rivers, he delivered the Indians to their villages near the eastern boundary of present Kansas. Here he procured horses and resumed his journey on September 1. By the 25th, Pike was at the Pawnee villages on the Republican River, where he learned that a Spanish party from New Mexico, intent on turning back the Americans, had penetrated to this point.

This counter expedition, led by Don Facundo Melgares, was very impressive, with 600 troops and over 2,000 horses and mules. Melgares had traversed the upper waters of the Red River, held a council with the Comanches, moved north of the Arkansas, and reached the Republican River. He had given Spanish flags and medals to the Pawnees, had taken American traders captive, and had told the Indians to turn back any Americans who attempted to penetrate beyond their villages. Melgares did not turn back Pike, as Viana had forced back Freeman on the Red River, simply because Pike had been too slow in reaching the Pawnee country. The Pawnees were more impressed with Spanish authority as represented by Melgares' imposing force than with United States power as evidenced by Pike's little party. So they tried to prevent the Americans from going farther. But the doughty lieutenant told them that he had been sent out to explore the western country and that "the young warriors of his great American Father were not women to be turned back by words." He determined to push on. "I had given orders," he records, "not to fire until within five or six paces, and then to charge with the bayonet and saber, when I believe it would have cost them at least one hundred men to have exterminated us, which would have been necessary." The opposition dissolved, and Pike proceeded to the Big Bend of the Arkansas. Here he made two canoes of cottonwood logs and buffalo skins, in which six of the men descended the river and returned to the States.

Following the homeward trail of Melgares, Pike and the remainder of his men made their way up the Arkansas. On November 15 they glimpsed the Rocky Mountains, and eight days later reached the site of Pueblo, Colorado. Though it was late November and snow covered the ground, Pike set out with three companions for the summit of the great peak that now is named for him. The distance, in the rarefied atmosphere, deceived him, as it has many another since. Two and one half days of marching and climbing brought him only to a point on the first range, near the summit of Mount Miller (since named for one of his companions). Here they "encamped in a cave, without blankets, victuals or water." The next day Pike records:

27th November, Thursday.—Arose hungry, dry, and extremely sore, from the inequality of the rocks, on which we had lain all night, but were amply compensated for toil by the sublimity of the prospects below. The unbounded prairie was overhung with clouds, which appeared like the ocean in a storm; wave piled on wave and foaming, whilst the sky was perfectly clear where we were. The summit of the Grand Peak [Pike's Peak] which was entirely bare of vegetation and covered with snow, now appeared at the distance of fifteen or sixteen miles from us, and as high again as what we had ascended, and would have taken a whole day's march to have arrived at its base, when I believe no human being could have ascended to its pinical [pinnacle].

So Pike returned to his camp on the Arkansas.

He now moved up the river to the mouth of the Royal Gorge, or Grand Canyon of the Arkansas, and, detouring to the north, explored South Park and the upper Arkansas. Returning to the Royal Gorge campsite, he constructed a log shelter, left two men here with the exhausted horses and part of the baggage, and with the remaining men traveled southward on foot in search of the Red River. Although enduring great hardships, they crossed the high Sangre de Cristo Range, traversed the San Luis Valley, and erected (in early February, 1807) a little log fort near the southern boundary of present Colorado. From here Dr. Robinson, a civilian who had accompanied the expedition, set out for Santa Fe, bearing a commission to collect a debt owed to William Morrison of Illinois. On February 26, 100 Spanish troops appeared at the fort and requested Pike to accompany them to the New Mexican capital.

Pike found that he was practically a prisoner. His maps and papers were taken from him. He was escorted to Chihuahua, was detained there for several months, and finally was deported through Texas, being released at Natchitoches on the Louisiana border on July 1, 1807. But though prevented from making and keeping notes, he was able by close observation to store his mind with valuable information regarding conditions and resources of the far Southwest. These data he incorporated in his report, published in 1810. So keen was the interest in the region and in the information presented that the book quickly went into English, French, German, and Dutch editions. Pike was to meet his death in the War of 1812.

Attention of the nation was soon absorbed by the international difficulties that culminated in the War of 1812, and further official western explorations were delayed. But with peace established in 1815, and with interest in the western fur trade growing, the government turned again to far western matters. In 1817 Major Stephen H. Long, of the topographical engineers, selected a site for a fort on the Arkansas River. Here Fort Smith was erected. In the same year, Long was sent up the Mississippi to choose locations for military establishments. Two years later, Fort Anthony was established by Colonel Henry Leavenworth at the mouth of the Minnesota (St. Peter's) River.

The establishment of these posts was but part of a general plan formulated by Secretary of War John C. Calhoun and President Monroe for protection of the fur trade and control of the western Indians. Another part of the plan, and the grandest—at least in conception and in preparations—was the so-called Yellowstone Expedition. This was to ascend the Missouri, make scientific explorations of the region, and establish a fort at the Mandan villages or at the mouth of the Yellowstone River. It was intended that this military post should overawe the Indians, frighten away the British traders, and open a trade route to Oregon and perhaps even to China. President Monroe and the country generally expected important results from the venture. The military phase of the undertaking was placed under Colonel Henry Atkinson, the scientific side under Major S. H. Long. Unfortunately, transportation of men and supplies was attempted in steamboats, and the experiment proved unsuccessful. The whole season was spent in reaching the Council Bluffs, a few miles above present Omaha. Here Camp Missouri (later known as Fort Atkinson and as Fort Calhoun) was established. The ensuing winter spent here was a miserable one, about 100 men dying of scurvy.

In the meantime Congress, disgusted at the progress made, investigated the project and refused to vote the funds necessary for its completion. As a sort of apology to the public, two minor expeditions were organized. One of these, led by Captain Magee, of the rifle regiment, opened a route from Camp Missouri to Fort Anthony (later, Fort Snelling) on the upper Mississippi. The party set out on July 2, 1820, and in 23 days had reached the site of present St. Paul, Minnesota. The other expedition, under Major Long, was sent to the Rocky Mountains.

With 19 men mounted on horses and supplied with a few pack animals, Major Long started from the Missouri River on June 6, 1820. At the Loup River, in central Nebraska, he visited the Pawnee villages, which together contained some 5,000 Indians. Fields of corn, beans, and pumpkins were being tended by the squaws, and around the towns from 6,000 to 8,000 horses were grazing. Two French guides were obtained here. Major Long journeyed up the north side of the Platte to the forks of that stream, and then followed the South Platte toward the mountains. He made rather regular marches of about 25 miles per day, passed large herds of buffalo, and occasionally saw bands of wild horses. On June 30 he caught his first glimpse of the mountains (present Long's Peak). He reached the site of Denver on July 5, and the next day arrived at Platte Canyon. After exploring a few miles into the mountains, he returned, moved south up Plum Creek, and crossed the divide to Fountain Creek. From Manitou Springs, near present Colorado Springs, Dr. James, botanist and chronicler of the expedition, made a successful ascent of Pike's Peak (July 13–14), discovering high-altitude species of plants and animals.

Continuing southward, the expedition reached the Arkansas River, ascended it to the Royal Gorge, and then descended it to the vicinity of present La Junta, Colorado. Here the party was divided, Captain Bell and 11 men continuing down the Arkansas, while Major Long and the nine others turned southward to seek the source of the Red River. After crossing the head of the Cimarron, the latter group continued southward and found a stream in such a position that it was believed to be the Red River. Down its course they made their way, suffering considerably from heat, violent storms, lack of food, and encounters

MAJOR LONG'S COUNCIL WITH THE PAWNEE INDIANS
(FROM THE OFFICIAL REPORT OF THE EXPEDITION.)

with Comanches. Then, to climax all, the river was found finally to empty into the Arkansas, and thus proved to be the Canadian. The elusive head of the Red River was still unexplored. Pike, Freeman, and Long, all had failed to find it. Captain Bell's party had suffered difficulties too, in the descent of the Arkansas, losing important manuscripts and at times being lost themselves. But in middle September the two branches of the expedition were united at Fort Smith, present Arkansas.

One of the important consequences of the expedition was the unfavorable impression its reports gave of the region traversed. Wrote Major Long: "In regard to this extensive section of country between the Missouri River and the Rocky Mountains we do not hesitate in giving the opinion that it is almost wholly unfit for cultivation, and of course uninhabitable by a people depending upon agriculture for their subsistence." He thought it might, however, serve a useful purpose as a frontier barrier, "to prevent too great an extension of our population westward, and secure us against the machinations or incursions of an enemy." On his map the high plains region was labeled the "Great

American Desert." This designation was carried over into the maps and schoolbooks of the country and for half a century persisted in the minds of the people. Large areas have since become agricultural land, while other sections are still desert.

BIBLIOGRAPHY

For discussions of the Louisiana Purchase, see the following: Binger Hermann, *The Louisiana Purchase and Our Title West of the Rocky Mountains, . . .* (Washington, 1900); J. K. Hosmer, *The Louisiana Purchase* (New York, 1902); C. F. Robertson, *The Louisiana Purchase and its Influence upon the American System* (in American Historical Association Papers, I); T. M. Marshall, *A History of the Western Boundary of the Louisiana Purchase, 1819–1841* (Berkeley, 1914); and E. S. Brown, *Constitutional History of the Louisiana Purchase* (Berkeley, 1920). More general works dealing with the subject are: Henry Adams, *History of the United States during the Administrations of Jefferson and Madison* (9 vols., New York, 1909–1911); Edward Channing, *History of the United States* (6 vols., New York, 1906–1925); Allen Johnson, *Jefferson and his Colleagues* (New Haven, 1921); Edward Channing, *The Jeffersonian System* (New York, 1906); Cardinal Goodwin, *The Trans-Mississippi West* (New York, 1922).

An important account by one of the negotiators of the treaty is: Barbé-Marbois, *Histoire de la Louisiane et de la Cession de cette Colonie par la France aux États-Unis de L'Amérique Septentrionale, . . .* (Paris, 1829, and English translation, Philadelphia, 1830). Important documents are found in *American State Papers, Foreign Relations, II,* and *Public Lands, I;* and in *State Papers and Correspondence bearing upon the Purchase of the Territory of Louisiana* (in *House Executive Documents,* No. 431, 57th Cong., 2nd Sess.). Copies of pertinent papers and documents are reproduced and an interesting account given in Volume II of Alcée Fortier, *A History of Louisiana* (4 vols., New York, 1904).

Data on Monroe's connection with the Purchase are found in D. C. Gilman, *James Monroe* (Boston, 1883). Biographies of Jefferson contain material on both the Louisiana Purchase and the Lewis and Clark Expedition. Among these are: H. S. Randall, *Thomas Jefferson* (2 vols., New York, 1858); J. T. Morse, Jr., *Thomas Jefferson* (Boston, 1883); D. S. Muzzey, *Thomas Jefferson* (New York, 1918); T. W. Hirst, *Thomas Jefferson* (New York, 1926).

Secondary accounts of early western explorations are the following: E. W. Gilbert, *The Exploration of Western America, 1800–1850* (New York, 1931); R. G. Thwaites, *A Brief History of Rocky Mountain Exploration, . . .* (New York, 1914). A popular account of the most famous expedition is Eva E. Dye, *The Conquest; the True Story of Lewis and Clark* (Chicago, 1902). See also the popular account, with numerous illustrations, O. D. Wheeler, *The Trail of Lewis and Clark, 1804–1904* (2 vols., New York, 1904). The first full-length biography of Pike is W. E. Hollon, *The Lost Pathfinder, Zebulon Montgomery Pike* (Norman, 1949).

A number of first-hand accounts of the Lewis and Clark Expedition are available. The first one to be published was the *Journal of the Voyages and Travels of a Corps of Discovery, . . .* (Philadelphia, 1807), by Patrick Gass, a member of the expedition. Seven years later Nicholas Biddle assem-

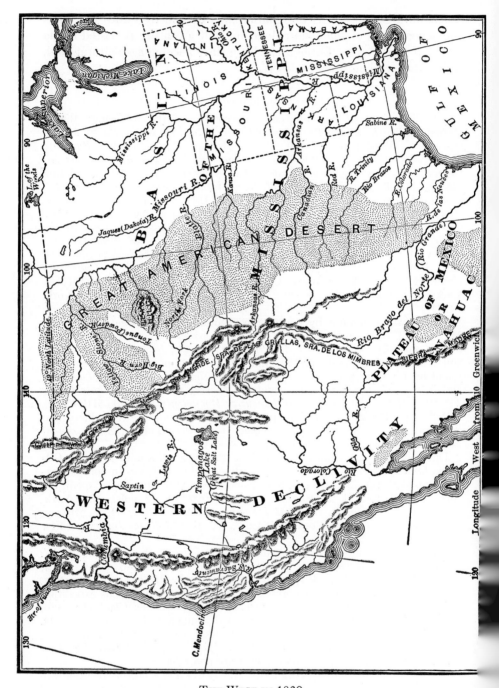

THE WEST IN 1820

(From W. M. Thayer, *Marvels of the New West*, page 220.)

bled from the various original journals his *History of the Expedition under the Command of Captains Lewis and Clark,* . . . (2 vols., Philadelphia, 1814). This and the Gass journal have gone through a number of subsequent editions. Elliott Coues, *History of the Expedition under the Command of Lewis and Clark* (4 vols., New York, 1893), was in some respects more satisfactory than the earlier versions. The most complete publication is R. G. Thwaites (ed.), *Original Journals of the Lewis and Clark Expedition, 1804–1806, Printed from the Original Manuscripts* . . . *and the Journals of Charles Floyd and Joseph Whitehouse,* . . . (7 vols. and an atlas, New York, 1904–1905). More recently Lewis's journal of his trip down the Ohio in 1803 and the complete journal of Sergeant Ordway have come to light. These were published by the Wisconsin Historical Society: M. M. Quaife (ed.), *The Journals of Captain Meriwether Lewis and Sergeant John Ordway Kept on the Expedition of Western Exploration, 1803–1806* (Madison, 1916). We have a recent biography of Lewis in C. M. Wilson, *Meriwether Lewis of Lewis and Clark* (New York, 1934).

The best edition of the Pike journeys is the one extensively annotated by Elliott Coues and entitled *The Expeditions of Zebulon Montgomery Pike, to Headwaters of the Mississippi River, through Louisiana Territory, and in New Spain, during the Years 1805–6–7* (3 vols., New York, 1895).

For the Long expedition, we have Edwin James, *An Account of an Expedition from Pittsburgh to the Rocky Mountains,* . . . (3 vols., Philadelphia, 1823). This work was reprinted as Volumes 14 to 17 in R. G. Thwaites, *Early Western Travels, 1748–1846* (32 vols., Cleveland, 1904–1906). There is a chapter on "The Yellowstone Expedition of 1819–20" in H. M. Chittenden, *The American Fur Trade of the Far West* (3 vols., New York, 1902, and new edition, 1935).

Accounts of the Dunbar-Hunter and the Freeman expeditions are found in I. J. Cox, "Explorations of the Louisiana Frontier, 1803–06," in the *Annual Report of the American Historical Association for the Year 1904* (Washington, 1905), 151–174.

12

ANGLO-AMERICAN OCCUPATION
OF LOUISIANA

T HE PURCHASE of the Louisiana
Territory increased the area of the United States by approximately
100 per cent. Indeed, its boundaries were not defined, and Jefferson
hardly knew how much of the trans-Mississippi West to claim, although
subsequently, on the basis of France's pretensions prior to 1762, he
claimed Louisiana as extending east of the Mississippi to the Perdido
River and the Rio Grande on the west and south. On October 30,
1803, a Congressional act authorized the President to take possession
of the new acquisition; and shortly thereafter Jefferson appointed
Governor William C. C. Claiborne, of the Mississippi Territory, and
General James Wilkinson as commissioners to receive the transfer of
New Orleans and its contiguous settlements from the French authorities.

But France must first secure its release from Spain, for Spanish
officials were yet in charge. It was not at all certain that the Spaniards
would move out, for the king had protested its sale to the United
States. Napoleon assured the American government, however, that
the treaty terms would be faithfully met; and a short time later the
Spanish minister at Washington informed the American Secretary of
State that his sovereign had thought it proper to withdraw his former
protest and that no opposition to American control would be offered.
At noon on November 30, therefore, the Spanish commissioners,
Governor Salcedo and the Marquis de Casa Calvo, ordered the Spanish
flag hauled down from its lofty pole in the center of the public square
at New Orleans, and formally surrendered control and the keys of
the city to M. Laussat, the French commissioner. But French tenure
was of short duration. On December 20 the final act of transfer was
consummated when Laussat gave way to Claiborne and Wilkinson;
the American flag was raised, the cannon at the near-by forts boomed
a salute, and the band struck up the air of "Hail, Columbia."

At St. Louis the transfer was equally ceremonious. On March 9, 1804, the upper part of Louisiana was formally delivered by the Spanish lieutenant-governor to Major Amos Stoddart, commissioned as French representative, in which capacity on the following day he presented St. Louis and the district to the United States. Moreover, he was to remain as the American military commandant and civil administrator. In his first proclamation he sought to offer the same assurances to his people as Claiborne had given the Creoles of New Orleans. He expressed his confidence in their patriotism and submission to the new regime, and congratulated them on being elevated from the rank of colonial subjects to free citizens of a great nation.

THE NEW FEDERAL DOMAIN

Although Spain relinquished all claim to Louisiana, the West Florida district lying south of the thirty-first parallel and west of the Perdido River and Bay was retained. The part of this district lying between the Mississippi and Pearl rivers was erected into the "Government of Baton Rouge" and administered by Lieutenant-Governor Don Carlos de Grandpré. The area included the posts of Manchac, Thompson's Creek, and Bayou Sara, near which was a considerable sprinkling of English and American settlers, who by their revolutionary plots were to cause the Spanish governor no end of anxiety.

The basis for settlement of the Louisiana Territory had already been laid by France and Spain, as previously discussed. Consul Daniel Clark at New Orleans reported to the Secretary of State in 1803 that the total population of Louisiana, including West Florida and the ports of Pensacola and Mobile, was approximately 49,500. New Orleans, with about 8,000 souls, was the most populous town. Then followed Mobile and its environs with 810, Pensacola with 404, and finally Baton Rouge and Galveston with 1,760. Upper Louisiana had 6,028 inhabitants, of which St. Louis was a border post of about 1,000 people. In this area settlements were generally along the Mississippi from the southeastern corner of the present state of Missouri to New Madrid, and from the mouth of the Ohio north to Cape Girardeau. And some 300 settlers settled the area about 50 miles from the confluence of the Arkansas and the Mississippi up the Arkansas. Generally the French and Creoles constituted a majority of the inhabitants in the towns, the Americans contenting themselves with isolated claims along the streams away from the towns; therefore, commerce and trade were generally in the hands of the former. St. Geneviève, where a considerable number of Anglo-American lead miners were located, was an exception.

The French, Creole, and Spanish inhabitants of the Louisiana Territory in 1803 were strikingly different in manners and customs from the Anglo-Americans in Kentucky and Tennessee or the English of the Natchez district. Alcée Fortier, in his *History of Louisiana,* quotes from the diary of John F. Watson, who arrived in New Orleans on May 26, 1804, as to his impressions of New Orleans and its people. The city was a bustling, wide-awake town, "that even now surpasses Philadelphia," from which he came. Here were oddly attired buccaneers and seamen, slovenly Spaniards, western trappers, homeseekers, and adventurers, and smartly dressed businessmen—all lending to the homogeneity of a remote community. The Place d'armes (public square) was daily a scene of interest and business transactions, where the challenges of shrill-voiced hucksters and auctioneers blended with the discordant noises of creaking, clumsy, wooden-wheeled carts, braying mules, and shouting urchins. At the wharves all was confusion amidst the thumping and jouncing aboard ships unloading. Watson noticed four flatboats in the river from Charleston on the Ohio, laden with flour, which brought a good price. The neat brick buildings, generally plastered over with mortar, lent an air of stability to the town, although only a few were more than one story in height or were well shaded. In the residential district, back from the river, were the less desirable frame structures, some little more than shanties. And in wet weather the streets were quagmires, necessitating travel by log sidewalks.

Society was greatly influenced by the Church, as practically all the French and Creoles were devout Catholics. Watson noticed that the "carnival" commenced on January 5, 1805, and was a period of great processions and entertainments. The scourging of Christ, His crucifixion, ascension, and other Biblical scenes were elaborately re-enacted by the priests and devout worshipers.

The ladies of New Orleans seldom appeared except at evening; and then generally by sitting at their doors or by walking along the levee. Those who shopped or moved about the streets during the day were accompanied by male companions, usually fathers or brothers; although some rode alone in a *volante* (two-wheeled cart), managing their own team. Indeed, more often than not the lady drivers must be content with a mixed team of horses and mules, three or four abreast, and generally driven at a gallop. Customarily the ladies would not call upon newcomers of their own sex, but expected to be visited by them first. Nor could a young gentleman visit his lady friend often unless he declared himself as an intended suitor. But perhaps the most novel of all customs was the *sherri-varries,* an occasion of "mobbing" the house of a widow when she married, whereupon a public donation was demanded. The constituents of the storming party were grotesquely and ludicrously disguised, and the former husband in effigy was brought along in a coffin riding beside that of the living spouse. When the donation was made, the crowd would disperse. Edward Livingston was sherri-varried later, and when he invited his visitors to partake of his "prepared cheer," they politely retired, after they had noisily shouted to him their good wishes for many years of happiness.

Quite obviously a people whose traditions and customs were so radically different from those of the United States, of which they were now a part, could little understand regulations and changes brought in by their new governor. The French and Creoles of New Orleans, and even some of the Anglo-Americans who had earlier infiltrated, were suspicious and resentful of Claiborne's motives and acts. Many believed that he would ignore their rights and even treaty stipulations guaranteeing them against American exploitation. Former French and Spanish officials encouraged them in these beliefs. Indeed, Laussat charged that neither Claiborne nor Wilkinson could speak French and were therefore incapable of understanding problems which confronted them. Under such circumstances the French and Creoles challenged every important act of their new governor. A Court of Pleas of seven judges was set up on December 30, 1803. Its civil jurisdiction extended over cases not exceeding $3,000 in value, with the right of appeal to the governor when the amount in litigation rose above $500. The court was also to have jurisdiction in criminal cases in which the punishment was not to exceed $300 and 60 days' imprisonment. This was a cause of popular concern, for it was charged that Claiborne favored newly arrived American citizens in appointment to judgeships, and that even court proceedings were in English.

Also, features of the Congressional act of March 26, 1804, to organize the new acquisition did not meet with popular approval. It divided Louisiana into two parts—the "Territory of Orleans" and the "District of Louisiana," with the latter attached to Indiana for judicial purposes. This was highly objectionable to the Creoles, for Louisiana had always been an administrative unit, and this seemed the first step in its reorganization in violation of treaty promises (1803). New Orleans citizens felt particularly incensed because of the federal attitude toward slavery. The importation of slaves was prohibited, except by American citizens who should come to settle in the territory with such slaves as they had previously owned in their former domiciles. Louisianans had in the past maintained a lucrative slave trade; now it was to cease. Was this not a discrimination against them, and in favor of the Anglo-Americans? Furthermore, they complained that the franchise was denied them under the new regime. Section IV of the territorial act had provided a Legislative Council, but its members were to be appointed by the President.

And any one of the three territorial judges would constitute a court, instead of two, as provided by the Ordinance of 1787. The Louisianans even complained that Claiborne's action in establishing the "Bank of Louisiana" should be regarded with suspicion. Had they not already suffered during the Spanish and French regimes from the issuance of too much paper money? What assurance could the governor give them that it would not be so now? Moreover, might not the bank prove to be an agency for legalized robbery? In fact, unrest was daily made evident by turbulent street crowds, the members of which shouted their denunciations of the new governor and his assistants.

When President Jefferson named the territorial Legislative Council, four of the appointees refused to serve; consequently, the others held back without either accepting or declining. For more than two months Claiborne faced an administrative impasse. Fortunately, in issuing commissions, the President did not know the Christian names of the nominees, and therefore sent blank forms for Claiborne to fill in. In the exigency, therefore, Claiborne substituted the names of four other Louisianans, and the Council was finally ready to start its work. The President later approved of Claiborne's action. The Council now divided the Territory into 12 counties, with an Inferior Court for each, composed of one judge; and before adjourning, it created a committee to prepare a territorial civil and criminal code.

With the passing of time most of the fears and grievances of the Louisianans were dissipated; anticipated dangers and discriminations did not materialize. Claiborne was a wise governor and worked unselfishly and constructively to allay popular unrest. The courts were disposed to render justice impartially; the New Orleans bank proved to be a safe depository for public funds and did not flood the country with worthless paper money; and the native citizens were given fair consideration with appointments. Perhaps the Louisianans found most satisfaction in the new territorial act of March 2, 1805. By its terms the demands of the French and Creoles were not entirely met, but Congress now authorized them to establish a government in all respects similar to that of the Territory of Mississippi. They were to choose 25 representatives for their lower house, and an upper branch (the Legislative Council) was to be selected by the President from a list presented by the territorial House of Representatives. And the "District of Louisiana" was now erected into the Territory of Louisiana, with the "first grade" of territorial government administered by a governor and territorial judges, as had been done during the early days of the Northwestern Territory. General James Wilkinson was selected as the first governor; he held office until he was succeeded by Meriwether Lewis at the close of the year 1806.

ORLEANS' EASTERN AND WESTERN BOUNDARIES

While these political changes were occurring west of the Mississippi, the Anglo-American settlers of the Baton Rouge country were demanding annexation to the United States. It will be remembered that West Florida had been settled largely by English, Scotch, Irish, and American immigrants during the period of British control from 1763 to 1783. Even after the region was again transferred to Spain, English-speaking colonists continued to enter the country. When Louisiana was acquired by the United States in 1803, the West Florida settlers had expected that their district would be included. And since it was not, in 1805 they rose in revolt. But the plans of the revolutionists failed, largely because of dissension among the leaders and the timely arrival of Spanish reinforcements. Governor Grandpré arrested the Kemper brothers, who had been the foremost leaders of the movement, and sought to spirit them out of the country; but as they were passing Point Coupée in the Mississippi on board a Spanish ship, they were recaptured by Lieutenant Wilson of the American army and sent before a Mississippi court for a hearing.

But the spirit of revolution would not down. Other immigrants had swelled the total number of Anglo-Americans within the district, and there was a general feeling that the Spanish government at Baton Rouge was too weak to care for their interests. Consequently, again in 1810 they rose in revolt, under the leadership of John Rhea, Andrew Steele, and others, and aided by recruits from Mississippi. The Spanish garrison at Baton Rouge surrendered, and, together with the civil officials, was allowed to withdraw to Pensacola. On September 26, 1810, delegates from the various parts of the district met in Baton Rouge in convention and declared their independence, maintaining that under Spanish control their lives and property were not protected, and that they had taken this means to safeguard them. Shortly thereafter the convention adopted a constitution for the "State of Florida," and appointed Fulwar Skipworth as governor. It next presented a formal application, through its president, John Rhea, to the Secretary of State of the United States, asking for admission to the Union. In the application the delegates asked "that this commonwealth . . . be immediately acknowledged as an integral part of the American Union," and requested a prompt reply, "since our weak and unprotected situation will oblige us to look to some foreign government for support, should it be refused. . . ." But President James Madison had no intention of granting the request, for the American government had not abandoned its claim to this territory. Congress asked the President to take immediate possession. Accordingly, on October 27, 1810, he issued a proclamation announcing that Governor Claiborne was empowered to incorporate the revolted area within the Territory of Orleans. On December 7 following, Claiborne, while returning from the eastern seaboard, stopped in Mississippi long enough to call on Governor Holmes for troops, which were furnished. With these he then advanced to St. Francisville and raised the United States flag. Disgruntled leaders opposed his actions, but a majority of the settlers gladly accepted annexation. On April 14, 1812, Congress added this district to Louisiana, and subdivided it into the parishes of Feliciana, East Baton Rouge, St. Helena, St. Tammany, Biloxi, and Pascagoula. A few days later the region from the Pearl to the Perdido was added to the Mississippi Territory, and still later General Wilkinson occupied Mobile.

The Louisiana-Texas boundary on the west was also in dispute. Spanish officials in Texas claimed the country west of Natchitoches, and early in 1806 Spanish troops were sent to Adaes, 14 miles west of Natchitoches, to establish a border post. A force of 600 men, well supplied with stores and ammunition, under Governor Antonio Cadero, also moved out to the Trinity River and there awaited other troops coming from Nuevo Leon under Don Simon Herrera. The combined army then moved still farther eastward and occupied Nacogdoches. This aroused the fears of Louisiana officials, and on January 24, 1806, Major Porter at Natchitoches informed the Spanish commandant at Nacogdoches, Don Rodriguez, that he intended to protect the rights of American citizens as far west as the Sabine; that he intended to distribute patrols through the said territory to prevent armed men not under the authority of the United States from advancing east of that stream; that he would repel invasion by pursuing and arresting invaders; but that, although he should sever all military communication, he would not seek to break peaceable intercourse between the settlements of Bayou Pierre and Nacogdoches. The Spaniard replied that his eastward advance was not designed as an encroachment on American territory, but that he intended to patrol the country as far east as the Arroyo Hondo, seven miles west of Natchitoches, which he recognized as the provisional boundary. Governor Claiborne, alarmed at this turn of affairs, dispatched militia reinforcements to the west; and General Wilkinson arrived on September 24 to assume personal command.

In spite of Porter's warning, a short time prior to Wilkinson's coming, Herrera, with 1,200 men, occupied a position on the Bayou Pierre; but when Wilkinson's force marched out to meet him, he withdrew. Wilkinson now established his headquarters on the east bank of the Sabine, and the Spanish occupied the west side, positions they held for several weeks. But bloodshed was avoided, for on November 6, 1806, the two commanders agreed to withdraw and leave the settlement of the boundary controversy to their respective governments. Wilkinson's men felt outraged; they believed that "money and not the sword had terminated the campaign."

And there were good reasons for believing this rumor. In October, emissaries of Aaron Burr visited Wilkinson's headquarters at Natchitoches to ascertain his views relative to the proposed western conspiracy. But after the ubiquitous general listened attentively to their plans, he sent them away with promises and evasive answers. Then when Wilkinson arrived on the Sabine, he dispatched Major Walter Burling, his aide-de-camp, to interview Governor Cordero and to arouse his fears concerning the proposed Burr venture. Burling was to advise that only Wilkinson, by a proper disposal of American troops, could save Spanish territory from occupation. Wilkinson could meet all the unusual demands thereto, if he were given $300,000 by the Spanish government. The New York *Spectator* of June 10, 1807, published a letter from New Orleans in which the author claimed that Cordero "furnished Wilkinson shortly with $120,000 *which were sent from San Antonio upon mules*"; but that, in spite of later efforts on Wilkinson's part, no other portion of the remaining $180,000 was forthcoming.

THE BURR-WILKINSON CONSPIRACY

The boundary controversies between the United States and Spain assumed even more alarming proportions in 1806 with the disclosure of the Burr-Wilkinson plot. Aaron Burr, Vice President of the United States, was a New York politician. On July 11, 1804, because of treasonable election charges against him, he killed Alexander Hamilton in a duel at Weehawken, New Jersey. Immediately after the duel he hastened back to Washington, where because of his official position he was secure from arrest on a charge of murder (which undoubtedly would have been brought against him had he remained either in New York or in New Jersey). But when his term of office expired on March 4 of the next year, he quietly rode out of the District of Columbia toward the west, for beyond the Alleghenies not only was dueling widely recognized as a means of settling points of honor among gentlemen, but popular antipathy for Hamilton made possible the recognition of Burr as a hero.

No student of American history has ever been able to present the composite whole of Burr's western plot, if, indeed, there was one. To the British minister in Washington, Anthony Merry, he could offer a Mississippi Valley colonial empire for the trifling sum of $110,000 and the loan of a fleet with which to take New Orleans. When he visited New Orleans in the summer of 1805, he negotiated with the Creoles and mestizos of the Mexican Association for the liberation of Mexico from Spain. Yet his attitude changed, for shortly after his return to the East his emissary informed the Marquis of Casa Yrujo, the Spanish minister in Washington, of the grave danger of dismemberment of Spain's northern borderland, which Burr alone could and would prevent for a consideration!

One authority states that the "kaleidoscopic changes of his plans baffle consistent explanation"; and another believes that "to every hearer he told the story that he thought would interest." Undoubtedly both are correct. To the British he offered control of the Mississippi Valley; to Mexican nationalists, the overthrow of Spanish power in Mexico; to Yrujo, aid in frustrating a western dismemberment plot; to Wilkinson, the second position in a western confederacy; to Jackson and Clay, the annexation of a vast region to the United States; and to homeseekers, liberal land grants within an agrarian paradise. But through a maze of intrigues and promises is clearly seen the selfish ambitions of a man in desperate need of funds; for, when western contributions did not meet his immediate needs, he borrowed from his son-in-law, Joseph Alston, a wealthy planter of South Carolina, and Harmon Blennerhassett.

As before stated, Burr's emissaries had visited Wilkinson in October, 1806, had revealed the ramifications of the conspiracy, and had asked for the general's support. But Wilkinson now found it more profitable to desert his confederate. Since Burr had visited him at Fort Massac, he had broached the subject to his subordinates and had been met with a decided rebuff, and without the backing of his officers and men there was little chance of success. Moreover, he now found it profitable to play the role of hero. Why not sell his knowledge of the affair and his offer of services to the Spaniards! A remuneration of $300,000 was certainly more than he could hope to secure from his agreement with Burr. But having collected $120,000 of the promised Spanish donation, he now turned to the President of the United States. He evidently knew that Burr's exposure would incriminate him, for he made noisy demonstrations of his patriotism. He placed New Orleans under martial law; he secured the arrest of such prominent Burr emissaries as Dr. Erick Bollman, Peter V. Ogden, and Samuel Swartwout, and frowned on attorneys and judges who would secure them bail; and he stationed all his available troops in and about the city. All the while, he was writing President Jefferson concerning the advance of the invaders and declaring his intentions of arresting Burr.

Meanwhile Burr had found a thorny path. Where in 1805 his friends were legion, now they were few. Jefferson issued a proclamation on November 27, 1806, declaring that a western conspiracy existed to invade Spanish territory, and warned all law-abiding citizens against joining it. Also, orders were issued to commanders of every important post from Pittsburgh to New Orleans, calling upon them to seize all boats, stores, and military supplies of the conspirators. Burr was therefore compelled to hasten his departure. Still only two of the five boats Jackson had agreed to build were ready. But hundreds of men who otherwise might have supported the movement now held back. Burr's plan, therefore, was completely wrecked. The Governor of Ohio seized Burr's bateaux and stores near Marietta, although Blenner-hassett and his more than 30 followers found enough boats to permit them to escape down the Ohio River. On December 24 they met Burr's small force near the mouth of the Cumberland, and the combined party of less than 60 men began its descent of the Mississippi.

Burr also encountered legal difficulties. In Kentucky he was taken into court to explain his actions, and Henry Clay, his counsel, promptly secured his release. Then when he and his party reached Bayou Pierre, Burr was again arrested and brought before a grand jury. No ground for conviction could be found, but the judge bound him over to appear from day to day. Then Burr fled from the territory, but was again arrested a month later at Wakefield, Alabama. He was detained at Fort Stoddart for three weeks, and was then sent under a guard of six men to Richmond, Virginia. In the trial which followed, Burr was represented by Luther Martin, of Maryland, and three distinguished attorneys of Virginia. The foreman of the grand jury was the eccentric John Randolph; and the chief witness was General Wilkinson. Jackson also attended the trial as a witness and made a speech in which he denounced President Jefferson as a persecutor. Burr was tried before Chief Justice John Marshall and was acquitted after a sensational trial. The federal Constitution defines treason as making war against the United States or giving aid and comfort to the enemy in time of war, and the court was not convinced that Burr's preparations at Blenner-hassett came within this definition.

War in the Southwest

The War of 1812 greatly involved the West. Western troops gar-risoned exposed points along the frontier, marched under Harrison for the recovery of Detroit and the northwest, and made possible the American victory of the Thames and the end of Tecumseh's confed-eracy. In like manner, Southwestern militia marched with Jackson into the Alabama country to crush the power of the Creeks, and were at New Orleans to drive back the invading force of English under Sir Edward Pakenham. The end of the war, therefore, found two Western leaders—Harrison and Jackson—national heroes, both of whom were to play important political roles in later years.

Tecumseh's pre-war efforts to build up an Indian confederacy had succeeded in arousing the Western Creeks of Alabama to drive from their country the hated white settlers. On August 30, 1813, taking advantage of military crises elsewhere, they had attacked and massacred 547 settlers and soldiers at Fort Mims, near the junction of the Alabama and Tombigbee rivers. Border men in Tennessee and Georgia then rose in anger to exterminate their red enemies, and the war which followed took a toll of a fifth of the Creek warriors. Three weeks after the Fort Mims affair, the Tennessee legislature voted to raise men and money to aid the distressed Mississippi Territory settlements. Jackson, one of the two state major generals, marched at the head of the Tennessee troops into the Tallapoosa River country of what is now Alabama, and on March 27, 1814, inflicted a crushing defeat on the Creeks in the battle of Horseshoe Bend (in the northeast corner of present Tallapoosa County). Then, continuing his march, he occupied their sacred Hickory Ground near the confluence of the Coosa and Tallapoosa rivers, and erected Fort Jackson. Here on August 9 of the same year he concluded a treaty with the survivors whereby they agreed to cede nearly two-thirds of their lands in southern Georgia and what was later central Alabama.

During the course of the campaign Jackson had demonstrated unusual skill and daring in handling his turbulent troops. He had a quick temper which brought him into trouble on more than one occasion, but he had other redeeming traits which saved him during the trying days of the campaign. At Natchez, prior to the campaign, he had quarreled with General Wilkinson on a question of rank. Indeed, when he was named to lead the troops, he was suffering in bed from a bullet wound received in a brawl with the Benton brothers. Like Wayne during the Maumee Campaign, he was a strict disciplinarian in handling unruly frontiersmen. John Wood was shot for insubordination and assaulting an officer; and, at least for a part of the campaign, one part of his army was used to prevent the other from deserting when the period of enlistment had expired. Jackson's commissary broke down, and the angry leader charged General Cocke, the second in command, with carelessness. This led to a quarrel which in turn was transmitted to the officers of lesser rank. Yet in spite of all obstacles, Jackson maintained a strict control. William Graham Sumner, an early biographer, says that Jackson "was . . . able to enforce discipline and obedience, by measures which, as it seems, no other frontier commander would have dared to use."

The successful termination of the Creek campaign marks the beginning of Jackson's national popularity. On May 31 he was appointed a major general in the army of the United States, and was to succeed

Wilkinson as commander of the Seventh Military District (the South). Since Mobile had been occupied by his predecessor, it now became Jackson's headquarters, for it was rumored that the British planned its capture. Indeed, on September 14, 1814, the English attacked Fort Bowyer on Mobile Point, but were repulsed. A short time later they occupied Pensacola, with the consent, Jackson believed, of the Spanish officials stationed there; and it was reported that Spain was allowing English troops the use of East Florida as a base of operations. This angered Jackson, who asked the Secretary of War, John Armstrong, for permission to attack Pensacola. The Secretary wrote in reply that it would first be necessary for Jackson to ascertain whether Spain had voluntarily allowed the British to use her territory. Beyond this the Secretary was able to give Jackson little more attention, for the military problems elsewhere were considered of more pressing importance. In fact, already on August 24 the English under General Robert Ross had occupied Washington and burned most of the public buildings. So Jackson advanced on his own account and occupied Pensacola with a force of 3,000 men. The Spaniards surrendered the forts near the town, and the British blew up a post at Barrancas and sailed away.

Having driven the British from this point of vantage, Jackson believed that they would next attack New Orleans, so on December 2 he set up his headquarters in that city and began his preparations for receiving them. His cavalry under General Coffee and Major Hinds advanced from Pine Barrens, near Mobile, to Baton Rouge, where fresh horses and forage were to be had. His artillery was to follow by slower stages. Jackson made his preparations hurriedly. And well he might, for within seven days after his arrival it was reported that a large British fleet was off the mouth of the Mississippi and that British agents and patrols were exploring the approaches to New Orleans. Edward Livingston and Governor Claiborne were of much help to Jackson at this time: Livingston, by presiding over a New Orleans mass meeting in which he urged that all citizens offer themselves for service and contribute of their means; and Claiborne, by offering the American commander the use of state troops and by aiding him in other respects. Jackson not only accepted these services, but he also called on the Governor of the Mississippi Territory to furnish men and supplies, and he accepted the services of Jean Lafitte and gangs of buccaneers and adventurers of every color and hue. By the time Pakenham was ready to attack, therefore, a formidable army, though motley in composition, was ready to defend the city.

Undoubtedly Pakenham could have captured New Orleans had he acted promptly. But he allowed Jackson to complete his preparations, to build formidable works across a narrow strip of land between the

Mississippi and a large marsh bordering Lake Borgne. Moreover, the invaders became hopelessly confused in their movements. They lost their way, one party firing at another; they disobeyed orders and neglected ordinary precautions as they advanced. At one time two parties built redoubts out of the same mud, and cannonaded each other all day through a dense smoke. With the coming of night, the British works were battered to pieces and the cannon were dismounted, while the American redoubts were hardly damaged.

But at last the invaders were ready to deliver their main attack. On January 8, 1815, they sought to drive Jackson's force from its strong position, marching in deliberate order across an open plain. This was a fatal error. Later Major A. L. Latour said that the British were overconfident, and that they had thrown aside all caution, perhaps because they had remembered Winder's disgraceful retreat before an inferior British force near Washington. Two attacks of Pakenham's troops were repulsed by the deadly fire of Jackson's riflemen, and the survivors now withdrew. The British had lost more than 2,000 killed, wounded, and missing; the Americans, a scant 63. But Jackson's victory had no influence on the stakes of war, for already American and English commissioners had concluded the treaty of Ghent (December 24, 1814), two weeks before the battle was fought! Before the English could attempt another major move in the south, the news of peace was received, although a month later they captured Fort Bowyer in a second attack.

Post-War Developments

After Louisiana was acquired from France, the government of the United States sought to obtain the Indian titles to a part of the territory therein in preparation for the influx of Anglo-American settlers. Commissioners on November 10, 1808, concluded treaties at Fort Clark with the Great and Little Osage tribes whereby they ceded to the United States practically the whole of Missouri and Arkansas. Ten years later an additional cession of 7,492,000 acres in Arkansas was also made by these tribes. Then commissioners induced the Quapaws on August 2, 1818, to cede 26,698,560 acres in Arkansas and 2,492,000 acres in Louisiana, south of Arkansas, upon the Verdigris River.

Anglo-American settlers were not slow to take advantage of these cessions. For five years after annexation the limits of white settlement had extended little beyond the boundaries of French and Spanish occupation. But by 1809 Anglo-Americans were moving westward in noticeable numbers, most of them settling within the vicinities of Cape Girardeau, St. Geneviève, St. Louis, St. Charles, New Madrid, and the "post of the Arkansas." Indeed, by 1810 the population of the upper part of Louisiana (Territory of Louisiana) increased to nearly 21,000 souls, including 3,000 slaves. All these settled within the area now embraced in Missouri, except some 1,500, who located in Arkansas.

St. Louis now became a thriving outfitting and supply town, profiting greatly from the fur trade and from commercial intercourse with Santa Fe, as will be noticed later. As a matter of fact its inhabitants, together with those within its vicinity, clamored for a representative government; and Congress granted their request by an act of June 4, 1812, whereby the Missouri Territory was set up, with a legislature and a representative in Congress. The Territory was to extend from latitude 33° to 41°, and was to reach westward to the Spanish boundary. William Clark, the "Governor and Superintendent of Indian Affairs," had his seat of administration at St. Louis.

Up until 1815 the territory still retained a distinctively French culture. For example, St. Louis yet sprawled its long, narrow, and sometimes filthy streets, lined with frail and miserable tenement houses, along the river, relieved only here and there by a few large stone houses, plastered and whitewashed, as at New Orleans. In the rear were the more romantic circular stone forts, also plastered with lime. This and other towns within the territory were soon to change, however. The end of the war caused thousands of homeseekers to turn their eyes to the newly acquired region. Enterprising emigrants from Kentucky and Tennessee began to arrive in great numbers, to be joined west of the Mississippi by others from Ohio, Illinois, and Indiana, literally overrunning the French settlements. Consequently, the French quickly adapted themselves to the new order of things, learning new customs and taking up the industry and trade of their new neighbors. The region for 80 or 90 miles west of the Mississippi, within present Missouri, and at many points on the Missouri River, was soon occupied. Settlements and organized counties also appeared in northern Arkansas west of the St. Francis and upon the waters of White River. And emigration continued until the close of the year 1817, at which time the territorial jurisdiction had been extended over 20 large counties, comprising an aggregate population of 60,000 people.

On petition of the settlers along the Arkansas and White rivers a bill for the creation of the Territory of Arkansas came before the Committee of the Whole on February 17, 1819. But an amendment to exclude slavery from the region delayed its passage. Henry Clay accused its sponsors of "Negrophobia"; and protests of Southern representatives were so strenuous that the amendment failed. The measure was signed by President Monroe before Congress adjourned on March 4, 1819. The new territory extended from Louisiana on the south to the line of

36° 30′ on the north, and from the Mississippi on the east to the Spanish territory on the west. However, the Indian Territory was presently carved from its western part.

Timothy Flint visited Arkansas shortly after it had received territorial recognition. He was not greatly impressed with the region along the Arkansas and White rivers, for it was swampy and malarial. Yet Arkansas' population numbered "about ten thousand . . . in long and detached lines, the one along the Mississippi, called the St. Francis settlement; the other on the Mississippi below the mouth of the river, called Point Ohico settlement, the settlement on the waters of White River, a settlement far up the Arkansas, called Mulberry settlement, and settlements on the table land between Arkansas and Red rivers, called Mount Prairie." [1]

Along with an increase in population and organization of the new federal domain came a steady growth of river commerce. This, in turn, stimulated the rise of such Ohio and Mississippi towns as Pittsburgh, Cincinnati, St. Louis, and New Orleans. Cargoes brought by barges, keelboats, and flatboats to New Orleans during the first two decades of the nineteenth century would have totaled $150,000,000 in value. During this period 1,200 flatboats, to say nothing of other craft, were employed; and ships of seagoing size were also used. As early as 1761 a Philadelphia writer boosted Pittsburgh as a future shipping center. And ten years later Franklin and his associates assured Lord Hillsborough that when farmers occupied the area along the Ohio and Cumberland and became acquainted with the possibilities of transportation, "they will build schooners, sloops, &c., . . . suitable for the West-India or European markets." This was what occurred. More than one New Englander turned his attention to shipbuilding when once he had established a home in the Ohio country and had seen the profits to be made in river transportation. By 1803 it was not uncommon for seagoing ships to be launched at Pittsburgh, Marietta, and Cincinnati. And New Orleans was only an intermediate shipping point; the Atlantic seaboard, the West Indies, and Europe were visited by ships built upon the banks of the Ohio. Ships of 150 and 200 tons' burden docked at St. Louis, at New Orleans, or at Gulf and Atlantic ports, with cargoes of flour, flax, hemp, grain, and pork. But losses incident to grounding heavy vessels on sandbars and shoals brought a diminution of shipbuilding by 1808, not to be revived until the appearance of steamboats. Nicholas J. Roosevelt ushered in the new era in 1811, when he brought his steamboat, the *New Orleans,* from Pittsburgh to New Orleans. And in later years steam-propelled ships increased. In 1817 the *Etna*

---

[1] *Recollections,* p. 256.

proved its worth in two-way traffic by going up the river from New Orleans to Louisville.

BIBLIOGRAPHY

Material on the acquisition of Louisiana, its occupation by Anglo-Americans, and its economic, political, and social development is fairly adequate for student needs. Barbé-Marbois sought to justify France's sale of Louisiana in his *Histoire de la Louisiane et de la Cession de cette Colonie par la France aux États-Unis de L'Amérique Septentrionale; Précédée d'un Discours sur la Constitution et le Gouvernement des États-Unis* (Paris, 1829; English translation, Philadelphia, 1830). No thorough study of this early period would be complete without this account. Two exhaustive works on Louisiana are indispensable because of various and sundry details found therein. They are Charles Étienne Gayarré, *History of Louisiana* (4 vols., 4th ed., New Orleans, 1903), IV; and Alcée Fortier, *A History of Louisiana* (4 vols., New York, 1904), III, Part I, 1803–1861. Still others of value are C. F. Robertson, *The Louisiana Purchase and Its Influence upon the American System* (in American Historical Papers, I); Binger Hermann, *The Louisiana Purchase and Our Title West of the Rocky Mountains with a Review of Annexation by the United States* (Washington, 1900); François-Xavier Martin, *The History of Louisiana, from the Earliest Period* (2 vols., New Orleans, 1827–1829); James A. Robertson (ed.), *Louisiana under the Rule of Spain, France, and the United States, 1785–1807* (2 vols., Cleveland, 1911); and J. K. Hosmer, *The Louisiana Purchase* (New York, 1902). The region north of the Territory of Orleans is given attention in such works as Louis Houck, *History of Missouri, from the Earliest Explorations . . . until the Admission of the State into the Union* (3 vols., Chicago, 1908); Eugene Morrow Violette, *A History of Missouri* (New York, 1918); and John Hugh Reynolds, *Makers of Arkansas* (Stories of the States Series, New York, 1905). Works dealing with the general history of the United States but worthy of study because of their treatment of early Louisiana should be examined. Among these are Edward Channing, *History of the United States* (6 vols., New York, 1905–1925), IV; ——, *Jeffersonian System (American Nation, A History*, New York, 1906), XII; and Henry Adams, *History of the United States during the Administrations of Jefferson and Madison* (9 vols., New York, 1909–1911). Miscellaneous materials valuable for other reasons are Thomas Maitland Marshall, *A History of the Western Boundary of the Louisiana Purchase, 1819–1841 (Publications in History*, University of California, Berkeley, 1914); Everett S. Brown, *Constitutional History of the Louisiana Purchase* (Berkeley, 1920); W. J. Duane, *Narrative and Correspondence Concerning the Removal of the Deposits and Occurrences Connected Therewith* (Philadelphia, 1838); French Ensor Chadwick, *Relations of the United States and Spain* (3 vols., New York, 1909–1911); George P. Garrison, *Westward Extension (American Nation*, 1906), XVII; Cardinal Goodwin, *The Trans-Mississippi West, 1803–1853* (New York, 1922); and Thomas Marshall Green, *Spanish Conspiracy; a Review of Early Spanish Movements in the Southwest* (Cincinnati, 1891). Excellent articles on various subjects relating to early Louisiana are found in regional magazines for specialists, for example, the *Mississippi Valley His-*

torical Review, the *Journal of Southern History,* the *Southwestern Historical Quarterly,* and the *Missouri Historical Review.*

Biographies of men who were related one way or another with the acquisition and development of Louisiana during the period covered in this chapter are helpful in throwing much light on various phases of history. The administrations of Thomas Jefferson are well treated in the works of Adams previously mentioned, but H. S. Randall, *Thomas Jefferson* (4 vols., New York, 1858); F. W. Hirst, *Thomas Jefferson* (New York, 1926); and David Saville Muzzey, *Thomas Jefferson* (New York, 1918), present many personal details not found elsewhere. A few of the Jackson biographies are valuable for the same reason, for example, William Graham Sumner, *Andrew Jackson as a Public Man (American Statesmen,* Boston, 1882); James Parton, *Life of Andrew Jackson* (3 vols., New York, 1861); Marquis James, *Life of Andrew Jackson* (New York, 1938); and J. S. Bassett, *Life of Andrew Jackson* (2 vols., New York, 1911). The Burr-Wilkinson conspiracy is well taken care of in James Parton, *Life and Times of Aaron Burr* (2 vols., Boston, 1857); S. H. Wandell and Meade Minnigerode, *Aaron Burr* (2 vols., New York, 1925); Walter Flavius McCaleb, *The Aaron Burr Conspiracy* (New York, 1903); Royal Ornan Shreve, *The Finished Scoundrel* (Indianapolis, 1933); and Major James R. Jacobs, *Tarnished Warrior* (New York, 1938).

For documentary material, consult *American State Papers, Foreign Relations,* II, *Public Lands,* I, as cited in previous bibliographies; *Niles' Weekly Register,* 1811–1849; and *State Papers and Correspondence bearing upon the Purchase of the Territory of Louisiana* (in *House Exec. Docs.,* No. 431. 57th Cong., 2nd Ses.).

13

MOUNTAIN MEN AND THE FUR TRADE

T̲RAPPERS AND fur traders were the trail-makers of the frontier, the real pioneers of most of the trans-Mississippi country. Nor was this primacy of the fur men peculiar to the region west of the great river. The first Englishmen in New England, the first Dutchmen on the Hudson, and the first Frenchmen on the St. Lawrence were vitally interested in procuring furs. The advance guard of each nation's pioneers were the fur gatherers, lured ever westward into unknown lands.

The fine furs from the beaver, otter, fox, and such animals were the principal objectives, but buffalo robes and bear and deer skins were also gathered. The skins were usually obtained from the Indians through the barter of merchandise, but many were secured directly by white trappers and hunters. France, perhaps more vigorously than any other European nation, took to the fur trade, and consequently pushed rapidly into the West. And even after she had withdrawn from America, her sons remained, to continue in the forefront of the fascinating pursuit of skins.

The primitive forest and the life it fostered have had a constant lure for men. And once wedded to the wilds and having had the thin veneer of civilization rubbed off him, the typical fur gatherer was loath to return to the restrictions of town life. Instead, he continued year after year in the untamed country, facing the rigors of the elements, wild animals, and the frequently hostile Indians. The typical early trapper was a young man, strong, hardy, adventure-loving. He came from the frontier settlements, where book learning was rare, where physical strength and courage were the qualities prized. He dressed in what is perhaps the only original American costume—the fringed buckskin suit. He was a pioneer, but was hardly conscious of the fact. Opening fresh trails and discovering new lands were to him but part of the day's work, incidental to the business of trapping beaver or trading for

209

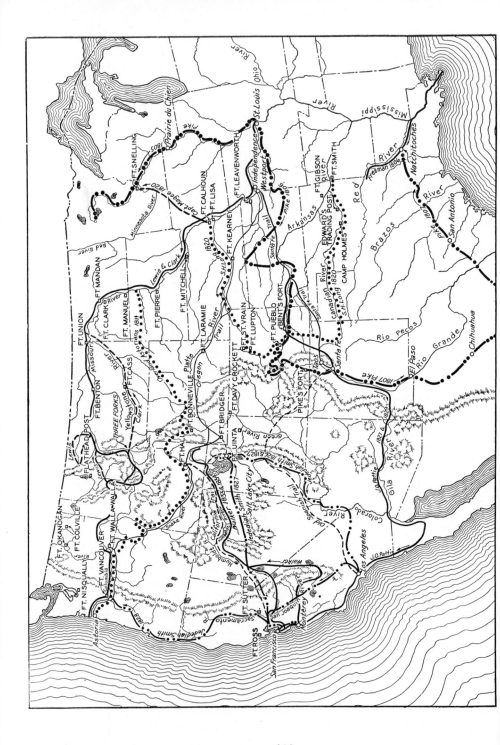

210

skins with remote Indian tribes. Inasmuch as a virgin territory was likely to yield the greatest return in pelts, there was thus a money reward for trail-blazing. It is to such adventurers that we are indebted for the first thorough exploration of the West. And the training they thus received equipped these men to become scouts and guides for official explorers and for the later covered-wagon emigrants.

Most of the trappers and traders in the trans-Mississippi West were in the employ of some fur company, and hence were directed in their general movements by the company officials. The exploration work accomplished may thus be studied by tracing the activities of the fur trade organizations that operated in this field.

Following the close of the French and Indian War (1763) the extensive French dominion in North America had been divided between England and Spain, with the latter nation acquiring title to the Louisiana Territory west of the Mississippi. Spanish attempts to continue the Frenchmen's fur business have been noted in Chapter 10, as has also the British trade penetration beyond the Mississippi. In fact, it was the British trader who became the real successor of the French in the region west of the Great Lakes. Loading the French boats with British-made goods and employing French and half-breed voyageurs to propel the crafts, these British fur gatherers soon were not only visiting the haunts of their predecessors, but were pushing beyond into untracked lands.

Outstanding in this activity was the North West Company, formed at Montreal in 1783. Scottish Highlanders dominated this organization, and the names of McKenzie, Henry, Thompson, McTavish, and McDonald are written large in the annals of Northwest exploration. The trading posts that Pike found in operation on the headwaters of the Mississippi in 1806 were North West Company "factories," and the British traders whom Lewis and Clark encountered in the Mandan country were "Nor'westers." These daring and vigorous Britishers were pioneers not only of western Canada, but of large areas of northwestern United States as well. Their competition was a matter of considerable moment to the Americans who were soon to operate in the northern field.

On the Upper Missouri and the Columbia

Following the Louisiana Purchase, Americans pushed into the western territory. The Missouri River was the great artery of the fur trade, and St. Louis was the principal emporium. Even before Lewis and Clark returned from their famous journey, their compatriots were ascending the Missouri and its tributaries in pursuit of furs. A little west of the Mandan villages of North Dakota (Bismarck), the returning American explorers met Joseph Dickson and Forest Hancock, who had left the Illinois country in 1804 and had already gathered peltry on the upper Missouri. John Colter, one of the Lewis and Clark employees, joined Dickson and Hancock, and in August, 1806, the three men loaded their traps in their canoe and headed up the river from the Mandan villages.

During the descent of the Missouri, from August 3 to 20, 1806, the Lewis and Clark Expedition met 11 separate parties of fur men ascending the Missouri. They were employing 20 boats loaded with trade goods and supplies. Some of these parties were planning to winter with the Arikaras, Sioux, Pawnees, and other tribes, and trade for peltries; others were to hunt and trap on their own account. Records of the fortunes and the journeyings of these various bands have not been preserved, if, indeed, they were ever made. In fact, most of the trappers were illiterate and could not have written an account of their wanderings even if they had considered it desirable to do so. This dearth of records applies to the whole period of exploration by the early fur men. Where one story of adventure and discovery has been preserved, dozens are forever lost.

It was probably some of these Americans that ascended the Missouri in the fall of 1806 who were in western Montana early the following summer. David Thompson, surveyor and trader for the North West Company, learned of their presence, and recorded that "the Americans, to the number of about 42, arrived to settle a military and trading post at the confluence of the two more southern and considerable branches of the Columbia." He also reported that they were preparing to make a small advance post, lower down the river, and that two of the men who had been with Lewis and Clark were of the party. The identity and membership of the American company are not definitely known.

In response to the favorable reports of Lewis and Clark regarding the fur resources of the region they had traversed, plans were laid in St. Louis for gathering pelts from the remote upper country. The most important expeditions to set out in the spring of 1807 were under the leadership, respectively, of Manuel Lisa and Pierre Chouteau. The first was a Spaniard, the second a Frenchman; both had been prominent fur traders during the Spanish regime in Louisiana Territory. At the mouth of the Platte River, Lisa met John Colter, floating down the Missouri. This adventurer, who had already made two journeys to the head of the Missouri, was induced to join Lisa and his men and to return to the upper country. His knowledge of the region to be visited was of great value to the party.

Both the Arikaras and the Mandans exhibited hostility to Lisa, but he craftily succeeded in passing their villages. Chouteau, who followed him, was not so fortunate, being stopped by the Arikaras. Lisa ascended the Yellowstone River, and at the mouth of the Big Horn established a trading post, Fort Manuel. Here the party spent the winter, men being sent out to various tribes to bring in the Indians to trade at the fort. Colter was one such emissary. He traveled south to the headwaters of the Big Horn, and appears to have been the first white man to view the wonders of Yellowstone Park—a region after-wards referred to as "Colter's Hell."

In the summer of 1808 Lisa returned to St. Louis with his furs and a favorable report of the resources of the upper country. Indian hostility was the primary difficulty to be feared. St. Louis businessmen, long interested in the fur trade, grew enthusiastic over the prospects. Rivals pooled their interests and organized the St. Louis Missouri Fur Company. The organization included Lisa, Chouteau, William Clark, Reuben Lewis (brother of Meriwether), Pierre Menard, Andrew Henry, and others. A large and well-equipped party was planned, one that could safely deal with Indian opposition.

In June, 1809, the company's first expedition set forth "with 172 men, nine barges and a canoe," and with sufficient merchandise to supply five or six trading posts. Upon reaching the Arikaras and the Mandans, the traders were accorded friendly receptions, the size of the party doubtless influencing the Indian attitude. After leaving traders and goods with the principal tribes on the Missouri, the main party pushed on to Fort Manuel. Profitable trapping and trading with the Crows were carried on during the fall and winter. In the spring, the fur men moved north to the Three Forks of the Missouri, and began erection of a fort there. In this rich beaver region, the trappers were making excellent catches and everything looked promising, when sud-denly the Blackfeet attacked the trapping party, killed five of the men, and made away with their horses, guns, traps, and furs. Preceding events may offer an explanation of the Blackfoot hostility: Meriwether Lewis had killed a Blackfoot Indian in 1806; John Colter had fought with the Crows against the Blackfeet the following year; Lisa had established his Fort Manuel and had begun trade with the Crows—hereditary enemies of the Blackfeet; and the British traders may have influenced the Blackfeet against the Americans. In any event, these Indians became the most persistent enemies of the Americans during the trapper period.

Indian attacks on Lisa's men continued during the summer of 1810, and the danger was so great that the trappers finally decided to abandon the region. Part of the men descended the Missouri with the gathered furs, while Andrew Henry led the others southward over the Continental Divide in the fall and built a post on the north fork (Henry's Fork) of

Snake River (present Idaho). Game was scarce and the winter severe. In the spring, Henry abandoned the post and returned to St. Louis. Fort Manuel, on the Big Horn, appears to have been deserted about the same time. The Missouri Fur Company had fallen short of the success anticipated, and in January, 1812, it underwent the first of a series of reorganizations. Lisa continued as the dominant figure, but the company did not prosper.

The war of 1812 disrupted the fur trade, especially in the upper Missouri country, where British influence was exerted over the Indians. It has been claimed that Lisa held the allegiance of the Sioux during the war, and that this prevented a possible loss of United States territory to England. After the close of the war, the Missouri Fur Company sent several expeditions to the upper Missouri country, but Blackfoot hostility again thwarted their efforts. The company continued in business for a few years longer, operating principally in the Omaha region, and then passed out of existence. It was the most important fur company operating from St. Louis during the first quarter of the nineteenth century.

During this period arose an important competing organization—the American Fur Company—destined for the leading role in the trans-Mississippi drama. It was organized by John Jacob Astor, one of the world's great fur merchants. As a German immigrant, Astor had come to America in 1784, and by the close of the century he had become the leading fur dealer in the United States. The favorable reports of the fur resources of the newly acquired Louisiana Territory induced him to enter this field. In 1808 he secured from New York State a charter for the American Fur Company. He now conceived a grand plan for conduct of the fur trade in the Far West. At the mouth of the Columbia River he would establish an important post, to which the furs of the vast Oregon country could be gathered. This depot would be supplied by ship from New York, and the same annual vessel would carry the accumulated pelts to China, whence the ship would return with Oriental goods to New York. A coastwise trade in Pacific Northwest waters was to be developed. Trapping on inland rivers and traffic with interior tribes were to correlate with other branches of the business; and overland communication and trade would be carried on from St. Louis by way of the Missouri River.

A subsidiary of the American Fur Company, known as the Pacific Fur Company, was organized in 1810 to manage this far western enterprise. A number of experienced British traders from Canada were induced to become partners in the undertaking, Astor providing the capital and agreeing to stand all losses for the first five years. Two expeditions were to be sent to the Columbia, one by sea and one by land.   In September, 1810, the first ship, the *Tonquin*, sailed from New York.   After rounding South America and touching at Hawaii, it reached the mouth of the Columbia in late March, 1811.   Here a trading post was begun and christened Astoria.   Meanwhile the *Tonquin* moved northward along the coast and opened trade with the Indians. Friction developed.   Indians allowed on board the vessel attacked and killed most of the crew.   Four men escaped to shore, but were later killed.   As the Indians again swarmed on deck, the sole white survivor fired the powder magazine, and the ship was blown to pieces.

The expedition from Missouri, known as the "Overland Astorians," left St. Louis with keelboats in March, 1811, under the leadership of Wilson Price Hunt.   Arrived at the Arikara villages in June, Hunt learned of Blackfoot danger ahead.   Therefore, trading his boats to Manuel Lisa for horses, and purchasing other animals from the Indians, he forsook the river.   Accompanied by 61 men, Price set out from the Arikara towns on July 18, having, as he reports, "eighty-two horses laden with merchandise, equipment, food and animal traps."   Avoiding the dangerous Blackfoot country on their right, the Astorians traveled due west across present South Dakota, touched southeast Montana, moved southwest across Wyoming, ascended the Wind River, and crossed the mountains to the headwaters of the Snake.   After building boats, they attempted to navigate this stream, but such obstacles were encountered that the effort had to be abandoned.   Over the desert region of Idaho they toiled.   The difficulties and hunger endured are graphically portrayed by Washington Irving in his *Astoria*.   The party divided, and the separate units made their way down the Snake, over the mountains, and down the Columbia.   Most of the men finally reached Astoria in January and February, 1812.   With struggle and suffering they had worked out a route through present Idaho and Oregon that was to become the western section of the great Oregon Trail.

In May, 1812, the second supply ship reached Astoria with new employees and an abundance of trade goods.   Plans were made for expanding the traffic with the Indians and for opening commerce with the Russians in Alaska.   A post was erected at the mouth of the Okanogan River in present northern Washington; trappers were sent to the Willamette River; and trading houses were built in the upper Columbia region.   A party was sent east by land in 1812 with reports for Mr. Astor.   These "returning Astorians," led by Robert Stuart, did some important exploration work.   After retracing in general the outbound route as far as present western Wyoming, they broke a new trail across the upper Green River valley, crossed the Continental Divide in the vicinity of South Pass, and descended the Sweetwater and then the

Platte to the Missouri. This route through the Wyoming and Nebraska region later developed into another section of the Oregon Trail.

The promising outlook for the Pacific Fur Company was suddenly altered by the War of 1812. Nor'westers brought news to Astor's men of the outbreak of war, and reported that a British warship was sailing for Astoria. Astor's partners in the Oregon country—probably influenced by their British citizenship and previous connections—now decided that it was hopeless to attempt to hold their ground. In October, 1813, they sold Astoria and all Pacific Fur Company interests in the region to the Northwest Company. Shortly after the sale, a British war vessel appeared before Astoria. It was the *Raccoon,* of 26 guns, commanded by Captain Black. Having sailed halfway round the world to no purpose, the vexed Captain gave vent to his displeasure when he saw the post: "Is this the fort about which I have heard so much talking? Damn me, but I'd batter it down in two hours with a four pounder." He took peaceful possession of the post and renamed it Fort George. The British fur interests now assumed control in the Oregon country.

In 1821 the long rivalry between the Hudson's Bay Company and the North West Company was ended when the former absorbed the latter. Fort Vancouver, on the Columbia River, opposite the mouth of the Willamette, became headquarters of the Hudson's Bay Company in the Oregon country. Here Dr. John McLoughlin, "the Father of Oregon," ruled for many years as Chief Factor. Trading posts were maintained in the upper Columbia region at Forts Walla Walla, Colville, and Okanogan. From the Columbia bases, fur gatherers penetrated farther south into present United States territory. Peter Skene Ogden, one of the notable brigade leaders, trapped the Snake River region regularly in the 1820's. He pushed on to Great Salt Lake, explored the Humboldt River and present Nevada, and trapped in the central valley of California. In 1837 the Hudson's Bay Company purchased Fort Hall on the Snake River in southern Idaho and maintained it for years as a British post. British traders went regularly to the rendezvous at Green River. Until the fifth decade of the nineteenth century, the great British company was supreme in the far Northwest.

THE FUR TRADE OF THE SOUTHWEST

A number of Americans, mostly of French extraction, had gone to the western border of Louisiana Territory and had entered New Mexico before Captain Pike reached Santa Fe. Two of these—Jean Baptiste Lalande and James Purcell—were interviewed by Pike, and the presence of others is reported in the Spanish records. Some of these early adventurers carried trade goods to the Indians and then continued to the Spanish settlements. Purcell, for example, had been with the Indians at the head of the South Platte River in present Colorado. One of the trading parties met by Lewis and Clark in the fall of 1806 was heading for the Platte River and intended to continue westward to Santa Fe. Whether or not it succeeded in this objective is not known.

From the Missouri Fur Company posts in the Upper Missouri country, Manuel Lisa sent men southward to barter in 1810. They contacted the Arapahoes, whom they found to be dealing regularly with the Spaniards of New Mexico. In 1811 Lisa sent another trading party, led by Jean B. Champlain and Ezekiel Williams, to the same region. They reached the upper Arkansas River and spent the winter hunting and trapping. Indians began to harass them, so the trappers separated. Some crossed the mountains westward, others went to Santa Fe, and the remainder stayed east of the mountains. All of the last-mentioned group appear to have been killed by Indians except Ezekiel Williams, who, after caching his furs, made his way down the Arkansas River and finally reached Missouri in September, 1813.

The next spring, Williams returned to the mountains and recovered his cached furs. He was accompanied up the Arkansas by Joseph Philibert and a company of trappers. No record of the wanderings of this band has come down to us, but the party must have met with some success, for the leader went back to Missouri and arranged to procure horses to bring down his furs. He doubtless carried to the frontier settlements a favorable report of the region, for another and larger party was organized by A. P. Chouteau and Julius De Munn of St. Louis to accompany Philibert westward in the fall of 1815. Enroute, Chouteau and De Munn purchased Philibert's outfit and the time of his men. For two years the new company operated on the headwaters of the Arkansas and Platte. The leaders took furs to Missouri in 1816 and brought back a party of 45 trappers. De Munn sought permission of the Spanish authorities to trap at the head of the Rio Grande and in other New Mexico areas, but, although he received a favorable reception at first, he was later ordered out of Spanish territory.

Finally, in May, 1817, Spanish troops came suddenly upon the Americans just as they were about to set out for home with their accumulated peltries. The Chouteau and De Munn party was escorted to Santa Fe, where the furs and property were confiscated and the men thrown into prison. After 48 days' confinement the men were released; but all their property was retained by the officials except one horse for each man. Upon their return to the United States, Chouteau and De Munn sought redress through their government for loss amounting to $30,000, but their claims were not paid until more than 30 years afterward.

The Chouteau and De Munn men must have trapped a large part of the area of present Colorado, and were doubtless the first American explorers of some sections of this mountain region. But no satisfactory account of their trapping and exploration has been preserved. However, one of these trappers, Bijou, accompanied Major Long to the mountains in 1820, and was able to give the official explorer descriptions of country far beyond the route of the government expedition's march. For example, Long records an accurate description of North Park, Colorado, although this picturesque, mountain-encircled area was many miles west of the Major's route. An account of a great trading council with the Indians in 1816, near the site of Denver, was also given by Bijou, and is similarly preserved in the Long report.

The unfortunate termination of the Chouteau and De Munn trapping and trading venture discouraged further American expeditions to the New Mexico border. In 1819, however, the Spanish-American boundary line in the Southwest was agreed upon, and some of the uncertainty and danger was thus removed. Then came the achievement of Mexican Independence in 1821, and the restrictive policy of Spain was replaced by one more favorable to American interests.

One of the first companies to profit from the new situation was led by Hugh Glenn and Jacob Fowler. Setting out from near the mouth of the Verdigris, this party followed the general course of the Arkansas to the site of present Pueblo, Colorado, from which point Glenn went to Santa Fe to obtain permission to trap in Mexican territory. After securing authorization, the party trapped the headwaters of the Rio Grande in southern Colorado.

Following Mexican Independence, trade between Missouri and New Mexico quickly developed, and the Santa Fe Trail soon became the famed highway for the "Commerce of the Prairies." (This subject will be treated in a subsequent chapter.) During the early years, the furs obtained in the Southwest constituted a considerable part of the trade carried over the Santa Fe Trail. Taos and Santa Fe quickly became bases for trapping and Indian trading operations. Such ventures were carried on primarily by Anglo-Americans, but Mexican citizens frequently participated. Supplies and trade goods could be procured in these New Mexican towns, and here also the pelts could be marketed, or at least sold for transshipment by the caravans to St. Louis. Taos soon developed into a favorite winter rendezvous for trapper bands. Here the men found respite from the rigors of a dangerous vocation and at the lively fandango saw paradise in the dark eyes of *señoritas*.

American trapper bands setting out from Santa Fe soon reached the Colorado and Green rivers in Utah. William Becknell, William Heddest, and Antoine Robidoux each led parties into western Colorado and eastern Utah in 1824. Robidoux continued in the region for two decades and earned the title "Kingpin of the Colorado River Fur Trade." He finally established trading posts in the region—one on the Gunnison River in Colorado and one on the Uinta in Utah. In later years he even transported goods to these forts over the rugged mountains in wagons, the first such achievement known. These early trappers were the pioneer explorers of much of the drainage areas of the Green and Colorado rivers.

New Mexico and Arizona were early searched for beaver sign. James Baird, of Missouri, who had gone to Santa Fe in 1812 and had suffered nine years' imprisonment for his intrusion, returned to New Mexico in 1822, became a Mexican citizen, and engaged in beaver hunting. Other Americans took up the pursuit. In fact, there were so many American trappers in the territory that in 1826 Baird protested to his newly adopted country, saying that "beaver is the most precious product which this territory produces," and avowing that during "a year and a half past they (the foreigners) have clandestinely extracted a large quantity of peltry exceeding $100,000 in value." "I have learned," he writes, "that with scandal and contempt for the Mexican nation a hundred-odd Anglo-Americans have introduced themselves in a body to hunt beaver in the possessions of this state and that of Sonora to which the Rio Gila belongs." "For fourteen years I have resided in the provinces," asserts Baird—neglecting to mention that nine of these were spent in jail—and being now a Mexican citizen he wants the "foreigners" excluded so that "we Mexicans may peacefully profit by the goods with which the merciful God has been pleased to enrich our soil."

But despite the protest, the large band of Americans—generally referred to as St. Vrain's Gila Expedition of 1826—was given permission to hunt beaver. Ceran St. Vrain, Miguel Robidoux, "Old Bill" Williams, Ewing Young, and James O. Pattie were among the better-known of the Americans in this company. Some of the men had been sent into the Southwest from the Council Bluffs on the Missouri in the fall of 1824 by Bernard Pratte, prominent merchant of St. Louis. In order to trap more effectively, the St. Vrain party broke into four divisions. Their routes and fortunes cannot be traced here, but we may say that, in trapping the Gila, San Francisco, and Colorado rivers, they visited most of present Arizona. Young Pattie says that his division followed the Colorado River almost its entire length and crossed from its headwaters over the mountain divide to the drainage of the South Platte. After trapping for some time east of the mountains, the division returned to New Mexico.

In the late 1820's several trapping parties reached California by way of Arizona. Ewing Young appears to have been one of the first Americans to reach the Pacific Coast by the Gila River route. In Young's party of 1829 was young Kit Carson, destined for fame as a Mountain Man. While this party was trapping in the San Joaquin Valley of California, it encountered Peter Skene Ogden with a brigade of Hudson's Bay Company trappers who had pushed down into this region from Fort Vancouver on the Columbia. Thus did the American trappers from the South meet the British fur men from the North in the central valley of Mexican California. During the winter of 1829–1830, Antonio Armijo's trading company of about 60 Mexicans made a round trip from New Mexico to Los Angeles, California. They moved across northern New Mexico and Arizona, forded the Colorado River at the "Crossing of the Fathers," and continued west and southwest to Los Angeles. In 1830–31 William Wolfskill led a party of American trappers over a route that was used regularly thereafter by annual caravans of pack animals carrying trade between Santa Fe and Los Angeles, and which became known as the Old Spanish Trail.

In the meantime, fur trade with the Indians of Oklahoma and the surrounding region had assumed considerable proportions. The beginnings of such traffic up the Red and Arkansas rivers date back to the French occupation in the early eighteenth century. During the Spanish regime, the business had continued on the French pattern; and after American acquisition of the territory, trade activity increased. Fort Smith, Arkansas, became an important center, and trading posts were presently established on the Arkansas, Canadian, and Red rivers. Traders were at the mouth of the Verdigris branch of the Arkansas in 1812. Here Nathaniel Pryor, of the Lewis and Clark Expedition, built a trading store and lived with his Osage wife, carrying on traffic with the Indians. From this point Hugh Glenn set forth on the trapping and trading venture of 1821, referred to previously. A. P. Chouteau, following the unhappy termination of his venture of 1817 at Santa Fe, came back to the States and ultimately established himself at the mouth of the Verdigris a little north of present Muskogee, Oklahoma. Here he won great influence among the Indians and became the outstanding trader of the region. "The mouth of the Verdigris," says Grant Foreman, "was the emporium of the Southwest; merchandise that came upstream by keel boat from New Orleans and Saint Louis was distributed from here." Regarding the business, Mr. Foreman writes: [1]

The Indian trade at the Verdigris was conducted for the sake of the furs, skins, and bear oil the Indians brought to the trading post. Wild bees were abundant, and honey and beeswax found a ready market. Wild horses, buffalo, elk, and deer ranged the prairies, and beaver, bear, wolves, otter, fox,

---

[1] Reprinted by permission of the publishers, The Arthur H. Clark Company, from Grant Foreman's *Pioneer Days in the Early Southwest.*

wildcats, panthers, turkeys, ducks, and swans were found in vast numbers. The Indians brought to the Verdigris the fruits of the chase and the trap, to exchange for the earrings, strouds, twists of tobacco, pipes, rope, vermilion, axes, knives, beads, cheap jewelry and bright-colored cloth, which constituted the medium of exchange.

Edward's Trading Post on the Canadian and Coffee's Trading Post on the Red were notable early business establishments. Other pioneer institutions of the region, reflecting activity in other lines, were the various Government Indian Agencies; the Union, Dwight, and Asbury Missions; and the military forts—Gibson, Towson, Holmes, Wayne, and Arbuckle.

MOUNTAIN MEN AND THE EXPLORATION OF THE CENTRAL ROCKIES

We turn now to the trapper activity that resulted in the first thorough exploration of the central Rocky Mountain region. Into this area were to come bands of energetic and hardy American frontiersmen, typical sons of Kentucky and Missouri, with a large admixture of Frenchmen and a sprinkling of other nationalities. With their bronzed faces and long hair, it was difficult to distinguish one from another, or all from a band of Indians. In a beaver or a coonskin cap and a fringed buckskin suit gaily decorated with dyed porcupine quills or bright glass beads, the trapper was proudly dressed. Or in slouch hat, calico shirt, and cotton overalls, he was equally at ease. With powder horn, bullet pouch, muzzle-loading rifle, and knife, he was self-supporting and independent. For money he had little need; primitive barter supplied his simple wants.

Most fur men were without book learning, but they were educated for the life they led. They could read the tracks of moccasins, the sign of beaver, and the trace of travois; they could mold their bullets from bars of lead, and strike a fire with flint and steel. A skin lodge (tepee) furnished the fur trader winter shelter, while for summer nights a buffalo robe was spread beneath the stars. A horse to ride, one to carry his trappings, others for his squaw and children (had he married a native woman), and he could journey wherever trails led, or did not lead. He gloried in the name of "Mountain Man."

An early leader in the central Rocky Mountain region was William H. Ashley of Missouri. Having formed a partnership with Andrew Henry—formerly of the Missouri Fur Company—he launched a trade venture on the upper Missouri in 1822. Following two seasons of disaster and severe losses in this region, Ashley sent a small detachment across present South Dakota. This group, led by Jedediah Smith and Thomas Fitzpatrick, broke a trail to the south of the overland Astorians' route and reached the Wind River country of present Wyoming in the fall of 1823. After trapping here, they crossed the Continental Divide at South Pass and found excellent beaver grounds on the upper Green River. The following spring Fitzpatrick returned to St. Louis by way of South Pass and the Platte River, and apprised Ashley of the rich country found and of the practicable land route to it. Ashley organized a party in the fall of 1824 and led it to Green River. Dividing his men into "brigades," he sent these in various directions to trap beaver, and appointed a place where all were to assemble in early July, 1825. Here pelts would be delivered and supplies replenished.

Thus was inaugurated the trapper *rendezvous* in the central Rockies, the first of a series of 16 such summer gatherings. The rendezvous became the most picturesque and typical fur trade institution of the mountain region. To it came fur company caravans from the East, laden with equipment and supplies for hired trappers, and with attractive goods for trade with Indians and independent fur men. The rendezvous was the great occasion of the year for the trapper. Here was opportunity for barter and for recreation. Races and contests of all kinds were arranged; gambling and drinking were indulged in. Beaver skins were money, and with these hairy banknotes all primitive wants could be satisfied. White trappers with Indian wives bedecked their spouses with bright cloth and gewgaws. Most of these Mountain Men were of the openhanded sort who in a few days of prodigal living squandered the earnings of a year. Indian bands came in, set up their lodges, and participated in the wilderness fair. Indeed, the rendezvous was a market day, a fiesta, a carousal, all in one.

General Ashley prospered in the mountain fur trade, and retired, a rich man, in 1826, selling his business to three of his employees— Jedediah Smith, William Sublette, and David Jackson. These partners carried on through four years, captaining fur brigades, exploring the Rocky Mountains and the Pacific Coast for beaver, and annually bringing trains of supplies to the appointed rendezvous. The earlier supply caravans were pack trains, but in 1830 wagons were used—the first on the Oregon Trail. The numerous journeys of the various trapping bands cannot, of course, be followed here. Suffice it to say that they combed the region from Canada to Sonora and from the eastern base of the Rockies to the Pacific Coast.

Of more than passing interest are the exploring achievements of one brigade leader—Jedediah Smith, sometimes called "the Knight in Buckskin." Carrying Bible and rifle and accompanied by hardy companions, he blazed important pioneer trails. From the rendezvous at the Great Salt Lake in 1826, he turned southwest and opened a route to Los Angeles. After journeying north through California to the Sacramento Valley, he turned east, crossed the snow-covered Sierras and the parched

deserts of Nevada—on approximately the route of the present Lincoln
Highway, or U. S. 30—to join in the Bear Lake rendezvous, northeast
of Great Salt Lake. Following this gathering he retraced his trail to
California in 1827, and from the Sacramento broke a land route northward to the Columbia. On the Colorado River ten of his men were
killed by Indians; on the Umpqua in Oregon he was again attacked, his
furs were stolen, and all his companions save two murdered by the
Indians. John McLoughlin, the kindly factor of the Hudson's Bay
Company at Fort Vancouver, recovered the stolen furs and then bought
them from the American. Smith made his way back to the Wind River
of present Wyoming. Here, on Christmas Eve, 1829, he wrote his
brother a letter, from which we quote an extract:

> It is that I may be able to help those who stand in need that I face every
> danger. It is for this that I traverse the mountains covered with eternal
> snow. It is for this that I pass over the sandy plains in heat of summer,
> thirsting for water, and am well pleased if I can find a shade, instead of
> water, where I may cool my over-heated body. It is for this that I go for
> days without eating, and am pretty well satisfied if I can gather a few roots,
> . . . Pray for me my brother, and may He before whom not a sparrow falls
> without notice, bring us in His own good time together again. . . . Let it
> be the greatest pleasure we can enjoy now, when our parents are in the
> decline of life, to smooth the pillow of their age, and as much as in us lies,
> take from them all cause of trouble.

Smith returned to Missouri and led a wagon train to Santa Fe in
1831. While ahead of the caravan alone, seeking water for his train,
he was pounced upon by Comanches and his career ended at the age
of 32. In an unknown spot on the Cimarron Desert were thus left to
bleach and crumble the bones of one of the most admirable characters
and one of the greatest trail-blazers of the Far West.

In 1830 Smith, Jackson, and Sublette had sold their mountain fur
business to another group of seasoned trappers—Fitzpatrick, Bridger,
M. G. Sublette, Fraeb, and Gervais—who adopted the firm name of the
Rocky Mountain Fur Company. Thus far this company and its
predecessors had had the central Rocky Mountain country largely to
themselves, save for a little competition from Peter Skene Ogden's
brigade of Hudson Bay Company men pushing down from the Columbia
and a few trappers coming up from the Taos country. But now came
a more formidable rival. Astor's powerful American Fur Company,
which had heretofore confined itself largely to the upper Missouri
River country and to the regions north and east, decided to exploit the
area of the central Rockies. With ample financial backing and an
efficient organization for marketing furs, it had distinct advantages, and
was finally able to crush the Rocky Mountain Fur Company, absorb
its leaders, and take over its territory.

Other independent organizations also entered this central field. In 1831 Gantt and Blackwell brought out 70 men to trap the region of the upper Arkansas and the Platte. Nathaniel J. Wyeth and his New Englanders reached the Rockies in 1832; and Captain B. L. E. Bonneville, late of the United States Army, with 110 well-equipped men, reached Green River the same year. Sinclair, with a party from Arkansas, and other minor groups swelled the numbers at the great rendezvous of 1832. Bent and St. Vrain operated on the upper Arkansas, Sublette and Campbell on the North Platte. The field was now overcrowded, the competition ruthless. Beaver became scarce, trapping less profitable, and the fur companies were self-ruined.

Although most of these fur organizations failed as business ventures, some of them performed achievements of far-reaching importance. One such was the work of a detachment of Bonneville's men. Sent westward from the rendezvous in 1833 to seek new beaver country, this band, led by Joseph R. Walker, followed the Humboldt River across present Nevada, crossed the Sierras, and entered California. They thus opened a direct and practical route that was later to become the great emigrant highway—the California Trail, branching from the Oregon Trail at Fort Hall, present Idaho.

Not only were the fur resources being depleted by overtrapping, but a change in styles helped to doom the beaver trade. The silk hat was designed, and in the early thirties it began to supplant the high top beaver headgear in the fashion centers of the world. With the falling price of pelts and an increasing scarcity of beaver, this branch of the business dwindled toward extinction. Many of the trappers left the country; others changed occupations. From beaver pelts, fur men turned to buffalo robes, which soon became the chief article of far western commerce. The coming of wagons aided this development on the high plains at the foot of the central Rockies, where no navigable streams exist. Buffalo robes, too bulky and cheap for carriage on pack animals, could be profitably handled by wagon train.

Methods of the fur trade changed. Whereas beaver skins had been garnered largely by white trappers, tanned buffalo robes were obtained by trade with Indians. So the rendezvous gave way to the trading post. Some of these forts were built of logs, others of adobe. Forts Bent and Pueblo were established on the upper Arkansas, Forts Lupton and St. Vrain on the South Platte, Fort Laramie near the North Platte, Forts Bridger, Davy Crockett, and Uintah on the Green or its branches, and Forts Hall and Boise on the Snake River of Idaho. Among the trade items found in old inventory lists from fur posts are the following: looking glasses, finger rings, wrist bands, ear bobs, glass beads of all colors, bells, powder horns, battle axes, scalping knives, blankets, calicoes, ver-

nilion, powder, lead, and alcohol. Whiskey was ever potent, in barter
is otherwise, and much trade was conducted on the basis of one pint of
whiskey for one buffalo robe. The more responsible fur companies
ried to eliminate the liquor trade, and the United States Government
passed prohibition laws against it, but it persisted none the less. The
Arapahoes, in an interview with Colonel Dodge in 1835, thus listed the
desirable things of this world: first, whiskey; second, tobacco; third,
horses; fourth, guns; fifth, women.

FORT LARAMIE, FAMOUS TRADING POST
(DRAWING MADE BY A. J. MILLER IN 1837.)

The American Fur Company, as indicated above, triumphed over its
competitors in the central Rocky Mountain region during the 1830's.
Previously it had become an important power in the trade of the Missouri River country. Following the War of 1812 and the loss of
Astoria, it had confined itself largely to the Great Lakes region. But
in 1822 it established a Western Department at St. Louis and entered
the Missouri River trade. With ample backing and aggressive leadership, it rapidly forged ahead, forcing out or absorbing its competitors.
In 1828 it built at the mouth of the Yellowstone a trading post that
came to be known as Fort Union.

Kenneth McKenzie, the capable leader here, demonstrated his ability
by winning the friendship and trade of the heretofore hostile Blackfeet.
In their country he established Fort McKenzie, near the mouth of the
Marias River, in 1832. Fort Cass, at the mouth of the Big Horn,
served the Crows. Fort Clark in present North Dakota and Fort Pierre
in South Dakota were among the most prominent American Fur Com-

pany posts in the upper country. Numerous other trading posts were located on the upper Missouri and its tributaries.

In 1831 the American Fur Company first employed steamboats on the upper river. In that year the *Yellowstone* came to the South Dakota region; the next year it reached Fort Union. Thereafter steamboats were an important feature of the company's operations; and finally (in 1859), they were to reach as far as Fort Benton, Montana, near the Great Falls of the Missouri. Astor retired from the company in 1834; but with such vigorous leaders as Pierre Chouteau, Jr., Kenneth McKenzie, and Ramsey Crooks, the business was continued with characteristic efficiency.

A number of the early fur men of the West have become famous; scores are well known. One could begin with Astor and Ashley, and list Bridger, Bonneville, Bent, and Beckworth; Carson, Clyman, Crooks, and Colter; Drips, Dougherty, Day, and Dickson—and continue thus through the alphabet to Walker, Work, Wyeth, and Williams.

The Mountain Men engraved their names in the topography of the West. Mountain peaks, passes, and ranges, and rivers, lakes, and canyons commemorate their names. Towns and counties have been christened in their honor. Many of the Mountain Men were "bad actors," fugitives from law and civilization; while others were specimens of the best in rugged manhood. With them a man was rated by his strength and skill, his courage and integrity. The open country, the freedom from restraint, the thrill of adventure, tied them to the wilds. Some were heroic, some brutal; most were adventurous, many picturesque. Together they pushed forward the frontier. Their paths have become our highways; their campfire ashes, our cities. As explorers and trail breakers, they have won rank among our pioneers. Says Chauncey Thomas, "The map of the West was drawn on a beaver skin."

BIBLIOGRAPHY

The best general account of the western fur trade is H. M. Chittenden, *The American Fur Trade of the Far West* (3 vols., New York, 1902, rev. ed., 1935). An excellent treatment, though more limited in scope, is H. C. Dale, *The Ashley-Smith Explorations and the Discovery of a Central Route to the Pacific, 1822–1829* (Cleveland, 1918). Other general works are C. A. Vandiveer, *The Fur Trade and Early Western Exploration* (Cleveland, 1929); Isaac Lippincott, *A Century and a Half of Fur Trade at St. Louis* (St. Louis, 1916); A. C. Laut, *The Fur Trade of America* (New York, 1921); ———, *The Story of the Trapper* (New York, 1902); Douglas MacKay, *The Honourable Company: A History of the Hudson's Bay Company* (Indianapolis, 1936); Katherine Coman, *Economic Beginnings of the Far West* (2 vols., New York, 1912); Washington Irving's *Astoria* and his *Bonneville;* Grant Foreman, *Pioneer Days in the Early Southwest* (Cleveland, 1926); Bernard De Voto, *Across the Wide Missouri* (Cambridge, 1947).

Among the important journals which supply source material are the following: Elliott Coues (ed.), *The Manuscript Journals of Alexander Henry and of David Thompson* (3 vols., New York, 1897); J. C. Luttig, *Journal of a Fur-trading Expedition on the Upper Missouri, 1812–1813,* edited by Stella M. Drumm (St. Louis, 1920); Osborne Russell, *Journal of a Trapper, or Nine Years in the Rocky Mountains, 1834–1843* (Boise, 1921); E. Coues (ed.), *The Journal of Jacob Fowler* (New York, 1898); Frederick Merk (ed.), *Fur Trade and Empire, George Simpson's Journal* (Cambridge, 1931); A. H. Abel (ed.), *Chardon's Journal at Fort Clark, 1834–1839* (Pierre, 1932); W. S. Lewis and P. C. Phillips (eds.), *The Journal of John Work* (Cleveland, 1923); R. B. Sage, *Scenes in the Rocky Mountains and in Oregon, California, New Mexico, Texas and the Grand Prairies, . . .* (Philadelphia, 1846); E. Coues, *Forty Years a Fur Trader: The Personal Narrative of Charles Larpenteur, 1833–1872* (2 vols., New York, 1899); W. F. Wagner (ed.), *Adventures of Zenas Leonard, Fur Trader and Trapper, 1831–1836* (Cleveland, 1904); F. G. Young (ed.), *The Correspondence and Journals of Captain Nathaniel J. Wyeth, 1831–1836* (Eugene, 1899); C. L. Camp (ed.), *James Clyman, American Frontiersman, 1792–1881* (San Francisco, 1928); R. G. Thwaites (ed.), *Early Western Travels,* Vols. V, VI, VII, XIII, XVIII, XXI, XXII, XXV, and XXVIII, respectively, the journals of John Bradbury, H. M. Brackenridge, Alexander Ross, Thomas Nuttall, J. O. Pattie, John B. Wyeth and John K. Townsend, Prince Maximilian, and T. J. Farnham. Another important publication is W. A. Ferris, *Life in the Rocky Mountains,* edited by P. C. Phillips (Denver, 1940).

Of biographical works dealing with the fur trade and Mountain Men, we list the following: E. L. Sabin, *Kit Carson Days, 1809–1868* (2 vols., New York, 1935); M. S. Sullivan, *Jedediah Smith, Trader and Trail Breaker* (New York, 1936); L. R. Hafen and W. J. Ghent, *Broken Hand, the Life Story of Thomas Fitzpatrick* (Denver, 1931); A. H. Favour, *Old Bill Williams, Mountain Man* (Chapel Hill, 1936); W. H. Ellison, *The Life and Adventures of George Nidever, 1802–1883* (Berkeley, 1937); Charles Kelly, *Old Greenwood* (Salt Lake City, 1936); H. L. Conard, *"Uncle Dick" Wootton, the Pioneer Frontiersman of the Rocky Mountain Region* (Chicago, 1890); Stallo Vinton, *John Colter, Discoverer of Yellowstone Park* (New York, 1926); C. W. Mackenzie, *Donald Mackenzie, "King of the Northwest"* (Los Angeles, 1937); K. W. Porter, *John Jacob Astor, Business Man* (2 vols., Cambridge, 1931); J. C. Alter, *James Bridger, Frontiersman, Scout and Guide* (Salt Lake City, 1925); R. G. Montgomery, *The White-headed Eagle: John McLoughlin, Builder of an Empire* (New York, 1934); W. B. Douglas (ed.), *Three Years Among the Indians and Mexicans, by Thomas James* (St. Louis, 1916); T. D. Bonner, *The Life and Adventures of James P. Beckwourth* (New York, 1856); C. Kelly and M. L. Howe, *Miles Goodyear, First Citizen of Utah, Trapper, Trader and California Pioneer* (Salt Lake City, 1937); Stanley Vestal, *Mountain Men* (Cambridge, 1937); Nolie Mumey, *The Life of Jim Baker, 1818–1898* (Denver, 1931); F. F. Victor, *The River of the West* [life of Joe Meek] (San Francisco, 1870).

Many articles on the fur trade, the results of recent research, are to be found in the various State Historical Society magazines and publications.

I4

THE ACQUISITION OF OREGON

In tracing the history of the
Oregon country, we must turn back, for the early phases of the story,
to developments that took place before the days of Lewis and Clark
and the Astorians. The earliest contacts with the region, those of the
Spaniards, have been noted previously, in Chapter 5. Their fear of
the Russians had been instrumental in effecting the occupation of California, and had continued to cause the Spaniards concern about the
territory north of their occupied area. But more disturbing, as the
last quarter of the eighteenth century began, was English intrusion in
Northwest waters.

By Sea to the Oregon Country

The Parliament of England having offered £20,000 as a reward for
discovery of a western entrance to a strait around North America, Captain James Cook set out from England in July, 1776, in search of such
an embouchure. After spending much time in southern waters, this
famous English mariner sailed northward, and in January, 1778, discovered the Hawaiian Islands. Two months later he reached the
American coast in about latitude 44°, and began a careful search for a
strait. Upon landing at Nootka Sound, on Vancouver Island, he was
visited by Indians eager to barter.

The articles which they offered for sale [says the official record] were
skins of various animals, such as bears, wolves, foxes, deer, raccoons, pole-
cats, and martins, and, in particular, that of the sea-otter, which are found
at the islands of Kamtschatka. Besides the undressed skins, they also
brought garments made of them, and another sort of clothing made of the
bark of a tree, or some plant like hemp; weapons, such as bows, arrows, and
spears; fishhooks, and instruments of various kinds; wooden vizors of many
different monstrous figures; a sort of woolen stuff, or blanketing; bags filled
with red ochre; pieces of carved work, beads, and several other little orna-
ments of thin brass and iron, shaped like a horse-shoe, which hung at their
noses; and several chisels, or pieces of iron fixed to handles. From their

possessing such metal, we inferred that they had either been visited before by some civilized nation, or had connections with tribes on the continent, who had communication with them. But the most extraordinary of all the articles which they brought to the ships for sale, were human skulls and hands, not yet quite stripped of the flesh, which they made our people plainly to understand they had eaten; and, indeed, some of them had evidently marks that they had been upon the fire. For the various articles which they brought, they took in exchange knives, chisels, pieces of iron, and tin, nails, looking-glasses, buttons, or any kind of metal. Glass beads they were not fond of, and cloth of every kind they rejected.

After spending a month here, Cook sailed northwestward, rounded the Alaskan peninsula, and in August reached the "western extremity of all America." He named the point "Cape Prince of Wales." After passing through Bering Strait and finding his way blocked by ice, he turned back to winter in Hawaii. Here he was killed by the natives in February, 1779.

Under Captain Clerke, who succeeded to the command, the voyage was resumed by the English adventurers. They returned to the North Pacific, touched at Kamchatka, and then sailed for China. At Canton they found a most excellent market for their Nootka furs. "Skins which did not cost the purchaser sixpence sterling, sold for one hundred dollars," one of the men reported. The crew were eager to return to "procure another cargo of skins, by which they might be enabled to make their fortunes." But the officers refused, despite entreaties and threats of mutiny.

The discovery of this ready market for sea-otter pelts and other furs opened up a new commercial field. It created a keen interest in the North Pacific, and stirred rivalry among a number of different nations. English ships, naturally, were first to engage in the profitable traffic. In 1785, James Hanna, with a quantity of gewgaws, procured in the Oregon country 560 otter skins, which at Canton brought him over $20,000. During the next two years more ships, captained by Meares, Strange, Portlock, Dixon, and others, arrived to stock up with American furs. Some of these navigators made important geographical discoveries, and Meares erected a trading post in the Oregon region. In 1788 came the vanguard from the United States under Captains Robert Gray and John Kendrick of Boston.

Spain was greatly aroused by these foreign intrusions into territory that she claimed by right of discovery. In 1789 the viceroy of New Spain sent Martinez with a naval vessel to the Northwest Coast. He destroyed Meares' trading post, replaced it by a Spanish fort, took some English trading vessels into custody, and sent one of these to Mexico. When news of the seizures reached Europe, England was indignant. She demanded restitution and compensation and the famous "Nootka Sound Controversy" resulted.

Spain had now reached the highwater mark of her territorial dominion, and was about to take her first step backward—the beginning of a retreat that was to end only with her complete withdrawal from the continents of North and South America in 1898. England dictated terms of the Nootka Sound settlement in the Treaty of 1790. Spain relinquished exclusive claim to Pacific Coast territory north of her occupied area, and admitted the right of other nations to trade in this region. She agreed to restore Meares' fort and to compensate English traders for Spanish seizures. In a subsequent treaty (1794) England and Spain agreed that neither nation would maintain permanent establishments in the region. During the years of controversy, both nations sent navigators to the Northwest waters, and a thorough exploration of the coastline resulted. The most notable contribution in this field was that of the Englishman Captain George Vancouver. Vancouver made a remarkable map of the coastline from San Diego, California, to Cook's Inlet, Alaska. He circumnavigated the island named for him, and explored the numerous inlets and islands along the coast.

After wintering at Nootka and obtaining a cargo of furs, the New England Captain Robert Gray sailed the *Columbia* to China in 1789, and then continued around the world, reaching his home port in August, 1790. Bostonians were thrilled with the achievement and were intrigued with the promising commercial opportunities. New ventures for those remote waters were straightway launched by the canny merchants and seamen of New England. Captain Gray immediately undertook a second voyage.

Traders along the Oregon coast found that barter was most profitable with Indians who had not previously traded with white men and who, consequently, were not aware of the value attached to furs. So the venturesome merchants sought out inaccessible places and new tribes. Thus, exploratory work was fostered and discoveries were rewarded with commercial profit. It was while ferreting out such strange places that Captain Gray, in May, 1792, ran into a bay that proved to be the mouth of a great river. He christened it "Columbia" after his good ship. It had previously been discovered by the Spaniard Heçeta.

Yankee seamen swarmed to the Northwest Coast. And as England became involved in the Napoleonic Wars, Americans won ascendency. Russian traders, inadequately provided with ships, soon arranged for New Englanders to carry much of the Russian traffic across the Pacific. Before 1800 the American ships had thus come to dominate the trade of the North Pacific, and they were to maintain this hegemony for more than two decades. Indians along the coast became so familiar with New Englanders that they came to use *Boston* as a generic term for "white man." Sea otter were obtained along the California coast as well as farther north. And the shrewd New Englanders were presently supplementing their fur trade by selling "Yankee notions" to the Spaniards of California.

OVERLAND TO OREGON

While hardy seamen were exploring the Northwest Coast and exploiting its fur resources, equally hardy adventurers were pushing overland to the Oregon country. By land, as by sea, Englishmen preceded Americans. The pioneer approaches take us back to the great Hudson's Bay Company, chartered in 1670, and to the North West Company, which succeeded to the French territory and trade in the Great Lakes region and the country to the west. The competition of those powerful rival companies sent traders and explorers pushing across Canada toward the Pacific. The Nor'westers were usually in the lead. Their outstanding early explorer was Alexander Mackenzie. In 1789, he reached Great Slave Lake, and from its western end found a stream flowing westward. Perhaps it would lead him to the Pacific Ocean. But as he followed the stream, it veered to the northwest; and when its mouth was finally reached, he found himself on the shores of the Arctic Ocean. "River Disappointment" he christened the stream, but the name was appropriately changed to Mackenzie River, to honor its discoverer and explorer.

Upon finding the northern ocean filled with ice, Mackenzie concluded that no practicable Northwest Passage existed. He returned over the long waterways to Montreal, and then crossed the Atlantic to Scotland. He arrived just in time to catch the excitement of the Nootka Sound Controversy and the redoubled interest in the fur trade of the far Northwest. Now he was more eager than ever to open a land route to the Pacific Coast. He returned to Canada, pushed inland to Lake Athabasca, and after an ascent of Peace River, reached the Canadian Rockies in the late fall of 1792. The next spring he crossed the mountains and reached a river which, from its southern course, he thought to be the Columbia. When he had descended it for some days, the numerous cataracts in the wild gorge induced him to forego further navigation. He followed a westward trail, and on July 22, 1793, stood on the shores of the Western Sea. He had achieved the first crossing of the continent north of Mexico. After returning to Europe and writing an excellent account of his voyages and journeys, he was knighted for his exploratory work.

Mackenzie's route to the Pacific was difficult, if not impracticable, so the North West Company took no immediate steps to develop it as a pathway of commerce. But the launching of the Lewis and Clark expedition by the United States spurred the British company to action. Simon Fraser, following up Mackenzie's pioneering, crossed the Rocky Mountains from Peace River, and in 1806 built trading posts on Stuart Lake and Fraser Lake. The next year he succeeded in navigating to its mouth the western-slope river which Mackenzie had thought to be the Columbia. It proved to be another river, that now known as the Fraser. The North West Company began development of the fur trade of the region, and, reminiscent of old Scotland, named the district New Caledonia (now British Columbia).

In the meantime other Nor'westers had discovered the headwaters of the Columbia and had begun to exploit the fur resources of that region. David Thompson and Duncan M'Gillivray are said to have crossed the Continental Divide from the Bow River branch of the Saskatchewan and to have reached the upper Kootenai River in 1801. As to this there is some dispute. But in 1807 Thompson was certainly on the Kootenai and other upper branches of the Columbia. It was here that Indians told him of the 42 Americans—referred to in the preceding chapter—who had arrived in July, 1807, to build a post at the confluence of two southern branches of the Columbia. "This establishment of the Americans," reports Thompson, "will give a new turn to our so long delayed settling of this Country, on which we have entered it seems too late." Between England and the United States, a contest for the Oregon country was on; and no one saw the issue more clearly than the learned partisan of the North West Company, David Thompson—astronomer, ornithologist, fur trader. For a time, however, Thompson appears to have devoted himself more to development of the fur trade than to finding a river route to the sea. In 1808 he was on the Kootenai River in present northern Idaho. The next year he pushed a little farther south, to Lake Pend Oreille, built a post upon this lake, and then ascended Clark's Fork to establish another post at Thompson's Prairie, present Montana.

News came of Astor's project for a post on the Oregon coast. The North West Company was at once concerned. To the land beyond the Rockies, said the British leaders, the Americans "have no pretensions by Discovery either by Water or Land, the right in both cases clearly belonging to Great Britain by the discoveries of Cook, Vancouver, and Mackenzie. No establishment of the States on that River [the Columbia] or on the Coast of the Pacific should therefore be sanctioned." Thompson was directed to push through to the coast and establish a fort at the mouth of the Columbia. Difficulties intervened and delays resulted. When he finally reached his destination, on July 15, 1811, the Stars and Stripes were already flying from Fort Astoria. But the primacy of the United States on the lower Columbia was to be short-lived, as was indicated in the preceding chapter. The War of 1812 terminated the Astor venture on the Pacific Coast.

However, American claims to the Oregon country were not surrendered. The Treaty of Ghent provided for the restoration of territorial conquests made during the war, and under its provisions Astoria was returned to the United States. As to other claims of the two nations relating to the Oregon country, no settlement was reached. Instead, a "Joint Occupation" agreement was signed in 1818. Under its provisions the region was to be open to the citizens of both countries for a period of ten years.

JOINT OCCUPATION AND BRITISH PREDOMINANCE

The United States and Great Britain were not the only claimants to territory in the American Northwest. Spain and Russia, by virtue of their discoveries, had sound claims of long standing. But these two countries were soon to be eliminated from the contest for Oregon. In 1819 a boundary between the territories of Spain and of the United States was agreed upon. On the Pacific slope this line ran along the forty-second degree of north latitude, the present boundary between California and Oregon. Spanish claims to territory north of this line were ceded to the United States, and Spain was thus eliminated from Oregon.

Russia was next to withdraw. In 1821 the Czar issued a *ukase*, or decree, asserting ownership to territory extending south as far as the fifty-first parallel. Secretary of State John Quincy Adams protested vigorously against the validity of any such claim, and prepared a statement that was incorporated into the Annual Message of President Monroe in 1823. In discussing "the respective rights and interests of the two nations on the northwest coast," Monroe declared:

In the discussions to which this interest has given rise and in the arrangements by which they may terminate, the occasion has been judged proper for asserting, as a principle in which the rights and interests of the United States are involved, that the American continents, by the free and independent condition which they have assumed and maintain, are henceforth not to be considered as subjects for future colonization by any European power.

Thus was a vital part of the famous Monroe Doctrine given expression. But proclaiming a principle is something quite different from having it recognized and honored by other nations. And so it was with this pronouncement. Happily for the young Republic, Great Britain made common cause with the United States in opposing the Russian territorial pretensions. And, of course, it was England's power rather than our Doctrine that blocked the Russian advance. By treaties with the United States and with England in 1824 and 1825,

Russia accepted parallel 54° 40′ as the southern boundary of Russian America. The Oregon country now had definite northern and southern boundaries. And this vast region, between parallels 42° and 54° 40′, was in joint possession of the United States and Great Britain. More than two decades were to elapse before the area was divided, and in that interval important developments took place that were decisively to affect the final division.

For about 20 years following the joint occupation agreement of 1818 —which was renewed in 1827 for an indefinite period—British interests were dominant in Oregon. Some few Americans interested themselves in the faraway land, but they received little encouragement or support from their fellow citizens during the early years. In 1820 Representative John Floyd advocated in Congress "the expediency of occupying the Columbia River." Two years later his proposal was considered in the House, but the opposition was overwhelming. Said Congressman Tracy of New York: "Nature has fixed limits for our nation; she has kindly interposed as our western barrier mountains almost inaccessible, whose base she has skirted with irreclaimable deserts of sand." Bills relating to Oregon were offered in successive sessions of Congress, but their support was not adequate to gain passage.

In the meantime the British hold on the region was becoming more firm. The Hudson's Bay Company and the North West Company were consolidated under the name of the former in 1821. Doctor John McLoughlin became chief factor on the Pacific Coast, where his long beneficent rule earned him the title "King of Oregon." Large of stature, distinguished in bearing, firm yet kindly in administration, he was freely accorded authority, even beyond that of his official position. The Indians called him "White Eagle," a name suggested by his snowy locks and the features of his face. He established Fort Vancouver on the Columbia, nearly opposite present Portland; and made it headquarters for the Company in Oregon. A strong stockade, 20 feet high, enclosed the principal buildings. From this central depot the fur brigades went forth each year. Under such experienced and efficient leaders as Ogden, Mackay, and Douglas, hundreds of trappers and traders not only covered the Columbia and the Frazer basins, but penetrated south and east into territory of the present states of California, Nevada, Idaho, Montana, Wyoming, and Utah.

From scores of forts and camps scattered throughout this wilderness empire of half a million square miles, peltries were gathered in to Fort Vancouver. Supply ships from London came regularly to this great depot on the Columbia to stock the large warehouse and to sail away richly laden with valuable furs. When Jedediah Smith was at the fort in 1828, he reported that 30,000 beaver skins, valued at $250,000, in addition to large quantities of other furs, had been brought to the post during the preceding year.

While fur trade was the principal concern of the Hudson's Bay Company, McLoughlin attended as well to the development of a local food supply. He caught and cured salmon and encouraged farming. Potatoes, peas, and other vegetables were first grown, and then wheat, barley, and oats. Presently fruit trees were introduced. The first cattle were brought from California, the first pigs from Hawaii. Horses, sheep, and goats were imported. And to expedite the stocking of the country, McLoughlin forbade the slaughter of any cattle during the early years. The Company established a flour mill and a saw mill. By 1828 sufficient wheat was grown to supply the local needs, and soon flour was being sold regularly to the Russians in Alaska. The Company's mechanics made barrels for the flour and salmon and built boats to ship them in. As voyageurs grew too old for the exacting life in fur brigades, they were induced to turn to farming. When the first American settlers reached Oregon, they were helped in establishing themselves. The kindly McLoughlin, at the risk of rebuke from higher officials, lent seed wheat and cows to the needy, though these Americans might well have been viewed as intruders and dangerous competitors.

AMERICANS MOVE INTO OREGON

Following Astor's withdrawal from Oregon, American entries by land into the region were for some years unimpressive. Occasionally fur gatherers crossed the mountains and trapped in the Oregon country—an area which then extended from the Continental Divide to the Pacific Coast. Parties from the Rocky Mountain Fur Company worked the Snake River country in the 1820's. Captain Bonneville entered present Idaho in 1832, and pushed on to Walla Walla. Wyeth built Fort Hall on the Snake River in 1834, visited Fort Vancouver, and planned the development of salmon fisheries on the Columbia. But his project failed, and he sold his fort to the British company. American trappers and traders met with little success in the far Northwest; effective methods were used against them. For example, Peter Skene Ogden, leader for years of the Snake River brigade, was directed to trap to extinction the beaver on the southern fringe of Oregon, and thus leave a "fur desert" that would keep the Americans out. Although fur men from the United States made little headway in Oregon, others of their fellow citizens were to meet with better success. Missionaries and pioneer settlers were to win ground in the Pacific Northwest.

The opening of the missionary field was prompted by the visit of a delegation of Flatheads or Nez Percés to St. Louis in 1831. These

Indians, with an exceptional interest in religious matters, had journeyed eastward to learn more of the white man's religion and to visit William Clark (of the Lewis and Clark expedition), whom they remembered as the "Redhead Chief." News of the visit spread through the country and lost nothing in the telling. Religious leaders heard a cry of benighted souls seeking Christian light. They broadcast the "Macedonian call" in the religious press, and appealed for funds and volunteers.

The Methodists were the first to respond, with Jason Lee accepting leadership of the first mission. This pioneer missionary band joined the trapper caravan of 1834, and journeyed with it to the Green River rendezvous and thence to Oregon. At Fort Vancouver Dr. McLoughlin received the missionaries gracefully, recommended the Willamette Valley as a suitable location, and gave assistance by lending cattle and seed for planting. The next year the Presbyterians entered the field, sending out Samuel Parker and Marcus Whitman. From the Green River rendezvous, Dr. Whitman returned to the States for reinforcements. In the spring of 1836 he brought his bride and Mr. and Mrs. Spalding into the mission field. Thus did the first white women cross the Rockies and enter Oregon. This party brought a wagon as far as Fort Boise, present Idaho, the first to make wheel tracks on such a stretch of the Oregon Trail. The missions founded by these Protestant churches developed farms and cattle ranches as well as churches and schools. In fact, their success was more marked in the material than in the spiritual realm. Finally Jason Lee concluded that missionary efforts might more profitably be directed to the incoming whites than toward the backward Indians.

The Catholics, who had been first with missions in most American frontier areas, yielded primacy in Oregon. But their efforts, even here, quickly supplemented Protestant beginnings. In 1838 Fathers Blanchet and Demers, escorted by a Hudson's Bay Company brigade, crossed Canada and reached Oregon. The Cowlitz, Walla Walla, Colville, and other missions were soon active centers. From St. Louis in 1840 came the best known of the Catholic missionaries in the region— Pierre Jean De Smet, S. J. He established missions in Coeur d'Alene and the Bitter Root country of present Idaho and western Montana.

Devoted as were the missionaries—the Whitmans suffered martyrdom—and important as were the missions they founded, yet their chief role in the development of Oregon was in directing attention to the country and inducing migration thither. In 1837 Reverend Samuel Parker reached New York, having sailed around Cape Horn from Oregon. The next year he published a book on his travels and missionary experiences. In 1838 Jason Lee returned to the East, toured through the States, and from pulpit and lecture stand sang the praises of Oregon and made stirring appeals for men and money. He gathered a company of over 50 persons—men, women, and children—and sailed with them from New York in 1839. Another party, responding to his glowing entreaties, was organized in Illinois. Styling themselves the "Oregon Dragoons," and bearing a flag with the motto, "Oregon or the Grave," these 19 young men set out across the plains for Oregon in 1839. Most of these adventurers turned back before reaching their destination, but Thomas Jefferson Farnham persisted to the end. He appears, however, to have been more interested in writing a book than in staying on the Pacific Coast. After visiting California and Hawaii, he returned to the United States and gave his story to the world. It was an interesting and popular book that swelled the enthusiasm for the Far West and promoted emigration.

Among the most ardent of Oregon promoters was Hall J. Kelley. In the early 1820's this Boston schoolteacher was writing letters, newspaper articles, and pamphlets; making maps; devising plans for emigration societies; and petitioning Congress for aid—all to the end that the United States assert and make good her right to Oregon. In 1833 he set out for his Promised Land, by way of Mexico and California. From the latter province he journeyed by land in company with some Americans driving horses to Oregon. The party's leader, now entering a new and final phase of his career, was Ewing Young, whom we have previously met as a fur trader in the Southwest and a pioneer on the Old Spanish Trail. Kelley's reception and treatment at Fort Vancouver were not up to his expectations, and when he left Oregon, in 1835, it was with embitterment toward the Hudson's Bay Company. Though his subsequent writings reflected this attitude, enthusiasm for the region did not wane. His activity was a potent factor in promoting the American settlement of Oregon.

In 1838 the Oregon Emigration Society was organized at Lynn, Massachusetts, and began publication of *The Oregonian* to promote interest and enlist recruits. Soon emigration societies were formed in Pennsylvania, Ohio, Illinois, Indiana, Michigan, and Missouri. A variety of factors aided the cause. Hard times brought on by the Panic of 1837; a desire to escape ague in the Mississippi Valley; opportunity visioned by poor whites to achieve social equality in a new land; adventure; patriotic zeal to win Oregon for the United States; alluring economic opportunities; the very momentum of the westward movement—all were to contribute in swelling the ranks of westbound emigrants.

The overland migration of actual settlers bound for the Pacific Coast did not begin until 1841. The few Americans in Oregon before this time were those connected with the missions, and some retired trappers. The pioneer band of settlers, comprising nearly 70 persons, left the Missouri frontier in early May, 1841, and moved westward over a route soon to be famed as the Oregon Trail.

From Independence, the early "jumping-off place," this trail took a northwest course to Fort Kearney at the southern bend of the Platte River. It then followed this stream and its north branch to Fort Laramie. Continuing up the North Platte and the Sweetwater fork, the trail passed Independence Rock and Devil's Gate and crossed over famous South Pass, the "gateway to Oregon." After traversing the Green River Valley and touching at Fort Bridger, it turned northwest by Soda Springs to Fort Hall on the Snake River. It now followed this stream, passed Fort Boise, traversed the Grand Ronde Valley, crossed the Blue Mountains to Whitman's Mission, descended the Columbia River, and led into the Willamette Valley.

It was a long trail, extending some 2,000 miles over prairies, mountains, and deserts. Six months were required for a journey over it by the covered wagon emigrants. But time and distance, hardship and danger, were but small deterrents to hardy homeseekers who set their faces to the West. Through the succeeding 25 years thousands upon thousands of pioneers were to trek the Oregon Trail and its branches to found western commonwealths. The thousands of wagons that carried those intrepid bands were to wear deep and enduring a trail from the Big Muddy to the Western Sea.

Across stretches of unplowed prairie and over projecting hills, traces of the century-old road are still visible. Perhaps the most impressive remnant to be seen today is on the North Platte River near present Guernsey, Wyoming. Here on a sandstone base, numberless hoofs of horses and oxen, endless grinding wheels, have cut a wagon-width four feet deep in the solid rock. Even the grooves on the side walls scratched by the high wheel hubs are clearly discernible. It is a mute yet eloquent record.

That first emigrant band, of 1841, divided into two parts at Soda Springs, modern Idaho, half heading for California and half for Oregon. The latter group abandoned its wagons at Fort Hall, and with belongings packed on horses and mules made its way to Whitman's Mission and to the Columbia.

The year 1842 saw a party of over 100 men, women, and children journey over the trail. Dr. Elijah White, former missionary to Oregon and now newly appointed United States Indian Agent for that country, was leader. Upon arriving at the Willamette Valley, this company doubled the number of Americans in Oregon. Dr. White brought disconcerting news from mission headquarters in Boston—orders to discontinue certain Presbyterian missions. Whitman resolved to petition for a reconsideration, and accordingly made an overland midwinter journey back to Boston. It is likely that he had other motives also, political and patriotic, for he visited Washington, and to Secretary of War Porter advocated the establishment of military forts along the Oregon Trail. Although his heroic ride did not "save Oregon," as some have contended, it was none the less helpful in winning for the United States territory in that region.

Since others already had been working toward the same end, the American tide was swelling. In 1838 the missionary colonists on the Willamette had formed a simple government and drawn up a petition asking the United States to extend its authority over the country. The death of Ewing Young in February, 1841, emphasized the need for governmental machinery; for this early trader and pioneer stockman of Oregon had died without known heirs and without having made provision for the disposition of his considerable estate. His neighbors met and selected a judge to handle the case, and at the same time chose a committee to draft a constitution and laws. The plan for a government did not materialize, largely because of opposition by French Canadians, former employees of the Hudson's Bay Company.

The next political move of consequence resulted from a concerted effort to exterminate the predatory animals that were attacking the settlers' herds. This led to the creation of a provisional government at Champoeg on May 2, 1843. "We the people of Oregon Territory," so runs the preamble of the organic law, "for purposes of mutual protection, and to secure peace and prosperity among ourselves, agree to adopt the following laws and regulations until such time as the United States of America extend their jurisdiction over us." This has a familiar ring, being an American expression of the Social Compact theory that has echoed along the frontier from Plymouth Rock to the Willamette.

The governmental effort at Champoeg was greatly aided, if not saved, by the large influx of Americans. The "Great Migration" of 1843 comprised 1,000 persons. A census taken in eastern Kansas and reported in *Niles Register* showed 121 wagons, 698 oxen, 296 horses, and 973 loose cattle. There were 260 men, 130 women, and 610 children—making nearly five children to each woman in the train. It was decidedly a family migration. The election of officers, as witnessed by Matt Field, was conducted in interesting fashion:

> The candidates stood up in a row behind the constituents, and at a given signal they wheeled about and marched off, while the general mass broke after them "Lick-a-ty-split," each man forming behind his favorite, so that every candidate flourished a sort of tail of his own, and the man with the

longest tail was elected! These proceedings were continued until a captain and a council of ten were elected.

By the year 1843 the methods of overland travel had been well worked out. No one has given us a better picture of train routine than an emigrant of that year, Jesse Applegate, in his "A Day with the Cow Column":

It is four o'clock A.M.; the sentinels on duty have discharged their rifles—the signal that the hours of sleep are over; and every wagon and tent is pouring forth its night tenants, and slow-kindling smokes begin largely to rise and float away on the morning air.

Sixty men start from the corral, spreading as they make through the vast herd of cattle and horses that form a semi-circle around the encampment, the most distant perhaps two miles away. . . .

By five o'clock the herders begin to contract the great moving circle and the well-trained animals move slowly toward camp, clipping here and there a thistle or tempting bunch of grass on the way.

In about an hour five thousand animals are close up to the encampment, and the teamsters are busy selecting their teams and driving them inside the "corral" to be yoked. The corral is a circle one hundred yards deep, formed with wagons connected strongly with each other, the wagon in the rear being connected with the wagon in front by its tongue and ox chains. . . . From six to seven o'clock is a busy time; breakfast is to be eaten, the tents struck, the wagons loaded, the teams yoked and brought in readiness to be attached to their respective wagons. All know when at seven o'clock, the signal to march sounds, that those not ready to take their proper places in the line of march must fall into the dusty rear for the day. . . .

It is on the stroke of seven; the rushing to and fro, the cracking of the whips, the loud command to oxen and what seems to be the inextricable confusion of the last ten minutes has ceased. Fortunately every one has been found and every teamster is at his post. The clear notes of the trumpet sound in the front; the pilot and his guards mount their horses, the leading division of wagons moves out of the encampment, and takes up the line of march, the rest fall into their places with the precision of clock work, until the spot so lately full of life sinks back into that solitude that seems to reign over the broad plain and rushing river as the caravan draws its lazy length toward the distant El Dorado. . . .

[The wagons] form a line three quarters of a mile in length; some of the teamsters ride upon the front of their wagons, some walk beside their teams; scattered along the line companies of women and children are taking exercise on foot; they gather bouquets of rare and beautiful flowers that line the way; near them stalks a stately gray hound or an Irish wolf dog, apparently proud of keeping watch and ward over his master's wife and children.

Next comes a band of horses; two or three men or boys follow them, the docile and sagacious animals scarce needing this attention, for they have learned to follow in the rear of the wagons, . . . not so with the large herd of horned beasts that bring up the rear; lazy, selfish and unsocial, it has been a task to get them in motion, . . .

[After some five hours of traveling the train makes the noon halt at a place chosen by the pilot.] As the teams are not unyoked, but simply turned loose from the wagons, a corral is not formed at noon, but the wagons are drawn up in columns, four abreast, . . .

It is now one o'clock; the bugle has sounded, and the caravan has resumed its westward journey. It is in the same order, but the evening is far less animated than the morning march; a drowsiness has fallen apparently on man and beast; teamsters drop asleep on their perches and even walking by their teams, and the words of command are now addressed to the slowly creeping oxen in the softened tenor of women or the piping treble of children, . . .

The sun is now getting low in the west and at length the painstaking pilot is standing ready to conduct the train in the circle which he has previously measured and marked out, which is to form the invariable fortification for the night. . . . Within ten minutes from the time the leading wagon halted, the barricade is formed, the teams unyoked and driven out to pasture.

Everyone is busy preparing fires of buffalo chips to cook the evening meal, pitching tents and otherwise preparing for the night. . . .

All able to bear arms in the party have been formed into three companies, and each of these into four watches. Every third night it is the duty of one of these companies to keep watch and ward over the camp, and it is so arranged that each watch takes its turn of guard duty through the different watches of the night. . . .

It is not yet eight o'clock when the first watch is to be set; the evening meal is just over, and the corral now free from the intrusion of the cattle or horses, groups of children are scattered over it. . . . Before a tent near the river a violin makes lively music, and some youths and maidens have improvised a dance upon the green; in another quarter a flute gives its mellow and melancholy notes to the still air, which as they float away over the quiet river seem a lament for the past rather than a hope for the future. . . .

But time passes; the watch is set for the night, the council of old men has broken up and each has turned to his own quarter. The flute has whispered its last lament to the deepening night, the violin is silent and the dancers have dispersed. Enamored youths have whispered a tender "Good night" in the ears of blushing maidens, or stolen a kiss from the lips of some future bride—for Cupid here as elsewhere has been busy bringing together congenial hearts. . . . All is hushed and repose from the fatigue of the day, save the vigilant guard, and the wakeful leader who still has cares upon his mind that forbid sleep.

He hears the ten o'clock relief taking post and the "all well" report of the returned guard; the night deepens, . . . the last care of the day being removed, and the last duty performed, he too seeks the rest that will enable him to go through the same routine tomorrow.

This was a day with one Oregon-bound company of 1843. But it might as well have been any day of 25 other summers, with any of hundreds of other companies bound for California or Utah or other states of the West. We present it here as a type picture of the emigrant train west-bound.

Yet no day was an exact duplication of the preceding one. There was always the unexpected to vary the monotony. Wind storms and rain storms, buffalo stampedes and Indian scares were frequent enough. The loss of animals and the breaking of wagons were trag-edies indeed, while births and weddings and deaths were special occa-sions of gladness or of sorrow. Rivers in flood were to be forded, teams must be doubled over sand patches and across deep gullies. Food supplies occasionally ran short and starvation threatened. But, on the whole, for the young and the strong, the trip was a delightful excursion. For others it was a long ordeal that tried their souls. The pioneer mother endured most. It is the figure in sunbonnet and ging-ham that looms through the years as heroine of the great trek.

We cannot here follow the caravans of succeeding years, but may say that in general the number of emigrants increased annually. As early as 1844 some people on the Missouri frontier felt that the "Ore-gon fever" was becoming a dangerous disease. "By next spring, a year, I think the mania will run out," writes a correspondent in the *Missouri Republican.* "At least, I do not perceive how it can keep up much longer. . . . In truth, no man of information, in his right mind, would think of leaving such a country as this, to wander over a thou-sand miles of desert and five hundred of mountains to reach such as that. It is wrong in the people of St. Louis to encourage this spirit of emigration."

But this was a discordant note in the national chorus. The general voice of the people sang a pean in praise of expansion. During the year 1844, the refrain was taken up by the political parties, and much oratory was loosed in behalf of the annexation of Texas and the occu-pation of Oregon. Indeed, "Fifty-Four Forty or Fight" became a campaign slogan with the Democrats. Following their victory, Presi-dent Polk, in his inaugural address, asserted that our title to the whole of Oregon "was clear and unquestionable," and that our people were preparing to perfect that title by occupation of the land. That Great Britain had a claim to the region served to stimulate rather than retard American emigration. The net result was a migration of 3,000 in 1845, equal to all that had gone before. American settlers were now clearly predominant in Oregon. And it was their presence that consti-tuted our principal weapon in the diplomatic duel with Great Britain. In 1842 Secretary of State Webster had been inclined to accept the Columbia River as a boundary between British and American territory in Oregon, but fortunately this was not incorporated in the Webster-Ashburton Treaty. John C. Calhoun, as Secretary of State in 1844, did not press the boundary question, correctly perceiving that time, with its influx of American settlers, was all on our side.

In the meantime Congress was concerned with the Oregon question. In the session of 1845–1846, the Senate Committee on Post Offices and Post Roads recommended establishment of a mail line from Missouri to Oregon, emphasizing the effects it would have "in strengthening the bonds of friendship and union between the people of the East and West; in affording the means of acquiring information of the Oregon, so as to promote emigration to those regions, and ultimately to control the vast trade of the Pacific Ocean." Accompanying the Committee report was a glowing description of Oregon, its resources and its possibilities, written by William Gilpin of Missouri. Gilpin, later to become the first Governor of Colorado, had accompanied Fremont to Oregon in 1843 and had returned to the States the following year. In this report, of which 3,000 extra copies were ordered printed by Congress, Gilpin said in part:

> The American population of Oregon nearly reaches 10,000. They have seventeen flour and saw mills; 20,000 head of cattle; the crop of 1844 and 1845 exhibits 100,000 bushels of surplus wheat; . . . Half a dozen years ago the Willamette was occupied by beaver and eagles; it now exhibits an American republic, with a government, agriculture, mills, and commerce. . . . There is already a great American commerce in the Pacific Ocean, and most of that in the vicinity of the mouth of the Columbia River. . . . Are this mighty commerce, and this brave, agricultural people, to be consigned forever to a melancholy banishment from home? Is government to do more than this, by keeping up a harassing diplomatic game, to tantalize our people in their remote and isolated position?—to sour them by unrelenting neglect, . . . I pray that Congress may not let the voice of western commerce blow by on the wind, but rather gather its prayers and complaints, and cover its feebleness with substantial legislation, aid, and protection.

Many of the senators thought the mail route proposition impracticable, if not visionary. Calhoun spoke strongly against it. Webster, according to Gilpin, closed his denunciation of the measure thus:

> What do we want with this vast, worthless area? This region of savages and wild beasts—of deserts of shifting sands and whirlwinds of dust—of cactus and prairie dogs? To what use could we ever hope to put these great deserts, or those endless mountain ranges, impenetrable and covered to their very base with eternal snow? What can we ever hope to do with the Western coast—a coast of three thousand miles, rockbound, cheerless, uninviting and not a harbor on it. What use have we for this country?

In December, 1845, President Polk asked Congress to serve notice on England of termination of the joint occupation agreement pertaining to the Oregon country. His request was acceded to, and the required one year's notice of abrogation was given. The diplomats now took their pens in hand and began to spar with their quills. England long had held for the Columbia as a southern boundary, while the spell-binders of Polk's party, with more alliteration than logic, had blustered "Fifty-Four Forty or Fight." Inasmuch as the United States was engaging in a war with Mexico in 1846, she was hardly in position

to "take on" Great Britain at the same time. So when England proposed a continuation of the forty-ninth parallel across the Rockies and
to the Pacific Coast, the United States accepted the compromise line.
Thus was the great Oregon country divided on what is generally considered a fair and equitable basis. The treaty was signed by the
United States in June, 1846.

At the next session of Congress a bill was introduced to provide a
Territorial government for Oregon. But the slavery question was in-
jected into the discussion, inasmuch as the constitution of the provisional government of Oregon had declared against slavery. So the
Congressional session closed without enactment of the bill. The succeeding session might have accomplished no more, had it not been for
a tragic occurrence in Oregon. Dr. Marcus Whitman, his wife, and
seven other persons were massacred by the Cayuse Indians at the
Whitman mission on November 29, 1847. This brought on an Indian
war that taxed the resources of the young country. Oregon leaders
felt that the neglect of the national government was in part responsible
for the tragedy. They prepared a ringing memorial to Congress and
put it in the hands of Joe Meek, early trapper and picturesque pioneer.
With nine hardy mountaineers he set out on March 4, 1848, and in 72
days was in St. Louis. The story of the massacre and of the need for
military aid was flashed to the country.

Said the Oregon memorial to Congress:

Having called upon the government so often in vain, we have almost
despaired of receiving its protection; yet we trust that our present situation,
when fully laid before you, will at once satisfy your honourable body of the
necessity of extending the strong arm of guardianship and protection over
this distant, but beautiful portion of the United States' domain. . . . The
Indians have shouted the war whoop, and crimsoned their tomahawks in the
blood of our citizens. . . . we have a right to expect your aid and you are
in justice bound to extend it. . . ."

The bill creating Oregon Territory was passed in August, 1848.
President Polk appointed Joseph Lane Governor and Joe Meek United
States Marshal. The new officials set out for the Territory by way of
Santa Fe and California. On March 2, 1849, they arrived at Oregon
City, and the following day the Territorial Government was proclaimed.

BIBLIOGRAPHY

For general accounts of Oregon and the Northwest Coast, see: J. W.
Caughey, *History of the Pacific Coast of North America* (New York, 1938);
Joseph Schafer, *A History of the Pacific Northwest* (New York, 1918);
H. H. Bancroft, *History of Oregon* (2 vols., San Francisco, 1886); H. H.
Bancroft, *History of the Northwest Coast* (2 vols., San Francisco, 1884);
C. L. Skinner, *Adventurers of Oregon* (New Haven, 1921); A. C. Laut,

The Conquest of Our Western Empire (New York, 1927); G. C. Davidson, *The North West Company* (Berkeley, 1918); Douglas Mackay, *The Honourable Company, A History of the Hudson's Bay Company* (Indianapolis, 1936); G. W. Fuller, *A History of the Pacific Northwest* (New York, 1931); R. C. Clark, *History of the Willamette Valley* (1927); C. H. Carey, *A General History of Oregon prior to 1861* (2 vols., Portland, 1935–1936); O. O. Winther, *The Great Northwest* (New York, 1947).

Detailed accounts of early explorations are the following: James Cook and James King, *A Voyage to the Pacific Ocean,* . . . (4 vols., London, 1784); John Ledyard, *A Journal of Captain Cook's Last Voyage to the Pacific Ocean* (Hartford, 1783); George Vancouver, *A Voyage of Discovery to the North Pacific Ocean* (3 vols., London, 1798); Alexander Mackenzie, *Voyages* . . . *to the Frozen and Pacific Oceans* (2 vols., London, 1801); Elliott Coues (ed.), *The Manuscript Journals of Alexander Henry and David Thompson* (3 vols., New York, 1897); Frederick Merk, *Fur Trade and Empire; George Simpson's Journal* (Cambridge, 1931).

An excellent collection of documents relating to Oregon is assembled in A. B. and D. P. Hulbert's *Overland to the Pacific* series, Vols. III-VII (Denver, 1933–1937). See also C. B. Bagley (ed.), *Early Catholic Missions in Old Oregon* (2 vols., Seattle, 1932).

For the diplomatic contest of 1790, consult W. R. Manning, "The Nootka Sound Controversy," in the American Historical Association *Annual Report of 1904.* See also H. M. Stephens, "The Conflict of European Nations in the Pacific," in Stephens and Bolton (eds.), *The Pacific Ocean in History* (New York, 1917).

The following biographical volumes relate to men prominent in the Oregon story: F. V. Holman, *Dr. John McLoughlin, the Father of Oregon* (Cleveland, 1907); E. E. Dye, *McLoughlin and Old Oregon* (Chicago, 1900); C. J. Brosnan, *Jason Lee, Prophet of the New Oregon* (New York, 1932); Myron Ells, *Marcus Whitman, Pathfinder and Patriot* (New York, 1909); A. B. Hulbert and D. P. Hulbert, *Marcus Whitman, Crusader* (2 vols., Denver, 1936); E. Laveille, *Life of Father De Smet, S. J.* (New York, 1915); C. M. Drury, *Henry Harmon Spalding* (Caldwell, Idaho, 1936); F. W. Powell (ed.), *Hall J. Kelley, on Oregon* (Princeton, 1932); A. J. Allen, *Ten Years in Oregon; Travels and Adventures of Doctor E. White and Lady West of the Rocky Mountains* (Ithaca, 1848); F. F. Victor, *The River of the West* [Life of Joe Meek] (Hartford, 1870).

The *Quarterlies* of the Oregon and the Washington Historical Societies carry much valuable material on the Northwest region. See also the *Pacific Historical Review* and the *Canadian Historical Review*.

15

THE SANTA FE TRAIL

Iꜰ ᴏɴᴇ seeks the origin of the Santa Fe Trail, he will find its path-breakers among the earliest white men to venture into the Southwest. Coronado, on his return from fabled Quivira in 1541, probably traversed a portion of what was to become the Santa Fe Trail. The French Mallet brothers were trail-makers along the upper Arkansas and into New Mexico in 1739. Pedro Vial did pioneering on the route in 1792–1793. Z. M. Pike traveled portions of the trail in 1806. These are but the more famous of the early explorers who stirred the dust of the great highway. Their achievements have been recounted in previous chapters. We are concerned here primarily with the opening and development of overland commerce between the United States and the Spanish-Mexican Southwest. Efforts to launch such a trade were undertaken immediately following the Louisiana Purchase.

Eᴀʀʟɪᴇꜱᴛ Aᴍᴇʀɪᴄᴀɴ Eꜰꜰᴏʀᴛꜱ ᴛᴏ Oᴘᴇɴ Tʀᴀᴅᴇ

The first commercial venture of which we have record was that of William Morrison, prominent merchant of Kaskaskia, Illinois. Early in 1804 he sent Jean Baptiste Lalande with an assortment of trade goods to find his way to Santa Fe and to test the market there. Lalande reached his destination and disposed of his goods, but remained in Santa Fe. Here Captain Pike met him in 1807.

The returning Lewis and Clark expedition met a trading party ascending the Missouri on September 17, 1806. Sergeant John Ordway reports, "about 2 o'clock P.M., we met a large boat commanded by one Capt. McLanen [McCallan] loaded down with Marchandize about 15 hands and an Intrepter & Clark [clerk]. they are bound for the Spanish country by way of River platte to the panies [Pawnee] Indians and purchase horses and cross the Mountains leaving their goods on this Side and git the Spaniards to come and bring their silver

& gold and trade it for goods as they are full of money and no goods among them of any account. and if Mr. McLanen has Success this voiage no doubt but that trade will be advantageous to the United States hereafter."

Of the same party Captain William Clark records: "Capt. McClellin informed us that he was on rather a speculative expedition to the confines of New Spain, with a view to introduce a trade with those people." This is doubtless the same expedition that General Wilkinson urged Pike to frustrate. We have no further record of the party, and are ignorant as to whether or not it reached its destination. A similar venture is said to have been undertaken by Manuel Lisa and Jacques Clamorgan the next year, with Louison Baudoin in command of the party. The fortune or fate of this party is likewise unknown.

In the fall of 1809, J. McLanahan, Reuben Smith, and James Patterson set out from Missouri to open trade with Santa Fe. Not only was this advance repulsed, but the Missourians were imprisoned and detained in New Mexico for two years.

Father Miguel Hidalgo, the priest of Dolores, raised the banner of Mexican independence and rang the liberty bell in September, 1810. When news of the early success of the Revolution reached the United States, Americans on our western frontier visioned the abolition of century-old Spanish trade restrictions. In expectation of such a longed-for culmination, Robert McKnight and a small party set out from Missouri in the spring of 1812. But the patriot priest had already faced the firing squad, and his head was hanging in an iron cage as a warning to all rebels. The rumbles of the uprising had hardly reached the far-northern province of New Mexico; and when the Americans arrived in Santa Fe, they were given the usual reception. Indeed, their entertainment was more prolonged than usual, for nine years were to pass before they would be freed from prison. And then their release came only because the Mexican Revolution had finally succeeded. With Independence accomplished by Iturbide in 1821, a new era was inaugurated in the Southwest. The development of the Santa Fe Trail and its prairie commerce was now possible.

OPENING THE TRAIL TO SANTA FE

Outstanding in this new commercial development was William Becknell, who has been called the "Father of the Santa Fe Trail." This title is a little presumptuous; for, as is evident from data presented heretofore, the Trail had many forebears. But Becknell was the first to employ wagons, and "after he opened the Trail, it stayed open." In the fall of 1821 he had reached Santa Fe with trade goods on pack animals and had been given a hearty welcome. After selling his merchandise at a gratifying profit, he made a midwinter journey back to the United States and immediately prepared for a return trip. With 21 men and three wagons, he set out from Missouri in May, 1822. He followed a course that came to be the principal route of the Santa Fe Trail, including the crossing of the Cimarron Desert. He reached Santa Fe on November 16. Other parties led by Cooper, Heath, Baird, and Chambers also traversed the trail in 1822. Major Stephen Cooper led a company to Santa Fe in 1823. It comprised some 30 traders. In New Mexico their dry goods were exchanged for "four hundred jacks, jennies and mules, a quantity of beaver and a considerable sum in specie."

The year 1824 witnessed the first extensive use of wagons and a marked expansion of the commerce to Santa Fe. The traders assembled in the frontier town of Franklin, Missouri, in early April to organize the year's expedition. On May 16 the caravan set forth. A few days later the men adopted a constitution and rules, and elected a corps of officers with Augustus Le Grand as Captain. The company, as reported in Mr. Marmaduke's diary, then consisted of 83 men, with 24 wagons and carts, a small cannon, and 200 horses. The train reached the Arkansas River on June 10, and arrived at Santa Fe on July 28. The market was good and the trading brisk. The merchandise brought in, valued at some $30,000 in Missouri, was disposed of for $180,000 in gold and silver and for furs valued at $10,000. This was one of the most profitable ventures in the history of the Trail.

The overland commerce to Santa Fe was now well launched, with promise of continuance on a good financial basis. But there was danger from hostile Indians en route, and uncertainty as to customs duties at Santa Fe; hence, those interested in the traffic were anxious for the blessing and protection of the national government in this new field of international trade. They petitioned for assistance, and Senator Benton of Missouri took up the cause of his constituents. They asked for the establishment of a garrison at the crossing of the Arkansas, the marking of the trail, and the assurance of unmolested passage over it through treaties with the Indians. Congress responded on March 3, 1825, with an appropriation of $30,000 for marking the road and securing Indian concessions.

Three commissioners were thereupon appointed to survey and mark the road and to treat with the Indians. On July 4, 1825, they left Franklin to begin the work. In general, they followed the wagon tracks of previous caravans and marked the road with mounds of stone or of earth. On August 10, they met the assembled Osages in a hickory grove on the Neosho River, at a place ever since known as Council Grove. Six days later a similar council was held with the Kansas tribe. The chiefs and head men agreed that the road being surveyed should "when marked be forever free for the use of the citizens of the United States and of the Mexican Republic, who shall at all times pass and repass thereon without any hindrance or molestation."

By the middle of September the Commissioners had reached the international boundary on the Arkansas River. In the following summer (1826), consent of the Mexican government having been obtained, the trail was surveyed and marked over Mexican territory from the Arkansas Crossing to Taos. Joseph C. Brown, the official surveyor, has left in his field notes an accurate and detailed description of the road (reproduced in A. B. Hulbert, *Southwest on the Turquoise Trail*).

The interest manifested by the national government in the overland commerce was very gratifying to the traders. The merchandise carried in 1825 was double that of the preceding year, and that of 1826 was treble that of 1824. The number of men, wagons, and goods showed a rather steady increase to the year 1828. In the meantime Indian danger was growing, and consequently demands for military protection were increased. The Osages and Kansas were generally peaceful, but the Comanches and Kiowas farther west were threatening. In 1828 trader caravans returning from Santa Fe suffered severely from the Indians. Three men were killed; the first company was robbed of nearly 1,000 head of horses and mules; and the second company lost all of its animals, and the men were forced to abandon their wagons and walk home. A storm of protests broke forth. The Missouri legislature sent to Congress a memorial reciting the losses sustained and the dangers apprehended, and demanded military protection. In response, a bill was introduced in Congress, but it failed of passage.

With the inauguration of President Jackson, however, in March, 1829, executive action was taken. Four companies of infantry were ordered to accompany the traders over the trail as far as the international boundary. Major Bennett Riley led this military escort. Within six hours after the traders crossed into Mexican territory, however, they were attacked by Indians. Apprised of the situation by a rider, Riley hurried to the rescue and then continued two more days with the caravan. He now returned to the north side of the Arkansas and encamped to await the return of the traders. About the middle of October the returning train arrived, accompanied by a detachment of Mexican troops. It was generally conceded that the escorts had saved the caravan.

The Westerners now asked for a cavalry escort, and the matter went before Congress. There was much debate but no action. So the traders finally decided to rely upon themselves, "without waiting longer on our dilatory and *speech-making* Congress." The expedition of 1830, with 104 men and 70 wagons, was larger than usual. With an efficient organization it made the trip safely. Government protection of the traffic was sought for another year or two, but without success. After 1832 we hear little about Indian danger. The traders had come to rely upon themselves, and had learned that by uniting into one strong caravan, directed by an efficient organization of a military character, they could withstand any Indian force likely to be encountered.

THE ROUTE

The Santa Fe Trail became one of the great historic highways of America. Much of the trade originated in St. Louis, went westward by boat to outfitting points on the river, and thence took the overland route to Santa Fe. During the early years the wagons set out from Franklin, but throughout most of its existence the trail was considered as beginning at Independence and ending at Santa Fe. It is remarkable how nearly the trail approaches a straight line from the Big Bend of the Missouri to the capital of New Mexico. The old road was considerably more direct than the present railroad. There were branches and in some places alternate routes on the wagon road, the wet or dry condition of the terrain often dictating the variations. In dangerous Indian country there were series of parallel tracks, as several wagons traveled abreast to better bunch the company for defense. When ruts were worn deep or rough, new tracks were broken. Thus it developed that in places the trail was a mile or so wide.

There were four fairly distinct divisions of the trail. The first extended over the well-watered prairie country from Independence to Council Grove and was comparatively free from Indian danger. The second, from Council Grove to the Arkansas River crossing, brought a botanical and climatic change from the humid prairie to the arid plains. This territory was roamed by Pawnees and Comanches, who were a constant menace to the caravans. The third division, on the direct route, was the Cimarron Desert. This was a high, dry, and desolate plain, with one stretch of over 60 miles without water. This was Kiowa and Comanche country. The fourth section extended from the Desert to the end of the trace. The country was still dry and barren, improving somewhat as the grass plains and the cedar-covered hills east of Santa Fe were reached.

West of the Cimarron Crossing of the Arkansas was the Mountain Branch of the Santa Fe Trail. This followed the Arkansas to the vicinity of Bent's Fort (near present La Junta, Colorado), then turned southwest up Timpas Creek, crossed Raton Pass, and intersected the "cutoff," or main trail, on the upper Canadian. Here the road forked again, one branch leading to Taos and the other to Santa Fe. The Mountain Branch was longer than the main route, but it was better watered and therefore safer. It was the older route, but was less frequently used in later years. Since it touched at Bent's Fort, it had advantages for those participating in the mountain fur trade.

METHODS AND CHARACTER OF CARAVAN TRAVEL

Travel over the trail took on a regular form and procedure, with an effective routine. Early in May the traders would assemble in Independence; and the place was soon a-bustle with the loading of wagons, the procuring of teams, and the laying in of supplies. Fifty pounds of flour, 50 of bacon, 20 of sugar, and 10 of coffee was the usual provision for each man. When the buffalo range was reached, fresh meat could be had. Employees were paid from $25 to $50 per month and rations. The vehicles employed, variously known as Conestoga, Pittsburgh, and Santa Fe wagons, were usually drawn by four span of mules or four yoke of oxen. In the later years five or six span or yoke were frequently used with wagons carrying loads of 5,000 pounds. The freight rate was figured at ten cents per pound.

The usual company comprised men from every class and grade of society—aristocratic merchants, capitalistic freighters, American and Mexican mule-skinners and bullwhackers, tourists and health-seekers. "The most 'fashionable' prairie dress," writes Josiah Gregg, early historian and author of the *Commerce of the Prairies,* "is the fustian frock of the city-bred merchant furnished with a multitude of pockets capable of accommodating a variety of 'extra tackling.' Then there is the backwoodsman with his linsey or leather hunting-shirt—the farmer with his blue jean coat—the wagoner with his flannel sleeve vest— besides an assortment of other costumes which go to make up the picture." There was diversity in the weapons. The frontier hunter kept his rifle, the sportsman preferred a double-barreled fowling piece, while most of the men carried pistols and knives.

The traders generally traveled in detached parties until they reached Council Grove, where they assembled, organized the caravan, and elected officers. Here, in the last hardwood grove, they procured hickory timber for extra axle-trees and for other wagon repairs that exigencies might demand.

At Council Grove the real, organized caravan travel began. A graphic picture of the setting out, of the scene that was to be repeated daily for weeks, is drawn for us by the early prairie traveler and outstanding chronicler of the Trail, Josiah Gregg:

The familiar note of preparation, "Catch up! catch up!" was now sounded from the captain's camp, and re-echoed from every division and scattered group along the valley.

The uproarish bustle which follows—the hallooing of those in pursuit of animals—the exclamations which the unruly brutes call forth from their wrathful drivers; together with the clatter of bells—the rattle of yokes and harness—the jingle of chains—all conspire to produce a clamorous confusion, which would be altogether incomprehensible without the assistance of the eyes.

"All's set!" is finally heard from some teamster—"All's set!," is directly responded from every quarter. "Stretch out!" immediately vociferates the captain. Then, the "heps!" of drivers—the cracking of whips—the trampling of feet—the occasional creak of wheels—the rumbling of wagons—form a new scene of exquisite confusion, which I shall not further attempt to describe. "Fall in!," is heard from head-quarters, and the wagons are forthwith strung out upon the long inclined plain, which stretches to the heights beyond Council Grove.

As the caravan moved westward, it extended for about a mile when the wagons were in single file. The huge train moved slowly, seldom averaging more than 15 miles a day, the length of the march being determined in part by the location of springs, creeks, and suitable camping places. At night the wagons were usually drawn into a circular corral, suitable for defense. Guards were always posted, each man taking his regular turn at watch.

Thus for two to three months was the general routine maintained while the train crept slowly along the trail. Uncertainty as to water on the dry stretches, dangers from Indian attacks, losses of animals, breaking of wagons, storms and stampedes, and accidents of every variety broke the monotony of the long march.

At last the tedious journey neared its end. There was now a new interest. The most lowly bullwhacker combed his hair and washed his face in anticipation of meeting bright *senoritas* in the New Mexican capital. Even the mules pricked up their ears and pushed harder against their collars as Santa Fe came in view. And the ancient Spanish town, drowsing with half closed lids through most of the year, wakened and thrilled with animation. *"Los Americanos! Caravana!"* rang from the flat tops of the dirt-roofed houses and echoed through the adobe town. Children and grownups crowded the crooked streets to welcome the caravan and join in the celebration. The arrival of this train of prairie schooners was like the coming in of a fleet to port, and briny tars were never more eager for a fling than were the bronzed bullwhackers of the plains.

CHARACTER AND EXTENT OF THE BUSINESS

The canny traders, some of whom had preceded the wagons to the capital in order to make preliminary arrangements as to customs duties and sales, now entered their goods at the customs house. The tariff rates were high and were a never-ending annoyance. But there were usually ways of reducing these exactions by bribery of officials or by sundry smuggling devices. It was a common saying that "the duties on American goods went one-third to the traders, one-third to the officials, and one-third to the Mexican Government."

The merchandise was now offered for sale, from stores or from the wagons. If the market was dull or overstocked, part of the caravan continued to Chihuahua or even deeper into Mexico. The goods freighted to Santa Fe were largely dry goods and hardware. Augustus Storrs, early freighter, reported to Congress the following as the principal varieties: "Cotton goods, consisting of coarse and fine cambrics, calicoes, domestic, shawls, handkerchiefs, steam-loom shirtings and cotton hose. A few woolen goods, consisting of super blues, stroudings, pelisse cloths, and shawls, crapes, bombazettes and some light articles of cutlery, silk shawls and looking glasses. In addition to these, many other articles, necessary for the purpose of an assortment."

The principal articles returned to the United States were specie, livestock, and furs. Sometimes wool and coarse Mexican blankets were taken. Beaver skins and buffalo robes were the leading peltries procured, most of these having been gathered by American trappers and traders from the region north of Santa Fe. The droves of livestock consisted of horses, jacks, jennets, and mules. Indeed, Missouri won pre-eminence in the mule-raising industry through the Santa Fe trade. Most important in the return cargo, however, was specie. During those early decades when this overland trade flourished, the United States was suffering a great shortage of metallic money. As a debtor nation, with little local production of gold or silver, we paid our foreign trade balances with difficulty, and domestic business languished through lack of currency. Varieties of paper bills and issues of "wildcat" banknotes passed as money. Into a melee of such depreciated and unstable currencies, the coming of sound Spanish and Mexican silver dollars was most welcome. In fact, the specie brought in by the Santa Fe traders placed Missouri on a sound money basis while most of the rest of the country was on a paper standard. Senator Benton's well-known predilection for hard money, which won him the sobriquet of "Old Bullion," is explained by the results of the commerce over the Santa Fe Trail. In a statement to Congressman Cross of Arkansas in 1840, Captain A. Harris said: "The state of Missouri is at this day the soundest in the Union in her monetary affairs. She is filled with specie; and the interior Mexican states have supplied it."

The magnitude of the Santa Fe trade is not impressive if compared with modern figures of merchandise turnover. But considering time, place, distance, transportation facilities, and importance to the country, the record looms large. The first Santa Fe Trail historian prepared in 1844 statistics of the traffic, which we reproduce herewith.

GREGG'S TABLE ON THE SANTA FE TRADE

Years	Amount of Merchandise	Wagons	Men	Proprietors	Taken to points other than Sante Fe	Remarks
1822	$ 15,000		70	60		Pack animals only used [except Becknell's wagons].
1823	12,000		50	30		Pack animals only used.
1824	35,000	26	100	80	$ 3,000	do. and wagons.
1825	65,000	37	130	90	5,000	do. do.
1826	90,000	60	100	70	7,000	Wagons only henceforth.
1827	85,000	55	90	50	8,000	
1828	150,000	100	200	80	20,000	3 men killed, being the first.
1829	60,000	30	50	20	5,000	U. S. escort, 1 trader killed.
1830	120,000	70	140	60	20,000	First oxen used by traders.
1831	250,000	130	320	80	80,000	Two men killed.
1832	140,000	70	150	40	50,000	Party defeated on Canadian. Two men killed, 3 perished.
1833	180,000	105	185	60	80,000	
1834	150,000	80	160	50	70,000	2nd U. S. escort.
1835	140,000	75	140	40	70,000	
1836	130,000	75	135	35	60,000	
1837	150,000	80	160	35	80,000	
1838	90,000	50	100	20	40,000	
1839	250,000	130	250	40	100,000	Arkansas expedition.
1840	50,000	30	60	5	10,000	Chihuahua expedition.
1841	150,000	60	100	12	80,000	Texan-Santa Fe expedition.
1842	160,000	70	120	15	90,000	
1843	450,000	250	350	30	300,000	3rd U. S. escort. Ports closed.

It will be noted that for the 22 years covered, the annual value of merchandise carried (in Missouri prices) averaged $130,000, or nearly $3,000,000 for the period. For two decades, an average of about 80 wagons and 150 men were employed annually. During the early years, most of the men were traders, undertaking the venture on their own accounts; but the number of proprietors steadily decreased in the later years, and a large majority of the men were simply employees. The business was always hazardous and marked with uncertainty. To the ordinary risks of transportation must be added the often capricious exactions of venal customs officials. The rates were frequently changed by the Mexican Congress or President, and specific articles were placed on the prohibited list. The duties were generally about 60 per cent ad valorem, but for a time a fixed impost of $500 was placed on each wagon, irrespective of its size or contents. Inasmuch as this ruling tended to increase the size of the loads and to reduce the quantity of cheap items, it was soon abandoned. But despite all risks and handicaps, the business usually showed satisfactory returns. H. M. Chittenden states that "the net profits rarely exceeded forty per cent, and were frequently as low as ten per cent. There were of course occasional instances of actual loss."

Those interested in the trade early attempted to obtain a "drawback" of tariff duties on goods imported from Europe and freighted overland to Mexico. The first commercial treaty between the United States and Mexico, concluded in 1831, contained a "most favored nation" clause and seemed to open the way for such an arrangement. The delegation in Congress from Missouri and Arkansas took up the fight in behalf of bills providing such concessions for the overland commerce. It was not until 1845, however, that their efforts finally succeeded. The law then provided that rebates might be secured on imported merchandise when it was re-exported through Missouri or Arkansas to Mexico. Inspectors were placed at Independence and at Van Buren to administer the act. But the measure came too late to be of much assistance to the traders. The next year the war with Mexico occurred, and an American army took possession of Santa Fe. Under the Treaty of Guadalupe Hidalgo, New Mexico became a part of the United States, and the former tariff barrier was removed. Since the price of goods dropped accordingly, the traders were not particularly benefited.

With American acquisition of the Southwest in 1848 and the discovery of gold in California the same year, far-reaching changes resulted. The Santa Fe Trail, however, suffered no diminution of importance under the altered conditions. Indeed, it carried a heavier traffic than ever before. Population increased with agricultural and mining development. Army posts demanded supplies that must be hauled across the plains. The heavy freighting continued into the post-Civil War period and to the coming of the railroad. In its later years, however, the Santa Fe Trail lost much of the early distinctive character that wove flavor and romance into its name. It became just one of several western highways. But all concede that the Santa Fe was the first great Trail of the West.

BIBLIOGRAPHY

The early classical account of the Santa Fe Trail is Josiah Gregg, *Commerce of the Prairies* (2 vols., New York, 1844, and numerous subsequent editions). A good, recent popular history is R. L. Duffus, *The Santa Fe Trail* (New York, 1930). See also the following: Henry Inman, *The Old Santa Fe Trail: the Story of a Great Highway* (New York, 1897); H. M. Chittenden, *The American Fur Trade of the Far West* (3 vols., New York, 1902); J. J. Webb, *Adventures in the Santa Fe Trade, 1844–1847*, ed. by R. P. Bieber (Glendale, Calif., 1931); Katherine Coman, *Economic Beginnings of the Far West* (2 vols., New York, 1912); Stella M. Drumm (ed.), *Down the Santa Fe Trail and into Mexico; the Diary of Susan Shelby Magoffin, 1846–1847* (New Haven, 1926); Thomas James, *Three Years Among the Indians and Mexicans*, ed. by W. B. Douglas (St. Louis, 1916).

Original diaries and other documents relating to the Trail are assembled in A. B. Hulbert, *Southwest on the Turquoise Trail; the First Diaries on the Road to Santa Fe* (Denver, 1933). A number of original journals may be found in the *Missouri Historical Review*, as follows: "Journals of Captain Thomas Becknell" (January, 1910); "M. M. Marmaduke's Journal" (October, 1911); "Major Alphonse Wetmore's Diary of a Journey to Santa Fe" (July, 1914). In the same quarterly is a series of articles on the economic phases of the trade by F. F. Stephens, entitled "Missouri and the Santa Fe Trade" (July, 1916–July, 1917).

16

ANGLO-AMERICANS IN TEXAS

THE EARLIEST Anglo-American intrusion into Texas is not a matter of record. It is probable that traders had crossed the Sabine during the period of migration to Natchez, as noted in Chapter 12. In 1804, 15 Anglo-Americans lived in the Nacogdoches district, one claiming to have been a resident for 30 years prior to the purchase of Louisiana. H. Yoakum, a mid-nineteenth-century Texas historian, believed that these intruders were lured by a spirit of "inquiry and progress," who "came first in search of wild horses, of cattle and of money." As early as 1791 Edward Murphy acquired a land grant on the Arroyo Hondo, and seven years later admitted to partnership Samuel Davenport, a Mr. Smith of New York, and William Barr of Pennsylvania. As a rule, these early comers were traders, adventurers, or ranchers, some of whom occasionally traveled as far west as the Comanche country.

ERA OF THE FILIBUSTERS

The opportunity for adventure and the lure of a vast unknown region caused more than one restless frontiersman to turn his attention to the undeveloped country beyond the Sabine. Here was a land of wild horses and game, of fabled gold and silver mines, and of opportunities for trade with Indians and Mexicans not found east of the Mississippi. Nor was the land without its attractions for the prosaic rancher or farmer. Sparkling streams, forests of stately pine and oak, billowing and far-reaching stretches of grass-carpeted prairieland, and rich river bottoms were spoken of by explorers and travelers. Texas adventure and wealth were common topics of conversation at Natchez and at New Orleans, and recruits for filibuster intrusions were never lacking.

Philip Nolan was among the early Anglo-Americans in Texas. He was described by a contemporary as a man of striking personality and

257

erudition. Since 1785 he had been engaged in trade between Natchez and San Antonio, although there is reason to believe that Spanish officials considered his interests other than trade. On February 6, 1797, James Wilkinson had recommended Nolan to Governor Gayoso de Lemos as "a child of my own raising, . . . a powerful instrument in our hands." Moreover, Wilkinson "was deeply interested in whatever concerned him," and he confidently asked for him the governor's "warmest protection." Perhaps this recommendation was of little value, for undoubtedly few Spaniards believed in Wilkinson's sincerity. Certainly Nolan was carefully watched as he went to and fro.

Nolan's reputation was evidently known east of the Alleghenies, for on June 24, 1798, Thomas Jefferson wrote to him in behalf of the Philosophical Society of Philadelphia inquiring about the herds of wild horses in Texas. Nolan was absent on one of his Texas trips when the letter arrived, but his friend, Daniel Clark, Jr., replied that the trader was qualified to give him the desired information. Furthermore, he assured Jefferson that his belief would be staggered by what Nolan could tell him relative to the numbers and habits of the horses, and of Texas and its people. Presently Nolan was in Philadelphia for a conference with Jefferson, bearing a letter of introduction from Wilkinson, and a short time later he was back in Natchez preparing for his last expedition.

In October, 1800, Nolan led a party of 20 men (including five Creoles and a Negro slave) from Natchez. Prior to his departure Governor Winthrop Sargent and Judge Peter B. Bruin, of the Mississippi Territory, were asked by the Spanish consul at Natchez to detain the adventurers, but when Nolan presented a passport procured from Don Pedro de Nava, commander general of the Eastern Internal Provinces, he was allowed to proceed.

Nolan crossed the Mississippi at a place known as Walnut Hills and took a westerly course to the Washita. A Spanish force sent out to intercept and turn him back did nothing more than observe his movements, for Nolan's men were heavily armed. Beyond the Red River they came to a Caddo village, where they obtained some horses. Then they traveled westward for six days until they reached the edge of a great prairie, and thence across this for nine days more until they came to the Brazos, where they found deer, elk, buffalo, and "wild horses by thousands." Here they caught 300 mustangs and penned them in a pole corral, and here also they were visited by a friendly band of Comanches who invited them to visit the great Comanche chief, "Necoroco," on the south fork of the Red River. The invitation was accepted, and the adventurers spent a month in the Comanche camp. After the visit the hunters returned to their old camp.

Ellis P. Bean, a member of Nolan's party, states in his *Memoir*, "In about five days we arrived at our old camp." Since a part of the country through which the party rode was traversed by the Cross Timbers and another part was rough and broken, it is doubtful that they averaged more than 25 or 30 miles per day. This would seem to locate their camp on the Brazos somewhere west of present Fort Worth.

A second Spanish force of 150 men had followed Nolan, and on March 22, 1801, shortly after their return, the horse hunters were attacked and Nolan was killed in the early part of the fighting. Five Spaniards and one American who were guarding the horses were captured, leaving eleven others to keep up the unequal struggle. Finally the survivors were forced to surrender and were carried back to Nacogdoches and thence *via* San Antonio and San Luis Potosi to Chihuahua. In February, 1807, an order came from the Spanish king that one out of every five of those engaged in the fighting must die. Since now there were only nine prisoners, Mexican officials decided that the execution of one would meet the requirement. A Texas historian states that Ephraim Blackburn, a Quaker, was chosen by lot, although Bean does not give his name. The doomed man was hanged at Chihuahua on November 11, 1807. The other prisoners were sentenced to ten years at hard labor, and were placed in remote penal settlements, from which only one, Ellis P. Bean, survived to tell the fateful story.

The first two decades of the nineteenth century were a period of filibustering, perhaps engendered by unsettled political conditions in Mexico. The Spanish colonial empire was on the point of disintegration, as was evidenced by the Mexican revolution of 1810–1811. But Father Hidalgo, its leader, was finally defeated in January, 1811, captured, and executed. Bernardo Gutiérrez de Lara, one of the padre's adherents, however, escaped and made his way to New Orleans. We have observed that Nolan, Burr, and Wilkinson were early on the Southwestern scene; others soon followed. Jean and Pierre Lafitte were in the Gulf, in command of buccaneers, who not only captured and plundered Spanish ships, but also interfered with American trade.

New Orleans was the mecca of many restless and turbulent men, and here, in September, 1812, Gutiérrez met and entered into a conspiracy with Augustus Magee, formerly a lieutenant in General Wilkinson's army, to invade and conquer Texas. Gutiérrez was to be nominal commander, in order to attract the mestizo element to the invader's cause, and Magee was to hold the rank of colonel. The revolutionists crossed the Sabine at the head of a force of upward of 200 men and captured Nacogdoches. This victory greatly stimulated enlistments. Then the invaders, 800 strong, marched to Goliad, which, with its military chest and a great quantity of stores, they captured. Here Governor Manuel Salcedo and a superior force of 1,400 men besieged them. During the attack on the town, Magee died suddenly, which fact has led one authority to imply that he committed suicide. Salcedo was compelled to raise the siege about the end of February, 1813.

After Magee's death, Samuel Kemper succeeded to the command, and on March 29 following he inflicted a crushing defeat on the Spaniards in the battle of Rosillo, near San Antonio, in which Salcedo lost nearly 1,000 men in killed and wounded, and in which he and General Herrera were captured. Presently the revolutionists occupied San Antonio. Then the fortunes of the invaders began to decline. Many of the Americans abandoned the cause in disgust when, through Gutiérrez's secret instructions, Salcedo, Herrera, and 15 other prisoners were brutally murdered. But other recruits came forward, and presently the revolutionary force numbered upward of 3,000, and José Álvarez de Toledo succeeded Gutiérrez as commander. The new leader allowed his force to be trapped, however, in the battle of the Medina, by a strong force under the commander general, Joaquin de Arredondo. Less than 100 Anglo-Americans survived.

Toledo, who was among those to escape across the Sabine, then joined with Dr. John Hamilton to head another expedition into Texas; but the governors of Louisiana and Mississippi, under instructions from President Monroe, frustrated it. Later Toledo was pardoned for his revolutionary designs by the Spanish king and was appointed ambassador to the court of Naples.

Still another enterprise remains to be considered. In 1819 news reached Natchez that the American Secretary of State, John Quincy Adams, had negotiated a treaty with Don Luis de Onis, resident Spanish minister in Washington. Its terms were of far-reaching importance. At this time the public was much concerned over the outcome of Jackson's invasion of Spanish Florida two years earlier, and it had been feared that embarrassing complications would arise. Spain, however, was in no position to demand satisfaction; for, as stated, her colonial empire was falling apart, and she could not furnish enough troops to control her Florida Indians. Jackson was supported by the American government, and Spain was left with the alternative of surrendering Florida or of guaranteeing border protection. By terms of the treaty Spain ceded Florida with the understanding that the United States was to cancel all claims against Spain for damages up to the date of the treaty, and to assume payment of private claims not to exceed $5,-000,000. Spain also gave to the United States all rights she had in the Oregon country. But the part of the treaty which aroused the border settlers was that abandoning American claim to Texas. For the first time a southwestern boundary was drawn between the territories of the United States and Spain. It was to begin at the mouth of the Sabine and run up this stream to the thirty-second parallel; thence north to the Red River, which it followed to the hundredth meridian; thence north to the Arkansas and along its right bank to its source; thence due north to the forty-second parallel, and along that parallel to the Pacific.

When the terms of the treaty were made known, a protest meeting was held at Natchez early in 1819, and a filibustering force was quickly formed to invade Texas. The command was offered to General John Adair of Kentucky, but was not accepted. It was then bestowed on James Long of Natchez. Spanish authorities sought to halt the movement; but in June, Long, with less than 50 followers, succeeded in crossing the international boundary and in occupying Nacogdoches without serious opposition. Here he set up a provisional government, controlled by a council of which the redoubtable Gutiérrez was a member; and forthwith Texas was declared to be a free and independent republic. But more than declarations was necessary. Recruits had not responded as readily as on the occasion of the previous expedition. Therefore, messengers were dispatched to Galveston Island, where Lafitte had established his base of operations. The buccaneers were extended an invitation to join the invaders. The wily Lafitte replied that he wished "General Long" every success; but that the fate of others, better equipped than he, should be a warning against a land invasion unless it were undertaken by a considerable force. Still desirous of Lafitte's aid, Long now went to Galveston for a personal conference, but he had no better success. Moreover, in his absence Spanish troops arrived and sent his own followers helter-skelter for the Sabine.

Long managed to assemble the remnants of his force at Bolivar point (opposite Galveston Island), and a short time later allied himself with those seeking Mexican independence. With this encouragement, and with only 51 men, he captured Goliad in October, 1821, but he was not able to hold it. Presently he was forced to surrender to Colonel Pérez, and was sent as a prisoner to San Antonio and later to Mexico City. Although he had declared for the national cause, the Mexicans regarded him with suspicion and held him as a prisoner. He was later killed by a Mexican soldier, who claimed that Long had refused to recognize a challenge. Long's friends believed that he was deliberately murdered by order of Mexican authorities to rid themselves of a disturbing factor in their border relations. Long's men were given their liberty through the influence of Joel R. Poinsett.

ANGLO-AMERICAN COLONIZATION

The Adams-De Onis treaty line of 1819 by no means halted the Anglo-Americans' advance westward. Instead, what followed demonstrated strikingly the difficulty of imposing arbitrary boundaries. In fact, Spain was to a large extent responsible for Anglo-American intrusion. On September 20, 1820, a revolutionary Spanish *cortes* reversed a long-standing policy of exclusion by enacting a very liberal land law. But Spain was not to reap any benefit from the act, for in the next year Mexico established her independence, and three years later enacted a still more liberal measure. The consequent immigration resulted in an inevitable cultural conflict. Since the days of the Mayflower Compact, Anglo-Americans had been accustomed, if not obsessed, with the ideals of democracy; and individual freedom, engendered by border experiences, had found expression in self-government. Indeed, a Mexican inspector who visited Texas in 1828 was surprised to find that the incoming immigrants "travel with their political constitution in their pockets, demanding the privileges, authority, and offices which such a constitution guarantees." Mexican residents, however, found greater offense in the attitude of the new arrivals—they were assertive, blunt, and aggressive, and made little effort to hide their assumed superiority. In striking contrast, the Mexicans were illiterate, superstitious, ceremonious, obsequious, and sensitive, and were observers of tradition and paternalistic authority. Obviously such striking cultural differences of the two people constituted an ever-present source of friction.

The Mexican's political background was another source of trouble. For 300 years Spain had denied him the right of self-government enjoyed by his northern neighbor. The highest positions of church and state, and sometimes minor offices, were reserved for Spaniards; and even these, from the important post of viceroy to that of the lowly *alcalde,* were enshrouded with detailed regulations and permitted no self-expression. H. H. Bancroft states that from 1535 to 1813 only three Creoles (Spaniards born in America) became viceroys of Mexico, and that during the same period out of 754 holders of the highest civil and military positions in all Spanish America, only 18 were born in the New World. Thus, but few Creoles were ready to assume administrative responsibilities, and the Mexican electorate was ignorant of the complex functions of government as provided by their constitution. In view of these circumstances, no wonder revolution after revolution was to sweep over Mexico when the newly set up officials sought to put into operation a constitution patterned after that of the United States, and that military dictators were to find a fertile field for intrigue and selfish designs.

A quest for homesteads led thousands of Anglo-Americans to cross the Red and Sabine rivers, or to come to Texas *via* the Gulf. Under the terms of the United States land law of 1820 it was possible to purchase 80 acres for $100 plus survey registry fees. But for approximately $200, a *sitio* (4,428 acres) of Mexican land might be had. The new Mexican Republic had initiated a very attractive colonial program. Under the terms of the national law of August 18, 1824, foreigners were invited to settle under the Mexican flag; however, no settlement was to be made within 20 leagues of the national boundary or within 10 leagues of the coast without the concurrent approval of both the national and state governments. No individual was to hold title to more than 49,000 acres of land; and, to guard against an unwieldy foreign element in any state, the Mexican government reserved the right to stop immigration at any time. Practical details for the working out of the national law were left to the states. And on March 24, 1825, the legislature of Coahuila and Texas enacted a very liberal measure, permitting heads of families to acquire a *sitio* for the nominal sum of $30, payable to the state in four-, five-, and six-year installments. But other costs, for example, clerical expenses and surveyor fees, would raise the total amount to about $200. Colonization movements were also favored by the law in that agents, called *empresarios*, were to be given large tracts of land for the settlement of a stipulated number of settlers thereon, and each *empresario* was to be rewarded with land in proportion to the number of colonists brought to his grant (at the rate of five leagues of grazing land and five *labores* [885 acres] of farming land for 100 families settled). Premium lands in excess of 11 leagues thus acquired must be disposed of within 12 years.

Within six weeks after the state law was passed, the governor had let contracts to *empresarios* for the settlement of 2,400 families in Texas. Indeed, the significance of the law is thus stressed by Professor E. C. Barker: "By the end of 1829 there were contracts outstanding for nearly seven thousand families, and almost the whole area of Texas was covered by grants to *empresarios* which in effect removed the land from the control of the government for six years. For during the life of the contract no title could issue in the territory that it covered without the approval and recommendation of the *empresario*."[1]

Under the Spanish regime only one Anglo-American contract had been made. In the spring of 1821 Joaquin de Arredondo, commander general of the Eastern Internal Provinces, upon the recommendation of Governor Antonio Martinez of Texas, had granted to Moses Austin

---

[1] Barker, E. C., *Mexico and Texas,* Dallas, P. L. Turner and Company, 1928. 13.

an *empresario* contract to settle 300 families in Texas; and upon the death of the latter, before the colony could be established, his son, Stephen F., was allowed to promote it. The Austins had migrated from western Virginia to the Missouri country during the days of Spanish tenure, and in 1820–1821 had come to Texas with the endorsement of former Spanish officials. Before the terms of the contract could be met, however, Austin was told by Governor Martinez that it would be necessary for him to go to Mexico City and have his contract confirmed by the new government. He immediately acted upon this advice. When he arrived in the capital, he found conditions so disturbed that it was necessary for him to remain a year before the executive committee, which was set up after Emperor Iturbide gave way to a democratic regime, could act favorably on his request (April 14, 1823). Subsequent *empresario* contracts were awarded under the terms of colonization laws. At this time and for many years following, other *empresarios*—Haden Edwards, Green Dewitt, Frost Thorn, and General James Wilkinson—were also in Mexico City seeking similar contracts. Indeed, from October 6, 1825, until April 28, 1832, some 22 grants were awarded to various promoters who agreed to bring to Texas 8,941 families.

Empresarios who were instrumental in bringing colonists to Texas were such men as "Burnet, Zavala, Vehlein, Robertson of the Nashville Company, Milam, McMullen, McGloin, Hewetson, Power, and De Leon." A contemporary map of Texas showing various grants resembles a "crazy quilt." Few of the *empresarios*, however, completed the terms of their contracts, and their rights were thereby voided. Like early Atlantic seaboard leaders, some *empresarios* acquired lands for speculative purposes, and when buyers did not appear, their enterprises failed; or they did not succeed because the grantees did not have the necessary capital to develop them.

The liberal terms offered by Coahuila-Texas in 1825 greatly appealed to American adventurers, and after the Austin and Dewitt contracts had been in large part successful, speculation ran riot. Few cared to observe, or were wholly ignorant of, the full obligations of their contracts. Some believed that unsettled portions of the grant, when the contractor had fulfilled his agreement, became the property of the *empresario*, and that he was then at liberty to sell it in any way he wished, notwithstanding the fact that the law specified that it remain a part of the national domain; and more than one speculator sought to establish claim to grants long after they had lapsed. Much of the jobbing in land scrip was promoted by eastern stock companies which advertised extensively in England and Ireland. As late as November 5, 1836, an English newspaper reported that "land speculators have reached England. Virginia, Georgia, and Texas lands are in the market. Texas scrip sells for an English shilling per acre." A point in this connection of more interest, however, which this press item fails to mention, is that much of the Texas land offered for sale was on lapsed grants. For example, in 1829 Dennis A. Smith, a Baltimore broker, was authorized by an eastern stock company to sell 48,000,000 acres of such land between the thirty-second parallel and the Arkansas River, in what is now western Texas, eastern New Mexico, and parts of Colorado and Kansas.

One of the most interesting *empresarios* was Dr. John Charles Beales, who acquired grants embracing a large part of eastern New Mexico and western Texas, and who in 1833 attempted unsuccessfully to plant a colony on Las Moras Creek, a few miles above its confluence with the Rio Grande. A raiding band of wild Comanches massacred all but five of the survivors, after they had abandoned their colony and had started by ox-train for Matamoras, where they expected to embark for the United States.

There were not many roads in Texas over which the colonists could travel. Sometimes a blazed trail was made, and frequently there was no road at all. The *Camino Real*, or the Old San Antonio Road, however, was of some consequence. It ran from Natchitoches, Louisiana, to Nacogdoches, and thence on westward to San Antonio, and from there one might travel southward to the Rio Grande. Many colonists voyaged *via* the Gulf of Mexico, landed at Anahuac, Velasco, or Copano Bay, and thence journeyed inland to desired destinations. They came from many parts of the United States. Southern planters brought their slaves. For example, Colonel Jared E. Groce, of Virginia, who had operated plantations in South Carolina, Georgia, and Alabama, brought 100 slaves to the Brazos River country in January, 1822. There were also those of limited means, like Noah Smithwick of Hopkinsville, Kentucky, who came on a flatboat *via* the Mississippi to Louisiana and thence to Texas. And others journeyed from as far away as the New England states. But most of the newcomers were from the Southern states. All overland travelers, however, encountered much the same experience, thus described by Frederick Law Olmsted:

Before you come upon them you hear, ringing through the woods, the fierce cries and blows with which they urge on their jaded cattle. Then the stragglers appear, lean dogs or fainting negroes, ragged and spiritless, followed soon by the white covers of the wagons from the back of which may be seen, as the traveler approaches, the faces of tired children, black and white, and behind them further in, the old people and young mothers, whose turn it is to ride. . . . The masters are plainly dressed, often in homespun, keeping their eyes about them, noticing the soil, sometimes making a remark on the crops by the roadside; but, generally, dogged, surly, and silent. The women are silent, too, frequently walking to relieve the teams, and weary, haggard, mud bedraggled, forlorn, and disconsolate, yet hopeful and careful. The negroes, mud incrusted, wrapped in old blankets or gunnybags, suffering from cold, plod on, aimless, hopeless, thoughtless, more indifferent than the ox to all about them.

REVOLUTION AND INDEPENDENCE

The origin of the Texas war for independence may be traced to two basic causes. First, as has already been pointed out, marked cultural differences led to friction and misunderstanding. In addition, Mexican officials became increasingly alarmed because of the swelling foreign immigrant tide in Texas, particularly the Anglo-American, and sought to impose annoying regulations and restrictions. George P. Garrison is authority for the statement that in 300 years Spain had managed to people Texas with only 4,000 souls, while in one decade, 1820–1830, the population increased to five times that number, largely as a result of the Anglo-American settlements. Mexican officials fancied that they could see in this movement an imperialistic design on the part of the government of the United States. Obviously suspicion was unfounded. No doubt the annexation of north Mexican territory would have been pleasing to Adams, Jackson, and Van Buren, but there is no evidence that they officially sponsored the emigrant movement. The fertile, unoccupied cotton lands of the Brazos, the Colorado, and the Trinity bottoms constituted the lodestone, drawing the homeseekers; and hundreds of the new arrivals so disregarded Mexican regulations, as well as those imposed by *empresarios,* as to settle within areas not granted to anyone.

The "Fredonian Rebellion" of 1826–1827 greatly stimulated Mexican fears. On April 25, 1825, Haden Edwards, a newcomer, had acquired contract to a large area in eastern Texas, including Nacogdoches. Upon some of these lands had settled Mexican families and "certain of the villainous class" of Anglo-American intruders who were to cause him no end of trouble. The second article of his contract provided that early settlers who could establish valid claims to their holdings were to be recognized in their possessions and given privileges equal to those brought in under the terms of the contract. Soon after coming to his grant, therefore, Edwards announced that those who held prior grants must establish their validity, and that those who could not do so would be evicted and their holdings sold (at $520 a league). Immediately a period of confusion and chaos set in. Early Spanish land titles were resurrected by designing Mexicans to establish claim to choice lands within Edwards' grant, and Anglo-Americans were equally eager to evict Mexican squatters. Edwards was so frank in dealing with his Mexican subjects as to give offense both to the authorities of Texas and the early settlers.

The contract also conferred on the *empresario* administrative duties. In order to carry out this particular obligation, an election was called for December 15. The *empresario* put forward his brother-in-law, a Mr. Chaplin, as his candidate for the office of *alcalde,* and the old settlers named Samuel Morris. Although the election resulted in a victory for the new arrivals, Sepúlveda, the outgoing *alcalde,* championed the cause of the Mexicans, and appealed to Governor Saucedo of San Antonio to sustain him. The Governor was glad to do this, since he believed that Edwards had exercised dictatorial powers, not given him under his contract, in settling land disputes, and that in this particular instance he was also at fault. The Sepúlveda faction was also successful in having James Gaines, the brother-in-law of Morris, named as the officer in charge of the militia.

Under the new dispensation, the gulf between the two factions was both deepened and widened. Mexican troops, who committed many thefts in the neighborhood in which they were stationed, went unpunished; Morris usually sided with Mexican claimants in land disputes and generally used his office to forward his own interests; and many settlers, seeing that they had no protection under the new regime, abandoned their claims and returned to the States.

These unfortunate developments led to the abortive "Fredonian Rebellion." The eruption came when the provisional governor, Blanco, declared that the Edwards grant was annulled because of the *empresario's* ill-treatment of the early settlers. Edwards and his brother, Benjamin, launched a revolt, after they had secured the promise of aid from a band of Cherokee Indians who had settled near them. They confidently believed, too, that other Anglo-Americans, both in Texas and the United States, would come to their aid. But in this they were mistaken. The Mexicans won over the Cherokees, and Austin and his colonists not only refused to support the movement, but they offered their services to the Governor in putting it down. Mexican troops under the command of Colonel Mateo Ahumada, aided by a force from Austin's colony, in January, 1827, drove the rebels across the Sabine, and Edwards' holdings were given to David G. Burnet and Joseph Vehlein.

Although other Anglo-American contractors gave little or no encouragement to the Edwards faction, nevertheless Mexican officials viewed the disturbance with much alarm. The immigrants favored slavery, and this, too, rendered offense. By the decree of September 15, 1827, the Mexican constituent congress sought to achieve the general emancipation of slaves, but Texas officials and *empresarios* pretty generally ignored it. When in 1829 Vicente Guerrero, then dictator of Mexico, abolished slavery throughout the republic, Texans believed that Guerrero had in mind only the halting of Anglo-American immigration. Austin promptly protested, and General Teran supported him; consequently, the decree was suspended in Texas. Many Mexicans believed that the United States government fomented dissension in Texas, and later cited as proof the persistent effort of American diplomats to purchase Texas, particularly during the administrations of John Quincy Adams and Andrew Jackson.

Two years after the "Fredonian Rebellion," General Manuel de Mier y Teran was sent to Texas to survey the eastern and northern boundaries between Mexico and the United States. In reporting to his superiors, he pointed out that friction had developed between the two races, and that conditions were such as to develop a serious problem in this part of the nation in the near future. In 1829 he was made commander general of the Eastern States, and he then inaugurated a vigorous policy looking toward the bolstering up of the national authority. He also expressed his growing concern over the Texas problem. He saw a grave danger of Texas' being absorbed by the United States, and advocated certain measures to prevent such an occurrence. First he thought it was imperative that troops be garrisoned at strategic points among the Anglo-Americans. Also, he advised that a counter-colonization of Mexican families be carried out. This would insure Mexican control of political affairs.

Until December, 1829, the Mexican government maintained the *status quo* in Texas, but at this time Anastasio Bustamante seized the reins of government and reversed the national policy toward foreigners in keeping with Teran's proposals. Paving the way for this eventful program, Lucas Alaman, secretary of relations, presented a memorial to the Mexican Congress calling attention to the rising menace in the north. He asserted that there was grave danger of Texas' being annexed to the United States, and that incoming Anglo-Americans were promiscuously settling on public lands whether they were on *empresario* grants or not. In suggesting a remedial course, he recommended: (1) that Texas be made a penal settlement so that Mexican prisoners transported thereto could engage in farming and thus develop this part of the nation; (2) that the immigration of foreigners differing from North Americans in language, manners, and customs be sponsored; (3) that commerce between Mexico and Texas be encouraged in order that common economic interests might be established; and (4) that the general colonization law of 1824 be suspended in its applications to Texas, and that settlement of that department be placed under the supervision of the general government. It was plain enough that, if developments then taking place in Texas were allowed to run their course, the United States would intervene in behalf of its nationals. To bring the settlement of Texas definitely under Mexican control, therefore, a new land law was passed on April 6, 1830, as previously mentioned. It declared all contracts not yet completed, or those which were in opposition to the new enactment, suspended; and it also closed the doors to Anglo-Americans, although tacit approval was given to the introduction of other nationals as provided under Alaman's memorial. An exception was made, however, of Austin's, De Leon's, and Dewitt's grants. Even Mexican officials interpreted the law liberally and allowed immigrants then in transit to enter Texas.

But the national government was not to be thwarted in its intentions. According to the early colonization law of Coahuila and Texas, *empresario* contracts were valid for a period of six years from the date of issuance. Thus, some contracts had expired and others had about run their course. A new national law was now passed on April 28, 1832, having for its purpose the settlement of Mexican immigrants on the lands thus reverting to the state. Moreover, as an evidence of increasing tension, all state officials were instructed to guard rigorously against intrusions under the inhibitions of the law of 1830. Nor did the Mexicans stop here. General Teran stationed troops at strategic points in Texas, and tariff regulations were rigorously enforced.

War clouds now approached swiftly. Colonel John Davis Bradburn, an American in the Mexican revenue service, commanding at Anahuac, aroused the resentment of Texans by the arrest of Patrick Jack, W. B. Travis, and others, on charges of tariff violations, as well as by his truculence toward slaveholders. The settlers then armed themselves and drove the Mexican troops out of Texas. But fortunately they avoided the charge of treason. While they were attempting to drive Bradburn from Anahuac, they had, by the Turtle Bayou Resolution, supported the cause of Antonio Lopez de Santa Anna against the acting president, Bustamante. And now Santa Anna was successful! The new dictator, therefore, could not very well ignore this friendly gesture. In April, 1833, the Texans met in convention and voted to send Austin to Mexico City for the purpose of extending their good will to Santa Anna and to ask of him certain reforms, among which were separate statehood for Texas, modification of the unfriendly immigration feature of the law of 1830, and judicial reforms. Santa Anna received Austin with a show of cordiality, and even promised minor reforms; but he could give no encouragement as to separate statehood and other important considerations. However, he did persuade the congress to repeal the anti-immigration provisions of the law of 1830. At Saltillo, while on his way back to Texas, seemingly in a mood of disappointment,

Austin wrote a letter to the *ayuntamiento* (council) at San Antonio, advising it to organize a state government for Texas. The letter was intercepted, and Austin was arrested and sent back to Mexico City for several months' imprisonment. Even now the *empresario* did not despair. He advised his friends that he would soon be free, and that Texan demands were so reasonable that certainly in the near future the national and state governments must take cognizance of them. His forbearance was soon rewarded. The legislature of Coahuila and Texas allowed the Texans better representation, created new municipalities, thus providing for a greater measure of local autonomy, and made concessions as to court reforms.

Once again it seemed that peace was to crown patience. But these friendly overtures were shortly nullified by Santa Anna. By his plan of Cuernavaca of May 31, 1834, his dictatorial hand was revealed, for state legislatures were disbanded, governors deposed, and national government centralized.

Meanwhile Mexican troops under Captain Antonio Tenorio were again sent to Texas to resume the collection of port duties, and once more the Texans rose in arms to drive them out. On June 29, 1835, W. B. Travis, at the head of a determined force, compelled Tenorio to evacuate Anahuac and to withdraw his men from Texas. But the conservative colonists now became alarmed lest Mexican officials visit punishment on them for the rash acts of the radicals, and offered to make amends. The officials refused their overtures, however, unless they surrendered Travis and other leaders of the uprising. This the peace party refused to do, particularly when they learned that Santa Anna was planning to send considerable reinforcements to Texas. On October 15, colonial delegates assembled at Washington on the Brazos to consult on what to do in the new crisis. Shortly after the call for the assembly went out, Austin, who had been freed from prison, returned to Texas. He advised his friends to prepare for trouble, and threw himself into the task of uniting all factions. Some members of the convention wished to proclaim the independence of Texas, but others were not willing to go that far. Consequently, the delegates finally decided to pledge allegiance to the constitution of 1824 and to set up a provisional government with Henry Smith as governor, James W. Robinson lieutenant-governor, and Sam Houston as commander-in-chief of the army. Also, a council was created with one representative from each municipality. And before adjournment, Branch T. Archer, Austin, and William H. Wharton were appointed agents to seek aid from the people of the United States.

Presently the storm of war broke. On October 2, 1835, Colonel Ugartechea, commander of troops at San Antonio, attempted to seize a cannon at Gonzales which had been given the colonists for defense against the Indians. But a determined band of settlers forced him to return to San Antonio empty-handed. A month earlier, news had reached the thoroughly aroused colonists that General Martín Perfecto de Cos, brother-in-law of Santa Anna, had landed at Copano with 600 reinforcements for the Bexar troops. Hundreds of men now answered Austin's call to arms, and a force 1,000 strong marched on San Antonio. Just as the troops approached the city, Austin withdrew from the expedition to undertake his mission to the United States previously mentioned, and leadership was transferred to Edward Burleson. Cos soon found himself besieged, and presently San Antonio was stormed by a picked force of Texans under the immediate command of Ben Milam, which by December 8 had captured the Zambrano Row of adobe buildings facing the public square by boring from house to house through the walls. Three days later Cos surrendered and was allowed to leave Texas with those of his troops who wished to go with him.

Santa Anna now assembled a large army to reduce Texas. On February 12, he reached the Rio Grande with upward of 4,000 men, and 11 days later his advance guard occupied Alazan, overlooking San Antonio, in which Colonel W. B. Travis with a small force held the Alamo, an old mission now converted into a fort. Santa Anna's lines soon completely encircled the town, and all avenues of escape were closed. But a small relief column succeeded in eluding the careless Mexicans and in swelling Travis' force to 182 men. Still the defenders were too few to hope for final success. On March 6 the besiegers marched to the attack, signaling "no quarter," and presently the last of the Alamo defenders were slain.

Another strong Mexican force under General José Urrea advanced from the Rio Grande against San Patricio, where Colonel J. W. Fannin was assembling a force to attack Matamoros. While on the road, two small bodies of Texans were surprised and slaughtered, and presently Urrea's cavalry had occupied the town and was rapidly approaching Goliad, where Fannin's army of better than 400 men had stopped. Houston had ordered Fannin to blow up the fort at Goliad and retire; but before Fannin could carry out his instructions, Urrea arrived. On March 19 a desperate battle was fought about three miles from Coleto Creek, and the Texans were forced to surrender. Yet in the fighting they had lost only seven men and only 60 had been wounded, while between 200 and 300 Mexicans were slain or wounded. But the Texans were surrounded by a superior force and cut off from water. The terms of capitulation stipulated that the captured men should be allowed to return to their homes. Santa Anna set aside this agreement, however, and ordered Colonel Nicholas Portilla, commander of the garrison at Goliad, to put them to death. Therefore, on Palm Sunday, March 27, 371 prisoners, not knowing what fate was about to befall them, were marched out in three detachments in separate directions from Goliad and inhumanly massacred.

This cold-blooded butchery was avenged a short time later. Santa Anna was now so anxious to overtake the main Texas army under Houston that he left his main force to advance by slower stages, and in command of a picked body of more than 1,000 men he caught up with Houston at San Jacinto. But he had reckoned without his host! Houston turned on him with a force of 700 men and engaged him in the short but decisive battle of San Jacinto. Here on April 21 the Mexican troops, now increased to 1,500 strong, were attacked while they were taking their midday siesta. The vengeful Texans charged through the camp shouting, "Remember the Alamo! Remember Goliad!" The battle was quickly changed into a rout, and with the coming of nightfall all the Mexican soldiers except those who had escaped or been killed were captured. Houston reported 630 Mexicans killed, 208 wounded, and 830 captured. His own losses were 2 killed and 23 wounded.

While Santa Anna's army was yet besieging the Alamo, Texan delegates had assembled at Washington on the Brazos for an important convention. The invasion of large Mexican forces had brought about wild scenes of disorder and confusion. Mexican ruthlessness, as exemplified by atrocious deeds occurring during the filibuster era and as now threatened by the invaders, caused a general exodus. All roads leading toward the Sabine were thronged with the fleeing colonists' wagons and vehicles, heavily laden with household goods and women and children; and armed bands of men were hastening here and there to join this or that army of defense. So the convention found little encouragement for its work. At best, Washington was only a small village of ten or twelve log huts, and was now pretty well deserted. The delegates proceeded, however, with their work, although the arrival of a severe "norther" caused much discomfort. A log hut without doors and windows was the meeting place, and cotton cloth was stretched across the openings to guard against the cold. Moreover, wild rumors were spread that the Alamo had fallen and that Santa Anna's cavalry was approaching. Still the delegates remained at their post. Richard Ellis of Pecan Point on the Red River was elected president and a committee consisting of George C. Childress, James Gaines, Bailey Hardeman, Edward Conrad, and Collin McKinney presently had ready the draft of a declaration of independence which was unanimously adopted on March 2. In this instrument were recited the long-standing and immediate grievances of the colonists against the national government and against the military dictators, as well as the principles upon which the declaration was made.

After proclaiming their independence, the delegates remained to draw up a constitution and to provide for *ad interim* officers. The constitution which was presently made ready was patterned in part after that of the United States and in part after eastern state constitutions. A president, bicameral congress, a system of courts, elective officers— all were provided for, and proper safeguards for religion, education, property rights, and the electorate were made. The *ad interim* officers chosen were David G. Burnet, president; Lorenzo de Zavala, vice president; Samuel P. Carson, secretary of state; Bailey Hardeman, secretary of the treasury; Thomas J. Rusk, secretary of war; Richard Potter, secretary of the navy; and David Thomas, attorney general.

The battle of San Jacinto brought to an end the short but fiercely fought revolution. Santa Anna was captured a few hours after the battle, and was brought before Houston, with whom he agreed to an armistice. He realized that all was lost, and greatly feared that his captors would put him to death. He was anxious, therefore, to conclude peace terms. When news of victory reached President Burnet and his cabinet on Galveston Island (to which they had fled with the approach of Santa Anna's army), they hurried to San Jacinto, took charge of Santa Anna, and began with him a series of conferences which culminated in the Treaty of Velasco (May 14). The terms of the treaty provided for the withdrawal of all Mexican troops beyond the Rio Grande, for the cessation of hostilities, for Santa Anna's pledge that he would not again take up arms against Texas, and for the restoration of all property taken from the Texans. On the same day a secret pact was also signed whereby the Texan government agreed to send Santa Anna immediately to Vera Cruz upon the condition that he was to use his influence to secure Mexico's recognition of Texas' independence. The Mexican president, however, was not allowed to return to Mexico at this time. Instead, Houston sent him to Washington to confer with President Andrew Jackson.

The news of Texan victory was received joyfully by the refugees. Those collected at Nacogdoches, Natchitoches, and elsewhere now made preparations to return to their homes and begin the difficult task of bringing order out of chaos. Intricate economic problems must be solved, and the foundations of a new republic well laid. For aid in this work, a majority of those who had fought for freedom now turned to their great hero, Houston.

BIBLIOGRAPHY

A few of the nineteenth-century Texas historians wrote reliable accounts, but more than one during the period 1821–1856 were either under the influence of *empresarios* or later Texas and American land agents. Three of these, however, are worthy of consideration if read with discrimination. They are Mrs. Mary Austin Holley, *Texas: Observations, Historical, Geographical, and Descriptive* . . . (Philadelphia, 1833); David B. Edwards, *The History of Texas* . . . (Cincinnati, 1836); and Henry Stuart Foote, *Texas and Texans; or, Advance of the Anglo-Americans to the Southwest* . . . (2 vols., Philadelphia, 1841). Another, Rev. C. Newell, who came to Texas during the days of the revolution, adds much color and interesting detail to the general theme by his *History of the Revolution in Texas* . . . (New York, 1836). The English, too, were awake to Texas possibilities, and William Kennedy, in his *Texas: The Rise, Progress, and Prospects of the Republic of Texas* (London, 1841; reprinted by Molyneaux Craftsmen, Fort Worth, 1925), sought to attract British capital and emigrants. His reprint of the Le Grand and Beales journals adds interest to his volume.

The second half of this century was a period of better narratives, although here, too, are found unreliable works. Hubert Howe Bancroft, *History of the North Mexican States and Texas* (2 vols., San Francisco, 1883–1889) is perhaps the best and is excellent for its bibliography. J. M. Morphis, *History of Texas* . . . (New York, 1874) is somewhat stilted but presents fairly well the general picture. Another work giving large emphasis to this period is H. Yoakum, *History of Texas from the Settlement in 1685 to Its Annexation to the United States in 1846* (2 vols., New York, 1856; reprinted in large part in Dudley G. Wooten [ed.], *A Comprehensive History of Texas*, 2 vols., Dallas, 1898). Still another comprehensive and fairly dependable account is John Henry Brown, *History of Texas from 1685 to 1892* (2 vols., St. Louis, 1892–1893).

Serviceable narratives have likewise been written since 1900. Among these are George P. Garrison, *Texas; a Contest of Civilization (American Commonwealth Series*, Boston, 1903); E. C. Barker, *Mexico and Texas, 1821–1835* (Dallas, 1938); George L. Rives, *The United States and Mexico, 1821–1848* (2 vols., New York, 1903); Louis J. Wortham, *A History of Texas from Wilderness to Commonwealth* (5 vols., Fort Worth, 1924); Lewis N. Newton and Herbert P. Gambrell, *A Social and Political History of Texas*, ed. by E. C. Barker (Dallas, 1932); Carlos E. Castaneda, *The Mexican Side of the Texas Revolution* (Dallas, 1928); Cardinal Goodwin, *The Trans-Mississippi West (1803–1853)* . . . (New York, 1922); and R. N. Richardson and C. C. Rister, *The Greater Southwest* . . . (Glendale, 1934).

Fortunately, three excellent biographies of men who played important parts during the days of Texas colonization and revolution are available. Eugene C. Barker, *The Life of Stephen F. Austin, Founder of Texas, 1793–1836* (Nashville, Dallas, 1925) is more than a biography; it is a scholarly, well-documented study of Texas colonization and revolution. The same may be said of Marquis James, *The Raven, A Biography of Sam Houston* (Indianapolis, 1929). Here are both a character study and a stirring account of Western border days in Tennessee, Indian Territory, and Texas. Wilfred Hardy Calcott is the author of the third biography, *Santa Anna, The Story of an Enigma Who Once Was Mexico* (Norman, 1936), Part II of which includes the Mexican dictator's campaign in Texas. Older biographies of

Houston are Henry Bruce, *Life of General Houston (Makers of America Series,* New York, 1891); and W. C. Crane, *Life and Select Literary Remains of Sam Houston and the War of Independence in Texas* (Boston, 1893). Biographic sketches, diaries, journals, and articles on Texans and Texas over the period of the last 25 or 30 years have appeared in the *Quarterly* of the Texas Historical Association, or its successor, *The Southwestern Historical Quarterly* (Austin, 1897–1939), and occasional articles are found in the *American Historical Review* and the *Mississippi Valley Historical Review.*

Professor E. C. Barker has done an excellent work in collecting and editing the *Austin Papers.* Volume II, in two parts, found in the *Annual Report of the American Historical Association for the Year 1919* (Washington, 1924), covers the period 1789–1827 and is an indispensable source on the early trials of the first Texas colonists.

17

A NEW ANGLO-AMERICAN REPUBLIC

THE TEXAS Revolution, like a lode-stone, drew restless and talented men from many parts of the United States. Houston left the Indian Territory in 1832 and crossed the Red River into Texas to assume an important role in the eventful days to follow. As a lad 14 years of age, he had moved from Virginia to Blount County, Tennessee, and there had passed through the gamut of frontier experiences. He was with Jackson's army at Horseshoe Bend (March 24, 1814), later was appointed Indian agent and district attorney of Davidson County, served two terms in Congress, and then was elected governor of Tennessee. Presently he married Eliza Allen; but shortly he left her, resigned his governorship, and, in voluntary exile, went to live among the Cherokees of the West. Stephen F. Austin and Branch T. Archer were other Virginians who served Texas conspicuously: the former as colonizer, diplomat, military leader, and Texas secretary of state until his death in 1837, the latter as president of the consultation of 1835, a commissioner to the United States, and secretary of war in Lamar's cabinet. Mirabeau B. Lamar was a Georgian, formerly secretary of Governor George M. Troup, and later a newspaper editor. The East was represented by such men as David G. Burnet of New Jersey, Dr. Anson Jones and Sidney Sherman of Massachusetts, and the cultured Dr. Ashbel Smith of Connecticut. Indeed, every section of the nation contributed notable leaders, such as Thomas J. Rusk, William H. Wharton, Albert Sidney Johnston, and Memucan Hunt; and from Mexico came such patriots as Lorenzo de Zavala.

INTEREST OF THE UNITED STATES IN TEXAS

The surprising news of Santa Anna's defeat and capture reached the Mexican capital on May 15, 1836. Secretary of War José María Tornel ignored the President's armistice agreement with Houston, and wrote General Vicente Filisola to halt his retreat and reoccupy all points of vantage, stating that 4,000 reinforcements were being sent to his aid. But Filisola had no choice in the matter. In the beginning of his withdrawal, a deluge of rain had set in, and for weeks his troops had floundered along the muddy roads southward, dispirited and hungry, until at the time of receiving this order they were all south of the Nueces. He placed Tornel's dispatch before his generals assembled in conference, and they agreed that compliance was impossible, so the retreat was continued. On June 18 the tired troops reached Matamoros.

Meanwhile Austin, Archer, and Wharton had met with pronounced success in the United States. From every quarter came friends after news was received of the Texans' victory. On May 30, President Burnet commissioned James Collingsworth and Peter W. Grayson to ask the President of the United States to act as an intermediary for securing Mexican recognition of Texas independence. The commissioners were also to say that Texas desired annexation to the United States.

TRIALS OF A YOUNG REPUBLIC

On July 23, 1836, President Burnet called an election on the first Monday in September to choose executive officers, senators, and representatives. The voters were also to approve the constitution and the proposition of the annexation of Texas to the United States, which they did almost unanimously. Austin, Houston, and Henry Smith (the former provisional governor) were candidates for the presidency. The popularity of the hero of San Jacinto, however, made him the victor. Lamar was elected to the vice-presidency.

The stormy and stressful period of the republic was approximately a decade—March 2, 1836, to January 16, 1846. During this era the Texans were to employ a surprisingly efficient buckskin-log-cabin-homemade technique in meeting their problems, surrounded by poverty, danger, and perverse circumstances of large proportions. Still they were successful in welding an invigorating and wholesome culture. The constitution provided that the first president was to serve a term of only two years, and that others succeeding him should serve for three years each. Houston, therefore, was president until December, 1838, at which time he was succeeded by Mirabeau B. Lamar (1838–1841). Then Houston was returned for another three years, and was followed by Dr. Anson Jones, who finished out the period of the Republic. Houston and Lamar particularly were confronted with many puzzling problems. Mexico refused to recognize Texas independence, and Mexican troops were stationed along the Rio Grande ever ready to invade. Moreover, along the frontier the wild Comanches were troublesome and made imperative the maintenance of a large ranger force. It was likewise necessary to keep armed ships in the Gulf to guarantee uninterrupted trade with the United States, for Mexican war vessels hovered along the Texas coast. The army had gone for months without pay, and the soldiers were restless and turbulent. All these needs could be met only by an adequate revenue, and this was not to be had. The treasury was empty, trade was at a standstill, and money had disappeared from circulation. The country was filled with strangers from every quarter of the United States and from other parts of the world, and a new society must be molded out of the nebulous whole. Whether out of necessity there would come a military dictator or a constitutional president must depend much on the ability of Houston and on a solution of the revenue problem.

The army threatened to get out of hand. When General Houston went to New Orleans for medical treatment following the battle of San Jacinto, Rusk was left in temporary command of the army, to be succeeded a short time later by General Felix Huston, when Rusk accepted a cabinet post. Then President Burnet appointed Lamar to succeed Huston, but the soldiers were much displeased that the president had thus sought to take advantage of Houston's absence, and they refused to accept Lamar. Still later, after Houston was elected president, he named Albert Sidney Johnston, a West Point graduate, to command the army, but when the new appointee sought to supersede Huston, the latter challenged him to a duel, and in the affray Johnston was severely wounded and Huston retained his command. Moreover, the army had been increased in recent months to approximately 2,300 men by ne'er-do-wells, adventurers, and turbulent opportunists from the United States. Some of these were clamorous for the setting up of a military dictatorship, others for an invasion of Mexico; all were much concerned about their back pay and refused to be discharged. The situation at this stage of development was not without humor, for while the mutinous General Huston was before Congress asking for permission to invade Mexico (which the president had already disapproved), Houston stole a march on him by granting furloughs to all but 600 of the army.

During Houston's administration, the congress sought by various means to provide an adequate revenue. To make possible a foreign loan, the president was instructed to issue bonds of the republic in sums of $1,000 each, to an amount not exceeding $5,000,000, which were to bear 10 per cent interest and which were to be secured by public lands and the public faith. But little money was derived from their sale, and faith was hardly marketable. Then revenue laws were enacted by levying a moderate *ad valorem* tax upon property, an *ad valorem* upon imports (from 1 to 50 per cent), and a tonnage duty of

$1.25; but trade remained at a standstill, and no revenue was forth-coming from these sources. Then, to meet its needs and as a last resort, the government issued paper money which was receivable for taxes and tariff duties, but this money depreciated rapidly in value. Consequently, when Houston came to the end of his first administra-tion, the young nation was in urgent need of revenue, its debt had in-creased to more than $1,800,000, and there were few reforms to which the president could "point with pride."

Land speculator influence is seen in certain acts of the Texan con-gress. On December 16, 1837, the Texas Railroad, Navigation, and Banking Company was chartered with a capital stock of $5,000,000. The company was granted the right to connect the waters of the Sabine and the Rio Grande by means of internal navigation and railroads, and was given extensive privileges and rights. Indeed, Dr. Jones, who was a member of the congress at the time the charter was granted, later included it as one of three "corrupt acts."

1st, the Texas Railroad, Navigation, and Banking Company; 2d, the location of Houston as the seat of government; and 3d, the sale of Galveston Island. These three acts constituted a perfect "selling out" of Texas to a few individuals, . . . if it had been practicable to carry out the scheme [Texas Railroad, Navigation, and Banking Company], the public lands of the country would have been comparatively worthless. The company would have been the great "feudal landlord" of the whole, and held them all by a *feudal tenure*. Houston and Galveston were pretty respectable speculations by members of a legislature; but the other was a grabbing up of everything that was left.

Jones' "corrupt acts," however, were to cause no harmful results. The Texas Railroad, Navigation, and Banking Company was underwritten by eight stockholders, but Bancroft states that the payment of $1,-000,000 in specie before the bank could begin operations was a stumbling-block which fortunately overthrew the project. Although the seat of government was changed from Columbia to Houston by the act of December 15, 1837, partly because of the president's wishes, it soon thereafter was moved to Waterloo (Austin) on the Colorado. Finally, the sale of Galveston Island in small lots increased the popu-lation, and Galveston became a thriving seaport.

Both Houston's and Lamar's land policies were liberal. Both de-pended much on the sale of land to provide a revenue, and both failed. In 1836 the republic had approximately 180,000,000 acres of unappro-priated public land. The provisional government and the Convention had promised liberal land bounties to soldiers, and land scrip had been issued with a lavish hand. At the close of the revolution, therefore, the land system was in confusion. In 1837 the General Land Office, provided for in the constitution, was opened in Houston, and 11 district land offices were created. But, in spite of all efforts to validate only worthy claims, a lucrative traffic in forged land certificates soon sprang up. Laws were then enacted to provide liberal grants to immigrants, and the act of 1839 freed a settler's home and implements from judgments for debt. A report of the commissioner-general of the land office revealed that county boards had issued 10,890 certificates up to November 1, 1838, representing 26,242,199 acres, while the secretary of war stated that up to October 15, 2,990,000 acres had been given the soldiers as bounties. "The issues of land scrip amounted to 2,-193,000, of which scrip to the amount of 870,000 acres had been returned by the agents, and a portion representing 60,800 acres had been funded."

LAMAR'S COMANCHE AND MEXICAN POLICIES

Much of the republic's increased indebtedness (from $1,887,526 to $7,300,000) which occurred during the period 1838–1841 could not be charged to Lamar's policies. General conditions were bad, the occupation and the survey of vast tracts of the frontier had brought on Indian raids and massacres, and Mexico was now seriously threatening to reconquer Texas. When the second congress met at Houston on May 1, 1837, the president admitted that he had been unable to secure a loan in the United States because of unfavorable conditions (the Panic of 1837), and that no revenue had been received from the sale of land scrip. Economies had been practiced, but still the debt had increased and the financial obligations of the republic were heavy.

The election of 1838 brought Lamar and Burnet to the presidency and vice-presidency. Lamar's tariff policy was much like that of his predecessor, although personally he believed in free trade. He proposed a national bank, with liberal privileges, but congress was not disposed to grant him his wishes. Lamar also made an effort to encourage foreign investors in Texas bonds, but he accomplished little. As a European commissioner he appointed General James Hamilton, who had made considerable progress in negotiating with Messrs. J. Lafitte and Company, when a quarrel at Austin between Count M. D. Saligny and a local hotel keeper nullified his efforts. Saligny was the brother-in-law of the French minister of finance, and, when Saligny could receive no satisfaction from the Texas government as to his local grievance, he used his influence to prevent the loan. Diplomatic relations between France and Texas were then severed, but were restored in 1842. Moreover, little money was derived from imports, for treasury notes had been issued and reissued as fast as they came in in payment of tariff duties, and paper money continued to depreciate until it reached but a little better than ten per cent of its face value. Presently credit was exhausted.

Lamar had better success with his program for public education. Since early colonial days the Texans had been much concerned with the training of their children. Believing that schools were necessary in a successful democracy, Lamar now recommended a thoroughgoing public school system. Congress supported him by enactments in 1839–1840, setting aside four leagues of public land in each county for primary schools and academies, and 50 leagues for the establishment and endowment of two colleges or universities to be created later. Also, county boards were provided to organize school districts and to examine teacher applicants and to grant certificates. Thus was laid the foundation of the Texas public school system.

Much of the increased indebtedness of the republic during Lamar's administration resulted from his policy toward Mexico and the Comanche Indians, but partly, too, from other expenditures. According to the *Texas Almanac* for 1858: ". . . He had the frontier to protect—the seat of Government to remove on the extreme borders to Austin—to erect all necessary public buildings—to support the Government—pay our foreign ministers—provide for the army—keep the navy on the Gulf—extensive mail routes to establish—and to meet a multiplicity of demands. . . ." Hundreds of homeseekers now swarmed along the border, sent surveying parties well within the Comanche country, and began the occupation of what had been recognized as Indian lands. As a result, they precipitated a crisis not of the president's making. Futhermore, Lamar was to have difficulties with Mexico.

During Houston's administration, the Mexican government had been too busy with internal eruptions, a French embroglio, and its own domestic problems to give much attention to Texas. Rumors of Mexican invasion plans were perennial, but Houston adopted a "watchful waiting" policy and was rewarded by a period of peace. But Lamar was not content to "leave well enough alone." He initiated a hostile policy toward Mexico which was to have its repercussions far within Houston's second administration. As early as 1839 a considerable body of Texans, without the sanction of Lamar's government, had attempted to aid the north Mexican states to set up an independent republic on the Rio Grande, but were defeated in their effort. This brought Mexican hostilities against the Texans.

Already Texas claimed the Rio Grande as a boundary, and in 1841 Lamar, over the disapproval of his congress, sent to New Mexico a force of 270 men under the command of Colonel Hugh McLeod. The expedition was accompanied by three commissioners, by George Wilkins Kendall, of the New Orleans *Picayune*, and by adventurers and traders. The commissioners were to take the president's proclamation asserting his authority over that part of New Mexico east of the Rio Grande; but, if the New Mexicans would not accept Texas' claims, then the commissioners were to invite the citizens of Santa Fe to trade with them. But the invading force came to grief. It was misled, and for many days was lost on the Staked Plains without food, and finally its half-starved vanguard stumbled into San Miguel, more dead than alive. Governor Manuel Armijo of New Mexico took the Texans captives and sent them on foot 2,000 miles to Mexico City, where they were imprisoned. Later, through the efforts of influential friends, they were freed and allowed to return to their homes.

Presently Mexico retaliated. In January, 1842, General Mariano Arista renewed hostilities and threatened to put to the sword those Texans who did not return to Mexican allegiance. In March, when the Texans had allowed his threat to go unheeded, Mexican troops crossed the Rio Grande and occupied Goliad, Refugio, San Antonio, and Victoria, but they withdrew to Mexico when Texas troops appeared. Then eight months later another force, 1,400 strong, led by General Adrian Woll, captured San Antonio, but the Mexicans were once more forced to retire when the Texas militia appeared. When they retired, they took with them a number of prisoners, including a district judge and other court officers.

After Woll's withdrawal, upward of 250 Texans, thoroughly incensed because of Mexican depredations, refused to return to their homes as they were instructed to do by General Somerville, their commander. Instead, led by Colonel William S. Fisher, they attacked Mier, on the southern side of the Rio Grande, and had won a victory over a larger Mexican army when they were tricked into surrender by Colonel Pedro Ampudia, who made them believe that they were encircled by a superior force, and who promised them fair treatment. But the untrustworthy colonel confined his prisoners in "filthy apartments" until December 31, then started them under guard for the fortress of Perote *via* Matamoros. Forty leagues beyond Saltillo they attempted to escape, but after almost starving in the mountains, they were recaptured on March 15, 1843, and taken back to the scene of their mutiny. Here every tenth man of the 182 captives was executed, after which the march toward Mexico City was resumed. Later the survivors were placed in prison or made to engage in hard labor, but the United States minister, Waddy Thompson, finally obtained their release in March, 1844, and they were allowed to return to Texas.

Yet another unsuccessful expedition remains to be noticed. In the spring of 1842 Colonel Jacob Snively gained the consent of the Texas government to pillage Mexican trade passing over the Santa Fe Trail. In May following he encamped on the right bank of the Arkansas with 180 men to await the coming of a Mexican caravan from Missouri. He learned through his scouts that a force of 400 Mexican cavalry had arrived on the Mexican side of the Arkansas to escort the caravan on to Santa Fe. Immediately he crossed the river, attacked the Mexicans, and put them to flight. But then his troubles began. His men were not in agreement as to their future course, and about 70 of them under Captain Chandler recrossed to Texas soil. Snively now made a disturbing discovery. When the caravan approached the Arkansas, it was under an escort of 200 United States dragoons, commanded by Captain Philip St. George Cooke! Cooke learned of the Texans' presence and demanded that they give up their arms, since they were on American soil. The fact that he had brought along two field pieces of artillery made his demand seem all the more impressive. Snively protested that he did not believe he had entered American territory, but Cooke would accept no explanations. He compelled the Texans to surrender, but allowed them to keep ten muskets and to begin their 600-mile journey homeward. Fortunately, they soon overtook the Chandler party and continued with it back to Bird's Fort on the Trinity, where they arrived on August 6.

The Texas navy played a near-comedy role during this period of Mexican invasion and counter-invasion. During the period of the revolution, Texas ships had rendered valuable service by aiding the supply and troop movements and by capturing Mexican ships laden with war materials. But by April, 1837, only one, the *Brutus*, remained on the Gulf, and it was now destroyed by a storm. Others had either been captured or sunk by Mexican warships.

There was urgent need, however, to maintain the navy in order to keep trade lanes open and to prevent Mexican vessels from plundering Texas ports. So on January 10, 1839, the Texas congress sanctioned the purchase of the steamship *Zavala*, to be converted into a warship, and 16 days later enacted another law to buy an 18-gun ship, two brigs of 12 guns each, and three schooners of six guns each. Then, in November following, a contract was made with Frederick Dawson of Baltimore for the six ships. When the ships were delivered, they were put under the command of Commodore E. W. Moore and sent on blockade duty along the Mexican coast as far as Yucatan, which state, with that of Tabasco, had revolted against the central government. The support of the navy required a considerable expenditure, however, and the Texas government decided to lend it to the Mexican revolutionists upon the condition that they pay for its keep. This they readily agreed to do, and for several months it operated against the central government of Mexico. In May, 1842, the ships returned to New Orleans and Mobile for repairs; still later they were ordered by Houston to return to their Texas home port, but Moore refused, and, taking with him the *Austin* and *Wharton,* sailed once more for the Yucatan coast. Then, to dispose of the problem of mutiny, as well as that of mounting expenses, congress in secret session voted to sell the navy. But Moore would not surrender it! Popular feeling so strongly supported the commodore that finally, on February 5, 1844, the congress reluctantly repealed the sales act; and when Texas was annexed to the United States, the four remaining ships were surrendered to the American Navy.

Lamar's Indian policy also resulted in turmoil and war. On December 21, 1838, the Texas congress provided for the raising of a regiment of 840 mounted men for the protection of the frontier, and directed the issuance of $300,000 in promissory notes to outfit the same. Eight days later another regiment of 472 men was created and an additional $75,000 was granted for its use. The men were to serve for a period of six months. One authority states that "to these corps is ascribed the origin of the famous Texas Rangers." In January, 1839, 112 additional men were called into service, and $1,000,000 was appropriated for the protection of the frontier and for general military purposes.

Although the maintenance of these troops would heavily burden the republic, many Texans believed that the menace of Mexican and Indian inroads justified it. Previous to the enactment of the first law, the president was informed of the "Nacogdoches Rebellion," headed by Nathaniel Norris, Vicente Córdova, and others who had refused to accept Texas control. There were strong reasons to believe that Mexican agents were in conspiracy with the eastern Texas Indians to rise against the republic. Indeed, it was known that General Canalizo had appointed Manuel Flores to go among the Indians for the purpose of stirring them up against the Texans, and that he had been in communication with Córdova. But when a Texan force appeared under General Rusk, the revolutionists scattered. Since it was suspected that Chief Bowl and other Cherokee leaders living within the vicinity of Nacogdoches had encouraged the plot, and since the Texans were anxious to possess their lands, Rusk was now instructed to expel them. This he did after a hard fight in which the Cherokees lost 100 warriors, including Bowl. The Indians were forced to leave their homes and growing crops and find refuge north of the Red River.

But a far more dangerous Indian problem had appeared in the west. In March, 1840, 35 Comanches, including Chief Muguara, were killed in San Antonio in what was known as the "Council House Fight" when they surrendered only one of 13 white captives whom the Texans had learned other bands held in their camps and whom it was said the treaty Indians had promised to surrender. The Comanches then charged that the Texans had violated their plighted word, for the Indian emissaries had come to San Antonio under the Texans' assurances to conclude a treaty of peace. On August 4, therefore, a large war party attacked Victoria, but the attack was repulsed by the defenders. Then the Indians burned and plundered Linnville. Before they could retreat to their prairie homes, however, they were overtaken by a large force of Texans under General Huston and severely defeated. On October 24 Colonel John H. Moore with 90 Texans and 12 Lipan scouts defeated another war party on the Colorado River and slew 120 men, women, and children. Yet this did not bring the Indians to terms. When Houston was re-elected president, he found a knotty Indian problem awaiting him. But by a policy of "treaty and trade," he succeeded in bringing more than one of the hostile bands to terms.

With Houston's return to the presidency, a policy of retrenchment was inaugurated. Houston deprecated his predecessor's militant policy toward both Mexico and the Indians, and assured an anxious congress that his program would be one of conciliation. Since there was no money in the treasury, he recommended the issuance of $350,000 in exchequer bills, for the redemption of which 1,000,000 acres of the country formerly held by the Cherokees would be reserved. Congress allowed only $200,000 of the proposed issue, however, and provided that only gold, silver, and the new bills would be receivable in payment of duties and taxes. But the new issue declined in value so rapidly that by the end of the year it was worth only 25 cents on the dollar. Under the president's encouragement, the congress carried out certain economies. On December 11, 1841, many offices were abolished and salaries were reduced to less than one-half. Bancroft states that this principle was employed in all branches of government for "the payments made by the treasurer during Lamar's administration amounted to $4,855,215, while during the three years of Houston's second term, they amounted to only $493,175, and $17,907 disbursed on account of mail service and tax collecting." But, in spite of all economies, the Texas debt continued to mount until the end of the period of the republic.

AMERICAN-EUROPEAN RIVALRIES IN TEXAS

Soon after Texas was opened for colonization, the immigrants began to arrive, among whom were English, Irish, French, and German. The Irish established a small colony (San Patricio) a short distance south of San Antonio, and by 1831 Germans began to settle at San Felipe de Austin. Both Houston and Lamar saw the possibilities of European colonization and sought to encourage it, and the earlier Mexican *empresario* system was resumed with considerable success. Among those coming to Texas during this period to take advantage of the new policy was Henri de Castro, of Portuguese descent, a Consul for the King of Naples at the port of Providence, Rhode Island. He returned to France in 1838, became the partner of Lafitte, and took an active part in attempting to negotiate the loan for the Republic of Texas. In consideration of his services, Houston appointed him, in 1842, Consul General of Texas at Paris, and gave him large grants of land. Castro immediately set to work to recruit colonists in Alsace and in the Rhenish and Bavarian Palatinate, Baden, and Wurtemburg. In August, 1844, he landed at Galveston with 485 families and 457 single men, in 27 ships; and a short time later he established his colony (Castroville) on the Medina. Later other groups were located at Quihi, Vanderburg, and D'Hanis, all reflecting the quaint culture of Old World towns.

Meanwhile, the French charge d'affaires, Alphonse de Saligny, proposed that the Texas Congress enact a law to authorize a French company to settle 8,000 Frenchmen on 3,000 acres of land in choice tracts along the frontier. These colonists would be permitted duty-free import rights for 20 years, would not be taxed until 1848, could seek out and exploit mines and have exclusive trade rights with northern Mexican towns. The French company on its part would protect the border settlements against marauding Comanches by maintaining troops in not less than 20 forts from the Rio Grande to the Red River. Saligny lobbied boldly for his bill and in his suite at the Bullock Hotel served influential Texans (Houston, Dr. Anson Jones, James Mayfield, and others) French wines, Principe cigars, West Indies sweetmeats, and promises aplenty. Success seemed within his grasp. Then an aroused public opinion caused Texas congressmen to table the measure and thus avoid the danger of the occupation of Texas by French troops.

But an even more interesting movement was sponsored by a German emigration society called the *Mainzer Adelsverein,* composed of more than 20 of the leading princes and noblemen of Germany. The *Adelsverein* was chartered by the Duke of Nassau, but was directed primarily by his adjutant, Count von Castell. Prince Carl von Solms-Braunfels was appointed to lead the colonists to Texas. To provide a site for their Texas venture, the directors bought from Henry Francis Fisher, a Texas consul at Bremen, 3,000,000 acres of land on the San Saba River in western Texas.

In May, 1844, Prince Solms landed at Lavaca Bay with 150 families, who were then transferred in oxcarts to the Comal River. Here two leagues of land, upon which the colonists were to be settled temporarily, were acquired, since the Prince had learned that the lands bought from Fisher were beyond the frontier and roamed by the wild Comanches. Within the new settlement, called New Braunfels, each settler was given a town lot upon which to build his home and, near by, ten acres of land to cultivate, both independent of the land he was later to receive on the San Saba. These early comers were presently joined by hundreds of other colonists, many of whom had become afflicted with a deadly scourge. Starvation and death were everywhere, the dead were buried while their bodies were yet warm, and it was only by unusual fortitude, self-sacrifice, and adaptability that the others survived. Prince Solms was overwhelmed by his task, and proved to be unfitted for leadership. He was supplanted by C. von Meusebach, who moved further west with a part of the immigrants and established Fredericksburg (May 8, 1846) and other settlements in the Perdenales Valley. Within a decade thousands of thrifty Germans had joined the *Adelsverein* colonists in the region between San Antonio and the Perdenales frontier.

In 1844 Anson Jones stated that Solms-Braunfels was the stepson of the King of Hanover and cousin of Queen Victoria (*Republic of Texas*, p. 371). Frederick Law Olmsted, who visited Texas during the fifties, added that Prince Leiningen, the first *Adelsverein* emissary to Texas, was a half-brother of the Queen of England; and that there was an agreement between the British Government and the leaders of the *Adelsverein* whereby England was to give adequate protection to the immigrants, and the *Adelsverein* was to furnish 10,000 families for the colony. It is not probable that England had given considerable official sanction to the movement, but there are reasons to believe that Prince Solms and other German leaders had more than a casual interest in Texas. Even their charter of agreement stipulated that the proposed colony was not only to be a home for those leaving the fatherland, but was also to be developed into a commercial dependency.

German princes did not desire the annexation of Texas to the United States. On November 2, 1844, while at Galveston, Prince Solms wrote to President Jones as follows: "The Association requested me to write . . . to you . . . to get, as far as possible for you to give, a slight notice whether the probability is for the independence of our beautiful Texas; whether we may flatter ourselves with the hope of a man with enlightened views, like you, Dear Dr. Jones, at the head of the Government, or whether Texas should fall into the condition of a territory of the United States." Then a month later he addressed a second letter to Jones, complaining that Duff Green, United States

Consul at Galveston, was working vigorously for annexation of Texas to the United States, and warned: "I am repeatedly told that annexation will and must be a case of war between England and the United States."

Although England may not have been greatly concerned in the success of the *Adelsverein,* unquestionably she was interested in maintaining the independent status of Texas. The rich lands of Texas might furnish English factories a large percentage of the cotton they needed if British diplomacy could procure a "favored nation" treaty. France was no less interested, and joined England in recognizing the independence of Texas shortly after the government of the United States had taken the lead (March 3, 1837). Charles Elliott and Count de Saligny, representatives of England and France, busied themselves during their stay in Texas in building up close commercial agreements with the republic and in leading Mexico to recognize the independence of Texas. So long as Texas retained its present status, both nations would have unlimited opportunities of trade and commerce.

Although the President of the United States, Andrew Jackson, was willing to grant Congress its request to recognize Texan independence, he would not listen to Minister Wharton's proposal of annexation. He could see only embarrassment and war with other nations, including Mexico, as well as New England opposition, if the United States were to do this. After he left the presidency, however, he became a very ardent advocate for annexation, believing that Texas had demonstrated before the world her claim to independence from Mexico. But his successor, Martin Van Buren, was even less disposed to champion annexation than Jackson had been while in office, for already Eastern abolitionists were complaining of a "Southern plot" to extend their plantation system to the Southwest. Then in 1841 William Henry Harrison succeeded Van Buren as the first Whig president, but died within one month after entering office. Vice-president John Tyler, of Virginia, a poor Whig at best, now came to the presidency. He refused to listen to Clay's dictations, and vetoed the "Fiscal Bank" bill, whereupon the Whig members of Congress, by a manifesto, formally read him out of the party. All the members of his cabinet, except Daniel Webster, resigned, and he remained only long enough to conclude a treaty with Lord Ashburton relative to our northeastern boundary. Tyler, therefore, had to shape his Western policies without the support of the Whigs; and in doing so, he had to draw support from all "manifest destiny" advocates in Congress, whether they were Whigs or Democrats. Although in approaching this objective, he found little in common with Jackson and his party, still he could work with them in their proposal to acquire Texas.

Meanwhile a parade of Texas ministers—W. H. Wharton, Memucan

Hunt, Peter W. Grayson, Richard G. Dunlap, and Isaac Van Zandt—had passed in and out of Washington, almost all proposing annexation in season and out of season, but none meeting with noticeable success until Tyler's administration. When Webster resigned in 1842, Tyler called Abel P. Upshur, an ardent annexationist, to take over the duties of Secretary of State, but two years later Upshur's early death by accident brought John C. Calhoun to the State Department. Calhoun, like many another Southerner, could see England's intention of organizing Texas on a basis of free trade and labor, and was alarmed at Elliott's and Aberdeen's efforts to bring Mexico to recognize Texas independence on condition that the republic would never be annexed to the United States. The new Secretary of State, therefore, threw himself whole-heartedly into the work of bringing the Senate to accept an annexation treaty, but this it refused to do. Already Jackson (while president) and Van Buren had rejected annexation because of their fears of foreign complications and of Eastern opposition. Still, events were taking shape to aid Tyler and Calhoun in their efforts.

English diplomacy, as related to the American West, haunted more than one American expansionist during the period 1836–1845. Jackson, Tyler, and others had often pointed out to the voter the danger of having a foreign dependency spring up west of the Sabine, and of permitting England's claims to Oregon; and as the election of 1844 approached, the public was much concerned about both the Oregon and Texas problems. James K. Polk, the democratic candidate for the presidency, capitalized on this sentiment and stood for election on the slogans of "Fifty-Four Forty or Fight" and "Re-Annexation of Texas." Both Clay and Webster had jeopardized their chances of election by declaring that the Texas question should not be made a party issue, although Clay was unanimously nominated by the Whigs at their Baltimore convention (May 1). During the campaign Jackson used his influence for Polk, and declared himself heartily in favor of acquiring Texas. Had he not made two attempts (in 1829 and 1835) to purchase the province from Mexico, even raising John Quincy Adams' offer of $1,000,000 to $5,000,000, and demanding that Mexico also surrender the region between the parallels of 37° and 42° north latitude from the Rio Grande to the Pacific?

The Texas ministers in Washington had watched the growth of sentiment for annexation throughout the United States. And Van Zandt a short time prior to annexation had written his government:

The possibility of England's (as many believe) securing an undue influence in Texas, and thereby monopolizing her growing trade, seems to have touched the secret springs of interest so fondly cherished by northern manufacturers, and presented the question in a form hitherto unheeded. The West are intent on the occupation of Oregon, in order to wrest it from the grasping power of Great Britain—it is believed that the interest of the two questions of the annexation of Texas, and the occupation of Oregon, can be combined, securing for the latter the south and southwestern votes, and for the former some northern and the entire western vote.

This prospect swung thousands of voters to Polk, and he became President because of a popular demand to annex Texas and to occupy Oregon as far north as the southern boundary of Alaska. The Oregon boundary controversy was not settled until 1846, and then on the old forty-ninth parallel proposal; but meanwhile Tyler and Calhoun aggressively took up their Texas treaty proposal.

British diplomats now became gravely alarmed at this turn of affairs and persuaded Mexico to agree to a treaty (May 19, 1845) recognizing the independence of Texas on the condition that she would remain a separate republic. But the American President moved swiftly. He announced to Congress that a majority of the states during the recent election had declared in favor of acquiring Texas. Already in June preceding, the Senate had rejected the Texas admission treaty (by 16 yeas and 35 nays), and Texas proponents had become much discouraged. But annexationists, unable to muster a two-thirds majority for the ratification of the treaty, proposed a joint resolution of Congress, which requires but a simple majority for passage. It was speedily passed (132 to 76 in the House, 27 to 25 in the Senate).

Tyler signed the resolution on March 1 and two days later sent A. J. Donelson, Jackson's nephew, to Texas to secure the acceptance of Jones' government. Thus the Texan congress had the option of accepting admission to the United States or the Mexican treaty. By a unanimous vote it rejected Mexico's overture and accepted annexation. The conditions of admission were as follows: (1) Texas was to surrender her public buildings, works of defense, ports, and harbors to the United States; (2) the new state was to assume the republic's debt, but was also to retain its public lands to make this possible; and (3) four additional states might be carved from Texas with the consent of the original state. The new state took its place in the Union on January 16, 1846.

The achievements of the Anglo-Americans in Texas during the period 1821–1845 were far superior to those of the Spanish-Americans over a longer period (better than 200 years), not only in the occupation of vacant lands, but in the development of material resources and in cultural growth. Immigrants from the United States had been much concerned with the two pillars of society—schools and churches. Proposals made for a common school system and for higher education during Lamar's administration were not idle political gestures. Still, little was accomplished then in putting these ideals into practical operation, but the young nation had taken its first steps. A few years later the state constitution adopted provided for "free schools throughout the state" and required that the legislature should furnish means for their support by taxation of property. It was not until 1854, however, that the first free school was established at San Antonio. Moreover, in this year the school fund amounted to $128,688, when there was added an additional $2,000,000 from the amount received from the United States for the sale of the Santa Fe territory which Texas had claimed prior to 1850. Yet for 65,463 state pupils only $40,587 had been distributed, and other measures were necessary to make available adequate school funds.

Early colonists found the Catholic Church well established in Texas. As early as 1805 there were regular priests in at least three Texas stations. By 1830 there were several others at such places as San Antonio, Goliad, and Nacogdoches; and at each of these places there were also substantial properties in churches, missions, and lands. The three most important Protestant sects were the Baptists, Methodists, and Presbyterians. The Baptists had their official introduction to Texas in the person of Elder Joseph Bays, who preached at the home of Moses Shipman, on the Brazos, in 1825. Four years later a Sunday School was organized at San Felipe, and the first church in Austin's colony in 1833. Reverend Z. N. Morrell was perhaps the most effective minister of this denomination who came to Texas at this time. By 1848 state and county associations had been provided, and Baylor University chartered (1846). In 1824 Reverend Henry Stephenson, a Methodist minister, preached in Austin's colony. Seven years later a camp meeting was held at San Augustine; and thereafter converts to the Methodist faith swelled the church membership to such an extent that Bishop Waugh organized the Texas Annual Conference at Ruterville on December 25, 1840, at which time there were 44 local and itinerant preachers caring for the needs of 1,980 church members. The Presbyterians also appeared a short time later, first in the person of Reverend P. H. Fullenwider, who in the summer of 1834 held a camp meeting in Austin's colony. The first churches were formed by Reverend Hugh Wilson, John McCulloch, and William Y. Allen in 1838 at San Augustine, Independence, Galveston, and Houston; the Brazos Presbytery was set up in 1840, and the Austin Synod 11 years later.

Even though Texas was remote from Eastern cultural centers, it was not as benighted as some early writers would have us believe. The literary papers of many of her public men reveal a large degree of erudition, and home training of children was religiously pursued. Moreover, the incoming foreign immigrants likewise possessed cultural habits and a wide variety of vocations which were used to good advantage in their several communities.

The thrift of the Germans who settled at New Braunfels and at

Fredericksburg is well known. Often the Teuton farmer cultivated only 10 or 15 acres of land, but he usually lived in a neatly built house, the influence of which bespoke progressiveness and frugality. They, too, believed in schools and churches. For example, in 1878, A. H. Granger (*Southwestern Texas Guide*) evaluated the real and personal property of the Germans of Comal County at $1,230,940, and mentioned 6 churches and 19 schools. Ferdinand Jacob Lindheimer and Karl Daniel Adolf Douai, editors of the *Neu Braunfelser Zeitung* and the San Antonio *Zeitung*, were two journalists as able as any in Texas (such as the editors of the *Telegraph and Texas Register* published at Houston; and the *Northern Standard*, Clarksville). These folk were also lovers of art and music. Carl G. Iwonski, portrait painter, Richard Petri, whose favorite themes were Biblical pictures and Indians, and Herman Lungkwitz, a landscape painter, were artists of merit who had received their training in Europe. Frequent community singings (*saengerfeste*) and musical recitals also added interest and color to their border life.

BIBLIOGRAPHY

Biographies of Houston and Lamar pretty well tell the story of the Texas Republic. Marquis James, *The Raven; A Biography of Sam Houston* (Indianapolis, 1929), gives in considerable detail the problems, discusses somewhat the principal characters, and portrays incidentally the culture of Texas during the two administrations of Houston. Three studies on the life of Lamar deal at length with both his private and his political life. The first, Herbert P. Gambrell, *Mirabeau Buonaparte Lamar, Troubadour and Crusader* (Dallas, 1934), is the study of "a man's career." A second, Asa Kyrus Christian, *Mirabeau Buonaparte Lamar* (Austin, 1922), analyzes well the problems and policies of the second Texas president; and a third, a recent biography of merit, Philip Graham, *The Life and Poems of Mirabeau B. Lamar* (Chapel Hill, 1938), lays considerable emphasis on his literary attainments. Two substantial composite studies are also available: William C. Binkley, *The Expansionist Movement in Texas, 1836–1850* (Berkeley, 1925), and Justin H. Smith, *The Annexation of Texas* (New York, 1911). Others covering this period are as follows: George L. Rives, *The United States and Mexico* (2 vols., New York, 1913), II; Doran Maillard, *The History of the Republic of Texas . . .* (London, 1842); William Kennedy, *Texas: The Rise, Progress and Prospects . . .* (2 vols., London, 1841); Henry Stuart Foote, *Texas and the Texans* (2 vols., Philadelphia, 1841), II; and John Henry Brown, *History of Texas from 1685 to 1892* (2 vols., St. Louis, 1893), II.

Narratives relating to Lamar's Comanche and Mexican policies are R. N. Richardson, *The Comanche Barrier to South Plains Settlement* (Glendale, 1933); Frederick C. Chabot, *The Perote Prisoners . . .* (San Antonio, 1934); Thomas Falconer, *Letters and Notes on the Santa Fe Expedition* (New York, 1930); George Wilkins Kendall, *Narrative of the Texan Santa Fe Expedition* (2 vols., London, 1848; reprinted under editorship of Milo M.

Quaife, Chicago, 1929); and Thomas J. Green, *Journal of the Texan Expedition Against Mier* . . . (New York, 1845).
Two dependable books are available on the French and German colonies at Castroville, New Braunfels, and Fredericksburg. Rudolph L. Biesele, in his *History of the German Settlements in Texas, 1831–1861* (Austin, 1930), has left little to be desired. His account is well documented and reliable. A. B. Faust, *The German Element in the United States* (2 vols., Boston, 1909), is a general account with a brief sketch of the Texas movement. Then, a third volume, written by a German, Ferdinand Roemer, *Texas* (Bonn, 1849), is an interesting early appraisal of Texas. A general account explaining at some length British diplomacy in Texas is found in Ephraim Douglass Adams, *British Interest and Activities in Texas, 1838–1846* (Baltimore, 1910). Bernie Barnett Denton, "Count Alphonso de Saligny and the Franco-Texienne Bill," in *Southwestern Historical Quarterly*, XLV (October, 1941), No. 2, 136–146, throws new light on one of this Frenchman's Texas enterprises. Herbert Gambrell, *Anson Jones* . . . (Garden City, 1948), presents an excellent analysis of Texan diplomacy.

Reliable accounts of early Texas culture are few. Lewis W. Newton and Herbert P. Gambrell, *A Social and Political History of Texas* (Dallas, 1932), has a brief sketch, but since this volume is designed for use in high schools, it is necessarily a summary of this aspect of Texas life. The evolution of a school system is well handled in Frederick Eby, *The Development of Education in Texas* (New York, 1925). Other works reflecting here and there various phases of culture are Mrs. Houston, *Texas and the Gulf of Mexico* . . . (London, 1844), II; A. J. Sowell, *Early Settlers and Indian Fighters in Texas* (Austin, 1890); Frederick Law Olmsted, *A Journey Through Texas* . . . (New York, 1857); J. de Córdova, *Texas* [statistics, education, religion] . . . (Philadelphia, 1858). Churches and sectarian growth, both during and after the Republic, are found in Paul J. Foik (ed.), *Our Catholic Heritage in Texas, 1519–1836* (3 vols., Austin, 1936); Z. N. Morrell, *Flowers and Fruits in the Wilderness* (Dallas, 1886); Rev. William M. Baker, *The Life and Labours of the Rev. Daniel Baker, D. D., Pastor and Evangelist* (Philadelphia, 1858); J. M. Carroll, *A History of Texas Baptists*, ed. by J. B. Cranfill (Dallas, 1923); *The Catholic Presbyterian. An International Journal . . . Ecclesiastical and Religious*, I (Jan.–June, 1879), 282–289; and Rev. William Allen, *Five Years in the West* (Nashville, 1890).

Contemporary printed accounts, letters, and documents are fairly adequate and accessible. Among these are Anson Jones, *Memoranda and Official Correspondence Relating to the Republic of Texas, Its History and Annexation* (New York, 1859); *Niles Weekly Register*, frequent items on Texas during the period 1836–1849 (76 vols., Baltimore, 1811–1849); George P. Garrison, *Diplomatic Correspondence of the Republic of Texas*, in American Historical Association reports for 1907 and 1908 (2 vols., Washington, 1908, 1911); J. D. Richardson, *A Compilation of the Messages and Papers of the Presidents, 1789–1897* (10 vols., Washington, 1896–1908), IV; Thomas H. Benton, *Thirty Years . . . from 1820 to 1850* (2 vols., New York, 1889); *House Executive Documents*, No. 40, 25th Congress, 1st session, and No. 351, 25th Congress, 2nd session; and E. D. Adams (ed.), "Correspondence from the British Archives Concerning Texas," in the *Southwestern Historical Quarterly*, XV–XXI (for pagination, see index in *Southwestern Historical Quarterly*, XLI (July, 1937), No. 1, 1–82, as also citations to many articles on Texas during this period).

18

"THE COURSE OF EMPIRE"

T HE WIDE cultural differences of Anglo- and Spanish-Americans constituted an ever-present source of friction between the United States and Mexico, a fertile field for the seed of war. From 1821 to 1846 annoying commercial incidents had arisen. Not until 1831 would Mexico agree to a treaty, and then half-heartedly. Mexico's unfulfilled claims promises so provoked President Andrew Jackson that in February, 1837, he told Congress that they would "justify, in the eyes of all nations, immediate war." Two years later, however, Mexico agreed to a claims commission; but the subsequent amount agreed upon, except three payments, was still outstanding at the time of war. In 1845 the American minister, John Forsyth, found that the reason Mexico had allowed her payments to lapse was that her treasury was empty, that military expenditures in 1845 reached $21,000,000, while the total Mexican revenue amounted to only $10,000,000! Moreover, there were grievances other than commercial. For example, in 1835, 22 Americans in Mexico were arrested on a charge of fomenting a revolution and executed without trial.

On the other hand, the Mexicans were suspicious and resentful of Anglo-American imperialist designs. The United States government was accused of engineering the Texas revolution and subsequently of planning the annexation of north Mexican states; and James K. Polk's campaign slogan in 1844 of "Re-annexation of Texas" increased Mexican suspicions. The annexation of Texas in the next year was one cause, therefore, for the overthrow of the Herrera government and the elevation to power of General Mariano Parades y Arrillago.

War Clouds

As president *ad interim,* Parades was now in a position to defy the United States and to be acclaimed by his military friends. So Slidell was told that his mission of establishing friendly relations was fruitless, that Mexico could receive only a commissioner with *ad hoc* powers to negotiate solely on the Texas annexation and American claims problems; then, perhaps, a resident minister would be accepted. In spurning Slidell on March 12, 1846, Don Joaquin Castillo y Lanzas, Parades' minister of foreign affairs, did not "pull his punches." He charged that Mexico had been "despoiled, outraged, and contemned" by the United States, in order that Texas might be acquired, and that the Mexican government could no longer tolerate her insults!

Such an attitude could only mean war. Slidell's reply on March 17 was equally fiery. He pointed out that Mexico was willing enough to recognize the independence of Texas at the behest of England and France. Thereby, in the eyes of the world, she had relinquished further claim. But when the Texans had unanimously voted for union with the United States, Mexico had resurrected her pretensions to ownership to prevent annexation. Slidell stated bluntly that the United States was tired of quibbling; that if war came, Mexico must assume responsibility for it.

The Parades government had truthfully maintained that the region between the Nueces and the Rio Grande claimed by the United States had never belonged to Coahuila-Texas (1821–1836), and was at that time a part of Tamaulipas. So Slidell was told that Mexican troops would expel all intruders. This increased tension, for already on January 13, 1846, President Polk had instructed General Zachary Taylor to occupy the north bank of the Rio Grande. Previously when Taylor arrived at Corpus Christi, Texas, his temporary base, he learned that General Pedro Ampudia was concentrating troops at Matamoros to cross the Rio Grande. He therefore hastily occupied some high ground on the north side of the river opposite Matamoros. Ampudia demanded that he withdraw, but Taylor refused. Before the Mexican general could attempt other measures, however, he was superseded by General Mariano Arista, who now crossed the Rio Grande and sought to drive the American troops from the disputed zone. Thus the conflict was precipitated.

Already Polk had agreed with his cabinet that war was inevitable, and was engaged in writing a war message to Congress when news came that Arista's troops had ambushed an American patrol under Captain S. B. Thornton, had killed or wounded 16 men, and had captured the others. On May 11, 1846, Polk went before Congress and declared that war already existed by reason of Mexican aggressions. And, indeed, it had, for in sending Arista northward, Parades had urged: "It is indispensable that hostilities begin, yourself taking the initiative." Polk asked Congress to provide for the raising of volunteers and to vote a war chest. The House of Representatives promptly took up a bill already introduced, reshaped it, and passed it by a vote of 174 to 14; and on the following day (May 12) the Senate concurred by a vote of 40 to 2. The measure provided for the raising of 50,000 volunteers, for an appropriation of not more than $10,000,000, and for the completion of certain war vessels then under construction. Senate action was delayed by an angry debate. Whig senators and abolitionists could only see a war of aggression by Southern slaveholders, but the overwhelming vote of the House brought them into line.

Although Polk was correct in saying, "War exists . . . by the act of Mexico herself," there is little doubt that he was willing to use the conflict as a means to acquire Mexican territory. On May 13 he told his cabinet, "In making peace with our adversary, we shall acquire California, New Mexico, and other further territory, as an indemnity for this war, if we can." Indeed, Slidell had been instructed to settle all outstanding claims by Mexican recognition of the Rio Grande as a boundary, to offer $5,000,000 for New Mexico; and that, for the acquisition of Alta California (the present state of California), "money would be no object."

To follow in detail the campaigns of Generals Taylor and Winfield Scott would serve no purpose in this narrative. It is only necessary to say that within a period of 16 months Mexico was conquered. Arista crossed the Rio Grande and fought Taylor in the two desperate battles of Palo Alto and Resaca de la Palma, May 8–13, 1846, and was defeated in both. Then the American army captured Matamoros and pressed on to Monterrey, which was occupied after a three-day battle, September 21–23. "Old Rough and Ready" Taylor was now talked of as a likely candidate for the presidency on the Whig ticket in 1848. More than one Whig charged that Polk became alarmed at this possibility and conceived the plan of sending Major General Winfield Scott to "steal the show." Although he, too, was a Whig, he was not a presidential possibility. Taylor's farthest advance was at Buena Vista, where on February 22–23, 1847, he won an overwhelming victory over a Mexican army thrice the size of his own, under the command of Santa Anna. If Polk believed that Scott was less brilliant, he little understood the man. Scott captured Vera Cruz on March 27, 1847, and then began his march to Mexico City, defeating the Mexican troops opposed to him at Cerro Gordo, Contreras, Churbusco, Molino del Rey, and Chapultepec. On September 14 his victorious troops entered Mexico City, and Mexican commissioners asked for terms of peace.

CONQUEST OF NEW MEXICO

While Taylor's troops were on their southward march toward central Mexico, President Polk was consummating plans for two other expeditions recently agreed upon in a cabinet meeting. Less than a

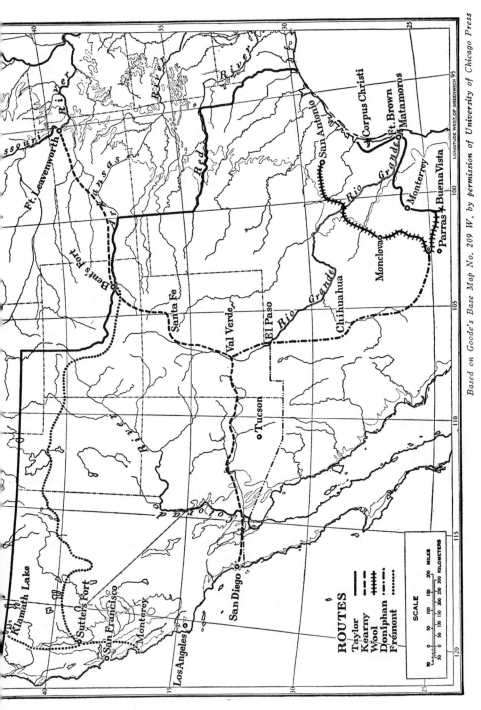

ROUTES
Taylor
Kearny
Wool
Doniphan
Frémont

SCALE
MILES
KILOMETERS

Based on Goode's Base Map No. 209 W, by permission of University of Chicago Press

THE MEXICAN WAR

week after his war message to Congress, a large caravan of Chihuahua traders had arrived at St. Louis *via* the Santa Fe Trail, bringing no less than $350,000 in specie to expend for merchandise. Western merchants could sense the importance of such a lucrative trade, valued by one contemporary authority at $1,000,000 or $2,000,000 annually. Indeed, the President had long since seen the growth of Mexican trade over this route, and now resolved to control it.

Colonel Stephen W. Kearny was instructed to assemble his "Army of the West" at Fort Leavenworth, and by June 30 he was ready to depart for Santa Fe. Kearny also sent a recruiting officer to the Mormon encampment at Council Bluffs, Iowa, where the Mormon leaders let him have a battalion of about 500 men. His force consisted of 2,700 men, most of whom were mounted. But he was also accompanied by a regiment of infantry and a train of wagons. He was to march over the Santa Fe Trail from Fort Leavenworth, on the Missouri River, to Santa Fe, approximately 800 miles distant. For the greater part of the way, his road lay over the plains—the age-old pasture of the buffalo and the hunting grounds of the wild Comanches and Kiowas. The weather was hot and water was scarce, yet the men endured the hardships of the journey without complaint. On September 8, 1846, in the St. Louis *Republican* appeared an interesting item from George B. Clark, who had just arrived from Santa Fe, stating that when he left Bent's Fort on the Arkansas, Kearny's troops had reached that point. They had lost about 100 horses on the march, and the "whole regiment was on half-rations." But he observed that "they were still in good spirits and willing to go ahead."

On August 3 Kearny left this point for Santa Fe, and ten days later had approached the Mexican settlements. The New Mexican governor, Manuel Armijo, had learned of Kearny's approach, and with an army 3,000 strong had occupied an eminence commanding a canyon through which lay the road to Santa Fe. Some time prior to the start of Kearny's march, James Magoffin, "a man of mind, of will, of generous temper, patriotic and rich," because of the influence of Thomas Hart Benton was commissioned by President Polk to accompany Kearny. Magoffin "knew every man in New Mexico and his character, and all the localities, and could be of infinite service to an invading force." With a staff officer, he now volunteered to visit Armijo to persuade him to offer no resistance. Armijo was not hard to persuade, for he had little taste for conflict. But Magoffin had more difficulty with Colonel Juan de Archuleta, the second in command. "He was of a different mould from the governor," said Benton, "and only accessible to a different class of considerations—those which addressed themselves to ambition." In a separate conference Magoffin informed him that Kearny would occupy only that part of New Mexico east of the Rio Grande, and suggested that he issue a *pronunciamiento* to take the western half for himself. Kearny would offer no objection, he believed. Archuleta eagerly accepted the suggestion, and presently the Mexican army was withdrawn to Santa Fe. Armijo fled from the country, traveling southward toward Durango with a caravan of Missourians. George F. Ruxton, an Englishman, met him between Chihuahua and Durango. "I stopped and had a long chat with Armijo," said he, "who, a mountain of fat, rolled out of his American dearbon [wagon], and inquired the price of cotton goods in Durango, he having some seven wagon-loads with him, and also what they said, in Mexico, of the doings in Santa Fe, alluding to its capture by the Americans without resistance. I told him that there was but one opinion respecting it expressed all over the country—that General Armijo and the New Mexicans were a pack of arrant cowards; to which he answered, 'Dios! They don't know that I had but 75 men to fight 3,000. What could I do?' "

On August 18 the United States troops passed through the same defile that the Mexicans had recently abandoned, and a few hours later entered Santa Fe. Then, marching with his troops to the governor's palace, Kearny hoisted the Stars and Stripes, and on the following day proclaimed to the assembled natives that the American army had come to establish a free government, to protect the people, and to absolve them from a government which had forsaken them.

Kearny's men found little in Santa Fe to arouse enthusiasm. One wrote: "This is the most miserable country I have ever seen. The houses the people live in are built of mud, one story high, and have no flooring. They sleep on the ground, and have neither beds, tables, nor chairs." Another complained that Santa Fe offered none of the pleasures of a rich and voluptuous city, and that it was inhabited by half-civilized people, in the midst of a barren and uninhabited country. But it was not entirely without interest. The *ricos* (wealthy class) were small in number and powerful, dominating the serf-like *peones*. A strange environment, quaint manners, customs, and attire, occasional *bailes* (formal balls) and *fandangos* (common man's dances), and cock-fights were quite interesting to the soldiers. But when the newness of their experiences wore off, they became restless and were anxious to move on.

A part of the army was not to be disappointed, for Kearny had instructions to send one column to Chihuahua and to march with another to California, where he was to become military governor. But before departure, he must consolidate his gains and make provisions for a satisfactory New Mexican administration. General Sterling Price was to be left in command of the troops; and on September 22, Kearny promulgated a code of laws for the new territory, which Colonel A. W. Doniphan and Willard P. Hall had prepared. He also guaranteed a democratic regime to the New Mexicans, and declared his intention of holding the department "with its original boundaries (on both sides of the Rio Grande), as a part of the United States, and under the name of the Territory of Mexico," thus laying a part-basis for the heated controversy over the region east of the Rio Grande shortly to arise between New Mexico and Texas. Furthermore, he assured the New Mexicans that it was the purpose of the United States government to provide a free government similar to that in any other United States territory; and that soon he would call upon all citizens to cast their ballots for representatives to the territorial legislature. For the present Charles Bent was to be their governor.

These measures were not inaugurated too soon, for already rumblings of a revolution were heard. Kearny acted promptly. Accompanied by 500 infantry, 100 dragoons, and adequate artillery, he immediately set out for the south, the scene of the purported rebellion. Bernalillo, Albuquerque, Isleta, Peralta, and other towns were visited; but everywhere the Americans were accepted with a show of friendship, and they finally returned to Santa Fe to report that the New Mexicans were peaceably inclined.

On September 25, when it seemed that order was established in New Mexico, Kearny, accompanied by 300 dragoons under Colonel E. V. Sumner and Lieutenants W. H. Emory and W. H. Warner of the Topographical Engineers, left Santa Fe for California. Emory and Warner were to make observations on the feasibility of building a railway across this approach to the western coast, and in later years their report became a handbook for more than one California-bound emigrant. Kearny followed the old Coppermine trace down the Rio Grande to Socorro, and thence westward *via* the arid valley of the Gila River, through present Arizona. A short distance out of Socorro Kearny met a detachment of United States troops under the recently commissioned Lieutenant Kit Carson bound for Santa Fe carrying dispatches announcing the successful establishment of American control of California. This news was quite pleasing to Kearny. Much against his will, Carson was now detached from his small command to go with Kearny to California, and Sumner was sent back to Albuquerque with all but 100 dragoons. With these Kearny now hastened on westward with Carson as guide.

But hardly had he reached his destination before the long-rumored uprising in New Mexico came. Its instigator was Archuleta, who was disgruntled because Kearny had ignored his claims to the control of

New Mexico west of the Rio Grande. Price quickly mobilized his available forces and marched on Taos, the center of the disturbance. In the revolt, the Mexicans had killed Governor Bent, Sheriff Lee, Circuit Attorney J. W. Leal, Captain Burgwin, and about 20 other prominent officials. Archuleta was in southern New Mexico at the time the northern districts rose in revolt, but the revolutionists had their firebrand in Pablo Montoya, who styled himself "Santa Anna of the North." With the appearance of Price's troops (January 24, 1847), the revolutionists took refuge in an adobe church at Taos. Artillery employed by the soldiers made little impression on the thick walls of the building, so ladders were used and finally an entry was gained. The revolt was now at an end. Archuleta was soon notified by his confederates of the failure of the revolt, and fled the country. Upward of 150 revolutionists were killed and wounded, and Montoya and others were hanged for high treason—being tried by a makeshift court without jurisdiction.

Meanwhile the Chihuahua column was ready to move. Magoffin was sent on ahead to prepare the way for peaceful entry as he had done when Kearny's troops approached New Mexico. According to Benton, he attempted to win Mexican friends by lavish entertainment. "He was a social, generous-tempered man, a son of Erin; loved company, spoke Spanish fluently, entertained freely, and where it was some cost to entertain—claret, $36.00 a dozen, champagne, $50.00." But the Mexicans were suspicious of his mission, arrested him, and with the approach of Doniphan, sent him off to Durango for confinement until the end of the war.

Doniphan met with no great hindrance. From Valverde he marched southward *via* the dreaded *Jornada del Muerto*, El Paso, and thence to Chihuahua. At *Brazito* (Little Arm) on the east side of the Rio Grande near El Paso, he defeated a Mexican force of 1,000 men under General Ponce de Leon; and before the walls of Chihuahua he overwhelmed another, 4,000 strong, under General José A. Heredia, and occupied the city on March 2. Meanwhile General John E. Wool with 2,940 cavalry and infantry had also advanced from San Antonio, Texas, southward *via* Presidio del Rio Grande, Monclova, Parras, and Agua Nueva, a difficult journey of 300 miles within Mexico through a barren country covered with chaparral, greasewood, cactus, and mesquite. Presently both forces joined with that of General Zachary Taylor.

CALIFORNIA'S "BEAR FLAG" REVOLUTION

Professor R. N. Richardson points out that during the period 1825–1845 there were only two California administrations that were not beset by conspiracy and revolt. The *Californios* (native Californians of Spanish blood) were ever jealous of Mexican control and ready to oppose arbitrary exactions. In 1842 the Mexican government sent to California as governor Manuel Micheltorena, who was accompanied by a small force of ex-convicts to keep the peace. But the soldiers were little interested in law and order; presently they began annoying depredations against the Californians, who in turn besieged the governor with their complaints.

A short time previously, Commodore Thomas A. Catesby Jones, in command of the United States Pacific squadron, sailed into the harbor of Monterey and seized the town, acting upon the belief that the United States was at war with Mexico. When later he learned that war had not been declared, however, he hauled down the American flag, fired a salute to the Mexican colors and sailed away. The Mexican government authorities, as well as the local officials, were highly indignant at this "invasion," but were somewhat mollified when the United States made prompt apologies.

While the Californians were yet angry because of Jones' act, a local revolt headed by a former governor, Juan Bautista Alvarado, and the Commander General, José Castro, threatened to unseat the new governor. Micheltorena issued a decree to draft the American settlers into service. But he was not entirely successful; many of them volunteered to go with the revolutionists. In the desultory fighting and marching and countermarching which followed, there was little loss of life. A half-day's furious cannonading by rival batteries at Cahuenga Pass resulted in no fatalities. Presently the Americans, most of whom were hardy pioneers, became impatient with so much Mexican knight-errantry and refused to fight on either side. Thus deserted, Micheltorena had no other element upon which to rely, and finally withdrew from the country. Pio Pico now assumed the governorship and established his capital at Los Angeles; and Castro, in charge of the troops, occupied Monterey, where he could keep a watchful eye on the customs house.

But Pio Pico was also to have a stormy administration. On June 24, 1845, by order of President Polk of the United States, secret and confidential instructions were given to Commodore J. D. Sloat. "If you ascertain with certainty that Mexico has declared war against the United States," ran his orders, "you will at once possess yourself of the port of Saint [sic] Francisco, and blockade and occupy such other ports as your force may permit." Sloat's "force" consisted of five vessels, which for months had been kept on the California coast, ready and watchful. The commodore with two men-of-war was at Mazatlan, at the entrance of the Gulf of California; two ships were stationed off

Monterey; and another was at San Francisco. On July 7, 1846, when news came of Taylor's campaign along the Rio Grande, the period of waiting was ended. Promptly Sloat weighed anchor and sailed for Monterey, and a month later seized that place, raised the American flag, and issued a proclamation (in both English and Spanish) announcing that "Henceforward California will be a portion of the United States." On July 9, San Francisco was formally occupied, as was Los Angeles, the provincial capital, on August 13. Then four days later Commodore Robert F. Stockton, who succeeded Sloat, announced to the local citizens at Monterey that "The flag of the United States is now flying from every commanding position in the Territory, and California is entirely free from Mexican dominion. The Territory of California now belongs to the United States."

In May, 1845, shortly before Sloat had been given his instructions, Captain John C. Frémont, of the United States Topographical Engineers, had been dispatched by the Secretary of War to survey a new emigrant route to Oregon, and January, 1846, found him in California. He first visited the United States consul, Thomas O. Larkin, who went with him to call on Commandant Castro. Frémont informed the commandant that he was in California on a mission of peace. The latter was suspicious and asked if he had not invaded with a large force of United States troops. Frémont answered that he had not; he had with him only a few "hired men" (62 mountain men, the most of whom had been left beyond the settlements) to supply game and to afford him protection against the Indians. He had come westward, he said, to find a shorter route to Oregon than that generally followed by emigrants, and for other "scientific purposes." Winter had caught him in the mountains, and he had come to Monterey to request the privilege of making a winter camp in the San Joaquin Valley, where his hunters could find game and his horses would have grass. Castro gave the desired permission, and Frémont subsequently led his small band of 62 men to the Salinas River, about 30 miles from Monterey.

Hardly had he become settled in his new camp, however, before he received news that Castro was raising a force to attack him. About the same time, too, Larkin sent a messenger to his camp bearing a letter, warning that he had better leave the country, as Castro was attempting to arouse the people against him. Since the commandant had appeared amiable and friendly on the occasion of his recent visit, Frémont could hardly credit this news; but from the top of a nearby "sierra" (Hawk's Peak), looking through his field glass, he could see many horsemen assembling near the town, and others riding rapidly here and there. Now thoroughly alarmed, he fortified his camp and raised the American flag. Presently Castro approached with his troops but did not attack. He contented himself merely with a show of force, and then remained in the vicinity to await reinforcements.

On March 10 Frémont abandoned his camp and started for Oregon, traveling by easy stages. Hearing of the Americans' departure, Castro posted a notice in a Monterey billiard room informing the inhabitants that a band of highwaymen *(bandoleros)* "under Captain Frémont of the United States army" had entered Monterey, and that he and 200 patriots had expelled them and sent them into the back country. He asked that all patriotic citizens be on the alert for any similar invasion. The governor sought to make much of the debauchery of Frémont's men, and stated that three inebriates had called at the home of his uncle, Don Angel Castro, and had insulted Señorita Castro. When news of the affair was brought to Larkin, he made inquiry of the offended Don Angel and was told that three of Frémont's party had visited his *rancho* to buy beef. One was drunk and asked Señorita Castro to drink with him. Don Angel remonstrated, and, when serious altercation threatened, the drunken man's companions forcibly took him from the house. Thereupon Don Angel, now in the role of a local *alcalde,* mounted his horse and rode to Frémont's camp to demand satisfaction. He made formal complaint and demanded the payment of a fine of five dollars. Frémont received his visitor courteously, listened to his grievance, and, according to Larkin, paid him twice the amount asked. Concerning his reception by the Castros, Frémont later wrote to his wife: "The Spaniards were somewhat rude and inhospitable below, and ordered me out of the country after having given me permission to winter there. We retired growlingly before a force of three or four hundred men, and three pieces of artillery. . . . I did not dare compromise the United States." But he failed to add that, by raising the American flag over his fortified position, he had already done so.

On May 6 Frémont had reached Klamath Lake. "Here," said a contemporary, "he found mountains of the Sierra Nevada in front covered with snow, and himself and party surrounded by hostile Indians." In this condition of affairs he determined to return by the river Sacramento. He had heard that Castro was assembling a force at Sonoma to attack him and to destroy the American settlements on the *"Rio de los Americanos"* (American River). Two days later a local resident brought him word that an American officer was seeking him, so he immediately retraced his steps and met Lieutenant A. H. Gillespie, whom the President had sent to California to deliver a message to him and letters to Sloat and Larkin. Gillespie's actions were to have an important bearing on Frémont's next move, as now appears.

On November 3, 1845, after ordering Taylor to the Rio Grande and while Taylor was waiting with his army at Corpus Christi (five states having furnished him with most of his troops), Polk sent Gillespie as a personal agent westward with messages for Sloat, Larkin, and Frémont. He was sent to Vera Cruz, and thence traveled through Mexico to Mazatlan in the disguise of a merchant. After an interview with Sloat, he then proceeded to Monterey and called on Larkin. The contents of the Larkin letter are not known, for Gillespie later said that, before landing in Mexico, he destroyed it, having first committed it to memory. After delivering his message to Sloat, he then went in search of Frémont. "I was directed by Mr. Buchanan [Secretary of State] to confer with Colonel Frémont," he later explained, "and make known my instructions, which, as I have previously stated, were to watch over the interests of the United States, and counteract the influence of any foreign agents who might be in the country with objects prejudicial to the United States. I was also directed to show Colonel Frémont the duplicate of the dispatch to Mr. Larkin, telling him it was the wish of the Government to conciliate the feelings of the people of California, and encourage friendship towards the United States."

Immediately Frémont retraced his steps to California and visited the American settlements on the Sacramento River. Meanwhile Gillespie got in touch with the American warship at San Francisco; and its commander, according to the later testimony of Gillespie, "with great kindness, promptness and energy, furnished me with all the supplies he could spare from his vessel, as also having supplied Captain Frémont with a small sum of money." What these supplies were, the Lieutenant did not say, but it is probable that they consisted of guns and ammunition, as well as food and clothing. Gillespie conveyed them up the Sacramento, and on May 13 rejoined Frémont.

On June 11 Ezekiel Merrit and a mounted party of 12 settlers (undoubtedly aided by Frémont) surprised and captured a Mexican force of 15 men who were driving 200 horses to Castro's camp. Four days later, at daybreak, they seized the military post at Sonoma, together with 9 brass cannon, 250 muskets, and other arms and ammunition. Here also they took as prisoners several officers of rank—General Mariano G. Vallejo, his brother, Captain Salvador Vallejo, and others. In these hostile acts, Frémont lent encouragement, if not open aid. Then, fearing attack from the Mexicans, he traveled eastward to the American settlements to ask for assistance, but presently a courier arrived with the report that Castro was crossing San Francisco Bay to take Sonoma and to wipe out his small band. On June 23, Frémont started for Sonoma with 90 mounted men, traveling night and day, and reached his destination, 80 miles distant, at two o'clock on June 25. He arrived none too soon. Castro's vanguard of 70 dragoons under

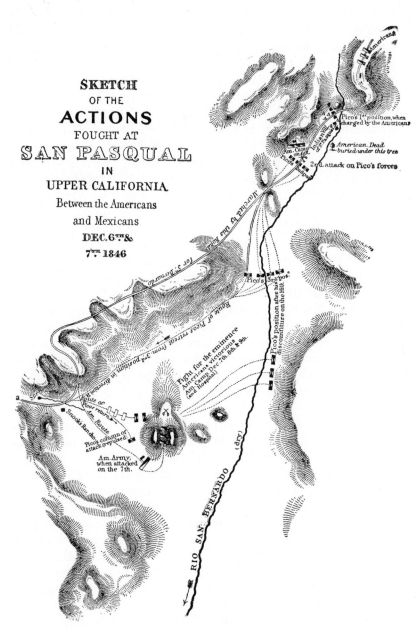

SKETCH
OF THE
ACTIONS
FOUGHT AT
SAN PASQUAL
IN
UPPER CALIFORNIA
Between the Americans
and Mexicans
DEC. 6ᵀᴴ &
7ᵀᴴ 1846

(FROM BREVET MAJOR W. H. EMORY, *Notes of a Military Reconnaissance, from Ft. Leavenworth in Missouri, to San Diego*, WASHINGTON, 1848.)

Joaquin de la Torre had crossed the bay, and these were attacked and defeated by 20 mounted riflemen of Frémont's command. The Americans were more than anxious to capture the commander of the Mexican force, for they had just learned that he had taken two of Frémont's dispatch carriers, who, "being bound to trees, were cut to pieces alive with knives."

Presently Frémont cut the bridges behind him. On July 4 he called the revolutionists together at Sonoma and addressed them. He advised that they declare their independence of Mexico and help him drive Castro and his followers from the country. This his listeners promptly did, raising over the town a flag carrying a red star and a bear, thus launching what was subsequently dubbed the "Bear Flag Republic." Having recruited from among them a force of 150 mounted men, Frémont started in pursuit of Castro. But before he had advanced far, he received an order from Commodore Sloat to come to Monterey. It is little wonder that the poorly armed and indifferently led Mexicans fled before him, for they had great fear of the trappers and mountain men who made up his command. On July 20 a local resident of Monterey thus reported to the editor of the Alexandria *Gazette:*

Colonel Frémont's party arrived here yesterday, having had some pretty hard fighting with the Mexicans and Indians. They number about two hundred, and are the most daring and hardy set of fellows I have ever looked upon. They are splendid marksmen and can plant a bullet in an enemy's head with their horses at full gallop. They never think of eating bread, but live upon meat all the time. They never sleep in a house but upon the ground, and with a blanket around them, their saddle for a pillow, and a rifle by their side.

On July 22, 1846, before Frémont had reached Monterey, Commodore Stockton had assumed command of the United States naval forces on the West Coast. Three days later he sent a warship, the *Cayane,* southward with the "California company of mounted riflemen" under Frémont to San Diego to land south of Castro's retreating force, but the pursued halted and occupied a strong position near Los Angeles. Consequently, Stockton, a few days later, sailed in the *Congress* for San Pedro, where he landed his "gallant sailor army" for an assault on Castro's position. But when he approached within 12 miles, the Mexicans "ran for the city of Mexico"; and on August 13, having been joined by Frémont and Larkin, Stockton entered Los Angeles *(de Nuestra Señora La Reina de Los Angelos).* Thus the conquest of California was complete. Only minor revolt in southern California challenged American control, but it, too, was quickly suppressed. In December Kearny arrived, having come *via* the Yuma route. During the latter part of their march, his troops had suffered greatly in crossing

308 "THE COURSE OF EMPIRE"

the 90-mile barren waste of what is now the Imperial Valley, and were little prepared for their unfriendly reception by the Mexicans. But after the latter were repulsed in the battle of San Pasqual, no more trouble was encountered, for presently a relief column of 215 sailors and 80 marines in charge of Lieutenant A. F. V. Gray arrived and escorted them to San Diego.

Although the Mexican uprising was soon suppressed, dissension presently appeared in American ranks. Acting under his previous instructions, Kearny demanded of Stockton that he desist from all further efforts to organize a civil government. The latter replied indignantly that his own authority was supreme. Frémont sided with Stockton, and soon thereafter the commodore appointed him governor and commander-in-chief. On February 15, 1847, the controversy was settled when Kearny received confirmation of his authority. He now ordered Frémont to bring to Monterey all the public records, but the latter, not knowing of Stockton's new instructions, refused. Thus he became technically guilty of insubordination, and was later tried and convicted. Attempting to maintain the traditional *esprit de corps* of the army, President Polk approved the sentence but remitted the penalty. Frémont now felt that he had been grossly mistreated, and resigned his commission.

Justin H. Smith, the Mexican War historian, characterized Frémont as an adventurer and political opportunist. This may be true, but it is equally certain that his efforts were largely the cause of the success of the "Bear Flag" revolution. It is more than probable that Mexico would have lost this part of her domain even had she remained at peace with the United States. And permanent separation of California from Mexico ultimately would have led to its annexation to the United States.

TREATY OF GUADALUPE HIDALGO

When news reached Washington late in October, 1847, of brilliant American victories in Mexico, a wave of popular enthusiasm swept the country. Almost immediately the national press urged the incorporation of the whole of Mexico into the United States. This greatly alarmed Northern abolitionists, for throughout the South not only was there sentiment for the absorption of Mexico, but also for the extension of slavery thereto. The Charleston *Courier* expressed its satisfaction that "Every battle fought in Mexico, and every dollar spent there, but insures the acquisition of territory which must widen the field of Southern enterprize and power for the future." The "Southern enterprize" concept was amplified somewhat by a Georgia paper, the *Fed-*

eral Union, which explained that "New York, the great emporium of commerce must be shorn in part of her greatness. Exchange, usually in her favor, must now be reversed, and in favor of New Orleans, where the supplies are furnished the army." And in view of the fact that the South was becoming overcrowded with slaves, the *Mobile Herald* suggested that, "by taking new territory in the direction of Mexico," a new field of exploitation could be opened.

Yet the imperialistic demands were not entirely of Southern origin. In the President's cabinet, the Secretaries of State and Treasury, James Buchanan and Robert J. Walker, advocated annexation of the whole of Mexico. *Niles' Weekly Register* (LXXIII, 113) quoted the Washington *Union* in praise of Mexico as a land of opportunity for the United States, in favor of "occupying that beautiful country," and urged the whole press of the Union to join the chorus so that "we shall see the Aztec and American eagles clasping wings, and our Yankee boys swapping knicknacks with the Americanized Rancheros for gold!" Such Northern politicians as Dickinson of New York and Hannegan of Indiana were just as ardent in their championship of imperialism. On the other hand, John C. Calhoun, the acknowledged champion of Southern interests, was opposed to acquiring the whole of Mexico. He believed that it was inconsistent with the avowed object of the war, and "a departure from the settled policy of the government."

There were certain other advocates, in both the North and South, for the acquisition of only a part of northern Mexico, in addition to New Mexico and California; and among these was President Polk. In August, 1846, he asked Congress to appropriate $2,000,000 to be used in carrying on peace negotiations with Mexico, obviously to be employed in purchasing additional territory. Benton charged that Polk was to use a part of this money to bribe Santa Anna to work for peace and territorial cessions to the United States, and pointed out that already the American warships in the Gulf had allowed him to go unmolested from Cuba to Mexico. Soon after the President had made his request, an appropriation bill was introduced in the House of Representatives by James J. McKay of North Carolina. Northern members became alarmed that the expenditure proposal might be of Southern origin, and David Wilmot of Pennsylvania offered a proviso that "neither slavery nor involuntary servitude" should ever exist in any part of the territory so acquired, "except for crime, whereof the party shall first be duly convicted." Although Southern representatives attacked the rider and sought to prevent its passage, it was accepted by a vote of 85 to 79 and sent to the Senate. But before it could be acted upon here, Congress adjourned. At the next session, in

December, again Wilmot proposed his amendment, but after a hard fight it was voted down.

Meanwhile, on April 15, 1847, President Polk had dispatched Nicholas P. Trist, Chief Clerk of the Department of State, to join General Scott and to negotiate a treaty of peace with Mexican commissioners. Trist arrived at Vera Cruz early in May and immediately apprised Scott of his presence. But the latter felt greatly affronted. He wrote Trist that Secretary of War W. L. Marcy was attempting "to degrade" him, and to promote a "clerk" of another department. He insisted that he alone was empowered to treat with the Mexicans. For this he was called to task by the irate Marcy. But in a subsequent letter, in amplifying his Trist statement, Scott explained that a few months past Thomas Hart Benton had boasted that, if he were chosen by the President to lead the army of invasion, he would also be intrusted with power to conclude a treaty. Thus, it seemed logical that if Polk had made such a promise to Benton, he should likewise clothe the present commander with peace-making powers. So for several weeks there was carried on an angry correspondence in which not only Trist and Scott, but also Marcy and Buchanan, took part. With some asperity, in his first reply to Scott, Trist had insisted that he would not engage in a war of words; he had been sent on a different mission. But presently Scott twitted him by writing that he had received from him 30 pages of letters, which he had not time to read. Yet naïvely he stated in the next paragraph that their import was "a farrago of indolence, conceit, and arrogance!"

This war of words caused Pork and Buchanan great concern, for it might defeat the purpose of Trist's mission, and finally the former ordered his bellicose agent to abandon his assignment and return home. Trist had been equally offensive to Polk, as is thus manifested in the latter's *Diary* (III, 300–301): "His [Trist's] dispatch is arrogant, impudent, and very insulting to his government, and even personally offensive." But in the meantime Trist had joined Scott's forces, and soldier and diplomat presently effected a reconciliation.

Had Trist obeyed his instructions and returned to the United States, there is little doubt that ultimately Mexico would have fared far worse than under the proposed American peace terms. On this point Julius Klein writes: "Had a certain train left the City of Mexico on the 4th of December, the future of America would have been changed." He refers here to a train which would have conveyed Trist from the Mexican capital to the coast, bound for the United States. E. G. Bourne gives strength to this assertion in another study, in which he traces the growth of the movement for the annexation of Mexico.

As charged by Benton, it is more than probable that President Polk and General Scott arrived at a secret agreement with Santa Anna whereby he was to use his influence for peace and for the United States annexation demands, although Polk indignantly denied complicity. Scott later admitted that he had made certain secret disbursements "to purchase valuable information"; and Wilfrid Hardy Calcott writes that, as Scott approached Mexico City, he "called upon his secret service funds for an advance payment, reported to have been $10,000, 'to overcome the resistance of members of [the Mexican] Congress.'" Trist, who was with Scott at this time, lends credence to this assertion by saying: "Last night, a letter was received from the intended recipient of the million [$1,000,000 was the amount reported to have been offered Santa Anna], showing that the business is rapidly and satisfactorily maturing." It may be added, however, that such an expenditure was of no material consequence; for, after Scott occupied Mexico City, Santa Anna resigned his provisional presidency, and Mexico came perilously close to the brink of anarchy.

When Scott approached Mexico City, he halted, and agreed to an armistice with Santa Anna (August 27–September 7, 1847) in order that Trist might negotiate with the Mexican commissioners. But Trist's terms were not acceptable. He demanded the cession of the disputed territory between the Nueces and the Rio Grande, of both Upper and Lower California, and of New Mexico. The Mexicans countered with a proposal to make the international boundary begin in Corpus Christi Bay; thence to the mouth of the Nueces and up the middle of this stream to its source; thence west to the eastern boundary of New Mexico, and northward along this line to the thirty-seventh degree of latitude; and thence west with that parallel to the Pacific. They likewise promised not to colonize the region beyond the Rio Grande and the Nueces.

When Trist announced the failure of negotiations, Scott resumed his advance and captured Mexico City. In the meantime, various documents had been issued by the Mexican authorities, indicating that Mexico was not ready for peace. One was a protest of representatives of the states of Mexico, Jalisco, and Zacatecas, signed by Valentin Gómez Farías and his colleague deputies, declaring that, under existing circumstances, "the City of Mexico would not allow the necessary freedom in its discussions and deliberations, if congress should assemble in that city, and that it would not comport with the dignity of the republic that its representatives should deliberate there on this matter [treaty cessions]." At the same time the Mexican Secretary of State issued a circular to the states of Puebla and Mexico, calling for a levy *en masse*, "in order that they may attack and harass the enemy with whatever weapons each may conveniently procure, whether good or bad, by fire and sword, and by every practicable means which it is possible to employ in the annihilating of an invading army." But cooler heads ultimately prevailed. A provisional government was set up under the resourceful Peña y Peña; Trist once more met the Mexican commissioners at Guadalupe Hidalgo; and on February 2, 1848, an agreement was signed. By its terms the international boundary was along the Rio Grande to New Mexico and thence westward *via* the Gila River to the Colorado; and from thence along the divisional line of Upper and Lower California. The United States thus gained undisputed control over Texas as far south as the Rio Grande, and acquired New Mexico and California, for which it agreed to pay $15,000,000 and assume the payment of all American claims against Mexico, totalling $3,208,315. In addition, the United States was given the right of transit and passage across the Isthmus of Tehuantepec. For three weeks after the treaty was presented to the United States Senate, ratification was delayed. Trist was denounced for his insubordination, and more than one Northern Senator could see only a Southern plan to extend slavery in the annexation of so much territory. But finally on March 16, the President ratified the treaty after the Senate had approved it by the requisite two-thirds majority. Thus, at a war cost of 12,000 lives and more than $100,000,000, the United States had acquired a domain approximately two and one-half times as great as France.

BIBLIOGRAPHY

There are several general studies on the westward movement which have concise chapters relating to the Mexican War period. Among these are R. E. Riegel, *America Moves West* (New York, 1930); Frederick L. Paxson, *History of the American Frontier, . . .* (Boston, etc., 1924); Cardinal Goodwin, *The Trans-Mississippi West . . .* (New York, 1922); and R. N. Richardson and C. C. Rister, *The Greater Southwest* (Glendale, 1934).

Justin H. Smith, *War with Mexico* (2 vols., New York, 1919), and George Lockhart Rives, *The United States and Mexico, 1821–1848* (2 vols., New York, 1913) yet remain the two most thorough accounts, although both should be supplemented by parallel reading in J. S. Reeves, *American Diplomacy under Tyler and Polk* (Baltimore, 1907). N. W. Stephenson, *Texas and the Mexican War* (in *Chronicles of America*, XXIV, New Haven, 1921) is decidedly a more readable and less voluminous narrative, and dependable.

Earlier accounts are also helpful. J. Frost, *The Mexican War and Its Warriors* (New Haven, etc., 1850) presents a fair composite picture of the entire war movement, as does also Edward D. Mansfield, *The Mexican War: A History of Its Origin* (New York, 1848). William Jay, *A Review of the Causes and Consequences of the Mexican War* (Boston, 1849) is violently anti-Southern, but it is valuable as a presentation of the abolitionists' point of view. Thomas Hart Benton, *Thirty Years' View . . .* (2 vols., New York, 1889), II, is the typical "manifest destiny" perspective. Captain

W. S. Henry, *Campaign Sketches of the War with Mexico* (New York, 1847) is in large part a diary kept by the author while accompanying Taylor's army, and has much of interest on the routine experiences of the army of occupation. In this class, two republished accounts are Ralph P. Bieber (ed.), *Marching with the Army of the West, 1846–1848*, by Abraham Robinson Johnston, Marcellus Ball Edwards, Philip Gooch Ferguson (in *Southwestern Historical Series*, IV, Glendale, 1936); ————, *Journal of a Soldier under Kearny and Doniphan, 1846–1847*, by George Rutledge Gibson (*ibid.*, Glendale, 1935).

The conquest of New Mexico and California is the basis for several reliable narratives. H. H. Bancroft, *A History of California* (7 vols., San Francisco, 1884–1890), V; ————, *History of Arizona and New Mexico* (New York, 1889); and ————, *North Mexican States and Texas* (2 vols., New York, 1889), II, are storehouses of information relating to the Southwest before, during, and after the Mexican War. William H. Emory, *Notes of a Military Reconnaissance from Fort Leavenworth in Missouri to San Diego in California* . . . (Washington, 1848) is a full official report of General S. W. Kearny's expedition, and an excellent description of the southern overland route to California. More writers, however, have exploited the Doniphan expedition, a few accounts of which are Colonel John T. Hughes, *Doniphan's Expedition and the Conquest of New Mexico and California* (Cincinnati, 1847; reprinted in W. E. Connelly, *War with Mexico*, Topeka, 1907); Stella M. Drumm, *Down the Santa Fé Trail and into Mexico; The Diary of Susan Shelby Magoffin, 1846–1847* (New Haven, 1926); Frank S. Edwards, *A Campaign in New Mexico with Colonel Doniphan* (London, 1848); and Adolphus Wislizenus, *Memoir of a Tour to Northern Mexico, Connected with Colonel Doniphan's Expedition in 1846 and 1847* (Washington, 1848). George F. Ruxton, an Englishman who traveled from Mexico City to Santa Fe *via* Chihuahua during the early days of the war, made interesting observations on the condition of the region through which he passed in his *Adventures in Mexico and the Rocky Mountains* (London, 1849).

Robert G. Cleland, *History of California, the American Period* (New York, 1922) is a well-balanced work on California. John Walton Caughey, *History of the Pacific Coast of North America* (New York, 1938) is a newer work, and contains a chapter on "The Acquisition of California." A popular one-volume work is Rockwell and Nellie Van de Grift Sanchez, *A Short History of California* (New York, 1929). Earlier accounts are Samuel H. Willey, *The Transition Period of California* . . . *1846–1850* (San Francisco, 1901); J. O. Thornton, *Oregon and California in 1848* (2 vols., New York, 1849); E. Bryant, *What I saw in California* (New York, 1848); J. M. Cutts, *The Conquest of California and New Mexico* (Philadelphia, 1847); and Walter Colton, *Three Years in California* (New York, 1850).

Helpful biographies, recollections, and diaries are Wilfrid Hardy Calcott, *Santa Anna, The Story of an Enigma Who Once was Mexico* (Norman, 1936); Frank C. Hanighen, *Santa Anna, The Napoleon of the West* (New York, 1934); Clarence R. Wharton, *El Presidente, A Sketch of the Life of General Santa Anna* (Houston, 1924); Waddy Thompson, *Recollections of Mexico* (New York, 1846); Justin H. Smith, *Polk and California* (Extracts from Massachusetts Historical Society *Publications*, December, 1916–January, 1917); Milo Milton Quaife (ed.), *The Diary of James K. Polk during His Presidency, 1845–1849* . . . (4 vols., Chicago, 1910); William Starr

Myers, *The Mexican War Diary of George B. McClellan* (Princeton, 1917);
P. S. G. Cooke, *Conquest of New Mexico and California* (New York, 1878);
F. S. Dellenbaugh, *Frémont and '49* (New York, 1914); John Charles
Frémont, *Memoirs of My Life . . .* (New York, 1887); J. R. Fry and R. T.
Conrad, *Life of Z. Taylor* (Philadelphia, 1847); *General Taylor's Life,
Battles and Dispatches* (Philadelphia, 1847); O. O. Howard, *General Taylor*
(New York, 1892); E. D. Mansfield, *General W. Scott* (New York, 1852);
and M. J. Wright, *General Scott* (New York, 1894).

Julius Klein, "The Making of the Treaty of Guadaloupe Hidalgo, on
February 2, 1848," in the *University Chronicle*, VII, Berkeley, 1905, No.
4, was the James Bryce Historical Prize essay for 1905, and is one of a few
well-written sketches of this period. Others include Clayton Charles Kohl,
Claims as a Cause of the Mexican War (in New York University Series of
Graduate School Studies, No. 2, New York, 1914); Robert Glass Cleland,
"The Early Sentiment for the Annexation of California: An Account of the
Growth of American Interest in California, 1835–1846," in *Southwestern
Historical Quarterly*, XVIII (Austin, 1915), Nos. 1, 2, 3.

The march of the Mormon Battalion is discussed in Daniel Tyler, *A Concise History of the Mormon Battalion in the Mexican War* (Salt Lake City,
1881); and Frank Alfred Golder (in collaboration with Thomas A. Bailey
and J. Lyman Smith), *The March of the Mormon Battalion* (New York and
London, 1928).

Documentary sources on the Mexican War are fairly accessible. *Niles'
National Register*, Vols. LXIX–LXXI, contains various contemporary news
items, letters, and narratives on every phase of the war, as do also House
and Senate documents. Other printed source materials are also available,
such as Justin H. Smith, "Letters of General Antonio Lopez de Santa Anna
Relating to the War between the United States and Mexico, 1846–1848," in
Annual Report of the American Historical Association for the Year 1917
(Washington, 1917); George P. Garrison, *Diplomatic Correspondence of the
Republic of Texas* (2 vols., Washington, 1908, 1911); and *Messages of the
President of the United States, with the Correspondence, Therewith Com-
municated, between the Secretary of War and other Officers of the Govern-
ment, of the Subject of the Mexican War* (in *House Executive Documents*,
30th Congress, 1st Session, No. 60, 2 vols.).

19

CALIFORNIA BECOMES AN AMERICAN STATE

$\mathcal{T}$HE STORY of the beginnings of settlement in California and a brief account of development in the region before 1800 were presented in a previous chapter. The chain of impressive missions, the presidios and pueblos established there, continued their slow but steady growth during the early years of the succeeding century. Hundreds of Indians lived at the missions, watching the flocks and herds, tending the orchards and fields. With thrifty husbandry the friars directed the labor of their neophytes and built up the material resources of their establishments. The hundreds of acres of cultivated land and the thousands of head of stock about the more prosperous missions appear to controvert the vows of poverty to which the missionaries had subscribed. And toward this accumulated wealth avid eyes were turned.

PASTORAL CALIFORNIA

The original intention of the Spanish government in authorizing and aiding missions was to convert the natives into peaceful, law-abiding, taxpaying subjects; while the missionaries were intent on saving their souls and raising them in the scale of civilization. The government looked upon the mission as a temporary institution that would quickly achieve its objective in a given area and then move on to new frontiers. Accordingly, the initial regulations provided a ten-year period for the operation of a mission, after which the settlement was to be converted into a civilian town with the natives as citizens. But in California, as elsewhere, practical experience proved that the desired result could not be attained in the period specified, and so the missions were continued decade after decade.

While the Indians made some progress toward civilization, they were still children in respect to mental and social development; and to hold

315

them to their tasks physical discipline was necessary. This restraint was incompatible with the principles of freedom with which the new Republic of Mexico was imbued. And so after 1822 a stronger sentiment developed for the secularization of the missions—for the breakup of the holdings and the distribution of the property. Persons primarily concerned over the freeing of the Indians were joined by individuals interested in the breaking up of the missions and the resultant opportunities for appropriating land and livestock. Between the sentimental republicans and the unscrupulous land-grabbers, the demand became so insistent that it finally succeeded.

The Mexican decree ordering secularization of the 21 missions of California was issued in 1833. It provided that secular priests should replace the missionaries in caring for the spiritual welfare of the Indians, but no adequate provision was made for disposal of the mission property. To Governor Figueroa fell the difficult task of executing the decree. Thinking persons in the region recognized that the change ought to be effected gradually, and that sudden emancipation of the Indians would be disastrous. The able Governor stretched the law as much as he dared, and arranged for its gradual execution. He emancipated such Indians as were best fitted for liberty, and allotted them land, stock, implements, and seed. He secularized the first ten missions in 1834, giving orders that half of the property be divided among the resident Indians and the remainder be placed in the hands of an administrator at each mission. Indians were forbidden to sell their land or chattels. Administrators were appointed for six more missions in 1835 and for the remaining five the following year. Figueroa died in 1835, and the problem of secularization was thereafter in less capable hands. To make matters worse, a series of political upheavals encouraged graft and inefficiency. Many administrators, left to their own devices, enriched themselves and their friends, while other individuals preyed on the childlike natives and defrauded them of their holdings. The Indian pueblos that supplanted the missions were failures. Many of the natives, freed from mission discipline, refused to work, squandered their property, and fled to the wild frontier tribes or sank to degradation about the settlements and ranches. Others hired themselves to ranchmen and became virtual slaves on the *ranchos*. Finally, just before the American conquest of California in 1846, the remains of the once glorious missions were auctioned off to private purchasers. The Indians decreased rapidly, and the remnants were to be practically trampled out of existence in the days of the gold rush.

During the early decades California had been primarily a missionary province; and at the end of the Spanish regime (1821), the mission property comprised the major part of the wealth of California. The missionaries opposed the giving of land to individual white settlers; but with the establishment of the Mexican Republic, a new policy was inaugurated. Liberal inducements were offered to settlers by the government. By the law of 1824, Mexicans of good character, and foreigners who would accept Catholicism and become naturalized, might acquire free 11 square leagues of land (almost 50,000 acres). Mexican officials also undertook to promote settlement by making California a penal colony. Over 100 convicts were sent there in 1826 and 80 more in 1830. Designing persons launched a colonizing project to utilize mission land. Yerba Buena (later to become San Francisco), Sonoma, and a few other towns were started. On land grants given to individuals numbers of large ranches developed.

The establishment of these ranches was the most notable development in California during the Mexican period (1822–1846). Horses and cattle were borrowed from the missions to stock many of these places, and in time almost every Californian had a ranch. Those holdings devoted to stock raising were called *ranchos,* those utilized for growing crops were *haciendas;* and the two were frequently combined. Some of these estates were of modest proportions, while others contained approximately 100,000 acres. Francisco Pacheco owned 90,000 acres, stocked with 14,000 cattle, 500 horses, and 15,000 sheep. Henry D. Fitch owned 14,000 cattle, 1,000 horses, and 10,000 sheep. Abel Stearns grazed 30,000 cattle; Mariano Vallejo had a princely domain; Sutter received a full grant of 11 square leagues. The land on which have risen the cities of Oakland, Berkeley, and Alameda was once but part of the ranch of Don Luis Peralta. W. H. Davis states that over 1,000 land grants were given by California governors during the Mexican period, and that on them grazed over 1,000,000 head of stock. Cattle raising was now the chief industry of California. In the absence of fences, the *rodeo,* or round-up, was developed for gathering, separating, and branding the stock. At intervals slaughterings occurred; men rode through the herds and killed the animals by a thrust of the knife in a vital part of the neck. Then came skinners and butchers to take the hides and cut up the meat into strips for drying. The tallow was melted and run into bags made of hides.

Although secondary to cattle, sheep were of importance for wool and mutton. On hand looms the wool was made into coarse cloth and blankets. Hogs were raised solely for their lard, which was used principally in soap-making. Some flax and hemp were grown and converted into ropes and textiles.

The farming was primitive. Plowing was done with an iron point attached to a forked pole. Grain was cut with sickles; and the bound sheaves, after being placed on a fenced plot of hard ground, were threshed by the tramping of cattle. By winnowing in the breeze, the grain was separated from the chaff. Stone pestles and mortars were at first used for grinding the wheat, but crude grist mills were later introduced.

Manufactured goods and luxuries were largely obtained through foreign commerce. New England whaling and fur-gathering vessels early touched at the California coast to get fresh food supplies. They found there an eager demand for Yankee notions, and a flourishing trade developed despite governmental prohibitions. The Californians offered hides and tallow at very attractive prices, and these commodities soon became the principal articles of export. Richard Henry Dana, who visited the region as a young man, has left us an excellent account of the hide and tallow trade in his *Two Years Before the Mast*.

The large *ranchos* were patriarchal establishments that were nearly self-sufficient. Each produced the food needed for the family of the *ranchero* and for the many Indian servants in the house and fields. The dwelling houses were usually built of adobe, with plastered walls and dirt floors. Many were embowered with blooms and surrounded with lovely gardens and orchards. Little furniture was in evidence, but the women lavished attention on the beds, which were usually covered with elegant lace or silk spreads. The women were skillful seamstresses.

Much attention was paid to dress. The well-to-do *ranchero* was quite a dandy, with knee breeches of velvet or satin, silk vest, short jacket embroidered with gold and silver thread, a red satin sash about his waist, and a wide sombrero tipped jauntily on one side of his head. His spirited horse was gorgeous with embroidered trappings, elaborate bridle, and a handsome saddle with mountings of silver. An American in 1829 describes the dress of the women as consisting of "a chemise with short embroidered sleeves, richly trimmed with lace, a muslin petticoat flounced with scarlet and secured at the waist by a silk band of the same color, shoes of velvet or blue satin, a cotton rebozo, or scarf, pearl necklace and earrings, with the hair falling in broad plaits down the back."

Amusements were important in the life of the Spanish Californians. Hunting of bears, elk, and wild horses was a favorite sport. Bull and bear fights, in which these two animals fought each other to the death, were a popular form of entertainment. Horse racing and cock fighting were enjoyed. Picnics, frequent and prodigal, were followed by singing to the accompaniment of strumming guitars. But dancing was the favorite form of amusement. Every notable event, from births to official ceremonies, was celebrated with a dance. Guests from miles around would gather at a *rancho,* and the festivities would frequently last for days.

California during this pastoral period has been variously pictured. Some have portrayed it as an adorable Arcadia, where life was simple and easy, no one was hurried, and everyone was happy and satisfied. Women were beautiful, men were bold; life was a succession of merry-making, love-making, and lavish hospitality. Distance has, of course, lent enchantment to the scene. To the early Anglo-American, the picture was less romantic. He reports the typical Californian of that day as a "dirty, idle, shiftless, treacherous, tawdry vagabond dwelling in a disgracefully primitive house, and backward in every aspect of civilization." Between the extremes the truth lies. Foreign visitors generally expressed surprise at the backwardness of the people in a land of such rich resources, but they uniformly testified to the personal charm of the people and to their boundless hospitality.

Early Anglo-American Intrusions

The earliest foreigners reached California on trading vessels. Though the trade was illegal, it flourished; and though foreigners were forbidden to enter Spanish territory, some flaunted the law and remained in the enchanting land. When the province changed from Spanish to Mexican hands, the hostility toward foreigners was mitigated somewhat. And as Americans married into California families and became naturalized citizens, their illegal entry was forgiven. Although the first intruders came by sea, others soon followed by land. Jedediah Smith led his band of Rocky Mountain trappers to southern California in 1826 and returned the following year. He opened two land routes across present Utah and Nevada—one from Salt Lake to Los Angeles, and one from the Sacramento region to the Great Salt Lake. The James Ohio Pattie party of trappers reached San Diego early in 1828. Some of the men remained in the region and became permanent residents of California. These initial companies of American fur gatherers were followed by others under such leaders as Ewing Young, William Wolfskill, and Joseph R. Walker.

By the middle thirties the American intruders were present in sufficient numbers to cause some alarm in Mexican officialdom. At the same time a new generation of Californians was rising—the first "native sons"—who were proud and ambitious. Why should not some of these able men be placed in official positions? They were becoming critical of Mexican leaders and Mexican methods of government. Foreign residents fanned the discontent and emphasized the neglect and ill treatment that California had suffered under Mexican rule. In

1836 Juan Bautista Alvarado, a 27-year-old Californian, led a revolt and made himself governor of "the free and independent sovereign state of Alta California." Alvarado gladly accepted the aid of the Tennessee hunter, Isaac Graham, and his motley following of ex-sailors and reformed trappers. Though the quickly won independence was short-lived, Alvarado cleverly retained his executive position and continued as governor while the "sovereign state" returned to its provincial status. But when once established and safely backed by the Mexican government, he forgot the American aid that had helped him rise, and became suspicious of the foreigners. Rumors reached him that the Americans were planning an uprising, and he feared that the recent revolution in Texas might be duplicated on the Pacific Coast. So in 1840 he had Graham, his one-time confederate, and 100 American and English residents arrested for plotting an insurrection. The men were tried and some were sent to Mexico, but all were ultimately released. The incident did not allay suspicions; instead, it increased ill will.

Among the foreigners who came to California before 1840, none was destined for greater fame than Johann August Sutter. This Swiss had come to the United States, traversed the Oregon Trail, sailed to Hawaii, and then landed in California in 1839. With his magnetic personality, his tactful ways, and his sheaf of favorable recommendations, he impressed Governor Alvarado, who invited him to become a Mexican citizen and select a tract of land for development. Sutter chose a princely domain in the Sacramento Valley far in the interior and well removed from possible interference. Here he built Fort Sutter, and rapidly developed New Helvetia (New Switzerland).

By 1840 the population of California was still sparse and the extent of immigration meager. The total population amounted to less than 6,000 (exclusive of Indians), and of these the foreigners numbered fewer than 400. A large majority of the latter had come by sea. But a new birth was imminent. The destiny of the region was in the womb of white-topped wagons.

In 1841 the first avowed homeseekers made their way to the Pacific Coast. They were prompted to the venture by glowing stories brought back to Missouri by fur gatherers. California was pronounced a "perfect paradise, a land of perpetual spring." The country was free from chills and fever, an important boon to Missouri Valley sufferers. "There never was but one man in California who had the ague," said trapper Robidoux. "He was from Missouri and carried the disease in his system. It was such a curiosity to see a man shake with the chills that the people of Monterey went eighteen miles into the country to watch him."

The factors listed in a previous chapter as operative in promoting emigration to Oregon applied with equal force to California. In fact, the first Pacific-bound company was to split into two equal parts at Soda Springs, present Idaho, half going to Oregon and half to California.

The California contingent was led by Captain John Bartleson, with John Bidwell as secretary and historian. Having traversed the well-known Oregon Trail along the Platte, over South Pass, and to the Soda Springs on Bear River, the party now faced the most dangerous part of the journey. They had no guide, and the country was but little known. From some trappers they learned that Mary's (the Humboldt) River was the life-saving stream along their proposed course. If they went too far south, they would lose themselves in the dry and barren desert; if they struck too far north, they would be lost in trackless deserts and canyons. Joseph R. Walker's band of Bonneville trappers had reached the Humboldt River eight years before, and had safely reached the Pacific Coast. The emigrants hoped to do as well. Thirty-two men, one woman, and a child set bravely forth. They skirted the Great Salt Lake and the dry salt desert. Tormented with thirst and fearful of disaster through delay, the emigrants deserted their wagons and packed a minimum of essentials on the backs of their mules and oxen. Finally, on September 23, they reached the Humboldt. Along this stream to its sink they made their way, turned southwest, and ascended Walker River into the Sierra Nevada. The difficult crossing of the high mountains was finally accomplished, and the weary, foot-sore emigrants reached the California Valley. They found succor near Mt. Diablo at the ranch of Dr. John Marsh, Harvard graduate and notable American frontiersman. They had opened an emigrant path, had blazed the California Trail.

Another company (some 25 persons), composed in part of home-seekers and in part of traders, made its way to California in the same year (1841) by a southern route. It is known as the Workman-Rowland Company, and was assembled at Santa Fe. Part of its members had recently journeyed over the Santa Fe Trail; others were American traders who had resided for some years in New Mexico. They set out from the frontier outpost of Abiquiu in September, driving along a flock of sheep to serve as food. They traveled on horseback and with pack animals, following the well-marked Old Spanish Trail, the trader route between Santa Fe and Los Angeles. Two months of travel brought them safely through Cajon Pass and to southern California. Rowland presented to the Mexican officials a list of the Americans and declared his intention to comply with the law of the region.

Each year thereafter, emigrant bands journeyed overland to California. But during the remaining years of Mexican jurisdiction, the companies were comparatively small; the heavy American migration was directed toward Oregon and Texas, in an effort to win those debatable areas for the United States. The Chiles-Walker party of 1843 was the first to bring wagons overland to California. Led by the Mountain Man, Joe Walker, the main band, upon reaching the Humboldt Sink, continued southward and finally crossed the Sierras in the vicinity of Owen's Lake and Walker's Pass.

A small party from Oregon came to California in 1843. It was led by Lansford W. Hastings, of the Oregon emigration of the preceding year. He was to return to the States in 1844 and publish the following year a guide book that was to aid travelers and direct homeseekers to California.

Early in 1844, John C. Frémont led his band of explorers into California. He had made a trip over the Oregon Trail to South Pass in 1842, and the following year had gone to Oregon. From the Dalles in late November, 1843, he turned south by way of Klamath and Pyramid Lakes, and with great hardihood effected a crossing of the Sierra Nevadas in midwinter. After recuperating at Sutter's Fort, he moved south through California and followed the Old Spanish Trail eastward. He circled and named the Great Basin of Nevada and Utah. The report of this expedition, published as a government document, was to serve as a guide to Oregon and California emigrants.

A few of those trekking the Oregon Trail in 1844 were met at Fort Hall by old Greenwood, carrying a recommendation from Captain Sutter in favor of settlement in California. The most important group taking Sutter's advice was led by Elisha Stephens. It took an almost due westward course after reaching the Sink of the Humboldt, following up the Truckee River, from the vicinity of present Reno, crossed the mountains by a course generally paralleling the railroad, and reached Sutter's Fort. This came to be the principal route of the California Trail.

Of the westbound emigration of 1845, California received an accession of some 250, coming in at least five distinct companies. Special efforts were made at Fort Hall to divert Oregon-bound emigrants to California. As a result, the homeseekers who came overland to California in 1846 probably equaled those of the five preceding years. The Truckee River route was the favorite trail. Ex-Governor L. W. Boggs of Missouri and his family were California-bound this year. Edwin Bryant, in his *What I Saw in California*, gives the principal contemporary account of the year's emigration. The Donner party, however, is most famous, because of the tragedy it experienced.

This group, under the leadership of George Donner, left the main emigrant trail at Fort Bridger, present southwestern Wyoming, to take a cut-off route to the south of the Great Salt Lake. It was recommended by L. W. Hastings and was reported to be 200 miles shorter than the regular route to the north of the Lake.

Great difficulties were encountered in making a road over the mountains to the Salt Lake, and a precious month's time was consumed in accomplishing it. Then came the hot and barren salt desert. The crossing was a terrible ordeal in which many of the animals perished. But by middle September the party finally reached the Humboldt and continued in the regular trail beside it.

The delay caused by taking the "cut-off" was to prove fatal. The company was caught in an early snowstorm of the high Sierras. Day after day the snow fell. All the cattle perished, buried under the trees where they sought shelter. At the place now known as Donner Lake, the men hastily constructed some crude cabins. Days passed with no prospect of relief. In late December, a band of 15 men and women volunteered to try to cross the mountains on snowshoes. Their six days' rations were soon exhausted. After having been without food four days, they were snowbound a week. Four died and the others lived on their flesh. Four others perished before the remnant of the party, at the end of 32 days, reached the settlements. Relief parties were immediately organized and sent to the rescue. In the meantime, the main Donner party in their "little dark cabins under the snow" were suffering death and the starkest tragedy. The terrible story need not be detailed here. Suffice it to say that 36 of the original party of 87 perished in the Sierra snows.

The year 1846 witnessed the Bear Flag Revolution and the American conquest of California, which were treated in the preceding chapter. While the military were in control, and before the treaty between Mexico and the United States had been signed, occurred the most famous event in California history—the discovery of gold.

Gold Discovery and the Forty-Niners

The finding of gold at Sutter's Mill, an event known to every American schoolboy, set the world aflame. James W. Marshall and workmen erecting a sawmill for Captain Sutter on the south fork of the American River made the initial find. The contemporary record is that of Henry W. Bigler, then lately discharged from the Mormon Battalion of the Mexican War.

Monday 24th this day some kind of mettle was found in the tail race that looks like goald. first discovered by James Martial, the Boss of the Mill.

Sunday 30th clear and has been all the last week our metal has been tride and prooves to be goald.

Marshall told Sutter of the find, and together they tried to keep it a secret. But news of such import could not be confined. Sam Brannan strode into San Francisco swinging his hat in one hand, a bottle of gold dust in the other, and shouting, "Gold! Gold! Gold! from the American River." The electrifying news was carried to other settlements, and the stampede began. Laborers left their jobs, merchants their stores, sailors their ships. The powerful magnet of gold drew all classes toward it with irresistible force. The area of the gold discov-

SUTTER'S MILL, THE SCENE OF THE GOLD DISCOVERY
(FROM A PAINTING BY NAHL, IN THE POSSESSION OF A. ROMAN.)

eries spread rapidly. By May, diggings were being worked for 30 miles along the river. Then rich placers were found along other streams coming down from the Sierra Nevadas. The story of the gold discoveries spread beyond the bounds of California. Goldseekers came down from Oregon, up from Mexico. The news was carried to the Atlantic seaboard.

Thomas O. Larkin, American Consul in California, dispatched on June 1 official news that reached Washington in mid-September. Governor Mason made a tour of the diggings during the early summer and in August sent his report to Washington, together with a little box of sample gold. His was a glowing story of men making from $10 to $50 a day with pick, shovel, and pan, and of a region fabulously rich in gold. Mason's report was incorporated in President Polk's Message to Congress on December 5, 1848, and was published widely in the newspapers of the country.

The response was immediate. Between December 14, 1848, and January 18, 1849, 61 vessels sailed from Atlantic seaports carrying their eager passengers toward the land of gold. Alluring stories went the rounds of the press, losing nothing in the telling. At crossroads and the general stores, the tales were repeated. Around thousands of hearth fires throughout the winter, plans were laid for overland journeys to California, come grass in the spring.

Foreign countries quickly contracted the gold fever. By January, 1849, mining and trading companies were being formed in England and in various other European countries. The Far East was stirred. Chinamen began to arrive in California early in 1849, and their numbers were to increase annually during the fifties. In Australia and New Zealand men fought for passage on California-bound ships.

But the largest proportion of the goldseekers was to come from the United States. Numerous routes by land and by sea were available. Many of the argonauts took passage on sailing vessels and made the long voyage—six months or more—around Cape Horn. Some sailed to Mexican ports, made their way across Mexico, and trusted fortune to provide passage on West Coast vessels. A large number sailed to the east coast of the Isthmus of Panama, made their way over the disease-infected isthmus by boat and on mule back, and then caught passage on Pacific steamers and sailing vessels.

The United States Government had made contracts for mail transportation in ocean steamers from New York to Chagres and from Panama to California and Oregon. The service on the West Coast was undertaken by the Pacific Mail Steamship Company. Its first vessel, the *California*, left New York in October, 1848, before the gold excitement had gripped the country. But after rounding the Horn and upon reaching Peru, the gold fever was encountered, and the rush for passage began. Panama was swarming with goldseekers when the ship arrived there. Although having accommodations for but 100, the *California* took on 400. Says H. H. Bancroft: "Many a one, glad to make his bed in a coil of rope, paid a higher fare than the state-room holder; for storage tickets rose to very high prices, even, it is said, to $1,000 or more." The scramble was even fiercer for passage on the company's other steamers, the *Oregon* and the *Panama,* when they reached the isthmus in March and May, respectively.

The overloaded *California* reached San Francisco safely on February 28, 1849. Thereupon, the whole crew, except the engineer, dashed away in response to the siren call of gold. When the *Oregon* arrived at the Golden Gate, the captain anchored her under the guns of a man-of-war and arrested the mutinous crew. "The refractory sailors were kept in irons until they submitted to accept an increase of pay from $12 to $112 per month." The vessel was thus enabled to make her return voyage, carrying the mail. The ocean service *via* Panama was soon established on a regular monthly schedule, thus providing the most speedy travel facilities to and from California.

But the largest number of goldseekers came by land. For inhabitants of the Mississippi Valley, overland travel afforded the most feasible opportunity. The poorer classes found it easier to organize companies and gather teams and wagons and food supplies than to raise the money required for ocean passage.

Several land routes were available. From the Texas region a number of trails converged at El Paso, whence travelers might continue westward to Tucson and along the Gila to San Diego and Los Angeles, and thence to the Sacramento region.

Fort Smith, Arkansas, became a great gathering place for overland emigrants. Here the Government provided a military escort under Captain R. B. Marcy to pilot and protect the emigrants along the Canadian River route to Santa Fe. From the New Mexico capital certain parties moved down the Rio Grande some distance and then followed either the Colonel Kearny or the Captain Cooke route across New Mexico and Arizona. Others turned north and west to follow the Old Spanish Trail to the Pacific Coast. Several parties of forty-niners, especially some Cherokees, broke a path northwest from Fort Smith, and on the Arkansas River struck the Santa Fe Trail, which they followed some distance into present Colorado. They then turned north to the South Platte River, crossed the Continental Divide at Bridger's Pass, and intersected the Oregon Trail near Fort Bridger. This route was called the Cherokee Trail.

The heaviest overland emigration of 1849, however, was over the Oregon and California Trail—along the Platte, over South Pass, and across Nevada by way of the Humboldt. Some of the travelers on this route, especially those who started late, turned southwest upon reaching Salt Lake City, and followed the safer Mormon Trail to Los Angeles. Some, however, who tried short cuts across Death Valley suffered hardships. All of the trails had numerous branches, short cuts, and alternate routes.

With the earliest signs of spring in 1849, eager goldseekers moved toward the frontier outfitting towns of Independence, Fort Smith, and other eligible points. Their attitude is well expressed in the *Arkansas Democrat:* "Who will sit quietly at home in the States, pining in penury when fortunes are to be had merely for the labor of picking them up in California, the fact being now established that there is gold enough for all?" Numerous incredible reports as to the amount of gold available went the rounds. And the repetition made people believe them. Said one man: "I believe I'll go. I know most of this talk is wildly exaggerated, but I am sensible enough to discount it and to disbelieve absurd stories. In fact, if I don't pick up more than a hatful of gold a day I shall be perfectly satisfied."

Some of the emigrants calmly provided themselves with all necessary equipment and supplies for a journey known to be long and exacting; others assembled a little food and clothing and hurriedly set forth, depending on Providence and their fellow-travelers for unforeseen needs. The merchants in the outfitting towns were not blind to their business opportunities. Said an observer at Van Buren, Arkansas, in April, 1849: "The California emigration has been the source of immense profit to the citizens of Arkansas, and should be encouraged by the press, the public men, and every one. They have left at this point, about $60,000 for oxen, horses, mules, bacon, flour, etc., etc., and probably as much more at Fort Smith."

The forefront of the gold rush along the Oregon Trail is thus reported from Fort Kearney on May 18, 1849:

The ice is at last broken, and the inundation of gold diggers is upon us. The first specimen, with a large pick-axe over his shoulder, a long rifle in his hand, and two revolvers and a bowie knife stuck in his belt, made his appearance here a week ago last Sunday. He only had time to ask for a drink of buttermilk, a piece of ginger-bread and how "fur" it was to "Californy," and then hallooing to his long-legged, slab-sided cattle, drawing a diminutive yellow-top Yankee wagon, he disappeared on the trail toward the gold "diggins." Since then wagons have been constantly passing. . . .

Every state, and I presume almost every town and county in the United States, is now represented in this part of the world. Wagons of all patterns, sizes and descriptions, drawn by bulls, cows, oxen, jack asses, mules and horses, are daily seen rolling along towards the Pacific, guarded by walking arsenals.

George A. Smith, writing from Iowa on May 28, says that about 12,000 wagons had crossed the Missouri below Council Bluffs. "The world is perfectly crazy after gold," he remarks. "It is estimated that 40,000 men are on their way overland in search of the yellow dirt."

To the ordinary hazards of overland travel was added this year the dreaded cholera. It struck without warning, terrifying its victims. A strong man might be well in the morning and be buried by nightfall. The water holes became infected, and the poor emigrants, drinking from the clear, cool pools instead of from the running—though warm and muddy—water of the Platte, spread the contagion. Fresh graves soon circled the springs and sloughs and lined the trail. It was estimated that the deaths averaged one and one-half per mile for the entire distance from the Missouri River to Fort Laramie.

The deaths of men and of animals and the breaking down of over-loaded wagons necessitated the abandonment of all kinds of equipment and supplies. Such wreckage strewed the trail for hundreds of miles, especially as it approached South Pass, where the road became rougher and the grass scarcer. Many gave up their wagons and resorted to pack animals. And as the emigrants pushed westward, difficulties did not diminish. The alkali deserts of Nevada levied heavy toll, especially on the weakened animals. And finally there was the high range of the Sierra Nevadas to surmount. Late arrivals were caught in the snows. Several rescue parties, organized by the California miners, were sent to relieve their fellow citizens. The government expended $100,000 in aiding the sufferers.

The westbound throng of 1850 was even larger than that of the preceding year. The official register at Fort Laramie had by August 14 recorded "39,506 men, 2,421 women, 609 children, 23,172 horses, 7,548 mules, 36,116 oxen, 7,323 cows, 2,106 sheep, 9,927 wagons; deaths en route, 316." It was stated that not more than four-fifths of the travelers registered, so the total emigration was estimated at about 55,000.

Cholera again raged on the trail. One correspondent counted 40 graves in 60 miles. On June 7 he saw "three wagons with only one man able to sit up, originally twelve; six dead and buried, four dying of cholera . . . sixteen out of seventeen of one train were sick; another buried seven, and five or six sick, one dying."

Wreckage similar to that strewn along the road in 1849 again cluttered the trail. Franklin Langworthy writes from the Sweetwater region:

Large numbers are leaving their wagons, and packing upon their animals. Horses, mules and even oxen are used for packing. The wagons are generally broken in pieces by their owners and used for fuel before they leave the ground. The number of vehicles that share this fate it would be impossible to calculate. Thousands of fine trunks, boxes and barrels are burnt for cooking purposes. Property that cost one hundred dollars in the states, is none too much to make one comfortable fire in an evening. The number of carcasses of dead animals increases as we proceed.

An overflowing of the Humboldt River in 1850 compelled the emigrants to travel on the barren uplands, thus lengthening the journey and starving the animals. Stock died in such numbers that the effluvia from the putrefying bodies was quite annoying. All in all, the emigrants of 1850 endured sufferings among the most severe in the annals of overland migration.

In the meantime, the influx of settlers was rapidly transforming California. The mining area was broadening. Supply towns, such as Sacramento and Stockton, were developing into cities; and San Francisco was emerging into a unique metropolis. Among the scores of camps that sprang into existence in the mining country were many with picturesque names. There was Whisky Bar, Skunk Gulch, Hangtown, Git-up-and-git, and Hell's Delight. The auriferous district covered a large area of foothills; and the Mother Lode, a remarkable metalliferous vein, extended for a distance of about 70 miles.

The first mining had been done along the streams. Free gold was found as dust, scales, or small nuggets along the river bed, the best "diggins" being located at or near bedrock. The pay dirt in dry diggings on flats and benches was commonly found in territory that had been the bed of some prehistoric stream. Inasmuch as water is the essential factor in placer mining, ditches were dug and the water was diverted from the streams to the dry areas.

Pick, shovel, and pan were the essential tools of mining, to which were soon added rockers, sluices, and other home-made devices for recovering the gold. In panning, one put some of the gold-bearing gravel into a pan, added water, shook the pan to induce the heavy particles of gold to settle to the bottom, poured out the water, scraped off the sand and gravel, and gathered the yellow gleanings from the bottom of the vessel. The same principle was employed with the rocker or cradle. The sluice, a favorite device, was a long wooden trough with strips of wood nailed across the bottom. Through this sluice, inclined at an angle, a stream of water was directed, and into it was shoveled the gravel. The swift current carried off the sand and small pieces of rock, while the heavy gold settled to the bottom of the sluice and was caught in front of the wooden crosspieces. Periodically, a "clean-up" of the sluice was made for recovery of the gold.

Mining was hard work. Wielding a pick and shovel is never easy, but in the mines additional factors made the labor more exacting. Miners worked long hours, sometimes at a feverish pace in anticipation of rich finds. Along the streams they worked all day in water that was usually ice-cold and that reached to their knees or even to their hips. The men were generally their own cooks, and the diet was neither choice nor varied. Pork, beans, flapjacks, stewed dried apples, and coffee were the regular fare, and variety consisted primarily in omission of one or more of these items. The hard life soon weeded out the weaklings. A strong back and iron muscles rated a man as superior, and there developed in the camps a democracy based on physical prowess. Contests of strength, endurance, and speed were favored.

As one might expect, the amusements were rude but hearty. The saloon and the dance hall never lacked patrons, but the typical miner was generous and good-hearted. No one in distress was left uncared for; any humanitarian cause won instant support.

The mining camps were not without law and order. Although the miners were intruders on public domain, there was no hesitation on that account. They assumed their right to exploit nature's resources, and considered gold to be the property of the finder. But experience and common sense soon evolved certain rules as applicable to the new conditions. In the absence of established law the men of a camp or district assembled in true Anglo-Saxon style and adopted laws for the district. These fixed the size of claims, the requirements for holding a claim, procedures for settling disputes, punishments for crimes, and so forth. Trials under these rules were speedy, with technicalities ignored and plain justice dispensed. A simple and practical democracy was created and administered.

ACHIEVEMENT OF STATEHOOD

It was well that the early miners provided laws and regulations of their own, for several years were to elapse before a satisfactory general government was in operation in California. Following occupation by the armed forces of the United States in 1846, the military had assumed control. Commodore Robert F. Stockton, as commander-in-chief, maintained the supremacy of the military, but endeavored to continue the Mexican system of law in civil matters. Alcaldes were continued in office, or new ones were appointed; and these functioned as the principal agencies of local government in the Spanish towns. With such an arrangement the Anglo-American inhabitants were increasingly dissatisfied; and soon they were demanding legal and governmental institutions of the English type.

Upon the ratification of the Treaty of Guadalupe Hidalgo on May 20, 1848, California became United States territory. Colonel Richard B. Mason, ranking officer in the region when the news of peace was received, continued as the *de facto* head of a quasi-civil government under military rule. Now followed an anxious period while everyone waited for Congress to provide a regular Territorial government. That august body seldom hurries. The session of 1848 came to a close without action, and the short session of 1849 ended with the same achievement. In the meantime, various meetings were held and resolutions were adopted favoring the creation of a provisional government, elected by the people themselves, without awaiting Congressional authorization. The San Francisco district created such a government in February, 1849.

At length, on June 3, 1849, General Bennet Riley, now acting-governor, issued a proclamation appointing a day for selecting delegates to a constitutional convention. Various local organizations endorsed the move. The convention, which assembled at the old capital of Monterey September 3, 1849, was a body of 48 young men, the average age being but 36. The majority were Anglo-Americans, with a worthy representation of native Californians. The convention decided to proceed forthwith to the creation of a State government, rather than provide for a Territorial organization. By October 13, the constitution was completed, including a prohibition of slavery. The document was quickly printed in English and in Spanish, was submitted to popular vote on November 13, and was ratified almost unanimously. A Governor and a legislature were elected, and representatives to Washington chosen. Without awaiting Congressional action as to admission to the Union, the legislature proceeded with its functions. In a session that lasted throughout the winter, necessary laws were enacted and the agencies of government established.

In the meantime California representatives to Congress had presented their cause and a petition for statehood. The slavery controversy was the all-absorbing issue there; but Clay's compromise plan, one part of which provided for California statehood, was finally adopted. With the affixing of President Fillmore's signature to the California measure, there entered the sisterhood of states one that William H. Seward referred to as "the youthful queen of the Pacific, in robes of freedom gorgeously inlaid with gold."

But even after statehood was achieved, the regular agencies of government were not always able to control affairs and administer justice. The gold rush had brought in a large body of lawless characters— "Sydney Coves" from the penal colony of Australia, border ruffians from the Missouri Valley frontier, renegades from Mexico and from Chile. In San Francisco, life and property became so unsafe that the better element of the citizenry finally had to act in self defense. A Vigilance Committee, organized in 1851, effected some timely hangings and established order. The same methods were employed again in 1856. Vigilante justice on the California pattern, as discussed in Chapter 26, was subsequently resorted to in other mining camps of the Rocky Mountains as occasion demanded.

BIBLIOGRAPHY

Good general accounts of California in the days of the American conquest are: R. G. Cleland, *A History of California; the American Period* (New York, 1922); R. D. Hunt and N. V. Sanchez, *A Short History of California* (New York, 1929); J. W. Caughey, *California, the Romance of a Great*

State (New York, 1940); S. E. White, *The Forty-niners* (New Haven, 1918); and Josiah Royce, *California* (Boston, 1886).

Larger works are the following: H. H. Bancroft, *History of California* (7 vols., San Francisco, 1884–1890); Z. S. Eldredge, *History of California* (5 vols., New York, 1915); T. H. Hittell, *History of California* (4 vols., San Francisco, 1885–1897).

On more limited topics, see: O. C. Coy, *Gold Days* (Los Angeles, 1929); Joseph Ellison, *California and the Nation, 1850–1869* (Berkeley, 1927); E. P. Houghton, *The Expedition of the Donner Party* (Chicago, 1911); John Bidwell, *Echoes of the Past about California* (Chicago, 1928); Cardinal Goodwin, *The Establishment of State Government in California, 1846–1850* (New York, 1914); Bayard Taylor, *Eldorado, or Adventures in the Path of Empire* (2 vols., New York, 1850); Carey McWilliams, *Southern California Country* (New York, 1946); G. W. Read and Ruth Gaines, *Gold Rush; the Journals, Drawings, and Other Papers of J. Goldsborough Bruff* (New York, 1944); J. H. Jackson, *Gold Rush Album* (New York, 1949).

The following biographies and books of reminiscences are useful: E. G. Gudde, *Sutter's Own Story* (New York, 1936); Julian Dana, *Sutter of California* (New York, 1934); J. A. B. Sherer, *The First Forty-niner* (New York, 1925); Jeremiah Lynch, *The Life of David C. Broderick* (New York, 1911); G. D. Lyman, *John Marsh, Pioneer* (New York, 1930); Horace Bell, *Reminiscences of a Ranger* (Santa Barbara, 1927); Harris Newmark, *Sixty Years in Southern California, 1853–1913* (Boston, 1930); W. L. Manly, *Death Valley in '49* (New York, 1929); Walter Colton, *Three Years in California* (New York, 1852); W. H. Davis, *Sixty Years in California* (San Francisco, 1889); R. L. Underhill, *From Cowhides to Golden Fleece* (Stanford University, 1939); S. B. Dakin, *A Scotch Paisano; Hugo Reid's Life in California, 1832–1852* (Berkeley, 1939). See also the *California Historical Quarterly*, the *Pacific Historical Review*, and the *Huntington Library Quarterly*.

Overland journals of trips to California have been published by the score and are too numerous for listing here. A composite journal, arranged by A. B. Hulbert and published as *Forty-niners* (Boston, 1932), may represent that group of sources. See also the California historical societies' publications.

20

THE MORMONS AND SETTLEMENT OF THE GREAT BASIN

In the settlement of the Great Basin region, a new element enters as the prime motive force; religion caused the migration to Utah. The early years of the nineteenth century were marked with religious enthusiasm, punctuated with revivals and controversies, and characterized by the launching of religious sects and social utopias. Among these newborn and ardently espoused organizations none was so unique in its origin or so important for the history of the West as was the Mormon Church.

RISE OF THE MORMONS

The Mormon sect, or, more properly, the Church of Jesus Christ of Latter-Day Saints, was organized by Joseph Smith at Fayette, New York, on April 6, 1830. The founder claimed a direct revelation from heaven, with divine authorization and direction in the establishment of his church. In the same year, Smith published a unique book which purports to be the history of the inhabitants of America before the days of Columbus. The original record, he asserted, had been kept on thin gold plates by the ancestors of the American Indians. The location of the plates having been revealed to Smith, he made a translation of the inscriptions, and this he issued as the Book of Mormon. Intermingled with the record is much religious doctrine, which has given the volume a sacred character for those who accept it. The Mormon theory respecting the aboriginal inhabitants of America gave the new sect a special interest in the Indians and, consequently, in the West.

Immediately upon its organization, the sect began the aggressive proselyting that has ever since characterized it. The result was a rather rapid increase in membership. Among the earliest of its missionaries were those sent to preach to the Indians. This activity resulted in the removal of headquarters from New York to Ohio, and later to Missouri.

Joseph Smith, accepted by his followers as a prophet, announced a revelation designating Jackson County, Missouri, as the "Land of Promise," the new Zion for his modern "Children of Israel." The Latter-Day Saints began to gather to the frontier town of Independence. Within two years, there were 1,200 of them in the county. They came so rapidly and exhibited such zeal in their new religion that the older inhabitants of the region took alarm. Friction soon developed. The Saints asserted that God had selected this choice land for their inheritance, and that they would ultimately possess it. They were industrious and rapidly accumulated land and property. The Missourians feared that the newcomers would gain political control and might dispossess the original settlers. Other factors contributed to the antipathy. The Mormons announced that theirs was the only true religion. They were clannish; they opposed slavery. Soon there were acts of violence.

In July, 1833, several hundred citizens assembled at Independence "to take some effectual means to rid themselves of their fanatical neighbors." They issued an address containing demands that no more Mormons enter the county, and that those already there depart without delay. Compliance being refused, attacks were made on men and property. The net result was a forced removal of the Saints. Most of them crossed the Missouri River to the northward and found refuge in Clay County. Soon the older residents here were filled with fear. In 1836, they forced the Mormons to move farther north. Here the story was repeated. In October, 1838, a band of ruffians fell upon the little Mormon settlement at Haun's Mill and massacred 18 persons. Fighting at various points resulted. Governor L. W. Boggs thereupon decided to solve the problem. To General J. B. Clark of the militia he issued an order in which he said: "The Mormons must be treated as enemies, and must be exterminated or driven from the State, if necessary, for the public peace." The outcome was the forced exodus of the Saints from Missouri.

The Mormons moved, in 1839, to Illinois, where they were at first welcomed. Smith chose an eligible site in a bend of the Mississippi, and here established the city of Nauvoo. To insure protection for life and property, the Mormon leaders decided to utilize political power. The close numerical equality between Whigs and Democrats made this possible; it gave the newcomers the balance of power, and thus enabled them to secure from the legislature a very liberal charter for their principal city. This instrument made the city a government practically independent of state control. In addition, it created a military organization known as the Nauvoo Legion and made it independent of the regular state militia. Joseph Smith, as Mayor of the city, General of the Nauvoo Legion, and President of the Mormon Church, was supreme in his rapidly growing domain. A municipal university was projected, and a Temple built. The people were advised and directed in temporal as well as in spiritual matters. Ardent missionaries preached the new religion throughout the States and in Europe, and hundreds of converts gathered to the new Zion. A beautiful city emerged, and about it a productive farming area. The growth was so rapid that within five years of its founding Nauvoo had a population of 15,000, and was the largest city in Illinois.

The Prophet now turned to national politics. Having submitted to the political leaders of the country interrogatories as to their policy toward the Mormons, and having received unsatisfactory replies, Joseph Smith, in February, 1844, announced his candidacy for President of the United States. His platform advocated territorial expansion; creation of a national bank and branches; abolition of slavery by 1850, with compensation to the slaveholders from the sale of public lands; reduction of the size of Congress; and authorization for the President on his own volition to suppress mob violence in the states. The campaign was launched, devoted Elders volunteering to stump the country on the dual missions of electioneering and proselyting.

In the meantime, difficulties were brewing. The Mormons became overconfident, and their neighbors suspicious. Citizens of other cities grew jealous of the special priviliges and powers granted to the citizens of Nauvoo. Voting almost as a unit, and having played one of the principal political parties against the other to gain advantages, the Saints were soon turned upon by both Whigs and Democrats. Many people believed, according to Governor Ford of Illinois, that the Mormons "entertained the treasonable design, when they got strong enough, of overturning the government, driving out the old population and taking possession of the country, as the children of Israel did in the land of Canaan." Critics and enemies in Missouri circulated defamatory reports of the Mormons and thus increased the opposition against them in Illinois.

Then internal difficulties arose. Some excommunicated Mormon leaders started the *Nauvoo Expositor,* and in this sheet vigorously attacked and slandered the Prophet and his associates. Mayor Smith and the city council declared the press a nuisance and ordered its destruction. The Mormon leaders were now charged with curtailing the freedom of the press, and thus being hostile to the principles of American liberty. The owners of the suppressed paper joined anti-Mormon leaders and adopted resolutions which "appealed to the citizens of

Illinois, Missouri and Iowa to co-operate with them in exterminating the hated Mormons." Writs were obtained for the arrest of Smith and his accomplices, and a large body of men assembled under a militia officer to effect the arrest. Governor Ford intervened. The Prophet and other leaders, after giving themselves up to the authorities on the pledge of the Governor that they would be protected from mob violence, were lodged in Carthage jail. On June 27, 1844, a mob of several hundred men broke into the jail and killed Joseph Smith and his brother Hyrum.

The murder of the founder of Mormonism did not bring a collapse of his church, as many had expected. Instead, he became enshrined as a martyr, with his influence more potent, perhaps, than ever. There was some question as to the succession of authority, with a number of claimants to leadership. But Brigham Young, head of the Council of Twelve Apostles, came to the fore and was accepted as leader by most of the Saints.

Opposition to the Mormons continued. In January, 1845, the legislature repealed the charter of the city of Nauvoo and deposed its officers. Violence was renewed, and the demand for expulsion of the Mormons grew more insistent. Finally, in September, 1845, the Twelve Apostles promised that their people would vacate the city early the following spring. During the winter, preparations were made for the removal. Homes and land were disposed of, but at great sacrifices, under the condition of forced sale. What was realized from real estate and improvements was converted into wagons, horses, cattle, and supplies. Early in 1846 the exodus began.

Many of the Mormons did not accept Brigham Young's leadership or follow him westward. The largest body of those who remained behind was later to be formed into the Re-organized Church of Jesus Christ of Latter-Day Saints, with the son of Joseph Smith, founder of the original church, as President. This group of Mormons established itself at Independence, Missouri, and has remained principally in that locality. Inasmuch as this branch and lesser offshoots did not figure in the settlement of the Great Basin, we shall not trace their history here.

THE WESTWARD TREK

The first detachment to leave Nauvoo, some 1,600 persons, crossed the Mississippi on the ice. The severe February weather and the lack of shelter entailed great suffering in the temporary camp established at Sugar Creek, Iowa. Many of the Saints went down the river to St. Louis, or scattered to other towns to seek refuge and employment. The main body was to push westward across Iowa, with an ultimate destination in the Rocky Mountains. In early March the first contingent set forth. Snow and cold caused difficulties at first, then came rain and mud. After thaws or heavy rains it was sometimes impossible, for days at a time, to proceed.

A party was sent in advance to select the route and camping places, to make bridges, and to open roads. Several permanent camps were established, where some members of the lead parties remained, built log cabins, dug wells, plowed the land, and planted crops. Later companies reaped the harvests and found shelter in the cabins prepared for them. Garden Grove and Mount Pisgah were the most important of these provident way stations. No Indian difficulties were encountered, and the vanguard reached the Missouri River, at Council Bluffs, in June. During the summer and fall other companies reached this point, which was to be the terminus of travel for the year 1846. On the national stage, events had occurred that altered Mormon plans.

President Polk, in his first Annual Message to Congress, on December 2, 1845, had asserted our right to the Oregon country. He also recommended that "a suitable number of stockades and blockhouse forts be erected along the usual route between our frontier settlements on the Missouri and the Rocky Mountains" to protect the Oregon-bound emigrants. The Mormons were anxious to procure a contract from the government to build such stations while en route over the trail. Such employment would give them desperately-needed money. When there was talk of war with England over Oregon, the Mormons, in January, 1846, officially avowed their loyalty: "Should hostilities arise between the government of the United States and any other power in relation to our right of possessing the territory of Oregon, we are on hand to sustain the [claims] of the United States to that country. It is geographically ours; and of right no foreign power should hold dominion there; and if our services are required to prevent it, those services will be cheerfully rendered according to our ability."

The difficulties with Great Britain were settled peaceably, but war came with Mexico. Instead of employing the Saints to build forts on the Oregon Trail, the national government was to offer them enlistment in the military detachment that was to march to New Mexico and California.

When expulsion from Nauvoo was imminent, the Mormons had begun the study of possible places for settlement. They considered Texas, British Columbia, California, and the Rocky Mountain region. Paramount in their minds was the idea of reaching an uninhabited area where they could practice their religion unmolested and where the ever-recurring difficulties with neighbors would be obviated. They studied Frémont's reports and the writings of other explorers and travelers. By the time the Saints crossed the Mississippi, early in 1846, they had decided to migrate to the country west of the Rocky Mountains, their exact destination not yet determined. Thus were they heading for a region owned by Mexico. It was with a willingness to give the Mormons aid, and with a desire to conciliate them and prevent the possible transfer of their allegiance to a foreign power, that the federal government offered them an opportunity for military service. Col. S. W. Kearny was authorized to enlist approximately 500 Mormon men and march them to Santa Fe and then to California, where they were to be discharged.

A recruiting officer visited the Mormon camps strung across Iowa. The rank and file were at first suspicious, but Brigham Young assured them: "The President of the United States has now stretched out his hand to help us and thank God and him too. It is for us to go and I know you will go. . . . I think the President has done us a great favor by calling upon us." The necessary men were raised and were formed into the Mormon Battalion. This was hardly the kind of aid the Saints had hoped for, as it took from the migrating camps young and able-bodied men, but it did give means of support to destitute families, as the men were given in advance a $42 allowance for clothing. Having raised their quota of volunteers, the Mormons readily obtained federal permission to settle upon the territory along the Missouri River in the vicinity of Council Bluffs. They established their main settlement on the west bank of the river, and named it "Winter Quarters." It was located at Florence, on the northern outskirts of present Omaha. For shelter, some of the people built log cabins; others lived in their wagons or in tents. The poorly housed and inadequately fed emigrants suffered greatly from sickness. Malaria and scurvy took a terrible toll. Six hundred deaths were reported in and about Winter Quarters before winter set in, and at times there were hardly enough able-bodied men to attend to the burials. The little Mormon cemetery at Florence, now appropriately marked by an impressive monument, contains scores of nameless graves.

As the dreary winter dragged to its end, preparations were completed for continuing the journey. Brigham Young issued instructions concerning the formation and conduct of the several parties that were to journey westward. They were to be organized into hundreds, fifties, and tens, with a captain over each division. Each company was to travel in compact form, armed and prepared for defense against hostile Indians. At camping places the wagons were to be drawn into an oval corral. Night and morning, at the sound of the bugle, all were to assemble for prayers. The Sabbath was to be observed, and divine service held. A small, well-organized "Pioneer Band," led by Young himself, was to push ahead, mark the trail, and select the destination. Exerting both temporal and ecclesiastical authority over his followers, President Young was accorded unquestioning obedience and was able to direct what was perhaps the most orderly and efficient migration that ever trekked the trail. Provision was made also for the keeping of adequate records.

The Pioneer Band that set forth in middle April, 1847, comprised 143 men, 3 women, and 2 children. They traveled in 72 wagons and had 93 horses, 52 mules, 66 oxen, 19 cows, 17 dogs, and some chickens. In the covered wagons were plows and other farming implements, seed grain, and a year's supply of provisions. An odometer to measure the distance traveled was invented and used. As far as Fort Laramie, the route taken was along the north bank of the Platte, on the opposite side of the river from the regular line of travel. This route, which was to be used by the Mormons throughout most of the covered wagon years of their overland travel, came to be known as the Mormon Trail. From Fort Laramie to Fort Bridger, they were to follow the regular Oregon Trail, and from the latter post take the route of the Donner Party to the valley of the Great Salt Lake.

Just before reaching Green River, the vanguard met Samuel Brannan, journeying eastward from California to meet them. Brannan was the leader of a party of Mormons in New York, who, when the expulsion from Nauvoo was imminent, had chosen the water route for their westward journey. They had chartered the *Brooklyn,* of 450 tons, and had laden it with farm implements, a printing press, schoolbooks, equipment for flour mills, and miscellaneous supplies. With 238 passengers on board, the ship sailed from New York on February 4, 1846, and reached San Francisco Bay on July 31. Although the water route around Cape Horn was long, the voyage had been completed by the time the overland travelers had crossed Iowa.

Arrived in California, a portion of the Mormon colonists had moved to the Stanislaus River and started the town of New Hope. From here Brannan had journeyed eastward to meet the main body of Saints. He tried to convince Brigham Young that the New Zion should be established in California, but the wary President thought otherwise. Young wanted isolation. He was seeking a respite from what he considered religious persecution; and a desert region, with the hardships its subjugation would entail, would serve his purpose. So Brannan, his proposal rejected, returned to the Pacific Coast, where he was to remain as an important California pioneer. But most of his colonists, impelled by religious motives, later joined their co-religionists in Utah.

In crossing the Wasatch Mountains west of Fort Bridger, President

Young became ill with "mountain fever." Just as his carriage reached the summit of "Big Mountain," where the first glimpse of Salt Lake Valley was possible, he rose from his bed—so it is reported—gazed earnestly into the distance, and said, "This is the Place." His followers are inclined to accept this as an instance of divine inspiration. The expression has become a Utah slogan.

The Beginnings of Utah

The official entry into the Salt Lake Valley (in 1847) occurred on July 24, thereafter to be known as "Pioneer Day." The surrounding mountains and the great lake in the distance were beautiful, while the immediate plain, which was chosen as the site of the future city, was dry, barren, and uninviting. But the pioneers set to work. Water was diverted from a creek, and the ground flooded to facilitate plowing. This was the beginning of extensive irrigation by Anglo-Saxons in the West.

The Ute and Shoshone Indians having given some trouble, it was decided to build the first houses in the form of a fort. A rectangular enclosure was constructed, in part of adobe walls and in part of log houses arranged in a solid row. The doors and windows of the houses faced the interior court, while the back of each room was pierced with a loophole. The roofs were made of brush and earth. Before winter set in, four additional companies, numbering some 1,500 persons, reached Salt Lake Valley. Most of these new arrivals found shelter in the Fort and in the extensions of it that were built. Here, during the first winter, two schools were maintained for the pioneer children. Most of the settlers lived in the Fort during the first year, but a few moved out to lay foundations of near-by towns.

There was one settler in the Great Basin when the Mormons arrived —Miles M. Goodyear. This red-headed Connecticut Yankee, as a boy of 19, had joined the Whitman-Spalding missionary party of 1836. At Fort Hall he had left the Oregon-bound group and had taken up the life of fur-trapper and trader with the Indians. In 1845 he had established himself on the Weber River, near the Great Salt Lake. Here he built a picket stockade with a log house in each corner, and called the place Fort Buenaventura. With a pack train laden with furs and buckskin, he had traveled in the fall of 1846 to southern California, where he sold his buckskin to Frémont to clothe the American soldiers. Returning with stock, Goodyear went to the Oregon Trail on Bear River (western Wyoming) to trade his California horses for worn-down emigrant horses and cattle. Here the Mormon pioneers had met him in early July, 1847, and had been advised by him as to the character of the country in the Salt Lake region. Soon after the Mormons reached their destination, an exploring party called at Goodyear's trading post. The visitors were interested in the vegetable garden and especially in the growing corn, for as yet there was doubt as to whether corn would mature in the region. The Mormons soon began negotiations for Goodyear's holdings, the squatter claiming that he held his land by virtue of a Mexican land grant. A deal was concluded in November, 1847, by which Goodyear yielded to James Brown the fort and the fictitious title to about 200 square miles of land, together with 75 cattle, 75 goats, 12 sheep, and 6 horses for the sum of $1,950. On the tract, the city of Ogden was built.

Having chosen a location for his people, and having given instructions for the conduct of affairs, President Young returned to the Missouri River in the fall of 1847 to superintend the next season's emigration. He realized that to succeed in that isolated region, the settlers must be as nearly self-sufficient as possible. Accordingly, in the "General Epistle" of December, 1847, Young instructed the Saints as follows:

Come immediately and prepare to go West, bringing with you all kinds of choice seeds, grains, vegetables, fruits, shrubbery, trees, and vines— everything that will please the eye, gladden the heart or cheer the soul of man, that grow upon the face of the earth; also the best stock of birds, beasts or fowl of every kind; also the best tools of every description; machinery for spinning and weaving, and dressing of wool, cotton, flax, and silk; or models or description of the same by which we can construct them; and the same in relation to all kinds of farming utensils and husbandry, such as corn shellers, grain threshers and cleaners, smut machines, mills and every implement and article within your knowledge that shall tend to promote the comfort, health, happiness, or prosperity of any people.

In November, 1847, the Mormons had sent an expedition southwest from Salt Lake to explore a route to California and to procure cattle and seed grain. The men followed the general course of the Old Spanish Trail, suffered somewhat from shortage of food, but reached their destination safely. From Californians they obtained cattle, mares, grain, and seeds of various kinds, which they brought back to Utah. The expedition was to be followed by others that thoroughly explored the country along the route and selected sites for settlements.

The planting of seeds in Salt Lake Valley by the pioneer Mormon band in 1847 had occurred so late that crops did not mature. But the following spring opened with promise. Five thousand acres of land were under cultivation. Then, onto the green fields of wheat descended myriads of crickets. They were devouring everything, and the colonists fought desperately to stay the destruction. When every effort seemed ineffectual, there came from the lake great flocks of sea gulls.

They gorged themselves with crickets, and then feasted again. Thus, part of the crop was saved and the people were rescued from impending famine. Thereafter the gull was accorded an almost sacred character. The sea gull monument in the Utah capital of today commemorates the birds' timely service to the pioneers.

In September, 1848, Brigham Young returned to Utah, bringing with him some 2,500 emigrants. With this increased population and a reduced crop—because of crickets and frosts—a shortage of food during the ensuing winter and spring caused considerable suffering.

In the meantime, Salt Lake City had been platted and surveyed. As laid out, it had the same large blocks and wide streets that characterize the city today. Each ten-acre block was divided into eight lots. Beyond the city limits, the farming land was subdivided into fields of 5, 10, and 20 acres, the smaller tracts being nearest the city. Each family was given a city lot for home building—protection demanded they house compactly—and a field tract. The settlers were exhorted to till the soil industriously. Canals were built co-operatively, and irrigation water was brought to each man's land. The first fences, of pickets and adobes, were community enterprises. In fact, co-operation and unity were the keynotes of Mormon policy and the primary causes of success.

Desert conditions forced the settlers to make adaptations to a harsh environment. Most noteworthy was the utilization of irrigation for the growing of crops in this semi-arid land. Such use of water was foreign to their previous experience farther east. The new use of streams—to supply ditches for watering the land—placed added importance upon the limited water supply of precious creeks and thus gave rise to a new concept of law pertaining to streams. The discarding of the doctrine of "riparian" rights and the adoption of the principle of "appropriation" of water (as discussed in Chapter 35) was inaugurated by the Mormons and subsequently adopted and elaborated by other pioneers and states of the Rocky Mountain area.

Pioneering was difficult in this isolated and semi-arid region. Discouraged settlers wanted to move on to the Pacific Coast. Then came the discovery of gold in California, to give an added lure to the land beyond the Sierras. But Brigham was adamant; he insisted that the right place had been chosen. To quell discontent, he made a public announcement:

We have been kicked out of the frying pan into the fire, out of the fire into the middle of the floor, and here we are and here we will stay. God has shown me that this is the spot to locate his people and here is where they will prosper. . . . We will extend our settlements to the east and to the west, to the north and to the south, and we will build towns and cities by the hundreds and thousands, and Saints will gather in from the nations of the earth. . . .

Take courage, brethren. . . . Plow your land and sow wheat, plant your potatoes. . . . The worst fear that I have about this people is that they will get rich in this country, forget God and his people, wax fat, and kick themselves out of the church and go to hell. This people will stand mobbing, robbing, poverty, and all manner of persecution, and be true. But my greatest fear for them is that they cannot stand wealth.

Almost to a man, the Saints complied with Brigham's request and remained in the Great Basin. This notable response is attributable to the religious zeal that characterized the Mormons. Submission to ecclesiastical authority was to them a prime virtue—the surest guarantee of temporal success and of celestial salvation. Temporary benefits should not outweigh eternal welfare.

EMIGRATION AND COLONIZATION

To develop the Great Basin area successfully, to make it an inland empire, Young and his associates needed more people. Thus, proselyting was increased. More missionaries were sent throughout the United States and to the various countries of the world. Not only was Mormonism preached with vigor, but converts were urged to flee to the Zion in the Rocky Mountains before the calamities came that were to be meted out to the wicked in the rest of the world. The response was immediate; the success, marked. Most of the conversions were among the poorer classes, and many converts were unable to finance a removal to Utah. To meet this situation, Young instituted the "Perpetual Emigration Fund" in 1849. Money contributed to this fund was lent to needy emigrants, who were to repay the loan as soon as possible after arrival in Utah. With the aid of this revolving fund, 1,100 Saints were enabled to migrate to their Zion during the succeeding five years.

Since other eager hundreds were clamoring for assistance, and funds were inadequate, Young decided on a new method of emigration across the Plains. He set forth the plan in a letter of September 30, 1855, directed to the head of his missions in Europe:

I have been thinking how we should operate another year. We cannot afford to purchase wagons and teams as in times past. I am consequently thrown back upon my old plan—to make hand-carts, and let the emigration foot it, and draw upon them the necessary supplies, having a cow or two for every ten. They can come just as quick, if not quicker, and much cheaper . . . they can beat any ox train crossing the plains. . . . I can promise them that they will be met with provisions and friends far down on the plains, perhaps as low as Laramie, if we get their names in time.

The plan was put into operation at once; five companies were to travel the Plains by hand-cart the next season. After the emigrants crossed the ocean in sailing vessels, they went by train to Iowa City, where hand-carts, made of hickory and oak, were prepared. These were similar in size and shape to the two-wheeled carts used today by street sweepers. On these tough vehicles the emigrants piled their clothing, bedding, and utensils, and set forth on their 1,200-mile trek to the Promised Land. A few ox-drawn wagons were sent along to carry the heavier supplies. The first two companies comprised together 497 persons, with 100 hand-carts and five ox-drawn wagons. The journey was hard and long, but the Saints, buoyed with religious enthusiasm, endured their hardships rather cheerfully. The chorus to their hand-cart song ran as follows:

> Some must push and some must pull
> As we go marching up the hill;
> As merrily on the way we go
> Until we reach the valley, oh.

The first three companies made as good time as did the usual ox-trains, and reached their destination safely. But the other two companies of this year were to suffer terrible disaster. Late in sailing from England, and delayed in getting their carts, they did not leave Iowa City until late July. The horrors of their journey cannot be traced here. Caught by snow in central Wyoming, with a shortage of food, with inadequate clothing and bedding, their condition can be imagined. Supplies were rushed to them from Salt Lake City; otherwise all might have been lost. For many starving and exhausted souls, rescue came too late. Over 200 persons of the 1,076 in the two companies perished. This was the largest single tragedy of overland migration in the West.

Hand-cart travel continued on a reduced scale during the four succeeding years, but no more companies set out late in the season. By 1861 the settlers in Utah had sufficient stock to provide wagon transportation. Thereafter, trains left Salt Lake City in the early spring, traveled to the Missouri River, and returned the same season with emigrants and supplies. The hand-cart plan was now abandoned. Ten companies had trekked to Utah in this manner. Three thousand souls had measured the distance with their footsteps, and 662 hand-carts had creaked the dusty miles.

Established in the center of a vast unoccupied area, with a steady stream of emigrants coming to his retreat and a devoted body of co-religionists eager to obey his every order, Brigham Young was in an admirable position to build up the empire he visioned. And the Mormon leader was no visionary; he was, above all, a man of practical affairs, with a genius for mobilizing men and resources toward the accomplishment of his purposes. His achievements in the Great Basin mark him as the West's greatest colonizer.

Exploring parties were sent forth in every direction to find eligible streams and springs where settlements could be established. Having decided upon a location, Brigham would issue a "Call" to settlers to migrate to the designated place, there to develop farms, build their homes, and found a town. Sometimes he selected a good, experienced leader and let him choose his associates in the new venture; at other times, he named in detail the families selected for the new settlement. To the faithful, the "Call" was regarded as a divine injunction that they should obey, no matter how great the sacrifice. Compliance was their duty—their part in "building the Kingdom of God on the earth."

In making up the personnel of these colonizing parties, Young and his leaders selected such individuals as would tend to make the community self-sufficient. For most settlements, farming and stock raising would be the principal occupations; but care was usually taken to include in each town-founding company a schoolteacher and such useful tradesmen as a carpenter, a blacksmith, a mason, a shoemaker, and so forth. Machinery for a sawmill and a grist-mill, needed tools, and implements were usually taken to a settlement at the time of its founding. Newly arrived immigrants from Europe, especially those with no experience in farming, were distributed among the communities where their training could be best utilized, or where from experienced farmers they could learn proved methods and adapt themselves to the new life.

Some of the more remote outposts were called "Missions." In their objectives, they were not unlike the early Spanish missions in the Southwest. As frontier institutions, they were expected to convert and civilize the Indians, hold the aborigines in control, and serve as a nucleus of white settlement. Persons "called" to such missions or to found new towns felt obliged to remain until "released," or until called elsewhere. Hence the persistence and stamina that were frequently exhibited in facing deterrent conditions and in subduing inhospitable lands.

When organizing the "Provisional Government of the State of Deseret" in 1849, the Mormons proposed boundaries of imperial proportions. The territory embraced all of present Utah and Nevada; parts of Wyoming, Colorado, New Mexico, Arizona, Idaho, Oregon, and California; and the port of San Diego with a liberal piece of the California coast. The Saints set about forthwith to establish themselves in the far reaches of the proposed domain. Within six years they had founded San Bernardino in California, Genoa and Las Vegas in Nevada, and had thriving settlements on the Salmon River in Idaho and in the Green River Valley of Wyoming. In addition, the far corners of present Utah had been occupied. During the first ten years in their new home, the Mormons founded 100 new towns. During the 30 years of Young's rule, says Dr. M. R. Hunter, 360 settlements were established by the Mormons, including 25 in Arizona and a number in Idaho. Subsequently the Mormons were to undertake colonizing ventures in Canada and in old Mexico.

The first extensive entry of non-Mormons, or "Gentiles," into Utah came during the Civil War. Troops, enlisted in California, were distributed along the overland trail. Colonel Patrick E. Connor, in command of these soldiers, set up headquarters at Camp Douglas, on the eastern outskirts of Salt Lake City. The Mormons and the soldiers were distrustful of each other at first, and serious conflict was narrowly averted.

Connor was anxious to promote mining in the region, not only to uncover mineral wealth, but to induce the entry of non-Mormons. He guaranteed protection to prospectors and even ordered that "soldiers of the several posts be allowed to prospect for mines, when such course shall not interfere with the due and proper performance of their military duties." Connor himself discovered several mines and organized mining companies and mining districts. After his release from the army in 1866, he pursued mining interests in the region. He has been called the "Father of Utah Mining." In succeeding years rich districts were opened and large productions of gold, silver, and copper resulted. The property at Bingham Canyon is one of the great copper mines of the world.

The coming of the railroad brought a large non-Mormon element to Utah. The number of Gentiles has steadily increased. Approximately half the populations of the two largest cities (Salt Lake and Ogden) and a majority of the citizens of several mining towns are Gentiles. The former antipathy between the two elements is disappearing.

GOVERNMENT AND FEDERAL RELATIONS

The pioneer settlers in Utah were primarily a religious body, and their first government was ecclesiastical. The Mormon Church had evolved a rather elaborate system of government, with numerous administrative and judicial officers. To these the people looked for advice, or appealed for settlement of disputes. A complete theocracy or theo-democracy existed. The system seemed to fit the needs of the early settlers, especially during the period of the Mexican War, when jurisdiction over the Great Basin area was in doubt. After cession of the region to the United States, there was need for political organization.

In March, 1849, a convention assembled in Salt Lake City and adopted a constitution for the "Provisional Government of the State of Deseret." The name of the proposed state was taken from the Book of Mormon, and meant "Honey Bee." From this has come the bee-hive symbol in the Utah state seal. The preamble to the constitution of 1849 reads:

Whereas, the Congress of the United States has failed to provide a form of government for the territory so acquired [from Mexico], or any portion thereof; and whereas, civil government and laws are necessary for the security of peace and prosperity of society, your committee begs leave to recommend the adoption of the following constitution until the Congress of the United States shall otherwise provide for the government of the territory hereinafter named and described.

The extensiveness of the area desired for the proposed state has been indicated above. Election of officers was held forthwith, Brigham Young being chosen governor, and other high church officials being elected to other important posts. A legislature convened and enacted laws needed in the new commonwealth. It memorialized Congress to approve its actions, recognize the state constitution, and admit Deseret into the Union. A delegate journeyed to Washington and presented the petition. Congress considered the matter, but finally decided to recognize a Territorial status rather than admit to statehood. Congress did not accept the name proposed, but instead created the Territory of Utah (named for the Ute Indians) on September 9, 1850. Nearly all of present Nevada, the western third of Colorado, a corner of Wyoming, and all of present Utah were included in the new Territory. By a series of subsequent reductions, Utah territory was to be cut to its present size.

President Fillmore selected a corps of Territorial officials, with Brigham Young as governor. Three of the other appointments went to Mormons, three to non-Mormons, or "Gentiles." As the Saints had hoped for Mormon officials throughout, friction soon developed. Most western Territories experienced some conflict between the outside and the home appointments to Territorial offices, but in Utah the strong antagonisms of religion increased the friction. Some of the Gentile appointees were of small caliber; on the other hand, they were placed in a difficult role. For, while there was theoretically a separation of church and state in Utah, in reality the church was supreme. Loyalty was to the church first, and to the state afterward. Even in the matter of property rights, disputes were usually taken to ecclesiastical rather than to civil courts. This un-American practice naturally offended the Gentile judges. Some of these, during the early years, gave up their offices, left the Territory, and issued strong denunciations of the Mormons. Friction continued, with bitter charges and countercharges.

The matter reached a climax in 1857. Judge W. W. Drummond, having fled from Utah, issued a statement justifying his resignation.

"The Mormons look to Brigham Young," he said, "and to him alone for the law by which they are governed . . . federal officers of the Territory are constantly insulted, harassed and annoyed by the Mormons, and for these insults there is no redress." W. M. F. Magraw, a previous contractor for the mail service from Missouri to Utah, issued a stinging arraignment of the Mormons. Indian Agent T. S. Twiss reported that the Utahans were making settlements on Indian land in violation of the law.

The administration at Washington considered the various reports and decided to do something about the matter. The law must be respected and obeyed in Utah. Political considerations and the influence of contractors are said to have had a bearing on the final decision. In any event, Young was replaced as governor, and a military force was dispatched with the new executive to uphold his authority. Twenty-five hundred troops and their extensive supply trains set out for Utah. General W. S. Harney was at first placed in command, but was later replaced by Colonel Albert S. Johnston.

News of the approach of the army caused consternation among the Mormons. They feared that enemies of their religion had won the ear of the government and were coming out to destroy them. So they marshaled their resources, began drilling troops, and planned a defense of their homes. Small detachments were sent out to attack and destroy the army supply trains as they approached the mountains. Winter set in before the United States army reached the Salt Lake Valley, and the troops were quartered for the winter in the vicinity of Fort Bridger, present western Wyoming. In the meantime, Colonel T. L. Kane assumed the role of mediator. He went from New York, by way of Panama, to California, and thence to Utah, where he conferred with Young. He then continued eastward to the army headquarters and induced Governor Cumming, the newly appointed executive, to go to Utah unaccompanied by the troops. In the Utah capital, Cumming was recognized as the new governor. Fears of the Mormons were finally allayed; the troops entered Salt Lake City in the summer of 1858 without opposition; and a presidential pardon was issued to the Utah citizens. The military expedition, sometimes called "Buchanan's Blunder," had cost the government fully $15,000,000.

One of the effects of the "Utah War" was abandonment of the more distant Mormon colonies. Upon hearing of the army's approach, Young had ordered the Saints from San Bernardino and other far-flung settlements to leave their homes and hurry to the defense of Zion. The colonists did not return to these outposts.

An event which was largely a by-product of the coming of "Johnston's Army" was the "Mountain Meadows Massacre"—the worst stain on Utah history. The tragic story cannot be detailed here, even were it possible entirely to separate the true from the false statements as to who was responsible or what actually occurred. Suffice it to say that a California-bound party of about 140 emigrants, from bitter anti-Mormon districts of Missouri and Arkansas, was attacked in September, 1857, by Mormons and Indians at the Mountain Meadows in southern Utah. After having surrendered under a flag of truce, all of the emigrants save 17 small children, were deliberately murdered. The perpetrators of the horrible crime went unpunished for years. Finally, one of those involved—John D. Lee—was tried and convicted. He was executed at the scene of the tragedy 20 years after the slaughter occurred.

From the earliest years in Utah, the settlers endeavored to win statehood for their Territory. But Congress would not consent, the most persistent objection being based on the practice of polygamy among the Mormons. Polygamy is said to have been advocated by Joseph Smith before his death and to have been practiced by some of the Mormon leaders while in Illinois. But it was not until 1852 that the system was publicly announced and advocated. From the first entry into Utah, Young had felt the need of population increase. Hence his emphasis on proselyting and emigration, as indicated above. The desirability of large families was also emphasized; in fact, the rearing of such was urged as a religious duty. The polygamy doctrine fitted well into the scheme. As advocated and practiced by the Mormons, it did not mean profligacy. Outside the bonds of marriage, sexual irregularity was very rare, and was vigorously condemned. But men who could provide the necessary economic support were urged to marry two or more wives and rear additional families, especially as there were more women converts than men. A natural antipathy toward polygamy—no woman wanting to share her husband with another—was overcome in part by the teachings of ecclesiastical authorities, by assurance that plurality of wives was in accord with Bible teachings and divine revelation, and that personal sacrifice in complying with the system would be rewarded in heaven.

But polygamy was an anachronism in the modern world, an affront to the social life of America. Generally condemned throughout the world, it soon became the most widely known feature of Mormonism. More and more was the federal government urged to take a hand in the matter and force abandonment of the practice. So long as Utah remained a Territory, the national authority had supreme control over all branches of government. There was no inclination on the part of Congress to relinquish this control and grant statehood so long as the offensive practice persisted.

An "Anti-Polygamy Society" was formed by the "Gentile" women of Salt Lake City in 1878. They charged the Mormons with the practice of a great crime under the cloak of religion. The cry was taken up throughout the country, and with such vigor that Congress, in 1882, passed the Edmunds Law, providing a fine and imprisonment for anyone guilty of polygamy. Federal marshals and courts began vigorously to prosecute offenders. Finally, the Mormon Church capitulated; and, in the "Manifesto" of 1890, President Wilford Woodruff directed all Mormons to "refrain from contracting any marriage forbidden by the law of the land." The long-standing cause of friction being removed, Utah was admitted to the Union as a state in 1896, after almost 50 years as a Territory.

BIBLIOGRAPHY

The literature for and against the Mormons is voluminous, but most of it is so biased as to be undependable. The following list is a selection from the more dependable historical works: W. A. Linn, *The Story of the Mormons* (New York, 1902); T. B. H. Stenhouse, *The Rocky Mountain Saints* (New York, 1873); O. F. Whitney, *History of Utah* (4 vols., Salt Lake City, 1892–1904); L. E. Young, *The Founding of Utah* (New York, 1923); L. H. Creer, *Utah and the Nation* (Seattle, 1929); E. E. Erickson, *The Psychological and Ethical Aspects of Mormon Group Life* (Chicago, 1923); H. H. Bancroft, *History of Utah, 1540–1886* (San Francisco, 1889); J. W. Gunnison, *The Mormons or Latter-Day Saints in the Valley of the Great Salt Lake* (Philadelphia, 1856); Andrew Jensen, *Church Chronology* (Salt Lake City, 1914); Daniel Tyler, *A Concise History of the Mormon Battalion* (Salt Lake City, 1881); R. F. Burton, *The City of the Saints* (London, 1861); O. G. Hammond (ed.), *The Utah Expedition, 1857–1858; Letters of Captain Jesse A. Gove* (Concord, N. H., 1928); *William Clayton's Journal* (Salt Lake City, 1921); J. C. Alter, *Utah, the Storied Domain* (Chicago, 1932); B. H. Roberts, "History of the Mormon Church," in the *American Historical Magazine* and the *Americana*, vols. IV–IX (New York, 1909–1914); W. R. Harris, *The Catholic Church in Utah* (Salt Lake City, 1909); C. D. Harris, *Salt Lake City, a Regional Capital* (Chicago, 1940); A. L. Neff, *History of Utah, 1847 to 1869* (Salt Lake City, 1940); Vardis Fisher, *Children of God, an American Epic* (New York, 1939); Nels Anderson, *Desert Saints, the Mormon Frontier in Utah* (Chicago, 1942); Wallace Stegner, *Mormon Country* (New York, 1942).

The following biographical works have value: H. M. Beardsley, *Joseph Smith and His Mormon Empire* (Boston, 1931); M. R. Werner, *Brigham Young* (New York, 1925); S. Y. Gates and L. D. Widtsoe, *The Life Story of Brigham Young* (New York, 1930); J. H. Evans, *Charles Coulson Rich; Pioneer Builder of the West* (New York, 1936); Reva Stanley, *A Biography of Parley P. Pratt: the Archer of Paradise* (Caldwell, Idaho, 1937); J. A. Little, *Jacob Hamblin* (Salt Lake City, 1881); Charles Kelly and M. L. Howe, *Miles Goodyear, First Citizen of Utah* (Salt Lake City, 1937); *A Friend of the Mormons* [Papers of T. L. Kane] (San Francisco, 1937); Fred B. Rogers, *Soldiers of the Overland, Being Some Account of the Services of General Patrick Edward Connor and his Volunteers in the Old West* (San

Francisco, 1938); Fawn M. Brodie, *No Man Knows my History, the Life of Joseph Smith, the Mormon Prophet* (New York, 1946); Reva Scott, *Samuel Brannan and the Golden Fleece* (New York, 1944); M. R. Hunter, *Brigham Young the Colonizer* (Salt Lake City, 1940).
See also the *Utah Historical Quarterly.*

21

IOWA AND MINNESOTA

$\mathbf{M}$INES AND furs brought the first white men to Iowa. Frenchmen early visited the region, as noted previously; and in the days when Spain ruled the Louisiana country, Julien Dubuque, a French-Canadian, operated lead mines in the vicinity of the present town of Dubuque. Two other Frenchmen had small establishments on Iowa soil before 1800. Basil Giard received from the Spanish Governor a grant of 5,000 acres of land in present Clayton County, some distance above Dubuque. Louis H. Tesson operated a trading post for several years in the southeast corner of Iowa, at the site of present Montrose. Various fur gatherers carried on their trade in the Iowa country during those early years, but they were temporary occupants.

After Dubuque's death in 1810, the Fox Indians refused to let any other white men work the lead mines which the Frenchman had exploited. Other Indians of the region opposed white entry, so the Iowa country remained in Indian possession. In the extreme southeast corner of the present state, in the section known as the Half-breed Tract, a few white men and half-breeds were permitted to settle in the 1820's. But before the important Black Hawk cession of 1833, there were probably less than 50 white men in Iowa.

The Settlement of Iowa

During the first three decades of the nineteenth century a great stream of west-moving homeseekers had poured across the Alleghenies, and spread over the lush region north of the Ohio and south of the Great Lakes. More than half a million Americans were living in Indiana and Illinois by 1830, and many of these were already looking across the Mississippi with covetous eyes at the deep, rich soil of Iowa. Thus far, Indian treaties and United States troops had held back the settlers, but the white tide was rising ominously. Settlers crowded into the lead-mining region of northern Illinois and southern Wisconsin before the Indian title to the land had been surrendered. The cleared ground and the cornfields about the Sauk and Fox village at Rock Island appealed to frontier farmers. When these pushed in, the Indians objected, and the Black Hawk War of 1832 began. Black Hawk and his warriors were soon subdued and not only were pushed across the Mississippi, but were forced to cede a strip on the west side of the river approximately 50 miles wide and extending from the northern boundary of Missouri to the vicinity of Prairie du Chien, Wisconsin. This important cession, which went into effect on June 1, 1833, opened the way for the settlement of Iowa.

The land could not as yet be legally acquired, for federal laws stipulated that survey and formal sale of lands should precede entry by settlers. But the spirit and genius of the frontiersmen went counter to such enactments. Settlers rushed in ahead of the surveyor and the federal land office to occupy choice locations. Feeling that possession was nine points of the law, they left the legal title for subsequent acquisition. They knew that Congress had on previous occasions forgiven intruders on the public domain, and had granted them the privilege of "pre-emption," that is, the right to buy ahead of the auction and at the minimum price the lands upon which they had illegally squatted. The practice was becoming so common that settlers had little to fear.

In the summer of 1833 the movement into Iowa began. From Illinois and states farther east the pioneers made their way toward the Black Hawk Purchase. Writes one of these homeseekers: "The roads were literally lined with the long blue wagons of the emigrants wending their way over the broad prairies—the cattle and hogs, men and dogs, and frequently women and children, forming the rear of the van—often ten, twenty and thirty wagons in company." On the bank of the Mississippi, they awaited their turn to be ferried across. The first ferries were hand-rowed flatboats, which were to be displaced later by steamboats. At the crossings, towns sprang up—Fort Madison, Burlington, Keokuk, Davenport, and Dubuque. From these points the emigrants spread westward, taking up land and founding towns. Pioneers who came by boat up the Mississippi landed at the river towns to swell the groups of homeseekers. In 1836 the population of Iowa was 10,000; two years later it was 23,000, and in 1840 it was 43,000. The Panic of 1837 induced many persons to migrate to this virgin country, where they could start anew. The normal movement from Indiana and Illinois was augmented by the exodus of those seeking to escape taxation made oppressively high by the late orgy of spending and borrowing for internal improvements.

In 1836 Dubuque, with a population of about 1,000, had 250 houses, including 15 dry goods stores. Two years later it boasted a bank, three hotels, three church societies, a theater, a lyceum, two academies, a printing press, and several "elegant brick mansions."

Iowa was widely and favorably advertised in the newspapers of the country. A correspondent of the *Buffalo Journal* wrote in March, 1839:

Taking into consideration the soil, the timber, the water, and the climate, Iowa territory may be considered the best part of the Mississippi valley. The Indians so consider it, as appears from the name which they gave it. For it is said that the Sioux (Sac) and Fox Indians, on beholding the exceeding beauties of this region, held up their hands, and exclaimed in an ecstasy of delight and amazement, "I-O-WA," which in the Fox language means, *"this is the land."*

Newspapers in the Iowa towns were not reticent or unduly modest in their claims. This report in 1840 is typical: "Burlington is the largest, wealthiest, most business doing and most fashionable city, on or in the neighborhood of the Upper Mississippi. . . . We have three or four churches, a theatre, and a dancing school in full blast."

The inflow of population brought pressure for further removal of the Indians. In 1837 the Sauks and Foxes were induced to cede a strip to the west of the Black Hawk Purchase; and in 1842 they gave up a large tract farther west, which embraced the major part of central and southern Iowa. The white acquisition in the southern part of the state was extended to the Mississippi in 1846; and five years later title to the remaining Indian lands in Iowa was relinquished by the red men.

With Indian claims settled and the resources of the region publicized, the emigrant stream continued to flow into Iowa with accelerated motion. During the 1840's the population showed an average increase of 15,000 per year, and by 1850 it had reached a total of 192,212. The earliest settlers came from the adjoining states of Illinois and Missouri, but soon they were coming from farther fields. The influx of long-distance emigrants was materially aided by the improved facilities for river navigation. By 1840 steamboats were regularly plying the Ohio and the Mississippi, and homeseekers could travel quickly and rather cheaply from Pittsburgh to the river ports of Iowa.

GOVERNMENT AND GROWTH

As indicated above, the first settlers went into Iowa in disregard of the federal land laws. Government surveyors did not begin work in the region until 1836, while land offices were not opened and land offered for sale until 1838. Inasmuch as the early squatters would be unable for some time to acquire legal title to their holdings, they took measures in the absence of a specific pre-emption law to insure ultimate acquisition of legal title. The squatters in a given area formed a Claim Club, or Association, electing a President, a Secretary or Recorder of Claims, Adjusters of Claims, and so forth. Each member of the Club reported the boundaries of the land he had appropriated, submitting this description for entry in the Record Book of the Club. In case of a dispute between two or more claimants, the contest was settled by the adjusters. Subsequent sales and transfers of claims were duly entered in the book. Thus was the record kept until the land had been surveyed and the day had arrived for the official sale.

According to the law, the land was to be sold at auction to the highest bidder, and collusion was to be punished. But this legal procedure was in conflict with the frontiersman's concept of justice. He felt that the pioneer who took up land, built a cabin, and broke the sod was performing a valuable service for his country, one for which he should be rewarded, not penalized. It would be a travesty on justice, he felt, if after the pioneer had taken up his land and improved his homestead, it were possible for some outside speculator to come to the official land sale and outbid the squatter for the land he had improved. To preclude such a possibility was the primary purpose of the Claim Club.

On the day of the public sale, the members of the Club attended in a body, exhibiting such show of force as would insure conduct of the sale in the manner their interests prescribed. The federal official, in due form, offered the tracts for sale to the highest bidder. The Secretary of the Club, on behalf of the occupier, bid the minimum price, $1.25 per acre. If all went as scheduled, no other bids were made, and the squatter thus acquired title to his farm. On occasion, some ignorant stranger or daring speculator offered a bid, whereupon he was suddenly made aware of his offense against community ethics. There were instances where floggings and other tangible sanctions were invoked to enforce compliance with the code. The movement of settlers into Iowa was so rapid that the surveyors and the land office were unable to keep pace with it. So the Claim Club continued to function with the advancing frontier. Over a hundred of these organizations were formed in Iowa. The principle for which they stood was finally embodied into law, when a general pre-emption act was passed by Congress in 1841. The pioneer settler was now guaranteed the first opportunity to buy the land upon which he squatted, and the Claim Club thereafter served primarily as an organization to settle disputes and to keep a record of claims until official titles were issued.

Upon the admission of Missouri to statehood in 1821, the region north of that state had been left without government. The few people who settled in this Indian territory managed very well without regular officials, their sense of justice caring for problems as they arose. One such instance occurred at the Dubuque mines in 1834. Patrick O'Connor killed a fellow miner, and the inhabitants of the district felt that the murderer should stand trial. "I'll not deny that I shot him," said O'Connor, "but ye have no laws in the country and cannot try me." The settlers were unwilling to let an absence of laws defeat justice. So after a jury was chosen, an orderly trial was conducted; the defendant was found guilty and was sentenced to be hanged. The condemned man was placed in a cart, driven under the gallows, and executed. From the crowd of witnesses a collection was gathered to defray the expenses incurred.

In 1834 Congress extended the western boundary of Michigan Territory to the Missouri River, thus providing government for the settlers in present Iowa. Dubuque and Des Moines counties were thereupon created in the Black Hawk Cession lands west of the Mississippi. In 1836 the western part of Michigan Territory was formed into Wisconsin Territory. About half of the population of the new Territory then lived west of the Mississippi in present Iowa. The Wisconsin Territorial legislature of 1837 met at Burlington, holding its sessions in the Methodist Church. This was the first legislative body to convene in present Iowa.

The Territory of Iowa was created from the western part of Wisconsin in 1838. Its original boundaries extended to Canada and comprised not only the present state, but most of Minnesota and large parts of the Dakotas of today. Robert Lucas, a former governor of Ohio, was appointed the first governor. The question of a Territorial capital was hotly debated in the first session of the legislature, with dozens of hopeful and aspiring towns seeking the designation. Finally, the legislature decided to lay out a new city in Johnson County, call it Iowa City, and make it the capital. A man was employed to plow a furrow from Dubuque to Iowa City, a distance of 100 miles, this line to direct emigrants to the new city. The cornerstone of the capitol was laid July 4, 1840; in 1842 the stone building was in use.

In typical Western fashion, the citizens of Iowa Territory began at once to talk of statehood. The proposal for calling a constitutional convention was submitted to the electorate in 1840 and again in 1842, but was lost on both occasions. The thought of the extra taxation necessary to support a state government was apparently the deciding factor. But with a continued growth of population, the proposition gained favor. In February, 1844, the advocates of statehood passed a bill through the legislature providing for a constitutional convention. The fundamental document, framed and then submitted to Congress, would have extended Iowa farther north than does the present state. Congress agreed to grant statehood, but at the same time reduced the size of the proposed state, omitting the western portion and thus cutting Iowa from frontage on the Missouri River. The proposed reduction in size was hotly opposed by the citizenry, who at two successive elections in 1845 defeated the constitution with the restricted boundaries. The next year a new convention drafted another constitution, which in the main was similar to the one of 1844. Congress made a slight alteration, fixing the boundaries as they exist today. With Iowa's acceptance of this change and of the altered constitution, the new state was admitted to the Union in 1846.

At this time most of the people lived in the eastern part of the state. As immigration continued and the frontier pushed westward, the demand increased for a more centrally located capital. Finally, in 1857, a new constitution was adopted and the capital was moved to Des Moines. Iowa City was placated by being made the seat of the state university. By this time the prejudice against banking institutions had been so mitigated that the new constitution permitted the creation of banks, whereas the former one had forbidden them.

By 1840, Iowa was beginning to produce a surplus of food. Numerous flatboats, laden with all kinds of produce, floated down to St. Louis. Corn soon became the principal crop, and farmers found that conversion of corn into pork was most profitable. Travelers noted that the roads were alive with hogs, each pig being "fifteen or twenty bushels of corn on four legs," transporting itself to market. There was "one universal squeal all along the Mississippi." In 1840 the corn crop of Iowa was 1,406,000 bushels; the number of hogs, 105,000. At the end of the decade corn production was 8,600,000 bushels and the hogs numbered 323,000. Wheat was as important as corn in 1840; but during the succeeding decade it rapidly lost its relative importance. Corn became king, and king it has remained through a century of agriculture. The popular song was to be:

> Io-way, I-o-way,
> That's where the tall corn grows.

In the early years surplus Iowa products were shipped out by water. Clothing, household goods, farm implements, and such items also came in by boat. Inland water routes were utilized with small steamers especially designed for shallow streams. In the fifties some 40 light-draft sternwheelers were in operation on the Des Moines River. During the short but romantic period of inland waterway supremacy, St. Louis was the great distributing point and market for early Iowa.

That primacy was soon to be challenged by Chicago. The railroad age was beginning.

In 1850 there was not a mile of railroad west of the Mississippi. But in the country at large, enthusiasm for rails was rising and spreading, and road construction was making real headway. In 1854 the Chicago and Rock Island reached the Mississippi, opposite Davenport.

The next year the great river was bridged at this point, and a railroad was pushed westward as far as Iowa City. The Illinois Central also reached the river, opposite Dubuque, in 1855. Chicago was bidding against St. Louis for the products of Iowa farms. Aspiring railroads began to challenge the supremacy of the steamboat in the transportation of both freight and passengers. In Iowa the principal early railroads ran east and west. The state was spanned in 1867 by the Chicago and Northwestern, which crossed the Mississippi at Clinton and reached the Missouri at Council Bluffs. Two other lines across the state were completed in 1869.

Although there was a great migration to Iowa during the 1840's, the influx of the next decade was even more imposing. The population figures, which stood at 43,000 in 1840, increased to 192,212 in 1850 and to 674,913 in 1860. The improvement in transportation facilities by water and then by rail encouraged the migration. More and more were the settlers coming from the northern tier of states, with large numbers from distant New England. In 1850 there were only 5,535 New Englanders in Iowa—about three per cent of the population. They were outnumbered by native Southerners about six to one. By 1856 the ratio was three to one, and shortly the Northern element was predominant.

A large immigration from foreign lands began to come to Iowa in the late forties and early fifties, although their numbers were proportionately less than those going to the neighboring states of Missouri, Illinois, Wisconsin, and Minnesota. Some of these foreigners came as unique organizations, such as the group of Trappist monks from Ireland, the French Icarians, and the German settlers at Amana. Each of these three groups had community ownership of property. But most of the immigrants came as did American homeseekers, to buy farms and to improve their condition by private initiative. In 1860 there were 106,081 foreigners in Iowa. Of these, Germany contributed more than any other country, with Ireland in second place. Others ranked in the following order: English, Canadians, Norwegians, Scotch, Dutch, Swiss, and French. The Census of 1890 showed 324,669 persons from foreign countries in Iowa's total population of 1,911,896. Germany was still in the lead, contributing more than a third of the foreign-born. The European immigrants soon learned the language

and accepted the customs of their adopted country, yet frequently
they made distinctive contributions characteristic of the land of their
birth.

THE BEGINNINGS OF MINNESOTA

The first entry of French fur men into the Minnesota region and
their displacement by the British traders have been noted previously.
The United States had acquired the region east of the Mississippi at
the close of the American Revolution, and had purchased the land to
the west of the river in 1803. But despite these titles, the British
traders continued to control the Indians and to exploit the fur resources of the northern country. This condition was changed soon
after the close of the War of 1812. Congress passed a law in 1816
which provided that licenses to trade with the Indians within the
territorial limits of the United States should be confined to American
citizens. To enforce this law and to protect both Indians and American
traders, Fort Crawford was established in that year at Prairie du
Chien, Wisconsin. Three years later Fort Snelling (first called Fort
St. Anthony) was established at the mouth of the Minnesota River. It
became an important frontier post. Some of the officers brought their
families here; and in 1823 John Marsh, who was a Harvard graduate
and was later to become a prominent pioneer of California, taught
school here.

President Monroe personally selected, as the first Indian Agent to
be sent to Fort Snelling, Lawrence Taliaferro (pronounced "Tolliver"),
a member of an old Virginia family of Italian extraction. For 20
years he was to be the most important civil official on the upper Mississippi. With him he brought a number of Negro slaves to Minnesota.
The Indians called them "black Frenchmen." One of these servant
girls he later gave in marriage to Dred Scott (of the famous legal
case), performing the ceremony himself. In dealing with the Indians
Taliaferro was upright and dependable; with the traders, strict and
incorruptible. He was able to win the Indians in the Minnesota wilds
from British influence. Within two years he had induced the chiefs
to surrender 36 medals of George III and 28 British flags. In return
he gave them American flags and "Peace and Friendship" medals
carrying a bust of the President of the United States.

The whole of present Minnesota was Indian territory prior to 1837,
and was not officially open to white settlement. But despite the
absence of legal authorization, a few people had already come into
the region and settled about Fort Snelling, carrying on trade with the
Indians and the soldiers. A French trader named Faribault was one
of the first to settle near the fort, at Mendota. He built a log cabin

there, choosing the site because of the protection Fort Snelling afforded. Other fur traders brought their employees and families to the location, and Mendota grew into a little town. The American Fur Company, which during the 1820's had won an almost complete monopoly of the fur trade of the region, established its headquarters for the Sioux trade at Mendota. In 1834, this company sent Henry Hastings Sibley to manage its business here. For 30 years Mendota was to be his home. Here he built the first stone house in Minnesota, a building that still stands and now serves as a museum. Throughout his lifetime, says W. W. Folwell, in his *History of Minnesota*, Sibley was "easily the most prominent figure in Minnesota history."

Among the earliest settlers to enter Minnesota and take up farming were some Swiss colonists from Canada. This strange entry requires an explanation. Lord Selkirk, one of the principal stockholders in the great Hudson's Bay Company, acquired from that organization a large tract of land south and west of Lake Winnipeg. His plan was to establish here colonies of evicted Scotch peasants and others. But the settlers who came to the region, beginning in 1812, were not welcomed by the North West Company fur traders, who looked upon them as intruders from the rival Hudson's Bay Company. Friction developed, and blood was shed. Selkirk continued to reinforce his colonists. In 1817 he brought in 100 Swiss and Italians who recently had been mercenary soldiers in the British army. He sent agents to Europe to recruit colonists. A company of Swiss mechanics and tradesmen, induced to come to the colony through glowing accounts of the Red River valley, arrived in 1821. The conditions and prospects here were so disappointing that five families immediately set out for the United States. They traveled up the Red River and down the Minnesota, and upon reaching Fort Snelling were permitted to settle in the vicinity. Two years later other Swiss families came from the Selkirk settlements. In 1826, following the occurrence of a flood in the Red River, 243 colonists, mostly Swiss, left the Pembina settlement. Upon reaching Fort Snelling, some of the refugees settled in the vicinity of the fort, while others pushed on down the river. By 1840 about 700 persons had reached Fort Snelling from the Red River settlements. About half of these remained permanently in Minnesota, becoming "the earliest settlers in the oldest towns of the state within a radius of twenty miles of Fort Snelling."

The military authorities soon objected to the presence of civilians on the military reserve about Fort Snelling. The settlers were burning up the timber, and some of the traders were supplying liquor to the Indians and the soldiers. Presently orders came from Washington for a survey and designation of the military tract, and for the expulsion of all civilians. The final removal occurred in 1840, the evicted squatters moving beyond the boundary of the reserve and settling on the east bank of the Mississippi. To serve the Catholics among these settlers a little log church, called the Chapel of St. Paul, was built in 1841. The village that grew up about the church took the name from the chapel. Such was the beginning of the capital of Minnesota.

In the meantime, the Indians had been induced to make their first cession of land in Minnesota other than the site of Fort Snelling. The Chippewa and the Sioux signed treaties in 1837 whereby they gave title to the triangular delta between the Mississippi and the St. Croix rivers, and were to receive annuities as remuneration. A desire to have access to the magnificent pine forests on the upper reaches of the St. Croix had been the primary objective of the whites in negotiating the Chippewa treaty. In fact, while negotiations were in progress at Fort Snelling in late July, 1837, some astute persons set out in a birch-bark canoe and reached the falls of the St. Croix, where they forthwith established a claim on the Wisconsin side of the river. Two years later the first sawmill on the St. Croix was put into operation about 20 miles below the falls, at Marine. The manufacture of lumber at Stillwater was begun in 1844. The excellent location for handling logs and the access to good forests and to down-river markets gave Stillwater decided advantages. It grew rapidly, and the enthusiastic citizens were certain that their city would become and remain the metropolis of the region. Most of the supplies for these lumbermen in the early years were brought up the Mississippi and the St. Croix in steamboats. When presently the agricultural possibilities of the country west of Lake St. Croix were demonstrated, some food was obtained locally. As early as 1839 farms in the area were started near Afton and Cottage Grove, but initial productions were small.

The Falls of St. Anthony on the Mississippi were early recognized as a valuable water power resource. But until completion of the treaty of 1837 with the Sioux, the falls were on Indian land. Upon receipt of the news at Fort Snelling in July, 1838, that the Senate had ratified the treaty, a contest for the land adjoining the falls took place. Franklin Steele finally emerged with the coveted prize. When the public land sale took place in 1848, he obtained legal title to this land, on the east side of the river. He thus acquired control of the water power east of the middle of the stream. In 1847 he had built a dam across the east channel and erected a sawmill. When the mill went into operation the next year, lumbermen began to build homes in the vicinity. The town of St. Anthony, platted in 1849, came into being. Some settlers from Stillwater and St. Paul moved to the new town. Lumbermen came from distant Maine and made their homes here.

By the year 1849, when Minnesota Territory was created, the region had received but very limited development. Lumbering and the fur trade were the leading industries, with Stillwater, St. Anthony, and St. Paul as the principal villages. Furs and lumber were floated down the Mississippi to markets in St. Louis and elsewhere. Cargoes of pork, flour, and other supplies came upstream. The first steamboat had reached Fort Snelling in 1823, and others came at irregular intervals thereafter. By 1847 a regular line of steamers was serving St. Paul.

The supply trade to this port was augmented by traffic to and from the Red River towns of the north. Settlers in the Pembina region found that St. Paul was their best and nearest supply depot and shipping point. So each spring a caravan of carts creaked across Minnesota, carrying their loads of furs and skins for the outside world. After disposal of the pelts at St. Paul, supplies of miscellaneous merchandise were purchased for the homeward journey. The two-wheeled Red River cart, made wholly of wood and rawhide and pulled by a single ox, carried a half-ton load. For years the cart caravan continued this northern commerce. Always the arrival of this picturesque train, and the evening camp of these *bois brûlés* in their semibarbaric costumes, were features of never-ending interest, especially to Americans newly arrived at St. Paul.

TERRITORY AND STATE

All of present Minnesota was embraced in Wisconsin Territory upon the latter's creation in 1836. Two years later, when Iowa Territory was formed, that part of Minnesota west of the Mississippi went to Iowa. Part of that portion east of the river, which remained in Wisconsin, was opened to settlement as a result of the Indian treaties of 1837. The pioneers who came into this triangular section, the first area in Minnesota to be officially opened to white settlers, soon began to think of a separate government. In 1846 a bill was introduced in Congress proposing the establishment of Minnesota Territory, but the national lawmakers considered the population too sparse to justify such action. When Wisconsin became a state, in 1848, its western boundary was contracted and the Minnesota region was excluded. The settlers left without government in this no-man's-land were alarmed at being thus neglected or ignored. In August, 1848, their representatives assembled at Stillwater, prepared a memorial to Congress pleading for the early organization of Minnesota Territory, and chose Henry H. Sibley as a delegate to represent their interests in Washington. Some of these ingenious citizens living west of the newly drawn Wisconsin boundary contended that the part of the former Territory not included in the new state of Wisconsin continued its existence as Wisconsin

Territory. On that assumption they held an election in October, 1848, and chose Sibley as delegate to Congress from Wisconsin Territory. No one appears to have inquired into the fact that Sibley was not a citizen of Wisconsin, his home being west of the Mississippi at Mendota, on land that from 1838 to 1846 had been part of Iowa, and in 1848 was unorganized and unceded Indian territory. But Sibley was a well-dressed gentleman, eloquent, and with a commanding personality, so the Congressmen ignored technicalities, gave him a seat in their body, and voted his salary. A bill for the creation of Minnesota Territory was debated in Congress in January, 1849, and was enacted on March 3 following. The boundaries as drawn included all of present Minnesota and that portion of the Dakotas east of the Missouri and the White Earth rivers. The region had a bona fide population of less than 4,000 at the time. Alexander Ramsey was appointed the first governor of the Territory.

When the chief executive took up his residence at St. Paul in June, 1849, the capital was "just emerging from a collection of Indian whiskey shops and birch-roof cabins of half-breed voyageurs." But this seat of government of a promising Territory immediately took on new life. James M. Goodhue had shipped a newspaper press to St. Paul, and on April 28, 1849, issued the first number of the *Minnesota Pioneer*. He visioned a great future for the town and Territory, and in the columns of his paper spread his glowing gospel. Other newspapers of the country called attention to the opportunities in the new land, and a ready response came from farmers, lumbermen, merchants, and land speculators. The sawmill at St. Anthony and others farther up the Mississippi and along its tributaries turned out lumber for the new settlers. Lumber camps sprang into busy life, and farmers followed the lumbermen.

As yet, however, the growth in Minnesota was seriously hampered. The Indians must give ground before Minnesota could achieve its real development. Thus far only the delta area between the Mississippi and the St. Croix was open to settlement, but everyone was confident that further concessions from the Sioux would bring an early opening of the region west of the Mississippi. Governor Ramsey and other leaders turned their attention at once toward this objective, but the attempt to obtain a treaty in 1849 did not succeed.

In 1851 the leaders of various tribes were assembled to meet the United States commissioners. An understanding having been reached for "taking care of" the various white traders and half-breeds, these influential persons gave active encouragement, and the chiefs were induced to sign the proffered treaties. The Sioux agreed to give up their land east of the Red River-Lake Traverse-Big Sioux line, except for very small reservations. Much of present Minnesota and part of Iowa were thus ceded to the whites. As each chief signed the treaty, someone "pulled his blanket," led him a few feet away, and directed him to sign another document, resting on a barrel head. This was the "traders' paper," which directed that a large amount of the Indians' money be paid to traders and half-breeds in satisfaction of various debts and claims. It is doubtful that the Indians realized what they were signing. From this unfair sowing the whites were to reap the whirlwind later in the Sioux uprising of 1862—to be treated later. Northern Minnesota was claimed by the Chippewa. By treaties signed in 1854, 1855, and 1863, most of this country was ceded by them to the whites.

The treaties approved by the Sioux in 1851 were amended somewhat by Congress. These alterations were accepted by the Indians in 1852, the treaty was proclaimed by the President in 1853, and the first of this land was legally opened for settlement in 1854. But eager white men did not wait for these later formalities before rushing onto the coveted soil. In 1851 they began crossing the Mississippi into the "Suland." They opened roads, staked claims, cut timber, and built houses. The Indian Agent tried to hold them back; but since he was refused military assistance from Fort Snelling, his efforts were futile. It was estimated that 20,000 white men had invaded the region by 1852. Of them, in a contemporary message, Minnesota's Governor Ramsey said:

They bring with them to the wilderness, which they embellish and advance, maxims of civil liberty, not engrossed on parchments, but inscribed in their hearts—not as barren abstractions, but as living principles and practical rules of conduct. They cost the government neither monthly pay, nor rations—they solicit no bounty—they expect no hospital privileges—but they make the country, its history and its glory.

The governor was urging the extension of the pre-emption privilege to settlers on unsurveyed land. This boon was to be granted the squatters in Minnesota by Congressional action in 1854. But already the settlers had come by the hundreds, confident that legal title to the land they claimed would be forthcoming. They organized Claim Clubs, and by these extra-legal devices insured ownership of the land squatted upon.

The valley of the Minnesota River was especially attractive. This was the region referred to as "the prettiest country lying wild that the world can boast of, got up with the greatest care and effort by old dame Nature ten thousand years or more ago." Here such towns as Le Sueur, Shakopee, and Mankato were begun in 1854. In this year St. Anthony had a population of 2,500 and St. Paul boasted 7,000 to 8,000, with brick warehouses, stores and hotels, and wharves that accommodated some 300 steamers annually. The land across the river from St. An-

thony was part of the Fort Snelling reservation until 1852. But prior
to this time, and in disregard of military regulations, some settlers had
squatted on the land. The first house had been built in 1850, and others
were soon added. The hamlet developed into Minneapolis, which was
ultimately to spread to the east side of the river and absorb St. Anthony.

The year 1854 witnessed the "Great Railroad Excursion," in celebration of the completion of the railroad to Rock Island. Many distinguished persons attended. At the rail head the visitors embarked in
five steamers and ascended the river to St. Paul. In addition to being
a gala affair, it advertised Minnesota and demonstrated the accessibility
of the new region. The next year saw such a flood of immigrants pour
into Minnesota that the packet companies were hardly able to handle
the traffic. Steamboats navigated the Minnesota River, 119 arrivals of
such craft at St. Paul being noted in 1855 and 292 in 1857. The capital
city became so crowded that many newcomers had to camp in the
streets. "Fence in a prairie fire! Dam up Niagara! Bail out Lake
Superior! Tame a wolf! Civilize Indians! Attempt any practical
thing; but not to set metes and bounds to the progress of St. Paul!"
Thus wrote one of the city's newspaper editors in 1854.

The influx to Minnesota from 1855 to 1857 was almost unprecedented
on the frontier, the population of the Territory reaching 150,000 in the
latter year. The heavy immigration made a ready market for all produce. Speculation in farm lands and town lots ran riot. From 1854
to 1857 there were 700 towns platted in Minnesota. Then suddenly the
great boom-bubble burst. The Panic of 1857, severe throughout the
entire country, struck especially hard in Minnesota, where so much was
being built on credit and hope. Money was drawn out of the territory
by Eastern creditors. Banks were closed; business was at a standstill.
St. Paul temporarily lost almost half its population. But here, as elsewhere, the people muddled through, and confidence was eventually
restored.

In February, 1857, Congress had passed an Enabling Act for Minnesota, defining boundaries for the proposed state practically as they
exist today. When the delegates to a constitutional convention assembled at St. Paul in the following July, the partisan feeling between
Republicans and Democrats was so strong that the convention split into
two factions. Each began to draft a constitution of its own; but compromise committees were presently appointed, and the two branches of
the convention finally adopted identical constitutions. On October 13,
1857, the electorate ratified the instrument and elected state officials.
Minnesota was admitted to the Union on May 11, 1858.

By 1860 the population of Minnesota stood at 172,023. Two-thirds
of the number were native-born Americans. Of these, the largest

proportion had come from the middle Atlantic area, those from the Middle West were second in number, and those from New England ranked third. The foreign-born numbered 58,728, with the principal nationals ranking as follows: Germans, 18,400; Irish, 12,831; Norwegians, 8,425; and Swedes, 3,178. Despite the Civil War and serious Indian troubles, Minnesota grew during the 1860's. This growth was in part due to the state-directed stimulation of foreign immigration. Pamphlets were printed and agents were employed to direct the immigrants to Minnesota. The Census of 1870 recorded a population of 439,706 for the state. Of the 160,697 foreign-born, Scandinavians now led with 59,390; Germans came second with 48,457. By 1880 the Scandinavians had increased to 107,768, the Germans to 66,592, and the total population to 780,773. Ten years later the Scandinavians numbered 215,000, in a foreign-born population of 467,000.

In 1862 the first railroad was built within the state, a short line connecting St. Paul and Minneapolis. Other lines, soon constructed, aided in the settlement of the prairie country inland from the rivers. Prior to 1870 most of the settlers lived in the southeastern part of the state; then came occupancy of the southwestern portion and the Red River Valley. Wheat was at first the principal crop, but corn was in time to exceed it in value. Cattle-raising and dairying were also to assume great importance. Although wheat-growing spread westward into the Dakotas, Montana, and Canada, Minneapolis maintained her primacy as the great milling center. The lumber industry steadily increased in the region about 1905. In the northern part of the state, in the decade of the 1890's, iron ore became the leading resource, and Minnesota soon was producing more iron than all the rest of the United States.

BIBLIOGRAPHY

For a comprehensive history of Iowa, consult Benjamin F. Gue, *History of Iowa from the Earliest Times to the Beginning of the Twentieth Century* (4 vols., New York, 1903). A readable and more recent work is I. B. Richman, *Ioway to Iowa* (Iowa City, 1931). See also W. J. J. Harsha, *The Story of Iowa* (Iowa, 1890); J. A. James, *Constitution and Admission of Iowa into the Union* (Baltimore, 1900); B. F. Shambaugh (ed.), *Documentary Material Relating to the History of Iowa* (3 vols., Iowa City, 1897–1901); Cyrenus Cole, *A History of the People of Iowa* (Cedar Rapids, 1921); Johnson Brigham, *Iowa: Its History and its Foremost Citizens* (Chicago, 1915); Franc B. Wilkie, *Davenport, Past and Present* (Davenport, 1858).

For special phases of Iowa history, see: B. M. H. Shambaugh, *Amana that Was and Amana that Is* (Iowa City, 1932); Jacob Van der Zee, *The British in Iowa* (Iowa City, 1922); ————, *The Hollanders of Iowa* (Iowa City, 1912); B. E. Mahan, *Old Fort Crawford and the Frontier* (Iowa City, 1926); W. J. Petersen, *Steamboating on the Upper Mississippi; The Water*

Way to Iowa (Iowa City, 1937); B. F. Shambaugh, *The Old Stone Capital Remembers* (Iowa City, 1939); B. F. Shambaugh (ed.), *Iowa Economic History Series* (5 vols., Iowa City, 1912–1928); B. F. Shambaugh (ed.), *Iowa Applied History* (6 vols., Iowa City, 1912–1930); Melvin Gingerich, *Mennonites in Iowa* (Iowa City, 1939).

Among valuable reminiscences and biographical sketches the following may be listed: Cyrenus Cole, *I Remember, I Remember; A Book of Recollections* (Iowa City, 1936); T. H. Macbride, *In Cabins and Sod-Houses* (Iowa City, 1928); John Todd, *Early Settlement and Growth of Western Iowa, or Reminiscences* (Des Moines, 1906); Louis Pelzer, *Henry Dodge* (Iowa City, 1911); J. C. Parish, *Robert Lucas* (Iowa City, 1907); J. A. Swisher, *Leonard Fletcher Parker* (Iowa City, 1927).

The files of the *Iowa Journal of History and Politics,* the *Annals of Iowa,* and *The Palimpsest* are full of valuable articles upon the history of Iowa.

The following may be listed as the larger histories of Minnesota: W. W. Folwell, *A History of Minnesota* (4 vols., St. Paul, 1922–1930); R. I. Holcombe, *Minnesota in Three Centuries* (4 vols., New York, 1908); Theodore Christianson, *Minnesota: The Land of Sky-Tinted Waters . . .* (5 vols., Chicago, 1935).

An excellent popular, yet authentic, history is T. C. Blegen, *Building Minnesota* (Boston, 1938). See also M. V. Carney, *Minnesota, the Star of the North* (Boston, 1918).

Among the early volumes relating to the state, the folowing may be cited: E. D. Seymour, *Sketches of Minnesota, the New England of the West* (New York, 1850); J. W. Bond, *Minnesota and its Resources* (New York, 1853); Lawrence Oliphant, *Minnesota and the Far West* (Edinburgh, 1855); J. F. Williams, *History of the City of Saint Paul* (St. Paul, 1876); and E. D. Neill, *The History of Minnesota* (4th ed., Minneapolis, 1882).

The following volumes of biography and reminiscence contain local history of value: S. J. Buck, *William Watts Folwell, . . .* (Minneapolis, 1933); T. C. Blegen, *The Unfinished Autobiography of Henry Hastings Sibley* (Minneapolis, 1932); F. A. Day and T. M. Knappen, *The Life of John Albert Johnson* (Chicago, 1910); Paul De Kruif, *Seven Iron Men* (New York, 1929); G. M. Stephenson, *John Lind of Minnesota* (Minneapolis, 1935); Hans Mattson, *Reminiscences: The Story of an Emigrant* (St. Paul, 1892); C. O. Van Cleve, *Three Score Years and Ten, Life-Long Memories of Fort Snelling, Minnesota, . . .* (Minneapolis, 1881).

For special phases of Minnesota history, consult the following: M. L. Hansen, *Old Fort Snelling, 1819–1858* (Iowa City, 1918); W. Anderson and A. J. Lobb, *History of the Constitution of Minnesota* (Minneapolis, 1921); A. L. Chetlain, *Red River Colony* (Chicago, 1892); Mildred Hartsough, *The Twin Cities as a Metropolitan Market . . .* (Minneapolis, 1925); C. B. Kuhlmann, *The Development of the Flour-Milling Industry . . .* (Boston, 1929); E. V. Robinson, *Early Economic Conditions and the Development of Agriculture in Minnesota* (Minneapolis, 1915); and H. M. Larson, *The Wheat Market and the Farmer in Minnesota, 1858–1900* (New York, 1926).

The Collections of the Minnesota Historical Society and that organization's publication, *Minnesota History: A Quarterly Magazine,* are mines of historical information pertaining to the "North Star State."

22

THE WEST AND CIVIL CONFLICT

Except for Texas, the tier of southern states immediately beyond the Mississippi River, and Kansas, the trans-Mississippi West was little interested in the slavery controversy. In 1861 most of the vast region between these states and the Sierra Nevadas was an unsettled wilderness. But there were a few islands of occupation—the mining region of Colorado, Utah, and the Rio Grande Valley—where emigrants had ventured far beyond the well-settled area. Wherever they settled, problems incident to local development, stock-raising, mining, or transportation claimed their attention. Therefore, these Westerners were little concerned with Negro bondage and the cotton economy, except here and there throughout the West where a few Negroes were held as slaves. Yet, in spite of their lack of interest, by 1861 almost every Western state or territory had been forced to align itself either with the North or the South.

SLAVERY AND EXPANSION

East of the Mississippi national expansion had early followed lines of longitude, except that influenced by the Ordinance of 1787; but even here most of the Northwestern Territory was north of the Pennsylvania-Maryland boundary, the existent demarcation line between free and slave states. In the rapid development of the public domain, both the anti- and pro-slave states had sought to win new states for their respective causes. The result was that in 1820 there were as many free states as slave, with a consequent equal balance of power in the United States Senate. But in the House of Representatives the South was outvoted 105 to 81. Although Southern lawmakers were disturbed because of this Northern advantage, they felt fairly secure so long as they could maintain parity in the Senate. And just here was the germ of rivalry, for after every new territorial acquisition, each section sought to control the states created therefrom.

368

This tendency was revealed when the first territories carved from the Louisiana Purchase asked for statehood. Southerners were not the first to threaten secession. Anti-slave leaders looked askance on the purchase of Louisiana, for the Creoles of the lower Mississippi delta were slaveholders; and when the Territory of Orleans sought admittance to the Union as the State of Louisiana, Representative Josiah Quincy of Massachusetts voiced a threat of secession. But he could not muster sufficient strength to defeat the Louisiana bill. Then in 1818 Missouri was ready for statehood. Again Eastern opposition was aroused. Representative James Tallmadge of New York offered an amendment to a Missouri bill prohibiting the further introduction of slaves into the proposed state and requiring that children of slaves, after reaching the age of 25, should be free. Six weeks of bitter debate followed, in which the press, religious leaders, and state politicians took part. Never before had the nation been so aroused over the slavery issue. Southern congressmen offered stubborn opposition to the amendment, and finally a compromise was effected, primarily as a result of the efforts of Senator Henry Clay of Kentucky. Maine was also ready for statehood; and since obviously it would be admitted as a free state, the basis for a sectional settlement was laid. The substitute plan now offered and enacted into law admitted Missouri as a slave state and Maine as a free state, and henceforth all states carved from the Louisiana Purchase, north of 36° 30′, should enter the Union as free states.

To the aged Jefferson, the debate on the Missouri bill was like "a fire bell in the night," as it was to many another far-sighted statesman. And well they might be alarmed, for this was the beginning of an era of sectional bitterness and strife. Every movement made by pioneers along the southwestern border was jealously watched by anti-slave politicians, who feared a "Southern plot." Such to them was the Texas colonization movement and the Texas revolution. They were convinced of this when, shortly after Houston's victory at San Jacinto, Texas was offered in annexation to the United States. President Andrew Jackson would not support the Texas offer, but he did recognize her independence on March 3, 1837. With this encouragement, during Van Buren's and Tyler's administrations, Texan diplomats sought annexation, but all to no avail. Undoubtedly one reason for their failure was that New England Abolitionists were threatening disunion if Texas were admitted. On March 3, 1843, John Quincy Adams of Massachusetts and 12 other anti-slavery Whig members of Congress issued an address to the non-slaveholding Commonwealths, hinting broadly of a slaveholders' conspiracy and threatening the secession of New England if Texas became a state of the American Union.

Presidential aspirants approached the election of 1844 warily, for both the Oregon and Texas problems loomed large on the political horizon. In the Pacific Northwest, the United States claimed 54° 40' as its northern boundary; but England would not accept it, nor would she compromise on the forty-ninth parallel. Since the Texas annexation issue was involved with slavery, it was even more fraught with political danger. Both Martin Van Buren and Henry Clay, candidates for the Democratic and Whig nominations, respectively, sought to sidestep the Texas issue by asserting that annexation might provoke war with Mexico. But the impatient voters turned from them. The Democratic convention chose James K. Polk of Tennessee as its presidential candidate, and launched a vigorous campaign on the slogans "Fifty-four Forty or Fight" and "Reannexation of Texas." Since they had no outstanding "manifest destiny" candidate, the Whigs chose Clay. He, before the campaign closed, saw that Polk had struck a popular note, and tardily announced himself in favor of annexation, but it was too late. Many of his former adherents then turned to James G. Birney, the Liberty party candidate; and the Democrats won the election. As previously noticed, shortly before Polk was inaugurated, Texas entered the Union as a result of a joint-resolution procedure.

But in the West the slavery issue would not down. Every advance of the frontier and every accession of territory increased the intensity of sectional rivalry. In 1847 David Wilmot's proposed amendment to a House appropriation bill would have closed the doors of the Mexican Cession in the face of the Southern planters. But after a stormy battle it was voted down. Texas particularly had cause for complaint against the federal government. President Polk had supported her claim of the Rio Grande as a southern and western boundary, but his successor, Zachary Taylor, was not favorably disposed; and Texas officials, Judge Spruce M. Beard and Robert S. Neighbors, who came to Santa Fe to organize western counties, were sent home by federal military commanders with curt reminders that New Mexico was under their control until other instructions were received. This pleased the New Mexicans, who had refused to recognize the Texas claims and who were clamoring for territorial organization. Moreover, the South was still concerned with the question raised by Wilmot. How should the Mexican Cession be organized? Would the Southerners, who had supported the Mexican War so generously, be allowed to carry slavery into states and territories carved from the ceded territory? Signs of the time indicated the contrary, for already California was demanding admittance to the Union on a free state constitution, and the Mormons of Utah were hostile to slavery.

The sectional clash of 1850, therefore, shook the very foundations of the nation. Leaders in Congress realized that a crisis was at hand, and that civil war might engulf the nation unless the matter was settled. The storm broke on January 29, 1850, when Clay proposed to the Senate a series of compromise resolutions that in the main ultimately was adopted.

The North had its firebrands in Chase of Ohio and Seward of New York, while the South was ably represented by Davis of Mississippi and others. The "Great American Triumvirate"—Clay, Calhoun, Webster—made their last great speeches in Congress. In his address of February 5 and 6, Clay warned that the sections must seek a common ground of understanding. Even the state legislatures, he said, were like "twenty-odd furnaces in full blast generating heat and passion and intemperance." Calhoun also warned of impending disaster, but largely because of Free Soil agitation; he declared that the South would be satisfied with nothing less than a stoppage of anti-slavery propaganda. In his brilliant March 7 speech, Webster called upon both sections to end their antagonisms, or else disunion would come. Free Soilers were disappointed. They had expected Webster to support their cause, but instead he had pled for compromise. James Russell Lowell wrote of his "mean and foolish treachery"; and John Greenleaf Whittier likened him to the fallen Lucifer, and advised his former friends to regard him with "pitying tears, not scorn and wrath."

During the angry resolutions debate, on July 9 President Taylor died and Millard Fillmore succeeded him. The new President favored compromise; consequently, a series of measures was presently introduced. One of these was the "Omnibus bill," covering the Western aspects of the controversy, but it failed of passage. Finally, separate enactments accomplished the same purpose. California was admitted to the Union with a free state constitution; New Mexico and Utah were given territorial recognition, leaving the problem of slavery to be settled later on the principle of popular sovereignty; and the public debt of Texas was to be assumed by the federal government, in return for which the United States would acquire the Texas claims north of the 31° and 36° 30′ parallels and west of the one hundred and third meridian. Two other measures did not greatly concern the West: a more stringent fugitive slave law was enacted, and the slave trade, but not slavery, was prohibited in the District of Columbia.

Once more the nation rejoiced that another crisis had been successfully met, and hoped that it might be the last. But hardly had the rumblings of the recent storm subsided, before others could be heard. The Pacific surveys, provided by a congressional appropriation of

$150,000 in 1853, had revealed the feasibility of four transcontinental railway routes. Naturally, both sections desired the eastern terminus of any line built. But Secretary of War Davis favored the southern-most one. So once more the Free Soilers advanced to the attack. They charged that the Secretary, being from Mississippi, had allowed his sectional bias to motivate his choice, and that he had proposed a road which would become a line of projection for Southern interests. Davis acknowledged that the central route was shorter, but he pointed out that the undeveloped Great Plains part of it presented an insuper-able barrier. Any road built over this region would not only violate Indian treaty rights, but would also offer poor prospects to its builders, for profits must come in large part from local freight and passengers.

This objection to the central route was strong, but there were North-ern proponents who were not willing to regard the undeveloped terri-tory, stretching from Texas to Canada and from Missouri to the Rockies, as a permanent barrier. Among these was Stephen A. Doug-las of Illinois. He not only wanted his state to share in the transconti-nental traffic of the proposed railroad, but he was anxious that Chicago, his home town, become its eastern terminus. Already Douglas had proved his skill as a railway politician by securing for his state the Illinois Central Railroad, connecting the Lakes with the Gulf. Now to substitute the central transcontinental route for the southern, as pro-posed by Davis, would indeed enhance his political fortunes as well as the material welfare of his state. James Ford Rhodes believed that Douglas was primarily concerned with winning Southern support for the Democratic presidential nomination in the forthcoming election, and other American historians have agreed with him; but the late Professor Frank Hodder of Kansas has pretty well proved that Doug-las' interest was primarily economic.

His chairmanship of the Senate territorial committee enabled him to accomplish his purpose. Moreover, shortly after Davis had made his report, Commissioner George W. Manypenny had negotiated new trea-ties with the Indians of the central plains area. Now there remained only the opening of the territory to settlement; and this was what Douglas proposed to do in his Nebraska bill. He knew, of course, that Southern members of Congress favored Davis' proposal, and would frown on any movement to organize an anti-slave territory, even though it should come from the region acknowledged as free soil under the Compromise of 1820. To overcome these objections, therefore, he resorted to a political master-stroke. He would win sufficient Southern support to his bill by proposing the repeal of the Missouri Compromise and by requiring that the proposed territory be settled on the basis of popular sovereignty, as had been done in the New Mexico and Utah bills.

A storm of opposition now greeted him. Free Soilers and Abolitionists charged that he was guilty of "undoing the sectional truce of 1820," of reopening an old wound that had long since healed. But he was not swerved from his purpose. When his Nebraska bill met with stubborn opposition, he then proposed two territories—Kansas and Nebraska, divided by the fortieth parallel. But he still sought the repeal of the Compromise of 1820 and the substitution of popular sovereignty. In the turbulent debate which followed, he was able to parry

Based on Goode's Base Map No. 209 W, by permission of University of Chicago Press

TERRITORIAL AND STATE BOUNDARIES, 1850–1860

every verbal thrust of his Northern foes—Benjamin Wade, Salmon P. Chase, Charles Sumner, William H. Seward, and Edward Everett. In spite of stern opposition, Alexander H. Stephens in the House and Douglas in the Senate successfully piloted the bill through the political storm, and President Franklin K. Pierce signed it.

The day of compromise was now over. Horace Greeley wrote in the *New York Tribune* that President Pierce and Douglas had made more Abolitionists in three months than William Lloyd Garrison and Wendell Phillips could have done in half a century. Seward dramatically accepted the gauge of battle which he believed that Douglas and pro-slave congressmen had insultingly thrown down before the North, and sent out a call to all lovers of freedom to rally to the anti-slave standard. Soon after the enactment of the measure both the anti- and pro-slave factions made preparations to invade and to take control of Kansas, and it was just here that the popular sovereignty theory was to prove untenable—Kansas was taken from the realm of normal settlement. Eli Thayer and many another Abolitionist were soon organizing Emigrant Aid Societies along the Atlantic seaboard, all committed to the task of settling Kansas. But General David R. Atchison and the western Missouri settlers stood ready to repel them. Because of these outside influences, popular sovereignty failed, and the basis of conflict was laid.

Presently anti-slave immigrants established their first settlement on the Kansas River at Lawrence, while the pro-slave immigrants founded Atchison on the left bank of the Missouri. The latter revealed their hostility to the former by announcing in their *Squatter Sovereign* that they would "lynch, hang, tar and feather, and drown every white-livered Abolitionist who dared to pollute the soil of Kansas."

The anti-slave settlers were undoubtedly in the majority when the first governor, Andrew H. Reeder of Pennsylvania, arrived in October, 1854, and could have elected a territorial delegate to Congress in a fair contest. But in November the Missourians, expecting Free Soil trickery, marched into Kansas 1,700 strong and elected John W. Whitfield as territorial delegate to Congress. Then on March 30, 1855, a pro-slave legislature was chosen. But 6,320 votes had been cast in the election, and the census taken shortly before the election showed a population of only about 8,500! Here again Missouri's determination to take Kansas for the South was manifest.

But the battle had hardly begun. From the east, north, and south came recruits for the rival forces. The setting up of the Topeka free state government, the sacking of Lawrence, the John Brown murders, and the marching and counter-marching of rival bodies of armed men were a few of the evidences of chaos; and a parade of territorial governors and acting governors—Reeder, Daniel Woodson, Wilson Shannon, J. W. Geary, Robert J. Walker, F. P. Stanton, and James W. Denver—was proof enough of political instability. Douglas spurned a slave-state constitution because of an evident election fraud, but he would not accept another proposed by Dr. Charles Robinson and other free state leaders. The pro-slave faction was better organized, however, and finally won. In 1858 the deadlock was broken by the English bill, which proposed a resubmission of the Lecompton (pro-slave) Constitution to popular vote. The anti-slave settlers now revealed a numerical superiority by rejecting it by a vote of 11,300 to 1,788. Then in January, 1861, they won a more decisive victory when Kansas was admitted as a free state. But Douglas, too, had won; in the next year Congress enacted its Union Pacific Railroad law, which authorized a road over the central route, as discussed elsewhere in this book.

OUTBREAK OF WAR

By 1861 the crescendo of sectional controversy had reached the deafening roar of war. The rise of a militant anti-slave party (Republican), the Dred Scott decision of the Supreme Court, the Lincoln-Douglas debates of 1858, the John Brown raid on Harper's Ferry, and Lincoln's election in 1860 were all indicative of an impending civil conflict. And soon after the election, amidst wild excitement, the South Carolina convention enacted its secession ordinance. By February 1, 1861, that state's lead had been followed by six other Southern states, including the two trans-Mississippi states of Louisiana and Texas. Governor Sam Houston had strongly pled with Texas politicians to refrain from such an extreme measure, but he was forced out of office, and a state convention voted for secession 166 to 7. The ordinance then was presented to the voters, who likewise ratified it by an overwhelming majority.

Even before the Texas convention assembled, steps had been taken to force the withdrawal of federal troops. Along the irregular Texas frontier about 2,000 men were stationed in isolated posts, which the department commander, D. E. Twiggs, a Southern sympathizer, now proposed to surrender. But rumors to this effect reached the ears of his superiors, and he was superseded by Colonel Carlos A. Waite. By the time the latter had arrived at headquarters in San Antonio, however, the surrender agreement had already been made, and there was little more he could do than to comply with its terms. The posts north of San Antonio were turned over to Colonel Henry McCulloch on February 17, 1861; and those farther south, to Colonel John S. Ford. Troops leaving the state were to retain their sidearms and were to be furnished with transportation facilities to the Texas coast, where they were to embark. Federal authorities refused to recognize the agreement, so the Texans used this as a pretext to hold as prisoners of war the troops who had not yet left the state. The military supplies which fell into the hands of McCulloch and Ford were valued at $1,500,000.

Arkansas joined the Confederacy on May 6, and it was confidently expected that Missouri would do the same. But the secession convention called by a pro-slave governor was nationalist in sentiment. It not only declared for the Union but also deposed the governor. St. Louis and other important towns were presently in Northern hands, largely because of the aggressive leadership of Francis P. Blair, Jr., and Captain Nathaniel Lyon.

The Five Civilized Tribes in Indian Territory were greatly influenced by pro-slave states; and among them, too, were numerous Negro slaves. It is not surprising, therefore, that they also decided to go with the South. When Albert Pike and General Ben McCulloch arrived in the spring of 1861 to negotiate with the Cherokees, John Ross, principal chief, refused the Southern offer, saying that the Indians were not interested in the white man's war. But after the commissioners had signed treaties with the Creeks, Choctaws, Chickasaws, and Seminoles, Ross reluctantly agreed to do the same. Opoth-le-yo-hola, a warlike Creek chief, refused to support the Southern cause, and fled with a part of his people and Union Cherokees to Kansas. In May, 1861, Colonel W. C. King crossed the Red River from Texas and occupied Fort Arbuckle and other former federal posts, the garrisons of which had already retired to Kansas.

Farther west the Confederates met with little encouragement. Lincoln's newly appointed governor, William Gilpin, arrived in Colorado on May 29, 1861, and aggressively set to work to organize the Union forces. On the previous April 24, Southerners had hoisted a Confederate flag in Denver, but Northern sympathizers hauled it down. Gilpin not only stabilized the maintenance of federal power in the territory, but troops which he presently dispatched southward enabled General E. R. S. Canby in New Mexico to defeat a formidable Confederate invasion. Colorado and Kansas retained a large part of their own troops to meet the Indian danger, as will be noted in Chapter 29.

Southern California had been settled largely by pro-Southern people, but the state as a whole evinced little bias, North or South. As threats of secession grew in frequency, and as both anti- and pro-slave factions wooed California, there grew up a movement to establish an independent Pacific republic. Governor John B. Weller proposed such a step to the legislature in January, 1860; and Representative John C. Burch told Congress that California, Oregon, New Mexico, Washington, and Utah should constitute the "youthful but vigorous Caesarian republic of the Pacific." Northern sentiment in upper California was active. On May 11 a tumultuous mass meeting was held in San Francisco, and drew up anti-secession resolutions; and a few days later the legislature voted its support of Lincoln.

New Mexico's organic act made possible the introduction of Negro slavery; but at the outbreak of the Civil War there were few slaves. Some Negroes had been brought in from time to time by Indian officials and military officers; but an unfavorable climate and soil, plus a legalized Mexican peonage, made Negro slavery impractical. Nevertheless, there was much slavery sentiment. The New Mexico legislature in 1859 restricted the residence of free Negroes in the territory, and two years later enacted a slave code (sponsored by Miguel Otero, the New Mexico delegate in Congress), providing for the protection of property in slaves.

People of Arizona were pro-Southern in sentiment. Here a separate territory movement had been agitated for several years; and until this was consummated in 1863, the region, including southern New Mexico, composed Doña Ana County with its seat at Mesilla. The Arizonans complained that both New Mexico and the federal government had failed to provide adequate protection against the Apaches, and that they had not been given proper representation in the territorial legislature. The Tucson *Arizonian* and the Mesilla *Times* both encouraged secession and bitterly assailed the Union. Thus, as will presently appear, with southern California, Arizona, and southern New Mexico in sympathy with the pro-slave cause, the ground for one of the most astonishing campaigns of the Civil War period was laid.

WESTERN CAMPAIGNS

Since the major military movements of the Civil War were east of the Mississippi River and had little influence on the West, it will serve no purpose to review them here. It is sufficient to say that the bifurcated invasion of the South launched by the North forced General Robert E. Lee to surrender in 1865. Although there were no major army movements in the West, yet there were minor war activities of interest and significance. After Lyon defeated Governor Jackson's troops on the outskirts of St. Louis, the discomfited state executive and his commander, Sterling Price, withdrew to the southern part of the state to join other troops sent up from Arkansas, after which General Earl Van Dorn succeeded to the command. On March 7 and 8, 1862, he encountered General S. R. Curtis and a considerable Union force in the battle of Pea Ridge, but was defeated and forced to retire. This was the only important engagement in which a large body of Indians took part. Major Albert Pike had organized a Confederate force of Cherokees under Brigadier General Stand Watie which saw service in this engagement. Opoth-le-yo-hola and a Creek contingent, however, presently joined Kansas troops in an invasion of Oklahoma.

In September, 1864, Price again invaded Missouri with 15,000 men. His objective was St. Louis; but when he found it strongly held, he turned aside to occupy Jefferson City, the capital. Federal troops soon made his position untenable and forced him to withdraw from the state, and Missouri was henceforth free from important military activity.

The control of the lower Mississippi was of great importance to the Federal government. Consequently, a naval expedition under Flag Officer David G. Farragut, commanding the west Gulf blockading squadron, appeared in the lower Mississippi, ran the gauntlet of fire from Forts Jackson and St. Philip, and on April 25, 1861, captured New Orleans, which was occupied soon thereafter by General Benjamin F. Butler's troops. But Butler's administration was so harsh that in 1863 General N. P. Banks was sent to supersede him. No sooner had Banks arrived than he laid plans for the conquest of Texas. Already, in December, 1862, Galveston had been occupied by United States troops (later recaptured). In September of the next year, Banks launched a campaign against Texas via Sabine Pass, Beaumont, and Houston, but it was defeated and turned back to Sabine Pass. Then in the next month a Federal force occupied Brownsville; but after a few months, it, too, was driven away. Confederate success in holding Texas was of great importance, for this state had not only furnished Southern armies with more than 50,000 men, but it had also sent eastward vast quantities of cotton, grain, meat, and other much needed supplies.

The Sibley invasion of New Mexico was a part of the most ambitious military plan undertaken by the Confederacy in the West. But its ramifications were visionary. As early as the midsummer of 1861, M. H. MacWillie, a citizen of Mesilla, had urged President Jefferson Davis to send a force of Cherokees and Choctaws up the Canadian River into New Mexico. "The stores, supplies, and munitions of war within New Mexico and Arizona are immense," he advised, "and I am decidedly of the opinion that the game is worth the candle." That Davis was impressed is revealed in Brigadier General Henry Hunter Sibley's later instructions. After he had occupied the New Mexico forts, he was to secure "all the arms, supplies, and materials of war."

Yet this was not the ultimate objective. One of Sibley's officers, Major T. T. Teel, later stated that Sibley informed him that his plan was the conquest not only of New Mexico, but of California, so that there would be an outlet for slavery. Then, "if the Confederates succeeded in occupying California, New Mexico, and Arizona, negotiations to secure Chihuahua, Sonora and Lower California, either by purchase or by conquest, would be opened. . . ." Later Colorado also would be taken. Thus, with the gold and silver of California, Nevada, and Colorado in Confederate hands, the Union would find its advantage of factories, foundries, and railways of little consequence. Colonel James Reily, second in command, as well as Sibley's personal agent at Chihuahua, wrote to John H. Regan, in January, 1862: "With Sonora and Chihuahua, we gain Southern California, and by a railroad to Guaymas render our State of Texas the great highway of nations." The Confederate representative in Mexico City, J. T. Pickett, could boast, "The Spaniards have now become our natural allies, and jointly with them we may own the Gulf of Mexico and effect a partition of this magnificent country." All of these predictions were undoubtedly based on the assumption that Mexico in the hands of the French invader was helpless, and, indeed, was on the point of disintegration. Yet undoubtedly they were not regarded seriously by the Confederate President. To him, the occupation of Colorado, New Mexico, Arizona, and California was of greater importance.

Among the United States officers who left New Mexico in 1861 with Colonel Loring was Major Sibley, previously mentioned. And although he tarried in Texas, his final destination was Richmond, where he arrived shortly. While in the Confederate capital, he conferred with President Davis about the conquest of the Southwest; and in less than a month he was again back in Texas with a commission of Brigadier General to recruit a mounted brigade for the invasion of New Mexico.

Even pre-war circumstances seemed to favor Sibley's ambitious scheme. Alexander M. Jackson, the Territorial Secretary of New Mexico, was a personal friend of Jefferson Davis and an ardent pro-slave man. Colonel W. W. Loring of North Carolina was in command in New Mexico in 1860, and there is some evidence that he connived with the Secretary of War, John B. Floyd, also a pro-Southerner, to accumulate vast quantities of military supplies in New Mexico so that they would fall into Confederate hands in the event of war. Some of Loring's officers and troops were also pro-Southern, and left the Territory to join the Confederates upon the outbreak of war. Unionists charged that Loring planned to surrender the New Mexico military posts to the Confederates. The southernmost of these was Fort Fillmore, across the river from Mesilla; others were Fort Thorn at Rincón, Fort Craig near Valverde, Fort Albuquerque (the principal depot), and Fort Marcy, near Santa Fe. Isolated posts were also in danger of capture—Fort Stanton, near the Capitan Mountains; Fort Union, at the base of the Gallinas, in northeastern New Mexico; and Fort Garland, in southern Colorado. But Loring was forced to resign his command and leave the department before his purported plan could be consummated.

Colonel John R. Baylor's invasion of southern New Mexico was probably not an initial part of Sibley's plan, but it was undoubtedly accepted as such before his Mesilla government collapsed. Advancing from Fort Bliss, near El Paso, with four companies of troops, in July, 1861, Baylor occupied Mesilla, where already a Confederate flag had been flown. Also, preceding his coming, a convention had been held which had adopted a resolution declaring that the Mesillians would not recognize the "Black Republican administration." Colonel Lynde, the commander of near-by Fort Fillmore, and about 450 troops, were captured by Baylor before they could withdraw to Fort Stanton. This post, too, was taken a short time later. At Mesilla Baylor learned of the recent visit of a party of California Confederates on their way to the East. Among these was Brigadier General Albert Sidney Johnston, who shortly as leader of the Confederate army was to meet General U. S. Grant on the field at Shiloh. At Mesilla also Baylor proclaimed himself Governor of Arizona (embracing southern New Mexico and Arizona), and on January 18, 1862, the Confederate Congress supported him by enacting an organic law for the new territory.

Sibley left San Antonio in November, 1861, with two and one-half regiments of troops, but it was not until February 18, 1862, that he appeared before Fort Craig, where with 1,750 men he confronted General E. R. S. Canby's 4,000 Union defenders (only 1,000 of whom were regulars). Sibley was victorious and drove the Federals within their fortifications, but he could not take the fort. He did not tarry long, however, for soon he was on the march toward the north. He took Albuquerque and Santa Fe without serious opposition, and then moved on Fort Union. The Federal troops were preparing to retire from this post also, when news reached them that Colorado troops under Colonel J. P. Slough were marching to their relief. The advance guard of these presently came in contact with Sibley troops at Apache Canyon, a short distance east of Santa Fe, and a sharp engagement was fought. Although Sibley drove the Coloradoans from the field, the Pike's Peakers destroyed his baggage train, and he was forced to retire. Canby allowed the Confederates to leave the Territory, for he realized that his own position was none too secure.

Meanwhile California troops were also on their way to relieve the hard-pressed Unionists of New Mexico. By June 7 General James H. Carleton with about 1,200 troops occupied Tucson, from which point a small cavalry force was sent on to New Mexico. With their appearance the Confederate tenure in Mesilla ended. Then a few weeks later the main California column arrived, and Carleton succeeded Canby to the command of the department. Another California column, augmented by several Nevada companies, was sent to Utah, ostensibly to guard the mail and telegraph lines, and was stationed at Camp Douglas near the outskirts of Salt Lake City. Mormon leaders protested their presence and later showed signs of hostility; but after the arrival of Governor James Duane Doty, in June, 1863, conditions were greatly improved, and Utah remained reasonably quiet for the remainder of the Civil War.

In the tier of Western states farther north there was little division of sympathy. Nebraska, Iowa, and the upper Mississippi Valley states furnished thousands of soldiers for the Northern army, as well as millions of bushels of corn and wheat. Oregon sent few troops eastward, since it was thought proper to retain all her available strength to meet any hostile move that England might make against the Northwest. "Battle-born" Nevada, so called because it was set up as a territory in 1861, was organized as a state three years later to give the Lincoln administration added strength in Washington. The state legislature deprived Southern sympathizers of the right to vote in elections, and enacted other laws to support the North.

A Confederate Exodus

It is not improbable that chaotic conditions in Mexico had caused Pickett and Sibley to propose the annexation of north Mexican states. Ever since the Mexican War the region south of the Rio Grande had been afflicted by military and political adventurers bent on exploiting the country. And since the Catholic Church was the richest institution in this poverty-stricken land, those in authority took a heavy toll from its treasury. This practice greatly aided Napoleon in his plan to rebuild a vast colonial empire in America. He could now appeal to French Catholics to aid him in throwing off the shackles of their Mexican brethren, and to French merchants and traders by holding out the prospects of rich profits in trade and development. Moreover, President Benito Juarez had played into his hands when in 1861 he suspended payment on foreign debts. In the autumn of 1861 a conference was held in London, and England, France, and Spain agreed to intervene in Mexico to force recognition of foreign obligations. But when Mexican promises satisfied England and Spain, they withdrew their fleets in 1862. Napoleon, however, turned to the task of overthrowing the Juarez regime. Under General Louis Elie Frederick Forey and Marshal François-Achille Bazaine, 35,000 French troops fought their way to Mexico City, where Bazaine organized a French-controlled government. In a mock election an empire was decreed and a hand-picked committee of Mexican Imperialists was sent to Austria to offer the throne to Archduke Maximilian. The Archduke accepted the throne, and in June, 1864, arrived with his beautiful wife, Carlota.

The United States Secretary of State, William H. Seward, had protested Napoleon's coup, and had watched closely subsequent developments. He obviously understood that Maximilian was Napoleon's puppet and resolved to end the French menace as soon as the Civil War ended. In 1865, therefore, General P. H. Sheridan was dispatched to the Rio Grande with an army of 52,000 men, while Seward demanded of Napoleon that he withdraw his troops. Since a failure to comply with Seward's demand would result in war with the United States and his ultimate forcible expulsion, Napoleon reluctantly consented, notifying Maximilian that he could no longer support him. But the stubborn Emperor refused to withdraw and was presently captured and shot by the Mexican Nationalists.

While he was yet in power, Maximilian maintained friendly relations with the Confederacy. Indeed, his north Mexican officials allowed large quantities of military supplies to be exported to Texas. On February 1, 1865, H. Flanigan, an Arkansas Confederate, wrote that "large amounts of clothing have already been distributed and trains are bringing supplies from Mexico"; and General Lew Wallace on the same day reported to Grant that he could stand on his boat and count at least 100 vessels of all kinds lying off Bagdad (a Mexican port contiguous to the Texas coast). "Neither the port of New Orleans nor that of Baltimore," he grumbled, "can present today such a promise of commercial activity."

In view of these friendly relations with the Imperialists it is not surprising that in 1865 the western Confederates looked to Mexico as a refuge. As early as February 1, 1865, General E. Kirby Smith had sent a personal agent, Robert Rose, to Mexico to inquire of Maximilian whether or not he would accept Confederate enlistments. Rose was instructed to say that 9,000 Missourians and not less than 10,000 Southerners from other states, all "daring and gallant spirits," would "gladly rally around any flag that promised to lead them to battle against their former foes." Smith was probably too generous in his estimates. Yet General Joseph O. Shelby led 1,800 well-armed troops across the Rio Grande shortly after the Confederate surrender, and General P. H. Sheridan reported that 10,000 ex-Southern soldiers had assembled at Matamoras. Former Confederate governors, members of Congress, judges, and generals were prominent among those who fled, but they came largely from the Southwestern states of Louisiana, Arkansas, Missouri, and Texas.

Although Maximilian would not enroll these refugees in his army, he launched for them a large-scale colonization scheme under the Imperial Commissioner of Immigration, M. F. Maury, formerly of the Confederate Navy. Military colonies were to be established along the railway between Vera Cruz and Mexico. The first and only settlement made was named Carlota in honor of the Empress. It was located near Cordova, in a beautiful mountain valley where nature was garbed in perpetual spring. A tract of 500,000 acres of confiscated land was given to the exiles, and presently a thriving community had sprung up. Grist-mills and sawmills were built, a newspaper (the *Mexican Times*) was published, supply stores were erected, and the surrounding valley was laid off in farms. Within a few months Carlota received such illustrious citizens as E. Kirby Smith, Sterling Price, J. B. Magruder, James E. Slaughter, John B. Walker, J. O. Shelby, and other ex-Confederate officers, as well as former governors, senators, representatives, and judges.

But the proposed "Eden" presently became the valley of despair. During the early stages of the movement former Southern leaders wrote of it in glowing terms to friends in the United States. General Sterling Price stated that his neighbor, Mr. Fink (a scientist), cultivated 80 acres in coffee with ten hands and sold his previous year's crop for $16,000. "His coffee field is shaded with every variety of fruit trees, in full bearing, and the walk, fringed with pineapple, is the most beautiful sight I have ever seen." Others spoke of varying climates that could be had by climbing the slopes of the mountains, of rippling streams, and of semi-tropical fruits which grew in great abundance. But the colony did not last. Resentful Nationalists and peons jealously watched its activities, and their smoldering hatred presently flared when the ex-Southerners with guns and clubs sought to force the peons to work their fields. Nationalists, mountain outlaws, and peons then retaliated by a night attack on Carlota, and the settlers were dispersed. Some sought safety in nearby Cordova, some took ship for Southern gulf ports, and some trekked back across the Rio Grande. But it is more than probable that the enterprise was already in a fair state of disintegration. Settlers, pining for their old homes, were deserting, for it was apparent that the Maximilian regime was doomed. So, with the destruction of Carlota, no other colony was attempted within this area.

There were other earlier colonial endeavors. In 1862 William M. Gwin of California sought to organize a Southern colony in Sonora, but it did not materialize. And on December 9, 1865, the *Mexican*

Times announced that Generals Hardeman and Terry had arrived at Jalisco to purchase a hacienda for colonization purposes; that a "Mr. Mitchell" had begun a settlement on the Rio Verde, near San Luis Potosi; and that a "Mr. Lloyd of England" had arrived with colonists to settle on a site between Vera Cruz and Mexico City. But none of these efforts bore large results, and it is safe to say that at least a majority of those who had sought Mexico as an asylum were all presently back across the Rio Grande to share in the work of reconstruction.

BIBLIOGRAPHY

There is no lack of standard works which treat of slavery and expansion, and the list that follows is by no means exhaustive. Others of equal reliability could be used. James Ford Rhodes, *History of the United States Since the Compromise of 1850* (9 vols., New York, 1893–1922), I, is generally sound and readable. John W. Burgess, *The Middle Period, 1817–1858* (*American History Series*, New York, 1897), reviews in broad outline the debates in Congress over the Compromises of 1820 and 1850 and the Kansas-Nebraska Bill of 1854, and has a well-balanced chapter on the popular sovereignty struggle for Kansas. Three volumes of the American Nation Series treat at great length the various aspects of the sectional problem: A. B. Hart, *Slavery and Abolition* (New York and London, 1906), Theodore Clarke Smith, *Parties and Slavery, 1850–1859* (New York, 1906), and French E. Chadwick, *Causes of the Civil War* (New York, 1913). Although H. E. von Holst, *Constitutional and Political History of the United States* (8 vols., Chicago, 1881–1892), III, is not generally reliable, it has a fair explanation of the slavery adjustment in New Mexico and Utah. A better general authority is James Schouler, *History of the United States of America Under the Constitution* (7 vols., New York, 1893–1913), especially Vols. VI and VII. Other books of merit are W. E. Dodd, *Expansion and Conflict* (Riverside Series, Boston, 1915); A. C. Cole, *The Irrepressible Conflict, 1850–1865* (*A History of American Life*, New York, 1934), VII; William B. Hesseltine, *A History of the South, 1607–1936* (New York, 1936); George F. Milton, *The Eve of Conflict* (Boston, 1934); P. O. Ray, *Repeal of the Missouri Compromise* (Cleveland, 1909); S. B. Dixson, *True History of the Missouri Compromise and Its Repeal* (Cincinnati, 1899); R. F. Nicholas, *The Democratic Machine, 1850–1854* (New York, 1923); R. J. Bartlett, *John C. Frémont and the Republican Party* (Columbus, 1930); A. W. Crandall, *Early History of the Republican Party* (Boston, 1930). The late Professor Frank H. Hodder's new approach to the Kansas-Nebraska Bill is explained in his two articles, "Genesis of the Kansas-Nebraska Act," in Wisconsin State Historical Society *Proceedings, 1912*; and "The Railroad Background of the Kansas-Nebraska Act," in *Mississippi Valley Historical Review*, XII (June, 1925).

The Autobiography and Reminiscences of Theophilus Noel (Chicago, 1904), and J. Ross Browne, *Adventures in the Apache Country; A Tour Through Arizona and Sonora* (New York, 1869), give in considerable detail the turmoil and confusion in New Mexico and Arizona during the Civil War. Samuel J. Crawford, *Kansas in the Sixties* (Chicago, 1911) and F. L. Paxson, *History of the American Frontier, 1763–1893* (New York, 1924), have chapters on Civil War movements on the Great Plains, particularly Indian troubles and guerrilla activities. Memoirs, diaries, and journals similarly worthy of mention along with Noel's account are Francis Richard Lubbock, *Six Decades in Texas* (Austin, 1900); Anson Mills, *My Story* (Washington, 1921); W. W. Mills, *Forty Years at El Paso, 1858–1898* (Chicago, 1901); Raphael Pumelly, *My Reminiscences* (2 vols., New York, 1918), I; Albert D. Richardson, *Beyond the Mississippi, 1857–1867* (Hartford, 1867); R. H. Williams, *With the Border Ruffians, 1852–1868* (London, 1907); and William Clark Whitford, *Colorado Volunteers in the Civil War* (Denver, 1906).

The several volumes of Bancroft's *Works*, previously listed, are of great value in piecing together the Civil War movements in the Western states and territories. The Confederate-Mexican relations are given in James Morton Callahan, *The Diplomatic History of the Southern Confederacy* (New York, 1922). But this work should be used along with J. Westlake, *Foreign Relations of the United States during the Civil War* (Cambridge History, New York, 1910); with William Beckles, *John Slidell and the Confederates in Paris* (New York, 1932); with the Civil War diplomatic correspondence found in *The War of the Rebellion: A Compilation of the Official Records of the Union and Confederate Armies*, Series 1, Vols. I, IV, IX, XV, and L (Parts 1 and 2), and Series 4, Vol. I; and with J. Fred Rippy, *The United States and Mexico* (New York, 1935).

State histories of merit other than those given in Bancroft's *Works* are Charles F. Coan, *A History of New Mexico* (3 vols., Chicago and New York, 1925); Leroy R. Hafen, *Colorado, the Story of a Western Commonwealth* (Denver, 1933); Frank C. Lockwood, *Pioneer Days in Arizona* (New York, 1932); Effie Mona Mack, *Nevada; A History of the State from the Earliest Times Through the Civil War* (Glendale, 1936); and Lewis W. Newton and Herbert P. Gambrell, *A Social and Political History of Texas* (Dallas, 1932).

Fortunately, articles in periodicals and publications of learned societies add many details to an otherwise partly obscure picture of the war in the West. Among these are R. S. Cotterill, "Southern Railroads and Western Trade," in *Mississippi Valley Historical Review*, II (March, 1917); W. Clement Eaton, "Frontier Life in Southern Arizona, 1858–1861," in *Southwestern Historical Quarterly*, XXXVI (January, 1933); William Henry Ellison, "The Movement for State Division in California, 1849–1860," *ibid.*, XX (October, 1926); "The New Mexico Campaign of 1862," in *Magazine of American History*, XV (February, 1886); "Letter from John T. Pickett to Manuel de Zomacona, Mexico, September 16, 1861," in *Hispanic American Historical Review*, II (1919); Charles W. Ramsdell, "The Natural Limits of Slavery Expansion," in *Southwestern Historical Quarterly*, XXXIII (October, 1929); Ralph Emerson Twitchell, "The Confederate Invasion of New Mexico, 1861–1862," in *Old Santa Fe*, III (January, 1916); Charles S. Walker, "Cause of the Confederate Invasion of New Mexico," in *New Mexico Historical Review*, VIII (April, 1933); H. L. Wilson, "Buchanan's Proposed Intervention in Mexico," in *American Historical Review*, V (July, 1900); and W. H. Watford, "Confederate Western Ambitions" in *Southwestern Historical Quarterly*, XLIV (October, 1940).

Little has been written on the Confederate exodus to Mexico following the surrender of General E. Kirby Smith. The *Personal Memoirs of General Philip Henry Sheridan* (Providence, 1888), II, has a brief reference to the movement, with more attention to the Maximilian affair. The fullest account yet written is John N. Edwards, *Memoirs, Reminiscences, and Recollections* . . . *also a Report of Shelby's Expedition to Mexico* (Kansas City, 1889), although it is not entirely trustworthy. A more reliable study, although only a sketch, is J. Fred Rippy, "Mexican Projects of the Confederates," in *Southwestern Historical Quarterly*, XXII (April, 1919). For diplomatic correspondence, letters of the refugees, and other papers related to the movement, consult *Senate Executive Documents*, No. 11, 38th Cong., 1st sess.; *House Executive Documents*, No. 1, Part III, 39th Cong., 1st sess.; and *War of Rebellion: Official Records*, Series I, XLVIII, Part I.

23

THE SOD-HOUSE FRONTIER

$\mathbb{F}$OR SIX years prior to the Civil War, middle-border men had become so embittered by sectional controversy that by 1865 they were resorting to acts of rapine and plunder which would not have been countenanced during saner moments. In Arkansas and Missouri were pro-slave men, both in and out of the army, not pleased with the Emigrant Aid Society conquest of Kansas, and who awaited only a call to arms to renew the conflict. Free state radicals, too, would welcome such an opportunity, for they remembered the several pre-war clashes with the "ruffians." Thus, the Arkansas and Missouri guerrillas were hardly more lawless than "Jim" Lane's nondescript Union troops.

In 1862 Lane and his "Red Legs" raided the Missouri border. Then, in retaliation, on August 20, 1863, William C. Quantrill at the head of 300 guerrillas sacked Lawrence and killed 180 citizens, a majority of whom had not shared in the Missouri raid. But Kansas was in no position to "throw the first stone." Here, too, lawless men were abroad, as may be seen in Lieutenant George Williams' report to the Commissioner of Indian Affairs, D. N. Cooley. Williams, at Fort Larned, charged that Kansas men—merchants, military officers, Indian agents, and traders—were in league with gangs of cattle thieves. He affirmed that such organizations had "induced men by the hundreds to go down into Indian Territory to steal and drive out cattle and horses"; that they had been engaged in this practice since 1862; and that they had stolen no less than 300,000 cattle.

The testimony of other federal officers stationed within the state to a large extent supported Williams' charges. Therefore, the dawn of general peace ended only sectional strife; local outlawry continued, as will be noted in Chapter 34. Yet unsettled conditions did not prevent the westward surge of immigrants taking advantage of the Homestead Law of 1862, and whose entry was facilitated by the building of the Union Pacific Railroad and other similar lines.

EARLY KANSAS AND NEBRASKA

As has been seen, Kansas territorial political problems caused the rise of pro-slave and free state elements, which ultimately found lodgment in the Democratic and Republican parties. By July, 1860, the Republicans took control of the Wyandotte convention, and proposed to Congress a free state constitution, but it did not receive approbation. On January 29 of the next year, however, Kansas was created as a free state, reaching from Missouri to the Rocky Mountains and from the thirty-seventh to the fortieth parallels, a commonwealth of 81,318 square miles.

In 1861 the Territory of Nebraska was shorn of much of its extended jurisdiction when portions of it were given to the new territories of Colorado and Dakota, and in 1863 by the formation of Idaho Territory. Four years later Nebraska followed Kansas into the Union. Its length was 412 miles (from Iowa to the Rockies) and its breadth 208 miles, comprising a total area of 75,955 square miles. And, in spite of border turmoil and strife, prospective settlers came. With the outbreak of the Civil War, Kansas had a population of 107,-206 and Nebraska 28,842. The settlers had not ventured far from the Missouri and Kansas rivers. Millions of fertile prairie acres yet awaited the coming of settlers.

So the dawn of the post-war era found Kansas and Nebraska in their economic and social swaddling clothes. In Kansas, Leavenworth City, Wyandotte, Atchison, and Lawrence were among the well-established, thriving towns. In 1827 Fort Leavenworth had been founded on the west side of the Missouri River, 31 miles above the mouth of the Kansas. It was a great frontier depot for other military posts on the Santa Fe, Utah, and Oregon routes, and the general rendezvous for troops proceeding to the western forts. Consequently, many civilians were employed about the post—at one time, 1,000 artisans and traders. These, with trappers and traders and their families, in 1834, founded Leavenworth City, three miles below the post. The town grew rapidly after 1854. Farther south, on Marmaton River, Fort Scott grew from a turbulent pro-slave village in 1861 to a young post-war city.

Farther down the river, at the mouth of the Kansas, was Wyandotte, a town of 3,000; and 46 miles above Leavenworth City was Atchison, which claimed the distinction of being the eastern terminus of the Overland Stage to the Rocky Mountains. An 1865 visitor found it prosperous; when the grass started in the spring, the place was so thronged with the teams of overland emigrants that one could scarcely cross the streets. It was the principal point on the Missouri from which freight was forwarded to Colorado, Utah, Montana, and other western territories. George A. Crofutt estimated the volume of Atchison's overland trade. There were loaded here 4,480 wagons, drawn by 7,310 mules and 29,720 oxen; and the freight amounted to 27,000 tons. To handle this business, a force of 5,600 men was employed. Assuming that freight shipped from other border towns—Kansas City, Leavenworth, St. Joseph, Omaha, and Plattsmouth—was as great, Crofutt believed that 8,960 wagons, 14,620 mules, 59,440 oxen, 54,000 tons of freight, and 11,200 men employed would have approximated the figures on the enormous Kansas and Nebraska transportation movement.

Lawrence, the scene of pre-war turbulence and the Quantrill raid, had emerged as a bustling town of 5,000 people, proud particularly of its Elridge House (hotel), reputed to be "by far the finest building in Kansas." In Lawrence, perhaps, was the first Kansas sod house, built for religious services. It was made of long poles united at the top, intertwined with sticks, twigs, and hay, and sodded over. Erastus D. Ladd of New England read his first Kansas sermon in this building. The first school was taught by a New Englander, Edward P. Fitch, of Massachusetts.

There were also other Kansas towns which promised much for the future. Topeka, on the Kansas River, about 25 miles west of Lawrence, had been the free state capital. But it had lagged behind its free state neighbors, previously mentioned. In 1865 its population was only about 1,000. Its first hotel had been a small log cabin, erected near the ferry to have the advantage of a transient trade. The earth floor was covered with prairie grass, on which as many as 24 people found a night's repose, while a twenty-fifth stretched himself on a load of hay outside. This structure was also used for religious services, and here Reverend S. Y. Lum, a Congregational minister, preached the first sermon in Topeka. Near by was a crude shanty (a " shake") used as a school building and presided over by a Miss Harlan (later Mrs. J. F. Cummings); and in November, 1855, W. W. Ross of Ohio printed in Topeka the *Kansas Tribune*, 30 numbers having already been issued at Lawrence. Thirty-five miles from Leavenworth was Lecompton, a town of 600 inhabitants, at which, in August, 1855, the territorial capital was located. Other small towns were Ossawatomie, at the confluence of the Pottawatomie Creek and the Osage River; Grasshopper Falls, about 30 miles northwest of Lawrence; and Manhattan and Waubaunsee, near Fort Riley (at the junction of the two main branches of the Kansas). Waubaunsee was colonized from New Haven, Connecticut, by an Emigrant Aid party to whom Sharp's rifles were subscribed at a church meeting.

Although Nebraska had a late start, it, too, could boast of thriving young towns. An 1865 visitor listed Brownsville, Nebraska City, Plattsmouth, Nemaha City, Bellevue, Florence, Saratoga, Fontenelle, Mt. Vernon, St. George, Columbus, and Omaha as towns worthy of mention. Omaha, on the Missouri River opposite Council Bluffs, was the capital and the largest, with a population of 9,000.

Still, in 1865 most of Kansas and Nebraska remained a part of the unoccupied frontier. In this year a traveler, while making his way across Kansas to Denver, found the border country alive to the homesteading movement. "Upon the eastern bank of the Great American desert," he wrote, "Kansas already contains a population sufficient to form a state. Eastern Nebraska and Dakotah are rapidly filling up. Here are, altogether, about 160,000 square miles to be made into new states, and this is all that remains of our public domain." But part of this area was yet the hunting grounds of Indians and the range of buffaloes. Much of the Kansas-Nebraska topography had a general sameness—a rolling, grass-carpeted plain. To transform it into farm land, the homesteader usually hitched several oxen to his plow, for the turf was thickly matted and hard to break. Kansas had two classes of lands: first, the timber and rich alluvial river and creek bottoms (for example, the Missouri, Kansas, Neosho, and Arkansas) were estimated at 10,000,000 acres, and were much sought for farming; second, in the central and western parts of the state, the prairie upland was a far-flung expanse, undeveloped except here and there where hardy ranchers grazed their cattle well within the Indian country.

Most of Nebraska, too, was a high plain, divided almost in half by the Platte. This stream had been a western line of travel, followed by early Oregon and California emigrants, and now became a post-war line of projection for the occupation of Nebraska. So Nebraska could boast of no lofty mountains and hills; its bottom lands and its plains were generally level. But early immigrants found it attractive. The broad prairies appeared like the waves of the ocean suddenly arrested in their swell and changed to soil and rock. Yet in remarkable contrast was a comparatively small tract known as the *Mauvaise Terre* (Bad Land) in the western part of the state, 90 miles long and 30 wide, produced by powerful agencies of degradation. When viewed from afar, this region seemed like some deserted town, its chrome and red prismatic and columnar masses resembling residences and public buildings. But upon a near approach these imposing forms of architectural beauty resolved into masses of rocks with labyrinthine defiles, within which were excellent sites for ranches.

The Federal Homestead Act of May 20, 1862, favored Northern homeseekers over Southern. By its terms the head of a family, or a man who had reached the age of 21 years (who was a citizen, or who had filed his citizenship papers), and who had never borne arms against the United States Government nor given aid and comfort to its enemies, was entitled to homestead 160 acres from the public domain. Since Southern men had borne arms against the government and had also given aid and comfort to the Confederacy, they were barred. This exclusion of Southern homesteaders was noticed by Kansans. In 1878 the Superintendent of Public Instruction said that shortly after the war it seemed as if the state was "to become a grand camp of the Union soldiers." The Timber Culture Act of 1873 also stimulated immigration. It provided that a man, or the head of a family, could acquire 160 acres of public land on condition of his planting 40 acres in trees and caring for it seven years. As will be noticed elsewhere, this not only hastened the occupation of the Kansas and Nebraska plains, but it also resulted in the growing of splendid forests of cotton-wood, oak, box-elder, maple, walnut, and other trees.

Still another movement was important in peopling this area. The Union Pacific Act of July 1, 1862, and its amendatory law two years later gave momentum to the operation of the land laws by providing means of transportation to the border country. The Union Pacific Railroad extended from Omaha through the center of Nebraska, and in 1863 it began to sell portions of its lands acquired by federal grant. The Burlington and Missouri River Railroad in the following year did the same. During the post-war period, the Missouri, Kansas and Texas; the Atchison, Topeka and Santa Fe; and the Kansas Pacific also promoted immigration to derive the same benefits. These later railroad land sales made possible to some degree Southern penetration of the Middle Border; but, on the whole, Kansas and Nebraska immigrants still came from those states north of the parallel of 36° 30'.

It is little wonder that the Indians fought desperately to retain the Kansas-Nebraska country. Grazing the grassy plains were countless thousands of bison. And equally appealing to the incoming settler-hunter were deer, antelope, sage hens, prairie-chickens, quail, and turkey. But covering much of the country were the "towns" of prairie-dogs which were to cause the homesteaders no end of trouble.

UNIQUE PROBLEMS

Along the Middle Border, settlers employed new techniques in adapting themselves to the country. Homesteaders found the wood and water problem ever present. Cottonwood, elm, willow, hackberry, and ash grew sparsely along the streams, and occasionally copses of cedar about escarpments and eroded terrain; but seldom was timber of sufficient size and quantity to supply building needs. In certain areas not even firewood was to be had; consequently, the settler burned buffalo "chips" (excrement) and grass. Moreover, the land was semi-arid, and there were few springs or perennial streams. On the high plains the larger streams were sand-filled, and their waters were bitter or salty. So the homesteader's usual quest for wood and water was unsatisfied here. In 1873 Henry Howe noticed the scarcity of timber in western Kansas, but he said that there was enough rock for building purposes. This was untrue. In much of the prairie country no stone could be found. Indeed, Howe must have seen this; for as he moved westward over the Kansas Pacific Railroad, he noticed along his line of travel "subterranean houses" (dugouts) and adobes in eastern Colorado. The dugout, he said, was an excavation, some 10 feet wide, 20 long, and 6 or 8 deep. Over this were timbers, put up like rafters, and the whole was covered with prairie sod.

The first Kansas and Nebraska settlers generally built sod houses and dugouts, either because they were too poor to provide a frame or brick structure or because of the inconvenience of hauling lumber from a distant town over the roadless prairie. Since they knew little about sod building, the first sod houses erected leaked badly during occasional periods of rainy weather. But later they were improved. Mrs. Emily Haines Harrison, who in 1866 with her nephew, Henry M. Tucker, and her son, Waldo, built a sod house on the Saline River, in Ottawa County, Kansas, tells of the discomforts of the early type. The roof of their "soddy" leaked so much that it was necessary for Tucker to hold an umbrella over Mrs. Harrison while she fried pancakes. W. E. Webb, who visited the Kansas-Nebraska border in 1872, watched a sod house turn to mud during a heavy rain.

Community structures (schoolhouses and churches) were also made of sod. William D. Street, in writing of Kansas border conditions, says that "schoolhouses of rude pattern, built of logs or sod, sprang up everywhere," and were used for devotional exercises on Sunday. A community sod-house building day was as much of an occasion for Great Plains people as was that of an Eastern log-raising. "The site being decided upon," writes Street, "the neighborhood gathered with horses, plows, and wagons. A piece of virgin sod would be selected, the sod-breaking plow would be started; the sharp share would cut the grass roots and slice out a long piece of the sod from two to four inches in thickness, by twelve to fourteen inches in width." From these slices were cut bricklike segments to build the walls. Window and door frames were made of poles, and openings were covered with buffalo or cow hide. Brush was laid over pole rafters, and the whole, covered with sod and sand, packed down. But in parts of the country,

Courtesy of Phillips Collection, University of Oklahoma

(1)

Courtesy of Phillips Collection, University of Oklahoma

(2)

EARLY WESTERN HOMES SHOWING THE INFLUENCE OF ENVIRONMENT
(1) THE DUGOUT; AND (2) THE SOD HOUSE

dugouts were used for churches and schoolhouses, particularly where but few settlers lived within a community, or where the prairie sod was not sufficiently matted. Both types were comfortable in winter and saved the lives of many Kansas and Nebraska homesteaders during blizzard visitations of the seventies and eighties, a fact which was proved by the greater proportion of deaths among those who sought shelter in flimsily constructed frame and log houses.

Numerous other problems taxed the ingenuity of the early settler. In much of the country water for household use could not be had in the saline or alkali ("gyp") streams, and there were few springs; consequently rivers and creeks often bore the names of Saline, Salt, Gyp, Croton, or Bitter. In parts of the plains, by 1890, deep wells were bored and windmills were imported; in others, cisterns or ground-tanks must suffice. Sometimes in the settler's yard stood a water wagon or sled, the barrels covered with unsightly, dirty duck cloth. Tank water was drunk by both man and beast, and presently "prairie fever" (typhoid) swept the country, causing many deaths. The home-steader resorted to various expedients to settle and purify muddy tank water, for example, by the use of alum, or by boiling; in time the latter method was found to be the cheapest and safest.

Although there were few trees to clear from the land before plowing, it was necessary for the farmer to destroy the prairie-dogs (by poisoning with arsenic), whose tepee-shaped embankments of sub-surface homes dotted the prairies. Then, once the tender shoots of corn, of wheat, or of other crops showed above the ground, it was equally important that he guard them against all kinds of rodents and grasshoppers. Grasshoppers were most destructive. Indeed, there are many early gloomy narratives of the havoc they wrought: but occasionally one finds others written in a lighter vein. In 1877 a western editor thus described a grasshopper about to lay its egg by comparing it with a map of Florida: "Consider the Ocean and the Gulf represent the ground. That portion of the State above the 30th degree of latitude is the upper part of the body; that below is the tail end; and the point below the 26th degree is bored into the ground; and the string of little islands called the Keys and Tortugas represent the eggs."

At intervals of from eight to ten years grasshoppers invaded the prairie farm lands in vast clouds so dense as to darken the sun, and in smaller swarms more frequently. They would destroy growing crops, and even eat the leaves and young shoots of trees. Near Court House Rock, on the Nebraska frontier, in 1855, General Harney observed that a grasshopper cloud filled the air and that the insects were an inch deep on the ground. In 1868, P. McVicar, the Kansas Superintendent of Public Instruction, reported: "The periodic inundation of

Courtesy of Phillips Collection, University of Oklahoma

Courtesy of Phillips Collection, University of Oklahoma

TYPICAL PIONEER SOD SCHOOLHOUSES COMMONLY USED THROUGHOUT THE
GREAT PLAINS AREA, 1856–1885

grasshoppers took place earlier this year than last, and consequently found vegetation young and tender. They ate and destroyed more than half the corn; also vegetables, including the potato crop." But to balance against this disaster he noticed that the tide of immigration continued with unabated interest, and that the incoming farmers were settling the upland prairies where a few years previously it was thought only ranchers could live.

The grasshopper invasion of 1877 is graphically described by the *Annals of Kansas:* "This visitation . . . was the most serious of any in the history of the State. The grasshoppers reached from the Platte River on the north to northern Texas and penetrated as far east as Sedalia, Missouri. On August 28, Governor Thomas A. Osborn of Kansas called a special session of the legislature to provide relief; and the legislature authorized the counties to issue 'relief bonds' and voted a $7,500 'grasshopper fund.' "

Blizzards, drouths, and hot winds were also destructive. Kansas was often mentioned in the Eastern press as the "Drouth and Grasshopper State," and the average editor remembered that Nebraska was its neighbor! All roads leading toward the border were usually dotted with covered wagons, in prosperous years moving westward, in lean years eastward. Thus an undirected movement of selection was apparent. Many adapted themselves to the country and became hardy plainsmen; others sought new homes elsewhere. Those who remained learned that they could cultivate 75 or 100 acres of prairie land in wheat or other crops, where on an Eastern farm they could hardly till 25 or 30. Western land was freer from weeds and crabgrass. Consequently, the plains farmer learned that he could sustain the impact of an occasional crop failure and still "get along," since the harvests of good years were bountiful. Moreover, by seed selection, crop adaptation (the planting of drouth-resisting milo-maize, kaffir corn, and Russian wheat), frequent stirring of the soil, and by late planting to avoid sandstorms, a new farming technique was evolved.

THE RUSH FOR FREE LAND

The farmers' rush for free prairie land was the last dramatic episode in the disappearance of the Great Plains frontier. In 1866 D. F. Drinkwater, Secretary of the United Press Association, wrote from Topeka: "Kansas in town and country has made rapid progress since I was here last fall. . . . It is estimated that since last January the accessions to the population of the State cannot be less than a hundred thousand. Should the census be taken today there would probably be a showing of at least 240,000 as the population of the State." In 1868 Governor Samuel J. Crawford resigned his executive chair to Lieutenant

Governor N. Green, in order to help Sheridan solve the Indian raiding problem and thus aid in the settler occupation of western Kansas. And at the conclusion of the campaign (1868–1869), homeseekers rushed forward to claim the arable lands abandoned by the Indians. Should one have traveled westward from Junction City over the Kansas Pacific Railroad in 1872, he would have noticed an unprecedented border expansion. In 1870 the farthest limit of western settlement was Brookville, then a mere railroad station; but two years later it had reached nearly 100 miles beyond, to the upland prairies. At Wilson there were scarcely six houses in 1870; in 1872 there were over 30, and not far from 50 farms, each of from 80 to 160 acres. At Bunker Hill there was nothing in 1870; but two years later there was a colony of 200 souls. Fossil was entirely unoccupied in 1871; one year later there were over 100 houses and 500 inhabitants. About the same time, a visitor wrote of similar progress in Nebraska, along the line of the Union Pacific. "Settlements," he said, "are springing up rapidly. Even the lapse of a few months makes a perceptible difference to the eye of the passing traveler."

DISTRIBUTION OF LAND AREAS
(Deduced from the Census of 1880)

States and Territories of the New West	Land in Farms			Land Not in Farms	Total Land Area
	Improved	Unimproved	Total		
Kansas	10,739,566	10,677,902	21,417,468	30,870,532	52,288,000
Nebraska	5,504,702	4,440,124	9,944,826	38,813,574	48,758,400
Oregon	2,198,645	2,016,067	4,214,712	56,303,688	60,518,400
Washington	484,346	925,075	1,409,421	41,393,779	42,803,200
Colorado	616,169	549,204	1,165,373	65,167,427	66,332,800
Utah	416,105	239,419	655,524	51,946,076	52,601,600
Wyoming	83,122	41,311	124,433	62,323,567	62,448,000
Montana	262,611	143,072	405,683	92,592,717	92,998,400
Idaho	197,407	130,391	327,798	53,617,802	53,945,600
Nevada	344,423	186,439	530,862	69,702,738	70,233,600
Arizona	56,071	79,502	135,573	72,133,227	72,268,800
Dakota	1,150,413	2,650,243	3,800,656	90,727,344	94,528,000
New Mexico	237,392	393,739	631,131	77,743,269	78,374,400
California	10,669,698	5,924,044	16,593,742	83,233,458	99,827,200
Totals	32,960,670	28,396,532	61,357,202	886,569,198	947,926,400

By 1880 the approximate line of settler occupation was the ninety-eighth meridian. At this time Kansas had 104 counties, only 26 of which were unorganized; and its population had increased to 849,978. In 1879 Nebraska had 68 organized counties, four unorganized, and a population of 456,812 (including Indians). By 1883 Kansas had become the leading corn-producing state, with Nebraska also in the running. In March of the next year, the United States Department of Agriculture reported a yield of 158,976,828 bushels for Kansas and

67,856,863 for Nebraska, with Kansas averaging 36.7 bushels per acre. Wheat, oats, and other grains also yielded large returns. At this time, however, Kansas had only 21,417,468 acres in cultivation, less than one-half the total area of the state; and Nebraska had 9,944,826 acres in farms and 38,813,574 acres not in farms.

The infiltration of foreign immigrants added uniqueness to the Kansas and Nebraska social patterns. German and Swedish towns, strongly reflecting Old World architectural design, dotted the prairies; and new crafts, customs, and techniques were introduced. Railroads capitalized on foreign immigration to dispose of their land grants. A case in point was the work of the immigration bureau of the Atchison, Topeka and Santa Fe, under the superintendency of A. Z. Touzalin. Touzalin saw the possibility of European sales, and appointed C. B. Schmidt as a foreign agent. The latter, in the summer of 1873, visited the German colonies along the shores of the Caspian and Black seas of southern Russia, and succeeded in getting more than 1,900 settlers to migrate to western Kansas. This was the beginning of an exodus which by 1905 brought more than 60,000 Germans from Russia, Germany, and Austria to new homes in western Kansas. L. P. Brockett [1] estimated the foreign influx after 1870 as one-fifth of the whole Kansas immigration, including Mennonites and their co-religionists from Russia, Germans, Scandinavians, French, Italians, English, Scotch, Welsh, and Irish. "With these," he said, "have also come large numbers from all the Atlantic States, Mexicans, and, of late, Negroes, making their exodus from the Southern States to Kansas, as pre-eminently the land of freedom."

Omaha, Leavenworth, and other cities profited by the new immigration. Each became a racial melting-pot, as a Leavenworth municipal election of 1877 revealed. George Ummethun, a German, was named mayor; Colonel Moonlight, a Scotchman, city marshal; Con Cartan, an Irishman, the weightmaster; Christian Beck, a Dane, a street commissioner; and Dr. Victor Bicert, a Frenchman, the city physician. Foreign-born members of the council were S. F. Burdett, an Englishman; M. A. Wohlfrom, an Alsatian; John O'Brien and Owen Duffy, Irishmen; and Martin Smith, a Prussian.

The end of the Red River Indian campaign (1874–1875) and the coming of railways hastened the disappearance of the southwestern Kansas frontier. The Missouri, Kansas, and Texas Railroad, building from St. Louis, reached Denison, Texas, on the Red River in 1872, with branch lines from Parsons, Kansas, to Junction City, Kansas; and from Holden, Missouri, to Paola, Kansas. About the same time

---

[1] *Our Western Empire,* 882.

the Atchison, Topeka and Sante Fe was projecting its line approximately over the old Santa Fe Trail; and the Kansas Pacific was affording the Texas cattle drovers excellent shipping points at Abilene and Ellsworth. Other new Kansas railway towns—Wichita, Dodge City, Wellington, Sheridan, and Wallace—also became important trade and outfitting centers, and their neighboring prairies were checker-boarded with improved ranches and farms.

Nebraska enjoyed much the same experience. Its western prairies were largely unoccupied until the end of the Sioux wars (1876–1877) and until railways had provided easy access. The Union Pacific, as previously noticed, was the main east-west route, with Omaha as its eastern terminus. But south of the Platte, most of the roads were connected with the Burlington and Missouri Railroad, the main line of which commenced at Plattsmouth, on the Missouri (across which a bridge was built to make connection with the Chicago, Burlington and Quincy of Iowa), with a branch line from Omaha joining the main line at Oreapolis (Concord), four miles west of Plattsmouth. The line then followed the Platte to the mouth of Salt Creek, and thence to Lincoln, the new state capital; and thence, through Lancaster, Saline, Fillmore, Clay, Adams, and Kearney counties to a junction with the Union Pacific at Kearney, in Buffalo County. Omaha was perhaps most benefited by railway building, claiming a population of 30,518 in 1880. But in 1867 its honor as Nebraska's capital was to be taken by the new town of Lincoln, when the South Platte settlements secured the appointment of a legislative committee to move the capital within their midst, and Lincoln was named. The new town had a population of 13,004 in 1880. Nebraska City was not far behind, with 10,000 people; and Plattsmouth, Brownville, Fremont, and Peru were other Nebraska towns ranging in population from 2,500 to 5,000.

Laying the Cultural Foundations

Kansas and Nebraska immigrants brought to the frontier cultural traditions as well as worldly goods; and, soon after they had planted communities and towns, they built churches and schoolhouses. Printing presses, too, were established. The *Kansas Magazine* (1872–1873) represented the best in the midwestern literary field, devoting space to poetry, fiction, and travel. In 1877 F. G. Adams reported to the Kansas Historical Association that 156 newspapers were serving the state. Those in Nebraska were proportionately numerous. The Bellevue *Palladium* (November, 1854) was the first newspaper published in Nebraska; the second was the Omaha *Arrow* (1854). Others were the Nebraska City *News*, the *Nebraska Farmer* (Brownville), the Brownville *Advertiser*, the Omaha *Herald* (later combined with the

Evening World as the *World-Herald*), and no less than a dozen others begun by 1875. The editors seemed motivated by optimism and a boom spirit which was sweeping the prairies. They filled their columns with glowing speculations concerning the possibilities of town building, the development of agrarian paradises, and the establishment of advanced centers of culture.

Common schools were given increasing attention. In 1879 Nebraska was divided into 2,856 school districts for the convenience of its 123,411 scholastics; but there were 173 districts which had no schools, either because of a lack of funds, or of teachers. And there were only 1,242 districts which could offer a six-month term. Problems of textbooks, maps, blackboards, and other needs vexed superintendents; and the poverty of homesteaders made the average attendance poor. If the teacher could train the pupil to read, write, and cipher, border parents were satisfied. Only 73,956 of the 123,411 children of school age were enrolled in 1880, but at least a beginning had been made.

Aside from grammar schools, there were a few high schools at Omaha and other large towns; a normal school at Peru; a university at Lincoln, endowed with 130,000 acres of land, which was supplemented by an annual state appropriation of $25,000; and an institute for the deaf and dumb at Omaha and one for the blind at Nebraska City. Moreover, there were colleges under denominational control, such as Doane College at Crete, Saline County; Nebraska College at Nebraska City; Creighton College at Omaha; and a Methodist Episcopal College at York, in York County.

By 1880 Kansas had 39 towns of 1,000 or more population, Leavenworth and Topeka leading with 16,550 and 15,451, respectively. These urban communities readily turned to the task of building churches and schools. In 1878 Kansas employed 6,359 teachers to give instruction to 188,884 pupils. But here, too, poor attendance (113,000 pupils) exemplified frontier individualism. Many of the towns supported grade and high schools, and four conducted normal schools with about 800 teacher-pupils. Besides these, the institutions of higher learning included an agricultural college at Manhattan, a university at Lawrence, and eight other colleges maintained by religious denominations. Kansas churches had an aggregate membership of 135,713, or nearly one-fifth of the entire population, and their properties were evaluated at $2,037,497.

By 1900 the "sod-house" frontier was no more. Frame, stone, and brick structures had supplanted "shanties," "soddies," dugouts, and adobe houses, or were in a fair way of doing so. The countless herds of bison, deer, and antelope had been destroyed, but on the prairies were many thousands of horses, mules, cattle, and sheep. Where in 1870 the rancher's cattle grazed the free range now were many prosperous farms; and what during the mid-century had been the favorite resorts of the wild Indians were now the sites of rapidly growing villages and towns. Once the pioneer had depended on wild game and the products of his own field and garden for food, but now he could obtain canned fruits and vegetables at nearby groceries, and his family could be clothed in "store-bought" garments. A liberal land law, Western enterprise, and railroads had largely wrought the change. Railroads had been substituted for cattle trails and overland paths of commerce and travel. Indeed, on the Kansas and Nebraska prairies a hardy culture had taken root. When nurtured by hard work, resourcefulness, and perseverance, it was to develop into one of the sturdiest plants of the Nation's garden. And in the future, the farmers were to be more concerned with agrarian crusades and social welfare than with grasshoppers, wild Indians, and free homesteads.

BIBLIOGRAPHY

State publications are indispensable in a study of post-war Kansas and Nebraska. Among these are the Kansas State Historical *Collections*, I–XIX (Topeka, 1881–1934), and the Nebraska State Historical *Collections,* I–XXII (Lincoln, 1885–1936). The annual messages of the governors and the reports of minor state officials should also be examined.

For a brief year-by-year Kansas chronicle of great value, see D. W. Wilder, *The Annals of Kansas, 1541–1885* (Topeka, 1886). And to add varied detail to many of these events mentioned by Wilder, consult *The Kansas Magazine,* I–IV January, 1872, to October, 1873); or *State Board of Immigration, Nebraska; A Sketch of Its History, Resources, and Advantages It Offers to Settlers* (Nebraska City, 1870).

Other early accounts relating to overland travel, railway building, land laws, immigration, and social and cultural growth are Alexander Majors, *Seventy Years on the Frontier* (New York, 1893); John W. Barber and Henry Howe, *All the Western States and Territories* (Cincinnati, 1867); Henry Howe, *Historical Collections of the Great West* (Cincinnati, 1873); Albert D. Richardson, *Beyond the Mississippi . . .* (Hartford, 1867); Samuel Mintern, *Travels West* (London and New York, 1878); Samuel Bowles, *Our New West* (Chicago, 1869); John W. Clampitt, *Echoes from the Rocky Mountains* (Chicago, 1888); and L. P. Brockett, *Our Western Empire; or the New West Beyond the Mississippi* (San Francisco, 1881).

Travelers and early settlers within the Kansas-Nebraska country during the post-war era have left narratives depicting the various aspects of border life. Among those on Kansas, A. T. Andreas, *History of the State of Kansas* (Chicago, 1883) is still regarded as among the best, both as to its general narrative and as to its treatment of county organization and growth. A few others are John N. Edwards, *Noted Guerrillas, or the Warfare on the Border* (St. Louis, 1877); W. F. Pride, *A History of Fort Riley* (n.p., 1926); Evan Jefferson Jenkins, *The Northern Tier; or Life Among the Homestead Settlers* (Topeka, 1880); F. W. Giles, *Thirty Years in Topeka;*

a Historical Sketch (Topeka, 1886); L. W. Springs, *Kansas* (American Commonwealth Series, Boston, 1885); and John N. Hollaway, *History of Kansas* (Lafayette, Indiana, 1868). Those worthy of mention on Nebraska are A. B. Hayes and S. D. Cox, *History of the City of Lincoln* (Lincoln, 1880); J. A. Barrett, *History and Government of Nebraska* (Lincoln, 1891); H. Johnson, *History of Nebraska* (Omaha, 1880); Alfred Sorenson, *Early History of Omaha* (Omaha, 1876); and A. T. Andreas, *History of the State of Nebraska* (3 vols., Chicago, 1882).

Twentieth-century general studies on Kansas are William Elsey Connelley, *History of Kansas, State and People* (5 vols., Chicago, 1928); Bliss Isely, *Four Centuries in Kansas; Unit Studies* (Wichita, 1936); Anna Estelle Arnold, *History of Kansas* (Topeka, 1914); Charles P. Beebe, *Kansas Facts: A Year Book of the State* (4 vols., Topeka, 1928–1933); and Noble Lovely Prentis, *History of Kansas* (ed. and rev. by Henrietta V. Race, Topeka, 1909). Volumes limited as to time and locality are Leola Howard Blanchard, *Conquest of Southwest Kansas . . .* (Wichita, Kansas, 1931); William E. Connelley, *Quantrill and the Border Wars* (Cedar Rapids, Iowa, 1910); Samuel J. Crawford, *Kansas in the Sixties* (Chicago, 1911); Richard Cordley, *Pioneer Days in Kansas* (Boston, 1903); Everett N. Dick, *The Sod-House Frontier, 1854–1890 . . .* (New York, 1937); Stuart Oliver Henry, *Conquering Our Great American Plains; a Historical Development* (New York, 1930); John Ise, *Sod and Stubble; the Story of a Kansas Homestead* (New York, 1936); Paul A. Jones, *Coronado and Quivira* (Lyons, Kansas, 1937); Thomas Allen McNeal, *When Kansas Was Young* (New York, 1922); Adolph Roenigk (ed.), *Pioneer History of Kansas* (Lincoln, Kansas, 1933).

Recent studies of Nebraska are G. E. Condra, *Geography of Nebraska* (Lincoln, 1906); J. S. Morton and others, *Illustrated History of Nebraska* (3 vols., Lincoln, 1905–1906); A. E. Sheldon, *History of Nebraska* (Lincoln, 1913); J. Sterling Morton and Albert Watkins, *History of Nebraska* (3 vols., Lincoln, 1913).

24

THE MINING FRONTIER

G REAT STRETCHES of high plains and plateaus of the West were passed over and ignored by pioneers who set their faces for Oregon and California. Though too barren or too precipitous to invite settlement based on farming or grazing, this rejected land ultimately was to be carved into several states. In the rugged reaches of the Rocky Mountains and the Sierra Nevadas treasure vaults of mineral wealth awaited discovery. In mining, no favors are asked. Expose a rich vein, and man will reach it, no matter how formidable the obstacles! The earliest of these areas to reveal precious metals and induce occupancy were those of present Colorado and Nevada. Gold discoveries in these two regions were simultaneous, and in several respects the developments were parallel.

"PIKE'S PEAK OR BUST"

That gold existed in the central Rockies had been rumored for decades. Early Spaniards had been lured into the mountains north of New Mexico by visions of gold. James Purcell had told Captain Z. M. Pike, at Santa Fe, of finding gold on the headwaters of the South Platte. Early trappers and fur traders told of mineral discoveries. Rufus B. Sage repeated the story that in one of their battles the Arapahoes, when out of lead, used gold for bullets.

It remained for the discoveries in California to whet the American appetite for gold and to stimulate interest in prospecting. A party of Cherokees, California-bound in 1850, paused to pan some gravel in Colorado streams. They found "color" near the site of present Denver; but the amount of dust was too meager to detain them long, and they hurried on to the brighter fields of California. After returning home, however, they recalled with greater favor the prospects at the eastern base of the Rockies. Captain John Beck, one of these Cherokees, having returned to the Indian Territory of present Oklahoma, published a proposal for the organization of a party to prospect thoroughly the eastern slope of the central Rockies. W. Green Russell and other friends in the gold region of North Georgia, where the Cherokees had formerly lived, agreed to join the project. Parties were organized in Ray and Bates counties, Missouri, for the same purpose.

In the spring of 1858 the various groups made their way westward. By the time they had ascended the Arkansas River, traveled northward, and descended Cherry Creek to the South Platte, the combined parties numbered slightly more than 100 men. Several days of prospecting on affluents of the South Platte were sufficient to convince most of the gold seekers that they had come on a fool's errand. Early in July, all but 13 turned toward home. This baker's dozen, under the leadership of W. Green Russell, an experienced Georgia miner, determined to make a more thorough search of the region. Several days later, Russell found "pay dirt" at the mouth of Dry Creek, on the southern outskirts of present Denver. News of these "good diggins" was carried east by travelers, and was presently expanded into reports of a new Eldorado.

Another party of gold seekers had been organized at Lawrence, Kansas, early in 1858. It was formed in response to stories told by Delaware Indians who had accompanied a military expedition to the West during the preceding summer, and who reported the discovery of gold in the vicinity of Pike's Peak. This Lawrence party made its way up the Arkansas, being about ten days behind the pioneer Cherokee-Russell company. The Kansas group went directly to Pike's Peak, and after prospecting the region unsuccessfully, turned south to the Sangre de Cristo Mountains of present southern Colorado. While they were here, news came of discoveries on the South Platte, and toward that section they hastened.

The amount of gold discovered during the summer of 1858 at the base of the Rockies was very meager. But color had been found at various places, and the more optimistic felt that important mines would soon be uncovered. Most of the prospectors returned home in the fall, some with the intention of coming again next spring, but a few determined to winter in the new country.

In the meantime, news of the Russell discoveries of July had been carried eastward, and accounts were appearing in the Kansas and Missouri newspapers. The *Lawrence Republican* of September 2 told of the arrival of a man with three ounces of gold "which he dug with a hatchet in Cherry Creek and washed out with a frying pan." It was reported that from $5 to $20 per day could be made by a man with pick and pan. The stories were told and retold, published and republished, gaining in size with the telling. Excitement ran high. "It must be a second California, a new Eldorado." Since Pike's Peak was the principal known point of geography, the name was attached to the gold country. To the "Pike's Peak gold mines" the eager ones must go at once, lest by spring all the richest ground be claimed by others. So a number of parties journeyed to the mountains in the fall of 1858. The principal gathering point was the mouth of Cherry Creek, where the town of Denver was founded. Pueblo, Boulder, and some other towns also were started in 1858.

During the winter a number of men returned to the East. Some were empty-handed and declared the mines a humbug; others brought small quantities of dust in goose quills and exhibited these in drugstores, newspaper offices, and saloons. Glowing stories went the rounds of the press. The public was eager for good news, especially in view of the widespread disasters that had come with the Panic of 1857. Men who had lost their all in the crash, with everything to gain and nothing to lose, could afford to take a chance. Avidly they read every bit of heartening news. And the frontier newspapers gladly printed all favorable reports, realizing that a large migration meant prosperity for themselves and for the outfitting merchants of the border towns along the Missouri River.

Extensive preparations were made for a large spring emigration to the Pike's Peak gold country. Merchants in the Missouri River towns laid in supplies—sacks of flour, sugar, beans, and coffee; stacks of bacon sides and hams; cases of canned goods; bales of overalls and shirts; large boxes of boots and shoes; shovels, picks, and pans. Ox yokes and chains, harnesses and saddles, wagons and carts, wagon bows and covers, and extra axletrees were crowded into sheds and heaped into piles in the yards of outfitters. Newspapers were full of sage advice on the proper tools for mining, outfits for travel, and routes to be taken. Guidebooks presented maps of routes and travel information. Some of these pamphlets directed emigrants to special cities and trails. There were three principal routes across the plains: one up the Platte, one up the Arkansas, and a third up the Smoky Hill River. Each was to draw its adherents, but the Platte River trail won the greatest favor.

With the first appearance of spring grass, the rush began. Every boat coming up the Missouri was loaded with gold seekers. Each party assembled its equipment and supplies, and eagerly set forth. There were all kinds of conveyances, from the ponderous covered wagon to the two-wheeled cart. Many went on horseback; some tramped on foot with their packs on their backs. "Pike's Peak or Bust" and similar slogans were scrawled on the covers of prairie schooners. Through April and May the motley caravan pushed westward, thousands of hopeful Argonauts seeking the golden fleece.

When the vanguard of the fifty-niners reached Denver, at the mouth of Cherry Creek, they found the little loghouse town still waiting for a gold discovery that would justify its existence. No gold veins had been found, and the poor placers were not paying for one-fourth of the labor expended on them. With the increasing arrivals, matters developed toward a crisis. Daily, scores came who had made the long journey in the belief that the sands of Cherry Creek were yellow with gold. After a few days of hard work panning gravel for a few cents' worth of gold dust, the newcomers were disillusioned. Disappointment turned to disgust. Covered wagons were turned back over the prairie trails, and embittered gold seekers sent forth the cry of a "Pike's Peak humbug." There were threats of lynching for the enthusiasts who had spread the false reports of gold.

> Hang Byers and D. C. Oakes
> For starting this damned Pike's Peak hoax

was often repeated with much feeling against two of those who had issued guidebooks. The great tide of gold seekers had surged to the foot of the Rockies, had broken against the mighty wall, and the back flow with strong current was now sweeping eastward. It is estimated that 100,000 gold seekers set out from the Missouri River in the spring of 1859, that 50,000 reached the mountains, and about half of these returned home immediately.

Development of Colorado

At this critical juncture, discoveries—made in the high mountains—saved the situation from collapse. On May 6, 1859, John H. Gregory found the outcropping of a rich lode, or vein, of gold-bearing quartz near present Central City. When lodes were discovered, a stampede to the hills began. The heartening report from Gregory Gulch was carried eastward across the plains by a newly launched stagecoach line. Active mining camps sprang up in the narrow gulches. Horace Greeley visited them in June. "As yet," he observed in a letter to his *New York Tribune,* "the entire population of the valley sleeps in tents or under booths of pine boughs, cooking and eating in the air. I doubt that there is as yet a table or chair in these diggings, eating being done around a cloth spread on the ground." The gold-seekers scurried like ants about their giant hills. Gold was found on upper Boulder Creek and on the Blue River to the west of the Continental Divide. From the placers in South Park, a miner wrote: "The gold is in scales nearly as large as watermelon seeds, smooth and very bright yellow, worth 25 cents to $1.30 each."

The mining activity in the mountain camps created business for the supply towns at the eastern base of the chain. Denver forged ahead, with Boulder, Canon City, and Golden as close competitors. Supply trains from the East came in with stocks of merchandise and food, mining tools, sawmills, and printing presses. The first newspaper in the region, the *Rocky Mountain News*, having made its appearance at Denver on April 23, 1859, continued to report the gold discoveries and to boost the country. With lumber from the sawmills, frame structures displaced log houses. Agriculture had its beginnings with truck gardens supplying vegetables to the miners. Some of the pioneers, vision-

GREGORY GOLD DIGGINGS, COLORADO, MAY, 1859
(FROM A. D. RICHARDSON, *Beyond the Mississippi*, PAGE 181.)

ing surer returns from farming than from mining, took up land along the streams and formed "claim clubs" to insure title to the lands squatted upon. Toll roads were built up the canyons and over the hills to the various mining camps.

In the fall of 1859 many of the miners returned to their eastern homes, but others decided to winter in the new country. On October 3 the first school in the region opened at Denver, with O. J. Goldrick, a picturesque Irishman, as teacher. He had entered the pioneer town some weeks before, decked out in a high-top silk hat, broadcloth suit, and kid gloves, yet driving an ox team with the regular bull-whacker's whip. A rented log cabin with dirt roof served as schoolhouse. The day which marked the opening of school saw also the first theatrical performance in the Pike's Peak country. Col. Thorne's Star Company, having crossed the plains from Leavenworth, played *Cross of Gold* at Apollo Hall, Denver. This announcement appeared at the bottom of the handbills: "Front seats reserved for the ladies."

The spring of 1860 saw a large emigration to the Pike's Peak region, one better ordered than that of 1859. More men came with their families, planning to build permanent homes. Additional mines were opened and new sections of the country developed during this year. The acreage of farm lands increased considerably. The first United States mail to the region came in a coach and six. To facilitate business transactions, a private mint was established. The bright yellow coins, in denominations of $2.50, $5, $10, and $20, and containing a little more gold than did the United States coins, soon became the accepted medium of exchange. For small amounts, gold dust was still given in payment. "A pinch," the amount picked up between the thumb and forefinger, counted as 25 cents, and this was usually considered the smallest change.

One of the most interesting features of early Colorado was the civic and political activity. The inborn Anglo-Saxon predilection for politics is nowhere better exhibited. A. D. Richardson, a journalist who visited Denver in 1859, wrote:

Making governments and building towns are the natural employments of the migratory Yankee. He takes to them as instinctively as a young duck to water. Congregate a hundred Americans anywhere beyond the settlements and they immediately lay out a city, frame a State constitution and apply for admission into the Union, while twenty-five of them become candidates for the United States Senate.

When the gold rush occurred, the land of present Colorado lay within the boundaries of four existing Territories—New Mexico, Utah, Kansas, and Nebraska. Indian title to the region had not been relinquished. But the pioneer Pike's Peakers showed little regard for Indian rights and were disinclined to acknowledge the jurisdiction of existing Territorial governments. From the beginning they visioned the creation of a new mountain state. As early as November, 1858, the handful of gold-seekers on Cherry Creek held an election and sent a representative to the Kansas legislature and a delegate to the national capital. Delegate Graham presented to Congress a petition praying the organization of a new Territory in the Pike's Peak region. In January, 1859, a bill was introduced for the creation of "Jefferson Territory," but it was given scant consideration.

Hopeful citizens assembled at Denver on April 15, 1859, proposed the creation of the "State of Jefferson," and issued a call for a constitutional convention to meet in June. They explained:

Government of some kind we must have and the question narrows itself down to this point: Shall it be government of the knife and revolver or shall we unite in forming here in our golden country, among the ravines and gulches of the Rocky Mountains, and the fertile valleys of the Arkansas and Plattes, a new and independent state? . . . Let us all unite as one in so great an object. . . . It is a glorious cause, and a feeling of pride as well as of duty should lead us to act in it.

When the delegates assembled in June, the future of the region was somewhat dubious, so the convention appointed committees and adjourned to await developments. Finally, in October, 1859, another convention assembled and in a three-day session drew up a constitution for Jefferson Territory. Two weeks later the document was ratified by popular vote, and a set of officers was elected. All of present Colorado and strips of present Utah and Wyoming were included in the generous boundaries of the provisional Territory. The General Assembly convened in November and enacted a set of laws. But the people were not united in supporting the new government. It was extra-legal and had no adequate means of enforcing its authority. When it attempted to levy and collect a poll tax, opposition against it crystallized. The Territorial government persisted; but since it was not yet ratified by Congress, it was more imposing on paper than in reality.

The effective governments in the Pike's Peak region before the creation of Colorado Territory, in 1861, were the local governments of mining districts and towns. These, too, were spontaneous and extralegal; but, operating in a small area, they were more successful. The miners in a given district, recognizing the need for law, would assemble in mass meeting, organize a district, elect officers, and enact needed rules and regulations. These local laws, simple and clear, were effective. They fixed the size of claims (usually 100 feet of frontage on a stream), provided methods for settling disputes, and prescribed rules for the trial and punishment of criminals. Justice was administered with dispatch. Crimes were usually punished by whipping, banishment from camp, or hanging. That democratic institution, the Mass Meeting, was the constitutional authority and the court of last resort.

Two sessions of Congress, those of 1858–1859 and 1859–1860, adjourned without providing a government for the pioneers of the Pike's Peak country. Finally, Colorado Territory was created, on February 28, 1861, with the same boundaries as those of the present State. President Lincoln appointed the Territorial officials, with Major William Gilpin, of Missouri, as governor.

Colorado's early Territorial years were filled with discouragements. The Civil War found the citizens divided in sentiment, and many partisans left the region to enlist in the armies, North and South. Some of the miners were lured away by the newer mineral discoveries in present Montana, Idaho, and Nevada. There was a decided slump in Colorado mining in the middle sixties. The placer deposits that had yielded the first gold were largely worked out. The ores on the lodes had become more and more refractory as the workings penetrated farther beneath the surface; and for the sulphide ores recently encountered, no practicable process was known whereby the values could be extracted. A general Indian war, begun in 1864, endangered the pioneers, absorbed their manpower, and boosted the cost of food and supplies. Crop failures, due to a grasshopper plague, brought distress. Finally, at the close of that first decade, the transcontinental railroad,

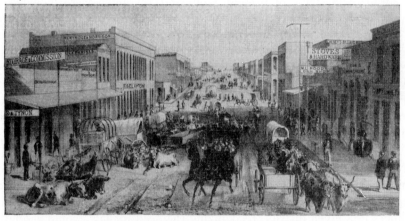

FIFTEENTH STREET, DENVER, IN 1865
(FROM A CONTEMPORARY SKETCH MADE BY A. E. MATHEWS.)

upon which the Colorado pioneers had placed great hope, chose a route not through Colorado, but through present Wyoming. Dark was the future of the state.

With the opening of the second decade, prospects brightened. The Civil War over, people in the East were now free to come to the West to build homes. Railroads were being extended beyond the Mississippi, affording swift and easy transportation for immigrants and their freight. A branch line was built from Cheyenne to Denver. Another railroad reached the Colorado city from across the eastern plains in 1870. The Indians of eastern Colorado had been moved away to reservations. Ways were being devised for the successful treatment of refractory ores, giving an impetus to mining. The rich agricultural resources of the region had been demonstrated and now invited further development. The Union Colony at Greeley was successfully launched, and other agricultural "colonies" began the co-operative development of irrigation projects and the founding of towns. Rich mines were opened in the high San Juan Mountains of southwestern Colorado. Wagon roads and railroads were pushed to the new mining camps.

With the rapid increase in population, the general development and improved outlook, demand for statehood grew. Congress was induced to pass an Enabling Act on March 3, 1875. Under its authorization a convention assembled, a constitution was adopted, and Colorado was admitted to statehood on August 1, 1876, as the "Centennial State."

The early statehood years were prosperous. Leadville opened her great silver vaults to enrich the state. Aspen and other rich camps augmented the silver stream and made Colorado famed as a mining region. The Utes were driven from the "Western Slope," and on their hunting grounds farms and towns developed. Cattle multiplied on the high plains to the east of the mountains, and cattle kings enjoyed their brief reign on the open range. During the decade of the seventies the population increased almost fivefold, and in the next decade more than doubled. Fortunately for Colorado, the great gold camp of Cripple Creek, developed in the nineties, helped absorb the shock dealt to silver by the earlier demonetization (in 1873) of the white metal. Mining in the state reached its peak in 1900, with the year's production of the precious metals totaling $50,000,000. Thereafter, the industry declined. But agriculture had a corresponding rise and soon far overshadowed mining production. The principal and enduring wealth of Colorado was in the soil.

THE WASHOE MINES

The first settlers within present Nevada came from the Mormon base at Salt Lake. In the spring of 1851 John Reese and his employees took a 10-wagon train of supplies and merchandise to the east base of the Sierra Nevadas and established a trading station in the Carson River Valley beside the California Trail. Some Californians crossed the mountains to participate in the trade with overland emigrants. Mormon settlers came in during the years 1851 to 1853 and took up land in the vicinity. Utah Territory, as created by Congress in 1850, extended west to the Sierras, and therefore embraced this region. Being separated by 500 miles of desert from Salt Lake City, the settlers in Carson Valley assembled in the fall of 1851 to form a simple squatters' government. The principal concern was for the survey and recording of land claims. In 1854 the legislature of Utah created Carson County in the western end of the Territory and made provision for a county government.

Inasmuch as some of the non-Mormon settlers were seeking annexation to California, Brigham Young sent more colonists to Carson County in 1855. As leader of the contingent went Apostle Orson Hyde, carrying also a commission as Probate Judge, signed by Governor Young. More colonists were sent the next year, and Judge Hyde laid out the first regular town in present Nevada. He named it "Genoa."

Farther south, on the Salt Lake-Los Angeles trail, a Mormon Mission was being established at the site of Las Vegas, a spot early named by the Spaniards for its beautiful meadows. William Bringhurst led a party of 30 men to the Las Vegas Springs in 1855. They were directed to preach to the Indians and to establish a way station. An adobe-walled fort, with dwellings inside, was constructed. Land was fenced with mesquite brush, and crops were planted. Some Indians were baptized; but their conversion was more formal than real, for in 1857 they swooped down upon the fields and carried off the ripe crops. The mission was thereupon abandoned by the whites. A blow equally disastrous came to the Carson County colonists the same year. When a federal army set out for Utah, Young directed the gathering-in of his Saints. The Mormon colonists, 985 men, women, and children, deserted their homes and farms in response to Brigham's call. "Nevada would have fared better had she kept her Mormon colonists," writes Dr. E. M. Mack, Nevada historian. "Their zeal and ability to develop virgin territory was ably demonstrated." [1]

Since the few people who remained in western Utah had a strong antipathy toward the Mormons, they held a mass meeting and petitioned Congress for a separate Territorial organization. They met in Genoa, proposed "Columbus" as the name for their territory, and sent a delegate with their memorial to Congress. With the "Utah War" on, the time seemed particularly opportune for winning Territorial status. A bill passed the House, but failed in the Senate. The pioneers in 1859 made another effort to establish a Territorial government. A constitution was drafted and adopted, but the government it proposed did not go into operation. For two more years the Nevada region was to continue without effective government. Utah authority in the region was defied, and the extra-legal local governments that rose were not generally recognized. This disorganized condition resulted largely from the entry of a new factor into the situation—a great mining rush. The discovery of the Comstock Lode in June, 1859, brought the influx of a horde of heterogeneous wealth-seekers who swept aside the half-completed government, subordinated the agricultural element and quiet

[1] Mack, E. M., *Nevada, a History of the State,* Glendale, Cal., Arthur H. Clark Co., 1936, 171.

life, and "replaced them with the new habiliments of a roistering, boisterous frontier mining society."

Placer gold in small quantities had been found at the eastern base of the Sierra Nevadas during the days of the early California discoveries. Returns had been small, but persistent miners continued to pan in the gulches, hoping for a real strike. As they worked their way up Gold Canyon and Six Mile Canyon toward Mount Davidson, the dirt became richer. Between the heads of these two ravines, about a mile apart, extended a great lode of silver awaiting discovery.

Among the miners in Gold Canyon was a shiftless, boastful fellow named Henry T. P. Comstock. Near the head of the canyon he and others staked and worked some rich claims, built several log cabins, and called the place Gold Hill. As the snow melted and ran off in the spring of 1859, water for the placer operations became scarce. So some of the miners in Six Mile Canyon went a short distance above their claims to dig a reservoir for collecting water from a spring. While excavating, they encountered a peculiar stratum that, upon being tested by two of the workers—Peter O'Riley and Patrick McLaughlin—proved to be a rich mineral vein. Comstock, upon hearing of the strike, visited the discoverers and informed them that he and others owned the spring and the ground about it. Not only did Comstock worm his way into a good share of the rich ground, but through his constant talk and his confident familiarity with veins and their courses, his name soon became attached to this greatest of veins in the history of American mining—the Comstock Lode.

The O'Riley and McLaughlin discovery was at first considered a gold mine. In the middle of the vein was a wedge of heavy bluish-black rock which hindered the placer work. Late in June some samples of this mineral were taken over the mountains to Grass Valley and Nevada City, California. The assay showed values of $3,000 in silver and $876 in gold per ton. The news was published and the first rush was on. Being located in the country of the Washoe Indians, the district was called the Washoe Mines.

In August the first consignment of ore was carried over the mountains on muleback, and was shipped to San Francisco. The yield after smelting was $114,000. The bars of white metal from the furnace were carried through the streets of the city. Excited crowds followed the exhibit. Everyone began to talk of the Washoe Mines. Many hurriedly made their way there, emigration continuing until snow closed the mountain passes. Early in the spring of 1860 the movement was resumed. Up the Sacramento River in crowded little steamboats, over the snow-clogged mountain trails, on foot, on horseback, and by wagon, the eager miners, gamblers, and numerous other types of humanity fought their way. Horses and mules were spoken for, days in advance. The stores, warehouses, and even the streets of the nearest California towns were piled with goods bound for Washoe. Cattle, hogs, and sheep were driven up the trails toward the new Eldorado. In the opposite direction came pack trains of mules bringing out the rich ore.

Since silver was new to most California miners, barren rock was as frequently claimed as silver veins. Soon the sides of Mount Davidson were bristling with location stakes and posted with crudely scrawled notices. Camps and towns sprang into existence. The principal of these, located high on the slope of the mountain, was soon called Virginia City. It is reputed to have been christened by Comstock's partner, "Old Virginia," who, while gloriously drunk, had stumbled from the door of his cabin and broken his bottle of whiskey. Rising on his knees and waving the bottle neck, he shouted, "I baptize this ground Virginia Town." In any event, the name was attached to the booming camp. "Frame shanties pitched together as if by accident, tents of canvas, of blankets, of brush, of potato sacks and old shirts, with empty whiskey barrels for chimneys; smoking hovels of mud and stone; coyote holes in the hillsides forcibly seized by men, pits and shanties with smoke issuing from every crevice; piles of goods and rubbish on craggy points, in hollows, on rocks, in the mud, on the snow"—this was Virginia City as viewed by a newcomer early in 1860.

During that year some 10,000 persons came into the district from California. Trails over the mountains were widened into roads, and stage lines and freight outfits crowded the routes. In providing food, drink, clothing, and shelter, the camps grew. Virginia City boasted two quartz mills, 10 livery stables, 25 saloons, and other facilities in proportion. The rich strikes kept people in a frenzy. Claims were staked in all directions, and prospectors brought in samples and sold "feet" along their mythical lodes to newcomers. Everyone was hopeful. Promoters invested the profits of their own frauds in the frauds of others. All were encouraged by the fact that in the real mines the width of the ore body increased as the shafts were sunk deeper.

In the summer of 1860 prospectors from Virginia City turned south and opened the Esmeralda mines a little southwest of Walker Lake. Others found mines in the Humboldt Mountains near present Unionville, while still others opened lesser districts in new sections. Two years later rich silver deposits were found beside the Pony Express trail on the Reese River, and the town of Austin sprang up. But the Virginia City region was the great mining district. The silver production here brought Nevada Territory into existence, and for years the history of the Comstock Lode was practically the history of Nevada (Spanish for "Snowy," named from its mountain range).

NEVADA BECOMES A STATE

Nevada Territory was created out of western Utah by act of Congress, March 2, 1861. Four months elapsed before the federal officials arrived. James W. Nye of New York, friend of Secretary of State William H. Seward, was appointed Governor. The member of the official family destined for greatest fame was Mark Twain, who accompanied his brother Orion Clemens, Secretary of the Territory. Twain was soon writing stories for the *Virginia City Enterprise*. A census showed a population of less than 20,000 in the Territory. The legislature, which met on August 31, 1861, passed the usual laws, regulating proceedings in civil and criminal cases, defining crime, prescribing punishments, and so forth. In view of present conditions, it may be interesting to note that those first enactments prohibited any theater, game of chance, or "noisy amusement" from operating on Sunday. Divorce was to be granted only on grounds of habitual drunkenness, extreme cruelty, and desertion. Marriage between a white person and an Indian, a Negro, or a Chinese was made a crime.

Nevada Territory, as created in 1861, was little more than half the size of the present state. The section lying south of the 37° of north latitude then belonged to New Mexico Territory. This was added to Nevada by Congressional Act in 1866. The eastern boundary of Nevada was twice moved eastward at the expense of Utah—from the 39th meridian west of Washington to the 38th in 1862, and to the 37th in 1866. The enlargement brought almost no additional population however.

Conflicting claims to footage on the Comstock Lode led inevitably to numerous lawsuits, and these were marked not only by great contests of legal talent, but by physical violence as well. The ground was so rich, the stakes so high, and the points of law so ill-defined, that the contests seemed endless. The 12 leading mines of the district were parties to 245 separate suits, and the cost of litigation has been estimated at $10,000,000.

The legal situation as regards mining property was very unsatisfactory. There was no national mining code and Congress was too busy with the Civil War to pay attention to such needs. Territorial judges, not of the highest caliber, were being presented with technical questions which they were incompetent to decide. Receiving meager salaries and determining the ownership of mines worth millions, these men were not always immune to bribery in its various forms. Development work on valuable properties was retarded through uncertainty of title. Representatives in Congress were advocating the sale at auction of mineral lands on the public domain in order to pay the cost of the Civil War. These conditions and dangers suggested to Nevada citizens the desirability of winning statehood. In the first Territorial legislature a bill was passed submitting the question of statehood to the electorate. Of the 8,162 votes cast in the consequent election, 6,660 were in favor of state government.

The majority in Congress, with an eye to future needs of the Republican Party, exhibited a willingness to admit new antislavery states. An "Enabling Act for the State of Nevada" was passed on March 3, 1863. In November of that year a convention assembled and drafted a constitution, but local politics brought its rejection at the polls. A bill for another enabling act for Nevada came before Congress in February, 1864. There was strong opposition on grounds of sparsity of population, the Territory having not over 20,000, whereas the quota for a Representative in Congress was then 127,381. But President Lincoln was strong for the Nevada bill. He wanted emancipation of slaves written into the United States Constitution, and he needed another free state to accomplish it. The freeing of the Negroes through a constitutional amendment would, in the opinion of Lincoln, have a moral effect on the rebellious states "equivalent to raising another army of a million men." He authorized Assistant Secretary of War Charles A. Dana to give the New York and New Jersey delegations the necessary political patronage to win their support. Thereupon the bill for Nevada's statehood was passed, and was signed on March 21, 1864.

Necessary steps to complete the set-up were taken with dispatch in Nevada. A constitutional convention assembled, and, in a 23-day session, it drafted a constitution that was accepted by the people. In order to be approved by the President in time to permit Nevada citizens' participation in the national election, the entire constitution was telegraphed to Lincoln. This telegram, the longest on record up to that time, cost $3,416.77. The President approved the document and proclaimed admission of the new state on October 31, 1864. On November 8 the Republican assistance to Nevada was rewarded by an overwhelming victory of that party at the first state election. Wrote Charles A. Dana: "I have sometimes heard people complain of Nevada as superfluous and petty, not big enough to be a state; but when I hear that complaint, I always hear Abraham Lincoln saying, 'It is easier to admit Nevada than to raise another million soldiers.'"

The product of the Nevada mines was an important factor in maintaining the financial stability of the nation during the Civil War period. In support of the Union cause, Nevada supplied a creditable number of soldiers. One of the most famous contributions to the Sanitary Fund, forerunner of the Red Cross, came from Nevada. A sack of flour, won in an election wager, was auctioned off for the benefit of the Fund, and was subsequently sold and resold dozens of times in various towns of the state. The amount raised finally totaled $275,000.

Senator William M. Stewart of Nevada obtained an appropriation from Congress in 1866 for the establishment of a mint at Carson City. By 1869 the institution was ready to turn out United States coins of various denominations and "trade dollars" for use in the Orient. The establishment of this mint was a recognition of Nevada's importance in monetary matters.

THE BIG BONANZA

The spectacular and colorful story of Virginia City and the Comstock Lode could fill volumes, but space permits only a brief mention here of a few of the striking features.

During its first decade Virginia City had experienced varying fortunes. It had suffered fire and flood and mine explosions; the ecstasy of new strikes; the long-drawn pain of failures. Some mines had paid handsomely; others were being worked through assessments on stockholders who were never to receive a cent in dividends. Between 1859 and 1872, 12 bonanzas, or rich ore bodies, had been found along the Comstock Lode. But the largest of all was yet hidden.

Four Irishmen—Mackay, Fair, Flood, and O'Brien—having acquired control of the Consolidated Virginia, which had suspended operations for lack of funds, decided early in 1873 to drive a drift at a depth of 1,167 feet. They soon cut the top of a rich ore deposit. Another drift, from beneath, struck the same body, 54 feet wide at this point. Here was the "Big Bonanza," the greatest in the history of the world's mining. It was to produce nearly $200,000,000 in bullion. The excitement in Virginia City, when the news was out, can be imagined. The boom on the San Francisco Stock Exchange sent shares skyrocketing. At the peak of hysteria, in January, 1875, shares of Comstock mines listed on the exchange were valued at $300,000,000.

The four men who struck the Big Bonanza were not the only millionaires produced by Virginia City mines. They were not the first— nor the last—kings of the Comstock. The great chest poured its treasure into California. Nevada silver built San Francisco's first great hotels, her first large banks; it erected the first mansions on Nob Hill and developed large real estate tracts. The Comstock won national and international fame. Its vast silver output shook the monetary systems of the world, upsetting the long-established ratio of gold and silver.

The great mining activity at Virginia City induced other important developments. Wood in large quantities was needed for the mines and the mills. The unusually large cavities caused by the taking out of the big lodes presented a new problem in the timbering of mines. To prevent the mountain from caving in, a plan of square sets was devised by Philip Diedesheimer. He built timber cribs, four by six feet square, which could be set one upon another to any required height. At one time over 70,000,000 feet of timber went annually into the caverns and drifts of the lode. The boilers supplying power for hoists and mills consumed 250,000 cords of wood in a year. Soon the eastern slope of the Sierras in the vicinity was denuded. Hungry axes and saws ate their way over the mountains to the California side. Hauling over roads was too expensive and uncertain. So great V-shaped flumes were constructed along the sides of the mountains and on high trestles across the canyons. On water turned into these flumes, logs and timbers were floated or slid to the Virginia and Truckee Railroad. In 1880 there were in operation ten such flumes with a combined length of 80 miles.

The providing of culinary water for Virginia City was a difficult problem. When local supplies from creeks and wells proved inadequate, engineers went 25 miles up the mountains to a supply source. In bringing the water to the city through 12-inch pipe, an inverted siphon with a dip of 1,720 feet had to be laid across Washoe Valley.

In the depths of some of the mines, working conditions were deplorable. The intense heat made it impossible for men to work more than a few minutes before they must retire to cooling stations. Here tubs of ice were kept and towels dipped in ice water were thrown over the workers' bodies. One of the companies used 2,000,000 pounds of ice in the cooling stations of its mines in a year. In the hottest spots miners worked with a spray of cold water directed upon them. Under these conditions it is little wonder that many men died of "miner's consumption." The miners worked in three eight-hour shifts, and the pay was usually four dollars per day.

The seepage of water into the mines necessitated expensive pumping operations. Indeed, as the mines deepened, the pumps were inadequate. Adolph Sutro conceived the plan of driving a four-mile tunnel from Carson Valley to strike the mines at the 1,800-foot level. This would drain the mines and permit carriage of ore through the bore. The mine owners agreed to pay a royalty of two dollars a ton on all ore mined after the completion of the tunnel. Sutro set to work with great determination. He appealed to Congress, to capitalists in New York and in Europe. In 1865, with a contribution of $50,000 from the miners, he began to drive the tunnel. Later he obtained over $2,000,-000 through the sale of stock at home and abroad. After years of struggle and disappointments his dream was realized with the completion of the bore in 1878. But, unfortunately, the great days of the Comstock had already passed. The main ore bodies had been mined. And, in addition, the price of silver was on the decline. Demonetization of silver had come through act of Congress in the "Crime of 1873." Government purchases of silver provided by the Bland-Allison Act of 1878 and the Sherman Act of 1890 were inadequate to maintain the price level. Then, with the Panic of 1893 and the repeal of the Sherman Act, silver mining was given a death blow. The great mines of the Comstock closed.

A number of other notable mining districts were opened in Nevada—Pioche, Tonopah, Goldfield, Rhyolite—and many others less enduring. In general, they were miniature models of Virginia City, and cannot be treated here.

Important as mining is, it is ephemeral in its nature. A body of ore can be taken from the ground but once, and all mines are destined for exhaustion. Roaring mining camps inevitably become ghost towns.

Resting on pillars of silver, Nevada has been resplendent and alluring. But the supporting pillars have been carried away to answer the calls of the market and to form the currencies of the world. Gradually other supports—products of the farm and range—are replacing those of silver. The Newlands Reclamation Project, the Lahontan Reservoir, and similar undertakings are putting to fuller use the limited waters of the state. Green fields have appeared on small patches of the desert. Railroads and highways and the mighty Boulder Dam are capital investments that help to maintain the "Sagebrush State."

BIBLIOGRAPHY

A good general account of mining in the United States is found in T. A. Rickard, *A History of American Mining* (New York, 1932). One of the early histories of Colorado and Nevada is H. H. Bancroft, *History of Nevada, Colorado and Wyoming, 1540–1888* (San Francisco, 1890).

For the Colorado region, the two earliest works devoted principally to mining history are: O. J. Hollister, *The Mines of Colorado* (Springfield, Mass., 1867) and Frank Fossett, *Colorado: a Historical, Descriptive and Statistical Work on the Rocky Mountain Gold and Silver Mining Region* (Denver, 1876). For general histories of the state, consult: L. R. Hafen, *Colorado, the Story of a Western Commonwealth* (Denver, 1933); J. C. Smiley, *Semi-Centennial History of the State of Colorado* (Chicago, 1913); Frank Hall, *History of the State of Colorado* (4 vols., Chicago, 1889–1895); J. H. Baker and L. R. Hafen, *History of Colorado* (3 vols., Denver, 1927); W. F. Stone, *History of Colorado* (Chicago, 1918); L. R. Hafen, *Colorado and Its People* (2 vols., New York, 1948); and A. T. Steinel, *History of Agriculture in Colorado* (Denver, 1926).

On the Colorado gold rush see L. R. Hafen, *Pike's Peak Gold Rush Guidebooks of 1859; Colorado Gold Rush, Contemporary Letters and Reports;*

and *Overland Routes to the Gold Fields*, Vols. IX to XI of the *Southwest Historical Series* (Glendale, 1941–1942). See the *Colorado Magazine* and *The Trail* for important historical articles.

The following popular books are devoted to Colorado mining development and mining men: G. F. Willison, *Here They Dug the Gold* (New York, 1931); L. C. Gandy, *The Tabors, a Footnote of Western History* (New York, 1934); David Karsner, *Silver Dollar, the Story of the Tabors* (New York, 1932); Frank Waters, *Midas of the Rockies. The Story of Stratton and Cripple Creek* (New York, 1937); E. W. McLean, *Father Struck It Rich* (Boston, 1936); C. C. Davis, *Olden Times in Colorado* (Los Angeles, 1916).

For biographical works on Colorado consult: J. A. Fisher, *A Builder of the West; the Life of William Jackson Palmer* (Caldwell, Idaho, 1937); E. C. McMechen, *Life of Governor Evans* (Denver, 1924); Elmer Ellis, *Henry Moore Teller, Defender of the West* (Caldwell, Idaho, 1941); Gene Fowler, *Timber Line; a Story of Bonfils and Tammen* (New York, 1933).

For general histories of Nevada, in addition to Bancroft, cited above, consult E. M. Mack, *Nevada, a History of the State from the Earliest Times through the Civil War* (Glendale, 1936); Myron Angel, *History of Nevada* (Oakland, 1881); S. P. Davis, *The History of Nevada* (2 vols., Reno, 1913). See also C. H. Shinn, *The Story of the Mine, as Illustrated by the Great Comstock Lode of Nevada* (New York, 1896); William Wright [Dan De Quille, pseud.], *History of the Big Bonanza* (San Francisco, 1876).

The following are recent popular accounts: G. D. Lyman, *The Saga of the Comstock Lode; Boom Days in Virginia City* (New York, 1934); C. B. Glasscock, *The Big Bonanza* (Indianapolis, 1931); Miriam Michelson, *The Wonderlode of Silver and Gold* (Boston, 1934); C. B. Glasscock, *Gold in Them Hills* (Indianapolis, 1932); G. D. Lyman, *Ralston's Ring; California Plunders the Comstock Lode* (New York, 1937); Richard G. Lillard, *Desert Challenge, an Interpretation of Nevada* (New York, 1942).

25

NORTHWEST TERRITORIES

T HE GOLD rush to California cost Oregon her leadership on the Pacific Coast. Prior to 1848 American interest had centered in the Columbia River country, and the major part of the emigration had gone there. But the discovery at Sutter's mill changed all that. California now monopolized not only the emigration from the East, but drew from Oregon as well. Over half the men in the Columbia Valley hurried away to the mines in 1848. The loss was but temporary. Presently miners, some with well-filled purses, began to return to their families. Calls came from California for the products of Oregon farms and forests. A new vigor was infused into the settlements on the Willamette, and California gold brought a welcome prosperity.

Alluring prices were offered for Oregon flour, meat, butter, eggs, fruit, and vegetables. There was great demand for lumber to supply building and mining needs, and for piling for San Francisco's waterfront. More land was put under cultivation in the Northwest, and more sawmills placed in operation. Roads were opened; steamboats plied the rivers. Coal was discovered at Coos Bay and on Puget Sound, and soon thousands of tons were being shipped annually to San Francisco. The gold rush led to the opening of southern Oregon. Settlement was begun there in 1850, when Jesse Applegate, outstanding explorer and pioneer, joined with others and began the colonization of the Umpqua Valley. Settlers went into the valley of Rogue River about the same time. Gold placers were discovered on a branch of this river in 1851, and a rush to the region brought in several thousand people. Many of these, however, found farming more profitable than mining.

By the middle fifties the people of Oregon were clamoring for statehood. The Territory had already been divided, the northern part being marked off in 1853 as Washington Territory (to be treated in

421

the following section). In 1856 General Lane, delegate to Congress, introduced a statehood bill for Oregon, but it failed of enactment. The next year a similar bill passed the House but failed in the Senate. Undaunted, the citizens of Oregon proceeded with their plans. The legislature submitted to the people the question of calling a constitutional convention. The proposal was carried in June, 1857, and the convention met in Salem in August. It drafted a constitution that was ratified in September, 1857. The state government went into effect in July, 1858, although formal admission to the Union was not effected until February 14, 1859.

WASHINGTON TERRITORY

The region north of Columbia River was controlled by Hudson's Bay Company when the first American settlers trekked to Oregon. Although the Joint Occupation Agreement with Great Britain permitted our citizens to enter any part of the Oregon country, the British fur men endeavored to keep the newcomers south of the great river. Indeed, England confidently expected that the Columbia would become the boundary line.

During the 1830's and 1840's, the Hudson's Bay Company, having broadened its activities beyond the fur trade field, did pioneering work of real importance for the future state of Washington. Fort Nisqually, established on Puget Sound in 1833, was soon devoting itself to farming and stockraising, and was becoming the base of colonization in the region. On the Pacific Coast the Hudson's Bay Company was operating under a special license, inasmuch as this region was beyond the boundaries of its original grant. When petitioning for a renewal of this license, Sir J. H. Pelly, head of the Company's affairs in London, stressed the Company's service to the mother country "in securing to it a branch of commerce which they are at present wresting out of the hands of foreigners, subjects of Russia and the United States of America." Sir George Simpson also wrote a letter to accompany the petition, in which he says: "The Possession of that country to Great Britain may become an object of great importance; and we are strengthening that claim to it . . . by forming the nucleus of a colony, through the establishment of farms and the settlement of some of our retired officers and servants as agriculturalists." The license was renewed.

The Hudson's Bay Company now organized a subsidiary corporation, the Puget Sound Agricultural Company, and placed all agricultural affairs in its hands. The herds of cattle and sheep were enlarged and improved. Dairying on a large scale was begun. At one time more than 200 cows were being milked at Fort Nisqually. Butter and cheese were exported to Russian Alaska and to Hawaii. Wool, hides, and tallow were generally shipped to England. Annual sales of grain amounted to as much as 15,000 bushels. A special group of colonists was brought out from the Red River settlements in 1841. While the flocks and herds on Puget Sound were increasing, the farms on the Cowlitz and at Fort Vancouver on the Columbia were being extended. And the British fur business was being carried on at Forts Walla Walla, Colville, and Okanogan, in present Washington, and at Fort Boise and Fort Hall in Idaho.

When certain Americans wanted to settle north of the Columbia, the efforts of British agents to keep them out served but to increase their desire. Such a one was Michael T. Simmons, a Kentucky-born Irishman. In July, 1845, he led a little party from Fort Vancouver to Puget Sound, where the men chose a site for settlement and then returned for their families. Two months later the colonists sailed down the Columbia to the mouth of the Cowlitz, up this stream to its forks, and thence made their way overland to Puget Sound. In the latter part of the journey they cut a road for their ox teams through 58 miles of forest. With Simmons and his family went four other families and two single men. These were the first Americans to make their homes on Puget Sound. Their settlement, which they called New Market, was located on the Des Chutes River at the head of Budd's Inlet, a little south of present Olympia.

The colonists obtained wheat, peas, potatoes, and ten head of cattle from the Puget Sound Agricultural Company, and supplemented their supplies with game from the forest, fish from the streams, and clams from the shore. From the Indians they learned where and when to take the clams and shellfish. The information developed into an adage: "When the tide is out, the table is set." The men made shingles and sold them at Fort Nisqually for clothing, blankets, and provisions. In the winter of 1846–1847, Simmons built a grist-mill at New Market, later known as Tumwater. He fashioned boulders into millstones and used the falls of the Des Chutes for power. Additional pioneers came in 1846 and 1847, increasing the American contingent. In August, 1847, Simmons and others formed the Puget Sound Milling Company, and built near the lower falls of the Des Chutes the first sawmill on the Sound. The machinery, obtained from the Hudson's Bay Company, previously had been used at Fort Vancouver.

In the meantime, in 1846, the international boundary had been fixed along the 49th parallel, and Americans were now assured that their homes were being built on United States soil. The Hudson's Bay

Company, the Puget Sound Agricultural Company, and all British subjects living south of the 49th parallel were, under the terms of the treaty, guaranteed their property rights in the region. Dr. McLoughlin had resigned from his position with the British company in 1845; he retired to his claim at the forks of the Willamette, became an American citizen, and was to spend the remainder of his life in futile efforts to defend his personal property rights from the attacks of persons whom he had befriended. McLoughlin was succeeded as chief factor by James Douglas, who presently moved the headquarters of the company to Victoria on Vancouver Island. Dr. William F. Tolmie was left in charge of business on the American side of the boundary, where large holdings of land and other property continued under his management.

The California gold discovery of 1848 drew men from the new settlements on Puget Sound as well as from the Willamette. When the census was taken in 1849, but 304 people were found north of the Columbia. Citizens of the United States numbered 189, foreigners 115; 231 males, 73 females. But gold-seekers soon began to return, bringing gold dust and, what was more important, news of a ready market for timber. San Francisco was crying for planking and piles to build wharves and lumber for houses. No section of the Northwest was better fitted by nature to supply this need than was the Puget Sound area. Here were excellent harbors for ocean-going vessels, falls to supply power for sawmills, and forests extending to the shore line. The lumber business was to flourish, and for years to be the leading industry of Washington.

In May, 1849, the Snoqualimich Indians decided to rid themselves of the white settlers. They attacked Fort Nisqually, but were repulsed. In August following, a detachment of the First Artillery arrived on the Sound and began the erection of Fort Steilacoom. Several Indians charged with the attack were tried, and two of them were convicted and hanged.

The federal Census of 1850 showed a population of 1,049 north of the Columbia River. The country east of the Cowlitz now formed Clark County; the region west was Lewis County. The principal centers of population were Forts Vancouver and Nisqually and the area at the head of Budd's Inlet. There were a few settlers along the north bank of the Columbia as far east as the Cascades, some on the Cowlitz, and a few on the coast as far north as Gray's Harbor. At the Vancouver and Nisqually posts the Hudson's Bay people still outnumbered the Americans.

In January, 1850, the brig *Orbit* had come into Puget Sound and had sailed as far as it safely could up Budd's Inlet. The boat was purchased by persons in New Market, and became the first ship owned on

Puget Sound. Colonel Simmons, after acquiring a controlling interest in the brig, sent it to San Francisco with a cargo of piles. In July, it was back with a load of general merchandise. Edmund Sylvester, who owned a half section of the land north of New Market and who had platted on this land the town of Olympia, offered Simmons two choice lots if he would build a store upon them. Simmons accepted, and built the store and a flourishing business. Another ship with a load of goods arrived at Olympia early in 1850, but not receiving the welcome expected, Captain Balch sailed away to find a location of his own. He selected a site a little north of Fort Nisqually, and laid out Port Steilacoom. The Hudson's Bay Company's Fort Nisqually now had two American competitors for the trade of the settlers and Indians.

The site of Seattle was explored and some claims were taken by John Holgate and others in 1850; but not until a little group of 24 colonists landed at Alki Point on November 13, 1851, were the foundations of the future metropolis laid. The first commercial employment of these men was the supplying of timber, a cargo of piles being loaded on a sailing vessel before the first homes were completed. These pioneers called their settlement New York. The next spring a majority of the settlers moved to the east side of the bay and started a town to which they gave the name of Seattle, a chief of the Suquamish tribe. At this time Dr. D. S. Maynard arrived, having been told by Chief Seattle that good fishing grounds were to be found on the Duwamish River and at Elliott Bay. The doctor developed a busy fishing camp in the southern end of the Seattle settlement. He employed Indian laborers, and exported many barrels of salt fish and fish oil to San Francisco. The town plot of Seattle was filed for record on May 23, 1853. Being well located, it grew to a population of 300 by 1855. Port Townsend at the head of the inlet to the Sound was also started in 1851 by pioneers who engaged in lumbering. Their business was given added impetus when two disastrous fires swept San Francisco in 1851 and brought new demands for wharf timbers and for lumber to rebuild the city. Though farms were developed in valleys back of the Sound, productions were meager, and for some years flour was imported from California. Lumbering continued as the dominant industry.

The Puget Sound settlers were nearly completely separated from those on the Willamette, the commercial trade of the former being almost entirely with San Francisco. This situation gave rise to a feeling of independence and to agitation for dividing the Territory. A newspaper called the *Columbian* was begun at Olympia in September, 1852, to advocate creation of a separate Territory north of the Columbia. On November 25 following, a convention assembled and prepared a memorial to Congress asking a separate government. The petition was sent to General Lane, Delegate to Congress. The Oregon legislature in January, 1853, adopted a similar memorial. Lane introduced in Congress a bill to create the Territory of Columbia from the northern part of Oregon. It was passed on February 10, 1853, but with the name changed to Washington Territory. The dividing line followed the Columbia River to the vicinity of Walla Walla, and thence along the 46th parallel to the Continental Divide. Isaac I. Stevens, engineer and West Point graduate, who had been chosen to survey the northern route for a Pacific railroad, was appointed governor. After exploring

Courtesy of State Historical Society of Colorado

WAGON TRAIN ENCAMPED ON STREET OF PIONEER DENVER, COLORADO

a practical route for a railroad, he reached Olympia in late November, 1853, and thereupon put into operation the Territorial government.

The new Territory had as yet a very limited population, a special enumeration of 1853 showing but 3,965 inhabitants. But in this year the Puget Sound area for the first time drew a considerable portion of the immigration to the far Northwest. A new road over the Cascade Mountains from the Yakima River to Olympia now made a more direct route available for covered wagon pioneers.

The Indian wars of the middle fifties retarded development in the Far Northwest. But early in the next decade came discoveries of gold —to be discussed presently. The influx of miners gave Washington a sudden population increase; but with the division of the Territory and the creation of Idaho in 1863, Washington lost much of what she had gained. During the seventies the population and the development of Washington increased gradually. The following decade, however, witnessed a striking change. Railroads came, and these furnished the needed stimulus to immigration and material development. New towns sprang up; old ones took on new life. Seattle began to develop a trade with the Orient that was to help make her the metropolis of the region. Big lumber interests began operations on a large scale. Shipbuilding assumed considerable proportions. Stock raising increased, and wheat farming expanded. Salmon and other fish became important articles of export. The population of Washington, which numbered 75,116 in 1880, increased to 349,390 by 1890.

"The Inland Empire"

East of the Cascade Range and west of the Rockies is an area of some 200,000 square miles drained by the Columbia and its affluents. Before the middle of the nineteenth century this vast region was uninhabited by white men, except for a few fur trading posts and missions. With lighter precipitation than that of the coastal plain, this interior land was generally pronounced unfit for white habitation. But Dr. Marcus Whitman, the pioneer missionary, had been more optimistic. In October, 1847, he wrote that "the interior of Oregon is unrivalled by any country for the grazing of stock, of which sheep is best." Within two months the good doctor was dead, massacred by the Indians he had tried to save, and the Indian war that followed brought soldiers rather than settlers to the Walla Walla region.

Governor Stevens, while surveying the northern railroad route in 1853, noted several sections of eastern Washington suitable for settlement—especially the valleys of the Spokane, Walla Walla, and Yakima rivers. The governor's treaties negotiated with the Indians soon thereafter were intended to open some of this territory to settlement; but an uprising in 1855, followed by several years of Indian war, again postponed the entry of white men. By the time the Indian danger was removed, a new attraction had been revealed to encourage white invasion. Gold was discovered.

Even before the outbreak of the Indian wars of the fifties, some gold had been found. In the thirties there were rumors of its presence, and in 1852 Angus MacDonald, Chief Trader at Fort Colville, northeast Washington, reported a discovery near his post. Other finds were made near the mouth of the Pend d'Oreille River. The discovery was celebrated by firing a field piece lashed to a boulder with buffalo thongs; and, no flag being available, a buffalo robe and a bear skin

were raised on a flagpole. The real rush to the Colville region occurred in 1855. Gold was found in many places, but not in large quantities. In 1857 discoveries were made on the upper Fraser River in British Columbia, and a stampede to the area began. Some 30,000 miners
from California went to the region in 1858, and others came from eastern United States. As the rush receded in 1859, gold-seekers spread in
all directions, prospecting as they went. They opened the rich Caribou
District in 1860. In the same year came discoveries on branches of
the Snake River in present northern Idaho.

E. D. Pierce found gold on the Clearwater branch of the Snake
River in August, 1860. But the prospectors he led to the region encountered hostility of the Nez Percé Indians. Some soldiers and the
Superintendent of Indian Affairs came in and smoothed the way for
the miners. By June, 1861, hundreds of gold-seekers were in the region, and the towns of Orofino and Pierce City had sprung into existence. At first the route of travel was up the Columbia to Fort Walla
Walla, and thence by pack-horses and teams to the mines. But steamers were presently ascending the Snake River to the mouth of the
Clearwater fork. Here the town of Lewiston, named for Meriwether
Lewis, was founded in June, 1861. It became a depot for supplies,
whence pack trains departed for the gold-bearing gulches. A wagon
road was immediately opened from Lewiston to Pierce City. By July
5,000 men were in the district. Some prospectors moved to the south
fork of the Clearwater and developed diggings there. By September
Elk City had been started and was claiming a population of 2,000.
Miners pushed south to the Salmon fork of the Snake River, where
gold placers were discovered and where Millersburg was founded in
October. Within a month there were 1,000 men at the Salmon River
mines. Perhaps the richest camp was Florence. Here one panful of
dirt yielded $500, and one man claimed recovery of $6,600 in a day's
work at Baboon Gulch.

The spring of 1862 brought a rush of gold-seekers. Boatloads of
Californians came up the coast and were joined by Oregonians for
the voyage up the Columbia. At The Dalles the enthusiasm of the
would-be miners was heightened by the arrival from the mines in
March of a pack train carrying 400 pounds of newly mined gold. Most
of the newcomers pushed into the mining region east of the Snake
River, but some went to diggings being opened on the Powder and
John Day rivers of eastern Oregon. In the late summer of 1862 gold
was found in the Boise Basin, some 70 miles east of Fort Boise. The
fame of the Salmon River and other mines of the region drew prospectors not only from the Pacific Coast, but from Nevada, Colorado,
and the eastern states. The experienced miners from the west coast

gloried in the name "yonder-siders," which Easterners applied to them. The converging of miners from various directions brought a population of some 20,000 to the new mining region by the autumn of 1862.

Furnishing supplies for miners was an important and large business. From camp to camp pack trains made their way, carrying flour, bacon, beans, picks, shovels, pans, and quicksilver. Some pack trains set out from Portland, others from The Dalles and Umatilla Landing. But Walla Walla became the great distributing center of the inland country. A military post had been established near the old Whitman mis-sion in 1856, and about it the small settlement of Walla Walla grew. The mining development gave it new life. From this central location trails radiated in all directions, pack trains going north to Colville and Kootenai, east to the Clearwater and Salmon, south to the Powder and

PACKING TO THE MINES IN THE ROCKY MOUNTAINS

the Boise. During the winter, feeding yards in the vicinity were filled with poor, scar-backed pack animals, while grizzled packers aug-mented the population and enlivened the new town. A military road from Fort Benton on the upper Missouri to Walla Walla was con-structed by Captain John Mullan between 1859 and 1862. With the discovery of gold in present western Montana in 1862, this road saw extensive use. Lewiston, established at the terminus of river naviga-tion and centrally located with regard to the Snake River country, was becoming an important commercial and social center. A line of four-horse coaches connected it with Walla Walla, and along the road farms were being developed. As the western emporium for the trade of the vast inland country, Portland was experiencing a rapid growth.

The agricultural development of the region east of the Cascade Mountains, begun before the major mining activity started, was greatly augmented by the miner influx. Several hundred settlers had gone into the Walla Walla Valley in 1859, following negotiation of the Indian treaty of that year. More came in 1860; and within the next six years, 750,000 acres of land in the valley were surveyed and most of these taken up for agricultural purposes. Wheat was the principal crop, but hay, wool, and vegetables were also produced. Into the beautiful valley of the Grand Ronde of northeastern Oregon settlers came in 1861 and 1862. La Grande became the chief town. Products of the farms went to miners of Boise, Owyhee, and other camps. The Yakima Valley east of the Columbia had a development that paralleled that of the Walla Walla.

Spokane, destined to become the metropolis of the Inland Empire, was founded late. Two cattlemen took up claims at the falls of the Spokane River in 1871. James N. Glover came the next year, soon acquired the claims at the falls, stayed on, and witnessed the growth of a modern city, of which he is generally considered the father. Spokane had a population of only 350 in 1880, but the coming of the Northern Pacific railroad the next year increased it to 1,000. With the mining development in the Coeur d'Alene to the eastward, the growth of agriculture, and the exploitation of the timber resources and hydroelectric power, Spokane assumed metropolitan proportions.

IDAHO TERRITORY

The mining development in eastern Washington during the years 1860–1862 was to give rise to a division of the Territory and the creation of Idaho. In 1859, when Oregon was admitted to statehood and her boundaries reduced to their present lines, Washington Territory was enlarged to embrace the rest of the Oregon Territory. Present Idaho and parts of Montana and Wyoming were thus included in Washington Territory of 1859. The miners in the eastern portion of this Territory in 1862 were loudly demanding a separate Territorial government. In every mining camp they circulated petitions addressed to the Washington legislature and to the United States Congress. The legislature failed to agree to the proposal, but Congress responded with remarkable alacrity. An act was passed and signed by President Lincoln on March 3, 1863. It created the Territory of Idaho, which embraced all of the present states of Idaho and Montana and most of Wyoming. The large area was retained only for a year, being reduced in 1864 by the creation of Montana Territory and the transfer of most of the present Wyoming region to Dakota Territory.

Fur trade activity in the Idaho region, the entry of missionaries, and the opening of the Oregon Trail have received treatment in earlier chapters. Reverend and Mrs. Henry H. Spalding, pioneer missionaries of Idaho, had established themselves on Lapwai Creek about 12 miles above the site of present Lewiston in November, 1836. Here they built a log house and opened a school for the Nez Percés. Reverend Spalding introduced agriculture and stock raising, planted apple trees, and erected a blacksmith shop and a gristmill. He even brought in a printing press (in 1839) and translated and published part of the New Testament in Nez Percé. Near by, William Craig, early mountain trapper, built a home for himself and his Nez Percé wife in 1846. He is referred to as Idaho's first permanent white settler. Father Pierre J. De Smet, famous Catholic missionary, visited Idaho in 1840. Two years later, Father Nicholas Point and others established near the southern end of Lake Coeur d'Alene the first Catholic mission in Idaho. It was moved in 1846 to the vicinity of the present town of Cataldo, where the historic "Old Mission" church was built.

In June, 1855, a colony of 28 Mormons established a mission in the Lemhi Valley of present eastern Idaho. They constructed a stockade and began farming. Other colonists arrived the next spring. In 1857 President Brigham Young visited the little settlement. Good crops of wheat, hay, and potatoes were raised this year. A gristmill was put into operation. But the promising settlement was short-lived. In February, 1858, Bannock and Shoshone Indians attacked the colony and killed some of the settlers. A few weeks later the colonists were recalled to Utah. But, despite this failure, the Mormons were destined to make the first permanent settlement in present Idaho, a party of Utah homeseekers founding the town of Franklin in April, 1860. They thought they were in Utah, but a subsequent survey of the boundary line placed the town in Idaho. Franklin was a typical Mormon settlement, with irrigated farms and a Meeting House for church services. Here the first school for white children in Idaho was conducted in the winter of 1860–1861.

But it was mining activity, as noted previously, that brought the first large immigration to the region and caused the creation of Idaho Territory. This mining development of 1860–1862, when the region was a part of Washington Territory, has been sketched above. In 1863 the most notable activity was in the Boise Basin. Placerville, Centerville, Hog'em (Pioneer), and Idaho City (Bannack) became busy centers. As the Indians of the region had exhibited hostility, a military post, Fort Boise, was established in July, 1863. It was located about 40 miles east of the old Hudson's Bay Company's Fort Boise, and, under the name Boise Barracks, is within the corporate limits of the present capital of Idaho.

For a time Idaho City was the metropolis of the Territory, with a population of 6,000 in 1864. It had well-filled stores, resplendent gambling saloons, a hospital, theater, churches, three newspapers, and a fire department. Placerville boasted a population of 5,000 and Centerville had 3,000. Pioneer City, with its 2,000, mostly Irish, was sometimes called New Dublin. In the extreme southwest corner of Idaho prospectors found gold in 1863, and a rush to this Owyhee district took place. The stampede, according to a California newspaper, was "a special forty-eight hour insanity." However, rich silver-bearing ledges were discovered, the camps of Boonville and Silver City sprang up, and a great production of mineral wealth ensued. "The miners of Idaho were like quicksilver," wrote H. H. Bancroft. "A mass of them dropped in any locality, broke up into individual globules, and ran off after any atom of gold in the vicinity. They stayed nowhere longer than the gold attracted them."

The early placer diggings were soon succeeded by lode mining. Arrastras were introduced, but presently were displaced by stamp mills for pulverizing the gold-bearing quartz. After removal of most of the pay dirt from the older placer workings, white men were willing to permit Chinamen to mine in the district, provided they pay a special tax of $6 per month. Half of this fee went to the Territory and half to the County, the sheriff being empowered to collect the levy.

Many of the new residents of Idaho had for years roamed the mining camps of California, Nevada, and Colorado. They had taken on prodigal habits and carefree dispositions. They patronized pleasures liberally, says an early historian, and had "no Puritan prejudices to overcome." Besides the usual mining camp attractions of gambling saloons, bawdy houses, and dance halls, there were also literary clubs and circulating libraries. Charitable projects were always generously supported. A novel sport that had great vogue in Idaho was bobsledding. "Sliding Clubs" were formed in the different towns, contests were arranged, and races were run with stakes as high as $2,500. In the winter of 1864–1865, when storms prevented the bringing in of supplies, and when prices soared in consequence, some of the miners raided food stores in Idaho City, and finally set fire to the town, seizing and carrying away provisions during the conflagration. The town was quickly rebuilt, with some improvements added.

Transportation facilities for the southern Idaho district were a primary concern. A new road up the John Day River and through Canon City to Boise was opened in 1864. A company was formed to build a road from old Fort Boise to Red Cliff, California, *via* Ruby City. A way was opened from the Washoe and Humboldt mines of Nevada to Southern Idaho. A tri-weekly mail in coaches from Salt Lake to

Walla Walla, by way of Fort Hall and Boise, was established by Ben Holladay in 1864.

During the 1860's and 1870's some mines were opened on the head-waters of the Salmon River in east-central Idaho, but the next decade was to witness far greater discoveries. Placers were found in the Coeur d'Alene district, and into this densely forested area hundreds of goldseekers trudged through deep snow early in 1884. Then quartz lodes were found. In August, 1885, N. S. Kellogg, a destitute carpenter turned prospector, was hunting his lost burrow. The story is that he heard the jackass bray far up the mountainside and went in pursuit. Near the animal he paused on a ledge to rest. His hand fell on a loose rock, which proved to be a piece of galena ore from a great dike of marvelous width crossing the mountain. He had found what became the Bunker Hill and Sullivan mine, one of the largest silver and lead mines in the world. The district was to produce over a quarter of a billion dollars and make 50 millionaires. Other rich strikes of these metals were made in the vicinity, and the district was to become one of the world's greatest producers of silver and lead. Unfortunately, the region was to become famous also for its bitter labor wars.

In the late 1860's cattlemen began to bring their herds to the Idaho region, and for more than two decades the open-range cattle business flourished. When sheep were introduced, bitter clashes ensued as a contest for the range developed. The problem was gradually worked out, however, when national forest reserves were established and the government assumed control of large areas through the granting of grazing permits.

Eventually, agriculture became the leading industry of Idaho. A volcanic-ash soil, rich in phosphorus and potash, brought remarkable crop yields. Today wheat is the principal product, but large amounts of other cereals, and of hay, potatoes, sugar beets, and fruits are produced. Much of the farming in the Snake River Valley is dependent on irrigation, but dry farming is carried on extensively in certain sections of the state. Agricultural progress has been contingent in large measure upon railroad building. The first line to enter Idaho (in 1877) was the Utah and Northern, which was built from Ogden, Utah, to Helena, Montana, by way of Pocatello and Blackfoot. The Oregon Short Line, following the general course of the Oregon Trail across Idaho, was constructed in the years 1882–1884. Branches built to various agricultural districts contributed greatly to their development. The Northern Pacific was built across the Idaho panhandle in 1880–1882, and the Great Northern crossed near the Canadian boundary in 1892. These roads provided a market for the mining, timber, and agricultural resources of the region. Following the mining flurry that brought Idaho into existence, the population decreased as the placers were worked out. In 1870 the population was but 15,000. By 1880 it had increased to 32,610. The next decade brought the number to 84,385.

MONTANA TERRITORY

The fur trade activity that resulted from the Lewis and Clark exploration of present Montana has been sketched in Chapter 13. Missionaries followed the traders. In 1841 Father De Smet and some Jesuit companions rode the Oregon Trail to Fort Hall and thence traveled northward to the Bitterroot Valley. Here, near the present town of Stevensville, they founded St. Mary's, the first mission in Montana. To Fort Colville, 300 miles away in present northeastern Washington, De Smet traveled and brought back seed wheat, oats, and potatoes to plant at St. Mary's. From this mother mission, priests went forth and established a mission on Coeur d'Alene Lake (Idaho) in 1842 and one on Pend d'Oreille River (Washington) in 1844.

At each of these Christian outposts the Indians were taught agriculture and the simple crafts. Father Ravalli, who arrived at St. Mary's in 1845, built a little sawmill there, fashioning the saws from old wagon tires. From Europe he obtained two small millstones, and with these set up a gristmill. The raising of cattle, hogs, and other domestic animals was begun. Seven thousand bushels of wheat and over 4,000 bushels of potatoes were raised on irrigated farms at St. Mary's in 1846. There were now 12 log cabins at the establishment and 40 head of cattle. Then difficulties began. Unprincipled white trappers came to St. Mary's. They debauched the Flatheads who had taken up the cross and plow. Enemy Blackfeet raided the settlement and drove off cattle. Finally, the Catholic fathers abandoned the mission in 1850, selling the buildings and improvements to John Owen.

Major Owen, as he was called, had come to Fort Hall with Colonel Loring's troops in 1849, had taken up trade with the Indians, and now, with his Shoshone wife Nancy, came to Bitterroot Valley and purchased St. Mary's for $250. Here he built a palisade of timbers and named it Fort Owen. Later the structure was rebuilt with adobe walls. The Major developed an important emporium, carrying on trade with Fort Benton on the Missouri, Fort Hall on the Snake, and The Dalles on the Columbia. He raised grain, brought in agricultural machinery, planted an orchard, and introduced better livestock. In 1856 he was appointed a special agent for the Flatheads.

The mission St. Ignatius, after having been maintained for 10 years on the Pend d'Oreille River, was moved in 1854 to a site south of Flathead Lake and about 35 miles north of present Missoula. Here the institution exerted great influence among a number of tribes. The Indians were induced to take up agriculture, 50 Indian farms being cultivated at the establishment in 1858. Flour was exported to the American Fur Company posts on the Missouri. Two sawmills were operated in the neighborhood. In the region lived a number of French Canadians who had married native women, adopted generally the Indian manner of life, and were engaged primarily in the fur trade. Some had a few cattle and did a little farming. Farther east, on the Missouri and the Yellowstone, agents of the American Fur Company and others were bartering with the Indians for skins and pelts. Fort Benton, built by Alexander Culbertson in 1846, was developing into an important trade center. About the forts and the missions gathered nondescript traders and hangers-on.

In 1853 Isaac I. Stevens explored a railroad route across Montana. The immediate building of a wagon road from Fort Benton on the Missouri to Fort Walla Walla on the Columbia, which he advocated, was prevented by the outburst of Indian war in the Northwest in 1855. After the Indians were quieted, Lieutenant John Mullan took up the road project in 1858. In the same year a steamboat ascended the Missouri as far as Fort Benton, thus correlating with the road project to form a practical, transcontinental route of travel. The Stevens survey and the Mullan road were important in opening Montana territory. They promoted gold discoveries, which were to start the real and rapid settlement of the region.

A member of the Stevens surveying party found a little gold in 1853 on a branch of the Hellgate River (Clark's Fork), some 50 miles east of present Missoula. Since the amount was meager, the surveyors did not become excited. But they called the stream Gold Creek. In 1857 John Silverthorne came in to Fort Benton with a buckskin bag containing $1,500 worth of gold dust. He did not reveal the location of his mine. Gold had been found previously at Fort Colville, Washington, and rumors were afloat that it existed in the Rocky Mountains to the eastward. Prominent among those to test the truth of such reports were the Stuart brothers, James and Granville.

Returning from California in 1857, the Stuarts were detained by sickness at Malad River, southern Idaho. Here they met a number of mountain traders who had come down from the Montana country to trade with emigrants on the California Trail. With these men they returned to the Beaverhead and Bighole valleys of present southwestern Montana. The following spring they went to Gold Creek to hunt for game and to learn if gold existed there. But losing some horses and having no proper tools, they did no mining. Instead, they continued with the mountain men, trading horses and cattle with emigrants and with Johnston's army. In 1861 they were again on Gold Creek. They whip-sawed lumber for sluice boxes and sent to Walla Walla for picks and shovels. Three other prospectors joined them in their little mining venture, but results were not encouraging.

In 1862 some men from Colorado set out for the mines on Salmon River. Joined by others, they made their way to Fort Lemhi, where 22 were induced to turn northeast to the Montana country. Some of these stayed at Fort Owen; the rest went to Gold Creek. Near here they found a rich placer in what they called Pike's Peak Gulch. In early August, 1862, John White and other prospectors discovered mines on Grasshopper Creek, a branch of the Beaverhead River (an affluent of the Jefferson Fork of the Missouri). About the same time J. K. Slack found placers on the head of Bighole River, and J. W. Powell located mines on North Boulder Creek. These discoveries on the upper reaches of the Missouri River drainage drew the miners from the Gold Creek and Deer Lodge mines on the Pacific side of the Continental Divide. A train from Minnesota, bound for the Salmon River mines, arrived in western Montana in August, 1862, and turned aside to the Beaverhead region. Several weeks later another Minnesota party, under government escort and bound for Washington, was similarly diverted. About 400 miners wintered at the Beaverhead mines and founded Bannock City, named for the Indians of the region.

In the spring of 1863 prospecting parties set out in all directions. One of these, having had the misfortune to be robbed by the Crows, was returning to Bannock when Fairweather, one of the men, found gold on Alder Creek. The placer was very rich. Claims were staked off and Barney Hughes was sent to Bannock, 65 miles to the west, for supplies. Hughes tried to keep the find a secret, but reticent prospectors in for supplies are watched closely. Two hundred men followed him back to Alder Creek. A mining district was organized in June, 1863. With many Southerners present, the principal camp was first called Varina, after the wife of Jefferson Davis, but this was soon changed to Virginia City. Within eight months after the initial discovery, 500 buildings stood on Alder Creek; and when Virginia City was a year old, it had a population of 4,000. Although the new camp was 400 miles from Salt Lake, 1,000 from Portland, and 1,400 from Omaha, the remoteness was of small consequence. The mines were rich, and gold wipes out distance. During the first three years, $30,-000,000 was taken from Montana's Virginia City district.

In the ridge near the Madison River gold and silver quartz veins were found. John Cowan, a gray-haired Georgian, having long prospected in vain, staked his final hopes on some ground in Little Prickly Pear Valley. Here, in Last Chance Gulch, he struck it rich. Hundreds of miners swarmed in, and Helena was founded in the fall of 1864. The district was to produce $16,000,000 in two decades. In the area about Helena—150 miles east and west, 100 miles north and south—rich mines were revealed in 1865 and 1866. The first steam quartz mill was put up at Bannock in 1863. Two years later hydraulic machinery was introduced. Both gold and silver lodes were being worked.

The mineral discoveries in the region and the resultant influx of population brought a demand for political organization. On May 26, 1864, Congress carved a new Territory from what was then Idaho and called it Montana. Sidney Edgerton, of Ohio, was appointed the first governor. When the first legislature met at Bannock in December, 1864, it chose Virginia City as the seat of government. The seal that was adopted showed the miner's pick and shovel and the farmer's plow against a mountain background, and the motto read *Oro y Plata* (Gold and Silver).

During the early years the miners of Montana did not rely entirely on regular officials for the administration of justice. A wave of lawlessness had swept the region, with criminal gangs and road agents making life and property unsafe. The most notorious group was the Plummer Gang, led by the gentlemanly legislator and sheriff Henry Plummer. His deputy sheriffs were his principal confederates. The better element of society organized as Vigilantes and meted out swift justice. Plummer and his chief lieutenants were brought to the gallows. Other criminals were rounded up. Jack Slade, of overland stagecoach fame, was hanged. During the month of January, 1864, 22 executions took place in Montana. Law and order were established.

The mining production of Montana, which reached a high of $18,-000,000 in 1865, began a gradual decline. In the middle seventies the output was down to $4,000,000. The more accessible ores had been mined, and in this remote region ores had to be rich to make their treatment profitable. New strikes in Colorado and Nevada lured away many Montana miners. Of the men who remained, a large proportion now turned to farming and stock raising.

Nutritious grasses of the region favored the rise of the latter industry. As early as 1866, John Grant, a pioneer stockman, ranged 4,000 head of cattle and over 2,000 horses. Stock was imported, and the natural increase helped to build up the herds. The Census of 1880 showed 489,500 cattle, 512,000 sheep, and 29,000 swine in the Territory. A Montana Wool-Grower's Association was organized in 1877, and the wool clip of the following year was 1,000,000 pounds. An effort to domesticate the native Rocky Mountain sheep was unsuccessful. Eastern Montana became a great cattle range, with Miles City as the principal shipping point.

The only markets for farm products during the early years were the mines. And as mining activity declined after the middle sixties, there was little profit for farmers. Recurring grasshopper plagues added discouragement. With the coming of railroads and a revival of mining, agricultural development was given impetus. The Utah Northern branch of the Union Pacific reached Helena in 1881, and the Northern Pacific was completed two years later. In 1883 Montana produced 745,000 bushels of wheat, 1,614,000 bushels of oats, and other field crops. In 1886, over 4,000,000 acres of land were reported under improvement. Lumbering, too, had become an important industry. The production from 98 mills was 150,000,000 feet in 1889. Some coal beds were exploited.

A mining revival in the eighties resulted from the success of deep mining and the discovery of rich copper and silver ores. Butte, which was a small placer camp in 1865, produced silver and copper worth $1,000,000 in 1880. Its output in 1888 was $23,000,000. Butte now had a population of some 30,000 and was claiming first place among the mining camps of the world. The Anaconda, first worked for silver, became the most celebrated copper mine in America. The combined mineral output of Montana for 1889 ($41,000,000) made it then the leading metal mining state of the Union. The population increased from 39,159 in 1880 to 132,159 in 1890.

The admission of the Northwest Territories to statehood will be treated hereafter, in Chapter 31.

BIBLIOGRAPHY

General works on the Northwest Territories are: H. H. Bancroft, *History of Washington, Idaho, and Montana, 1845–1889* (San Francisco, 1890); Joseph Schafer, *A History of the Pacific Northwest* (New York, 1922); J. W. Caughey, *History of the Pacific Coast of North America* (New York, 1938); and Lawrence Paladin, *Indian and White in the Northwest* (Lancaster, 1922).

Among early guidebooks and descriptive works, the following may be listed: A. N. Armstrong, *Oregon: Comprising a History and full Description of the Territories of Oregon and Washington* (Chicago, 1857); F. Fry, *Fry's Traveler's Guide: Descriptive Journal of the Great Northwestern Territories* (Cincinnati, 1865); J. E. Campbell, *Idaho and Montana Gold Region: The Emigrant's Guide Overland* (Chicago, 1865?); John Mullan, *Miners' and Travelers' Guide to Oregon, Washington, Idaho, Montana, Wyoming and Colorado* (New York, 1865); F. M. Thompson, *Thompson's Complete Guide to the New Gold Regions of Upper Missouri, etc.* (St. Louis, 1863); and J. L. Fisk, *Idaho; Her Gold Fields and the Routes to Them. A Hand Book for Emigrants* (New York, 1863).

For the history of Washington, consult E. S. Meany, *History of the State of Washington* (New York, 1909); C. A. Snowden, *History of Washington: The Rise and Progress of an American State* (4 vols., New York, 1909); Herbert Hunt and F. C. Kaylor, *Washington West of the Cascades* (Chicago, 1917). On the "Inland Empire," see G. W. Fuller, *The Inland Empire of the Pacific Northwest* (3 vols., Spokane, 1928); and N. W. Durham, *History of the City of Spokane and Spokane Country* (3 vols., Spokane, 1912).

For brief sketches of Idaho history, see C. J. Brosnan, *History of the State of Idaho* (New York, 1918); and W. J. McConnell, *Early History of Idaho* (Caldwell, 1913). Various phases of Idaho's story are presented in the following: W. T. Stoll and H. W. Whicker, *Silver Strike: the True Story of Silver Mining in the Coeur d'Alenes* (Boston, 1932); B. W. Briggs, *History of Teton Valley, Idaho* (Caldwell, 1926); J. B. Brown, *Fort Hall on the Oregon Trail* (Caldwell, 1932); C. S. Walgamott, *Six Decades Back* (Caldwell, 1936); A. L. Bird, *Boise, the Peaceful Valley* (Caldwell, 1934); Vardis Fisher (ed.), *Idaho Lore* (Caldwell, 1939).

On Montana history, consult: H. F. Sanders, *A History of Montana* (Chicago, 1913); Michael Leeson, *History of Montana* (Chicago, 1885); C. H. Miller, *An Illustrated History of the State of Montana* (Chicago, 1894); K. B. Judson, *Montana, the Land of Shining Mountains* (Chicago, 1913). See also Paul C. Phillips (ed.), *Forty Years on the Frontier as seen in the Journals and Reminiscences of Granville Stuart* (2 vols., Cleveland, 1925); Seymour Dunbar and Paul C. Phillips (eds.), *The Journals and Letters of Major John Owen, Pioneer of the Northwest, 1850–1871* (2 vols., New York, 1927); N. P. Langford, *Vigilante Days and Ways* (Boston, 1890); T. J. Dimsdale, *The Vigilantes of Montana* (Virginia City, 1866); G. R. Hebard and A. R. Brininstool, *The Bozeman Trail* (2 vols., Cleveland, 1922); C. B. Glasscock, *The War of the Copper Kings; Builders of Butte and Wolves of Wall Street* (Indianapolis, 1935); C. P. Connolly, *The Devil Learns to Vote; The Story of Montana* (New York, 1938); H. E. Briggs, *Frontiers of the Northwest* (New York, 1940); and M. G. Burlingame, *The Montana Frontier* (Helena, 1942).

The publications of the Historical Societies of Washington, Idaho, and Montana contain much valuable historical information.

26

OUTLAWRY AND VIGILANCE COMMITTEES

$\mathbb{F}$ROM EARLIEST times the American frontier was the home of two contrasting characters—the honest home-builder and the outlaw. He who sought home and fortune in the West found a friendly environment. If the settler exemplified energy, bravery, fortitude, honesty, candor, and hospitality, qualities held in high esteem, he was entitled to a full share of public honor and confidence. On the border his simple needs could be met if he were neighborly—if he showed a willingness to exchange labor, or salt for corn, or bacon for potatoes. There was little cause for thieving where all shared in exchange what they had in abundance for what they needed, or were inclined to procure necessities by their own industry. Courage was the chief frontier virtue, and each man who could shoulder a rifle was regarded as a citizen-soldier, to bear the responsibility of community defense equally with his neighbors.

It was logical for the desperado to seek a border retreat, for here he was not restricted by law courts and peace officers. During the late eighteenth century the region which separated western Pennsylvania from Virginia was not under either state's control, and for many years civil jurisdiction was withheld. Indeed, in much of the back country of these states, and in the Carolinas, Georgia, and the Kentucky and Tennessee country, there were few courts of justice. To these areas came, said an early writer, "men who are the pests of the human race, averse to labor, impatient of the wholesome restraints of law, or the courtesies of civilized life." In the absence of courts, sheriffs, and constables, they hoped to plunder and steal.

A majority of the border settlers were law-abiding, and it was only natural under such conditions for them to provide their own means of defense. Consequently, they evolved a *lex loci,* known more commonly as "lynch law," a vigilance committee procedure, quite removed from mob action of our own day. The average border settler accepted vigilante responsibilities; "their own consciences were a law unto themselves, and if they erred, it was human to err." Public opinion was the aggregate of individual judgment, and ruled in primitive judicial procedure, as on the Mayflower Compact theory. It would obviously follow that border justice was raw and homespun, and once in a while the innocent suffered, but generally it was effective. Under the cover of night, mounted, armed men struck terror in the hearts of miscreants. "Chief Justice Birch" would set up his tribunal under the forest canopy, and examine the acts of his erring subjects. The wrongdoer was tried with form and ceremony, and, as a matter of course, convicted. James Hall (in *Sketches of the West,* II, 88–92) wrote in 1834 concerning this form of primitive border justice, as did also John W. Monette 12 years later. Both pictured lawless conditions and vigilance committee methods much as they existed in the trans-Mississippi West during later years.

In vigilance committee trials, sentence was pronounced without delay and the penalty was inflicted without stint or mercy. Tied securely to a tree, the convicted criminal was made to feel the rod, if the "law of Moses" ("forty stripes save one") had been imposed; otherwise, the "old thirteen" of the border. If an old offender, the vigilantes often warned the culprit to leave the community, or perchance a coat of tar and feathers was given him, after corporal punishment had been inflicted. The murderer was dealt with more summarily; his life was the invariable forfeit.

THE CALIFORNIA VIGILANTES

Border communities west of the Mississippi were similarly infested with outlaws, and vigilance committees were organized. But after the Missouri and Arkansas frontiers were settled, a leap was then made to the Western Coast, and from here vigilante activity swept eastward. For example, in June, 1858, corruption and maladministration existed at New Orleans; and, taking their cue from the leaders of San Francisco, citizens organized a vigilance committee. The thoroughly alarmed mayor surrendered control to the secret tribunal; but in an election soon thereafter, the voters did not support the vigilantes.

California in 1851 was the first far western crucible in which vigilante methods were tested. One authority estimates that the goldfield polyglot population approximated a quarter of a million. "There were honest men and knaves, pious men and blasphemers, learned and ignorant, refined and brutish, humane and merciless. Every trade and profession was represented—lawyers, doctors, and preachers; thieves, murderers, and gamblers; bakers, bar-keepers, and butchers; loafers, highwaymen, and prize-fighters; horse-jockeys, bankers, peddlers, grocers, and blacksmiths—a human mess which even Mercury would closely eye before pitching them into Charon's boat." Most of these, thought Bancroft, were not desperadoes, but ne'er-do-wells who never took what they could not reach; and whose word was as good as their bond, because neither was worth anything!

English convicts from Australia ("Sydney coves"), who had "served their time" in penal colonies, were among the worst of San Francisco's social scum. Telegraph Hill, or Clark's point and vicinity, was their rendezvous—a general area called Sydney Town. Throngs of lawless men were habitués of the drinking, dancing, lodging, and gambling houses—places of lewdness, drunkenness, and strife. For the most trifling consideration they would commit murder or fire the town. Southwest of Sydney Town was Little Chile, and farther in the same direction, Chinatown. Spanish-Americans congregated about Dupont, Kearny, and Pacific Streets; and Chinese at the intersection of Sacramento and Dupont Streets. These two peoples furnished few desperadoes; rather, they were the early victims of the "Sydney coves." Presently the entire town was infected with the virus of outlawry. Murders were committed on the streets both day and night, and nightly debauch and riot caused honest citizens to bar their doors and windows. The "Sydney coves" were joined by outlaws of every nationality and degree of crime; and for systematic plunder they organized as the "Hounds." When one of their number was arrested and hauled before a court, his companions in crime furnished bail or false alibis in his behalf. Seldom would peace officers visit Sydney Town, the outlaw retreat, because they feared organized crime, if, indeed, some were not in league with the culprits; consequently, anarchy ran riot. One early writer believed the outlaw toll in California during the years 1849 to 1854 inclusive to have been 4,200 murders, 1,200 suicides, and 1,700 driven to insanity. Bancroft found that California was visited with 538 murders during the single year of 1855, and another observer affirmed that "at least one hundred murders had been committed within the space of a few months" prior to the organization of the vigilance committee. Still, said the latter, *not one criminal had yet been executed.*

On June 9, 1851, the vigilance committee was organized "for the protection of the lives and property of the citizens and residents of the city of San Francisco." They formed a constitution and selected a secret meeting place (the Rassette House). Among the prominent signers of the membership book were S. E. Woodworth, Sam Brannan, E. Gorham, and Frederick A. Woodworth. The first person arrested was one John Jenkins, a notorious "Sydney cove," who on June 10 had stolen a safe. About ten o'clock that night, the signal for the assembling of the committee was given—the tolling of the Monumental Engine Company's bell—and presently 80 members had hurried to the appointed place. After a session of two hours Jenkins was found guilty. When he was informed that he was to be hanged, he boasted that his friends would rescue him.

Meanwhile a large crowd had assembled before the Rassette House. Doubtful as to the sentiments of those assembled, President S. E. Woodworth appointed Sam Brannan to address them. From a nearby mound of sand, Brannan spoke to the milling crowd, picturing the general condition of lawlessness existing, and explaining the purposes of the vigilance committee. He told of Jenkins' crime and conviction, and asked for popular endorsement of the penalty assessed by the vigilantes. A majority of those present shouted, "Aye! Aye!" and many willing hands seized the rope attached to a Market Street wharf derrick to hoist the condemned man into the air. Thus, the first vigilance committee hanging was consummated. About a month later James Stuart, another Englishman, was executed for murder; and in August Samuel Whittaker and Robert McKenzie were found guilty of robbery, murder, and arson, and hanged to beams protruding from the Rassette House.

But numerous executions were unnecessary. The fate of Jenkins, Stuart, Whittaker, and McKenzie convinced lawless men that San Francisco was no longer a safe retreat. Many suspects, when warned by the committee, fled elsewhere, some to other territories and some to isolated gold districts. Sacramento, Stockton, San Jose, and other California towns likewise formed committees which pounced upon evildoers. Some desperadoes were hanged, some were lashed and branded, but the greater number were simply ordered to leave the community within a limited time. Moreover, town committees exchanged information as to the movements of the suspects, and thus made vigilante control more effective.

But the lesson of vigilance committee justice in 1851 was presently forgotten. The rush of hurly-burly days incident to the state's phenomenal development crowded out memories of San Francisco's evil times; and by 1855, scandals and murders had again become promiscuous. Also public work frauds—transactions of corrupt officials— aroused well-meaning citizens and drove them to action. As on the previous occasion, vigilante methods were invoked. James King, an outspoken editor of the *Bulletin,* devoted much space in his columns to local crime and fraud, and went so far as to name persons and places involved. In this manner he denounced Palmer, Cook & Company, one of the leading financial concerns of San Francisco. He boldly singled out for attack James P. Casey, a former inmate of Sing Sing, but now a county supervisor. While intoxicated, Casey waylaid King as he left his office and shot him. King's death brought immediate popular action. Under the leadership of such men as William T. Coleman and Clancy Dempster, a vigilance committee was formed. On June 20, 3,000 men surrounded the San Francisco prison and forced the jailer to surrender Casey, as well as Charles E. Cora, another murderer awaiting trial. Then the accused men were taken before the committee and sentenced to death. And, as in 1851, the executions were public.

The vigilantes energetically continued their work of ridding the community of the "Sydney Ducks" and other criminals, most of whom, when arrested, were turned over to the jurisdiction of the regular courts. Whereas convictions before Casey's and Cora's death had been few, they were now uniformly imposed. So once more the criminals staged a general exodus from California, and after 1855 there was little cause for vigilante intervention in criminal court procedure.

IN OTHER MINING FIELDS

Arizona, Colorado, and Nevada were the principal recipients of California's outcasts. Here one community was much like another. Raphael Pumpelly, manager of the Santa Rita Mine, wrote in 1861 that the entire population of Arizona, with the exception of a few Anglo-American miners and ranchers, was made up of outlaws— "escaped convicts from Australia, refugees from the San Francisco Vigilance Committee, and Mexican outlaws from Sonora." Yet Mesilla, being an agricultural community, was hardly as lawless as other Arizona and New Mexico towns. Even here, however, "dark-eyed prostitutes" and citizens who rejoiced at jail deliveries gave the town a notorious reputation.

Tucson was more typical. It was a collection of miserable, unpainted adobe huts. "The principal objects which met one's eye were sore-backed burros, coyote dogs, dirty children without underclothing, languid Mexicans, broken corrals, a few American stores, mescal shops dispensing fiery poison to Sonora miners and degraded Indians." In 1860 John Cremony, interpreter of the United States Boundary Commission, stated that Tucson's graveyard was the final resting place of 47 white men, only two of whom had died natural deaths; and two years later a traveler, J. Ross Browne, said that this town had caused him to realize what "Sodom and Gomorrah must have been." Here criminals from several nations—Anglo-Americans, Australians, and Mexicans—collected, thronged the dusty streets, frequented the dives, and fought pistol duels. A "Sydney cove," says one early visitor, "had a string of eighteen pairs of human ears which he had cut from the heads of men he had murdered." Sylvester Mowry explained conditions thus: "There is no law or protection from the government, every man redresses his own wrongs with pistol or knife or submits in silence."

By 1875, every important mining town east of the Sierra Nevada Mountains had felt the blight of outlawry, partly because of the influx of California outcasts. Near the Washoe Mountains in Nevada was a mining town with even more of the Pacific Coast *émigrés* than Tucson. When a drunken reprobate "christianed" it Virginia City, unconsciously he symbolized its future debauchery. "Washoe" (as Nevada was popularly called), wrote one, "is now to California what the latter was at one time to all the world beside—a receptacle for the vagrant, the vicious, the unfortunate, who hasten to find in the excitements and social license incident to frontier life, a condition congenial to their perturbed spirits and blasted hopes." And Bancroft, writing about 15 years later, added: "Of all places on the planet, it was then the paradise of evil-doers, as California had been in her day. From the frequency of assaults, assassinations, and robberies, together with the many minor misdemeanors and suicides, one would think that Washoe Valley had become the world's moral cess-pool, the receptacle of prison offal from every quarter." But vigilance committee action here was relatively unimportant, since soon the miners moved to other fields.

Similar conditions existed in Colorado and Montana. To describe them at length would serve little purpose. William Hepworth Dixon wrote of Denver during the gold-rush days: "According to the code in fashion here in Denver, murder is a comparatively slight offense." Albert D. Richardson agreed that it was bad, and that vigilance committee procedure was justified. Moreover, he found lawless conditions in Montana—at Bannock, Virginia City, and Helena. Captain O. M. Knapp in 1866 noticed the same at Santa Fe, although this was not strictly a mining town. There he refused to enter a gambling hall because "it looked like entering the door of hell."

Mining communities often declined in population once the minerals were exhausted, and therefore troubled themselves little with the problem of outlaw control. Others were more stable and evolved regular law courts and peace officers. But in transition, they depended on popular tribunals to keep order. Criminality in Montana up to 1865 was encouraged by Sheriff Henry Plummer of Bannock and Virginia City. Plummer had been a notorious ex-California criminal, who in Montana had so won the favors of the miners as to be elected sheriff. Presently he had organized a band of more than 100 desperadoes specializing in stage robbing. But there were enough well-meaning citizens to thwart his purposes. The first vigilance committee was organized at Virginia City when Nicholas Tiebalt was murdered. The vigilantes arrested five outlaws hiding in a herder's shack a short distance from the town. Under close questioning, one of these, John French, turned state's evidence, and all were released except George Ives and a petty thief, George Hilderman. The latter, however, was elderly and regarded as an imbecile, and received only a sentence of banishment. But Ives was hanged. Then followed numerous arrests, and occasionally a cringing outlaw would confess as to the guilt of himself and others, resulting in arrests and executions. In ones, twos, and fives, Plummer and his gang were run down, tried, and hanged. Presently, popular tribunals appeared in other mining communities. By February, 1865, the vigilante movement had gained such momentum as to comprise more than 1,000 members, each local unit well organized into companies with leaders, rituals, and passwords. They had under complete control the turbulent towns of Virginia, Bannock, and Nevada City.

A. D. Richardson was much impressed with the Helena popular tribunal in 1865. "Three days previously," he said after his arrival, "the people awoke one morning to find a notorious reprobate in a state of suspense—hanging dead from a tree limb, and labeled: 'Murderer.'" Here the favorite place of execution was an aged, dead tree in Dry Gulch, which the visitor said had been used so frequently as to be called "Tyburn." Up until this time the outlaws had murdered 125 people, and had robbed many more. But the vigilantes exacted an equally heavy toll of desperado lives, and by 1875 the most desperate criminals either had been hanged or had fled. A. K. McClure, writing from Montana in the autumn of 1867, credited John X. Beidler, formerly of Chambersburg, Pennsylvania, with being the principal leader of the Montana regulators. At this time, he said, "Fully three thousand perfectly organized men are at his back."

In Denver, as in many another town, there was little formality in organization and procedure. If a murder were committed, the culprit was arrested and tried summarily by the settlers *en masse*. Thus, in 1865 James Gordon, a notorious outlaw, was arrested for murdering a harmless German immigrant. The settlers were assembled, one was appointed presiding judge, another the prosecutor, and another attorney for defense. But the trial was brief. By acclamation the crowd voted the penalty of death. Gordon escaped, was recovered after an extended search, and ultimately was brought back to Denver and executed.

In some instances semi-legal recognition was given to the popular tribunals. In August, 1873, a Tucson grand jury upheld the vigilante execution of John Willis, Leonard Córdoba, Clement Lopez, and Jesus Saguaripa. The condemned men had murdered three Mexicans, and the jurors found that "the extreme measures taken by our fellow citizens . . . were necessary."

Lawlessness on the Southern Plains

Until after 1865 most of the southern plains were occupied by Indians; consequently, its outlaw problem was relatively unimportant during the gold-rush period. It had no bonanzas or Comstock lodes; but after 1865 it had its cattle kingdoms and boom towns, and these attracted all classes. Contiguous to the ranch country were ideal outlaw retreats, such as within the mountainous, semi-arid wastes of the Texas Big Bend country, the mesquite and brush-covered flats of the lower Rio Grande Valley, or the broken country of Indian Territory. King Fisher was an outlaw of the Rio Grande border who had at his beck and call a large band of ruthless thieves and killers. More than once supposed Indian raiders from north of the Red River were reported by Texans to be outlaws in Indian disguise. On this point Thomas C. Battey, a Quaker schoolteacher in the Kiowa country, wrote in 1873 that on one occasion a northwestern Texas sheriff informed him that twice in his official capacity he had called out posses to put down Indian depredators in his county, and in the ensuing skirmish one or two had been killed. Those slain on both occasions "proved to be white men, so thoroughly disguised with false hair, masks, and Indian equipage, as to readily be mistaken for Indians." Among other similar accounts, the St. Louis *Daily Republican* complained that "lawless and reckless men swarmed into the Indian Territory, adopting half-nomadic, half-predatory life of the red man, became a terror to all, and rendered life and property doubtful and insecure." Also, an 1873 issue of the Fort Smith *New Era* noticed that vigilantes from the Sugar Loaf and Scullyville country had pursued a band of outlaws into Indian Territory and had succeeded in killing six of them.

The Missouri, Kansas, and Texas Railroad terminus town of Denison, Texas, in 1875 was much like the Rocky Mountain mining towns in lawlessness. Edward King, a trained Eastern correspondent, thus described it:

Every third building in the place was a drinking saloon with gambling appurtenances, filled after nightfall with a depraved, adventurous crowd, whose profanity was appalling, whose aspect was hideous. Men drunk and sober danced to rude music in the poorly lighted saloons, and did not lack female partners. In vulgar bestiality of language, in the pure delight of parading profanity and indecency, the ruffian there had no equal. The gambling houses were nightly frequented by hundreds. Robberies were, of course, of frequent occurrence in the gambling halls.

This description might well have applied to Deadwood, Dodge City, Tascosa, Fort Griffin, or many another cow or railway town of the Great Plains. Charles M. Harger said that rowdyism was so prevalent throughout the plains area as to give rise to the expression, "There is no Sunday west of Newton and no God west of Pueblo." Typical of outlaw bands in other Great Plains states of the eighteen-seventies, Texas was infested with the "Peg Leg" stage robbers of Menard County; the "Jesse Evans" cow thieves of Lincoln County War notoriety; the "Dick Tutts" gang of Travis County; the "Bill Redding" cow and horse thieves of Llano County; the Taylors of Lampasas County; the "Bone Wilson" gang of Erath County; and the John Wesley Hardin and Sam Bass elements of central western Texas.

Eastern New Mexico shocked the nation in 1878 with its Lincoln County War. In this county legitimate ranches had been established shortly after the Civil War, adjoining which were lesser properties belonging to "rustlers" and "brand-burners," whose owners preyed on the cattle of neighboring ranches. The murder of a young Englishman, John H. Tunstall, on February 18, 1878, precipitated a range war. J. H. Tunstall and Company owned a large ranch. Near by was a rival organization, L. G. Murphy and Company or, as it was later known, J. J. Dolan and Company. Each organization employed gunmen and thieves.

Among these desperate men one day rode a young outlaw who was to become notorious as a gunman and killer. William Antrim, *alias* William Bonney, or still better known as "Billy the Kid," was a lad only 21 years of age. Presently he was at the head of a dozen men who set out to run down the murderers of Tunstall, who were thought to be employees of the Murphy ranch. Associated with "The Kid" were such desperate characters as Charles Bowdre, Tom O'Foillard, and Dave Rudabaugh, all of whom later died violent deaths. Governor Lew Wallace of New Mexico attempted to arrest the bloody feud by holding a midnight conference with the young leader. Wallace threatened to declare martial law and to punish all concerned in the disturbance if it were not stopped, but nothing came of his threat. Later "The Kid" was killed by Sheriff Pat Garrett, and the trouble presently came to an end.

A similar range disorder occurred during the late eighteen-eighties and the early nineties in Johnson County, Wyoming, within the region of the Powder River, Crazy Woman Creek, Tongue River, and the Big Horn Mountains. In order to break up brand-burning and rustling, the Wyoming Stock Association had black-listed all ranchers who employed thieves and gunmen. The rustlers, in turn, banded together to prey on the honest ranchers, and were presently joined by other outlaws driven from Montana by Granville Stuart and his vigilantes. Clashes between the thieves and ranchers were now frequent. The County Sheriff could afford the stockmen little protection, but Deputy United States Marshal Frank Canton arrested six of the thieves and brought them before Judge Sauffley's district court. The jurors, however, were so overawed that they returned an acquittal. Trouble came in 1891 when two rustlers, John Tisdale and Ranger Jones, were killed by unknown parties. Friends of the slain men charged that the crime had been committed by orders of the Stock Association; and in retaliation, during subsequent weeks, they committed numerous outrages.

Aroused to action in the spring of the next year, the stockmen of Johnson and neighboring counties organized an expedition under Major Wolcott. They marched into outlaw country, surrounded the K-C Ranch, believed to be rustler headquarters, and attacked. But only two desperadoes, Nate Champion and Nick Ray, were present, and these, refusing to be taken alive, were killed. Then, in turn, a short time later the ranchers were surrounded by more than a hundred rustlers at the T-A Ranch. For two days they withstood assault, although they were heavily outnumbered and might have suffered serious reverses had not troops from Fort McKinney appeared. Later martial law was declared, and soldiers were stationed at Gillette and on the lower Powder River. Then most of the outlaws left the country.

On the Great Plains one cow town was much like another. Along an unpaved street sprawled general merchandise stores, livery stables, blacksmith shops, cheap hotels, boarding houses, saloons, and gambling halls. In July, 1867, there was only one house in Cheyenne, Wyoming; in the spring of the next year, after the Union Pacific Railroad reached it, there were 6,000 inhabitants. William M. Thayer, writing later, stated that this population embraced scores of irresponsible men, "who frequented gambling halls, until the best citizens . . . rose in their might and appointed a vigilance committee." To an early visitor Abilene was "the wickedest town in the West." Yet it was hardly more lawless than Deadwood, Ogallala, Ellsworth, Tascosa, or Fort Griffin. R. M. Wright, a resident of Dodge City during the cattle-driving era, has well described his home town's wild days, when every man was a law unto himself, and when personal differences were generally settled by rifle or pistol duel. J. H. Runkle found Ellsworth about the same. Here acts of violence were subjects of common gos-

sip about the breakfast table.   In Texas, ranch towns were equally
bad. El Paso harbored outlaws from many nations.   Tascosa of the
Panhandle had more gambling halls and saloons than all other business
houses combined; and a rancher of the Clear Fork of the Brazos affirmed that Fort Griffin was so peopled with outlaws during the late
seventies that it was dangerous to appear on its streets during any
hour of the day unless one were well armed.

Within these towns assembled outlaws, gamblers, and horse and cattle thieves until they menaced the rights and interests of sober citizens,
as had been true in the early mining towns.   And as was also true
elsewhere, such conditions caused the rise of vigilance committees.
Fort Griffin was a noteworthy example.   A. B. Greenleaf, an Alabama
traveler in western Texas, found the body of a vigilante victim hanging
from a pecan tree near Fort Griffin, to which was penned this note:
"Hung for horse-stealing.   He said his name was William McBride,
but he was a liar as well as a thief."   A Dallas *Herald* correspondent
at Fort Griffin wrote on April 23, 1876, relative to the same affair, and
added: "A vigilance committee is now astonishing the authorities, both
military and civil, by the offhand way it does business.   Already suspicious characters have been ordered to leave or fare worse. . . .   As
long as the committee cleans out and strings up the right party or parties, it has the well wishes of every lover of tranquility."

But much of the country was prairie, and trees for hangings could
not be found.   Yet the vigilantes were resourceful.   Railroad bridges,
suspended ends of wagon tongues, or cross-beams of telegraph poles
were used.   De B. Randolph Keim described a Kansas execution at a
bridge in which the victim was suspended between the cross-ties, and
"was there left to shuffle off this mortal coil; which was more readily
done than to shuffle off the coil which had been prepared for him by
his peculiarly justice-loving fellow citizens."   And on July 4, 1875, the
Topeka *Commonwealth* reported the organization of a vigilance committee at Dodge City to break up a bold gang of horse thieves in the
Arkansas Valley, prophesying that "the telegraph poles will be found
ornamented some of these days."

Not in every community were the vigilance committees above re-
proach.   In some instances decisions were precipitously made and
injustices were done.   But generally they aided western society in
salvaging many communities.   In this connection, Richardson found
at Helena, Montana, that "these vigilantes have executed no man of
whose guilt there was reasonable doubt; and they rendered life and
property far safer than is usual in new gold regions."   It was a tribute
to the good sense of the Westerner, too, that as soon as regularly
established courts and officers protected life and property, he ceased
to support primitive popular tribunals.

In state, county, and town, efficient officers did much to make unnecessary the continuance of popular tribunals. The Texas Rangers rendered spectacular service. According to J. H. Beadle, with the appearance of the Rangers in western Texas, after the Indian wars, "eight hundred robbers and desperadoes fled the state in a body." On the Ranger roll of honor were many brave men, such as John B. Jones, Bill McDonald, and George W. Arrington. More commonly than not, town marshals were also daring men and expert marksmen with the pistol or rifle. Among those yet remembered by western people are "Wild Bill" Hickok of Hays and Abilene, Kansas; "Red" Hall of Denison, Texas; and Wyatt Earp of Tombstone, Arizona. Frank Canton of Johnson County, Wyoming, and Pat Garrett of Lincoln County, New Mexico, were among the best-known sheriffs.

Early western courts were often as arbitrary and as irregular in procedure as vigilance committees. Some professed a semblance of legality; others were impatient of legal restraints and technicalities. Judge Roy Bean's "Law West of the Pecos" was little more than a vigilance committee. Bean exercised authority far beyond that permitted in his cherished *Revised Statutes of Texas*. Still he was little more beyond the bounds of written law than Justice of the Peace Jim Burnett at Charleston, Arizona, who usually held his court wherever he happened to be and who collected his fines at the point of a double-barreled shotgun. One authority states that he fined a desperado, Jack Harrer, "twenty head of three-year-old steers," and collected. Just as novel was the ruling of a Texas Panhandle judge who refused to admit evidence presented by a defending attorney because he would not cover a $10 bet on the prosecutor's point of law. Jeff Jenkins, an early Kansas settler, writes of an occasion when the County Judge was ill, and the attending attorneys elected a pro tem. judge.

But, in spite of the vigilance committees' problems and semi-regular courts, the western pioneers finally brought order out of chaos. California by 1861 was as law-abiding as any other trans-Mississippi state; and in other mining-field commonwealths two decades later, citizens were actively engaged in solving their crime problems. The bona fide settler was interested not only in establishing ranches, farms, towns, schools, and churches, and in building railroads and telegraph lines, but also in establishing law and order. In fact, his record in clearing the West of organized bands of desperadoes and thieves exemplifies a sturdy quality of citizenship not surpassed elsewhere. There were times when popular tribunals temporarily got out of hand, but the Westerner's sense of justice was an excellent stabilizer, and soon legal sobriety again appeared.

BIBLIOGRAPHY

John W. Monette, *History of the Discovery and Settlement of the Valley of the Mississippi* . . . (New York, 1846), II, contains an interesting discussion of trans-Alleghany popular tribunals. The standard work of the trans-Mississippi region is H. H. Bancroft, *Popular Tribunals* (2 vols., San Francisco, 1887). Other volumes treating wholly or in part with lawlessness in California and in the Rocky Mountains mining communities are Thomas J. Dimsdale, *The Vigilantes of Montana* (Virginia City, Montana, 1921); Stewart Edward White, *The Forty-Niners* (Chronicles of America, XXV); Mary Floyd Williams, *San Francisco Committee of Vigilance of 1851* (Berkeley, 1921); James A. B. Scherer, *"The Lion of the Vigilantes," William T. Coleman, and the Life of Old San Francisco* (Indianapolis, 1939); Nathaniel Pitt Langford, *Vigilante Days and Ways* (Chicago, 1923); Isabelle L. Bird, *A Lady's Life in the Rocky Mountains* (New York, 1879); William M. Raine, *Famous Sheriffs and Western Outlaws* (New York, 1929); Frank C. Lockwood, *Pioneer Days in Arizona* (New York, 1932); R. N. Richardson and C. C. Rister, *The Greater Southwest* (Glendale, 1934); Albert D. Richardson, *Beyond the Mississippi, from the Great River to the Great Ocean* (Hartford, 1867); George F. Ruxton, *Adventures in Mexico and the Rocky Mountains* (London, 1849); and J. H. Beadle, *The Undeveloped West* (Philadelphia, 1873).

Books relating to the range country of the Great Plains are W. P. Webb, *The Texas Rangers; a Century of Border Defense* (Boston, 1935); R. M. Wright, *Dodge City, the Cowboy Capital* (n.p., n.d.); Edward King, *The Southern States of North America* (London, 1875); Thomas C. Battey, *A Quaker Among the Indians* (Boston, 1875); Jeff Jenkins, *The Northern Tier, or Life Among the Homestead Settlers* (Topeka, 1880); E. D. Nix, *Oklahombres* (St. Louis, 1929); Edward Everett Dale (ed.), *Frontier Trails; the Autobiography of Frank M. Canton* (Boston and New York, 1930); Maurice G. Fulton (ed.), *Pat Garrett's Authentic Life of Billy the Kid* (New York, 1927); W. R. Eisele, *The Real Wild Bill Hickok* (Denver, 1931); William Elsey Connelley, *Wild Bill and His Era* (New York, 1933); and William Hepworth Dixon, *New America* (London, 1867).

Articles in early popular magazines lend color and interest to a study of western law and order. Those of particular merit are James E. Pilcher, "Outlawry on the Mexican Border," in *Scribner's Magazine*, X (July–December, 1891); Charles Michelson, "The Vigilance of the West," in *Munsey's Magazine*, XXV (1901); William Raine, *"Billy the Kid,"* in *Pacific Monthly*, XX (1908); J. T. Botkin, "Justice was Swift and Sure in Early Kansas," in *Kansas State Historical Collections*, XVI (1923–1925); Theodore Roosevelt, "Sheriff's Work on the Ranch," in *Century Magazine*, XXXVI (1888); Timothy Nelson Stephens, "Influence of Lawyers on Development of Law as It Now Exists Among English-Speaking Peoples," *ibid.*, XIV (1915–1918); and Joseph Nimmo, Jr., "The American Cow-Boy," in *Harper's Magazine*, LXXII (1886). Studies in journals of scientific societies are C. C. Rister, "Outlaws and Vigilantes of the Southern Plains, 1865–1885," in *Mississippi Valley Historical Review*, XIX (March, 1933); Thomas F. Turner, "Prairie Dog Lawyers," in *Panhandle Plains Historical Review*, II (1929); W. P. Webb, "George W. Arrington," *ibid.*, VIII (1935).

27

OVERLAND COMMUNICATION
AND TRANSPORTATION

$\mathbb{B}$ACK OF the projection of lines of communication and of regular travel into the trans-Mississippi West lay a long period of evolution in methods and facilities. When the first white men landed on the Atlantic seaboard, there stretched westward for a thousand miles an almost unbroken forest. Through this shady maze, pioneer white men were to make their way slowly and with difficulty. In this vast wilderness area the rivers formed the natural and practical routes of travel. Connecting these, especially across divides separating the headwaters of two streams, the shortest and most practical trail had been ferreted out by Indian footmen. White pioneers followed these Indian paths, widened them into pack-horse trails, later converted them into wagon roads, and finally were to make them into paved highways.

In utilizing the rivers as highways, the Indians developed two types of canoes—one type hollowed out from a solid log (the *pirogue*), the other made of bark stretched over a willow framework. The latter, being light, was readily carried over the portage leading from one river source to the next. The white pioneers adopted both kinds of canoes, and immediately began to build more pretentious craft. They early made barges and sailing vessels employing oars, poles, and sails as means of propulsion. Transportation being much faster and easier by water than by land, the early English colonists used boats almost exclusively for long trips and for inter-colonial trade. In fact, roads and wagons came but slowly. The saddle horse and the pack horse were the chief reliance during the early years of travel by land.

Early in the eighteenth century wheeled vehicles began to come into general use, but the mileage of roads was so limited that the use of carriages and wagons was largely confined to the towns. Before the American Revolution, stage coaches had made their appearance, and one that covered the distance from New York to Philadelphia in a day and a half was called the "Flying Machine." Contemporary stages running between Boston and New York were more than a week on the way. Except on routes connecting the principal cities, the pack animal was still the chief agency of land transportation. Seymour Dunbar, in his admirable *History of Travel in America,* speaks of the years 1750 to 1790 as "an age of pack-horse travel." In fact, such extensive pack-horse transportation systems were built up, especially on the frontier, that strong opposition developed against any improvement of wagon roads.

But despite the wide use of pack horses, there was introduced at this time the Conestoga wagon, destined to be important in the American westward movement. This huge blue and red vehicle from the Conestoga Valley of Pennsylvania was to remain in use for a century. With boat-shaped bed, higher at each end than in the middle, the body topped with a cloth cover supported by arched wagon bows that were so set as to accentuate the sway-backed contour, this wagon came to be the symbol of the westward advance. The ruts dug deep by its ponderous wheels marked the path for stagecoach and railroad. After this vehicle crossed the Mississippi, it was frequently called the "prairie schooner."

Ahead of the covered wagon in reaching the banks of the Mississippi were the river boats. First came canoes of explorers and traders; then followed flatboats down the Ohio, carrying homeseekers to new lands, or floating produce to a New Orleans market. Flat-bottomed keelboats ascended the great river and its branches, propelled by poles, oars, sails, and tow lines. But it remained for the steamboat to usher in the great days of water transportation. John Fitch launched his crude steamboat, the first to move in American waters, in 1786. The next year he offered it to the Congress of the Confederation, but the lawmakers and the people generally could not see the value of the invention or the great revolution it would produce. At least 15 other steamboats of various designs were built and tested during the next 20 years; but not until after Livingston and Fulton's *Clermont* of 1807 proved its ability did the era of commercial steam navigation begin.

In 1811 Nicholas Roosevelt, in conjunction with Livingston and Fulton, built a steamboat at Pittsburgh and ran it down the Ohio and the Mississippi to New Orleans. This stern-wheeled steamer, 116 feet long and 20 feet wide, cost $30,000 and had a capacity of 100 tons. It was the first steam craft to operate on waters of the Mississippi system. Similar boats were to follow, but for about 15 years flatboats and keel-boats remained the dominant craft. As steamboats increased they pushed farther and farther up the rivers. By 1823 a steamer had arrived at Fort Snelling, Minnesota; and in 1832 a steamboat reached the mouth of the Yellowstone. Comparable development was taking place on the various branches of the Mississippi and the Missouri. Before the steamboat reached its heyday in the Mississippi Valley, however, the steam railroad came to challenge the supremacy of water transportation. But before the first railroad spanned the trans-Mississippi West (in 1869), the region was to witness the development of other important overland precursors of the iron horse. To these we now turn.

EARLY COMMUNICATION WITH THE FAR WEST

The transportation facilities of the early western fur men—their keel-boats, bull boats, pack horses, and Red River carts—have been mentioned in a previous chapter. The covered wagons carrying the first homeseekers to Oregon, California, and Utah, and the prairie schooners employed in the caravan traffic over the Santa Fe Trail have also been given consideration. Our present attention is directed to the agencies and methods employed during the two decades preceding the completion of the first transcontinental railroad. It was during these years that periodic carriage of passengers, mail, and express on regular schedules was first extended to the Rocky Mountain region and the Pacific Coast. Overland freighting to military forts, mining camps, and interior towns now for the first time assumed great proportions.

The first regular United States mail service to the Pacific Coast was established on a water route in 1849. One line of steamboats carried the mail, express, and passengers from New York City to Chagres, on the Isthmus of Panama; another made the voyage from Panama to San Francisco. The crossing of the isthmus was effected by canoe and muleback travel until the Panama railroad was completed in 1855. The ocean steamers provided the fastest and easiest method of reaching California during the first decade following the gold rush. Operating on a semimonthly schedule, and making the trip from New York to the Golden Gate in from 25 to 30 days, the steamships gave generally satisfactory service.

The arrival and departure of these mail steamers were important occasions in San Francisco. A fortnightly summary of news was condensed in the "Steamer Papers" for transmission eastward on the outgoing boats. The approach of the incoming vessel was announced from Telegraph Hill, and long lines of expectant persons quickly formed before the Post Office window. Soon "extras" were on the streets with the latest, month-old news. The postage rate to the Pacific Coast for half-ounce letters was 40 cents until 1851, when it was reduced to 6 cents. It was raised in 1855 to 10 cents, and in 1863 was fixed at 3 cents, the rate being for the first time made uniform throughout the United States.

While the ocean mail was serving pioneers on the Pacific Coast, overland lines were being established to the Rocky Mountain region. During the first three years following the founding of Salt Lake City in 1847, the means of communication with the outside world were irregular and of a private nature. In 1850, a regular United States mail was provided, running from Independence, Missouri, to the Mormon capital. The service was monthly, and 60 days were allowed for the round trip. The mail was carried in a light wagon or on a packhorse. In 1851 a mail line was started between Salt Lake City and California. This, too, ran monthly, and the trips each way were to be made in 30 days. Part of the time the mail was carried over the usual emigrant road along the Humboldt River; but at other times, especially in the winter season, it went by way of the Mormon Trail connecting Salt Lake and Los Angeles.

Following the Mexican War and the cession of the Southwest to the United States, demand for a mail line came from our new citizens in the New Mexico region. A military express over the Sante Fe Trail was operated in 1849, and a regular monthly mail between Independence and Santa Fe was introduced the next year. Coaches or wagons were employed, and some provision was made for care of passengers and baggage. New Mexico was also served by another mail line in the 1850's. This ran monthly from San Antonio and El Paso to Santa Fe, and the trips were made in 25 days.

These four pioneer mail lines to Utah and New Mexico were far from satisfactory. The remuneration from the government was too small to insure adequate service. The carriers had to camp out at night to allow their animals to graze, as no way-stations were maintained, and no change of stock was provided. Snows in winter and mud in the spring made travel difficult and the carriage irregular. In addition, Indian depredations were suffered on all the routes during the early fifties. Men were killed, animals stolen, and property was destroyed. Upon appealing to Congress, the mail contractors were reimbursed for losses and allowed increased compensation.

During the fifties there was a growing public sentiment for improved communication and travel facilities between our coasts. Railroads had crept to the Mississippi, and men were devising plans for tying together our far-flung domain by bands of steel. The railroad aspects of this development are reserved for treatment in a subsequent chapter. Suffice it here to say that no scheme advanced had been considered at once practical and acceptable. So efforts were turned toward the improvement of wagon roads and the establishment of better stagecoach service across the western plains and mountains. Californians especially desired a through overland mail and adequate highways. A petition carrying 75,000 signatures, and bound in two splendid volumes, was sent by steamer to the national lawmakers in April, 1856. In February following, Congress appropriated $300,000 for the construction of a road from Fort Kearney *via* South Pass to the eastern boundary of California; $200,000 for one from El Paso, Texas, to Fort Yuma on the Colorado River; and $50,000 for improvements on the route from Fort Defiance, New Mexico, to the Colorado River, near the Mohave Indian villages.

ESTABLISHMENT OF THROUGH MAIL SERVICE

In the meantime, Congress was considering an improved overland mail service to California. Senator Crittenden of Kentucky, in voicing the typical opposition, pointed to the large expenditure involved. "Wait until your line can go a little further towards supporting itself," he urged. "It is out of season, out of time, inappropriate, extravagant, exaggerated in the highest degree." Supporters of the proposition denounced the ocean mail companies and the Panama railroad as gigantic monopolies that could be broken only by the establishment of a competitive overland service. They asserted that a stagecoach line, with stations every 10 miles, would give protection to emigrants and encourage settlement along the route. It would bind the nation together and help preserve the Union. On the Panama route our mail was at the mercy of a foreign power, they said, when it might far better be carried over our own soil. After extended debate the overland mail bill was finally enacted in March, 1857.

A contract was let in the following September to John Butterfield, William G. Fargo, and associates for a semiweekly mail at $600,000 per year. The law stipulated that the service be "performed with good four-horse coaches or spring wagons, suitable for the conveyance of passengers, as well as the safety and security of the mails." The route chosen by Postmaster General A. V. Brown of Tennessee ran from St. Louis and Memphis with converging lines to Fort Smith, Arkansas, and thence by way of El Paso, Tucson, Yuma, and Los Angeles to San Francisco. It was a long and roundabout course, but the Postmaster General defended it as the only feasible route, contending that the more direct ones farther to the north were impractical for year-round travel. The distance from St. Louis to San Francisco was 2,795 miles, and the schedule provided 25 days for making the

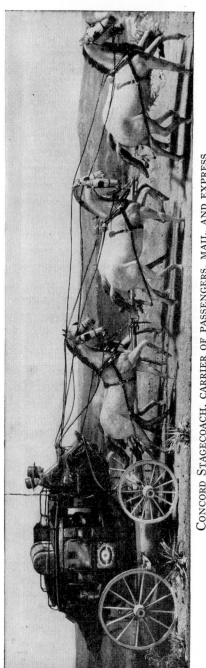

CONCORD STAGECOACH, CARRIER OF PASSENGERS, MAIL, AND EXPRESS
(FROM A MODEL IN THE STATE MUSEUM, DENVER.)

OX-DRAWN COVERED WAGON

458

trip. A year was allowed for construction of stations and general preparations. On September 15, 1858, the initial coach set out from each
end of the line. The first trips were made in a little less than 24 days.
Arrival of the first coach at San Francisco is thus described by a contemporary newspaper:

At a quarter after four o'clock the coach turned from Market into Montgomery street. The driver blew his horn and cracked his whip; at which the
horses, four in number, almost seemed to partake of his enthusiasm, and
dashed ahead at a clattering pace, and the dust flew from the glowing wheels.
At the same time a shout was raised, that ran with the rapidity of an electric
flash along Montgomery street, which throughout its length was crowded by
an excited populace. As the coach dashed along through the crowds, the
hats of the spectators were whirled in the air and the hurrah was repeated
from a thousand throats, responsive to which the driver, the lion of the
occasion, doffed his weather-beaten old slouch, and in uncovered dignity, like
the victor of an Olympic race, guided his foaming steeds towards the Post
Office.

The "Butterfield Overland Mail" was a marked success in operation.
Difficulties of travel over long stretches of uninhabited desert were
overcome. Stations were established at intervals of 10 to 15 miles,
and at those in hostile Indian country armed guards were maintained.
Supplies of hay, grain, and sometimes even water, often had to be
hauled long distances. The Concord coach, that remarkable vehicle
made by the Abbott-Downing Company of Concord, New Hampshire,
was used on the line. The coach body was swung on leather thorough-
braces in lieu of steel springs. A leather boot in the rear and one
under the driver's seat were provided for the mail, express, and baggage. The three inside seats would accommodate nine passengers,
while others might ride on the upper deck. But 25 days of continuous
riding, day and night, in a sitting posture was not very alluring, and
through passenger traffic was not heavy. Some of the travelers, however, asserted that the journey improved their health—a remarkable
style of bodily exercise. The through fare was generally $200, and
the customer was allowed 40 pounds of luggage. Cost of meals
was extra.

The overland mail line gradually gained in favor, until by 1860 more
letters were being sent over it than by the ocean steamer. Even in
England, sealed letter-bags for San Francisco and the English Pacific
Coast possessions were made up regularly to go overland between the
dates of sailing of the Panama steamers. The service on this line was
above serious criticism, but the *route* traveled was an object of constant complaint. Efforts were made time and again to have the contract cancelled or the line moved farther north. But not until the

outbreak of the Civil War brought interruption of service was the line moved to a more northern route.

In the meantime, the sectional conflict over eligible routes continued. Overland stagecoach lines were looked upon as precursors of the railroad, hence the great concern of various cities and sections as to routes taken. Northerners were especially incensed at the selection of a southern route for the great semiweekly stagecoach service. Because of its dip far into the South, they called this Butterfield line the "ox-bow route."

Finally, in response to demands that other sections be aided, the Postmaster General ordered improvements in service elsewhere and instituted new lines. He established semimonthly mail from San Antonio, Texas, to San Diego, California, in 1857, employing coaches and pack mules, with trips each way being made in less than 30 days. In 1858 he authorized a service from Kansas City to Stockton, California, by way of Santa Fe. In this instance the carriage of mail was a secondary consideration, the postal department assuming the role of explorer and advance agent of civilization. Service was to be performed in a six-mule wagon, and 60 days were allowed for the through trip. It appears that but two mails reached Kansas City over the line during the nine months' duration of the contract, and one Congressman charged that all the mail could have been carried in a man's hat. A semimonthly mail from New Orleans to San Francisco by way of the Isthmus of Tehuantepec was established in 1858, the trip being made in from 15 to 18 days. The service on the "Central Route," from Independence to Sacramento by way of Salt Lake City, was improved to weekly trips, with the remuneration proportionately increased. These four lines, added to the two already mentioned (the Butterfield route and the ocean mail *via* Panama), gave six mail lines to the Pacific Coast. Westerners generally were well pleased with Postmaster General Brown and the newly provided mail lines serving their section.

The country as a whole was not so unanimous in its approval, and Congressmen debated the question as to what the national policy in the matter should be. The postal service had been founded and for many years was conducted on the principle that it should be self-supporting. By the 1850's, many Congressmen did not subscribe to that theory. To them the service, especially in its western lines, should be primarily a pioneer of civilization, marking trails and keeping them open to travel, encouraging settlement, and acting as a precursor of the railroad. Said Senator W. H. Seward: "I regard the inland postal system as a great instrumentality for maintaining, preserving and extending this Union." Congressman Maynard added that "it is not merely the means of communication and correspondence but the great means of our civilization." Senator Toombs of Georgia, one of the chief exponents of economy, remarked: "The present Postmaster General [Brown] totes civilization in his mail bags and lets it out all over the Indian country going to the Pacific Ocean. . . . He says he has civilized two-thirds of the continent by his mail service." Senator Gwin of California responded: "I hope nobody will take spasms when I say that I am in favor of all the routes and always have been, . . . By keeping up these routes you will people all that section of country." And so the contest continued, with no clear-cut decision for either side.

In March, 1859, Postmaster General Brown died. He was replaced by Judge Joseph Holt, who immediately instituted a policy of retrenchment. Upon assuming office, he found that the six mail lines running to the Pacific Coast were costing $2,184,697 per annum, while the receipts amounted to only $339,747.34. This, in his opinion, was an indictment. He discontinued some lines, reduced the service on others, and made a saving of nearly $1,000,000 per year. Western Congressmen were soon fighting in behalf of a measure ordering a complete restoration of all curtailed service. But they failed by a small margin as Congress adjourned in June, 1859.

The Pony Express and the Overland Telegraph

While Congressmen debated on postal policy and extension of mail service, others were contending over the relative merits of the two principal overland mail routes—the Butterfield, *via* El Paso, and the "Central," *via* Salt Lake City. The former had been definitely favored by the Post Office Department, being given a more frequent service and much higher compensation. The latter was considerably shorter and was the favorite emigrant route of travel; but being farther north and crossing higher mountain ranges, there was grave doubt as to its practicability for year-round travel. Proponents of the Central route were confident that good service could be maintained during the winter months if the remuneration were increased to provide adequate stock and stations. However, the Post Office Department and Congress were skeptical.

The great freighting firm of Russell, Majors and Waddell was carrying the mail over the Central route on a semimonthly schedule in 1859. While in Washington the following winter, W. H. Russell, one of the contractors, discussed the situation with Senator Gwin of California. The senator maintained that it was necessary to demonstrate the practicability of the Central route for fast and regular travel before a satisfactory mail service would be authorized by the national law-makers. He suggested that Russell launch a swift overland express, and promised to obtain from Congress a subsidy to reimburse the firm for the undertaking. On January 27, 1860, Russell telegraphed this announcement from Washington: "Have determined to establish a Pony Express to Sacramento, California, commencing the 3rd of April. Time ten days."

Upon coming West, Russell found that his more practical partners were not enthused with the proposition. But because of his commitments, they finally agreed to support him. Preparations were pushed with vigor. Horses were purchased and distributed along the line. The best riders obtainable were employed. Stock tenders repaired to their respective stations with relay and extra animals. On the appointed day the starts were made from San Francisco and from St. Joseph, Missouri. Large crowds assembled to cheer the launching of "this new enterprise in this fast age." The arrangements were so well planned and executed that the express went through in excellent time. Receptions accorded the ponies along the route and at the opposite ends of the line were enthusiastic. An account of the arrival at the west coast we quote from the *San Francisco Bulletin:*

It took seventy-five ponies to make the trip from Missouri to California in 10½ days, but the last one—the little fellow who came down in the Sacramento boat this morning—had the vicarious glory of them all. Upon him an enthusiastic crowd were disposed to shower all their compliments. He was the veritable Hippagriff who shoved a continent behind his hoofs so easily; who snuffed up sandy plains, sent lakes and mountains, prairies and forest, whizzing behind him, like one great river rushing eastward.

The boat waited for the Pony Express at Sacramento until 5 o'clock, yesterday afternoon. The instant it arrived it came on board, and the Antelope put on all steam to accomplish an early trip. Meanwhile at the theatres it had been announced that on the landing of the boat there would be ceremonies of reception, music, jollification and some speeches. The California Band traveled up and down the streets waking all the echoes, fetching out the boys, and making the night melodious. Bonfires were kindled here and there on the Plaza and on the wharves. . . . The organized turn-out reached the foot of Broadway at midnight. With waltzes and Yankee Doodle, the airs of all the nations and several improvised black-oak dances, the spirits were maintained until near one o'clock when the Antelope came steaming down, wheeled, threw out her hawsers, was made fast and the glorified pony walked ashore.

The crowds cheered till their throats were sore; the Band played as if they would crack their cheeks, . . . the boys stirred up their bonfires and the speech makers studied their points. The procession reformed, opened right and left, and the pony, a bright bay . . . paced gaily up to his stand. The line closed again, the Band went ahead, the firemen followed with their machines, the center of attraction, the Hippagriff, came next, and citizens fell in behind. There was one lady on the ground. As the pony trotted into line, she tore the ribbons from her bonnet and tied them around his neck. All moved up to the Pony Express office. While the twenty-five letters that were brought were being distributed, the speech makers were proceeding to uncork the bottles of their eloquence. Their friends said "hear hear," but the boys would leave it to the pony. He considered a moment, eyed the ribbon around his neck, looked a bit sleepy, thought of his oats, and uttered a loud neigh. So the speeches were corked down again, the speech makers tied comforters around their throats, the Dashaways cheered hoarsely, the rag-tag-and-bob-tail took something warm, the morning papers went to press, the crowd to bed and the Pony to his stable. . . . Long live the Pony!

With stations every 10 to 15 miles for change of ponies, with wiry horses noted for speed and endurance, with riders picked for light weight, nerve, and stamina, the express made a name for itself. Over the high plains, the mountains and deserts, hardy riders found a path or made one. Day or night, in sunshine or storm, the precious mail went through. Each rider rode about 75 miles, changing mounts at each station. The mail was carried in the four pockets of a leather *mochila,* which fitted over the saddle and was transferred from pony to pony throughout the trip. The letters, before being placed in the pockets, were wrapped in oiled silk to preserve them from moisture, and the weight of each mail was limited to 20 pounds. Charges at first were $5 per half-ounce letter, but these were reduced finally to $1 per half-ounce. In addition, each letter had to pay the regular 10 cents government postage.

The express, at first a weekly, was soon increased to a semiweekly. The 10-day schedule was fairly well maintained during summer and fall, and by using the telegraph extensions at each end of the line, good time was made in the transmission of messages. In carrying the news of Lincoln's election, the Pony Express reached its maximum speed— precisely six days between the telegraph termini of Fort Kearney, Ne-braska, and Fort Churchill, western Nevada. As winter approached, the experiment was watched with great interest. The success of the pony might determine the route of a daily stagecoach mail, the through telegraph, and ultimately the railroad. In December the schedule time was extended to 15 days between St. Joseph and San Francisco, and to 11 days between the ends of the telegraph lines. Throughout the win-ter the Pony Express service was maintained, the actual time made between Forts Kearney and Churchill for the 22 midwinter trips aver-aging 13.8 days. As spring and summer came, the service improved and resumed its former speed.

Begun and operated as a private undertaking, the Pony Express was not self-supporting. An abortive effort was made in Congress in 1860 to subsidize it. But not until Southern leaders withdrew from Con-gress and the Civil War was imminent did supporters of the Central route win over proponents of the Butterfield line. A law was enacted March 2, 1861, providing for a daily overland stagecoach mail and a semiweekly Pony Express on the Central route, with the compensation for the joint undertaking fixed at $1,000,000 per year. The coach service was to begin on July 1, 1861, the stock and equipment of the Butterfield line being moved to the more northern route. The Pony Express was to continue until completion of the overland telegraph.

The electromagnetic telegraph that Professor Samuel F. B. Morse perfected in 1844 was being extended into the trans-Mississippi West in the 1850's. A line was run from St. Louis up the Missouri River to Boonville, the wire being fastened on trees most of the way. A glass insulator with a hole through it held up the wire. In 1858 the telegraph reached Kansas City. The next year C. M. Stebbins began to build from Missouri to Fort Smith, Arkansas, intending to follow the Butterfield mail route toward California; while other builders pushed a line eastward from Los Angeles. In California the telegraph had been built from San Francisco to Sacramento in 1857; and in October, 1860, it was completed from the former city to Los Angeles. The California legislature of 1859 pledged $6,000 per annum to the first telegraph connecting the state with the East, and $4,000 for the second such line. Congress, by Act of June 16, 1860, promised $40,000 per annum for ten years for carrying Government messages over a transcontinental telegraph.

Under these inducements work was begun along the Pony Express route in 1860, but the wire was run only to Fort Kearney from the east and to Fort Churchill from the west during that year. There was some question as to choice of a route across the Rocky Mountains. Edward Creighton, superintendent of the Western Union and Missouri Telegraph Company, went to Denver in the summer of 1860 and informed the people that if they would buy $20,000 in stock of the enterprise, the line would be run through Denver. The amount was not subscribed, so the telegraph took the regular emigrant and mail route *via* Fort Laramie and South Pass. The building of the line was pushed from both ends during the summer of 1861. The wire used was "No. 9 and No. 10 annealed." Across the treeless plains and the deserts, the bringing in and distribution of poles was the principal problem. The wires were connected at Salt Lake City on October 24, 1861. The day before, the *San Francisco Bulletin* commented:

Great epochs approach with moccasined feet—great events glide in with muffled oars. One of these great events, a grand epoch for California, is just at hand—the opening of telegraphic communication from New York to San Francisco. It comes without half the fuss that the Bactrian camels made—it makes no such stir, breeds no such celebration as the Atlantic cable laying begot, but to us it is more important by far than that famous project would have been even if it had not proved a failure. One of the wonders of the age is just about being revealed a perfect fact, and it scarcely makes as much sensation as a $1,000 fire would do.

THE DAILY OVERLAND STAGECOACH

The first coach of the daily overland mail left St. Joseph on July 1, 1861, and reached San Francisco on the 18th. No such demonstration greeted its arrival as had honored the first mail on the Butterfield route or the initial Pony Express. As a bearer of news it was being anticipated by the Pony Express, which in turn was soon to be replaced by the telegraph. But as a carrier of ordinary mail, express, and passengers, it was an important institution. Through the summer and fall the mail was carried with complete satisfaction; but as winter came on, snow and mud slowed down and almost stopped the service. South-

Courtesy of State Historical Society of Colorado

OVERLAND STAGE LINE RECEIPT

ern California, with its strong preference for the Butterfield route, came early and loud with its criticism. The daily overland mail on the Central route, according to the *Los Angeles Star,* was "a failure—a gigantic humbug and swindle." For a time most of the mail was sent by ocean steamers. The stagecoaches muddled along through the winter, and finally in June were able again to maintain their schedule. The contractors had become so involved in debt that their equipment, stock, and contract were sold at auction in March, 1862, to Ben Holladay.

The new proprietor was a good businessman, an effective executive. He reorganized the service and soon had the line running with efficiency and dispatch. In time he extended service to Idaho and Montana, established branches to various mining camps, and purchased competing lines. By the middle sixties he was operating nearly 5,000 miles of stage lines, and was known as the "Napoleon of the Plains." During Indian uprisings, stations were burned and coaches destroyed, but obstacles other than Indian attacks caused few interruptions in the service.

The administrative unit of the Overland Stage Line was the Division (some 200 miles), managed by an agent or boss. "It was not absolutely necessary that the division agent should be a gentleman and occasionally he wasn't," said Mark Twain. "But he was always a general in administrative ability, and a bull-dog in courage and determination." There were messengers who rode the coaches, and at each station were stock tenders and station keepers, but the really interesting and distinctive employee was the driver. His was a fascinating profession and one that was abandoned with regret. What the saddle was to the cowboy, the stage whip was to the driver. He hesitated to lend it even to his most intimate friend. Some whips had stocks ornamented with woven silk bands and silver ferrules. Some drivers were so expert in handling their whips that they could pick a fly off a lead horse with the lash while driving at a lively trot. Of the stage driver, Mark Twain observes:

> In the eyes of the station-keeper and the hostler, the stage-driver was a hero—a great and shining dignitary, the world's favorite son, the envy of the people, the observed of the nations. When they spoke to him they received his insolent silence meekly, and as being the natural and proper conduct of so great a man; . . . the *driver* was the only being they bowed down to and worshipped. How admirably they would gaze up at him in his high seat as he gloved himself with lingering deliberation, while some happy hostler held the bunch of reins aloft, and waited patiently for him to take it. And how they would bombard him with glorifying ejaculations as he cracked his long whip and went careering away.

The Concord coach was usually drawn by four or six horses, frequently arranged in well-matched teams. There were spans of white horses, black horses, beautiful bays, roans, buckskins, sorrels, and dapple grays. High-spirited animals were chosen for runs into and out of the principal towns, while mules were often used on sandy desert stretches. Stations for change of animals were maintained at intervals of from 10 to 15 miles. Every 50 miles or so there were "home stations," where the driver's route ended and where passengers could obtain meals. Ranches developed at some of the stations, but others had to be supplied with hay and grain hauled long distances. Several trains of wagons were kept busy distributing feed and supplies.

There was considerable passenger travel on the overland stages in the sixties. Fare from the Missouri River to California at the outbreak of the Civil War was $225; but as the greenbacks depreciated, the fare rose to about $500. Meals were extra. These cost from 50 cents to $2. The coaches were frequently crowded with nine passengers inside and as many on the top as could hold on. Writes one such traveler:

A through ticket and fifteen inches of seat, with a fat man on one side, a poor widow on the other, a baby on your lap, a bandbox over your head, and three or four more persons immediately in front, leaning against your knee, makes the picture, as well as your sleeping place for the trip.

Late in 1866 Holladay sold his entire overland mail and stagecoach business to Wells, Fargo and Company. This great organization absorbed other lines and continued efficient operation. The consolidation gave the company control of almost all the large express and stage lines between the Missouri River and the Pacific Coast. It was capitalized at $10,000,000. At this time the company expected a half-dozen years of through staging before the railroad would be completed, but in this it was disappointed, and it lost heavily in consequence. When the transcontinental railroad was finished in 1869, Wells, Fargo and Company had on hand more than $50,000 worth of surplus stagecoaches, which they closed out at one-third their original cost. Operation of shorter lines of stagecoaches continued, of course, in all sections of the West for many more years.

EXPRESS AND FREIGHT

The express business in America had its beginnings in colonial days, when the post rider took to carrying and delivering packages and executing various commissions. As time passed, many messengers and carriers came to make short runs on boats, stages, and the early railroads. In 1839 William F. Harnden, sometimes called the father of the express business, began to operate between Boston and New York. He was perhaps "the first man to undertake so long a carriage, and the first to build up a really extensive express service." When his line was extended to Albany, Henry Wells became his agent in that city. Competition soon arose, first in importance being that of Alvin Adams, who quickly built up his powerful Adams Express Company. These early expresses began carrying letters for less than the United States postage, and forced the government to adopt low rates in 1845. The express business experienced a remarkable growth. In 1850 coalitions resulted in the formation of Wells, Butterfield and Company and Livingston, Fargo and Company. These two thereupon organized the American Express Company. Thus far operations were east of the Mississippi.

Following the discovery of gold in California, an urgent need for mail and express service arose. The government was very slow in providing postal facilities, so private expresses came into being. In July, 1849, Alexander H. Todd organized an express line, the first of consequence in California. He visited the mines and took the subscriptions of those who authorized him to procure their mail, charging them a dollar each for entering their names on his list. He then went to the San Francisco post office and obtained the mail of his clients. For deliveries to the gold fields, he charged an ounce of gold per letter, and sold newspapers at $8 per copy. Such lucrative returns quickly brought competitors and a reduction of prices. Some of the mining camps were difficult of access, and wagon roads were slow in reaching them. The rainy season made many paths impassable for wagons, so for years the pack-mule express flourished, especially in winter. Daniel Dancer of Downieville was one of the famed packers. His mule train contained as many as 150 animals, with a rider for each 15. It was 12 years before a wagon reached the rich camp of Downieville, and during that time Dancer's mule team delivered anything from a sack of flour to a grand piano.

In the early 1850's express companies sprang up in California like mushrooms after a rain. Scholars have listed several hundred of them, many of the names having been revealed by the hand-stamps or franks on old envelopes. These early express franks, now the delight of modern philatelists, are the keys that unlock much modern history. The large express companies of the East were a little slow in extending their business to California, and, when they did come, confined themselves largely to the principal towns. This left the farther fields and remote camps to the small, independent expresses. Upon coming to California, the Adams Express and the Wells, Fargo Express developed important establishments there. At first, their business was largely carried by means of ocean steamship lines, but they soon developed stagecoach service to interior California. They brought merchandise of all kinds to San Francisco, and shipped gold dust to the East. The receiving and transfer of gold became an important phase of express company activity, and in some instances—especially in the case of Wells, Fargo—developed into a great banking business.

When the earliest stagecoach lines were projected across the trans-Mississippi West, express service was established on these overland carriers. And when mining camps and settlements sprang up in remote areas of the Far West, expressmen were ever first on the ground to open lines of communication. On them the pioneer settler depended until government mails were extended to the region. After the regular postal service came, the express lines devoted themselves primarily to the carriage of treasure and packages of prized merchandise. The "strong box," carrying money and valuables, was regularly placed in the boot beneath the driver's seat, and was guarded zealously. The same "treasure chest" was the objective of "road agents" who occasionally waylaid the stage. The integrity of express companies in earning the great confidence reposed in them, the hardihood of pioneer expressmen, the vigorous competition of rival lines in their race against time, the daring of drivers and messengers in guarding treasure entrusted to their care, have written romance and valor into a thrilling chapter of the West's history.

Overland freighting, though less spectacular than express carriage and stagecoach travel, was no less important. The caravan traffic to Santa Fe, following the first use of wagons on the trail in 1822, has been treated in a previous chapter. In 1830, wagons were taken over the Oregon Trail as far as the Rocky Mountains, and emigrant trains traversed that trail annually after 1841. Following Mormon settlement in the Great Basin, the transportation of supplies to that region assumed considerable proportions. But it was not until the fifties and sixties that overland wagon freighting took on the character of a big and well-organized business. As military forts of the West multiplied, the business of carrying supplies to these outposts in the Indian country showed a corresponding increase. And as new mining camps were opened in the Rocky Mountains, the calls for provisions and equipment made heavy demands on the transportation companies. As early as 1855 the hauling of merchandise to Utah employed 304 wagons and 3,210 oxen, the freight rate being 17½ cents per pound.

One of the earliest large freighting undertakings across the Plains was that occasioned by the movement of Johnston's Army to Utah in 1857. Russell, Majors and Waddell, the greatest carriers of the region, were employed in 1858 to haul supplies to the army in Utah. The rate agreed upon by the Quartermaster General varied with the time of year when deliveries were to be made. The price for each hundredweight per 100 miles ranged from $1.35 in summer to $4.50 in winter. Freight to Salt Lake City would thus cost from 19 to 50 cents per pound. This rate applied only to the first 10,000,000 pounds; the next 5,000,000 pounds would cost 25 per cent more—inasmuch as this would require the contractors to purchase additional stock. Alexander Majors, of the contracting firm, writes that his company employed 3,500 wagons, 40,000 oxen, 1,000 mules, and over 4,000 men in its transportation operations during 1858. The *Freedom's Champion* of

October 30, 1858, lists other overland freighters of that year who employed 775 wagons, 1,114 men, 7,963 oxen, 142 horses, and 1,286 mules, and carried 3,730,905 pounds of merchandise.

The equipment of Russell, Majors and Waddell greatly impressed Horace Greeley as the editor visited Leavenworth, Kansas, in May, 1859:

> Such acres of wagons! such pyramids of extra axletrees! such herds of oxen! such regiments of drivers and other employees! No one who does not see can realize how vast a business this is, nor how immense are its outlays as well as its income. I presume this great firm has at this hour two millions of dollars invested in stock, mainly oxen, mules and wagons.

The *American Railway Times* of January 26, 1861, reported that during the preceding year 18,000 tons of freight were carried from the Missouri River to the Rocky Mountains. One firm owned 15,500 oxen and sent out 51 trains of 26 wagons each; another sent 32 trains of the same size. Nearly 12,000 men, 8,000 mules, 68,000 oxen, and 6,900 wagons were employed in freighting on the Plains. By 1865, the amount of merchandise carried overland had mounted to approximately 125,000,000 pounds for the year. One liquor shipment to Denver in 1864 was carried in an 80-wagon train and comprised 1,600 barrels of liquor and 2,700 cases of champagne.

Alexander Majors, the prince of old-time freighters, gives in his *Seventy Years on the Frontier,* a good description of the wagon train and its conduct:

> The organization of a full-fledged train for crossing the plains consisted of from twenty-five to twenty-six large wagons that would carry from three to three and a half tons each, the merchandise or contents of each wagon being protected by three sheets of thin ducking, such as is used for army tents. The number of cattle necessary to draw each wagon was twelve, making six yokes or pairs, and a prudent freighter would always have from twenty to thirty head of extra oxen, in case of accident to or lameness of some of the animals. In camping or stopping to allow the cattle to graze, a corral or pen of oblong shape is formed by the wagons, the tongues being turned out, and a log chain extended from the hind wheel of each wagon to the fore wheel of the next behind, etc., thus making a solid pen except for a wide gap at each end, through which gaps the cattle are driven when they are to be yoked and made ready for travel, the gaps then being filled by the wagon-master, his assistant, and the extra men, to prevent the cattle from getting out. When the cattle are driven into this corral or pen, each driver yokes his oxen, drives them out to his wagon, and gets ready to start. The entire train of cattle, including extras, generally numbered from 320 to 330 head and usually from four to five mules for riding and herding. The force of men for each train consisted of a wagonmaster, his assistant, the teamsters, a man to look after the extra cattle, and two or three extra men as a reserve to take the places of any men who might be disabled or sick. . . . They walked by the side of

their teams, as it was impossible for them to ride and keep them moving with regularity. The average distance traveled with loaded wagons was from twelve to fifteen miles per day.

Oxen were generally preferred as draught animals. They were cheaper in price than horses and mules; they could subsist better on the grass along the trail; and they were not in such danger of being stolen by Indians as were horses. Ox teams seemed barely to move, as they made but two miles an hour.

By the sixties there were several manufactories supplying wagons. The common makes were the Studebaker, Schuttler, Bain, and Murphy. These were thimble-skein wagons. The strap-skein axles, using linch pin and tar, had recently been superseded by axles with cast-iron thimbles, using nuts and Frazer's axle grease. The investment in a single train was about $35,000.

The driver, known as the "bull whacker," was a rough and frequently a tough character, occupying a humble place in the scale of frontier society. Card playing and story telling were his principal forms of amusement on the road. Swearing was usually considered essential in the driving of "bull teams," but Majors, being very religious, attempted reforms. In calling for 1,500 teamsters in 1858, he published this in his advertisement: "The use of intoxicating liquors as a beverage, card playing and profane language are prohibited. Each man will be presented with a Bible and hymn book." One man reports that Majors paid him $10 for having refrained from swearing on a round trip to Santa Fe. The bull whacker, with whip in hand, walked on the left side of his team. His whip consisted of a hickory stock two feet long, a lash about 12 feet long, and a snapper about nine inches in length. With this "bull whip" he became very expert, whirling it about his head several times and then letting it fly straight to its mark. The crack of the whip sounded like a rifle shot.

The following are extracts from the instructions issued by Russell, Majors and Waddell to their teamsters in 1858:

See that the cattle get on the best feeding ground in the vicinity of the camp, and also that when turned out they have a sufficient guard by day and by night, and never to be left without a guard. In driving cattle to corral, men enough must be employed to encircle them, and drive them directly in, and when at a distance from camp, drive them very slowly, as fast driving injures them greatly. No man should begin yoking before the cattle have had two or three minutes to become quieted in, then all should enter and yoke in a quiet, gentle manner. First yoke the wheelers, and then chain them to the front wheel outside the corral, or hitch them to the tongue. Secondly, yoke the leaders and fasten them to the wagon, on the inside; then yoke the next leaders, and so on till the whole team is yoked and hitched up, when they will be taken out of the corral and hitched to the wagon. . . .

After leaving corral, do not travel more than a half to one mile before stopping eight or ten minutes for the cattle to breathe, particularly if the weather is warm and cattle very full. When you have selected a capable hand to lead the train, always keep him as leader. . . .

Drive the oxen into the corral in the morning as soon as the teamsters can see to yoke, and travel until about 10 A.M., varying an hour more or less, according to camping ground. Remain in camp 2 or 3 hours, and then make the evening drive. These rules are for conducting a loaded train. . . .

When arrived, turn out your cattle, put out your guard, and let the rest of the hands go to bed. This will give hands two meals a day, which is sufficient for men on the plains, as they eat hearty and have strong diet.

Colonel Henry Inman, in his *Old Santa Fe Trail,* states that the largest six-mule wagon-train that was ever strung out on the plains transported the supplies for General Custer's command during the winter of 1868. "It comprised over eight hundred army-wagons, and was four miles in length in one column or one mile when in four lines— the usual formation when in the field."

BIBLIOGRAPHY

The comprehensive treatment of transportation is the excellent work of Seymour Dunbar, *A History of Travel in America* (4 vols., Indianapolis, 1915). For accounts of mail and stagecoach service, see L. R. Hafen, *The Overland Mail, 1849–1869; Promoter of Settlement, Precursor of Railroads* (Cleveland, 1926); F. A. Root and W. E. Connelley, *The Overland Stage to California* (Topeka, 1901); William and G. H. Banning, *Six Horses* (New York, 1930); J. Holbrook, *Ten Years Among the Mail Bags* (Philadelphia, 1856); J. V. Frederick, *Ben Holladay* (Glendale, Calif., 1940); R. P. and M. B. Conkling, *The Butterfield Overland Mail, 1857–1869* (3 vols., Glendale, 1947).

The following books are devoted to the Pony Express: Arthur Chapman, *The Pony Express; the Record of a Romantic Adventure in Business* (New York, 1932); G. D. Bradley, *The Story of the Pony Express* (Chicago, 1913); W. L. Visscher, *A Thrilling and Truthful History of the Pony Express* (Chicago, 1908); H. R. Driggs, *The Pony Express Goes Through* (New York, 1935); L. P. Houck, *The Youngest Rider* (Boston, 1927). There are several good articles in the *Collector's Club Philatelist* on the Pony Express and on franks of the early express companies.

Much good data regarding western travel, by stage and otherwise, may be gathered from the following personal narratives: J. F. Rusling, *Across America; or the Great West and the Pacific Coast* (New York, 1874); Horace Greeley, *An Overland Journey from New York to San Francisco in the Summer of 1859* (New York, 1860); Samuel Bowles, *Across the Continent. A Summer's Journey to the Rocky Mountains, the Mormons and the Pacific States with Speaker Colfax* (Springfield, 1866); Bayard Taylor, *Colorado; a Summer Trip* (New York, 1867); A. D. Richardson, *Beyond the Mississippi* (Hartford, 1867); Mark Twain, *Roughing It* (Hartford, 1872); J. W. Clampitt, *Echoes from the Rocky Mountains* (Chicago, 1890); H. R. Egan, *Pioneering the West, 1846 to 1878* (Richmond, Utah, 1917); Demas Barnes, *From Atlantic to Pacific Overland* (New York, 1866); P. G. Lowe, *Five*

Years a Dragoon (Kansas City, 1906); James A. Little, *What I Saw on the Old Santa Fe Trail* (Plainfield, Ind., 1904); C. E. Young, *Dangers of the Trail in 1865* (Geneva, 1913).

Numerous handbooks for guiding travelers to various sections of the West were issued during the days of heavy migration. Most of these give advice as to equipment, supplies, routes of travel, and so forth. One of the most useful of these was R. B. Marcy, *The Prairie Traveler. A Handbook for Overland Expeditions* (New York, 1859). This must serve as a sample of others, too numerous to list.

For the history and romance of the express business, see A. F. Harlow, *Old Waybills. The Romance of the Express Companies* (New York, 1934); N. C. Wilson, *The Treasure Express. Epic Days of the Wells Fargo* (New York, 1936); E. A. Wiltsee, *The Pioneer Miner and the Pack Mule Express* (San Francisco, 1931); A. L. Stimson, *History of the Express Companies* (New York, 1858); Edward Hungerford, *Wells Fargo; Advancing the American Frontier* (New York, 1949); and Lucius Beebe and Charles Clegg, *U. S. West; the Saga of Wells Fargo* (New York, 1949).

The story of the telegraph is contained in J. D. Reid, *The Telegraph in America—Its Founders, Promoters and Noted Men* (New York, 1879). See also H. M. Porter, *Pencilings of an Early Western Pioneer* (Denver, 1929).

There is no good comprehensive work on western freighting as a whole. Various books treat phases of the subject. See Alexander Majors, *Seventy Years on the Frontier* (Chicago, 1893); W. F. Hooker, *The Bullwhacker. Adventures of a Frontier Freighter* (Yonkers-on-Hudson, N. Y., 1925); Henry Inman, *The Great Salt Lake Trail* (Topeka, 1910); *Life and Adventure of Alex. Toponce,* written by himself (Ogden, Utah, 1923); W. F. Hooker, *The Prairie Schooner* (Chicago, 1918); *Time Exposure; the Autobiography of William Henry Jackson* (New York, 1940); and R. W. and M. L. Settle, *Empire on Wheels* (Stanford, 1949).

Some excellent articles on overland freighting are assembled in the *Proceedings and Collections of the Nebraska State Historical Society,* Second Series, Vol. V. Others are found in Vol. I of the same series and in the *Transactions of the Kansas State Historical Society.* On the Conestoga wagon, see John Omwake, *The Conestoga Six-Horse Bull Teams of Eastern Pennsylvania* (Cincinnati, 1930).

28

THE PLAINS INDIAN PROBLEM

INDIAN REMOVALS

$\mathbb{T}$HE WHITE MAN'S STAGECOACHES
and wagon caravans on Great Plains roads and trails, as discussed in
the preceding chapter, were of much concern to the native Indians.
Their coming presaged the breaking up of an Indian "Canaan" created
by the federal government during the presidency of James Monroe.
Monroe had transmitted to Congress on January 27, 1825, a request
for the setting up of such an Indian country, saying that he was deeply
impressed with its "very high importance to our Union."

To implement the new program Congress created the Bureau of
Indian Affairs in the War Department (under a Commissioner) in 1832
and two years later passed the Indian Intercourse Act which forbade
any white person, without license from the federal government, to
trespass on Indian lands. Then came the removal of 92,664 Eastern
Indians (not counting small tribal elements in Maine, Massachusetts,
Connecticut, Rhode Island, Virginia, South Carolina and Louisiana)
to tier on tier of reservations, running from the Red River, west of
Arkansas and Missouri, to Green Bay, Wisconsin.

The Five Civilized Tribes (Cherokees, Creeks, Choctaws, Chickasaws, and Seminoles) were moved from their homes east of the Mississippi to reservations west of Arkansas Territory, a country soon to be
known as Indian Territory. And north of them, from Missouri to the
upper lakes region, were settled the Potawatomi, Sauk and Fox,
Winnebago, Menominee, Chippewa, and eastern Sioux tribes.

Beyond this stratification of Eastern Indians, the Great Plains comprised a second major part of the Indian "Canaan." Federal commissioners negotiated agreements with the native, nomadic tribes to
mark their ranges and to secure land cessions for the Eastern Indians.
William Clark and Auguste Chouteau had signed such a treaty with
the Quapaw on August 24, 1818, and similar treaties were signed by

the Osages in 1818 and 1825. Colonel Henry Leavenworth, with eight companies of dragoons, had sought to pave the way for a peaceful understanding with Southern Plains tribes—Comanches, Kiowas, Wichitas, and affiliated bands—on June 21, 1834, when he left Camp Rendezvous, eighteen miles from Fort Gibson, for the Wichita Mountains. In a conference with these nomads near present-day Fort Sill, he assured the red men that soon peace commissioners, with appropriate presents, would arrive to sign a treaty. In the next year Montfort Stokes and General Matthew Arbuckle met the Comanche, Wichita, and lesser tribal elements at Camp Holmes and concluded such a treaty, and a similar understanding was reached with the Kiowas two years later.

The powerful Sioux and other northern Great Plains tribes agreed to federal terms in 1825. Brigadier General Henry Atkinson and Major Benjamin O'Fallon, Indian Agent, met the Teton, Yankton, and Yanktonai bands at Fort Lookout; William Clark and Lewis Cass negotiated a still more important treaty with the Sioux and Oglala at the mouth of the Teton River and with the Sioux, Chippewa, Sauk and Fox, Menominee, Iowa, Winnebago, and lesser bands of Ottawa, Chippewa, and Potawatomi at Prairie du Chien. Each treaty was to conform to the new Indian policy.

But there was many a "Trail of Tears" before Indian removals were completed. Often the Indians' long and exhausting journeys, accompanied by hunger and sickness, caused great suffering and death, the Cherokees alone losing hundreds of men, women, and children in the trek from Tennessee to Indian Territory. In some instances they fought bitter wars with their white foes before they would accept their new assignments, such as the Black Hawk War of the Rock and Wisconsin rivers country and the Seminole War of Florida. Occasional feuds, arising over the question of removal, added confusion among the tribes; and the Great Plains tribes made a bad situation worse when they resented and fought against the new arrangements.

THE MINNESOTA SIOUX WAR

The rapid development of the Louisiana Purchase during the forties and fifties brought about the abandonment of the Calhoun-Monroe program of permanent Indian country and the break-up of the unrestricted tribal ranges, as is observed in what happened in Minnesota. Here, Indian claims were subordinated to the white man's needs. In 1837 the Sioux and Chippewas, always hereditary foes, had surrendered most of Wisconsin, the Sioux accepting the Mississippi as their eastern boundary; and the Chippewas, a new line beginning at the confluence of the Crow Wing and Mississippi and running north of Lake St. Croix to the north side of the Menominee holdings. Then, 14 years later, Governor Alexander Ramsey of Minnesota and Luke Lea, Commissioner of Indian Affairs, negotiated treaties with other Sioux bands whereby they gave up lands east of Red River of the North-Big Sioux line (the western boundary of Minnesota), for which they were to receive a large monetary consideration to care for the educational needs of their children, to buy agricultural equipment, and to have enough left to provide an annuity. But designing traders caused the unsuspecting chiefs to sign a "trader paper" along with the treaties. By this trick, the red men presently learned that the trader claims had absorbed their promised money grant. Furthermore, before the United States Senate could act on the treaty, white home-seekers, who by 1860 numbered 172,230, rushed into the ceded area.

These injustices divided the Sioux into two factions—the "blanket" Indians and the "farmers." Those of the first group felt that they had been robbed of their old homes, accepted their slender annuities grudgingly, scoffed at the domestic attempts of the "farmers," and refused to accept the government's friendly overtures. Moreover, they exerted an unwholesome influence on those who were following sedentary pursuits and who were attempting to make the best of their recent bargain. Thus, the general situation has well been likened to a powder-keg, awaiting a match to set off a terrific explosion. The lighted match was applied in 1862!

On August 17, 1862, at Acton, four young braves, while drunk, killed Robinson Jones, his wife, three other men, and a girl who would not give them food and more whiskey. Then they called upon Chief Little Crow to protect them. This he and his band did; and, of course, war followed, the "blanket" Indians and "farmers" joining forces. The Indians broke up into raiding parties, and a series of forays and massacres was begun from New Ulm to the Yellow Medicine River and about Fort Ridgely that was to claim during the seven days' outrages the lives of 737 white men, women, and children—all, authorities have agreed, because of the conduct of designing "government agents and the cupidity of the post traders."

Judge Flandrau led the survivors of the New Ulm devastated area to Fort Ridgely for protection. Then Governor Ramsey sent Brigadier General Henry Hastings Sibley up the Minnesota River in pursuit of the Indians. The hostiles were overtaken and defeated at Birch Coolie, Fort Abercrombie, and Wood Lake, in the last engagement of which Sibley took 2,000 prisoners and sent them to Fort Snelling for temporary confinement. The temper of the settlers was such that 400 warriors were then tried for murder, rape, and arson, and 300 were condemned to death. But President Lincoln pardoned all but 38 of the ringleaders, who were hanged on a single scaffold at Mankato on December 26, 1862.

Upward of 2,000 hostile warriors were yet in the field. Correspondence found in the *Official Records of the Union and Confederate Armies* (Series I, Vol. XXII, Parts i and ii) gives the interesting details of the campaigns which followed under Sibley and Brigadier General Alfred Sully. In 1863 Major General John Pope, the new federal department commander, sent Sibley up the Minnesota River with a well-equipped force to chastise the hostile Indians, and ordered Sully to march his cavalry from Sioux Falls up the Missouri to prevent warriors whom Sibley might defeat from crossing that river. But Pope later complained that Sully was overcautious and by his timorous movements spoiled any chance of complete success. Sibley overtook Little Crow's warriors (estimated at from 2,200 to 2,500) near the Missouri Coteau and put them to rout in the two battles of Big Mound and Dead Buffalo Lake; and, despite Sully's tardy movements, his cavalry defeated a part of the same Indians at White Stone Hill, about 130 miles above the Little Cheyenne. The Indian losses in killed and wounded and in horses and camp equipment were heavy. Later, Congress punished both the guilty and the innocent alike by confiscating the remaining Minnesota holdings of the Sioux, and moved the several bands to less desirable quarters near Fort Thompson.

On the Middle Border

In 1849 Congress transferred the Indian Office from the War Department to the Interior on the assumption that civilians could better sympathize with and understand the needs of the Indians than could military officers. Two years later, Thomas Fitzpatrick signed treaties with the plains Sioux, Assiniboin, Arikara, Grosventre, Crow, Arapaho, Shoshone, and Cheyenne tribes at Fort Laramie. Congress was to pay annuities to the several tribes, and they, in turn, were to allow the government to build military posts within their country and to project roads across it. In this agreement, the range of each was defined or accepted as it then was. That of the Cheyennes and Arapahoes embraced the region immediately east of the Rocky Mountains and between the North Platte and the Arkansas rivers.

The discovery of gold near the present site of Denver (1858), however, necessitated a drastic revision of this treaty. Thousands of gold-seekers, many perhaps impoverished by the panic of the preceding year, now started for the new goldfields. Approximately 100,000 emi-

grants crossed the plains to Pike's Peak in 1859. While at Fort Leavenworth in April, 1859, General W. T. Sherman wrote: "At this
moment we are in the midst of a rush to Pike's Peak. Steamboats
arrive in twos and threes each day, loaded with people for the new
gold region, . . . probably twenty-five thousand people have actually
gone." Many of the new arrivals who did not find gold occupied Indian lands and slaughtered wild game. This the warriors deeply resented. Anticipating trouble, federal authorities at Fort Wise on
February 18, 1861, forced the Arapahoes and Cheyennes to accept in
exchange for their princely range a comparatively small sand-waste
reserve near Fort Lyon in southeastern Colorado. But many of the
chiefs and warriors withheld their consent and chided those who had
accepted the white man's terms. War parties now began to pillage
isolated settlements and ranches, to steal horses, and to kill the settlers.
After a few months all service over the Overland Mail route was suspended, and immigrant trains were plundered. The federal government could offer little aid, for Civil War needs in the Eastern war zone
were great. Consequently, on June 24, 1864, Governor John Evans of
Colorado Territory directed friendly Arapahoes and Cheyennes on the
Arkansas River to go to Major Colley at Fort Lyon for enrollment and
protection, and sent messages to other tribes telling them to present
themselves at Fort Laramie, Fort Larned, and Camp Collins, for those
who remained on the warpath, or who joined the hostile bands, were to
be hunted down and destroyed.

Most of the roving bands refused. After destroying ranches and
the line of communication between Forts Lyon and Larned on the
Arkansas River Trail during July, 1864, they next attacked the Platte
Valley settlers. From Camp Sanborn eastward, for more than 300
miles, the country was soon in ruins, and Denver was isolated. In
August following, in the absence of adequate federal troops, Governor
Evans issued a proclamation calling on all citizens "to go in pursuit"
of the Indians "to kill and destroy"; and put into service two volunteer
regiments of state cavalry.

As the summer drew to a close, however, Indian thoughts turned to
peace. In the past they had made war during the summer when game
was plentiful and grass was green, but during the winter they would
often settle near military posts to receive government food and clothing. In a letter of August 29, Black Kettle, of the Cheyennes, wrote
that he and his fellow chiefs and warriors were ready for peace.
Major E. W. Wynkoop, military commander of Fort Lyon, then conducted a group of Cheyenne and Arapaho chiefs before Governor
Evans at Denver; and, in a conference on September 28 at Camp
Weld, Evans refused to accept the Indians' friendly overtures, telling

them that only Major General S. R. Curtis, in charge of this military department, had the right of peace-making. Colonel J. M. Chivington, who was present, also warned that he would make war until the Indians surrendered. Taking this cue, Black Kettle, White Antelope, and other chiefs of the Cheyennes and Arapahoes with 700 followers then came to Fort Lyon and offered to surrender to Major Scott J. Anthony, who had succeeded Wynkoop to the command of the post. Wynkoop had already given permission for the Indians to settle in peace near the fort. Anthony would not guarantee the Indians protection, but he made them surrender their weapons and leave the vicinity of the post, and later, according to the testimony of Black Kettle and others, promised them protection. Subsequently, he concluded that he had exceeded his authority, and returned the worn-out guns which the Indians had previously surrendered, and ordered them from the post. The Indians then moved 40 miles away and camped on Sand Creek.

Meanwhile Colonel Chivington led the Third Colorado Cavalry and a part of the First, from 900 to 1,000 strong, to Fort Lyon. Here he arrived in November, and immediately went into conference with Anthony. The latter urged that he destroy Black Kettle's camp. About daybreak, on November 29, therefore, Chivington's troops surrounded and attacked the Indians. Black Kettle sought to halt the attack by raising an American flag, then a white one, but was unsuccessful. The Indians, most of whom were defenseless, were driven from one point to another, and many (variously estimated at from 150 to 500) were slain. Private Stephen Decatur later testified before a military commission convened to investigate the affair that on the day following the battle, he walked over the battlefield "and counted 450 dead Indian warriors." Chivington sent Governor Evans a dispatch stating that he had lost 9 killed and 38 wounded; that he had "killed 500 Indians; destroyed 130 lodges; took 500 mules and ponies. . . ."

The Chivington attack is still a subject of controversy. More than 30 witnesses came before the military commission and gave contradictory testimony. Some affirmed that recent Indian outrages, as well as hostile demonstrations near Fort Lyon shortly before Chivington's arrival, had precipitated the attack of the troops. Moreover, they said, it was a battle and not a massacre. Yet others were equally positive that it was a cold-blooded butchery. John Smith, an Indian trader and Cheyenne friend, stated that during the attack, helpless men, women, and children were wantonly slain, while they were begging for mercy, that their brains were beaten out and their bodies mutilated. Rebuttal testimony, however, revealed that wearing apparel and scalps of white women and children were found in some of the lodges, evidences of Cheyenne complicity in recent Colorado raids.

Indian warriors who had escaped the massacre presently made their way to another Cheyenne camp on the Smoky Hill. From here they sent messengers to the northern Arapahoes and Sioux on the Solomon River bearing the news of the Sand Creek disaster and inviting them to a war of revenge. The latter were not hard to persuade, for news of Sibley's and Sully's campaigns had already caused them much concern. Soon, therefore, raids broke out along both the North and South Platte valleys. Ranches and stage stations were burned, cattle were driven away, and the telegraph line connecting Denver with the outside world was torn down. But Colonel Thomas Moonlight, who had succeeded Chivington in command of the district, put troops in the field to repair the telegraph and to safeguard the South Platte settlements. Farther north, however, the raids continued, with a pitched battle at Platte Bridge, in which the Indians defeated the soldiers. Twice Julesburg was sacked and a large quantity of flour, sugar, and other supplies was taken, and at nearby Fort Sedgwick 14 soldiers were ambushed and killed. Against these various hostiles, General Connor's Powder River Expedition of 1865 was to be directed (as mentioned on page 488), without success.

Once more the federal government sought to appease the wrath of the Indians. In October, 1865, William S. Harney, John B. Sanborn, and others met representatives of the Arapahoes and Cheyennes at the mouth of the Little Arkansas, and concluded a new treaty with them. The Indians were induced to abandon their old home and to accept a new reservation, partly in Kansas and partly in the Indian Territory, with the understanding that they could continue to hunt on their former range as long as the wild game lasted. This treaty, however, was never ratified by the Senate, and for the present they continued to occupy their old range. The Comanches and Kiowas were also assigned a hunting ground, including a large part of western Texas and western Indian Territory, which, too, was unsatisfactory and had to be abandoned two years later.

The "Peace Policy" and its Failure

Since the close of the Civil War, military officers stationed in the West had not been able to cope with the Indian problem. By General Order No. 118, on June 27, 1865, Lieutenant General W. T. Sherman was assigned command of the Division of the Mississippi, later named the Division of the Missouri. In 1867 the Great Plains part of the division was composed of the departments of the Missouri, Platte, and Dakota. By act of Congress on July 28, 1866, the aggregate force of the army was fixed at 54,641 men, consisting of ten regiments of cavalry, five of artillery, and 45 of infantry. To bring order out of chaos, Sherman found his available forces inadequate. For example, when Sherman took command of the Department of the Missouri (New Mexico, Colorado, Indian Territory, and Kansas) in 1868, the area under his control was more than 150,000 square miles, and yet he was allowed a total force of only 2,600 men—1,200 of cavalry and 1,400 of infantry.

In March, 1865, soon after the Chivington massacre, Congress sent a commission to the West to investigate recent border disturbances. Its members, in sub-groups, visited various areas of disturbance, and subsequently published their *Report on the Condition of the Indian Tribes*, fixing part of the blame for Indian forays on the "fire and sword" policy of the military. Then, partly to make amends, Congress created a "peace commission" (1866), composed of N. G. Taylor, Commissioner of Indian Affairs; J. B. Henderson, Chairman of the Senate Committee on Indian Affairs; and J. B. Sanborn and S. F. Tappan. A short time later, President Andrew Johnson also added three generals—W. S. Harney, A. H. Terry, and C. C. Augur—to represent the War Department, and, in addition, requested Lieutenant General W. T. Sherman to act with the commission, since he was in command of the Division of the Missouri.

The commission was to work toward four main objectives: (1) to remove, if possible, the causes of Indian wars; (2) to provide for the security of border settlements; (3) to make possible the uninterrupted building of western railways; and (4) to inaugurate an attractive plan that would cause the red men to abandon their roving life and accept restricted reservations. To accomplish these purposes, the Indians must be placed on two large reservations, one in the Sioux country and the other in the Indian Territory (present Oklahoma). Here they must be trained to become self-supporting and amenable to federal control. Obviously, success of the "peace policy" could be gained only by rigorous coercion, for the nomadic tribes were yet determined to retain their hunting grounds and nomadic customs. The Congressional act creating the "peace commission" also provided $500,000 to be expended by Sherman "in carrying out treaty stipulations, making and preparing homes, furnishing provisions, tools, and farming utensils, and furnishing food. . . ." In order to serve these purposes, on August 10, 1868, Sherman created two administrative districts within the Great Plains. That of the Sioux country, west of the Missouri, was put under the superintendency of Brigadier General W. S. Harney, and that of the southern plains under Colonel W. B. Hazen with headquarters at Fort Cobb, Indian Territory.

In October, 1867, the peace commission first applied the new "peace policy." The Arapahoes, Cheyennes, Comanches, Kiowas, and Katakas were called into council at Medicine Lodge Creek (in present Barber County), Kansas, where on October 21 the three last-mentioned accepted terms. They were given a reservation between the main Red River and the Washita, and from the ninety-eighth to the hundredth meridians (about 3,000,000 acres). The Cheyennes had hesitated to come to Medicine Lodge, for only recently Major General W. S. Hancock had led a strong military expedition into their country and had destroyed one of their villages, and memories of the Sand Creek affair were yet fresh. But since the Comanches, Kiowas, and Katakas had fared well, on October 28 they and the Arapahoes also concluded an understanding whereby they were assigned a reserve of approximately 4,300,000 acres between the Comanche-Kiowa reserve and the Cherokee Outlet.

Both Medicine Lodge treaties provided what the prairie nomads had repeatedly said they did not want—fixed homes, farms, agricultural implements, and white men to teach them how "to walk on the white man's road." Each year they were to be issued food and clothing and all things necessary to start them in their new life. The Indians, on their part, were to renounce all claim to their former ranges, to cease war on the frontier, to abandon promiscuous roving about in search of the buffalo, and to make restitution of stolen property or amends for wrongs done the white man. Not all southern plains chiefs were parties to these agreements, and those not signing, together with young warriors, now declared that the treaties were unacceptable and that they would not abide by them.

So the Texas, Colorado, Kansas, and New Mexico frontiers were devastated as of old. During the spring of 1868 band after band of Comanches and Kiowas raided in Texas and New Mexico, and a few forays were made south of the Rio Grande. In August, a party of Cheyennes and Arapahoes attacked the Saline and Solomon rivers settlements in Kansas and killed several men, women, and children. Sheridan was convinced that only a punitive policy would bring the warring tribes to terms. Since the numerous small roving bands could elude the cavalry during the summer months, he proposed to Sherman that an expedition be carried out against their fixed camps during the winter, after those peacefully inclined had been given a chance to settle on their reservations. On October 15, 1868, Sherman, who had just convinced a majority of the "peace commission" that a punitive campaign was necessary, gave his approval. Samuel F. Tappan, J. H. Leavenworth, E. W. Wynkoop, and other Indian champions condemned the proposed campaign and sought to create public sentiment against

Sherman and Sheridan, but in this they were unsuccessful. In a letter bristling with indignation, Sherman accused Tappan of "monomania," and said that renewed war by the Indians was inexcusable. They had been given food and clothing, he charged, and had been promised future security—all of which they had accepted, promising "peace" on their part, but later had committed many acts of rapine and plunder.

During the summer of 1868 Sheridan could do little more than remain on the defensive and send minor expeditions into the Indian country. From September 17 to 25 Colonel George A. Forsythe and a party of scouts were surrounded by a band of Cheyenne warriors under Roman Nose on the Arickaree Fork of the Republican River (near present Wray, Colorado), but he and his men were rescued by relief columns from Forts Wallace and D. A. Russell.

By November, however, at Forts Larned, Dodge, Hays, Lyon, Bascom, and Gibson, Sheridan had assembled well-trained troops and large stores of supplies for his winter campaign. Eleven troops of the Seventh Cavalry under Lieutenant Colonel George A. Custer and five companies of infantry under Major John H. Page, both commanded by Colonel Alfred Sully, marched southward from Fort Dodge and located Camp Supply at the confluence of Wolf and Bear creeks in northwestern Indian Territory; and Major General Sheridan arrived soon thereafter to accompany the troops on the campaign, although henceforth Custer was to have nominal field command. Sheridan had also accepted the services of the Kansas Volunteer Cavalry, and Governor S. J. Crawford had resigned his executive office to command it. This force, too, reached Camp Supply a few days after the post was established. Moreover, two other columns assisted in the campaign. One, composed of six troops of the Third Cavalry and two companies of infantry, under Colonel A. W. Evans, advanced from Fort Bascom, New Mexico, down the Canadian River; and the other, consisting of seven troops of the Fifth Cavalry under Brevet Brigadier General W. H. Penrose, was already in the field southwest of Fort Lyon. These converging columns from the north and west drove the roving bands in Colorado, Kansas, and the Texas Panhandle toward old Fort Cobb. Texas troops, however, were not employed in the encircling movement, since Texas was not a part of Sheridan's department; consequently, many a Comanche and Kiowa war band fled to the broken country along the headwaters of the Red, the Pease, the Wichita, and other Texas rivers.

While marching southward, Sully's scouts discovered a well-marked trail in the deep snow made by a marauding band of Indians; and after Camp Supply had been established, Custer was sent out to find and follow it. It led directly to Black Kettle's village of 60 lodges, which Custer surrounded and attacked at daybreak on November 27. Black Kettle was killed during the early moments of the assault, and by mid-afternoon the cavalry was in complete possession of his camp. In his report of the battle, Custer listed 103 warriors (including a few women and children) slain and 53 women and children captured. In addition, he captured and killed 875 horses and burned the village, together with the Indians' store of supplies. During the heat of the battle, however, Major Joel R. Elliott and 15 enlisted men went in pursuit of fleeing villagers, and were surrounded and slain by warriors who had recently arrived from other camps farther down the Washita.

By evening, Custer's position was untenable, for on the hills on either side of the river were hundreds of warriors from near-by villages. He therefore retreated to Camp Supply. Presently, the combined force of the Seventh Cavalry and the Kansas Volunteers moved down the Washita; and, as it neared the base of the Wichita Mountains, a large war party of Kiowas was encountered. Custer prepared to attack them, but Hazen sent a messenger from Fort Cobb to say that the Indians were peaceful. Sheridan later believed that the Kiowas had deceived Hazen, that they had committed recent depredations in Texas, and that, if they had been punished at this time, future disturbances would have been avoided. Still, Custer required that Satanta and other chiefs accompany him to Fort Cobb as a guarantee that their villages would follow; and when the Indians sought to escape, Satanta and Lone Wolf were arrested and put in the Fort Cobb guardhouse until their villages had arrived. In January, Sheridan, who had accompanied Custer's column, ordered a new post established on Cache Creek, near the eastern base of the Wichita Mountains, and named it Fort Sill in honor of a West Point classmate. Here he and Custer held a series of conferences with the Indians, with the result that most of the warring bands agreed to accept the reservations already set apart for them by the Medicine Lodge treaty. But subsequently it was necessary for Custer and his cavalry to bring in other sulking bands.

Two Indian battles were yet to be fought before the end of the campaign. On Christmas Day, while floundering through deep snow on the north fork of the Red River, Evans' column destroyed a Comanche village southwest of the Wichitas and drove its warriors in confusion toward the west. Then, on July 11 of the following summer, Carr's troops routed Tall Bull's "dog soldiers" (Cheyennes) and a small number of Oglala Sioux at Summit Springs (near present Sterling, Colorado) in the sand breaks of the South Platte and burned their village. Already in March, 1869, Sheridan had written Sherman that his winter campaign was a complete success and that the principal bands were on their reserves.

THE RED RIVER WAR, 1874–1875

Sheridan's belief that Hazen had made a mistake in protecting the Kiowas during the winter of 1868 was largely substantiated by later events. Several bands of the Comanches and Kiowas had escaped to the south during the early stages of the fighting and had not yet arrived at Fort Sill when in March, 1869, Sheridan left for his headquarters at Fort Hays. These bands now became the nuclei of new disturbances, which by 1874 grew into a second major war. But by the end of the winter campaign, Sheridan had evolved a definite *modus operandi*. He believed that permanent peace would not come until each warrior realized that he must answer for his misdeeds before the white man's court.

Attacks during the next four years were frequent along the Texas frontier, and once again the warring bands were subjected to a punitive campaign. For two years, however, it was difficult for Sherman (Sheridan's superior) to accept the accounts of atrocities which came to his St. Louis office from the distressed frontier. So during the summer of 1871, he, accompanied by Inspector General R. B. Marcy, visited the Texas border. With a small escort, he traveled from San Antonio *via* old Fort Mason and the posts of McKavett, Griffin, and Richardson. While he was at Fort Richardson (near Jacksboro, Texas), he heard that a large Kiowa raiding party had destroyed Henry Warren's wagon train 17 miles west of Jacksboro, and that 7 of the 12 teamsters were killed and their bodies mutilated. Sherman sent Colonel Ranald S. MacKenzie with all the available post cavalry in pursuit of the marauders, but the Indians succeeded in eluding him and in making their way back to their Fort Sill reservation. A few days later, Sherman arrived at Fort Sill and listened to Satanta's boastful admission that he had led the recent raid, although accompanied by other prominent chiefs. The three principal leaders, Satanta, Satank, and Big Tree, were now put under arrest and sent under a strong guard back to Jacksboro for trial before Judge Charles Soward's Thirteenth District Court. Satank attempted to escape a short distance from Fort Sill, and was shot. The other two Indians a few weeks later were tried and sentenced to be hanged, but the "peace policy" advocates protested the verdict, and the Texas governor, Edmund J. Davis, set it aside and sent them to the Huntsville penitentiary.

But Indian champions would not stop here. They maintained that Texas courts had no jurisdiction over the Indians. Reluctantly, two years later, the Texas governor allowed Satanta and Big Tree to return to their reservation on the condition that if they were again implicated in raids, they would be recommitted to prison. Sherman and Sheridan were greatly angered at this act of clemency, and the former wrote Davis that if the Indians resumed their raids and took scalps, he hoped the governor's would be the first taken. Presently, as Sherman and Sheridan had feared, the Indians renewed war. The Texas frontier was plundered, more than 60 settlers were slain, and the warriors had driven back to their reservation many horses, mules, and cattle. Satanta was arrested and returned to the penitentiary, but he committed suicide a short time later. The Secretary of the Interior now turned his charges over to the War Department for punishment.

Colonel C. C. Augur, commander of the department of Texas, soon put in the field all his available cavalry under Colonels George Buell and MacKenzie, operating northward from Forts Concho and Griffin. From the area north of the Red River, Lieutenant Colonel John W. Davidson was to move westward from Fort Sill with six companies of cavalry, three of infantry, and 44 Indian scouts; and Colonel Nelson A. Miles was to come down from Camp Supply with eight companies of cavalry, four of infantry, and three small field guns. Then, still another column of four companies of cavalry under Major William Price was to advance from Fort Union (Mora County), New Mexico, over Evans' old route toward Antelope Hills. Thus, the large bands of raiders were encircled by converging cavalry columns. Never before had such a large military force been put in the field against prairie Indians. Forty-six companies of cavalry and infantry (more than 3,000 men) were sent in pursuit of the marauders after all peaceful bands had been allowed to gather on their reservations for protection. Only 173 Kiowas, 108 Katakas, and 83 Comanches, however, claimed the protection of their agents by August 3, although there were 100 or more who came in later.

Fourteen pitched battles were fought during the campaign which followed. On October 9 Buell destroyed a large Kiowa camp on the Salt Fork of the Brazos; and eight days later, Captain A. R. Chaffee, of Miles' command, captured another near the Washita River. A month later, Lieutenant Frank Baldwin destroyed a Cheyenne camp on McClellan Creek (Wheeler County, Texas) and recovered two white captives (the German sisters). Then, on February 11, 1875, Buell struck a large Kiowa-Comanche camp near the Double Mountains (Kent County, Texas) and burned it, killing 11 warriors. Miles' and Davidson's columns were equally successful, driving the Indians before them onto the Staked Plains. Within the deep rock-ribbed Tule Canyon, the Indians had taken a strong position, but they were routed by 12 troops of cavalry under Colonel Miles. Chaffee led his men in the attack by shouting, "If any man is killed, I will make him a corporal." A few weeks later, Colonel MacKenzie's force, moving up from the headwaters of the Brazos, defeated another strong war party near the same site, and captured and killed more than 1,400 ponies.

By November 14, Sheridan was able to caution Secretary Delano: "It would be a good thing to ease down on the parties hostile at present." Indeed, by the middle of the summer of 1875 the spirit of resistance was broken. Seventy-five of the chiefs and head men responsible for the outbreak were now arrested, tried, and sentenced to imprisonment at a federal post near Saint Augustine, Florida. This brought to an end the long period of raids along the southern plains frontier. The imprisoned Indians were freed a few years later, however, and allowed to return to their people.

Sioux Wars, 1865–1876

The summary punishment meted out to the Minnesota Sioux by Sibley and Sully during 1862 and 1863 had its repercussions on the Great Plains Sioux, who were divided into the Brulé, Yankton, Yanktonai, Blackfoot, Hunkpapa, Sans Arc, and Miniconjou bands, distributed over the northern plains part of the Dakota, Montana, and Wyoming Territories. The northern Arapahoes and Cheyennes were in close alliance with them.

The Sioux were as powerful in the northern plains country as the Comanches had earlier been in the southern plains; they were 16,000 or 17,000 strong. By terms of the treaty of 1851 they were to allow the white man to build roads through their country and to travel over them, in which they erred, for presently long emigrant trains were passing over the Oregon Trail west of Fort Laramie. As early as August, 1854, a clash occurred between Fort Laramie soldiers and a small band of Miniconjous, resulting in the deaths of Lieutenant Grattan and his men. Colonel W. S. Harney in the following autumn conducted a punitive expedition along the Little Blue River and inflicted a crushing defeat on Little Thunder's Brulés. Still there was no general war, and the affair was important only in that it taught the northern plains Sioux for the first time to have respect for the military power of the white man.

During the Civil War period, Montana and Idaho mines attracted a large emigration, and Virginia City, Helena, and Bozeman became bustling mining towns. Governor Caleb Lyon estimated that the population of Idaho alone approximated 50,000, and said that the new arrivals had extended "their prospecting tours in every direction."

This, he believed, would make difficult the maintenance of peaceful relations with neighboring Indians. So long as the emigrants traveled to the goldfields *via* the Missouri River-Fort Benton route, or the Platte Trail to Fort Hall and thence by a roundabout approach to Virginia City, they did not seriously encroach on the Sioux country. But early in 1865, the federal government announced its intention to provide a more direct route from Fort Laramie northwesterly to the Big Horn Mountains, and thence east of the mountains to Bozeman, Montana (the Bozeman Trail). This would cross the headwaters of the Powder and Yellowstone rivers, the very heart of the Indians' favorite hunting and camping grounds. The foothills, said a visitor, "are all covered with a fine growth of grass, and in every valley there is either a rushing stream or some quiet babbling brook of pure, clear snow-water filled with trout, the banks lined with trees—wild cherry, quaking asp, some birch, willow, and cottonwood." Here the Indians found bear, buffalo, elk, deer, antelope, and other wild game in great abundance; and here roving bands of various tribes were accustomed to pitch their lodges.

The Sioux chief, Red Cloud, protested bitterly the proposed violation of his country; and, when his protests went unheeded, he opened hostilities. Presently General John Pope wrote that the Sioux had "been attacking everybody in their region of the country; . . . and only lately . . . in heavy force, Fort Rice on the upper Missouri."

For several years military leaders had urged that the Sioux be punished, but no great effort to this end had been made. Now, in the summer of 1865, General Grenville M. Dodge, in command of the Department of Missouri, sent against them three columns of troops commanded by General Patrick E. Connor. One, under Colonel Nelson Cole, was to move up the Loup Fork of the Platte, along the eastern base of the Black Hills, and on to a point on the Tongue River about 50 miles above the Yellowstone. A second, under Lieutenant Colonel Walker, was to march north from Fort Laramie, skirt the western base of the Black Hills, and meet Cole's command on the Tongue, while General Connor himself was to move with the third up the North Platte and thence across to the Powder River, upon which he was to establish Fort Connor. Then he was to move along the eastern base of the Big Horn Mountains and join the other two columns on the Tongue. But the expedition accomplished little. The first two columns suffered from lack of food and lost many of their horses, and were finally led into Fort Connor half famished. Connor fared a little better. Late in August he destroyed Black Bear's Arapaho village of 250 lodges and burned its winter supplies, but only a few Indians were killed. He was now recalled from the war zone to try peaceful measures.

Already, in October, 1865, Governor Newton Edmunds of the Dakota Territory and a peace commission had negotiated a series of nine treaties with as many bands of Sioux at Fort Sully. Peace was proclaimed, roads were to be permitted through the Sioux country, and agriculture was to be fostered among the Indians. Since game was rapidly diminishing, the government promised $15 per capita to purchase supplies, and $25 if the Indian should engage in farming. Then during March, 1866, General Dodge negotiated a temporary cessation of hostilities with the war bands within his department; and by June 1, 1866, at Fort Laramie, Superintendent E. B. Taylor, Colonel H. E. Manadier, Colonel R. N. McLaren, and Thomas Wistar concluded peace terms with the sullen Brulé and Oglala chiefs somewhat like those given the Fort Sully bands.

But the arrival of Colonel Henry B. Carrington with a large body of troops to open the Powder River road caused Red Cloud and Man-afraid-of-his-horses to withdraw from the conference and once more take the warpath. Carrington was to command the "Mountain District" of the Department of the Platte, and was ordered to garrison Fort Reno and to build other posts on the Powder, Big Horn, and Yellowstone rivers.

In July and August, 1866, Forts Philip Kearny and C. F. Smith were established within the Indian country. Sioux war bands gave the soldiers at these isolated posts much trouble by attacking woodcutters and other small detachments which might venture out from the posts. On December 21, 1866, they wiped out Captain W. J. Fetterman's entire command of 82 officers and men that had been sent from Fort Kearny to relieve a hard-pressed wood train. There is little doubt that this as favorably impressed the Sioux as the Sand Creek affair had disturbed the Arapahoes and Cheyennes, and caused them to assume an independent attitude when they were called to a new peace council.

In September, 1867, General Sherman and Commissioner Taylor of the "peace commission" sent runners throughout the Sioux country to invite the chiefs to a conference, but only a few came. Red Cloud sent word that so long as the government maintained the Powder River road and forts in their country, the Sioux would accept no overtures. The chief had his way. On April 29, 1868, a representative body of chiefs assembled at Fort Laramie. Much to the consternation and anger of the Montana miners, the government now agreed to withdraw troops from Forts Philip Kearny and C. F. Smith and to close the Powder road. Other terms provided that the principal Sioux country was to lie west of the Missouri River, in what is now western South Dakota; however, the Sioux were allowed to hunt on their old range, and some distance east of the Big Horn Mountains was considered as unceded Sioux country. The Indians, on their part, were to allow mail and wagon roads and railways to be built through their country and to permit "other works of utility and necessity."

The election of Grant to the presidency in 1868 brought Lieutenant General Sherman to Washington to assume Grant's former post as General of the Army. Sheridan was now given the rank of Lieutenant General, and he in turn came to Sherman's post as commander of the Division of the Missouri, with his headquarters at Chicago. Sheridan watched with growing alarm the gold-seekers' invasion of the Black Hills, for this engendered Sioux resentment. He believed that Sitting Bull's and Crazy Horse's small non-treaty bands were the nuclei about which a new Indian war would arise unless remedial measures were taken, but for more than a year his warnings to his superiors went unheeded. In his annual reports of 1874 and 1875, he had recommended the establishment of forts within the Sioux country, one at the mouth of the Tongue River and another on the Big Horn, from which he could keep watch on the hostile bands. But Congress delayed an appropriation, much to Sheridan's disappointment.

Sheridan's division prior to the general Sioux outbreak in 1876 consisted of the departments of Dakota, the Platte, the Missouri, Texas, and the Gulf, under the commands of Brigadier Generals Alfred H. Terry, George Crook, John Pope, E. O. C. Ord, and C. C. Augur, respectively. The departments of Crook and Terry embraced the Sioux country, and these officers were to inaugurate a new campaign against the hostile bands much like that of 1874–1875 against the southern plains tribes.

Perhaps the delay of a Congressional appropriation for the building of the recommended posts was due to Commissioner Edward P. Smith's assurance to the Secretary of the Interior that "a general Indian war is never to occur in the United States," because the non-treaty Sioux could not "bring three hundred men into the field." But persistent rumors of Sioux war preparations brought Inspector E. C. Watkins hurrying out to the Sioux country to investigate; and on November 9, 1875, he reported to Smith that the rumors were without foundation. He recommended, however, that the non-treaty bands should be made to accept government supervision. Both Smith and his superior, Secretary Chandler, approved Watkins' proposal, and sent runners to Sitting Bull's and Crazy Horse's bands to tell them that they must assemble on their already assigned reservations before January 31, 1876. If they refused, they were to be turned over to the War Department for punishment. The warriors spurned the warning and began to collect war supplies and to assemble on the Little Big Horn River to prepare for the forthcoming conflict.

Sheridan presently launched another "winter campaign." He was soon to learn, however, that winter campaigning on the northern plains was far more hazardous than on the southern plains. It was fortunate that the final transfer of control over the hostile bands from the Interior Department to the army for punishment was not effected until March, for the season had been unusually cold. On March 17, 1876, Colonel J. J. Reynolds advanced from Fort Fetterman, Wyoming, and destroyed a mixed Cheyenne-Sioux village of 105 lodges on the Little Powder River and captured the Indian horse herd. A March blizzard made further campaigning impossible, the temperature sinking to 28° below zero. Indeed, it was so cold that little effort was made to guard against an Indian counterattack, and on the following morning, before daybreak, the Sioux recovered their horses. Presently Reynolds returned to Fetterman. Sheridan decided to wait for warmer weather before he resumed the campaign, because the "wild storms of Dakota" were more than he had bargained for. Yet Reynolds' effort had beneficial results. One authority writes that "This village [which Reynolds destroyed] was a perfect magazine of fixed ammunition and supplies of all sorts," and that the wild bands were working in close agreement with the Indians at the Red Cloud and Spotted Tail agencies.

Two months later Crook and Terry were ready to move. On May 29, 1876, the former left Fort Fetterman with 20 companies of cavalry and infantry. On June 17 he fought a desperate battle with a large force of Sioux near the headwaters of the Rosebud. Thirteen warriors were killed. Crook's loss was nine killed and one officer and 23 men wounded. Likewise Terry had moved out from Fort Abraham Lincoln, North Dakota (near present Bismarck), with 18 companies of cavalry and infantry. On June 7, he arrived at the confluence of the Powder and Yellowstone rivers. From here he sent Major Marcus A. Reno with six companies of Custer's Seventh Cavalry to scout the region to the forks of the Powder and thence down the Rosebud. Meanwhile he moved his entire command up the Yellowstone and formed a junction at the mouth of the Rosebud with Colonel John Gibbon's 12 companies of cavalry and infantry which had advanced from Fort Ellis, Montana.

Presently, Terry sent Custer and his cavalry up the Rosebud until he intersected an Indian trail which Reno's command had found. Then he was to follow it until the camp of the hostile Indians was located, presumably at some point on the Little Big Horn. But he was not to attack. Instead, he was to swing farther south to prevent the Indians from slipping into the Big Horn Mountains when they were struck by Terry's column coming up the Little Big Horn.

Just why Custer did not wait the coming of Terry's command, after he discovered the Sioux camp, has never been satisfactorily explained. Some have thought that he was yet smarting under Grant's rebuke because he had dared to testify before a Congressional committee investigating trader frauds in the Sioux country, in which Orville Grant, the President's brother, was accused. Others affirm that his actions here reveal much the same foolhardy spirit that characterized him in the battle of the Washita eight years before. But both, or neither, of these explanations may have been true.

On the morning of June 25, Custer pushed down the valley of the Little Big Horn against the Indian village. Taking personal command of five troops of the Seventh, he marched down the right bank of the stream. Major Reno was given command of three troops and Captain Benteen three, both moving along the left bank of the river. Near noon, Custer's scouts reported that the Indians were in flight. Custer and Reno now sought to surround the village. But what they had supposed to be a few hundred Indians were later estimated at more than 2,500. Reno was overwhelmed and forced to retreat precipitately to a high bluff on the opposite bank of the river, where he was presently joined by Benteen; and Custer's command (265 men) was surrounded and annihilated. Then the Indians turned on Reno and Benteen, and might have destroyed them also had not Terry's column come up.

There is little doubt that the Little Big Horn disaster should be charged partly to a careless (or corrupt) agency control. For example, on July 22, 1876, Sheridan persuaded the Secretary of the Interior to transfer temporary control of all Indian agencies in the Sioux country to the military. A careful count was now made to ascertain whether agency Indians had aided Sitting Bull. The Indians at Red Cloud numbered only 4,760, almost one-half less than had been reported by the agent and to whom issues were made. At the Spotted Tail agency there were less than 5,000, and the agent here had issued supplies to, and had reported, twice as many. At the Missouri agencies, the situation was much the same—from one-half to one-third the number formerly reported. It was easy to see, therefore, the source of supplies and reinforcements of Sitting Bull and Gall's hostile bands encamped on the Little Big Horn.

The troops under Crook and Terry were now led a merry chase by the Indians, who for months managed to keep out of harm's way. On September 17, Captain Anson Mills with a part of Crook's troops captured a small village of 35 lodges, but he was unable to come up with the main Indian force. In October, the Sioux attacked a wagon train bound for a supply camp on the Tongue. Colonel Nelson A. Miles, recently arrived from Fort Leavenworth, then went in pursuit, and on

October 21 forced a village of 400 lodges (about 3,000 Indians) to surrender. Soon thereafter others came to their agencies and were disarmed.

Sitting Bull remained at large. When hard pressed, he and a band of irreconcilables fled to Canada. On October 17, 1877, he met General Terry and A. G. Lawrence in a conference at Fort Walsh, Canada, but he refused to return to the United States on the white men's terms. It was not until July 19, 1881, that he and his half-starved followers gave themselves up at Fort Buford, Dakota. Crow King, Rain-in-the-face, and Gall, other hostile leaders, had already agreed to accept the government "flesh pots."

But Sitting Bull shared in yet another disturbance—the Ghost Dance craze. This ceremony arose among the Paviotso Indians of Nevada in 1888, and was connected with the Indian Messiah doctrine. It spread rapidly among the western tribes until it numbered among its adherents nearly all the red men between the Missouri River and the Rockies. The Indian prophet was a young Paiute, known among his tribesmen as Wovoka, but called Jack Wilson by neighboring whites because he worked for a rancher named Wilson. Wovoka taught that the Great Spirit was to set aright the wrongs of his red people, to restore their hunting grounds and provide every want, and to reunite them with their departed friends and relatives. The Indians were to prepare for this restoration day by practicing songs and dances which the prophet would give them.

Although Sitting Bull had accepted a reservation, it was through his influence that the Sioux refused to sell their land in 1888; and it was now at his camp at Standing Rock agency and at his invitation that Kicking Bear organized the first Ghost Dance on the reservation. The Rosebud and Pine Ridge agencies also joined the movement, and the warriors were engaged in warlike demonstrations when Indian officials sought to stop the dances. Presently, troops under General Miles took the field, and the Indians fled to the badlands, swearing vengeance on those who would try to break up a ceremony approved by the Great Spirit. One important authority states that Sitting Bull encouraged them to resist. He claimed that he had been endowed with miraculous powers, and that his "ghost shirts" would protect the bodies of the red men against the soldiers' bullets. Presently, the Indian police sought to arrest him, and a fight followed in which Sitting Bull was killed by Sergeants Red Tomahawk and Bullhead. His son, Crow Foot, and several others, including six of the police, were also killed. Two weeks later, Miles' troops attempted to disarm hostile warriors at Wounded Knee, and the Indians resisted. But the rapid-fire Hotchkiss guns of the soldiers were too much for them. More than 200 of the village, the most of whom were women and children, were killed. Hopelessly

Base map from Hall, "Outline Maps and Graphs." Published by permission of the author and the publishers John Wiley & Sons, Inc.

MAJOR INDIAN RESERVATIONS AND RAILROADS, 1885

Indian tribes: (1) Quinaielt; (2) Yakima; (3) Colville; (4) Spokane; (5) Coeur d'Alene; (6) Lapwai; (7) Warm Spring; (8) Grand Ronde; (9) Umatilla; (10) Klamath; (11) Jocko; (12) Blackfeet; (13) Hoopa Valley; (14) Round Valley; (15) Pyramid Lake; (16) Walker River; (17) Maronge; (18) Agua Caliente; (19) Yuma; (20) Colorado River; (21) Hualpa; (22) Navajo; (23) Uintah; (24) Uncompaghre; (25) Fort Hall; (26) Wind River; (27) Crow; (28) Fort Belknap; (29) Fort Peck; (30) Fort Berthold; (31) Standing Rock; (32) Lower Bruce; (33) Pine Ridge; (34) Rosebud; (35) Yankton; (36) Lake Traverse; (37) White Earth; (38) Red Lake; (39) White Mt.; (40) Apache; (41) Cheyenne and Arapaho; (42) Kiowa and Comanche; (43) Chickasaw; (44) Creeks; (45) Choctaw; (46) Cherokee.

494

overwhelmed by numbers and faced with starvation unless they surrendered, other irreconcilables now returned to their agencies.

Thus, what in 1867 the President and Congress had hoped might be a peace policy had reverted to that of the sword. Not until the Indians had felt the nation's military might and had seen the futility of further resistance were they willing to surrender their vast hunting ranges and their nomadic ways and accept troop-controlled reserves and subsistence.

Pointing toward a new policy, the federal government refused to enter into new Indian treaties after 1871. Under the terms of the Dawes Act of 1887 the basis for Indian citizenship was laid. Land in severalty was to be granted to such individuals as the President might designate, to be held in trust for 25 years, after which time the holder was to have full title; and at the beginning of the probation period, the Indian was to be granted citizenship. Subsequent experience proved, however, that the trial period was too long, and that early citizenship was unwise. The Burke Act of 1906 was designed to correct these flaws. Under its terms, an Indian was not to be granted citizenship until he won full title to his property, individuals were to have full title when the President thought them worthy of it, and intoxicating liquors must not be given or sold to non-citizen Indians. Then, finally, in 1924, when one-half the eligibles had qualified for citizenship under the Burke Act, Congress extended citizenship to all.

BIBLIOGRAPHY

For dependable narratives on the evolution of a Western "Canaan" see Roy Gittinger, *The Formation of the State of Oklahoma* (in University of California *Publications in History*, VI, Berkeley, 1917); Grant Foreman, *Indian Removal* (Norman, 1932); and James C. Malin, "Indian Policy and Western Expansion," in University of Kansas *Bulletins*, 1921.

A wide range of substantial works are available on the Great Plains Indian problem after the Civil War. The army policy is defended in such well-known narratives as Alice Blackwood Baldwin, *Memoirs of the Late Frank D. Baldwin* (Los Angeles, 1929); Captain R. A. Carter, *The Old Sergeant's Story* (New York, 1926); ————, *On the Border with MacKenzie* (Washington, 1935); Charles J. Crane, *Experiences of a Colonel of Infantry* (New York, 1923); George A. Custer, *Life on the Plains, and Personal Experiences with Indians* (New York, 1876), expanded and re-edited by W. L. Hollaway *et al.* under the title of *Wild Life on the Plains and Horrors of Indian Warfare* (St. Louis, 1891); W. S. Hancock, *Reminiscences of William Scott Hancock* (New York, 1887); P. H. Sheridan, *Personal Memoirs* (2 vols., New York, 1904; W. T. Sherman, *Personal Memoirs* (2 vols., New York, 1890); H. H. McConnell, *Five Years a Cavalryman* (Jacksboro, Texas, 1889); George A. Forsyth, *The Story of the Soldier* (New York, 1909); W. S. Nye, *Carbine and Lance* (Norman, 1937); and George F. Price, *Across the Continent with the Fifth Cavalry* (New York, 1885).

Among the better narratives of Indian Bureau policies are Laurence F. Schmeckebier, *The Office of Indian Affairs, Its History, Activities, and Organization (Monograph No. 48,* of the Institute for Government Research, Baltimore, 1927); Lawrie Tatum, *Our Red Brothers and the Peace Policy of President Ulysses S. Grant* (Philadelphia, 1899); Thomas C. Battey, *A Quaker Among the Indians* (Boston, 1875); and Francis A. Walker, *The Indian Question* (Boston, 1874).

The American press had competent observers in the West during the Indian campaigns. One of these, representing the *New York Herald,* was De. B. Randolph Keim, who accompanied Custer's Seventh Cavalry to the Washita, and who wrote *Sheridan's Troopers on the Borders* (Philadelphia, 1885). Another was John R. Finerty, sent out by the *Chicago Times* to report on the Sioux Campaign of 1876 and who later wrote *War-Path and Bivouac, or the Conquest of the Sioux* (Chicago, 1890). Still others contributed much of interest to contemporary newspapers and magazines.

Other readable nineteenth-century accounts are I. V. D. Heard, *History of the Sioux War and Massacres of 1862 and 1863* (New York, 1863); L. E. Textor, *Official Relations Between the United States and the Sioux Indians* (Palo Alto, 1896); Stephen R. Riggs, *Mary and I. Forty Years with the Sioux* (Chicago, 1880); Fanny Kelly, *Narrative of My Captivity Among the Sioux Indians* (Hartford, 1872); Nelson Lee, *Three Years Among the Comanches* (Albany, 1859); *Record of Engagements with Hostile Indians with the Military Division of the Missouri, from 1868 to 1882* (Washington, 1882); and James Mooney, "Calendar History of the Kiowa Indians," in *Seventeenth Annual Report of the Bureau of American Ethnology, 1895–1896* (Washington, 1899), Part II.

R. N. Richardson, *Comanche Barrier to South Plains Settlement* (Glendale, 1933), George B. Grinnell, *The Fighting Cheyennes* (New York, 1915), and L. R. Hafen and W. J. Ghent, *Broken Hand, the Life Story of Thomas Fitzpatrick . . .* (Denver, 1931) are without rivals in their respective fields, and give in broad panorama the story of Indian wars and settlements. Other dependable studies of fairly recent issue are W. P. Webb, *Texas Rangers, a Century of Border Defense* (Boston, 1935); Stanley Vestal, *Sitting Bull, Champion of the Sioux* (Boston, 1932); George E. Hyde, *Red Cloud's Folk. A History of the Ogalala Sioux Indians* (Norman, Okla., 1937); Paul I. Wellman, *Death on the Prairie. The Thirty Years' Struggle for the Western Plains* (New York, 1934); W. C. Macleod, *The American Indian Frontier* (New York, 1928); Dennis Collins, *The Indians' Last Fight, or the Dull Knife Raid* (Girard, Kansas, n.d.); Frederick Logan Paxson, *The Last American Frontier* (New York, 1915); James T. DeShields, *Border Wars of Texas* (Tioga, Texas, 1912); Roy Gittinger, *The Formation of the State of Oklahoma* (in University of California Publications in History, VI, Berkeley, 1918; reprinted, Norman, Okla., 1939); and Carl L. Cannon, ed., *James Pike, Scout and Ranger* (Princeton, 1932).

For reminiscences, published journals, short articles, and personal sketches, the reader should consult regional historical magazines, for example, *Southwestern Historical Quarterly, New Mexico Historical Review, Oklahoma Chronicles, Annals of Iowa, Transactions and Reports of the Nebraska Historical Society, Contributions to the Historical Society of Montana, Colorado Magazine, Kansas State Historical Collections, Panhandle-Plains Historical Review,* and *West Texas Historical Association Yearbook,* most of which are listed in previous chapter bibliographies.

29

INDIANS OF THE MOUNTAIN REGIONS

AFTER JAMES W. MARSHALL discovered gold at Sutter's mill on the American River in California on January 24, 1848, treasure hunters from the area east of the Mississippi and from the first tier of states carved from Louisiana thronged every available trail and road leading to the West. Where formerly an occasional traveler or caravan had crossed the Indian country, now there were many.

Few emigrants respected the rights of the thoroughly aroused red men, across whose hunting ranges the caravans moved. Thousands of buffalo were slaughtered, sometimes the Indians were robbed and cheated, and proof is available that in more than one instance warriors and squaws were needlessly slain. But, on the other hand, smarting under real or imaginary wrongs, Indians were often the aggressors; they begged and stole from travelers and intruders, plundered their caravans, and frequently massacred and wantonly mutilated defenseless whites. This was particularly true of the Apaches of New Mexico and Arizona. Many activities of the new white intruders gave them much alarm. Not only were stage and wagon roads built through their country, and military and stage posts established, but claims of homesteaders were validated at the red man's expense.

EARLY APACHE RELATIONS

The western mountain region was not included in the national domain of the United States when the "permanent Indian country" policy was launched; consequently, Indians residing there were little influenced by the reservation break-up of the early fifties, as noted in Chapter 28. From the 49th parallel to the Mexican border was a vast semi-arid country of more than 450,000 square miles, inhabited by about 60,000 warlike Indians and by more than 100,000 others peacefully inclined. Almost all the mountain tribes were friendly toward the whites when the United States acquired this country from England and Mexico. But by 1865 those of the first group mentioned had been aroused to acts of war. A short-sighted federal policy, plus exploitation by designing traders and outlaws, was largely the cause.

The settlers' cruel treatment of the California "Diggers" is a notable example of subordinating Indian rights. Professor A. L. Kroeber groups the 150,000 nude and semi-nude western coast aborigines into seven families: Hokan, Penutian, Algonkian, Shoshonean, Athapascan, Lutuamian, and Yukian—all generally called "Diggers" by the forty-niners. During the rapid miner influx these tribes were brutally treated. Writing in 1862, Commissioner William P. Dole explained their plight. "The emigration began," said he, "and every part of the state was overrun, as it were, in a day. All, or nearly so, of the fertile valleys were seized; the mountain gulches and ravines were filled with miners; and without the slightest recognition of Indian rights, they were dispossessed of their homes, their hunting grounds, their fisheries, and, to a great extent, of the production of the earth, . . . and they were compelled to become vagabonds." H. H. Bancroft affirmed that California could not "grace her annals with a single Indian war bordering on respectability." That the "Diggers" declined in population from 210,000 in 1834 to 15,500 in 1900 is evidence enough of the white man's ruthlessness.

But the New Mexico and Arizona Apaches were more warlike. The Jicarillas (Ollero and Llañero) and their Athapascan cousins, the Navajos, were the most powerful bands living in the northern part of this country; and the Mescaleros (plains people of the east and mountain people of the west), the Western Apache (Coyotero, Tonto, Cibecue, and San Carlos), and the Chiricahuas were those dominant in the southern part. All depended much on thieving and plundering, either from each other or from their Mexican neighbors; and all were quite primitive and nomadic. The Mexicans of Chihuahua, Durango, and other north Mexican states had been their enemies since the days of the Spanish *conquistadores*. From Spanish-American *haciendas* and *ranchos* they had stolen many horses and captives. Although Mangas Coloradas, Cochise, and other celebrated chiefs expressed a sincere friendship for the United States and the American people, they said that the Spaniards and Mexicans had always been their enemies, and that they expected to continue their forays against them.

While passing through their country in 1846, General S. W. Kearny admonished the Apaches to follow paths of peace; and seven years later, Commissioner John R. Bartlett, of the United States-Mexican boundary survey, warned that the United States would not tolerate their capture of Mexican women and children. It is significant that during these early days the Indians had again and again affirmed their friendship for the new intruders, although they had suffered at their hands. In February, 1825, Sylvester Pattie's hunting party had killed in battle ten of their warriors, and three years later Ewing Young's trappers led another war band into a trap and slew many of them. Then, about 1835, a trader, James Johnson, violated a long-established friendship for Juan José, an Apache chieftain, and treacherously killed him to claim a reward offered by the Sonora government.

In later years other blunders and mistakes of the newcomers drove the Apaches to war. In October, 1860, Lieutenant George N. Bascom conferred with Cochise and lesser chiefs near the stage station at Apache Pass, Arizona, relative to the whereabouts of a Mexican captive boy. Bascom accused Cochise of capturing the boy, but the chief maintained his innocence. Moreover, the Indian promised that if the lad were held by any of his band, he would effect his release. But Bascom ordered his arrest. The proud chief angrily protested, and when his captors scoffed at his claims of friendship, he slashed the tent in which he was detained, and escaped. Bascom's act was a stupid blunder, for he later learned that the boy had been taken by another war band. In 1863 Mangas Coloradas also voluntarily surrendered to prove his friendship for the whites, and was later killed. Whether he was slain while he was attempting to escape or was murdered is yet a controversial issue. A general war followed, and for several years thereafter the Apaches were a scourge to the frontier.

The reader should not assume that the Apaches were faultless, nor that all bands were friendly. At best, they were primitive and cruel. For many generations they had raided and plundered the north Mexican states. Captain John C. Cremony declared that even the name of Mangas Coloradas, the most friendly of Apache chiefs during the early days of American control, was the "tocsin of terror and dismay." He combined the attributes of greatness with the ferocity and brutality of the bloodiest savage, and it was believed that "the actual slaughter or captivity of his victims would have amounted to thousands." Both he and Cochise could and had cruelly tortured and murdered innocent and helpless prisoners, and their names inspired terror among both Mexican and Anglo-American residents of New Mexico and Arizona.

Under the leadership of these chiefs, the Apaches made white tenure hazardous. They were intimately acquainted with every mountain fastness, canyon, and desert; they were adapted to their country's shortcomings and its wildness; they could adeptly climb precipitous cliffs and mountains, moving at incredible speed; and they could strike a peaceful valley one day and be safe from pursuit in their mountain fastness the next. By a system of smoke signals communicating from one mountain peak to another, they could acquaint wandering bands of the presence of an enemy. Since they moved in small bands, large-scale operations against them were impossible. Consequently, the Apaches were more than a match for an equal number of troops. They plundered stage stations along the Overland route, robbed ranches, and forced mines to cease operations; and during the Civil War period, they threatened to drive the white men from their country.

The United States Government found the Mexican Cession country hard to control, as a sketch of events in New Mexico will reveal. During the period 1851 to 1863, from 1,400 to 1,800 troops were distributed over the territory in Forts Union, Marcy, Defiance, Craig, Stanton, Fillmore, Bliss, and Sumner; and patrols were always out on escort service or protecting the settlements against marauding Indians. In 1851–1852 Colonel E. V. Sumner invaded the country of the Navajos; in 1854–1855 General John Garland operated against the Mescaleros, Jicarillas, and Utes; and still later, beginning in 1858, a series of expeditions were launched against the Navajos by Garland, Bonneville, Fauntleroy, Canby, Carleton, and other army officers. Canby pursued a severe policy. He warned hostile bands that they must accept unconditional surrender; that those who held out against the military would be given no quarter. This stern policy was continued until 1864, when most of the war chiefs were ready for peace. In the campaigns of 1863–1864, 143 battles were fought, and 664 Indians were killed, 227 wounded, and 8,793 captured. Colonel Kit Carson trapped more than 7,000 Navajos in a mountain canyon in northwestern New Mexico and forced them to surrender.

FRIENDLY TRIBES

The end of the Civil War brought a profound change in western Indian relations. The "peace policy," discussed more fully in Chapter 28, was applied in New Mexico and Arizona as elsewhere. A program of condensation of reservations and of strict federal control was to be substituted for the opportunistic policy of the pre-war period. Most of the non-Apache tribes of New Mexico and Arizona were friendly and caused the authorities little concern. Among these were the Pueblo Indians, living in their picturesque adobe villages. They generally spent their time in peaceful pursuits, as in making pottery and blankets, in herding their flocks, and in tilling their small patches of corn and vegetables. And occasionally their young men acted as scouts or guides for United States troops campaigning in New Mexico and Texas.

In western Arizona were several other peaceful tribal elements. Bancroft says that the Yumas were "worthless and harmless vagabonds"; many of their women were prostitutes; and both men and women were often plagued by venereal diseases. Drunkenness, gambling, and plundering were habits of long standing. This might also have been said of others. After the Civil War about 1,000 Yumas were domiciled on the California side of the Colorado River near Fort Yuma; and the Walapais and Yavapais (both Yuman) were sent elsewhere. Arizona settlers charged them with thieving and other outrages in 1866–1868. But, in turn, they were the "victims of several disgraceful outrages" at the hands of the whites. They broke out into open revolt in 1871, but were presently subdued. Two years later the Yavapais were settled on the San Carlos Reserve with the Apaches. About 600 Walapais were removed to Colorado, but they soon returned to their old haunts, destitute and starving. Until the government could make other provisions, the settlers supplied their wants. Finally, a tract of 2,000 square miles along the Grand Canyon Bend of the Colorado was allotted them.

The Mojaves, who had earlier manifested hostility to white traders occasionally crossing their country, were now also unwarlike. A band of 800, under their chief Iriteba, was settled with a smaller group of Chemehuevis on a reservation at Half Way Bend on the Colorado; and another band of more than 1,000 lived near Fort Mojave, shiftless and victimized by traders and whiskey peddlers. And under similar circumstances, the Havasupais and Moquis, both small bands, were put under reservation control: the former on Cataract Creek, and the latter near Fort Defiance.

Since the annexation of the Arizona country to the United States, the Pimas and Pápagos had been steadfast friends of the Anglo-Americans. In 1859 the Pimas and Maricopas were assigned a reservation on the Gila River, and here they had remained throughout the war period in 12 wicker-hut villages. After the Civil War, however, ill treatment at the hands of traders, whiskey peddlers, and itinerant Mexicans caused them to resort to depredations. But Indian commissioners met their grievances by enlarging their reservation on the Salt River below Fort McDowell. Since they were of the same race and language, the Pápagos were consolidated with them in 1876. Subsequently, both groups furnished warriors and scouts to military officers conducting campaigns against the Apaches. In 1885 the Pápagos numbered about 5,000 men, women, and children, 2,000 of whom were on their reservation, or near Tucson, and the others were ranging through *Papaguería,* north and south of the American-Mexican boundary.

APACHE RESERVATION PROBLEMS

It is unnecessary in this chapter survey to discuss each military campaign against the Apaches during the period 1865–1886, for there were many. Apache relations with the federal and territorial governments were hopelessly confused by rival policies of the War and Interior departments, punitive measures of the settlers, harmful influences of renegade Mexicans and traders, and by white homeseeker invasion of the Indian country. A parade of officials into and out of the territories added to the unsettled condition. From 1864 to 1886, 14 military commanders were sent to Arizona and 10 to New Mexico; and from 1864 to 1872, there were five Indian commissioners in Arizona and eight in New Mexico. Army officers maintained that the Indians must first be punished before they would accept their reservations and government subsistence; but Indian Bureau officials were equally positive of the merits of the "peace policy." Thus, the two worked at cross-purposes, thereby nullifying the success of a long-range program.

By 1865 a majority of Navajos had been brought to the Bosque Redondo on the Pecos River near Fort Sumner in New Mexico, after Carson had surrounded them in their mountain retreat. Their capture was hailed as a great victory by the New Mexicans, who thought they were now to have relief from long-continued raids. But the Navajos were not satisfied with their new home, and strove to return to their former home. They particularly disliked to reside on the same reservation with the Mescaleros, their enemies, and quarreled with them daily. In 1866 the dissatisfied Mescaleros harried the New Mexico and Texas Rio Grande settlements. Presently, General W. T. Sherman and Colonel S. F. Tappan, as members of Grant's peace commission, visited New Mexico. They decided upon the abandonment of the Bosque Redondo reserve, and permitted the Navajos to return to their former haunts. Ample compensation and removal expenses were allowed, and by July 23, 1868, more than 7,000 Navajos had arrived at Fort Wingate, near where their agency was established.

Their neighbors, the Jicarillas, numbering upward of 1,000, were settled with more than 1,500 Utes at Cimarron, east of the Rio Grande, and at Abiquiú, and finally at Tierra Amarilla. But in 1878 the two tribes were separated; the Utes were placed on a southern Colorado reservation, and the Jicarillas (in 1880) were removed to Fort Stanton to join their kinsmen, the Mescaleros, who had been sent there eight years previously. But neither tribe was yet ready to "walk the white man's road."

Until 1871 the southern Apaches, the Mimbres, Mogollones, and

Gilas had no reservation. But at this time they were collected in the beautiful and fertile Canada Alamosa Valley. Rations issued by their agent were insufficient, and presently the warriors supplemented their wants by raiding, often staying off their reservation for months. This caused the sorely stricken settlers to protest bitterly. So with the arrival of Vincent Colyer, a federal commissioner, on August 29, 1871, the Indians were assigned a new home at Tularosa, some distance northwest of Warm Spring *(Ojo Caliente)*. The Apaches objected strenuously to the change, and only about 500 agreed to move. The others fled to the mountains or joined their kinsmen, the Chiricahuas, in Arizona. Then, in the autumn of 1874, the government set up a new reservation for them at Warm Spring, and here they remained contentedly until 1877, joined at intervals by other refugee bands. But by March, 1877, it was evident that the Warm Spring agency had become a center for renewed raiding, its disgruntled warriors working in collusion with the Chiricahuas. In May following, therefore, 453 of its wards, Victorio among them, were removed to San Carlos, Arizona. Again the Indians protested, and again unreconciled warriors joined other pillagers off their reservations.

These outlaw Apaches joined the war bands of Victorio and Gerónimo, and of lesser chiefs, such as Nané, Loco, and Chatto. In addition, white outlaw depredations and ne'er-do-well encroachments on Indian country augmented the warriors' resentment. In 1874, several Mescalero chiefs protested to Agent W. D. Crothers that whites were stealing their horses. At the same time La Luz and Tularosa traders were selling intoxicating liquors to the Indians in spite of federal restrictions. Still later, in July, 1877, Texas outlaws raided the Fort Stanton reserve and drove off 13 Mescalero horses.

Victorio, next to Cochise and Mangas Coloradas, the greatest Apache warriors, soon became the leader of a composite war band of Mescaleros, Jicarillas, Mimbres, Mogollones, Gilas, and Chiricahuas, although the Mescaleros formed the nucleus. Again and again he left his Fort Stanton reserve to depredate north and south of the Rio Grande, until both United States and Mexican troops regarded him as the cause of their border woes. To capture or kill him in battle, therefore, became a much desired end. But from 1874 to 1880 he was able to outwit and outmaneuver all troops sent against him. One week he would harry the Texas Pecos Valley ranch country, and the next he would strike a peaceful Rio Grande Mexican settlement. A few times he stood for battle (for example, Ojo del Piño, Mexico; and Rattlesnake Springs, Texas), but generally he retreated before his enemy, to appear shortly at a distant point to ravage and to steal.

By the midsummer of 1880 approximately 2,000 United States and Mexican troops had taken the field against Victorio. Cavalry patrols were sent on long wearisome marches across arid wastes, through unfrequented canyons and mountains, but no Indians were encountered. In October, the crafty Victorio remained with his older warriors, women, and children in his Tres Castillos Mountain camp, and sent his younger braves north of the Rio Grande to harass the widely separated Texas settlements. While Colonel B. H. Grierson with his cavalry were chasing these, Colonel Joaquin Terrazas' troopers were joined by three fighting organizations from the United States—20 Texas Rangers, 68 Chiricahua scouts, and a detachment of Negro troopers commanded by Lieutenant Charles Parker. But Terrazas would not co-operate with the Americans, and ordered them to re-cross the Rio Grande, upon the excuse that the Chiricahua scouts were relatives of Victorio and might prove treacherous in battle. Twenty-four hours later, however, a messenger overtook the retiring Americans with the news that the Mexicans had fought and defeated the Indians in a box canyon. In the battle a Tarahumara Indian (Mauricio by name) had killed Victorio. The governor of Sonora later rewarded him with a nickel-plated rifle. A lesser chief, Nané, now assumed the leadership of the remnants of Victorio's band, but by 1882 the raiders were back on their reservations or they had joined Gerónimo's band.

There is little doubt that divided authority in Arizona and frequent military reorganizations affected adversely a constructive Indian policy. In 1865 the territory was attached to the military department of California of more than 2,000 men, with General John S. Mason in command; but in 1867 it became a separate military district, only to be joined to that of southern California two years later. In the next year General George Stoneman arrived to take command. Thus, the uncertainties of command, when coupled with the meddling of local authorities and citizens, made impossible effective military control.

Mason launched a campaign against hostile Indians soon after he took charge, and Arizona furnished him with four companies of territorial troops, two of which were composed of Pápagos. But little was accomplished. In 1866 Mason reported that 900 Chiricahuas, White Mountain, and other associated Apache bands were on a temporary reservation at Camp Goodwin. This was not greatly significant, however, for the Chiricahuas alone numbered above 2,000, and the other bands would have totaled more.

Stoneman, who succeeded Mason, accomplished little, and the Camp Grant Massacre of 1871 led to his dismissal. A short time previously hostile Indians had raided the San Xavier settlement and had driven away a large number of horses and cattle. The aroused citizens of San

Xavier and of nearby Tucson quickly took the marauders' trail. They overtook the Indians and engaged them in battle, killing a warrior and recovering a part of the stock. Jesus M. Elias, an influential Tucson Mexican, claimed to identify the slain Indian man as from Camp Grant, where only recently a band of Arivaipa Apaches had been temporarily located by Lieutenant R. E. Whitman. But the post commander maintained that the Indians had not left their camp. A short time later Elias and 42 Mexicans, W. H. Oury and five other Americans, and 92 Pápagos attacked the Camp Grant Apaches and killed 128 men, women, and children. The nation was profoundly shocked by this wanton slaughter, and President Grant demanded that the guilty be punished. Hostility of Arizona settlers against the Indians, however, was so pronounced that the court was influenced to free those tried. Popular indignation was now directed toward Stoneman. The recent massacre could not have happened, it was believed, under an alert administration; consequently, Stoneman gave way to Major General George Crook.

Crook arrived in Tucson in June, 1871, and summoned his field officers to council. He listened quietly to their advice, and later to that of Indian friends and foes, but said little to indicate what his policy would be. It soon became known, however, when he warned the Indians that he would punish those who remained on the warpath and aid those who followed ways of peace. "But he was kind," says Professor Frank C. Lockwood. "Children were not afraid of him; and there was no man—soldier or savage—so poor or ignorant that he could not gain access to him." [1] He was an indefatigable worker. With only a small escort or riding alone, he visited various parts of his command, parleying with the Indians, encouraging his men in long, arduous drill campaigns, and making new troop dispositions. At one council an attempt was made on his life by disgruntled Indians, but the would-be assassins were promptly disarmed and arrested. At another he admonished Miguel, Pedro, Alchisay, and other White Mountain Apache chiefs to follow peaceful pursuits, promising that they would be rewarded with government support. Order began to appear from the chaotic conditions, and Arizona citizens were optimistic for the future. But his work was interrupted by the arrival of Commissioner Colyer.

Within a year after Colyer's coming, the Indians had made about 50 raids, in which more than 40 citizens were killed. Yet Colyer was not slow in introducing his policy. He came directly from Tularosa, New Mexico, to Camp Apache, Arizona, where he established a reservation on September 7, 1871. Then on October 3 he set aside another for the

---

[1] Frank C. Lockwood, *The Apache Indians*, New York, The Macmillan Company, 1938, 188.

Apache-Mojaves at Camp Verde, and a short time later others at Beale Springs for the Hualapais and at Date Creek for another band of Apache-Mojaves. The commissioner kept his own counsel. He refused to take the advice of military officers, of agents, or of citizens, and for a short while suspended Crook's military operations. Meanwhile, he opened direct negotiations with the Indians, who were suspicious and noncommunicative.

But General O. O. Howard, President Grant's personal representative, who came a short time later, rectified some of Colyer's mistakes. Unlike the commissioner, Howard took the miners, ranchers, soldiers, and Arizona civil officers into his confidence. He informed them of the President's wishes and plans. He believed that the guilty should be punished and the innocent protected. This policy he also conveyed to the Indians at war. Through the efforts of Captain Thomas J. Jeffords, he succeeded in meeting Cochise in his stronghold, and in winning him for his peace policy when he promised the Chiricahuas a reservation embracing their favorite mountain resort. Moreover, through his recommendations, the Arivaipas were moved from Camp Grant to San Carlos; and the Indians at Fort McDowell, Date Creek, and Beale Springs were allowed to choose other reservations.

Meanwhile, Crook conducted a vigorous campaign against those Apaches who would not accept peace; and by the end of the winter of 1872, the most hostile Indians were asking for terms. Crook advised them to send their leading chiefs for a conference, and shortly the mountains were alive with swift Indian messengers, carrying the necessary summons. Calipun was the first to respond, coming with 300 head men of the hostile bands. He offered to surrender, saying that he was the spokesman for all the war tribes. But again, just as it seemed that Crook was on the eve of success, his efforts were frustrated; in March, 1875, he was transferred to the Department of the Platte to assist in rounding up the Sioux, as will be noted in the following chapter.

But much of the credit for establishing the basis for a sound Indian policy should be shared by another—John P. Clum, agent of the San Carlos Reservation. Upon his arrival in 1874 he inaugurated an Indian police and a self-governing body. Presently he had the friendship of Eskiminzin and other Apache chiefs and had won them to his new policy. He reduced Indian drunkenness by destroying their *tizwin* distilleries, and then he established discipline and order over a savage, turbulent people, thus proving to skeptics that a wise humane policy was best. That he was a man of iron nerve is proved by his firm policy and direct dealings. With no outside military aid, on one occasion his police arrested Pi-on-senay, a Chiricahua trouble-maker; and on another, the notorious Gerónimo, whom he confined on a charge of murder. However, Clum was not allowed the subsequent custody of the chief, who escaped to plague anew the frontier settlements. Clum's policy was so unusual as to arouse local criticism, and in 1877 the Indian Bureau at Washington released him. But he had laid well the foundation of a constructive policy.

After the death of Victorio, Gerónimo was the great leader of Apache outlaws. In 1882 Crook returned to Arizona and sought to resume his policy of exterminating the outlaws and of encouraging friendly Apaches by liberal grants of land and annuities. In May, 1883, Chatto's Chiricahua warriors were defeated in the Sierra Madre Mountains, and nine were killed and five captured. This had a sobering effect on others, and Gerónimo, Chatto, Nachez, and Loco presently returned to their reservation. But during the summer of 1885 Gerónimo and Nachez and half the Chiricahuas again escaped and resumed war. Shortly thereafter Colonel Nelson A. Miles superseded Crook, but the latter's policy was continued. Captain H. W. Lawton with a picked force of 100 seasoned troops was sent on a driving campaign against hostiles. The persistence of such officers as Lawton and Leonard Wood, and the daring of Lieutenant Gatewood finally brought success. At the risk of his own life, Gatewood went alone to Gerónimo's camp and persuaded the wily old chief to surrender. Gerónimo's band was followed across the Mexican boundary for 200 miles within the Yaqui country, and for five months the pursuit was kept up until the fleeing Indians were at last captured. Gerónimo and other war leaders were then sent to Fort Marion, Florida, for imprisonment, and the Arizona and New Mexico settlements had peace.

OTHER RESERVATION PROBLEMS

While the Indian Bureau was engaged in solving the Arizona and New Mexico reservation problems, it was similarly involved elsewhere. North of the Apache country were the ranges of the Utes, Paiutes, Snakes, and Bannocks, tribes of the Shoshonean linguistic family. The Mormons of the Great Basin found the Utes quite hostile. This powerful tribe occupied a large part of southern and western Colorado, almost the whole of Utah and Nevada, and ranged both sides of the Colorado River into Arizona and California. Closely allied with them were the Paiutes, a term, according to Frederick W. Hodge, used as a "convenient divisional" name for the tribes occupying southwestern Utah about the Beaver, the southeastern part of Nevada, and the northwestern part of Arizona. The Snakes and the Bannocks farther north made war on the Great Basin settlements. The Snakes ranged western Wyoming (meeting the Utes on the south), central and southern Idaho (except the Bannock country), northeastern Nevada, and a small strip of Utah west of the Great Lake. Their favorite resort, however, was the Snake River country of Idaho. The Bannocks lived in southeastern Idaho, along Portneuf River, a region through which trails to California and Oregon led.

Ute opposition to Mormon occupation of the Salt Lake Valley was increasingly bitter after 1847 because the new arrivals were driving their game into the mountains, were occupying much of their hunting range, and were threatening extinction of the tribe. In 1850 Ute hostility compelled Brigham Young to send an expedition against the tribe. They were severely chastised; 27 warriors were killed, and their women and children threw themselves on the mercy of the settlers. The Paiutes and Shoshones (or Snakes) also occasionally attacked the whites. On October 24, 1853, Captain J. W. Gunnison and five men of a surveying party of nine were killed by the Paiutes on the Sevier River; and on February 25, 1858, 250 Shoshones made a descent on the northern settlements, killing two settlers, wounding five, and driving off a large number of horses and cattle. Travelers passing through the region on their way to California were also trouble-makers. Thus Bancroft noticed that "In the summer of 1859 an emigrant party, en route to California, was surprised in the neighborhood of the Goose Creek Mountains and at least five men and two women were killed, the massacre being caused by the slaughter of two Indians who entered the camp for trading purposes."

Yet the Indian Bureau had promoted friendly relations. On December 30, 1849, the Utes signed a treaty with federal commissioners, agreeing to accept the settlers as friendly neighbors; and in 1856 and 1859 the Tabequache, Moache, Capote, Wiminuche, Yampa, Grand River, Uinta, and other Ute bands accepted reservations. But the swelling tide of homeseekers necessitated a return of tribal reserves to the public domain; and on March 2, these bands were moved to a Colorado reservation.

The Colorado Utes had much the same complaint as their Utah kinsmen. Incoming whites killed their game and overran their country. So in 1854 they leagued with the Jicarillas to make war on their enemies. But they were defeated by General Garland's troops in the battles of the Saguache Valley at a point some distance above present Salida. In the latter engagement 40 Indians were killed, others were captured, and horses, sheep, and supplies were taken. Consequently, the Utes accepted peace terms in September, 1855.

This did not end the Ute troubles. In 1868 gold and silver strikes in the San Juan Mountains brought many prospectors and treasure hunters, who demanded that the Indians abandon the country. So by the Brunot Treaty of September, 1873, federal commissioners restricted the Utes to the White River Agency and annuities. Still later, in 1878, their agent, Nathan Meeker, introduced agriculture, stock-raising, and schools among them. But the Indians had brooded over their wrongs, and they wanted no part of a culture whose exponents robbed them of their lands, killed their game, and mistreated their women and children. After a petty quarrel Meeker was assaulted by a sub-chief, and the surly attitude of others was such that he thought it wise to call for troops. When Major Thornburg and 190 men approached the reserve, they were warned away by the angry Indians. But Thornburg continued his advance. The warriors then prepared for resistance. On September 20, 1879, Thornburg's men were ambushed on the Milk Creek branch of the Yampa near the reservation's boundary, and the major and 13 of his men were killed. The survivors corralled the train, made breastworks of wagons and equipment, and sent out Joe Rankin, a scout, for reinforcements. The scout arrived at Rawlins 28 hours later, and presently General Wesley A. Merritt with 500 troops started southward. He was preceded, however, by Captain Dodge's colored troops from Fort Garland. The hostile warriors might have continued the struggle against their combined forces had not the head chief, Ouray, who had been away on a hunt and had only recently learned of the trouble, ordered them to desist. Then the troops advanced to the agency, where they found the bodies of Meeker and seven of his employees. The revolt came to an end, and the White River bands were presently moved to a Utah reservation.

The Bannocks and Snakes were also to taste of bitter defeat. On January 29, 1863, Colonel Patrick Edward Connor with California volunteers had destroyed a large Bannock village on Bear River in Utah. Five years later, the principal Bannock chiefs came to Fort Laramie and signed a treaty with General C. C. Augur. Yet there was others who remained sullen and defiant and did not accept the Fort Hall reservation as provided. In 1878 they took the warpath, but more than 1,000 were surrounded and captured by General O. O. Howard's cavalry. More serious trouble might have followed had not Washakie, head chief of the eastern Shoshones, remained quietly on his Wind River reservation.

A Nez Percé uprising of the Snake Valley was even more formidable. Its evident causes were the influx of gold-seekers and the government's failure to fulfill former treaty promises. By the treaties of 1855 and 1863, the Nez Percés had ceded much of their country and had been assigned the Lapwai reservation in Idaho. But here again some of the chiefs refused to accept their new home. Chief Joseph and his band continued to roam over the Wallowa Valley, ceded by the other chiefs. Then in 1873 President Grant gave them a reserve on the Wallowa, but later restored it to the public domain when they did not confine their wanderings to this area. In 1876 Secretary Zachary Chandler dispatched a commission to persuade Chief Joseph to accept government control, but it returned without success.

When all other measures had failed, and it became evident that force must be employed, Chandler turned the Indians over to General O. O. Howard. War followed. In August Chief Joseph abandoned the Salmon River country and crossed to the Yellowstone. There ensued a long, exhausting chase. Howard's troops followed the Nez Percés across Idaho and Wyoming into Montana, more than 1,300 miles, for 75 days, during which time a series of running fights occurred. When the pursued had reached the Missouri River, Colonel Nelson A. Miles, commanding the District of the Yellowstone, was ordered to head them off; and on October 3, 1877, he attacked Chief Joseph while camped on Snake Creek, killed 17 warriors, wounded 40 others, and captured 318 men, women, and children and 800 head of stock. General P. H. Sheridan later estimated Miles' loss at 20 per cent of the force engaged. On the next day the Indians surrendered, and a short time later the federal government transferred them to a small Indian Territory reserve. In 1885, however, they were allowed to return to their old country on the Collville reservation in northeastern Washington.

The Modocs in Tulé Lake and Lower Klamath Lake country of northern California had encountered much the same experience. They, too, had been assigned a desirable reserve. A part of the tribe continued to roam their former range around Tulé Lake, and resisted when the military sought to evict them. In March, 1873, they treacherously murdered General E. R. S. Canby and another peace commissioner sent to confer with them. Then, under Modoc Jack and Scar-Faced Charley, they took refuge in the lava beds along the boundary between California and Oregon, but they were overpowered by United States troops. In October, 1873, Modoc Jack and three other leaders were hanged at Fort Klamath, and Scar-Faced Charley and his followers were transferred to a small Indian Territory reservation.

BIBLIOGRAPHY

A majority of the early accounts of Indian wars lack balance and credibility. A few, however, are fairly dependable. Among these is J. P. Dunn, *Massacre of the Mountains, A History of the Indian Wars of the Far West* (New York, 1886), which covers in broad perspective red man–white relations. Also, the *Western Works* of Hubert Howe Bancroft are standard. Volume I of his five-volume group, *Native Races*, presents ethnic groupings, manners, and customs, and early history of the "Diggers," Apaches, Utes,

Shoshones, and Modocs. His seven-volume work on *California* (1886–1890) is likewise helpful, although it is designed primarily as a study of the Spanish- and Anglo-American occupation of that part of the western coast. Volumes IV, VI, and VII have sketches of Indian affairs. Moreover, Bancroft's single-volume works are similarly useful—for example: *Arizona and New Mexico* (San Francisco, 1889); *History of Nevada, Colorado, and Wyoming* (San Francisco, 1890); *History of Utah* (San Francisco, 1890); and *History of Washington, Idaho, and Montana* (San Francisco, 1890).

In the narratives of travelers in New Mexico and Arizona during the forties and fifties is found much of interest on the Apaches. General Stephen W. Kearny encountered the Apaches on his march to California, and Lieutenant W. H. Emory, who accompanied him, records his impressions in his *Notes of a Military Reconnaissance, from Fort Leavenworth, in Missouri, to San Diego, in California, Including Parts of the Arkansas, Del Norte, and Gila Rivers* (30 Cong., 1 Sess., *Senate Executive Documents*, No. 7, Washington, 1848). During the early fifties and late sixties we have John R. Bartlett, *Personal Narrative* (2 vols., New York, 1854), I; John C. Cremony, *Life Among the Apaches* (San Francisco, 1868); J. Ross Brown, *Adventures in the Apache Country; A Tour Through Arizona and Sonora* (New York, 1869); and James S. Calhoun, *Official Correspondence*, collected and edited by Annie Heloise Abel (Washington, 1915), all of which devote some attention to the Apaches.

The writings of important army officers and Indian officials throw much light on Apache relations after the Civil War, such as George Crook, *Résumé of Operations Against the Apache Indians from 1882 to 1886* (Washington, 1886); and *Personal Recollections of Nelson A. Miles* (Chicago, 1896). John G. Bourke, *On the Border with Crook* (Chicago, 1891) supplements Crook's *Résumé* and is generally trustworthy. The "peace policy" has a unique interpretation in Woodworth Clum's *Apache Agent, The Story of John P. Clum* (Boston and New York, 1936).

The reader should be careful, however, in the use of narratives of Indian apologists and "military might" exponents. For example, G. W. Manypenny, *Our Indian Wards* (Cincinnati, 1880); and Mrs. Helen Hunt Jackson, *A Century of Dishonor, A Sketch of the United States' Dealings with Some of the Indian Tribes* (New York, 1881) are highly colored and biased, and should be read with discrimination. This is also true of certain narratives of army officers, for example, James B. Fry, *Army Sacrifices; or Briefs from Official Pigeon-Holes* (New York, 1879).

Frank C. Lockwood, *Apache Indians* (New York, 1938) and Ralph H. Ogle, *Federal Control of the Western Apaches, 1848–1886* (Albuquerque, 1940) are the only trustworthy studies of the Apaches published within recent years, and their lists of chapter readings point the way to more intensive study. Other volumes relating to various phases of the Apache problem are as follows: Paul I. Wellman, *Death on the Desert* (New York, 1913); Herbert Welsh, *The Apache Prisoners in Fort Marion* (Philadelphia, 1887); Britton Davis, *The Truth about Gerónimo* (New Haven, 1927); C. C. Rister, *The Southwestern Frontier, 1865–1881* (Cleveland, 1928); and C. C. Raht, *The Romance of the Davis Mountains and the Big Bend Country* (El Paso, 1919).

Relating to Indian tribes farther north, Leroy Hafen and Francis Marion Young, in their *Fort Laramie and the Pageant of the West, 1834–1890* (Glendale, 1938) ably portray army post life and Indian border wars, as well as selected readings. Other books worthy of mention, dealing with the north-western tribes, are as follows: C. T. Brady, *Northwestern Fights and Fighters* (New York, 1907); O. O. Howard, *Nez Percé Joseph, An Account of his Ancestors, his Lands, his Confederates, his Enemies, his War, his Pursuit and Capture* (Boston, 1881), and ————, *My Life and Experiences Among Our Hostile Indians* (Hartford, 1907); and Jeff. C. Riddle, *The Indian History of the Modoc War and the Causes that Led to It* (n.p., 1914). Riddle was the son of the Modoc heroine of the war and presents the Indian viewpoint.

The "Digger" Indian problem is well treated in A. L. Kroeber, *Handbook of the Indians of California* (*Bulletin 78*, Bureau of American Ethnology, Washington, 1925); and brief discussions are found in the Bancroft volumes previously mentioned and in R. N. Richardson and C. C. Rister, *The Greater Southwest* (Glendale, 1934). The manners and customs and general history of the Hopis, Navajos, Walapais, and Havasupais are given in George Wharton James, *The Indians of the Painted Desert Region* (Boston, 1907).

Federal documentary materials are also available. Frederick Webb Hodge is the editor of a two-volume work, published as *Bulletin 30* of the Bureau of American Ethnology and entitled *Handbook of the American Indians North of Mexico* (Washington, 1907 and 1910), in which the various tribes are listed alphabetically, and in which each is identified, its range named, and a sketch presented. The *Annual Reports* of the Secretary of War and the Indian Commissioner, incorporating the sub-reports of border officials, interestingly portray the Indian problem and reveal the interdepartmental friction. For reports on Indian battles, consult *A Record of Engagements with Hostile Indians within the Military Division of the Missouri from 1868 to 1882, Lieutenant General P. H. Sheridan Commanding,* compiled at Headquarters of the Military Division of the Missouri from Official Records (Washington, 1882); and for treaties, reservation settlements, and names of commissioners, see C. J. Kappler (ed.), *Indian Affairs, Laws and Treaties* (57th Cong., 1st Sess., *Senate Documents,* No. 452, 3 vols., Washington, 1903).

30

THE COMING OF THE RAILROADS

THE NINETEENTH century had reached its halfway mark before a single mile of railroad was built beyond the Mississippi. And yet railroad development in America was well under way by 1850. Two decades of experimenting had brought considerable wisdom and skill to the problems of railroad construction, operation, and financing. For those early efforts, trans-Mississippi builders were the wiser and richer.

The earliest railroads had been propelled by horse power, and the cars were run on planks or wooden rails. Such equipment had long been employed in English coal mines, and a few rail lines—one of which carried stone for the Bunker Hill monument—were being operated in the United States before 1830. The application of steam motive power was to work a revolutionary change and rather quickly make the railroad an important agency of transportation.

On July 4, 1828, Charles Carroll, last surviving signer of the Declaration of Independence, turned the first spadeful of earth that inaugurated work on the Baltimore and Ohio Railroad. Little headway was made at first, and it was 1830 before the first 12 miles of road were opened. Twenty more years were to elapse before the Alleghenies would be conquered and the Ohio River reached. Other eastern cities projected lines westward to compete with the one from Baltimore in order to win a share of the trade of the middle western states.

At first railroads were built as local units to connect important cities or supplement water routes. Gradually the new agency became a competitor of canal boats and river steamers. Short sections of track were consolidated and connected into trunk lines. Wooden rails were covered with strips of iron and then were displaced by rails made entirely of iron. The great diversity in the widths of track—ranging from three to six feet—was gradually eliminated, and the English standard of four feet eight and one-half inches was generally adopted. The cars, first patterned after stagecoaches, soon assumed more ap-

513

propriate forms, with adaptations for such divergent uses as coaches, sleepers, and carriers of different kinds of freight.

During the 1830's and 1840's railroads were looked upon as public benefactions, as were hospitals or community buildings. Their promotion was a civic duty, and contributors to the cause were philanthropic citizens. Conventions were called to promote the enterprise and to develop enthusiasm. As early as 1836 such an assemblage met at Knoxville to discuss a "great southern railroad." In the late forties railroad conventions became epidemic. The gatherings at Memphis in 1845, at Chicago in 1847, and at St. Louis in 1849 were among the most important. The Camp Meeting technique, which had proved so efficacious in religious reformation, was now applied to railroad promotion. Vigorous exhorters waxed warm and eloquent, exuding enthusiasm as they preached a new salvation via the iron rail instead of by the sawdust trail. There were great "slayings," but the efforts were more productive of converts than of cash.

The problem of raising money for the grand projects, so alluringly described, still remained. Corporate financing in America was yet in its swaddling clothes, with no accumulations of capital adequate to undertake large enterprises. Advocates turned to governmental units for aid. Cities, counties, states, and the nation were asked to subscribe stock. All were finally induced to render aid. There were some precedents for national assistance. Rivers and harbors had been improved and the National Road built at federal expense. But strict constructionists at the White House and in Congress had generally resisted appeals for federal aid to promote internal improvements. States were less conservative. They not only voted state assistance, but authorized cities and counties to issue bonds to further railroad building. Railroads held a whip hand over these local communities, threatening to choose routes that missed particular counties and cities unless these political subdivisions bought stock in the road. One town was played against another to induce competitive offers of assistance.

EARLY RAILROAD BUILDING IN THE WEST

In the 1830's enthusiasm for railroad construction swept the Middle West, and numerous lines were chartered. Indiana, Illinois, Michigan, and other states voted funds, and some of these almost bankrupted themselves with their frenzied expenditures for internal improvements—principally canals and railroads. The Panic of 1837, brought on, or at least accentuated, by such policies, had a sobering effect, and induced most states to cease making internal improvements at their own direct expense.

Western railroad activity during the 1840's and 1850's centered about Chicago. Leaders in this city saw the strategy of their position at the head of Lake Michigan, and eagerly made the most of it. St. Louis and New Orleans, the principal competitors, had been built on water transportation, and the security which they felt led them for some years to underestimate the importance of rail connections. In 1852, both the Michigan Central and the Michigan Southern reached Chicago. With eastern connections established, the new city now looked toward the building of feeder lines from the West. Vigorous efforts were directed toward this achievement; for, when railroad lines should reach the Mississippi, Chicago could hope to attract to herself business that had been going down the river to older trade centers. The first step in this plan was taken when the Chicago and Rock Island reached the Mississippi in 1854, and within the decade three other lines had reached the great river. In 1853 a railroad was completed between St. Louis and Chicago; and by 1857 the Missouri city had established connections with the eastern seaboard, *via* Cincinnati.

In some respects, the Illinois Central was the most fortunate of the early Mississippi Valley roads. As projected, it was to run the length of Illinois north and south, and also across the state in its northern section. Stephen A. Douglas became its leading promoter, working actively in Congress to obtain federal aid for the enterprise. Through persistent efforts and by well-planned log-rolling, he succeeded. The assistance was in the form previously given to certain canal projects. By the Congressional Act of 1850, alternate sections of land in a 12-mile strip were given the State of Illinois to aid the undertaking. The railroad company would thus receive six sections of public land for each mile of track it built. The price of the remaining alternate sections, under this law, was raised to double the established minimum, or to $2.50 per acre; and the United States would thus lose no cash as a result of the contribution. This federal grant not only aided the building of the Illinois Central, but, what was perhaps more important, it set a precedent for subsequent gifts. In the next 20 years the United States government was to proffer 180,000,000 acres of land as grants in aid of railroad construction.

The first state west of the Mississippi to give assistance to railroads was Missouri. State bonds to the amount of $19,000,000 were issued and sold, the money obtained being lent to the railroads, with mortgages accepted as security. Almost no repayments were made to the state. One of the chief reasons for Minnesota's eagerness for statehood was her desire to promote railroad building. Upon admission, she issued $5,000,000 in bonds and lent the money forthwith to railroad companies. Here, as in Missouri, there were waste and fraud, the mileage of track being far from commensurate with the outlay. Banking difficulties in the 1830's had so impaired the credit of Arkansas that she was unable or unwilling to assist railroads prior to the Civil War. After that conflict her condition was even worse, but politicians succeeded in getting legislation in aid of railroad building. The bonds that were issued were later repudiated. The record of Texas is better. Having come into the Union in possession of all the public land within her boundaries, Texas was able to make attractive land grants to encourage railroad construction. She also made money loans. Fair results were obtained from the state's investments. Iowa gave very little state aid, probably realizing that her favorable location would bring roads without state expenditures. California gave assistance to the Central Pacific.

Where state aid was given, it was usually in furtherance of a plan that was local rather than national in its conception. Thus, the Missouri system centered at St. Louis; the Arkansas system, at Little Rock. The Texas roads were to converge at Galveston Bay. Iowa roads were to run east and west. Minnesota planned routes east and west and others centering at St. Paul. Railroad construction west of the Mississippi made slow progress in the 1850's, and even these meager efforts were brought practically to a stop by the Panic of 1857. Rail building was scarcely revived until after the Civil War, with the exception of the Hannibal and St. Joe, which was completed to the Missouri River in 1859, and the Missouri Pacific, which finally completed its track from St. Louis to Kansas City in 1865.

After the war, railroad development again attracted the attention it merited. Three main groups of lines were building. The first was the transcontinental group (which we shall discuss presently). The second embraced the "granger" roads built from Chicago and St. Louis to the Missouri River. These included the Chicago and Northwestern, which crossed Iowa and reached Council Bluffs in 1867, two other roads which were completed to the same point in 1869, and another line that was opened to Sioux City the next year. The third group connected the Missouri River with the Gulf of Mexico, two such lines being completed in 1873. One of these ran from Kansas City to Houston; the other was a combination of four roads that together joined St. Louis and Houston.

EFFORTS FOR A TRANSCONTINENTAL RAILROAD

Americans were dreaming of a railroad to the Pacific even before the land on the western coast had become part of the national domain. To most people it was a visionary scheme that would probably require a century or more for its realization. But as people talked and the country grew, the project came a little nearer the realm of practical affairs. Asa Whitney, a New York merchant who was interested in trade with China, was perhaps the most active of early advocates. After devoting much attention to possible schemes, he presented his own plan to Congress in January, 1845. It provided for the building of a railroad from a suitable point on the Great Lakes westward to the Oregon coast, upon what Whitney considered the shortest and most practicable route. He asked Congressional aid in the form of a grant of land 60 miles wide along the proposed line. The majority in Congress, considering the project impractical, were apathetic to it.

Whitney's proposal for a railroad on a northern route spurred Southerners to advocate lines favorable to their section. Colonel James Gadsden, at the Memphis railroad convention of November, 1845, proposed a southern route. Professor Foshey, of Louisiana, advocated a road that would traverse Louisiana and Texas and cross Mexico to Mazatlan on the Gulf of California. This would be less than 1,500 miles in length and would avoid the cold and the mountains on Whitney's route. General Sam Houston suggested a line from Galveston to San Diego, by way of the Gila River. This would be a still shorter line. One of the objections to the Southern proposals was that such roads would have to traverse Mexican territory. But control of Oregon also was as yet shared with a foreign power.

Whitney began a campaign of education. He toured the country on speaking engagements, visited legislatures, distributed promotion literature and railroad petitions, and lobbied in Congress. Before his plan, or any other, had gathered general acceptance, new developments had occurred that affected the situation. The title to Oregon was cleared. The Mexican War gave California and the whole Southwest to the United States. The discovery of gold quickly drew a large population to California and made San Francisco the leading city on the Pacific Coast. There was now real justification for a railroad, with a larger population to serve and with extensive traffic in prospect. But with these advantages came difficulties. Several routes were now available across United States territory; and among these, competition grew keener as the prize became greater. Whitney's project was placed before Congress session after session. It won many friends; but, as other plans and routes developed, his became less popular and was finally displaced in Congress in 1852.

"Pacific Railroad" projects, pushed with vigor during the late 1840's and the early 1850's, quite monopolized the Senate at the short session of 1852–1853. Senator Gwin of California in January, 1853, presented his plan for a trunk line to run from San Francisco eastward to Albuquerque and along the Red River. Toward the eastern end, branches were to diverge to Memphis, St. Louis, Council Bluffs, New Orleans, and Austin. At the west end a branch was to continue to Oregon and Puget Sound. The total estimated length of trunk and branches was 5,115 miles. The project was planned to satisfy all sections, but the result was, as Senator Cass remarked, "too magnificent" to be considered practical or to gain the necessary support. However, the discussions had shown the need of more accurate information on the subject. The Army Appropriation Bill of March, 1853, was amended to provide for the survey of such routes as the Secretary of War should deem advisable, under the mandate "to ascertain the most practicable and economical route for a railroad from the Mississippi River to the Pacific Ocean."

Secretary of War Jefferson Davis at once placed engineers in the field. The four principal routes surveyed were these: (1) the northern or Whitney route, between the forty-seventh and forty-ninth parallels; (2) Senator Benton's route, between the thirty-eighth and thirty-ninth parallels; (3) Senator Gwin's recommendation, along the thirty-fifth latitude line, and (4) the Gila or thirty-second parallel route. Fairly thorough explorations were made, and when the reports came to Congress, it was evident that several routes were practicable. The selection was thus thrown back into the lap of Congress.

In the meantime, Northern men were aware of the fact that routes favorable to their section were blocked by the unorganized Indian country, extending from the Missouri frontier to the Rockies and from Texas to the Canadian border. To remove this impediment, the Commissioner of Indian Affairs, G. W. Manypenny, was directed to negotiate new treaties with the tribes, and to win cessions of land that would permit railroad building through this country. Though not relishing the task, Manypenny undertook it in the summer of 1853, and wrung concessions from most of the tribes. Then came forward Stephen A. Douglas, rising railroad promoter, with a bill from his Senate Committee to create Nebraska Territory in the northern plains Indian country. To win the necessary Southern support, he espoused the principle of "popular sovereignty" and its application to the proposed Territory, permitted a division of the area in Kansas and Nebraska, and included a clause repealing the Missouri Compromise—thus opening the proposed Territories to Negro slavery.

The log-rolling tactics that had enabled Douglas to secure federal land grants for railroads in his Illinois Central law of 1850 succeeded also with his Kansas-Nebraska bill. But enactment of this measure in May, 1854, ended the truce that the Compromise of 1850 had purchased, and thus let loose the flood of slavery and sectional controversy that was to rise and swell until it broke all gates and inundated the nation. The "Little Giant" tried to calm the waters and save his railroad project. In January, 1855, he introduced a bill to create three Pacific railroads—northern, central, and southern. This passed the Senate by a close vote but failed in the House. It, like Gwin's bill, was too magnificent for practicability. To the general sectional conflict was added the rivalry of various cities—New Orleans, Memphis, St. Louis, Chicago, and others—each wanting to be the eastern terminus of the Pacific railroad. As the decade advanced, the project for a transcontinental railroad lost rather than gained ground; and the rivalry between overland routes was transferred to the stagecoaches on the western plains, as recounted previously in Chapter 27. Thus was the railroad project postponed until the coming of the Civil War, when the withdrawal of Southern Congressmen removed one group of partisans and made possible the passage of a railroad bill satisfactory to those who remained at Washington. The exigencies of the war, and the desirability of tying the West to the North, also were factors contributing to the ultimate result.

THE UNION PACIFIC AND THE CENTRAL PACIFIC

By an Act of July 1, 1862, Congress chartered the Union Pacific Company to build the eastern part of the first transcontinental railroad, and provided assistance for the Central Pacific Company to build the western end of the line. The national aid offered these two companies in the original act was a gift of ten sections of public lands and a government loan for each mile of track laid. The amount of the loan was fixed at $16,000 per mile across the plains area, $32,000 in the foothills and plateau region, and $48,000 per mile in the mountains. The assistance appeared to be generous, but in actuality it proved insufficient to induce the necessary investment of outside capital. Generally looked upon as a project that gave little promise of paying dividends to stockholders, the railroad undertaking did not appeal strongly to investors. Leaders in the enterprise thought that the easiest and surest way to success would be to obtain more favorable concessions from Congress. So they instituted an active lobby at Washington. In 1864, Congress doubled the land grant and relegated the government loan to the status of a second mortgage, thus permitting the railroad companies to borrow elsewhere on first mortgage. With these revisions enacted, the project was to succeed. Of the two companies that were to build this transcontinental line, the one at the western end was first to make headway.

The Central Pacific Railroad Company had been organized on June 28, 1861, and incorporated under the laws of California. Four Sacramento merchants—Leland Stanford, Collis P. Huntington, Mark Hopkins, and Charles Crocker—became the "Big Four" of the undertaking. Theodore D. Judah, a gifted engineer, who was largely responsible for interesting the others in the project, died in 1863, and thus failed to see culmination of the great work he had launched.

Californians long had been enthusiastic for a railroad connection with the East; but when a specific project was formulated and a definite route selected, unanimity ceased. San Francisco was jealous of Sacramento; Placerville feared that she would be sidetracked. Wells-Fargo and other stagecoach companies did not relish railroad competition, nor did the powerful Pacific Mail Steamship Company and the river steamboats. A host of wagon and pack-horse freighters and their numerous employees were belligerent. But Nevada's great Comstock Lode and the human ants that burrowed in it beckoned from the sunrise side of the Sierras. Fortunes expended in freighting over the mountains might well be diverted to help pay for the building of a railroad. So the Central Pacific leaders were encouraged. They divided assignments to duty. President Stanford was to attend to state legislation; Vice-President Huntington would be Eastern financial agent and congressional lobbyist; and Crocker and Hopkins would manage the local business and construction.

The California legislature, by Acts in 1863 and 1864, authorized the state and various counties to exchange bonds, to the sum of $1,650,000, for company stock. Interest on $1,500,000 of company bonds was to be borne by the state treasury for 20 years. President Lincoln obliged the builders by officially placing the western edge of the Sierras well out in the Sacramento Valley, thus making the $48,000 loan per mile apply to a stretch of low and easy grade. With the federal, state, and county aid and the money raised in the East by Huntington, the road made progress.

Costs were high, and prices rose as a result of the Civil War. Iron rails that at the mills had cost $55 per ton in 1861 rose to over $90. Freight rates around Cape Horn averaged $17.50 per ton, and over the Isthmus of Panama $50. By July, 1864, the rail head was at Newcastle, 31 miles from Sacramento. The next year brought the rails 12 miles farther. Then, despite the great physical obstacles which the mountain range presented, real building progressed. Crocker, Superintendent of Construction, exerted indomitable will and energy. Confronted with a wage strike among the Irish laborers, he employed Chinese. The Chinaman was a patient and steady worker, accepted $30 per month as pay, and boarded himself. With pick and spade, basket and wheelbarrow, he dug a path through the oak-covered hills and along the side of the densely-forested mountains. Visitors were impressed with the pig-tailed figures in their basket hats, blue blouses, and flapping pantaloons, shuttling back and forth trundling their wheel-barrows, or at mealtime squatting around their bowls of rice and pork. By the end of 1865, there were 7,000 Chinamen and 2,500 whites employed on the road.

Twenty-eight miles of difficult construction, at a cost of $8,290,790, were completed in 1866. In midsummer of 1867, the first locomotive crossed the Divide. The original federal act had authorized the Central Pacific Company to build only to California's eastern boundary, but the company leaders early set their hearts upon building the line across the easy desert stretches of Nevada. In 1866 they won the enactment of a congressional law authorizing them to continue the road eastward "until they shall meet and connect with the Union Pacific Railroad." A great contest ensued—a contest that was to end only when the rail heads met.

Let us now turn to the other actors in the drama—the Union Pacific forces pushing their rails westward from the Missouri. The Board of Commissioners named in the Union Pacific Act of 1862 had held a meeting at Chicago in September of that year and effected a temporary organization. At the first annual meeting of the company, in late October, 1863, 30 directors were chosen; General John A. Dix was named President and Thomas C. Durant Vice-President. Since General Dix never really assumed the duties of his office, Durant became the chief executive and financial agent. Ground was broken at the little town of Omaha on December 2, 1863, Governor Saunders of Nebraska wielding the spade. Practically no money was forthcoming, however, so grading was deferred for almost a year. New life came with the Congressional Act of 1864. Some money was obtained from New York banks. Contracts for grading were let. But not until July 10, 1865, was the first rail laid at Omaha; and by the end of the year only 40 miles of track had been completed. After three years of marking time, however, the Union Pacific was at last ready to stride.

With the Civil War over, ample labor was procurable. New financial support had come from Boston capitalists with the entry of the brothers Oakes Ames and Oliver Ames—the former a member of Congress from Massachusetts. Durant had devised a scheme whereby construction of the road could be pushed and, at the same time, leaders of the company could make their fortunes. He and his friends set up the Credit Mobilier of America as a construction company. Its stockholders were leaders in the Union Pacific Company, selected Congressmen, and others whose influence was needed. To this company the Union Pacific gave very lucrative construction contracts. Dividends on *railroad* stock might be long delayed or might never come, but large and frequent returns were to be made by Credit Mobilier. Its stockholders received annual dividends of about 100 per cent on a capital of $3,750,000 for approximately five years. These tremendous profits were gathered at the expense of the railroad itself, of the small stockholders, and ultimately of the government. The Credit Mobilier became a national scandal that did much to turn public sentiment against railroads and to induce the government by 1870 to cease giving aid to them. Similar to the Credit Mobilier was "Crocker and Company," the construction subsidiary operated by leaders of the Central Pacific. The lucrative and unjust construction contracts had one redeeming feature. They made for speed in building the first transcontinental railroad.

Although the topography of the plains country favored railroad building, other physical difficulties were present. Rails and supplies had to be shipped to Omaha by river boats. Even after the Chicago and Northwestern rails reached Council Bluffs in 1867, there was no bridge over the Missouri, and everything had to be ferried across the river to Omaha. Timber for ties was not to be had on the plains. So the cottonwoods along the Missouri River bottoms were cut into ties, hardened by a zinc treatment, and used. Numerous teams were employed in the grading operations, and hundreds of wagons were kept busy hauling supplies to the crews. During the year 1866, 260 miles of track were laid.

General "Jack" Casement, the "champion tracklayer of the continent," drove his doughty Irish crew at high speed. The scene at the end of track is thus described by a contemporary:

A light car, drawn by a single horse, gallops up to the front with its load of rails. Two men seize the end of a rail and start forward, the rest of the gang taking hold by twos until it is clear of the car. They come forward at a run. At the word of command, the rail is dropped in its place, right side up, with care, while the same process goes on at the other side of the car. Less than thirty seconds to a rail for each gang, and four rails go down to the minute! . . . Close behind the first gang come the gaugers, spikers, and bolters, and a lively time they make of it. It is a grand anvil chorus that these sturdy sledges are playing across the plains. It is in a triple time, three strokes to a spike. There are ten spikes to a rail, four hundred rails to a mile, eighteen hundred miles to San Francisco. That's the sum, what is the quotient?

On November 13, 1867, the tracks reached Cheyenne. During the year, 240 miles of road were completed. In crossing the plains, the builders encountered some Indian resistance to the iron horse invasion. But Colonel Grenville M. Dodge, chief engineer of the road, was an experienced military man, and many of the workers had seen service during the late war. So, when necessary, the railroad gangs became soldier brigades, dropping shovels for rifles and effectively defending their position.

As the road built westward, a succession of mushroom towns sprang up at the end of track. Tents and frame shacks blossomed into dance halls, saloons, and gambling dens, each with its gaudy allurements. The dregs of society that gathered here to prey on the workmen at the end of the day stamped the terminal town with a bizarre and blatant aspect, and gave it the sobriquet "Hell on Wheels." When the track nosed too far ahead of the town for easy access, the paraphernalia was moved to a new location. Frame houses were disjointed, and disreputable contraptions of rough lumber, canvas, and sheet iron were loaded on flat cars. Tables, chairs, and saloon bars, boxes, bales, and barrels, were piled on top, and the gamblers, sharpsters, and "girls" climbed aboard. "What had been Julesburg in the morning became Cheyenne at night."

The Central Pacific had its terminal bases—"the semicolons of railroad history"—but these were not counterparts of the roistering camps east of the Rockies. The Chinese workers were poor customers for whiskey peddlers, monte men, and their ilk.

The surveying parties, in their search for the shortest and most economical route, sidetracked the two principal centers of population in the mountain area—Denver and Salt Lake City. Though Coloradans and Utahans were sorely disappointed, they had no recourse but to build branch lines, and this they set about to do.

The great race between the Union Pacific and the Central Pacific gained momentum in 1868. The latter road had completed the work over the hard mountain section of its line, and the comparatively easy Nevada desert lay ahead. The Union Pacific, on the other hand, was just entering the mountain region. Both roads wanted to reach the Utah settlements and win their business. But the greatest spur to speed, perhaps, was the ruling that President Lincoln had given classifying the Nevada region as mountainous and thus making the $48,000 of government loan per mile applicable to that level country. Under such incentive both companies exerted themselves to the utmost. The laying of ten miles of track in a single day was the record finally reached. Each company surveyed its line and built grade far ahead of its rails, in the hope of winning more mileage and the consequent government subsidy. Thus, for some distance, the competitors' grades ran parallel. But Congress intervened, and decreed that the rails should meet at Promontory Point, a little west of Ogden, Utah.

So here, in the Sego Lily State, the final ceremonies were held. High officials and honored guests of both companies assembled. A polished laurel tie, bound with silver, was put into place. Rails were carried to

AFTER THE LAST SPIKE WAS DRIVEN, THE LOCOMOTIVES WERE MOVED CLOSER TOGETHER AND BOTTLES OF CHAMPAGNE WERE USED FOR CHRISTENING PURPOSES.

position. Special spikes were at hand—one of silver from Nevada; one of gold, silver, and iron from Arizona; silver and gold ones from Idaho and Montana; and two gold ones from California. As the speeches were made and the spikes driven, the telegraph flashed the news to the world and signaled the beginning of celebrations in scores of cities and towns throughout the nation. The two engines came nose to nose. The crowd yelled. The whistles shrieked. To President Grant at Washington went this official telegram:

> Promontory Summit, Utah, May 10, 1869.
> The last rail is laid, the last spike driven. The Pacific Railroad is completed. The point of junction is 1068 miles west of the Missouri River, and 690 miles east of Sacramento City.

The continent was spanned; the Indian country cut asunder. One epoch was ended; another had begun.

THE BUILDING OF OTHER MAJOR WESTERN RAILROADS

Before the final gold spike was driven on the first transcontinental railroad, other lines were pushing into the Far West. The first to make considerable progress was the Kansas Pacific, considered a branch of the Union Pacific, and accordingly given federal aid. Work on this road was begun near Kansas City as early as September, 1863, but for some years little progress was made. When Congress authorized a route through Denver, building was pushed. The rails reached the Colorado capital in August, 1870, and there connected with the Denver Pacific, a branch line that Coloradans had built to connect them with the Union Pacific at Cheyenne.

The Atchison, Topeka and Santa Fe had its beginnings in 1859, when Cyrus K. Holliday obtained a charter from the Kansas legislature for a railroad to run from Atchison on the Missouri to the new capital, Topeka. Holliday, the "Father of the Santa Fe," early dreamed of extending the rails to New Mexico, along the famous Santa Fe Trail. The railroad company received a land grant across Kansas, and by 1872 had built its line the length of that state. Here the land grant ended, and building ceased for some time. The Panic of 1873 did not affect this road so seriously as it did most other companies. Finances were reorganized, bonds were voted by two Colorado counties, and the rails were pushed westward, reaching Pueblo in 1876.

Here the Santa Fe came into competition with the Denver and Rio Grande, a narrow-gauge line that had been started at Denver in 1871 and had reached Pueblo the next year. This Colorado road, fathered by William J. Palmer, planned to build southward to Mexico City.

The gateway to New Mexico for both the Sante Fe and the Rio Grande was Raton Pass. The former road won the prize and began construction work in 1878. An equally keen rivalry to reach the rich mining camp of Leadville developed between the companies. The Royal Gorge of the Arkansas River was the key to Leadville, and this deep canyon was so narrow that but one road could traverse it. Here the Rio Grande finally won. A working arrangement was made by the rival roads whereby the Rio Grande agreed not to build south to El Paso, Texas, and the Santa Fe promised not to build into the Colorado mountains. After reaching Leadville in 1880, the Rio Grande connected with Salt Lake City in 1883, and in addition built numerous branches to Colorado mining camps. The Santa Fe built to Denver in 1887. Its transcontinental activity will be mentioned presently.

The Northern Pacific was chartered July 1, 1864, and was to take the Whitney and Stevens route from Lake Superior to Puget Sound. Its federal land grant was most liberal, providing 20 sections per mile of track through the states and 40 sections in the territories. But no loan of bonds was given. Hence, the raising of cash was a serious problem. Jay Cooke and Company, widely and favorably known through its effective handling of government bonds during the Civil War, was induced to become financial representative of the Northern Pacific. Jay Cooke himself took a personal interest in the project and was enthusiastic about the country to be traversed. He raised money here and in Europe, and actual construction was begun in 1870 at Pacific Junction, the point at which the intended branches from St. Paul and Duluth should converge. Satisfactory building progress was made, and the road reached the Missouri River at Bismarck in 1873. But the financial resources of the railroad company were exhausted, and Jay Cooke had strained his credit to the breaking point in bolstering the railroad. His banking house failed, and in so doing precipitated the disastrous Panic of 1873. Extravagant railroad building in the West had been an important factor in producing the panic. With the collapse of business and credit, many railroad companies failed, and practically all rail laying ceased.

The reorganization that brought about the completion of this northern road was largely the work of Henry Villard, German immigrant and journalist. He was made the representative of German capitalists who had invested heavily in the Northern Pacific and its ally, the Oregon Steam Navigation Company, which operated steamships on the Columbia. Villard obtained control of this navigation company and of the Oregon Railroad, already operating in the Columbia Valley. In possession of these, he controlled western extension of the Northern Pacific. Then he executed a bold stroke. In June, 1881, he obtained subscriptions to a "blind pool," and with the proceeds bought control of the Northern Pacific. Thereupon, he pushed construction on the road and, by utilizing existing transportation units, made a connection with Portland in September, 1883. The main line to Seattle was completed in 1887.

The Atlantic and Pacific Railroad was chartered July 27, 1866, to build along the thirty-fifth parallel. Its land grant was similar to that of the Northern Pacific, and no government bonds were given. There was a proviso in the act authorizing the Central Pacific railroad group of California, organized as the Southern Pacific, to build a line through California and connect with the Atlantic and Pacific at the eastern border of that state. The California road was to receive a federal land grant of 20 sections per mile of track. The Atlantic and Pacific failed in 1873, was reorganized as the St. Louis and San Francisco in 1876, but still was unable to make headway. Finally, that portion of its land grant west of Albuquerque was transferred to the Santa Fe, and this active company pushed the rails to Needles on the Colorado River. Here they were met in 1883 by the line built east from Barstow by the Southern Pacific.

The Texas and Pacific Railroad, chartered in 1871 to run along the thirty-second parallel, was the last of the land-grant transcontinental lines. Congress provided the usual gift of 20 and 40 sections of land, but this did not apply in Texas, where all public land was owned by the state. For the western end of the route, the Southern Pacific was authorized to build in California and to receive the customary land grant. The Southern Pacific ran its line to the Colorado River at Yuma, while the Texas and Pacific rail head was still in Texas. Unwilling to wait longer, the California railroad group obtained charters from Arizona and New Mexico and began to build eastward. Jay Gould, now in control of the Texas and Pacific, made an agreement with Huntington and his associates whereby the two lines should be joined at El Paso, and the western part of the land grant should be transferred to the Southern Pacific. The junction of the roads was effected in 1882, but Congress did not indorse the land grant transfer. The Southern Pacific, not satisfied with arrangements, decided to make its own line eastward to the Mississippi. Utilizing roads already built, it established through connections to New Orleans late in 1882. Says Dr. R. E. Riegel, "the decade of 1878 to 1888 saw the building of the greatest number of miles ever constructed in a similar period in the history of the United States." [1] A large part of this railroad building was on the western plains. In addition to American construction, there

---

[1] Riegel, R. E., *America Moves West*, New York, Henry Holt and Co., 1930, 509.

was completed in 1885 the Canadian Pacific, a strong road that became a competitor with lines in the United States.

After the decade of the 1880's several other roads were built through the American West. James J. Hill, one of the nation's railroad builders, ran his Great Northern from the Great Lakes to Puget Sound, completing the line in 1893. The Chicago and Northwestern connected with the Northern Pacific in Montana the following year. The Los Angeles and Salt Lake was completed in 1905 between the cities named. The Chicago, Milwaukee and St. Paul ran its line to Seattle in 1909. In 1911 the Western Pacific was completed between Utah and California, and by use of the Rio Grande to Denver and the Burlington to Chicago, another through line was pieced together. The numerous shorter lines and branches built in the West during the railroad epoch obviously cannot be treated in the space available here.

BIBLIOGRAPHY

A general treatment of western railroads is found in R. E. Riegel, *The Story of the Western Railroads* (New York, 1926). Accounts covering the entire United States are: John Moody, *The Railroad Builders* (New Haven, 1919); J. W. Starr, *One Hundred Years of American Railroading;* Slason Thompson, *A Short History of American Railways* (Chicago, 1925); and C. F. Carter, *When Railroads were New* (New York, 1926). In Seymour Dunbar's extensive *History of Travel in America* (4 vols., Indianapolis, 1915), a number of chapters are devoted to railroads. Popular accounts dealing largely with the West are Cy Warman, *The Story of the Railroad* (New York, 1905); and A. C. Laut, *The Romance of the Rails* (New York, 1929). G. L. Albright, *Official Explorations for Pacific Railroads, 1853–1855* (Berkeley, 1921), gives a good digest of the government surveys. On federal aid to railroads, see L. H. Haney, *A Congressional History of Railways in the United States, 1850–1887* (Madison, 1910); and J. B. Sanborn, *Congressional Grants of Land in Aid of Railways* (Madison, 1899).

For a sympathetic account of the Credit Mobilier, see J. B. Crawford, *The Credit Mobilier of America* (Boston, 1880); and for the opposite view, consult the *House Reports* numbers 77, 78, 81, 82, and 95 of the 42nd Congress, 3rd Session.

A popular account of the building of the first transcontinental railroad is presented in E. L. Sabin, *The Building of the Pacific Railway* (Philadelphia, 1919). The story of the Union Pacific may be found in the following: J. P. Davis, *The Union Pacific Railway* (Chicago, 1894); H. K. White, *History of the Union Pacific* (Chicago, 1895); and Nelson Trottman, *History of the Union Pacific* (New York, 1923).

For accounts of various other railroads, consult the following: G. D. Bradley, *The Story of the Santa Fe* (Boston, 1920); Stewart Daggett, *Chapters on the History of the Southern Pacific* (New York, 1922); I. W. Cary, *The Organization and History of the Chicago, Milwaukee and St. Paul* (Milwaukee, 1893); E. V. Smalley, *History of the Northern Pacific Railroad* (New York, 1883); C. H. Grinling, *The History of the Great Northern Railway, 1845–1895* (London, 1898); H. A. Innis, *A History of the Cana-*

dian Pacific Railway (London, 1923); R. C. Overton, *Burlington West, A Colonization History of the Burlington Railroad* (Cambridge, 1941).

Among biographies of special interest for railroad history, the following may be listed: E. P. Oberholtzer, *Jay Cooke, Financier of the Civil War* (2 vols., Philadelphia, 1907); J. G. Pyle, *The Life of James J. Hill* (2 vols., New York, 1917); Henry Villard, *Memoirs of Henry Villard* (2 vols., New York, 1904); J. B. Hedges, *Henry Villard and the Railways of the Northwest* (New Haven, Conn., 1930); *Oliver Ames, a Memoir* (Cambridge, Mass., 1887); G. T. Clark, *Leland Stanford* (Palo Alto, Calif., 1931); Oscar Lewis, *The Big Four: The Story of Huntington, Stanford, Hopkins, and Crocker, and the Building of the Central Pacific* (New York, 1938); J. R. Perkins, *Trails, Rails and War; The Life of General G. M. Dodge* (Indianapolis, 1929); George Kennan, *E. H. Harriman, a Biography* (2 vols., Boston, 1922); J. A. Fisher, *A Builder of the West; The Life of General William Jackson Palmer* (Caldwell, Idaho, 1939).

3 1

THE DAKOTAS AND WYOMING

Beginnings in the Dakota Country

Early French and American explorations and fur trade in the country of the Dakotas have received some consideration in preceding chapters. Regular trading posts had been established by the Northwest Fur Company on the Red River of the North before 1800, and a profitable fur trade was carried on there. Then in 1812 some of Lord Selkirk's Scotch colonists—previously mentioned in Chapter 21—began the first settlement in the Dakotas. These beginnings were at Pembina on the Red River, in the extreme northeast corner of present North Dakota. Here the colonists built log cabins and surrounded them with a stockade as a defense against Indians. Other settlers came to the region in succeeding years, but conflicts with the fur trading companies and numerous difficulties discouraged many and caused them to leave the colony. Others remained and sustained themselves by farming and by trade with the Indians.

The international boundary was not agreed upon in this region until 1818, when the line was fixed on the forty-ninth parallel. But not until the boundary was definitely surveyed by Major Stephen H. Long in 1823 was it known that the Pembina settlement was in United States territory. At that time the village contained about 350 inhabitants. The settlement grew slowly. When Major Samuel Woods visited it in 1849, coming over from Fort Snelling, Minnesota, to warn away British traders and to select a site for a military post, he found more than 1,000 people living in the Red River Valley south of the Canadian line. Farming was increasing, but fur trading was still the chief industry. The pelts were sent down the Red River to Winnipeg or were carried in two-wheeled carts to St. Paul, Minnesota, and thence sent down the Mississippi. In the late 1850's, steamboat transportation was established on the Red River. But progress was meager and development slow in the valley until the coming of the railroad.

The Missouri River, along its course through the Dakota country, had been the scene of much fur trading activity from the last quarter of the eighteenth century. A number of trading posts were established, and regular steamboat transportation was provided. In the middle fifties United States military forces came into the region to establish an outpost. White emigrants were thronging the Oregon Trail, and homeseekers were pressing into northwestern Iowa. As they came in contact with various tribes of the great Dakota (Sioux) nation, conflicts developed. The whites demanded that the government establish a military post on the Missouri River in the Dakota country.

Fort Pierre, early fur trading post on the right bank of the Missouri, was purchased by the War Department in 1855. During the summer of this year soldiers were sent up the river to the fort. General W. S. Harney, after defeating the Brulé Sioux near Ash Hollow on the North Platte of western Nebraska in September, 1855, led his troops overland from Fort Laramie to the post. Quarters were established at Fort Pierre and in the vicinity. During the winter the Sioux were contacted; and at a general council early in March, 1856, representatives of nine tribes signed a peace treaty with General Harney. The next year the post was abandoned, the troops being moved down the river to Fort Randall, near the southern boundary of present South Dakota.

Another area of the Dakota country to receive early permanent settlers was the southeast corner of present South Dakota. Development began here in 1857, 45 years after the beginnings at Pembina. Two land-development organizations, the Western Town Company of Dubuque, Iowa, and the Dakota Land Company from St. Paul, Minnesota, were the promoting agents. They began almost simultaneously the establishment of towns near the falls of the Big Sioux River. The Iowa group occupied their town site in June, 1857. Very shortly thereafter the Minnesota promoters arrived at the same point, took up land adjoining, and named their town site Sioux Falls City. Farther up the Sioux River the Minnesotans made town locations at Flandreau and Medary. In July, when Indian troubles developed, the would-be town builders deserted their claims. But late in August representatives of the Western Town Company returned to their location, bringing ample provisions. Each member of the party took up a quarter-section of land. Together they erected a stone house, a store, and a sawmill. On October 15, members of the Dakota Land Company returned. The region, within the bounds of Minnesota Territory, was organized as Big Sioux County, and a set of officers was appointed.

The spring of 1858 brought new settlers, including several women. But hardly had the newcomers arrived before serious Indian hostilities threatened. The pioneers decided to stand their ground. The two town companies joined forces at Sioux Falls and erected a fort of logs and sod. The walls were ten feet high and four feet thick. Wrote one of the defenders on June 17, 1858: "Mrs. Goodwin has made a large flag out of all the old flannel shirts we could find and we now have the stars and stripes proudly waving over Fort Sod. . . . All told, we number thirty-five men for defense, not including the woman, who can shoot as well as any man." The Indians did not attack the fort. Medary was abandoned. As a consequence of the Indian disturbances, the expected immigration to the region, upon which the town promoters had set great hope, did not materialize.

In response to white demands, the Indian Department negotiated with the Yankton Sioux in 1858 a treaty whereby most of southeastern South Dakota was ceded to the United States for $1,600,000, to be paid as annuities during 50 years. The Yanktons accepted a reservation and moved to it in 1859. Following the withdrawal of the Indians, a number of emigrants immediately crossed the Missouri River from Nebraska Territory in July, 1859. They started the towns of Vermillion, Yankton, Elk Point, and Bon Homme. Norwegian farmers settled in the rich bottom lands between the James and Vermillion rivers. During the ensuing year, churches and schools were organized in this district.

When Minnesota was admitted to statehood in May, 1858, the western portion of the former Minnesota Territory, extending to the Missouri River, was left without regular government. There were few inhabitants in the region, but they were politically ambitious. A mass meeting convened at Sioux Falls on September 18, 1858, and issued a call for an election to choose a Territorial legislature for the Dakota region. The procedure was rather typical of that employed in various frontier areas where there was a desire to impress Congress with the importance of a region. Dana R. Bailey, local historian, writes thus of the election:

With the thirty or forty souls who composed the population at that time, it required considerable ingenuity to arrange matters and the elections were conducted in a somewhat peculiar manner. We learn from one of the members that on the morning of the election the whole population organized into parties of three or four, elected each other judges and clerks of election, and then started off with their teams for a pleasure trip, and wherever a rest was taken, which occurred frequently, an election precinct was established and the votes not only of the party, but of their uncles, cousins, relatives and friends were cast, until as a result of the election the total of several hundred votes was rolled up and properly certified to.

A governor and a legislature of "Dakota Territory" were duly elected, and they memorialized Congress for the recognition of their Territory. But the national lawmakers were not sufficiently impressed. A second election was held at Sioux Falls in September, 1859; officers were chosen; and a second memorial was sent to Congress. The settlers in and about Yankton and Vermillion failed to co-operate in this political move at Sioux Falls, but sent their own petition to Washington asking a Territorial government. Again Congress turned a deaf ear. Not easily discouraged, the pioneers made a third effort. A convention assembled at Yankton in December, 1860, and prepared an earnest and lengthy memorial. Congress responded with the Act of March 2, 1861, which created Dakota Territory. On the night the news reached Yankton, says M. K. Armstrong, "hats, hurrahs and town lots 'went up,' to greet the dawning future of the Great Northwest."

DAKOTA TERRITORY

The new Territory was carved from portions of the former Territories of Minnesota and Nebraska. It extended from the forty-third parallel to Canada and from the western boundary of present Minnesota to the Continental Divide. Upon the creation of Idaho Territory in 1863, that part of Dakota Territory west of present North Dakota and South Dakota was made a part of Idaho. In 1864, upon the creation of Montana Territory, most of present Wyoming was attached to Dakota, where it remained until Wyoming was set up as a separate Territory in 1868.

The Territorial government of Dakota, as established in 1861, was headed by Governor William Jayne, friend, neighbor, and the family physician, at Springfield, of President Lincoln. He took up his residence at Yankton in June, an unpretentious log cabin becoming the executive mansion. A census, taken at his order, revealed a population of but 2,402 for the Territory. He called an election for September 16, 1861, to choose a delegate to Congress and a legislature. Several candidates for the delegateship appeared, and two newspapers were started in their interest. "After the election," writes historian Doane Robinson, "the newspapers suspended publication and the federal officers went home for the winter." The Governor returned to Yankton for the convening of the first Territorial legislature in March, 1862. To be present at the session, the delegation from the Red River settlements had come south, making part of their journey to Yankton by dog train. Regarding the governor's message, M. K. Armstrong, correspondent to the *Sioux City Register*, writes on March 25, 1862: "Three thousand copies were ordered printed in the English, French, German and Norwegian languages. No copies will be printed for some days, for want of help, type and paper." It is doubtful whether the foreign-language copies were issued. Laws of the usual variety were enacted.

In 1861 a number of homeseekers moved into southeastern Dakota, settling along the Missouri River and the Big Sioux. The following year others arrived, most of them coming in covered wagons. The crops of 1862 were bountiful, but just as they were being harvested came news of the terrible Sioux massacres on the Minnesota frontier. Many of the Dakota pioneers fled the territory, but others organized themselves as military units, built stockades, and prepared strong defenses. The precautions taken here and the vigorous military measures directed against hostilities in Minnesota saved the Dakota settlers from serious losses. The Indian uprising and the ensuing war, with its numerous campaigns, frightened away settlers and stopped further immigration for several years. In addition to Indian troubles, the pioneers who remained suffered crop losses from droughts and grasshoppers during most of the sixties.

The peace treaties signed at old Fort Sully in October, 1865, brought a cessation of military campaigns, but not a permanent peace. In 1868 the Indians agreed to the Fort Laramie Treaty. The section pertaining to Dakota set up all that area of present South Dakota west of the Missouri River as a great Sioux reserve. However, other land farther east was relinquished by the Indians and thus acquired for white settlement.

New settlers came to southeastern Dakota in 1868. The harvest of that year was good, and prospects began to brighten. Improvement continued through the following year. The Census of 1870 showed a population of 14,181. In 1872 the Dakota Southern Railway was built from Sioux City, Iowa, to Yankton, being aided by the issuance of Yankton County bonds to the amount of $200,000. A colony of Hollanders came to southern Dakota in 1872, settling near the Missouri River. Some German Russians came the next year. Yankton Academy, the first institution of higher learning in Dakota Territory, was organized in July, 1872. By 1874, 13 newspapers, including a German one, were being published in Dakota Territory.

Persistent rumors of the existence of gold in the Black Hills of southwestern Dakota Territory induced the national government in the summer of 1874 to send Lieutenant-Colonel George A. Custer to make a reconnaissance of the region. Scientists, scouts, and practical miners accompanied the soldiers. From French Creek, on August 2, Custer sent out this dispatch: "I have on my table forty or fifty small particles of gold in size averaging a small pin head, and most of it obtained from one pan." Other favorable reports followed, and the news spread rapidly. Prospecting expeditions were being excitedly organized when General Sheridan, on August 27, issued orders for the arrest of all trespassers on the Sioux Reservation.

Sheridan's order disrupted most of the prospecting parties, but the one led by John Gordon of Sioux City got through. It reached the Black Hills in December, and set about building a pine stockade on French Creek. In February following, Gordon and a companion made their way back to Yankton, carrying the yellow fruit of their mining operations. Sight of the dust produced another flare of the gold fever. Parties were formed to push into the new mining country. The one led by Gordon was stopped by United States troops; the outfits were destroyed, and the trespassers were taken across country to Fort Laramie on the North Platte and lodged in jail. The little party left in the stockade on French Creek was rounded up in April and marched off the reservation to Fort Laramie.

Then, in an effort to gauge the authenticity of the reports and to determine the value of the region, the government sent a second expedition to the Black Hills. It was led by Professor W. P. Jenny, of the School of Mines of New York. Accompanied by a large escort of cavalry and infantry, Jenny reached the Black Hills in early June, 1875. The prospectors, he reported, "poured by hundreds into the hills and accompanying me, gave me great assistance in prospecting the country." In August, General Crook assembled the miners at Custer City and asked them to leave the region until the Indian title could be extinguished. Some complied; others hid out in the hills.

In the meantime, the government, hard pressed to hold back its citizens, had asked the Sioux to sell the mineral country. A delegation of Indians was taken to Washington in May, 1875, but this effort and others that followed failed to get a cession of the desired area. Unable to obtain the land by treaty, the government made little pretense of further excluding the whites. Miners now rushed in by the hundreds. Camps were started and important towns founded. By March, about 10,000 men were in the vicinity of Custer City, in the southern part of the Black Hills. Here they set up a civil government on their own initiative. Rich diggings having been found in the northern portion of the Hills, a rush to that area began in 1876. Deadwood was laid out in April, and by September was a fully organized city.

An Indian war developed, as discussed in Chapter 28. In the meantime, Congress passed a law stipulating that no annuities should be paid the hostile bands until after the Black Hills region had been ceded. A commission visited the Sioux and induced them to give up the land; and the agreement, submitted to Congress, was enacted into law on February 28, 1877.

The rush to the Black Hills continued. Wagons freighted with mining tools, baggage, and supplies, creaked along newly opened roads to the new Eldorado. One route led from Cheyenne by way of Fort

Laramie; another came in from Fort Pierre on the Missouri River. Over the latter road the rate for freight was three cents per pound. Stage lines and expresses were established. With the Indian war on, miners and emigrants were harassed and some were killed. At times the settlements in the gulches became armed camps.

A movement for the creation of a new Territory in the Black Hills region had begun as early as August, 1876, and it gained momentum the next year. At the same time Wyoming was eager to annex the rich section. Cheyenne businessmen exerted themselves toward that end. In 1877 they issued *The Hand-Book of Wyoming and Guide to the Black Hills,* which emphasized the common interests of Wyoming and the new mineral country. But Dakota was fully determined to retain the gold area, and she did.

The Black Hills mining activity gave impetus to other lines of development in Dakota. Perhaps even more important than the mining stir was the coming of railroads. The northern part of the Territory was especially affected by the Northern Pacific, which began building westward in 1870. It reached the eastern boundary of Dakota early in 1872 and the Missouri River at Bismarck in the summer of 1873. Then came the great panic and the collapse of the railroad. Building ceased, and the stock of the road fell to but a fraction of its face value. Inasmuch as the railroad had received a large land grant from the government, some of the principal stockholders decided to accept land in exchange for their railroad stock and thus try to salvage something from their losses. This enforced interest in farming soon brought results. It was discovered that the Red River Valley was an excellent wheat country. Good yields were obtained, and expansive farms were developed. Homesteaders and other settlers moved farther out onto the prairie, and the country filled up rapidly. Within a few years the railroad was able to realize several million dollars from the sale of its land. And the wheat crop provided freight for the road. In 1879 the Northern Pacific was reorganized and began to build westward from Bismarck. It reached the Pacific in 1883.

In a similar fashion the Great Northern did much to develop the northern part of Dakota. James J. Hill, dynamo of the enterprise, began his railroad career in 1879 by buying the poor St. Paul and Pacific road. He built slowly at first, encouraging farmers to settle beside the railroad. Steadily he pushed westward across Dakota and Montana, reaching Butte in 1888 and the Pacific Coast in 1893. Many branch lines, or "feeders," were built north and south of the main line. Hill aided farmers in getting started, sending out thousands of blooded horses, cattle, and hogs. In the meantime other railroads were building into eastern and central Dakota Territory. Wheat was king, and agriculture was flourishing. Towns sprang up from the prairie sod.

The boom reached its climax in 1885, and thereupon a long reactionary period set in. The Territory had witnessed a remarkable population growth. The census count for Dakota Territory was but 14,181 in 1870; it had increased to 135,177 by 1880. The same area contained 539,583 inhabitants in 1890, and of this number 348,600 were in South Dakota and 190,883 were in North Dakota.

The rapid settlement of the northern part of Dakota Territory brought dissatisfaction with the location of the capital at Yankton. In 1883 the legislature appointed a commission to select a more appropriate location. Bismarck was chosen, and here the capital remained until the Territory was divided and formed into two states in 1889.

SETTLEMENT OF WYOMING

Although the territory of present Wyoming was visited by fur trappers at an early day and was traversed by thousands of pioneer emigrants bound for the Pacific Coast and Utah, it was late in receiving permanent settlers. Two trading posts—Fort Laramie and Fort Bridger—established by mountain traders, were subsequently purchased by the government. As military forts they persisted well into the settlement period and served as protectors of pioneer citizens. They were thus the earliest centers of continuing occupancy in the region.

In 1853 the Mormons started a colony in the Green River Valley of present southwestern Wyoming, founding Fort Supply some 10 miles south of Fort Bridger. They purchased Fort Bridger two years later. These Mormons engaged in farming and stock raising. Upon the approach of Johnston's army, on its march to Utah in 1857, the settlers deserted the region and set fire to their holdings. The army wintered here and established Camp Scott in the vicinity. In 1858, Fort Bridger was re-established as a military post, and was garrisoned by soldiers until its abandonment in 1890.

The Pike's Peak gold rush of 1859 and the mineral discoveries in Idaho and Montana during the early 1860's led prospectors to search the intervening Wyoming country. But no important finds were made there prior to 1867. In the summer of that year gold was found near South Pass on sources of the Sweetwater branch of the North Platte. Several hundred persons flocked to the diggings, and South Pass City was started. The Indians objected to the intrusion, and killed some of the prospectors. But despite the danger, additional miners came in and opened new camps. C. G. Coutant, Wyoming historian, writes [1]:

During the year 1869 the placers around Miners Delight and Atlantic produced a large amount of gold. The gravel in Meadow gulch in the next

[1] Coutant, C. G., *The History of Wyoming,* Laramie, Chaplin, Spafford and Mathison, 1899, 663.

two or three years yielded $100,000, Yankee gulch $50,000, Spring gulch $1,000,000 [?], Poor Man's gulch $30,000, Promise gulch $30,000, Smith's gulch, $20,000, Atlantic gulch $15,000, Beaver creek $10,000.

But as a whole, the district was disappointing, the ore being uneven and "pockety." In a few years most of the miners gave up hope and forsook the district.

The coming of the Union Pacific was to bring the first considerable population and start the settlement era in Wyoming. In July, 1867, the land agent of the railroad company came to the site of Cheyenne, set up a crude structure, and began selling town lots. A city government for the future capital was formed the next month. In September a mass meeting was held for the purpose of organizing a county. An election was set for October 8, 1867. On that day a delegate to Congress, a representative to the Dakota legislature, and a set of county officers were chosen. But the Dakota legislature did not recognize the unauthorized action. It created its own county government for the Cheyenne region, and appointed a set of officers. Two other counties were created by the Dakota legislature for the Wyoming country.

In the meantime Cheyenne was having a hectic life. Like newborn mining camps throughout the West, it had at first almost no law. During that winter of 1867–1868, when it was the end of the track for the Union Pacific, it contained the scum that drifted with the railroad. Some 6,000 people wintered in Cheyenne, and many of them did not love law and order. Robberies and assaults were of nightly occurrence, and the city officials were powerless. When the patience of the better element was exhausted, a vigilance committee was organized. The committee's first act, on January 11, 1868, was the capture of three men, whom they bound together, and to whom they attached a large canvas carrying this legend:

$900 stole; $500 returned; thieves, F. St. Clair, W. Grier, E. D. Brownville. City authorities please not interfere until 10 o'clock A. M. Next case goes up a tree. Beware of vigilance committee.

During the next six months, a dozen men were hanged or shot by the vigilantes; thereafter civil law was more operative in Cheyenne. As the end of track moved westward, it bore with it the lawless element to plague Laramie City, Green River, and other towns in turn. Each of these resorted to stern measures and soon established order.

Most of present Wyoming, as mentioned above, had been added to Dakota Territory in 1864. With the approach of the railroad, the creation of a new Territory was advocated. As early as 1865 such a measure was introduced in Congress, but was buried in a committee. The delegate chosen at the Cheyenne election of October 8, 1867, was

refused a seat in Congress. Presently he was joined by other representatives of Wyoming citizenry, mostly self-appointed, who lobbied in
Washington. One of these, Dr. Hiram Latham, presented a circular
in which he painted a glowing picture of the resources and future of
the region. The final outcome was the passage of a bill on July 25,
1868, which created Wyoming Territory, giving it the boundaries which
the state has today. President Johnson immediately nominated officials for the new Territory; but in view of the Reconstruction conflict
between the executive and legislative branches of the government, the
Senate would not confirm the nominations. Therefore, officers were
not appointed until in April, 1869, after President Grant had come to
the White House. John A. Campbell became the first governor. Perhaps the most famous enactment of the first legislature was the measure giving women the right to vote and to hold office. Wyoming was
first among the states in granting woman suffrage.

The railroad, with its shops and crews of workmen, was the principal
stabilizing force in early Wyoming, if, indeed, it were not the primary
excuse for the existence of the Territory. When the natural resources
of the region were gradually utilized, an increase in population resulted.
The first industry to be developed was the production of livestock.
Limited sections of the Wyoming range were tested in the late 1860's,
with encouraging results. The following decade saw the beginning of
extensive cattle ranches. Some of the early ranchers sold their holdings to Eastern or foreign capitalists; others pooled their resources and
formed companies. The big operator, after acquiring existing titles
and claims to a given section, would publish in a Cheyenne newspaper
his brand or brands and give a public announcement such as the following: "The Blank Cattle Company; home ranch on Little Beaver.
Our range extends from Wild Horse Creek north to Sheep Buttes, east
to Rocky Ridge and south to Pilot Knob." Claim to the described
area of the public domain was thus made, and all other cattlemen were
warned against trespassing. This was the unwritten law of the range,
but there was no legal title and "nesters" soon made trouble.

In the region there developed what Professor Louis Pelzer has called
"A Cattleman's Commonwealth." It was controlled by the Wyoming
Stock Growers' Association; and Cheyenne was its administrative and
social capital. This association, begun in 1873, made its rules regarding round-ups, disposal of mavericks, employment of detectives, and
other matters affecting the industry. It exerted great power in the
Territorial legislature. A Wyoming statute of 1884 specially recognized the "by-laws and rules" of the Stock Growers' Association, and
legally placed control of round-ups in that organization's hands. In
1885 the Association had 400 members, who owned 2,000,000 cattle.
Its detective service was maintained at a cost of $26,000 in 1886, and

in that year 2,276 mavericks were sold, netting the Association $25,605. The terrible winter of 1886–1887, with its blizzards and deep snow, wrought havoc on the open range. Thousands of cattle froze or starved. One company gathered, in the spring, but 100 steers out of a herd of 5,500. Some herds were lost completely. The prosperous and glamorous days of the range now came to a close. As the industry struggled to its feet after the disaster, new methods were evolved, with hay ranches, sheds, and fenced pasture-lands as parts of the new system.

The cattleman's domain already was being invaded by the home-steader. In the eighties, real progress was made in farming. Several large land-improvement companies were formed, and irrigation projects were developed in practically all of the river valleys. The Census of 1880 had listed but 2,000 acres of improved land in Wyoming. By 1889 some 5,000 miles of canals had been dug and 2,000,000 acres of land were under cultivation. Good crops of wheat, oats, barley, pota-toes, and other farm products were being produced. Towns based on irrigated agriculture were springing up in various parts of the Terri-tory. Dry-farming development was to follow later. But the popula-tion was still sparse. The count of 9,118 in 1870 became only 20,789 in 1880, and increased to 62,555 by 1890.

STATEHOOD FOR NORTHWEST TERRITORIES

Wyoming was carried to statehood largely on the wings of her more populous sisters. For some years northwestern Territories had been clamoring for statehood. But at no time from 1876 until 1889 had Congress been under the control of one party, except between 1881 and 1883. During that biennium, Dakota framed a constitution and asked for statehood, but the move was blocked, partly because Yank-ton County had repudiated her railroad bonds. During the next six years, Democratic opposition prevented admission. Growth of the northwest Territories during the eighties was such as would justify statehood. The five Territories—Washington, Idaho, Montana, Da-kota, and Wyoming—had more than trebled in population during the decade, rising from 302,851 in 1880 to 1,168,072 in 1890. Nearly 9,000 miles of railroad were constructed within their boundaries during the 10-year interval.

The Republican victory at the polls in the fall of 1888 brightened the prospects for these Territories. With their marked leanings toward the Republican Party, they would confidently look to it for favorable action. Seeing the handwriting on the wall, the Democrats introduced an omnibus bill, linking Democratic New Mexico with the Republican Territories of the Northwest. But the triumphant Republicans were

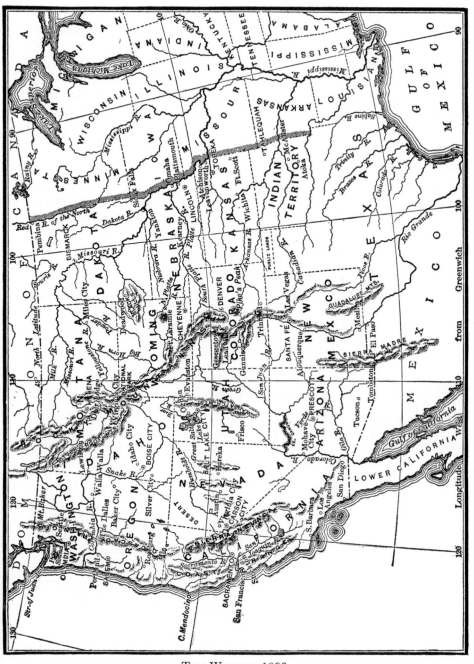

THE WEST IN 1890

(FROM W. M. THAYER, *Marvels of the New West*, PAGE 221.)

541

now in a position where they need make no concession. So they struck New Mexico from the list. They divided Dakota, taking cognizance of the divergent interests of the northern and southern sections. North Dakota, South Dakota, Washington, and Montana were authorized in February, 1889, to draft constitutions, and in the following November they were admitted to statehood. Idaho and Wyoming, having failed to secure enabling acts along with their sisters, drafted constitutions on their own volition. The national government accepted their efforts and admitted them to full fellowship in the summer of 1890.

BIBLIOGRAPHY

For general accounts of the Dakota country, see: M. K. Armstrong, *The Early Empire Builders of the Great West* (St. Paul, 1901); Edna L. Waldo, *Dakota: an Informal Study of Territorial Days* (Caldwell, Idaho, 1936); George W. Kingsbury and George M. Smith, *History of Dakota and of South Dakota* (5 vols., Chicago, 1915); Dana R. Bailey, *History of Minnehaha County, South Dakota* (Sioux Falls, 1899).

Upon South Dakota and its Black Hills area, consult: Doane Robinson, *History of South Dakota* (2 vols., n. p., 1904); C. C. O'Harra, *Handbook of the Black Hills* (Rapid City, 1924); Newton Jenney, *et al.*, *Geology of the Black Hills of Dakota* (Washington, 1880); John S. McClintock, *Pioneer Days in the Black Hills* (New York, 1939); Annie D. Tallent, *The Black Hills; or the Last Hunting Ground of the Dakotahs* (St. Louis, 1899); Peter Rosen, *Pa-Ha-Sa-Pah, or the Black Hills of South Dakota, A Complete History* (St. Louis, 1895); R. I. Dodge, *The Black Hills . . .* (New York, 1876); Jesse Brown and A. M. Willard, *The Black Hills Trails: a History of the Struggles of the Pioneers in the Winning of the Black Hills* (Rapid City, 1924).

The following references contain data on North Dakota: Lewis F. Crawford, *History of North Dakota* (New York, 1931); H. C. Fish and R. M. Black, *A Brief History of North Dakota* (Chicago, 1925); W. B. Hennessey, *History of North Dakota* (Bismarck, 1910); W. M. Wemett, *The Story of the Flickertail State* (Valley City, 1923); H. V. Arnold, *History of Old Pembina* (Larimore, 1917); ——, *Forty Years in North Dakota* (Larimore, 1921); ——, *Early History of Ransom County* (Larimore, 1918); R. M. Black, *A History of Dickey County* (Ellendale, 1930).

For accounts of Wyoming history, refer to the following: C. G. Coutant, *The History of Wyoming from the Earliest Known Discoveries* (Laramie, 1899); I. S. Bartlett, *History of Wyoming* (Chicago, 1918); R. E. Strahorn, *The Hand-book of Wyoming and Guide to the Black Hills and Big Horn Regions* (Cheyenne, 1877); H. H. Bancroft, *History of Nevada, Colorado and Wyoming, 1540–1888* (San Francisco, 1890); C. A. Guernsey, *Wyoming Cowboy Days* (New York, 1936); A. J. Mokler, *History of Natrona County, Wyoming* (Chicago, 1923); E. A. Stone, *Uinta County, its Place in History* (n. p., n. d.); Velma Linford, *Wyoming, Frontier State* (Denver, 1947).

See also the *South Dakota Historical Collections* (since 1902); the *South Dakota Historical Review* (since 1935); the *Collections of the State Historical Society of North Dakota* (since 1906); the *North Dakota Historical Quarterly* (since 1926); *Collections of the Wyoming Historical Society* (1897); and *The Annals of Wyoming* (since 1924).

32

RANGE CATTLE AND SHEEP INDUSTRIES

The "Wild Cattle"

Early Spanish *conquistadores* and colonists found bison, or "wild cattle," as they called them, in California and as far south as the Gulf plains; French trappers encountered them along the Saskatchewan in Canada; and during the eighteenth century, Anglo-Americans killed them far east of the Mississippi. But in 1865, their range was confined to the Great Plains; and there, while on their spring and fall migrations, they moved in two great herds—a northern herd and a southern one. The southern herd generally ranged from Kansas to western Texas; the northern herd, from Nebraska to the region well into Canada. The large concourse of gold-seekers passing over the Platte Trail had probably caused the division. In 1849, while journeying over this route, Captain Howard Stansbury noticed this, and wrote that hunters had formerly encountered herds along the Platte Trail, but that on this trip he had seen few. Hunters engaged in supplying his command with meat had traveled considerable distances both north and south of the trail before even strays were found.

Although Josiah Gregg, Captain Randolph B. Marcy, and other plains visitors prior to the Civil War had noticed that the buffalo herds were being reduced, the red and white hunters of the post-war period found millions in their old haunts. Available contemporary records would put the total number of buffaloes in the two herds at this time at about 15,000,000. Three years prior to Stansbury's expedition along the Platte, Colonel Alexander Doniphan struck the southern herd while marching over the Santa Fe Trail. His chief hunter, Thomas Forsythe, estimated the buffaloes he could see from the crest of Pawnee Rock at 300,000, and calculations of others with him ranged from 200,000 to 800,000. General P. H. Sheridan evidently encountered a part of the

543

same herd in 1868 while he was advancing from Fort Dodge to the Wichita Mountains, and he threw out flankers on either side of his marching column in order to protect his men and supply train.

During the plains Indian wars, in 1865–1876, the buffalo had been the warrior's commissary—his clothing, his food, and his lodge covering—and until the great herds were materially diminished, the nomadic tribes rejected reservations. Furthermore, not until then could the rancher claim the grassy plains for his domain.

Both before and after the Civil War, buffalo hunting was a rare sport, shared not only by Americans, but also by Europeans. In 1872 Sheridan entertained the Grand Duke Alexis of Russia in a hunt south of Fort McPherson, Nebraska; and a short time later an English peer was the guest of General John Pope. During the early seventies buffalo hunting was so popular that the Santa Fe, Kansas Pacific, and other railroads crossing the plains conducted hunting excursions at low rates. On these, passengers were given the privilege of shooting their game from car windows, and of buying drinks and food on the cars.

The plains Indians were greatly angered because of this wanton slaughter. At the Medicine Lodge council of 1867 Satanta bitterly assailed the government commissioners because they had done nothing to stop it; later, other chiefs confessed that it was only when the great herds had disappeared that they had accepted reservations and the white man's subsistence.

But when viewed in the large, the sportsmen were not responsible for the buffalo's disappearance. During the early seventies American and English tanneries discovered that buffalo leather could be used in the manufacture of harness, belting, shoes, and other things, and large orders were placed with Great Plains hunters. Then in parties of sixes and sevens, armed with large-caliber, long-range rifles, the commercial hunters started their work of destruction. By 1877 a Texas Congressman said that more than 500 hunters had pitched their camps on the prairies between the Red and Brazos rivers. In consequence, the mighty thunder of stampeding bison, fleeing before their pursuers; the booming of the heavy guns; the bellow of stricken animals; and the rumble of capacious wagons, piled high with hides, on their way to market—all proclaimed the bison's death knell.

Buffalo hides sold from $1 to more than $3 each, and it was not uncommon for a party of six men to kill and skin 50 or more in one day. The business was quite profitable. On January 4, 1877, the F. E. Conrad general merchandise store at Fort Griffin, Texas, announced its sales for the day at $4,000, of which $2,500 had been in guns and ammunition to hunters; and there were numerous other supply stores, from the Brazos to the Arkansas, similarly engaged. In two years,

1872–1874, 1,378,359 hides, 6,751,200 pounds of meat, and 32,380,650 pounds of bones were shipped to Eastern markets over the Santa Fe, the Union Pacific, and the Kansas Pacific railroads. In 1873 alone, 754,529 hides were sent eastward over the Santa Fe.

A Kansas hunter, John R. Cook, later wrote that his party made hay while the sun shone, "for we then had stacked up and drying 2,000 hides; 892 of them I had skinned and was so credited." Others were equally successful, and by 1880 the last of the southern herd was gone. General Nelson A. Miles, who witnessed a part of the destruction, later estimated that 4,373,730 bison were killed during the early seventies, while others placed the number as high as 5,500,000. From conservative estimates, it may be safely said that from 1870 to 1885 more than 10,000,000 bison were killed on the northern and southern plains. But the passing of the buffalo had beneficial results. General Sheridan had told the Texas legislature that it would herald the era of "speckled cattle," and his prophecy had come true. The millions of acres of the grassy buffalo range presently became the center of the more important range cattle industry.

THE RANGE CATTLE INDUSTRY

During the summer and fall of 1865 thousands of soldiers discharged from the armies of Lee, Johnston, and Smith arrived at their Texas homes, discouraged and disconsolate. Their cause was defeated, and they faced an uncertain future. Specie had disappeared from circulation; homes, farms, and business properties were in sad need of repair; and opportunities for employment were rare. Yet an occasional optimist found cause for hope. Food was in plenty; the spinning-wheel, the loom, and a bountiful supply of cotton, wool, and leather only needed industrious hands to provide clothing and shoes; and trade and industry would come in due time. Moreover, potential wealth could be seen in the Civil War accumulation of cotton, in the development of the public domain, and in the marketing of the tens of thousands of wild cattle that grazed the grassy plains.

Fat steers, worth only $6 or $7 in Texas, commanded as high as $40 or $50 in northern markets; and even cattle of the Texas breed brought an attractive price. Texans thought this fortunate, for any enterprising stockman could round up a herd, drive it northward, and find at the end of the trail the rainbow's pot of gold! But certain expenditures had to be made. It was not easy to find the means to finance a drive—to pay wages and to buy supplies, horses, and saddles. Furthermore, trail driving had its hazards. Thieves and wild Indians waited beside the trail to trap and rob unwary drovers; storms swept the prairies during the spring driving season, filling every stream and gully with flood waters; and frequent stampedes made uncertain the life of the night rider.

An unusual demand for beef at home and abroad gave the Texas cowman his opportunity, for only under such circumstances could he find a considerable market for his wild cattle. In 1865 the Chicago Union Stockyards was established, and this city became the center of the western meat-packing industry. Before the war wild Texas cattle had been slaughtered in great numbers for their hides only. But now their tough, strongly flavored flesh could also be sold to the slaughter houses.

When control of Texas was relinquished by the Spaniards to the Mexicans, and in turn by the Mexicans to the Anglo-Americans, there was left behind a scrawny, lean, long-horned type of cattle raised by the Moors for centuries past on the Andalusian Plains. These soon became acclimated to Texas, increased amazingly fast, and later inbred with those of other European stock brought in by Anglo-Americans. But in 1836 the Spanish-Mexican breed grazed about four-fifths of the settled but unplowed border country. The Federal Census of 1880 lists all Texas range cattle in four general groups: (1) the wild cattle of western Texas and New Mexico, brown in color with a light stripe down the back, with long, slim, blue horns and large and mealy noses; (2) the Texan-Mexican, varied in color, with patches of white, horns long and thin with a half-twist back, heads coarse and thin, bodies gaunt, and narrow hips; (3) "Spanish" cattle, with small, short horns, not so wild, and in colors black, white, brindle, brown, buckskin, and calico; and (4) the "curly-haired Texans," or "Chino," of larger build, well-formed, round, legs long, body heavy, and color a brownish buffalo. But whether the one type or the other, the average wild cow was not desirable for beef. Yet when fattened in stockyards or in northern pastures and cornfields, it was good enough to command a fair price.

Even before the Civil War, the Texas cattlemen had been enterprising. Shortly after the Texas revolution they drove many herds to Galveston, to New Orleans, and to other Gulf ports, from which they shipped to eastern and northern markets. By 1846 Edward Piper had driven a herd to Ohio; and soon after the discovery of gold and silver in California and Arizona, other Texans drove many thousands westward over the southern trail (San Antonio-El Paso-Tucson). But these pre-war drives by no means assumed the importance of those of the post-war period, when upward of 6,000,000 cattle moved over the northern trails.

The post-war Texas range cattle industry may be divided into two broad eras. The first, from about 1865 to 1885, was the period of the unfenced range when border ranchers "squatted" on the public domain; of wild, unbranded cattle; of lawlessness when outlaws and adventurers infested the border; and of the long drives. The second period, after 1885, was marked by the purchase and fencing of large ranch properties; of the coming of railways, providing better shipping facilities and obviating the necessary of the long drives; and of the introduction of improved breeds of cattle. This last period also was accompanied by less lawlessness. The organization of border counties provided the needed complement of law courts and peace officers, with the consequence that outlaws were convicted and imprisoned or were driven elsewhere. The Rangers, too, shared in this constructive service. In one year the Adjutant General of Texas published a list of more than 5,000 men wanted on criminal charges, many of whom were later captured.

During the first period, the vast Texas plains (carpeted with grama, mesquite, buffalo, and blue-stem grasses) comprised an area estimated by an 1870 writer at 152,000,000 acres. This immense region was watered by the Red, Trinity, Brazos, Leon, Colorado, San Antonio, Guadalupe, and Nueces rivers, and their tributaries. Here was the grazing ground of one-eighth of all the cattle of the United States, while the number of people residing in Texas was but one-eighteenth of our entire population. The extraordinary aspect of this Texas industry may be seen in comparative census figures from other states. New York, with a population of 4,000,000 in 1870, had 748,000 beef and stock cattle; Pennsylvania, with a population of 3,000,000, had 721,000 cattle of all kinds; Ohio, with about the same population, 749,000 cattle; while Texas, with only 500,000 people, had 3,000,000 beef cattle, 800,000 milch cows, and branded annually 750,000 calves.

The long trails to market and feeding grounds were broad and well marked. The East and West Shawnee trails followed the San Antonio-Fort Worth line to the Red River, thence through Indian Territory to Kansas City and Junction City, Kansas; the Chisholm Trail entered Indian Territory at Red River Crossing, and from thence ran northward to Abilene, Kansas, slightly east of the present Comanche-Chickasha line; and the Great Western Trail crossed the Red River at Doan's Store, through western Oklahoma via Camp Supply, thence on to Dodge City, at the southern terminus of the Santa Fe Railroad, where stock pens and shipping facilities were available, or still northward to Ogallala, Nebraska. The gradual westward movement of the cattle-shipping points (Abilene [1867–1871], Dodge City [1872 to about 1885], and so forth) was caused by the rapid farmer-occupation of the Kansas border. Farmers (Jayhawkers) met the trail herds at the Kansas border and forced the cowmen to turn back or to range their cattle on Indian lands. The farmers objected to the driving of cattle across their property and to the mysterious Texas fever brought by the cattle, which had such deadly effect on their own stock. Consequently, the cowmen had to find a new trail west of the occupied zone. Later, however, the cause of the fever was found to be a tick, and through "dipping" the cattle, the danger of transmitting fever to northern cattle was eliminated.

If the starting point was Fort Concho, or other places in midwestern Texas, the drive was generally over the Goodnight-Loving Trail from the Concho to the Pecos, a distance of more than 100 miles, and thence northward to the Rio Grande Valley and on to the grazing grounds of Colorado and Wyoming; or from New Mexico westward to Arizona and California.

To war-weary, poverty-ridden ex-soldiers, the opportunity for wealth and adventure in Texas was a stimulating elixir. From the press, from emigrant guidebooks, and from state and government publications came optimistic reports. Texas was a land where a poor man could acquire great wealth if he possessed initiative and enterprise! And land salesmen cited living examples of this—Colonel Richard King, John Hittson, John Chisum, and others.

"Before the Civil War," wrote a promoter, "King came to Texas possessing only a horse, a saddle, and ten dollars in cash. Now it is a hundred miles from his front door to his yard gate!" This enthusiastic statement was not far wrong. In 1870 the King ranch, on the Santa Gertrudes River in southern Texas, contained 84,132 acres and was stocked with 65,000 cattle, 20,000 horses, 7,000 sheep, and 8,000 goats. To manage this extensive property, King employed 300 Mexicans, for whom he furnished 1,000 saddle horses. Moreover, his enterprise was profitable, for he sold annually 10,000 beeves and branded 12,000 calves. Then, not far distant was the Robideaux ranch, owned by Mifflin Kennedy. It was on a peninsula reaching out into the Gulf, between the Rio Grande and the Nueces River, surrounded on three sides by water and guarded on the land side by a plank fence. Within was a vast range of 142,840 acres, grazed by 30,000 cattle. Along the plank fence, every three miles, were a cowboy shack and stock stables and pens.

Farther north were other ranches of large size owned by men who had worked their way up from poverty; and these, too, the emigrant guidebooks mentioned. On the Brazos River, in Palo Pinto County, was John Hittson's ranch, supporting 50,000 cattle. In 1850 Hittson was working as a day laborer in Rust County, Tennessee, clearing land to plant corn and wheat. "He knew," said a contemporary, "that it would take three score and ten years of a natural life to clear away the trees and wear out the stumps, and not fancying the doom of hard labor for life, he sold his land and with sixty Texan cows and nine brood mares turned his face toward the setting sun and the grass regions of the Brazos." In the new land of promise he had made a fortune—and all within less than 20 years. The Denver *Rocky Mountain News* (November 23, 1870) also noticed this success, and added that recently Hittson had acquired an extensive ranch on the South Platte upon which he was wintering 5,000 cattle, and to which, during the following season, he would drive 10,000 fat beeves to hold for market   West of Hittson's Texas ranch was another on the Concho River, equally extensive, upon which John Chisum ranged 30,000 head of cattle. But later he moved his stock to New Mexico below Ft. Sumner, where he controlled a property of 150 miles along the Pecos River. More than one Texas guidebook mentioned among the select ranches the O'Connor property on the San Antonio River, 20 miles below Goliad. In 1862 O'Connor owned 40,000 cattle, branded annually 11,-772 calves, and received $75,000 to $80,000 from the sale of fat steers.

Thus, the Texas prairies were a new land of promise. "Jack, Young, Throckmorton, Stephens, Callahan, Coleman, Brown, Tarrant, Erath, Comanche, Palo Pinto, Hill and Johnson counties are all great stock countries," said a booster. Yet these counties were but the eastern shore-line of a vast inland sea of grass, upon which many a range captain was to launch his flimsy bark. Along the border, Charles Rivers, James Brown, C. J. Johnson, S. E. Jackson, Robert Sloan, Samuel Vaughn, Martin Childress, and others ranched on a small scale, controlling properties of 20,000 acres or more and grazing from 4,000 to 15,000 cattle. It was also largely from these counties that in 1877 C. L. Carter, J. C. Loving, E. B. Harreld, and other cattlemen came to Graham to organize the Northwestern Texas Stock-Raisers Association (later the Southwestern Stock-Raisers Association) to enforce herd inspections, to drive out brand-burners, and to enact regulations for the spring round-up.

Texas ranch propaganda was partly based on fact. The rise to eminence of King, Kennedy, Hittson, and Chisum was convincing proof of what could be done earlier; but it was no future guarantee of the success of many other ranch investors. Like all "get-rich-quick" movements, a few encountered great success and many failed. The industry was soon swamped by would-be stockmen, by moderately well-to-do farmers who sold their property and gambled recklessly on large acreages, by foreign investors, and by adventurers. The small home-seekers also presently appeared to take advantage of Texas' liberal land law, thus restricting the free grass range. Also, by 1875 barb wire was introduced, and a movement of land-fencing began. Independent ranchers battled against great odds—cattle thieves; grasping newcomers who bought up and fenced in the once free range; the appearance of improved breeds of cattle on corporation-controlled ranches in Colorado, New Mexico, Wyoming, and other western states; a glutted market; and the droughts and hard times of the mid-eighties.

During the wild seventies and eighties the free-range industry was at its height. From 1866 to 1885 approximately 6,000,000 cattle were driven over the northern and western trails to Sedalia, Abilene, Dodge City, Wichita, Ellsworth, Denver, Tucson, and elsewhere.

JOSEPH NIMMO'S ESTIMATE OF ANNUAL DRIVES OF TEXAS CATTLE
(*Range and Ranch Cattle Traffic*, p. 28)

1866	260,000	1876	321,998
1867	35,000	1877	201,159
1868	75,000	1878	265,646
1869	350,000	1879	257,927
1870	300,000	1880	394,784
1871	600,000	1881	250,000
1872	350,000	1882	250,000
1873	405,000	1883	267,000
1874	166,000	1884	300,000
1875	151,618		

An increasing demand for beef during the seventies (caused by a considerable improvement in transportation and cold-storage facilities) and overcrowding of the southern plains brought about the rapid spread of the cattle industry. Surplus cattle were disposed of by packing and by shipping in refrigerated steamers to the Gulf states, to the Atlantic seaboard, and even to Europe. Presently cattle driven over the Goodnight-Loving Trail into New Mexico were often pointed on northward to the Arkansas River, crossing at Bent's old fort, and thence, along the eastern base of the mountains, through Colorado to the Union Pacific Railroad, and on to the great valleys and markets of Wyoming, Utah, Montana, Nevada, and the Pacific states. Of the 100,000 cattle driven over this route in 1870, Montana received 20,000, Wyoming 8,000, Idaho 11,000, Nevada 7,000, Utah 8,000, and California 10,000—a total of 64,000. The others were sold in New Mexico and Colorado. And in the same year more than 200,000 steers were driven over the Chisholm Trail to Abilene, Kansas. Railroads now enjoyed a lively business. Shipments by rail reached 60,000 head during September, or 3,333 carloads (111 carloads per day). These cattle were sent primarily to the cornfields of Iowa, Missouri, and Illinois to be fattened for market.

By 1880 Texas range-fed beef threatened to take completely the English market, and an English parliamentary committee sought to ascertain the reason why. It found that a free range and little expense in ranching enabled the plains cowman to undersell the English stock-raiser and to make extraordinary profits. This caused Scottish investors to seek the purchase of Great Plains ranches, and Edinburgh became an important investment center. In 1882 the Wyoming Stock-Raisers Association's *By-Laws and Reports* estimated that English and Scottish investments in the West, and largely in Wyoming and Texas, amounted to £6,000,000 (approximately $30,000,000). And on March 27, 1884, Representative N. W. Nutting of New York reported to Congress that foreign interests controlled more than 20,000,000 acres of Great Plains range lands and threatened to dominate the industry.

Although Nutting was unduly alarmed, foreign interests were great. The Scottish American Mortgage Company controlled extensive properties in Colorado, New Mexico, and Texas with its Prairie Cattle Company ranches. Its properties were in three divisions. The first, called the Arkansas, extended from the Arkansas River in Colorado on the north to the Colorado-New Mexico line on the south, comprising 3,500 square miles or 2,240,000 acres. The second, called the Cimarron, was in northern New Mexico, extending 84 miles from the Colorado line to the southern line of Mora County, an area of 4,032 square miles, or 2,580,480 acres. The southern division was on the Canadian River in the Texas Panhandle, in Potter and Oldham counties, 400 square miles or 256,000 acres. On these three properties ranged approximately 140,000 cattle. Still later, it extended its operations to South Dakota and Montana. Other English and Scottish investments were in the Espuela (Spur) Land and Cattle Company of western Texas, the Wyoming Ranches Limited, The Western Land and Cattle Company, with interests in California, Montana, and Wyoming, and the Swan Land and Cattle Company, with ranch lands in Wyoming.

Titled Europeans also sought adventure and wealth in the West. The Marquis de Mores, a French nobleman, built the town of Medora on the Union Pacific Railroad in western Dakota, and controlled large ranch properties near by. Farther south, in Colorado, a German, Baron von Richthofen, also engaged in ranching; and in Estes Park he had as his neighbor an English peer, the Earl of Dunraven. Although not of the English peerage, John George Adair owned a large estate at Rathdair, Ireland. In 1875 he established a brokerage business at Denver, and two years later he formed a partnership with Colonel Charles Goodnight in the JA Ranch of the Palo Duro Canyon of western Texas.

But important as were the foreign investments in western ranch properties, they did not equal those made by citizens of the United States. Indeed, the largest of all southern plains ranches was the XIT,

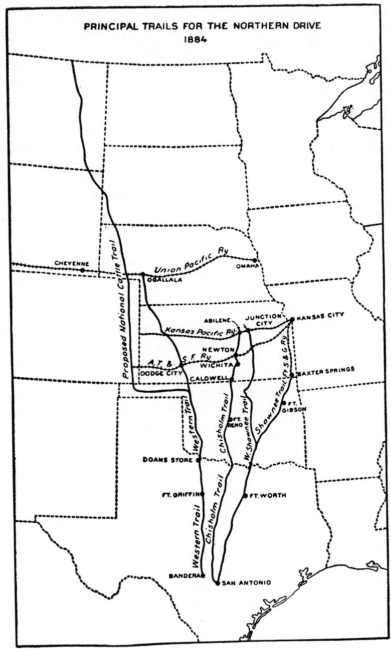

PRINCIPAL TRAILS FOR THE NORTHERN DRIVE, 1884

(From E. E. Dale, *The Range Cattle Industry,* Norman, Okla.,
The University of Oklahoma Press, 1930, page 62.)

552

financed by a Chicago syndicate which contracted to build the present Texas capitol in exchange for 3,050,000 acres of land in nine Texas Panhandle counties. This huge property required a fence of 781¼ miles in length, at a cost of $181,000. Other neighboring ranches were the Frying Pan, the Daniel Waggoner, and the Burk Burnett, all American-owned; and in other parts of the Great Plains, ranches owned by United States citizens were likewise in the predominance.

Shortly after the westward-building railroads had reached the grasslands of Colorado, Nebraska, Wyoming, and Dakota, Texas cattle were used to stock the central and northern plains. By 1883 stockmen had intruded on the Comanche-Kiowa and the Cheyenne-Arapaho reservations and the Cherokee Outlet, and the Cherokee Strip Live Stock Association had been formed at Caldwell, Kansas. In 1868 George A. Binkleman established a ranch on the Kiowa east of Denver, but presently moved farther north to the Republican. Soon others—F. P. Ernest, John W. Iliff, and Hittson—acquired ranches in Colorado; and by 1874 the Arkansas Valley, from Pueblo eastward for 100 miles, was occupied. When the Kansas Pacific Railroad reached Cheyenne about 1867, this town became an important livestock market to which numerous Texas herds were driven to stock Montana, Idaho, Utah, and Nevada ranches. Then the building of the Northern Pacific Railroad and other lines into western Dakota by 1880 led to rancher-occupation of this region. At this time the Federal Census thus indicates the number of cattle within the states and territories of this area: Kansas, 1,533,-133; Nebraska, 1,113,247; Wyoming, 521,213; Montana, 428,279; Dakota, 140,815; and Colorado, 791,492.

Northern plains stock-raisers, too, had well-known trails to market. The Montana drives began in 1874 with about 3,000 cattle, increasing during the following four years, respectively, to 5,000, 6,000, 10,000, and 22,000; and in 1879 the yearly drive comprised between 30,000 and 40,000. The principal trail was up the Yellowstone to Fort Custer; thence into Wyoming via Forts McKinley, Reno, and Fetterman to Pine Bluff, a railroad station 50 miles east of Cheyenne. Along this route was plenty of grass and water.

Moreover, the industry had now passed its experimental stage. By 1880 there was little free grass in Texas; and a decade later there was hardly more on the central or northern plains, and properties were generally bought or leased and substantial improvements made. The Texas Longhorn could no longer compete with the new breeds—Poled Angus, Hereford, Short Horn. Farming lands had been occupied, but still here and there were millions of acres unsuited for agriculture which were given to ranching. In brief, stock-raising was localized; thousands of small ranchers turned their attention to other pursuits; and the Texas Longhorn was presently seen only in state or federal parks.

SHEEP HUSBANDRY

In some respects, the sheep industry of the semi-arid mountain and plateau regions of the West developed along parallel lines with cattle ranching. It also started with a poor-quality animal, the *chaurros;* it had its princely ranches of thousands of acres; it had its long drives to market of 1,000 or more miles; and its improvements came through the bringing in of better breeds. But in other respects, the sheep industry was unlike the cattle industry. Its routine ranch life was strongly influenced by Spanish tradition and practice; it required primarily the services of footmen and not horsemen; and the cowman's general practices of round-up and branding, the sheepman found unnecessary.

When Juan de Oñate established the first Spanish settlement in New Mexico, his colonists drove into the Rio Grande valley more than 1,000 sheep; and presently this industry was of prime importance. In Texas, Arizona, and California it was the same. From 1769 to the close of the century, the *padres* at San Juan, Monterey, Los Angeles, and San Francisco imported sheep, goats, and cattle for the use of the missions, as did others in the Arizona country at Tubac and Tucson. And in 1776 Athanase de Mézières reported that a good beginning had been made in sheep husbandry at the Texas missions. Nowhere in the Southwest during this period were there flocks of improved sheep. Rather, only the foundation of the future Anglo-American industry was laid. The *chaurros,* found by the intruders after 1821, was a lean, gaunt sheep, producing from one to one and one-half pounds of coarse wool; and its flesh was tough and undesirable for mutton. But the Anglo-Americans soon improved their stock by cross-breeding and by bringing in Cotswolds, Southdowns, Shropshires, Lincolns, Merinos, and other high-grade animals, the mutton of which was finely flavored and the annual wool clip of which was five or more pounds per animal.

On some western sheep ranches, for example, the Callahan ranch of southern Texas, were four grades of employees. The lowest in rank was the *pastor* (shepherd), who kept watch over a flock of 1,000 or 1,500 sheep, assisted only by one or more dogs. Over two or three *pastores* was a *vaquero* (mounted rider), who selected the area to be grazed for the day and the watering places, and attended to other routine duties. A *caporal* (range boss) had charge over the divisional *vaqueros;* and overseeing the work of two or three *caporales* was the *majordomo* (superintendent). But the average ranch owner performed all these functions. In fact, a majority of the sheep ranchers owned but a few hundred sheep each.

Although the first Anglo-American intruders found within the mesquite, chaparral, and prickly-pear country of southern Texas a few herds of Spanish sheep, and engaged in ranching in a small way, they did not consider the industry of great importance. And, indeed, it was not until well after 1865 that sheep ranching developed on a large scale. Unsettled conditions constituted a serious handicap. During the 15 years of border forays which followed the Civil War, military commanders annually reported sheep rancher losses, both in property and lives. But the death of the Apache leader Victorio solved the last of the raiding problems and opened for grazing millions of acres formerly denied the ranchers.

Texas now asumed a position of first importance in sheep husbandry. From 1880 to 1884 state-owned sheep increased from 5,940,200 to 8,035,700, or approximately 33⅓ per cent. In cross-breeding experiments, western Texas sheepmen favored the Merino, although other breeds were imported. In 1879 Colonel John James, who owned a large ranch west of San Antonio, wrote that the reason why he and his neighbors favored the Merino was that it was a better herd animal, and that its mutton and wool were of high quality. He said that Mexican herders were generally employed at a salary of $12 per month with an additional $6 for food allowance. Therefore, with a few herders at low pay, handling large flocks of Merinos, opportunities for profit were great. He estimated that from 1,000 ewes a rancher could expect more than 800 lambs annually, besides an average of 5,000 pounds of wool. And with wool selling at above 30 cents per pound, it alone would bring more than $1,500.

Unlike Texas, New Mexico had no great let-down in sheep ranching during the period of transition from Spanish- to Anglo-American control. From 1821 to 1846 New Mexicans drove not less than 200,000 sheep annually from the Rio Grande Valley to Mexico. During this period about 20 wealthy ranchers (ricos) owned four-fifths of New Mexico's sheep. One of these, Colonel Chaves, in 1839 drove 75,000 sheep southward to Mexico. Later, in commenting on these southern drives, Chaves said that they would have totaled about 1,000,000 sheep annually, but he probably was too generous with his estimate. Although the poor quality of wool and mutton of the chaurros was not conducive to an active Anglo-American market, these southern drives evidenced a considerable Mexican trade. When the United States extended its control over New Mexico in 1848, therefore, the basis for the more important industry was laid. During the next 50 years sheep husbandry in New Mexico had an unprecedented growth. In

1880 the Federal Census listed 2,990,700 sheep in New Mexico. Immigrants from the United States improved the native stock; and later drove tens of thousands of Merinos to neighboring states and territories—as far west as California and as far north as Montana.

By 1865 New Mexican herders had driven their flocks into southern Colorado, and Las Animas, Huerfano, and Conejos Counties were grazed by thousands of long-legged, short-wool sheep. Then, with improvement and under aggressive Anglo-American leadership, ranches were pushed northward rapidly until the eastern plains region of the territory, from Las Animas to Weld County, was dotted. And with statehood in 1876, one contemporary authority estimated that Colorado owned 2,500,000 sheep, sold 7,000,000 pounds of wool, and had a crop of 1,000,000 lambs annually. But the sheepman had invaded the range claimed by the cowman; and, in the years to follow, serious clashes were inevitable.

California was also the recipient of many of these early drives. Soon after its gold rush, New Mexicans appeared with their herds, for mutton sold at a fabulous price. But it was not until 1853 that any thought was given to wool. In this year, however, W. W. Hollister devoted his attention to wool-growing on a southern California ranch. In San Francisco he found a ready market. Presently other ranchers engaged in raising flocks in which the qualities of both mutton and wool were cultivated; and many ships putting in at Pacific ports landed thousands of Cotswolds, Lincolns, and Shropshires to stock California ranches.

Conditions for sheep ranching within this area were favorable. The climate was salubrious, the soil was fertile, and ample fodder could be procured from near-by farms. In summer the shepherds drove their flocks to the hills, where pasturage was sufficient. Then when autumn rains had started, they returned to the foothills and plains, now covered with green grass. By 1875 Fresno, Los Angeles, Mendocino, San Joaquin, Colusa, Merced, and Sonoma counties each grazed from 100,000 to 300,000 sheep; and five years later 40,000 California Merinos were driven to New Mexico, and many other thousands to neighboring states and territories. The Governor of Utah was alarmed. He complained that the Californians had driven "immense herds . . . of fifteen, twenty, and thirty thousand sheep" onto his already overstocked territory; and that they would "poison and kill" the buffalo grass and leave the range bare.

But sheep ranching in Utah was already a major industry. Up to 1870 the New Mexicans with their flocks had entered from the south; and from the eastern states of Kansas, Nebraska, and Missouri, the Mormons had driven in large flocks over the Platte Trail.

Mormon lawmakers encouraged this movement by exempting sheep from taxation for the first few years. The immigrants also brought with them spinning wheels, looms, and cards, for they wished to be independent of Gentile industry. Thus, woolen manufacture and sheep husbandry were encouraged as twin industries. By 1882 Utah possessed 10 woolen mills, one of which was equipped with 3,000 spindles. Some of these were co-operative enterprises, for example, the Provo Manufacturing Company, reputed to be the largest woolen mill west of the Missouri River. Yet the mills used only one-fourth of the wool grown in the Great Basin; the remaining three-fourths was sent east, to be returned later as clothing and blankets.

From the inception of sheep ranching, the Mormons had imported improved breeds, although the Spanish Merinos predominated. In Millard, San Pete, and Emery counties in central Utah, and Juab, Utah, and Wasatch counties farther north were many ranches; and numerous flocks also ranged along the Colorado and Green River basins. Both Arizona and Nevada received a part of this overflow, but their sparse populations down to the end of the century would not support a large industry. From 1875 to 1880 Utah's wool clip was annually 1,500,000 pounds, the fleece averaging about four pounds for ewes and six for wethers.

Sheep ranching in Montana, Idaho, Dakota, and much of Washington and Oregon differed from that farther south in that ample provision had to be made by the ranchers for winter shelter and fodder. This requirement militated against numerous large ranches, although many small stockmen prospered. For example, in 1876, while the country was yet occupied by the Sioux, a Mr. Burgess drove a mixed Cotswold-Merino flock of 1,400 from California to Montana. He arrived at Miles City about the end of September (having consumed two seasons on the trip) and located on the Tongue River. In the following fall, however, he sold his sheep to George M. Miles, who later moved them to a point about 14 miles above the mouth of the Tongue. It was difficult to guard his flock against predatory animals and the cold of winter, with a consequence that he had little increase. But one year (1879) he was able to ship to a Philadelphia market 3,000 pounds of wool, for which he netted a profit of 32 cents per pound. This modest success caused others to invest in ranching. In 1879 many thousand sheep were driven to Montana from California, Oregon, and Washington, and were sold to those establishing small ranches. But, as in eastern Colorado, Montana, too, had been preempted by the cattlemen.

The cattlemen complained that sheep's cutting hoofs destroyed the range turf, and that cattle would not drink at a watering place where sheep had been. Moreover, they had little in common with the shepherds, many of whom were Mexicans. Along the range border, therefore, from Mexico to Canada, frequent clashes occurred. In western Texas, New Mexicans drove their flocks onto the Goodnight ranch, and aggressive cowboys promptly drowned 400 sheep in the Canadian River. A serious clash was imminent, but Goodnight and the shepherds agreed on a division of the range. In Arizona, Colorado, Nevada, Idaho, Wyoming, and Montana, the struggle was even more bitter; and thousands of sheep, and occasionally a cowboy or shepherd, were killed. During the eighties and nineties sheepmen controlled the Arizona range from Ash Fork to Seligman, and seriously encroached on the property of neighboring cattlemen. A range war followed, known as the Graham-Tewksbury Feud, in which 26 cattlemen and six sheepmen lost their lives. In Wyoming, cowmen expelled the shepherds who invaded their ranges, and drove more than 10,000 sheep into the mountains to be eaten by wolves; and near North Rock Springs, 12,000 sheep were plunged to their death over a cliff.

But in the end sheep ranchers gained the advantage. Prices of mutton and wool were decidedly more stable than those of beef, and sheep were more hardy than cattle. Moreover, each year the sheepman had the added advantage of a large lamb crop. By the end of the century, therefore, many cattlemen endured the ridicule of their fellows and invested in sheep. In consequence, sheep husbandry experienced a steady growth, while the cattle industry fluctuated. In 1903, Texas and the western mountain states owned more than 30,000,000 of the nation's 63,964,876 sheep.

THE COWBOY AND THE SHEPHERD

The cowboy represented regionalism more than did the shepherd. The latter was attired much like other men of his community, and lived an indolent, even-tenored life. But the cowboy was a range rider, a horseman, and showed to best advantage while mounted. Generally, he exhibited proficiency both in riding a broncho and in "bull-dogging" (throwing by hand) and branding a wild steer. His profession demanded arduous riding, quick thinking, a steady nerve, and sometimes reckless daring; therefore, he usually exhibited qualities of pride, self-sufficiency, and a love for adventure. His broadbrimmed hat, chaps, high-heeled boots, spurs, six-shooters belted about his waist, lariat, saddle, and slicker (raincoat)—all were indicative of an arduous, open prairie life. Indeed, a contemporary observer found him "above prettinesses and uselessnesses"; and believed that

NEAR THE NOON HOUR ON THE RANGE

"his costume was appropriate because it was harmonious with his surroundings."

It is not uncommon for the present-day student to regard the early range rider as an outlaw because the cow country was turbulent. In the absence of law courts and peace officers, undeniably the rancher often resorted to homespun methods to protect his interests, and turned to vigilance committees when his individual efforts failed. Most of the ranchers were intolerant of horse and cow thieves, and felt that these extra-legal measures were justified. But they heartily supported law and order and encouraged the organization of border counties. Occasionally, however, a cowman built up his herd by brand-burning and stealing, but such cowmen were black-listed by honest ranchers in their stock-raisers' associations. The average rancher was honest, ambitious, progressive, and given to hard toil. Moreover, his cowboys were usually of the same class, although he was not averse to employing a hand under an alias. Even the temperament of the seasoned rancher might exhibit great extremes. Wild orgies and drunken sprees at Abilene, at Dodge City, or at other turbulent cow towns were only once-in-a-great-while emotional outbursts, for at home he was generally sober, generous, cheerful, and hospitable. He had a profound respect for womanhood; he championed schools and churches, but not always because he felt personally benefited. He was ambitious and considerate for the welfare of his family and community. Generally, his own educational advantages had been meager; and on the ranch, books, magazines, and newspapers were scarce. But there were exceptions; some cowmen had been trained in the best of American and European universities.

So, in comparison with other western characters, the cowboy yet remains one of America's most colorful figures—a man on horseback, a plainsman, brave and adventurous. In this role he stands out in sharp contrast with the lowly shepherd of the mountain and plateau country. About the ranch, the cowboy's duties were varied—to rope wild horses and steers, to brand calves, to ride wild, bucking bronchos, to repair or to build fences, to line-ride his employer's ranch, and to fight wild Indians or outlaws whenever it became necessary. Yet writers of fiction have too often portrayed him as a "two-gun" man, "quick on the trigger," notwithstanding the fact that he is seen at his best while trailing a herd or engaged in the round-up. On the free range once or twice a year his services were needed when eight or ten ranchers would unite their 40 or 50 riders to engage in a series of round-ups, moving from place to place over the range to brand unmarked cattle and calves, to reassemble their own herds, and to turn homeward those from other ranges. All these several duties developed a cow country *esprit de corps* hardly paralleled elsewhere. The rancher was proud of his profession, sought to uphold its traditions of fair play and enterprise, and as a consequence became a border citizen of great worth.

The shepherd, with whom the cowman often clashed, was, during early years of sheep ranching, a Spanish-American, reticent, introspective, sensitive; but in later years the Anglo-American was so employed. The shepherd's task, assisted only by his faithful dog, was to guard his sheep and to lead them from one range to another. In performing this simple duty he generally led a lonely life, sometimes separated for long periods from his family and friends. Occasionally, a New Mexican would load his *aguage* (water-gourd) and supplies on a *burro* (ass) and start for a distant mountain slope or canyon with his sheep. Within these solitudes he would stay for weeks, or sometimes months, seeking one green pasture after another. Occasionally, a prowling wolf would disturb the sheep, but the faithful dog would drive it away or the shepherd would cast a firebrand in its direction.

During storms the sheep were held in their fold until it was safe to drive them to pasture. Sometimes during blizzards it was necessary for the shepherd to subject himself to much exposure in order to search for wind-swept areas in the snow where his sheep might graze. A Colorado blizzard on one occasion descended upon an unwary shepherd and his flock. The herder realized his desperate plight and sought to drive his flock homeward. But the fear-mad sheep ran before the wind toward a mountain gulch. The faithful shepherd would not desert them, and all plunged over the brink to their death in the deep snow. Thus, says a contemporary, "It was not in Palestine alone that it could be said, 'the good shepherd giveth his life for his sheep.' "

A visitor would find the same high quality of hospitality in the adobe or jacal shanty of the shepherd as in the more pretentious ranch home of the cowman. Many grateful travelers have left accounts of how, when necessary, generous shepherds shared their last morsels of *frijoles* (beans), *tortillas* (corn fritters), and mutton; and, on cold nights, warm beds near the fire. The life of the shepherd was not so adventurous and heroic as that of his illustrious contemporary, the cowboy, but it was equally important in claiming for the nation a semi-arid wilderness.

BIBLIOGRAPHY

An exhaustive study made of the Great Plains bisons during the days of the great slaughter is J. A. Allen, "History of the American Bison," in *Ninth Annual Report of the United States Geological and Geographical Survey*, . . . (Washington, 1875). But a more popular early account is Richard Irving Dodge, *Hunting Grounds of the Great West* (London, 1877).

J. R. Cook in his *The Border and the Buffalo* (Topeka, 1907) tells of his own day-by-day experiences as a commercial hunter. Modern writers have given little attention to the destruction of the great herds, but a few accounts worthy of mention are E. Douglas Branch, *Hunting the Buffalo* (New York and London, 1929); M. D. Garretson, *The American Bison, the Story of Its Extermination as a Wild Species and Its Restoration Under Federal Protection* (New York, 1938); C. C. Rister, "The Significance of the Destruction of the Buffalo," in *Southwestern Historical Quarterly*, XXXIII (July, 1929); ———, *The Southwestern Frontier* (Cleveland, 1928); *Report of the American Bison Society, 1924-25, 1926* (New York, 1927); Colonel Homer C. Wheeler, *Buffalo Days* (Indianapolis, 1925).

Every aspect of the range cattle industry is treated in the writings of early observers. The two most valuable accounts within this class dealing at length with ranching, cattle drives, markets, and growth of the industry are Joseph G. McCoy, *Historic Sketches of the Cattle Trade of the West and Southwest* (Kansas City, 1874; reprinted, Washington, 1932); and Joseph Nimmo, *Range and Ranch Cattle Traffic* (in *House Executive Documents,* No. 267, 48th Cong., 2nd sess.). Andy Adams, *The Log of a Cowboy* (Boston, 1903) is rated by one authority as the best single-volume work on ranching. Walter Baron von Richthofen, *Cattle Raising on the Plains of North America* (New York, 1885), presents a European's opinion, not entirely sound because of the author's lack of knowledge of general conditions. Consult also A. W. Lyman, "From Steer to Steak," in *Kansas Magazine,* II (April, 1872); and Charles M. Harger, "Trails of the Prairies," in *Scribner's,* XI (June, 1892). Sundry tables, data, and summaries concerning the growth of the industry are found in the Federal Census reports of 1880 and 1890, and in L. P. Brockett, *Our Western Empire, or the New West Beyond the Mississippi* (Philadelphia, 1881).

Edward Everett Dale, *The Range Cattle Industry* (Norman, Okla., 1930), is a well-documented study of the economic phases of the cattle industry. This writer's other contributions are "Those Kansas Jayhawkers, a Study in Sectionalism," in *Agricultural History,* II (October, 1928), No. 4; "The Cherokee Strip Live Stock Association," in Southwestern Political and Social Science *Proceedings,* March 24–26, 1924; and "The Cow Country in Transition," in *Mississippi Valley Historical Review,* XXIV (June, 1937), No. 1. Other well-known general works of merit are Ernest Staples Osgood, *The Day of the Cattleman* (Minneapolis, 1929); and Louis Pelzer, *The Cattleman's Frontier* (Glendale, 1926).

Books related to the cattle industry within the different parts of the West should be examined. For example, J. Frank Dobie, *A Vaquero of the Brush Country* (Dallas, 1929) is an excellent account of wild cattle round-ups along the Rio Grande; Ellsworth Collings, *The 101 Ranch* (Norman, 1937), treats of north Indian Territory ranching; and Ora Brooks Peake, *The Colorado Range Cattle Industry* (Glendale, 1937), traces the industry's rise and growth in this area. Within this class also are four excellent books on western Texas. J. Evetts Haley's two studies, *The XIT Ranch* (Chicago, 1939), and *Charles Goodnight, Cowman and Plainsman* (Boston and New York, 1936), are unexcelled for their vivid portrayal of ranch life. H. F. Burton, *History of the JA Ranch* (Austin, 1927), and W. C. Holden, *The Spur Ranch* (Austin, 1934), are also dependable.

A miscellaneous list of all writings related to the cow country would require more space than could be given here. But the following selected list is representative: J. Marvin Hunter (ed.), *Trail Drivers of Texas* (Bandera, Texas, 1923–1924); Frederic L. Paxson, "The Cow Country," *American Historical Review*, XXII (October, 1916); R. Adams, "Public Range Lands—A New Policy Needed," in *American Journal of Sociology*, XXII (November, 1916); C. G. Coutant, *History of Wyoming* (Laramie, 1899), I; John Duffield, "Driving Cattle from Texas to Iowa, 1866," in *Annals of Iowa*, XIV (April, 1924), No. 4; Will James, *Cowboys, North and South* (New York, 1924); P. A. Rollins, *The Cowboy, His Characteristics, His Equipment, and His Part in the Development of the West* (New York, 1924); Conrad Kohrs, "A Veteran's Experience in the Western Cattle Trade," in *Breeder's Gazette* (Dec. 12, 1912, Chicago); A. A. Hayes, "Cattle Ranches of Colorado," in *Harper's Magazine*, LIX (Nov., 1879); Clara M. Love, "History of the Cattle Industry in the Southwest," in *Southwestern Historical Quarterly*, XIX (April, 1916); and Theodore Roosevelt, "Ranch Life in the Far West," in *Century Magazine*, XIII (Feb., 1888), New Series.

Dependable studies on the inception and development of sheep ranching are few. Brockett's *Our Western Empire*, previously cited, has a fair chapter on the economic aspects of the industry; and in *Agriculture*, V, of the United States Census, 1880, are supplementary data related to the various states and territories. Bancroft's works on the western states and territories, as listed in other chapter bibliographies, are also reliable. Emigrant guidebooks are helpful when used with discrimination. Of this class are A. H. Granger, *Southern and Western Texas Guide for 1878* (St. Louis, 1878); and *New Mexico* (Santa Fe, 1890), published by the Bureau of Immigration. Current narratives are L. G. Connor, *A Brief History of the Sheep Industry in the United States* (in American Historical Association, *Report* for 1918, Washington, 1921); E. P. Snow, "Sheepmen and Cattlemen," in *Outlook*, LXXIII (April 4, 1903); and R. N. Richardson and C. C. Rister, *The Greater Southwest* (Glendale, 1934).

Two good recent studies are the following: Charles W. Towne and Edward N. Wentworth, *Shepherd's Empire* (Norman, 1945); and Edward N. Wentworth, *America's Sheep Trails; History; Personalities* (Ames, Iowa, 1948).

33

THE LAST SOUTHWESTERN

TERRITORIES

T HE CHEROKEES, Creeks, Choctaws, Chickasaws, and Seminoles supported the Confederacy during the Civil War; consequently, with the dawn of peace they were penalized by being forced to surrender the western half of Indian Territory. The Cherokees alone, being less pro-Southern, were allowed to retain nominal control of the tract surrendered (the "Outlet"). But the government reserved the right to settle thereon other tribal bands, and by 1880 only the "Oklahoma District" (north of the Chickasaw country) and the "Outlet" remained unoccupied by recently transferred Indians. Cattlemen, however, had made agreements with the Indians— for the most part, not recognized by the Indian Office—whereby their cattle were allowed to graze these lands. This was particularly objectionable to homesteaders whom federal authorities had denied entry thereon under the terms of the Homestead Law (1862). During the 1870's the protestants were unorganized and without effective leadership. Minor movements, headed by such men as C. C. Carpenter and James M. Bell, had been broken up by federal troops or agents within the country. By 1880, however, their camps along the Kansas-Indian Territory line were large, and able leaders had appeared.

INDIAN TERRITORY RUSHES

The most active boomer leader during the early 1880's was David L. Payne. Payne had run the usual gamut of frontier life. He had homesteaded a Kansas farm, had visited the goldfields of Colorado, had served on the frontier as scout and soldier during the Indian wars, had been an officer in the Federal army during the Civil War, had been a member of the Kansas legislature for two terms, and, in addition, a short time prior to 1879, had been an assistant doorkeeper of the House of Representatives in Washington.

The 1879 boomer agitation led Payne back to Kansas. Here was a field in which his restless soul could find satisfactory employment. During the years 1880–1884 he led several expeditions to the Oklahoma district. In April, 1880, he organized a small band of Kansas squatters and led it southward to the North Canadian River, 40 miles east of Fort Reno, but he was promptly escorted back to Kansas by federal troops under Captain T. B. Robinson. Three months later he was back with still another party, and was arrested and sent before a federal court at Fort Smith. He was fined $1,000; but he had no property against which an attachment could be made, and as soon as he was freed, he returned to Kansas to organize another settler invasion. In 1881 he headed a Texas party, crossed the Red River, and pitched his camp at Cache Creek, northeast of present Wichita Falls; but again he and his followers were expelled.

In 1883, at Wichita, Kansas, Payne organized an "Oklahoma colony," with himself as president, J. M. Steele as treasurer, and W. H. Osborn as secretary. A membership fee of $2 was charged (which was later increased to $6). This "colony," according to Professor Roy Gittinger, "was to become a vigilance committee to protect the rights of its members in an extra-legal, not to say illegal way." Colonel Edward Hatch estimated that Payne collected $100,000 in membership fees up to 1884. But he evidently spent the entire sum on his movement, for he died a poor man. It is probable that part of this amount was devoted to the establishment of the *Oklahoma War Chief,* the official newspaper of the boomers, which began publication at Caldwell, Kansas, on January 12, 1883.

On November 27, 1884, Payne died while dining with friends at Wellington, Kansas, and his mantle of leadership fell to his able lieutenant, W. L. Couch. The new leader was equally determined. In December he led a strong expedition to Stillwater Creek; and when troops appeared, Couch informed them that he and his men were prepared to fight for their rights. Fortunately, Hatch would not force the issue; but he so stationed his men between the boomer camp and Kansas as to turn back other parties as well as supplies. Thus isolated, in ones and twos the invaders presently retired.

Meanwhile the fight had been transferred to Congress. Here railway lobbyists joined hands with boomers and Western Congressmen in demanding the opening of western Oklahoma. But they were opposed by representatives of the Five Civilized Tribes, the cattlemen, and Indian rights advocates. For nine years the fight was hotly waged over resolutions, bills, and amendments to appropriation bills in one way or another affecting Indian Territory. In 1880 five or six measures proposing the allotment of lands in severalty to Oklahoma Indians were introduced, but each failed. In the next year Kansas Negroes organized the "Freedmen's Oklahoma Association," and appealed to Congress to allow them to settle in western Oklahoma. Although their request was endorsed by Indian Bureau officials, Congress was not disposed to grant it. As early as January 9, 1889, Representative Edward H. Rollins of New Hampshire had proposed a measure to organize the Territory of Oklahoma, which met a similar fate. But Rollins' bill was only the forerunner of others, the agitation of which finally brought success.

The first substantial boomer victory in Congress came when a rider was attached to the Indian appropriation act of March 2, 1885, authorizing the purchase of the Cherokee Outlet and the Oklahoma district (yet claimed by the Creeks and Seminoles). This amended bill, when coupled with the Dawes Act two years later, paved the way for final boomer success. The latter measure provided for the allotment of Indian Territory lands in severalty, except the lands of the Osages, Peorias, Miamis, Sac, and Fox, and the Five Civilized Tribes. The President was authorized to make the allotments whenever in his opinion it was for the good of the Indians. Surplus lands could then be purchased by the government. Two years later the Secretary of Interior, William F. Vilas, made an agreement with the Creeks whereby, for a consideration of $2,280,000, they released all claim on the Oklahoma district. On March 2 following, the Seminoles' claim was met by a payment of $1,902,000; and a provision of the appropriation bill incorporating the same authorized the President to open the district for white settlement.

By this authority, on March 23, 1889, President Benjamin Harrison issued a proclamation declaring that the "Oklahoma District" would be subject to homestead entry "at and after the hour of twelve o'clock noon, on the twenty-second day of April." The region to be opened was bounded on the south by the Chickasaw reservation, on the west by the Arapaho and Cheyenne lands, on the north by the Cherokee Outlet, and on the east by the small holdings of the Potawatomis and Shawnees, Iowas, Kickapoos, and Sac and Fox. To approach it from the south, Texas homesteaders must cross the Chickasaw country; and from the north, Kansans must travel through the Cherokee Outlet.

It is more than probable that the President had not anticipated a "run." Tens of thousands of eager home-seekers, only a small per cent of whom could be accommodated, were ready to capitalize on the generosity of their "Uncle Sam." From March 23 to April 22 every road through southern Kansas or from the Red River across the Chickasaw country was thronged with immigrant wagons; and towns like Caldwell, Wichita, and Arkansas City, Kansas; or Denison and Gainesville,

Texas, were crowded with jostling, good-natured strangers, all anxious to have the last report on "the promised land." By April, 1889, the Atchison, Topeka and Santa Fe Railroad had been completed across present central Oklahoma from north to south, *via* Arkansas City, Purcell, and Gainesville; and it now became a line of settler projection. Marion T. Rock stated that scenes about the Arkansas City Railroad station on Sunday night of April 21 reminded one of the surging crowd at the Philadelphia station during the Centennial of 1876; and that by noon of the next day, 15 trains, filled with passengers, were ready to start for Oklahoma.

Prior to the opening of the "Oklahoma District," prospective settlers were allowed to camp along the northern and southern boundaries, but soldiers maintained a watchful patrol to guard against "Sooner" intrusion before the time stipulated in the President's March 23 proclamation. Yet, in spite of every precaution, many "Sooners" evaded their watchful guards and were later found pre-empting favorite 160-acre tracts when once those who had abided by the President's proclamation came in. At the sites of Kingfisher, Guthrie, and Oklahoma City as early as ten o'clock on the morning of April 22, government inspectors found hundreds of "Sooners" engaged in surveying choice lots and in establishing business houses.

When army officers stationed at intervals along the boundaries sounded the signal for the start, an estimated 50,000 contestants began the run for homes, some on foot, some riding horses, and some in wagons, carts, buggies, or hacks. When the trains, whose speed was regulated with the conveyances of other contestants, disgorged their passengers, these joined the wild melee. Madly racing horses, careening vehicles, and excited contestants, shouting, cursing, yelling—all created an indescribable scene of confusion. Within a few hours, from the Cherokee Outlet to the South Canadian, the prairies were dotted with homesteaders, some engaged in staking claims and in erecting temporary shelters, and others in moving forlornly here and there looking for nonexistent homesteads. Thousands returned to their old homes, disappointed after weary months of waiting; other thousands journeyed back to Kansas and Texas or other states to await future land openings.

Along the Atchison, Topeka and Santa Fe Railroad, Guthrie, Oklahoma City, and Norman were established as tent towns within a day, and farther west Kingfisher was equally promising. Later, Guthrie was to have the advantage of being the capital of the new territory. No trustworthy population figures before 1890 on these towns are available. Estimates run from 3,000 to 15,000 for Guthrie and Oklahoma City, and considerably less for other new towns, such as Stillwater and Norman. At both Guthrie and Oklahoma City law-abiding citizens took control, and temporary governments were established. W. L. Couch was elected mayor of Oklahoma City and D. B. Dyer to the same office at Guthrie.

On May 2, 1890, Congress approved an organic act for the Territory of Oklahoma. The Territory consisted of seven counties, later named Logan, Payne, Kingfisher, Canadian, Oklahoma, and Cleveland of the Oklahoma district, and Beaver County of the present Oklahoma panhandle. Under terms of the federal law of 1887, additional counties were to be added from time to time after allotments had been completed on each reservation. Cattlemen had occupied the Public Land Strip (Oklahoma panhandle) shortly after the Civil War; and in 1887 they had sought to create the Territory of Cimarron, but had gained no encouragement from Congress. Therefore, to meet their needs, Congress now added the strip to the Territory of Oklahoma as Beaver County. George W. Steele of Indiana was named governor of the new Territory, and a secretary of state, a supreme court, and a Territorial legislature were soon created.

The new Territory now grew rapidly. During the period 1891–1895, four Indian reservations were opened to settlement. On September 22, 1891, 900,000 acres of the Sac and Fox, Iowa, and Shawnee-Potawatomi lands were occupied, adding two counties to the original seven; and in the next year the Cheyenne-Arapaho reservation of more than 4,000,000 acres was thrown open. But several months elapsed before all the lands of the Territory were claimed by homesteaders, since its western half was considered little suited for farming.

The Cherokee Outlet, together with the Tonkawa and Pawnee reservations of more than 6,300,000 acres, was the greatest of all openings, when on September 16, 1893, it is estimated that more than 100,000 people came in a mad scramble to claim its rich prairies. Federal officials had sought to obviate "Sooner" troubles by requiring that prospective homesteaders acquire registration certificates at booths located along the boundary. The rapidly increasing crowds of men, women, and children before each registration station, however, some of whom stood in line for many hours awaiting their turn, made this plan impracticable. Also, officials learned that registration certificates were being bought and sold.

The last run came in May, 1895, with the opening of the Kickapoo district of 200,000 acres. But from time to time the Territory grew by other additions. The Greer County region, between the two Red rivers, was taken from Texas and added to Oklahoma by a Supreme Court decision in 1896. In 1901 the Comanche-Kiowa-Wichita district was opened by lottery awards at Lawton and El Reno; and from 1904 to 1906 the Ponca, Otoe, and Missouri lands, the Big Pasture of the Comanches and Kiowas, and the Osage-Kaw country were disposed of by allotment or auction sale. Each opening had been made only after the reservation Indians had been awarded lands in severalty. Thus, by 1906, the Territory of Oklahoma had grown from the original six counties of the "Oklahoma Lands" and of Beaver (the Public Land Strip) into that region embracing the whole of present western Oklahoma.

THE OKLAHOMA STATEHOOD MOVEMENT

Governor Steele arrived at Guthrie on May 22, 1890, and promptly addressed himself to the task of launching his administration. Boundaries of the counties were run, their governments established, and a Territorial legislature was called to assemble in Guthrie on August 27. The census presently taken revealed that the counties of the Oklahoma district had a population of 57,435, the Public Land Strip 2,982, and Guthrie and Oklahoma City, the two largest towns, 5,884 and 5,086, respectively. Members of the legislature considered the Governor a "carpet-bagger," and engaged in petty quarrels with him, proposing two measures for the removal of the capital, the first to Oklahoma City and the second to Kingfisher, but the Governor vetoed both. Finally, in exasperation, Steele resigned his governorship and returned to his Indiana home. His successor, Judge A. J. Seay, who assumed the duties of office on October 18, 1891, was more acceptable to the legislature.

During the 16 years following the Organic law, the growth of Oklahoma Territory was unparalleled. Each opening of Indian lands had been quickly followed by white settlement. The Territory, except the cow country of the northwestern part, became pre-eminently a home of farmers. The prairie wilderness, over which there was Indian campaigning in 1874–1875, had been checker-boarded with 160-acre farms before the close of the century. Where only tall prairie grass and sagebrush had formerly grown, within a decade were innumerable fields of wheat and row crops. On each farm was a sodhouse, a dugout, and appurtenant barns, fences, and pens; and along the section lines were roads leading to markets. Agricultural development also encouraged railroad building. In 1894 there were only 382 miles of railroads within the Territory, but six years later the rails extended 783 miles.

The Territory's cultural growth was equally marked. Hardly had the first buildings appeared on the sites of Guthrie, Oklahoma City, Kingfisher, and other towns before subscription schools were inaugurated, and the legislature had promptly voted for rural schools. The Organic Act had provided that Sections 16 and 36 of each township should be reserved as an endowment for public schools; and in addition, Congress had set aside Section 33 for higher education. The first Territorial legislature established the University of Oklahoma at Norman, a teachers college at Edmond, and the Agricultural and Mechanical College at Stillwater; and subsequent enactments added teachers colleges at Alva and Weatherford, and a University Preparatory School at Tonkawa. Then, still later, shortly after statehood, the legislature provided for the eastern part of the state the teachers colleges at Tahlequah, Ada, and Durant, a University Preparatory School at Claremore, and the State School of Mines at Wilburton.

Other evidences of culture presently appeared. Literary societies, church organizations, and study clubs were promptly organized in each large town. On May 9, 1889, the first eight-column folio edition of the *Oklahoma Times* appeared on the streets of Oklahoma City, published by A. C. and W. W. Scott, and within the same year the *Oklahoma State Capitol* (Guthrie) was also printed. At Kingfisher, a non-railroad town west of Guthrie, Jacob V. Admire, receiver of the land office under President Harrison, soon published the *Free Press*. Newspapers also served the smaller towns. During these early years, George W. McClintock was to have the distinction of editing three Oklahoma newspapers—the first at Frisco (a colony of Civil War veterans), the second at Yukon, and the third at El Reno.

Indian Territory also grew rapidly in wealth and population, and clamored for statehood several years prior to the enabling act of 1906. The Missouri, Kansas and Texas Railroad, built from north to south through the Cherokee-Creek-Choctaw country, had greatly stimulated white settler penetration. Among the Five Civilized Tribes, lands were held in common, but any man could cultivate as many acres as he wished, provided that he did not infringe upon the rights of others. Many mixed-bloods and "intermarried citizens" had well-built farmhouses, cultivated fine orchards and large fields, and owned thousands of horses and cattle. But generally, the full-bloods were poor, living in log cabins and cultivating only a few acres. Yet each tribe maintained schools. The Cherokees adopted a compulsory school law and gave free textbooks to all pupils. By 1888 they had nearly 100 country schools, as well as a female seminary at Tahlequah, a male academy at Park Hill, and an orphanage at Grand Saline. The Creek system of education was not so good as that of the Cherokees, but the Chickasaws and Choctaws had fair systems of country schools and advanced academies and seminaries. Among the better schools supported by either the tribes or churches were the Tullahassee mission,

Worcester Academy, the Baptist and Presbyterian missions at Tahlequah, the Chickasaw Male Academy, the Female Seminary, New Hope Seminary for girls, Wheelock Academy, Spencer Academy, Armstrong Academy, and the two Seminole missions (Emahaka and Mekusukey). The number of white intruders within Indian Territory steadily increased. In 1880 there were reported to be 6,000, not including railway workers and other laborers whom the Indians had allowed to remain. By 1884 they had increased to 35,000, in 1890 to 120,000, in 1895 to 300,000, and in 1900 to more than 500,000. To care for the legal interests of a rapidly swelling population, in 1889 a United States Court was established at Muskogee, having jurisdiction over all cases in which United States citizens were interested when the amount involved was more than $100. But in political affairs white men within Indian Territory were allowed no rights, and by 1900 many demanded statehood. In such a movement the Indians saw the danger of being supplanted by their white neighbors, and by their "Sequoyah Convention" at Muskogee, in August, 1905, they proposed to Congress an Indian state separate and independent of Oklahoma Territory. But Congress refused the proposal.

Meanwhile, on March 3, 1893, Congress had created the Dawes Commission to persuade the Five Civilized Tribes to accept allotments and to throw open for settlement all surplus tracts. The tribes refused to treat with the commission, however; and three years later Congress enacted a new law authorizing the commission to make up the rolls of the Indians preparatory to allotments. Then in 1897 the Choctaws and Chickasaws agreed to accept individual allotments of their lands, upon condition that they should be free from all taxes for a period of 21 years from the date of allotment. The Cherokees and Creeks would not enter similar agreements until April, 1900, when the final step was taken laying the basis for statehood. Also, by the Dawes Act of 1893, tribal courts were abolished and the laws of Arkansas were extended over Indian Territory; and two years later a complete judicial change was made when three federal district courts were established.

Governor Seay had reported to President Cleveland that Oklahoma would soon be ready for statehood, and presently various proposals to create a single state or two states were made. Governor William C. Renfrow, who succeeded Seay, favored a single state, but many Indian Territory citizens asked for two, since it was believed that only in this way could they protect their interests. Too, they were averse to joining a territory in which the liquor traffic was legalized. Finally, in 1906 a provisional omnibus bill was enacted in which Arizona and New Mexico were to be organized as one state and Indian Territory and Oklahoma as another. Arizona and New Mexico would not consent to single statehood, however, so the act as finally approved on June 16, 1906, came to apply to Oklahoma and Indian Territory only.

Soon after the passage of the enabling act, Governor Frank Frantz issued a call for an election to choose delegates to a constitutional convention. One hundred and twelve delegates were to be chosen, 55 from Indian Territory, 55 from Oklahoma, and 2 from the Osage country. It was commonly believed that the new state would pass under Republican control, but such was not the case. Of the delegates selected, 99 were Democrats, 12 were Republicans, and 1 was an independent. Moreover, fears of Indian Territory politicians that delegates from Oklahoma would dominate the convention's proceedings proved groundless, for William H. Murray, an intermarried Chickasaw citizen, was chosen president, and other Indian Territory men were elected to responsible positions. The constitution presently proposed to the voters strongly reflected western liberalism. Among other things, it provided for the initiative and referendum, both as to laws and constitutional amendments; an eight-hour day on public works and in mines; elaborate provisions to control corporations under a corporation commission; and a four-year term for the governor, without the privilege of serving twice in succession.

On September 17, 1907, the state constitution was ratified, state prohibition of intoxicating liquors was approved, and Charles N. Haskell, the Democratic nominee, was chosen governor. The Democrats were successful not only in naming the governor, but also in electing four of the five Congressmen and a large majority in both houses of the legislature. Robert L. Owen and Thomas P. Gore, later named by Governor Haskell as Oklahoma's first Senators, were of the same party.

On November 16, 1907, President Roosevelt issued a proclamation recognizing Oklahoma as a new state, 104 years after the United States purchased it as a part of Louisiana.

Arizona and New Mexico

Arizona was a part of the cession acquired from Mexico by the Treaty of Guadalupe Hidalgo (1848) and the Gadsden Purchase (1853), although for more than a decade it was to remain a part of the Territory of New Mexico. It has already been observed that the country was ravaged by the fierce Apaches during the early days of the Civil War. But upon the arrival of Colonel Carleton's California column on June 2, 1862, a provisional military government was proclaimed, and peace and order followed.

Frank C. Lockwood states that the launching of Arizona's territorial government "came in a sort of a left-handed, *opéra bouffe,* yet very

American . . . [manner]." [1]   Federal recognition was gained largely because of Charles D. Poston's able work in Washington. According to Poston, there was no one in the capital in 1862 interested in Arizona affairs except General Heintzelman. But soon he had won to his territorial proposal President Abraham Lincoln, Benjamin Wade of the Senate Territorial Committee, and Representative Ashley of the House Committee. Ashley informed Poston that certain Congressmen, whose terms in the House would shortly expire, would vote for the bill if they could secure territorial appointment. Poston promptly acted upon this suggestion. He invited these "lame ducks" to an oyster supper, at which he gained their support for his measure, which, as enacted by Congress on February 24, 1863, provided that "All that part of the former Territory of New Mexico lying west of the thirty-second meridian, west from Washington," be erected into a separate Territory styled Arizona. Later, President Lincoln appointed John A. Gurley governor, Richard C. McCormick secretary, and John N. Goodwin chief justice. But Gurley died on August 18, and Goodwin was appointed to succeed him. Two associate justices, a district attorney, a marshal, and a surveyor-general were also named. Poston accepted the position of Indian agent. A short time later, however, he was returned to Washington as Territorial delegate.

On December 27, 1863, after a long, trying journey, the newly appointed officials arrived in eastern Arizona. During a severe snowstorm they held inaugural exercises at Navajo Springs, at which time they took the oath of office and Governor Goodwin wrote his first proclamation, providing for a preliminary census, creating judicial districts, and calling an election for members of the legislative assembly.

The Territory was sparsely populated, and for many years its capital was migratory. In July, 1864, it was moved from Fort Whipple to Prescott, a new town on Granite Creek a short distance southwest of the fort; then, three years later, to Tucson, where it remained until 1877; finally, it was changed to Phoenix, in the Salt River Valley. Tucson later sought to regain the seat of government, but in a political trade it received the University of Arizona instead. The first legislature enacted a general code of laws, prepared by Judge Howell and modeled after the California and New York codes; a Territorial seal was designed; mining laws were passed; and the counties of Pima, Yuma, Mohave, and Yavapai were created. (By 1900 nine others were added.)

But for several decades the territory grew slowly. In 1870 its population was only 9,658 whites and civilized Indians; and 10 years later

[1] Lockwood, Frank C., *Pioneer Days in Arizona,* New York, The Macmillan Company, 1928, 149.

it had risen to only 40,441. In 1880 its principal towns were Tucson, with a population of 6,000; Arizona City (Yuma), at the junction of the Gila and Colorado, with a population of 1,600; and Prescott, the capital and a mining town, on the Salinas, with 2,000. Ehrenburg, on the Colorado in Yuma County, was the chief shipping point for central Arizona; and here and there were other small villages, such as Florence, Sanford, Mineral Park, Hardyville, Wickenburg, and Phoenix, a small village in the Salt River Valley.

While Arizona's population was largely Anglo-American and Indian, that of New Mexico was principally Spanish-American and Indian. Therefore, the culture of the New Mexicans was strikingly different. The *ricos* (wealthy citizens) constituted the controlling class, living in comfortable homes, enjoying semi-medieval manners and customs, and dominating the political, social, and economic life of the country. Under them were the docile *peones* (serflike poor) who lived in primitive flat-top adobe huts and in humble circumstances, ignorant and contented. There was also a rudimentary industry. Well-kept patches of pepper, corn, beans, and melons, and orchards, irrigated from near-by streams, and small flocks of sheep, tended by their *pastores,* were evidences that the inhabitants were self-supporting. Occasionally, too, a native workman was skillful at making leather goods, carving into his object of workmanship intricate designs; others made jewelry and vessels of gold and silver, artistically embossed and engraved; and still others fashioned brilliantly colored *serapes* (cloaks), *rebosos* (shawls), *chaquetas* (jackets), and *calzoneras* (trousers) from wool and silk.

Prior to statehood the Catholic Church had furnished the chief educational opportunities, but by 1912 a definite public school system had been instituted. The total number of pupils enrolled in New Mexico schools during 1911–1912 was as follows: in the public schools, 61,027; in Indian schools, 2,085; and in private and sectarian schools, 4,252. There were 256 students of college rank and 1,411 below college rank enrolled in the University of New Mexico at Albuquerque, the Normal University at Las Vegas, the Agricultural and Mechanical College at Las Cruces, the Military Institute at Roswell, the Normal School at Silver City, and the School of Mines at Socorro.

Protestant schools had appeared, although they were small and indifferently attended. The Presbyterians supported schools at Truchas, Ranchos de Taos, Trementina, Taos, Chacon, Chemayó, Albuquerque, and Santa Fe; the Methodists at Albuquerque (three) and Farmington (for the Navajos); the Congregationalists at Marquez, Cubero, San Mateo, and Albuquerque; the United Brethren at Valverde, Alcalde, and Santa Cruz; and the Baptists, a small college at Montezuma.

Church membership also increased from 137,000 in 1906 to 210,000 in 1916, of which the Catholic increase was from 121,559 to 177,727. That the new emphasis put on popular education by the church and state had beneficial results is interestingly revealed by the greatly increased circulation of newspapers published in Santa Fe, Albuquerque, Las Vegas, Roswell, and Raton.

But for many years the growth of New Mexico had been slight. It had been created as a Territory (with Arizona included) on September 9, 1850, but its Territorial government was not inaugurated until March 1 of the next year. At this time the Territory's population consisted of about three-fourths Spanish-Americans and one-fourth Pueblo and other Indians, with a few Germans, French, and Americans —a total of 85,547. From 1864 to 1887, as is shown by Bancroft, the membership of the legislature was largely Spanish-American, and all business was transacted in Spanish, so that the journals and laws had to be translated into English for publication. Towns were small. For example, Santa Fe, the capital and oldest town, in 1880 had a population of only about 6,500. Albuquerque was next with 5,000; Las Vegas, Mesilla, and Silver City had from 3,000 to 4,000 people each; and Cimarron, Las Cruces, Mora, Placitas, Fernando de Taos, Ocate, Tomé, and San Marcial each could claim little more than 1,000.

The slow growth of the Territory was largely a result of the semi-arid nature of the country, but also because of its isolation. For many years after its acquisition from Mexico, its only connection with the outside world was by caravan or stagecoach. But by 1880 the Atchison, Topeka and Santa Fe Railroad had entered its northern border *via* Raton Pass, and had thence projected southward to Las Vegas and on westward to the Rio Grande, with a branch line to Santa Fe. The Southern Pacific had crossed the Colorado River at Yuma in 1879, and during the following year had built through southern Arizona to western New Mexico, *via* Tucson. By 1879 the 12 counties of Taos, Colfax, Mora, Rio Arriba, Bernalillo, Santa Fe, San Miguel, Valencia, Lincoln, Socorro, Grant, and Dona Ana had a combined population of 125,230, with Anglo-Americans rapidly supplanting the Spanish-Americans. After the appearance of railroads the Territory's growth was substantial. The increase in the ranching industry, the exploitation of mines, and the building of reclamation projects were other primary causes.

A move for statehood had appeared in New Mexico shortly after the Mexican War, and in Arizona in 1872, when Richard C. McCormick, Territorial delegate in Congress, made such a proposal. In 1893 ex-Governor John N. Irwin sought to prove Arizona's claim for statehood by pointing out that the Territory then had a population of 70,000, more than some of the Territories could claim at the time of admission to the Union, and that its resources in cattle, sheep, mineral wealth, and lumber made it amply able to care for its financial needs. In September, 1910, Governor Richard E. Sloan advanced even more substantial claims. He said that the Territory was fifth in size among the States of the Union. It was blessed with adequate rainfall, and had sufficient water to irrigate more than 1,000,000 acres of farmland. Already it had a population of about 200,000. As to its resources, in addition to other minerals produced, it led all states and territories in copper output; and it had 10,000,000 acres of forests. Its transportation problem was largely solved by the construction of more than 2,000 miles of railway. But most important, he contended, its heterogeneous citizenship had made adequate provision for an excellent public school system, a university, and two normal schools, and was served by 60 newspapers and magazines. New Mexico, too, was making similar claims.

Interestingly enough, both movements were for separate statehood. In 1902, during Miguel A. Otero's governorship, Senator Albert J. Beveridge, with his sub-committee on statehood, visited New Mexico. Between November 12 and 21, the committee held closed hearings in Las Vegas, Santa Fe, Albuquerque, Las Cruces, and Carlsbad; but those giving testimony were principally court interpreters, census enumerators, judges, teachers, justices of the peace, and other public officials. So when the committee returned to Washington, it was opposed to statehood. It recommended, however, that Spanish be required in schools and in official use. Its report now became the majority report of the Senate committee, four members of which favored statehood. Bernard S. Rodey, the New Mexico delegate, then introduced a bill in the next session of Congress, but it failed to pass.

A plan for joint statehood for Arizona and New Mexico was proposed in 1905, and Senator Beveridge supported it. From the two Territories there arose a mighty chorus of protest. M. G. Cunniff, a prominent Arizona Democrat, maintained that, although Arizona had not more than 150,000 people (25,000 of whom were Indians), it was not a half-Mexican community, as was New Mexico. He said that there was a larger proportion of college graduates among its population than in any other area of similar size in the West—engineers, lawyers, doctors, businessmen, and farmers. Moreover, he said, "I found well paid college and normal school graduates teaching bright children under sanitary conditions and according to modern methods. The schools in Prescott and Phoenix are as good as those in Boston." His most convincing argument, however, was that "Arizona is as different from New Mexico as Texas is. . . . In a state made of the two territories the 300,000 people of New Mexico would outvote the 125,-000 people of Arizona, and the new State would naturally assume the New Mexico tone."

The Arizona legislature voted unanimously against single statehood, and instructed J. F. Wilson, Territorial delegate, to say to Congress: "We insist that such is without precedent in American history. It threatens to fasten upon us a government that would be neither of, by, nor for the people of Arizona. . . . It humiliates our pride, violates our tradition, and would subject us to the domination of another Commonwealth of different traditions, customs, and aspirations." E. E. Ellinwood, United States District Attorney of Prescott, thus bitterly assailed joint statehood before a House committee: "If you cannot admit Arizona with its 113,000 square miles, with its resources, with its American population, leave us out. . . . For heaven's sake do not strike us in the face if you cannot help us up."

In New Mexico, sentiment against single statehood was also evident, although less pronounced. A letter from Governor Otero read before Congress on January 6, 1905, advanced the claim that "the great majority of the people of New Mexico" were opposed to joining New Mexico with Arizona. "This is not due to any innate animosity between the two Territories," he said, "but to the inherent difference in population, in legislation, industries, in contour, in ideals. . . . It would be the coercion of two populations, which are unlike in character, in ambition, and largely in occupation." The New Mexico legislative assembly strongly supported the governor. In a memorial sent to Congress, the council voted 10 to 2 and the house 21 to 3 against joint statehood.

Because of these protests, in January, 1906, Congress enacted a measure to permit the Arizona and New Mexico voters to express their will; and in November following, Arizona returned a resounding "No!" with New Mexico more favorably disposed. Arizona's vote was 16,265 against and 3,141 for joint statehood; and New Mexico favored it by a vote of 26,195 to 14,735. Congress was now convinced that joint statehood was inadvisable. The likelihood that Arizona as a separate state would send two Democratic Senators to Washington might have motivated a Republican majority. But the decided opposition in Arizona and New Mexico to joint statehood made slow the next step of Congress. It was not until June 20, 1910, that enabling acts were passed, and not until 1912 that the two states were admitted, with New Mexico a few weeks ahead of Arizona. The latter had incorporated in its constitution several liberal western reform ideas, for example, initiative, referendum, direct primary, and recall of judges. President William Howard Taft's legal training and experience caused him to object to the recall of judges, and he refused to issue a proclamation admitting the new state until the offending clause was stricken out, and Congress supported his demand. Finally, however, a new measure, excising the recall of judges, was enacted by Congress and approved by the President. But the new state was not to be denied; and in the next election the voters amended their state constitution restoring the principle of recall!

BIBLIOGRAPHY

Roy Gittinger, *The Formation of the State of Oklahoma* (University of California Publications in History, VI, Berkeley, 1917; reprinted, Norman, 1939) covers completely Indian Territory affairs, the openings of the various districts to white settlement, growth of the "twin" Territories, and the formation of the state. John Alley, *City Beginnings in Oklahoma Territory* (Norman, 1939) supplements Gittinger's account in adding interesting details of city organization, the "Sooner" problem, and political alignments. Other volumes related in one way or another to this period are E. E. Dale, *The Range Cattle Industry* (Norman, 1930); Angie Debo, *Rise and Fall of the Choctaw Republic* (Norman, 1934); E. E. Dale and J. L. Rader, *Readings in Oklahoma History* (Evanston, 1930); E. E. Dale and Morris L. Wardell, *History of Oklahoma* (New York, 1948); Morris L. Wardell, *A Political History of the Cherokees 1838–1907* (Norman, 1938); C. C. Rister, *Land Hunger: David L. Payne and the Oklahoma Boomers* (Norman, 1942); ——, *No Man's Land* (Norman, 1948); "Bunky" (Irving Geffs), *The First Eight Months of Oklahoma City* (Oklahoma City, 1890; reprinted, Oklahoma City, 1939); Gerald Forbes, *Guthrie: Oklahoma's First Capital* (Norman, 1938); Grant Foreman, *A History of Oklahoma* (Norman, 1942); Roy M. Johnson (comp.), *Oklahoma History South of the Canadian* (3 vols., Chicago, 1925); Dora Ann Stewart, *The Government and Development of Oklahoma Territory* (Oklahoma City, 1933); Joseph B. Thoburn and Muriel H. Wright, *Oklahoma, A History of the State and Its People* (4 vols., New York, 1929); Luther B. Hill, *A History of the State of Oklahoma* (2 vols., Chicago and New York, 1909), I; Seth K. Gordon and W. B. Richards (comps.), *Oklahoma Red Book* (2 vols., Oklahoma City, 1912); and Marion T. Rock, *Illustrated History of Oklahoma* (Topeka, 1890).

The spirit of the boomer and early settler movement is found in two pamphlets: *Proceedings of the Convention to Consider the Opening of the Indian Territory, Held at Kansas City, Missouri, February 8, 1888;* and *Oklahoma—Information for Congress—Don't Legalize Town Acts nor Give Them Any Force, Copies of Ordinances, Judgments, and Records* (Oklahoma City, 1889). W. B. Matthews, *Matthews' Guide for Settlers upon the Public Land* (Washington, 1889) is a typical guidebook.

Lansing B. Bloom, *New Mexico History and Civics* (Albuquerque, 1933), presents in compact form the essential facts covered in this chapter. More elaborate narratives are Ralph Emerson Twitchell, *Leading Facts of New Mexican History* (2 vols., Cedar Rapids, 1911); Charles F. Coan, *A History of New Mexico* (3 vols., Chicago and New York, 1925); George W. James, *New Mexico, the Land of Delight Makers* (Boston, 1920); and Colonel James F. Meline, *Two Thousand Miles on Horseback* (New York, 1867). The earliest standard work on both Arizona and New Mexico is H. H. Bancroft, *History of Arizona and New Mexico* (*Works*, XVII, San Francisco, 1889).

For Arizona Territorial problems and the statehood movement, consult Alex. D. Anderson, *The Silver Country of the Great Southwest* (New York, 1877); Robert P. Porter *et al.*, *The West from the Census of 1880* (Chicago, 1882); J. Ross Browne, *Adventures in the Apache Country* (New York, 1869); George W. James, *Arizona, the Wonderland* (Boston, 1917); Frank C. Lockwood, *Pioneer Days in Arizona* (New York, 1932); S. R. De Long, *A History of Arizona* (San Francisco, 1905); and J. H. McClintock, *Arizona, Prehistoric, Aboriginal, Pioneer, Modern* (Chicago, 1916).

The student should consult magazine articles contemporary with the statehood movement in Arizona, New Mexico, and Oklahoma. The following list is selective and not all-comprehensive: Charles Moreau Harger, "The Next Commonwealth," in *Outlook*, LXVII (February, 1901); Theodore R. Jenness, "The Indian Territory," in *Atlantic Monthly*, LXIII (April, 1879); H. B. Kelly, "No Man's Land," in *Kansas State Historical Collections*, IV (1886–1890); Hamilton S. Wicks, "The Opening of Oklahoma," in *Cosmopolitan*, VII (June, 1889); Helen C. Candee, "Social Conditions in Our Newest Territory," in the *Forum*, XXV (March-August, 1898); J. W. Babcock, "States Rights of Arizona and New Mexico," in *Independent*, IX (February 22, 1906); Editorial, "Arizona's Outlook in the Family of States," in *American Review of Reviews*, XLII (October, 1910); T. E. Farish, "Another View of Arizona," in *Nation*, XLVIII (May, 1889); Charles Moreau Harger, "Our Two New States," in *Outlook*, XCVII (January, 1911); and Theodore Roosevelt, "Arizona and the Recall of the Judiciary," in *Outlook*, XCVIII (June, 1911); and Marion Dargan, "New Mexico's Fight for Statehood, 1895–1912," in *New Mexico Historical Review*, issues of January and April, 1939, and April, 1940.

34

THE RISE OF WESTERN CITIES

GENERAL FACTORS AFFECTING URBAN GROWTH

ONE OF the striking developments of the West, as of the nation generally, was the phenomenal growth of cities during the last third of the nineteenth century. The growth of industry and commerce, the influx of immigrants, the expansion of transportation facilities, all contributed to the rapid rise of urban centers.

The Industrial Revolution, that wrought a transformation of Great Britain in the second half of the eighteenth century, came to America in the nineteenth to effect a similar change. The factory system of manufacturing, with its introduction of improved machinery, the utilization of steam power, and the mass production of goods, gave rise to industrial centers that challenged the primacy of older commercial cities. The greater production of industry provided new goods and more goods for commerce. Thus did industry and commerce join hands to build bigger cities.

America, with doors open wide to the politically oppressed and the economically depressed of other lands, received a great influx of immigrants. During the nineteenth century the population increase of the United States went as high as 35.6 per cent in the decade 1850–60, and for the second half of the century averaged about 25 per cent increase per decade. The great tide of immigrants, joined to the natural increase of resident citizens, brought a rapid occupation of the free land and a spectacular growth of cities.

With the disappearance of free land by about 1890, rural growth began to slacken. At the same time the marvelous improvements effected in cities augmented their lure. The expansion of industries created new jobs, and these were offered at alluring pay rates. Man, ever a gregarious animal, found more and more reasons for migration to the city. Entertainment was available in a wide variety range, from

580

Grand Opera to bar-room diversions, from art galleries and lyceums to prize fights and races.

As cities grew they provided such modern facilities as good water works, municipal transportation systems, improved sanitary facilities, electric light and power, and telephone service. Wealth accumulated, and brownstone mansions rose to exhibit the splendors of the more successful. Money and opportunities for advancement were abundant, so economic and social forces combined to lure people from rural areas to the urban.

As one studies the population figures of various cities he sees changes that are difficult to explain. Why does one city shoot ahead of another that has, apparently, equal advantages of site and resources? It has been said that under normal conditions a successful city is as much a matter of natural growth as a tree. But physical conditions alone cannot explain a city's rise.

Glenn Quiett has concluded that "natural advantages plus transportation facilities, plus aggressive men make cities." He argues that "Since most places that men select for the sites of their communities have some natural advantages and the coming of transportation is a matter that can be influenced by individuals, the formula can almost be reduced to the simple phrase, Men make Cities. Given the leadership of aggressive and far-sighted men and a tolerably favorable site for a city, transportation will come, business will come, population will come." [1]

A given region with such natural resources as productive soil, minerals, or lumber, must when settled have a commercial center that inevitably rises to urban proportions. Where there is no one location that is the inevitable site of the metropolis, various factors influence the final result. One of these is primacy of founding.

The first settlement to be started and to acquire a sizeable population has an advantage over other towns. Many people when coming to a particular region come to the largest center of population. New businesses, or branches of older business concerns seeking new locations, tend to come to the largest population center of the region. The better schools and more ample opportunities of economic and social life invite prospective residents to the larger city. Hence the region's largest town or city attracts settlers and business. Its bigness induces still greater size; the very inertia of growth produces more growth. "To him that hath is given" more.

Transportation facilities have ever been important factors in determining the location and the size of cities. At the crossroads of trade

---

[1] Glenn C. Quiett, *They Built the West; an Epic of Rails and Cities* (New York, D. Appleton-Century Co., 1934), p. 83.

and the breaks in transportation, cities have risen. Where goods had to be changed from one type of carrier to another—as from land to sea, from river boat to ocean vessel—labor must be at hand to effect the transfer. So cities rise on good harbors and near the mouths of great rivers. In the Old World and through early centuries, rivers and harbors determined the locations of cities, for water transportation was the chief reliance in the carrying trade of the world. Until well into the nineteenth century this form of transport continued as the great agency of commerce. But in the second half of the nineteenth century, and especially in Western America, railroads assumed the dominant role. They became so all-important to the existence and growth of cities that they were able to make or break new urban communities.

As a railway was projected into a territory, the rail company's representatives went ahead to negotiate with existing towns or to select sites for new ones. Towns within the general range of the proposed rail route were invited to vote bonds or to buy stock in the enterprise and to make gifts of land, sites for stations, or other concessions. And so necessary was rail transportation to a new town that it generally acceded to the railroad's demands. If the required assistance was not forthcoming the rail company would usually by-pass the town, select another site in the vicinity, and lay out a new city around its own depot. And this new town generally supplanted the older settlement.

The major part of the trans-Mississippi West was settled in the second half of the nineteenth century. Hence most of the cities in this area—and those that we shall especially consider here—had their real growth, if not their founding, after 1850. Only two cities of the region had achieved importance and size before the Civil War. These were New Orleans and St. Louis, with populations respectively of 168,675 and 160,773 in 1860. (While New Orleans is on the east bank of the Mississippi we include it here because it is the metropolis of a state that is predominantly in the trans-Mississippi area.) These two great cities were important in the national scene and dominant in Western America.

It is interesting to note the relative positions of the leading Western cities through the years, as reflected by their population figures in successive decades. The following table exhibits the successive positions of the three largest cities at the end of each decade. Before the Civil War, New Orleans, with its command of the internal commerce of the vast Mississippi Basin, held first place. By 1870 St. Louis, with its central position and its great transportation facilities by water and rail, came into first place. For six decades St. Louis maintained her primacy as the metropolis of the West. New Orleans held second place in 1870, San Francisco in 1880 and 1890, and Minneapolis-St.

CENSUS OF POPULATION OF THIRTY LEADING WESTERN CITIES

	1860	1870	1880	1890	1900	1910	1920	1930	1940
Albuquerque				3,785	6,238	11,020	15,157	26,570	35,449
Boise		995	1,899	2,311	5,957	17,358	21,393	21,544	26,130
Butte			3,363	10,723	30,470	39,165	41,611	39,532	37,081
Dallas			10,358	38,067	42,638	92,104	158,976	260,475	294,734
Denver	4,749	4,759	35,629	106,713	133,859	213,381	256,491	287,861	322,412
Des Moines	3,965	12,035	22,408	50,093	62,139	86,368	126,468	142,559	159,819
Fort Worth			6,663	23,076	26,688	73,312	106,482	163,447	177,662
Houston	4,845	9,382	16,513	27,557	44,633	78,800	138,276	292,352	384,514
Kansas City	4,418	32,260	55,785	132,716	163,752	248,381	324,410	399,746	399,178
Los Angeles	4,385	5,728	11,183	50,395	102,479	319,198	576,672	1,283,048	1,504,277
Little Rock	3,727	12,380	13,138	25,874	38,307	45,941	65,142	81,679	88,039
Minneapolis	2,564	13,066	46,887	164,738	202,718	301,408	380,582	464,356	492,370
New Orleans	168,675	191,418	216,090	242,039	287,104	339,075	387,219	458,762	494,537
Oakland	1,543	10,500	34,555	48,682	66,960	150,174	216,261	284,063	302,163
Oklahoma City				4,151	10,037	64,205	91,285	185,389	204,424
Omaha	1,883	16,083	30,518	140,452	102,555	124,096	191,601	214,006	223,844
Phoenix				3,152	5,544	11,134	29,053	48,118	65,414
Portland	2,874	8,293	17,577	46,385	90,426	207,214	258,288	301,815	305,394
St. Louis	160,773	310,864	350,518	451,770	575,238	687,029	772,897	821,960	816,048
St. Paul	10,401	20,030	41,473	133,156	163,065	214,744	234,698	271,606	287,736
Salt Lake City	8,236	12,854	20,768	44,843	53,531	92,777	118,110	140,267	149,934
San Antonio	8,235	12,256	20,550	37,673	53,321	96,614	161,379	231,542	253,854
San Diego	731	2,300	2,637	16,159	17,700	39,578	74,361	147,995	203,341
San Francisco	56,802	149,473	233,950	298,997	342,782	416,912	506,676	634,394	634,536
Seattle		1,107	3,533	42,837	80,671	237,194	315,312	365,583	368,302
Sioux Falls			2,164	10,177	10,266	14,094	25,202	33,362	40,832
Spokane				19,992	36,848	104,402	104,437	115,514	122,001
Topeka	759	5,790	15,452	31,007	33,608	43,684	50,022	64,120	67,414
Tulsa					1,390	18,182	72,075	141,258	142,157
Wichita			4,911	23,853	24,671	52,450	72,217	111,110	114,966

Paul from 1900 to 1920. Los Angeles jumped from third place to first in 1930 and has retained leadership since.

RANK OF CITIES AS TO SIZE

Year	First Place		Second Place		Third Place	
1860	New Orleans	168,675	St. Louis	160,773	San Francisco	56,802
1870	St. Louis	310,864	New Orleans	191,418	San Francisco	149,473
1880	St. Louis	350,518	San Francisco	233,950	New Orleans	216,090
1890	St. Louis	451,770	San Francisco	298,997	Minn.-St. Paul	297,894
1900	St. Louis	575,238	Minn.-St. Paul	365,883	San Francisco	342,782
1910	St. Louis	687,029	Minn.-St. Paul	517,152	San Francisco	416,912
1920	St. Louis	772,897	Minn.-St. Paul	615,280	Los Angeles	576,673
1930	Los Angeles	1,238,048	St. Louis	831,960	Minn.-St. Paul	735,962
1940	Los Angeles	1,504,277	St. Louis	816,048	Minn.-St. Paul	780,106

Many factors have had a part in determining the site and the rapid growth of Western cities. The net result, as reflected in population statistics, is shown in the accompanying table of thirty Western cities.

Two cities showed marked growth in the sixties. St. Louis increased from 160,773 to 310,864; and San Francisco jumped from 56,802 to 149,473. A number of towns—Kansas City, St. Paul, Portland, Little Rock, Des Moines, and Oakland—showed large proportional increases and were nursing metropolitan aspirations.

The decade of the seventies saw Minneapolis-St. Paul increase from 33,096 to 88,360; Topeka, from 5,790 to 15,452; Denver, from 4,759 to 35,629; Portland, from 8,293 to 17,577; and Oakland, from 10,500 to 34,555.

Boom conditions existed in many areas during the eighties. Leading cities achieved population increases as follows: Denver, 35,629 to 106,713; Kansas City, 55,785 to 132,716; Minneapolis-St. Paul, 88,-360 to 297,894; Omaha, 30,518 to 149,452; Los Angeles, 11,183 to 50,395; Dallas, 10,358 to 38,067; Portland, 17,577 to 46,385; Seattle, 3,533 to 42,837; Salt Lake City, 30,768 to 44,843; Des Moines, 22,408 to 50,093.

The Panic of 1893, and the depression years that followed, retarded growth of most cities in the nineties. Some actually lost population, but Los Angeles increased from 50,394 to 102,479; Butte, from 10,723 to 30,470; Seattle, from 42,837 to 80,671, and Portland, from 46,385 to 90,426.

The first decade of the twentieth century registered some rapid population increases, as follows: Fort Worth, 26,688 to 73,312; Seattle, 80,671 to 237,194; Spokane, 36,848 to 104,402; Oklahoma City, 10,037 to 64,205; Los Angeles, 102,479 to 319,198; and Oakland, 66,960 to 150,174.

Since 1910 the growth of most Western cities has been substantial, but not spectacular. The notable exceptions made increases from 1910 to 1940 as follows: Houston, from 78,700 to 384,514; Dallas, from 92,104 to 294,734; San Antonio, from 96,614 to 253,854; Phoenix, from 11,134 to 65,414; Oklahoma City, from 64,205 to 204,424; Tulsa, from 18,182 to 142,157; San Diego, from 39,578 to 203,341; and Los Angeles, from 319,198 to 1,504,277.

SOME LEADING WESTERN CITIES

No generalizations will apply to all Western cities. The factors accounting for rise and growth are so diverse that it is advisable to take a number of the leading cities one by one and give brief outlines of their development.

Kansas City. Nature chose the site for Kansas City. The Big Bend of the Missouri River was the starting place for the two great arteries of far western travel—the Santa Fe Trail and the Oregon Trail. Here, where the "Big Muddy" after flowing southward for a thousand miles suddenly turns eastward, was the natural break in transportation methods. Emigrants and commerce generally gave up river transport here and took to wagons. The bend of the Missouri thus became the gateway to the far West.

The rocky bluff that meets and turns the current of the mighty river provided an excellent and suitable location for a river landing. Here John C. McCoy, principal founder of the future city, landed trade goods for his store in 1834. Other men joined him to form the Kansas Town Company, but the hilly character of the land and shadows on the title retarded development until 1846. In that year the legal difficulties were solved and, what was even more important for the infant metropolis, the Mexican War began. The campaign for the conquest of New Mexico and California required great quantities of military supplies. These were disembarked at the landing beside the bluff. Kansas City was thus given its first great impetus to growth.

Before the military business had declined, another continent-shaking event occurred. Gold was found in California and the great rush of the gold-seekers was on. Kansas City continued as an important landing place and outfitting point; business houses multiplied; the city expanded.

The conflicts of the Civil War, including the Battle of Westport in her own back yard, retarded development in Kansas City. She lost population, while she saw a rival, Leavenworth City, gathering immigrants and business. The railroad had come to Missouri, in a line from Hannibal to St. Joseph. The fate of the two hopefuls, Kansas City and Leavenworth, would depend in large measure upon which would first have a railroad bridge across the Missouri. Kansas City won the race, an assurance of future greatness. Railroads now planned their routes to cross the vital bridge. When the span was completed, in 1869, four railroads on the east side of the river and three on the west were connected over the bridge. The great post-Civil War surge of emigrants into the West was now on; many thousands of them, by rail and by water, came through Kansas City. The town became a supply depot for settlers making farms in Kansas, for miners burrowing the mountains of Colorado.

Up from Texas came trail herds of longhorns. Leggy steers were squeezed into stock cars at Abilene and Dodge City for the haul to the Missouri River. Kansas City built stockyards on the bottom lands to care for the cattle. She became a livestock center as well as a railroad center. With the cattle came the flavor of the range. Kansas City became a "capital of cow towns," providing atmosphere for cowboys and two-gun men. Recreation centers appropriate to every station were provided, from the meanest brothel to the House of Lords gambling hall. The city was to retain its livestock trade, but to alter its character.

The refrigerator car promoted meat shipments just when growing cities about the country were swelling with people who could afford more meat in their diet. Packing houses sprang up in Kansas City beside the stockyards; then soap and glue factories were added. The city became also a great livestock market where cattle and hogs were sold, and where range cattle were bought by Kansas farmers for feeding. The horse and mule market expanded, and hogs assumed ever-increasing importance.

Steamboating on the river continued for a decade or so after the coming of the railroad, but the importance of water traffic was soon overshadowed by that of rail. Indeed, the city turned about: from facing north on the levee, it turned to face west upon the railroad center.

In unison with many other western cities Kansas City experienced a boom in the eighties. The growth of stockyards and transportation facilities was typical of other business expansion. The lumber business, which early developed, retained its importance. Agricultural implement trade grew to large proportions. The mail order business became a big branch of merchandising. A real estate boom struck the city. The price of city lots skyrocketed and new subdivisions were no sooner platted than sold. Annual real estate transfers, amounting to $5,000,000 in 1880, climbed to nearly $100,000,000 in 1887. The population, which was 55,785 in 1880, was nearly tripled by the end of the decade. Most of the new arrivals were from Northern states—a large part from Kansas. Thus was altered the former Southern character of the city.

Turkey Red wheat, introduced from Russia, thrived on the western plains. Trainloads of this hard winter grain came into Kansas City for shipment to the East. But the price of wheat was so low that most of it went to pay the railroad freight. Arthur E. Stillwell visioned and built a direct-line railroad—the Kansas City Southern—to the Texas coast. It cut the freight on wheat from 26 cents to 16 cents per hundredweight. Kansas City now became the country's leading winter wheat market. Stillwell next projected a railroad from Kansas City on the shortest route to the Pacific Coast—in Old Mexico. But he was unable to finish this Orient Line. However, when oil was discovered along the track, in Oklahoma and Texas, the black gold became freight for the railroad; and Kansas City, as a rail center for the Southwest, benefited. Oil brought tank cars and then refineries, adding wealth to the city.

The logical center of a large and rich agricultural area, Kansas City expanded while its trade territory grew more populous and productive. Having outdistanced its regional rivals, Kansas City drew the industries, the distributing agencies, and the people who are attracted to urban centers. Its position, size, and growth assured it continued pre-eminence and development.

San Francisco. Astride a peninsula and almost surrounded by water, San Francisco is a city of the sea. Set beside the Golden Gate, upon one of the great natural harbors of the world, she was to become a great commercial emporium.

Her beginnings date back to the historic year 1776, when the Mission Dolores and the *presidio* (fort) were founded by the Spanish pioneers. Later *Yerba Buena* (good herbs) grew up as a little village to accommodate the foreign traders. Here the *U.S.S. Portsmouth* landed on July 8, 1846, to raise the Stars and Stripes as a part of the Mexican War. Some three weeks later Sam Brannan disembarked his boatload of Mormons in the sleepy little town. The *Yerba Buena California Star,* which he started as the first newspaper in California, was to be the initial promotion sheet for publicizing the region.

Washington A. Bartlett, first American *alcalde* of Yerba Buena, changed the name of the town to San Francisco. This was an important move, for San Francisco Bay, discovered by Spanish explorers in 1769, was already well known. Identifying the town with the Bay, shippers directed their goods to San Francisco and the rising town had an advantage over competitors situated elsewhere on the Bay.

It was the discovery of gold in Sutter's mill race that suddenly transformed San Francisco from a village to a city. The first effect of the electrifying news was to make of San Francisco a deserted village, as the eager gold-seekers hurried away to the American River. But as the reports spread farther afield, a flood of argonauts came through the Golden Gate to make San Francisco their supply depot and trade center. Gold-seekers came from Oregon, Mexico, and Hawaii in 1848; but these were a token only. The rush of '49 brought in 40,000 excited men by sea in overloaded boats, by wagon and horseback routes across the mountains and plains of Western America.

Courtesy of Tom King

SAN FRANCISCO SKYLINE

A section of San Francisco's busy financial center looking toward Nob Hill. On the extreme right is the Standard Oil Building and in back of it the tower of the Russ Building, which is located on Montgomery Street—"The Wall Street of the West." In the distance are two of San Francisco's famous hotels, the Mark Hopkins and the Fairmont.

Little frame-built San Francisco bulged with the thousands who squeezed into the lodging houses and gambling saloons. Reckless men formed gangs and preyed upon the unprotected; incendiary fires gave opportunities for looting—in eighteen months San Francisco was swept by six fires. Then the better element of the citizenry roused to form vigilance committees who executed justice and established law and order.

As mining in California declined, agriculture rose to take its place. San Francisco continued as the trade center, with wheat, wines, and fruit becoming leading articles of commerce.

Theodore D. Judah and other prophets of the future began to plan and work for a transcontinental railroad. The western phase of the great project materialized under the energy of the "Big Four"—Stanford, Huntington, Crocker, and Hopkins. San Francisco basked in the wealth of ocean-going and rail-borne commerce and became the largest city on the Pacific Coast.

Begun as a city of gold, San Francisco was embellished later with silver. The world's greatest silver strike, the Comstock Lode, poured its wealth into the California metropolis. San Francisco and Virginia City in the '70s were twin cities, though separated by 300 miles. The California city financed and directed the mining; Nevada poured her white money into San Francisco. W. C. Ralston and his Bank of California associates dominated the Comstock. With Nevada silver they built the $6,000,000 Palace Hotel, the California Theater, the Mission Woolen Mills, a sugar refinery, and other industries. Adolph Sutro, who built the famed Virginia City tunnel that carries his name, took his wealth to San Francisco and invested it in Sutro Heights and other city developments.

The Big Four of the Central Pacific visioned even greater railroad triumphs. They built the Southern Pacific through California and across the Southwest; they extended a line north to Portland. They dominated the entrances to San Francisco and won control of the state —industrially, commercially, and politically. On Nob Hill, San Francisco, the railroad and mining magnates built residential palaces to exhibit their wealth. But much of their accumulations was finally to be employed in the creation of universities, libraries, and other cultural institutions.

San Francisco suffered the ordeal of earthquake and fire in 1906, but she rose from the ashes, strong and beautiful. Her growth through the years has been rapid, but without the spectacular booms that have characterized Los Angeles. The growth of the San Francisco area has been far greater than the city's municipal population figures indicate, for the thriving East Bay cities—Oakland, Berkeley, Richmond, and Alameda—are commercially but a part of the San Francisco metropolis.

Seattle. Twenty-four pilgrims—men, women, and children—landed at Alki Point on Puget Sound in November, 1851, to found a city. Within a month of their landing, and before they had built themselves shelters from the drenching rains, their first commercial opportunity came. A ship arrived from San Francisco seeking piles for wharf building, and the Puget Sound pioneers signed a contract to supply them.

Next spring some of the settlers explored the vicinity for a more eligible site for a city. With horseshoes tied to the end of a clothes-line they made soundings along the shore and found the deepest water along the east side of Elliott Bay. Here also were a dense forest, fertile soil, and springs of water. They staked claims and began the founding of Seattle. Good fishing grounds and the early establish-

Courtesy of Charles Laidlaw

SEATTLE, WASHINGTON

This is a striking air-view picture of Seattle with the city's harbor, Elliott Bay, in the foreground and its metropolitan business district spread out in the center. Towering in the rear left is beautiful Mount Baker, and to the right can be seen part of the twenty-six-mile-long Lake Washington, which forms the city's eastern boundary. In the left foreground is the ferry, Kalakala, on its way to Bremerton, home of the bustling Puget Sound Navy Yard, ship construction and repair hub of the North Pacific for the U. S. Navy.

ment of a sawmill aided the growth of the settlement. In 1853 Washington Territory was created and plats of Seattle were filed. In that year, also, Seattle had its first local wedding and built its first hotel.

Seattle needed more than lumber and shipping to become a metropolis. She needed wagon road connections with the interior. Because the early efforts to build a road over the Cascade Mountains did not succeed, overland emigrants continued to go to Oregon instead of to Washington. When railroads nosed across the continent Seattle was hopeful of becoming the western terminus of the Northern Pacific railroad. But Tacoma finally won the coveted designation. This was a stunning blow to Seattle; instead of being crushed, however, the vigorous citizens of Seattle determined to build their own railroad over the Cascades. On May Day, 1874, the citizens celebrated the holiday by rolling up their sleeves to cut down trees and build roadbed for construction of their own railroad toward Walla Walla. They then pledged themselves to give one day's work a week to further the project. By October, twelve miles of road had been graded. The next year the completed road to the Renton coal mines began to carry profitable freight. But requested aid from Congress did not come, and the Northern Pacific naturally favored Tacoma.

In 1881, when Henry Villard became president of the Northern Pacific, Seattle's hopes rose. Two years later a branch railroad connected Seattle with the Northern Pacific, but after Villard retired from the presidency in 1884, Tacoma interests stopped the running of trains on the Seattle branch. Seattle businessmen now threatened to build their own road to a connection with the Canadian Pacific. Then they began the building of a road from Spokane westward toward Seattle. Finally the great empire builder, James J. Hill, pushed his Great Northern railroad from St. Paul to Puget Sound. Before this project was consummated, Seattle was to undergo the ordeal of fire. In June, 1889, sixty blocks of the business heart of the city were razed. But phoenix-like a safer city, of brick and stone, rose from the ashes.

The Great Northern pushed westward and in July, 1893, trains were running over this road into Seattle. Hill constructed an excellent road, with lower grades, flatter curves, and a shorter line than other transcontinental roads. This enabled him to cut freight and passenger rates and give Seattle a commercial advantage over competing cities.

Next came an important steamship connection with the Orient. The Nippon Yusen Kaisha Company of Japan was induced to make Seattle the eastern terminus of its commercial line. Railroad connections with Canada were established.

In 1897 gold nuggets were brought to Puget Sound from Alaska. The bright news was flashed to the world and the adventurous and eager set their faces toward the Klondike. Seattle grasped her golden opportunity. She broadcast the news of gold and publicized herself as the natural gateway and outfitting depot for the new eldorado. Argonauts thronged her supply stores and crowded onto her Alaska-bound steamers. Business boomed in Seattle and her fame spread around the world.

The jealous and the skeptical had pointed to the topography of Seattle as a bar to any future greatness. The city was confined to a narrow strip of land between Lake Washington and Elliott Bay; high hills ran to the water's edge and left no level places for business streets and little available water front suitable for railroad tracks and factories. Engineer R. H. Thomson dreamed great dreams for his adopted city. He pushed to completion a great municipal water project and attached to it an electric plant. He laid out bicycle paths that became boulevards. Then he conceived a great project to remake the city's topography. He would tear down the hills and with the dirt fill in the tidal lands. He would re-grade and widen the business streets. With the backing of daring and farsighted citizens the expensive program was carried into effect.

Then a canal was projected to connect Lakes Washington and Union with Puget Sound. Years of promotion and effort finally brought state and congressional aid. After the canal was built Seattle could boast a fresh water harbor clear of tides and large enough to accommodate the fleets of the world. Keeping pace with navigation facilities were the railroad improvements that aided the city.

Lumber from the vast forests of the Northwest and wheat from the Inland Empire about Spokane sped along the rails to the Seattle wharfs, where waiting ships lay ready to carry these vital products to ports of the seven seas. The metropolis of an empire, gateway on the short route to the Orient, young and vigorous Seattle forges confidently ahead.

Los Angeles. "Whatever good things Los Angeles has obtained— and they are many—she has herself alone to thank for nearly all of them. Her railroads, her harbor, even that basic necessity, her water, have been brought to the City of the Angels by sheer force. . . . Originating in a few dry brown hills 30 miles from a harbor that was not a harbor, starting without a railroad, Los Angeles has shown the power of mind over matter by promoting herself into the great metropolis of the Southwest and one of the most beautiful cities in America." Thus does Glenn C. Quiett appraise a city's achievement. But granted the remarkable work of bold planners and consummate salesmen, we must recognize basic assets. Climate and situation are endowments of Nature, and these were the base and the capital upon which the structure was built. Los Angeles platted her climate into city lots and sold them to the people of the nation.

The beginnings and the early years of Los Angeles are decidedly unimpressive. Started in 1781 as the second *pueblo*, or Spanish town, in California, there were decades of sleepy existence ahead of it, with no indications for years that this straggling adobe village was one day to become the largest city in the trans-Mississippi West. The founding settlers were lured to the ground by free land, government subsidies in the form of livestock and farm implements, and by the promise of money bounties for five years. Despite this aid the colonists were largely dependent on nearby San Gabriel Mission for the first twenty years. By 1800 the pueblo contained but thirty adobe houses. But large ranches were being developed in the neighborhood and cattle were multiplying on the hills. Hides and tallow were exportable commodities which drew white sails to the harbor of San Pedro. The stacks of hides loaded onto Yankee clipper ships and carried around the Horn to New England were to make Boston the leather market of America.

The pastoral life about Los Angeles was to continue through the Spanish days and the succeeding period of Mexican rule (1821–1846). A few Anglo-Americans drifted in—some fleeing in sailors' costume from anchored ships; others putting aside the fringed buckskins and fur caps of mountain beaver trappers to don *bandos* and *sombreros*. The change in costume was usually caused by the attractiveness of the climate and the señoritas.

Then came the discovery of gold at Sutter's mill and Los Angeles became a way station for gold-seekers hurrying from the South and Southwest to the eldorado. Los Angeles acquired some gold from the northbound travelers and some from the returning miners. From the vineyards, that for years had been spreading out from Los Angeles, wine and brandy were shipped northward to cheer the miners in the gold camps. The mines provided also a market for the beef of the southern ranges.

The increasing trade of the Los Angeles area required the development of a seaport. The shallow beach at San Pedro was a poor excuse for a harbor, but it was the only one available and was the best in many miles of barren coast. It must be utilized and developed. Also, it must be recognized as an official port of entry, a consummation achieved by declaration of Congress in August, 1854. Citizens now began to dredge the shallow waters to form a harbor at the mouth of Wilmington Creek.

Vineyards, orchards, and farms continued to spread over an ever widening area. Farseeing men saw that the future of the region rested on intensive cultivation of the soil and the development of an adequate port. One of the first to visualize the possibilities of the port and work effectively to materialize his dream was Col. P. T. Banning. After operating a stage line from Los Angeles to San Pedro he successfully promoted the building of a railroad across the thirty-mile barrier. The road was opened in November, 1869. So successful was this enterprise that the citizens began to hope for a connection with the transcontinental railroad that had recently reached San Francisco.

The Southern Pacific was planning a railroad south from San Francisco, but its announced intention was to bypass Los Angeles and take a shorter route through the San Bernardino region. The builders let it be known that they might alter their plans and run the road by way of Los Angeles if the town and county would offer sufficient inducements—say $600,000 in bonds, with right of way and acreage for a depot. To the 7,000 citizens of the town it seemed a high price to exact, but to be bypassed would mean oblivion. So they voted the bonds. By the time these were due the valuation of the county had increased, partly because of the railroad, to $100,000,000 and the subsidy seemed small.

The arrival of the railroad in September, 1876, started a new era for Los Angeles. The town's growth was promoted when the Santa Fe railroad arrived in the next decade, and the resulting competition brought better freight rates. The railroads and citizens now began aggressively to advertise the climate and resources of southern California. Tourists and prospective settlers by the thousands flocked to the region and land values began to soar. Newly platted towns sprang up in the area and subdivision bred subdivisions to stretch the elastic boundaries of Los Angeles. Effective techniques for selling town lots were developed—brass bands, free lunches, colorful maps, and spirited ballyhoo. The boom of the eighties brought marvelous expansion, which the recession at the end of the decade affected only temporarily.

The navel orange, introduced from Brazil in 1873, soon began to transform the landscape and bring new wealth to southern California. Fast fruit express trains were now installed to satisfy the aroused demand of the country for this citrus fruit. The Los Angeles Chamber of Commerce and the California Fruit Growers Exchange built up the market for oranges and the facilities for their production and handling.

As the city and region grew, the need for harbor improvement became more urgent. A Congressional Commission studied the problem and recommended the development of San Pedro. Conflicts between rival interests were finally resolved, federal money was appropriated, a breakwater was constructed, and a great harbor that would accommodate ships of any size and draft was made. Over $50,000,000 was expended on this project before 1940.

The climate, the railroads, the rich horticultural area, the harbor— each contributed toward producing and supporting the growing population. But a shadow hung over Los Angeles—its future was endangered by lack of water; by 1900 the city was nearing the limit of its water supply. Then came the spectacular plan of city engineer

William Mulholland to build a 250-mile aqueduct across desert and mountain from Owens Lake. "If Los Angeles doesn't get this water now," he declared, "it will never need it." In six years' time the engineering feat was accomplished and in 1913 precious water from Mount Whitney flowed into Los Angeles. A city of 300,000 appeared supplied for its possible population limit of 1,000,000, but in a surprisingly short time the million was reached and more water was needed. Joining forces with the Imperial Valley and with other areas and interests, Los Angeles participated in projecting and building the great dam on the Colorado River. The subsequent construction of the giant aqueduct brought a bountiful supply of water.

A great financial landfall for Los Angeles was the discovery of oil in her own dooryard. The wealth of black gold tapped in the early 1900's presently produced forests of derricks. Millions of barrels of oil were produced annually. The wealth was reflected in mansions and industrial plants.

During the same years there sprang up the fabulous "movie" industry. The motion picture was quickly developed into the number one entertainment of America. The Hollywood suburb became more famous in foreign lands than its mother city. This "super-colossal" industry was almost unbounded in its worldwide influence.

During the depression of the 1930's, hordes of the destitute from other areas of the country deluged the comparatively favored land of southern California. Then came World War II, with its demands for rapid mass production of airplanes and other instruments and sinews of war. The Los Angeles pool of manpower, with oil and electric power available, formed an ideal combination for great industrial production.

The rise of Los Angeles to first place among the cities of Western America has been a spectacular achievement. In this metropolis is strikingly exhibited what can result from the bounty of Nature and the energy of Man.

Houston is the modern wonder city of Texas. Its manmade ship canal, the resources of its hinterland, and the aggressive optimism of its citizens have made it one of the great ports of the world. Begun as a real estate promotion of the Allen brothers back in 1836, its growth has been substantial during most of the subsequent years and reached boom proportions after 1900.

In the 1870's Galveston was the largest city in Texas. But nearby Houston, at the head of the Buffalo Bayou, was able to capture considerable traffic and to ship it on shallow-draft boats down the bayou to Galveston. With manufacturing and commerce increasing, it set about to deepen its life-line to the sea. A Congressional appropriation in 1899 made possible the transformation of the bayou into a channel

18½ feet deep.   Ten years later the ambitious city was working on a really deep-water ship canal.   By 1925 over $10,000,000 in federal funds had been spent in constructing a 30-foot deep channel for the 55 miles from the harbor to the outer bar.   Houston had brought the deep sea to the city, and the tonnage increase was phenomenal. Further widening and development of the channel have since been effected.   Industrial expansion, mushrooming up beside the channel, is one of the marvels of the city.   The price of frontage here, as of

SKYLINE OF A PORTION OF THE BUSINESS SECTION OF HOUSTON, TEXAS, LARGEST CITY IN THE SOUTHWEST.

Houston has a population of almost 508,000.   The city's metropolitan area has a population of approximately 780,000, largest in the South.   Houston is the South's largest industrial center, a major deepwater port, and an international air gateway.

city lots downtown, is the materialization of a mad real estate promoter's dream.

Houston had been designated the capital of the Texas Republic in 1837, but subsequently lost this distinction.   Nevertheless, Houston grew, becoming an important cattle port and lumber center.   During the Civil War it was notorious as a center for blockade runners.

By the 1890's Houston had sawmills, wagon and carriage factories, breweries, soap factories, mills for pressing cottonseed oil, and four railroad shops.   The flat marshy backlands were being converted into rice fields. Houston was shipping large quantities of rice, cotton, lumber, and cattle. In 1901 an oil well blew in at the Beaumont Field. Other fields were developed. Houston became an oil center and presently proclaimed itself the world's leading oil port.

With its ship channel for ocean-going vessels and the Intracoastal Waterway extending the length of the Gulf coast of the United States, Houston was well equipped to capture and hold water-borne commerce. Its railroad facilities were equally good, with feeder lines bringing in wheat from Kansas, cattle from Texas ranges, and oil from Texas and Oklahoma.

Following the outbreak of World War II, Houston's position and the natural resources of her area pushed her forward. A wealth of petroleum, natural gas, sulphur, lime (from oyster shells), and salt made possible the rapid development of the synthetic rubber and chemical industries. She claims distinction as the chemical capital of the nation.

Business expansion is rapid, and uncontrolled by regulations. The city is a powerful adolescent, conscious of strength and not yet ready to accept the calm modes and manner of sedate maturity.

Denver was born of a gold rush. The prospecting party that came to the foot of the Rocky Mountains in the summer of 1858 camped on June 24 at the point where Cherry Creek enters the South Platte River. Here, at the site of future Denver, and at various points in the region round about they found color in stream beds, but not in sufficient quantities to justify mining operations. A few days later they found a paying placer at nearby Dry Creek. News of this find, carried back East and expanded in the telling, produced a stampede. Although the big rush did not occur until the spring of 1859, a number of would-be miners hurried across the plains in the autumn of 1858. Some of these hopefuls formed a town company and started Denver. Founded on hope rather than substance, its existence was precarious until May, 1859, when the Gregory Lode was found near present Central City. This discovery in the mountains, some forty miles west of Denver, saved the situation and made Denver the principal depot for the mines. Other mines were opened and Denver maintained her position as the chief outfitting point for the gold region. But the placers were soon exhausted and the ore on the lodes became refractory as these veins were followed into the earth.

Mining in Colorado suffered a slump in the middle sixties. The Civil War and an Indian uprising also retarded Denver's growth. A fire in 1863 and a disastrous flood the following year added to the discouragements. But the town survived these ordeals and brighter days lay ahead. Agriculture in the surrounding region gradually developed; the Civil War ended; the Indian danger was removed; new mines were opened. Then the railroad came in 1870, two lines in fact—a branch from the Union Pacific at Cheyenne, and one from Kansas City.

Denver began to look up. Her population rose from less than 5,000 in 1870 to over 35,000 in 1880. Her favorable location and her priority in the region gave her command of the business and trade of the area.

Great impetus to her growth came with the discovery and development of the rich carbonate ores of Leadville. The silver from this great camp flowed into Denver. Wealth from the mines of the San Juan region, from Aspen, and other mining districts contributed to the upbuilding of the principal trade center of the region. The boom of the eighties was reflected in the growth of Colorado and its capital city. Denver's population tripled in the decade. The demonetization of silver and the Panic of 1893 burst the real estate bubble in Denver and brought bankruptcy to many of its citizens, banks, and businesses. But the timely rise of the great gold camp of Cripple Creek helped to save the situation.

After 1900 Denver depended less on mining and more on agriculture, as products of the farm in her trade territory outdid those from the mines. Then manufacturing overtopped mining and won a place second only to agriculture. As the largest city between Kansas City and San Francisco, Denver in 1910 prospered as the trade center of a large area. She was also gaining favor as a desirable residence city and as a center for tourists visiting scenic attractions in the Rocky Mountains.

World War II brought military training camps and war industries to the Denver area. The population continued to mount after the end of the war.

Minneapolis-St. Paul. The Falls of St. Anthony on the Mississippi River constitute a natural site for a great city. In fact, not one city but two were to grow up here. In 1820 Col. Snelling built at the confluence of the Minnesota and Mississippi rivers a military post that was soon called Fort Snelling. A steamboat reached it in 1823. Here at the head of navigation on the Mississippi the village of St. Paul sprang up. It became the capital of the Territory when Minnesota was organized in 1848, and has since retained political leadership. Its dominance continued into the post-Civil War period, with lumbering and trade as prominent activities. It built up great wholesale houses, and railroad enterprises centering there were destined to extend westward to the Pacific.

Minneapolis, the newer and now the larger of the "Twin Cities," has a hybrid name—*Minne,* Sioux for "water," and *polis,* Greek for "city." Its utilization of the water power of the falls launched it upon a manufacturing career. Sawmills and then flour mills brought expansion and by 1880 she had surpassed St. Paul in size.

Both cities were started by Yankees, but nineteenth-century immigration gave them their size and some of their distinguishing characteristics. St. Paul grew up during the heavy influx of Germans and Irish, is strongly Catholic, and Democratic. Minneapolis expanded later, during heavy Scandinavian immigration, and is Lutheran in religion and generally Republican in politics. St. Paul is conservative and deliberate; Minneapolis has a faster tempo and is more aggressive.

Courtesy of the Minneapolis Chamber of Commerce

SKYLINE OF MINNEAPOLIS, AS SEEN FROM LORING LAKE, ONE OF MINNE-
APOLIS' TWENTY-TWO LAKES AND LAKELETS.

The two cities look at each other across the Mississippi as rivals—usually friendly.

As western Minnesota and the Dakotas were settled, the great wheat production of these western prairies poured into Minneapolis to make her the milling center of the nation. Her primacy resulted not only from her location and water power, but also from the skill and ingenuity of the men engaged in the industry.

Located at the head of river navigation, the Twin Cities were well situated for water transportation. But with the coming of the railroad era their position was not so advantageous. Also, their position is unfortunate in relation to the great iron deposits of the Mesabi Range, only 150 miles away. That treasure takes the natural, easy route of the Great Lakes and goes to the mills of Chicago and Pittsburgh.

Up to and through World War I, Minneapolis was the flour milling center of the world. After the war, foreign markets collapsed and a scramble began for the domestic market. Control remained in Minneapolis, but plants sprang up in other locations, such as Buffalo and Kansas City. Today, Minneapolis mills produce less than half as much as they did thirty years ago. But Minneapolis-St. Paul remain the metropolis of a vast agricultural empire, extending west into Montana and south into Nebraska. Supplementing her milling industry, Minneapolis has developed many specialized light industries, such as precision machinery, and the manufacture of wearing apparel and package foods. The Twin Cities, with their suburban area, constitute a metropolitan center of about one million Americans.

BRIEFER SKETCHES OF REPRESENTATIVE CITIES

Brief sketches of a few additional cities will illustrate various features of Western urban centers.

Omaha was started at the western end of a ferry that transported western emigrants, mostly gold-seekers, across the Missouri River. The ferry company laid out a town site on the west bank in the summer of 1854. A post office was named before there was any settlement. Omaha had to fight for its place as capital of Nebraska Territory from 1855 to 1858 and retained the designation until statehood in 1867, when Lincoln was created on the virgin prairie.

The Pacific telegraph and the transcontinental railroad gave Omaha its real lead over other competitors along the Missouri River. Edward Creighton was prime mover in building the overland telegraph, which ran from Omaha, and was completed in 1861. The telegraph was forerunner of the railroad and gave Omaha an advantage over competitors as choice for the eastern terminus of the Pacific railroad. With the winning of this designation, Omaha's future was assured. By the time the golden spike was driven to mark the joining of the Union Pacific and the Central Pacific railroads, four railroads from the East converged at the river opposite Omaha.

The Union Pacific, in making Omaha headquarters of its company and business, linked itself with the new city. Omaha became a rail center and by 1900 three bridges spanned the Missouri at this point. Its commercial prominence has been supplemented by industrial development, including meat packing and machine shops.

Des Moines. The history of Des Moines has not been dramatic or spectacular. Originally it was a frontier fort, established in 1843 to stabilize the Indian frontier and protect the Sac and Fox Indians from encroachments of the whites and the Sioux. A town government was organized in 1851.

Navigation of the Des Moines River was an important factor in the growth of the city. Congress was induced to give alternate sections of land, in a five-mile strip on each side of the river, to aid in improving the channel, but in the long run the "internal improvement" move produced more grief than benefit.

Iowa's first capital was Burlington (1838–41); Iowa City had the designation from 1841 to 1857. Then in 1857 Des Moines was made the capital city, while Iowa City was designated the seat of the state university. Aided by the prestige of being the state capital, Des Moines grew steadily. To the first railroad, that came in 1866, others were added until seventeen radiated from the city. It became a whole-sale and retail jobbing center. Deposits of coal and clay induced industrial development. Business enterprise and stability made it an insurance center.

Salt Lake City was selected by Brigham Young and his Mormon band of wayfarers as their place of refuge. The Pioneer Band arrived July 24, 1847, and five days later began platting the city, with its broad streets and rectangular, ten-acre blocks. Construction began with erection of a fort of log cabins enclosing a city block.

Members and proselytes came in large caravans to swell the capital of this new Zion. The provisional State of Deseret was organized in 1850, and its General Assembly chartered Great Salt Lake City the next year. Irrigation was the basis of their farming, and cooperative enterprises the feature of their economic life. Missionaries brought converts from United States and Europe; the gold rush of '49 to California brought goods and trade to the city.

Johnston's Army came in 1857 and troops remained until the Civil War. Their presence provided a market for local produce. Home manufacturing was encouraged by the materially minded leader, Brigham Young. The telegraph came in 1861; the railroad to Utah in 1869. Thereafter growth was rapid.

As the ecclesiastical and political capital of the Mormon country, Salt Lake City has a large clientele. By 1900 a majority of the citizens were non-Mormon. Fort Douglas, established at the east border of the city, has been an economic asset. The discovery of rich mines, and of an enormous deposit of low-grade copper ore in the vicinity, has raised mining and smelting to a high place in the economy of the region. The presence of coal and iron has brought large steel mills to the area.

Portland. In 1843 A. M. Overton and A. L. Lovejoy camped on the site of Portland. Next day they projected a town there. Overton sold his share in the site to F. W. Pettygrove and the two partners established a store at the site. Lovejoy, a native of Boston, wanted to call the future city after his birthplace; Pettygrove was equally loyal to his home state of Maine and its capital city. They settled the controversy by the flip of a coin.

When Capt. John H. Couch brought the sailing vessel *Maryland* into the Columbia and Willamette he decided that Portland was the best site for a port. So he brought his family here in 1849, built wharves and warehouses, and established a regular shipping business. His choice, accepted by other sea captains, gave Portland its first important boost. The gold discovery in California created a demand for provisions from the fertile Willamette Valley, and the Pacific Mail Steamship Company made Portland its terminus.

Ambitious boosters improved their city's position and prospects by building wagon roads and establishing a ferry and river boat service. These radiating transportation lines helped make Portland the commercial metropolis of the Columbia Basin. The gold rush to Idaho and to western Montana in the early sixties augmented traffic on the Columbia and built up Portland as a supply depot. Strong contenders fought for routes and transportation facilities along the Columbia and by land. The Northern Pacific Railroad, under Henry Villard, finally won supremacy. Villard established Portland as the hub of railway and steamboat traffic in the Northwest. He made large investments in the city, spread promotion literature in Europe, and brought thousands of settlers to Oregon.

The shallow and dangerous Columbia River bar was a handicap to Portland's commerce. So the citizens raised money and won Congressional appropriations to deepen the channel. In 1887 the Oregon Short Line connection with the Union Pacific gave Portland another tie with the East. In the same year the Southern Pacific line provided a direct connection south to San Francisco.

After the Panic of 1893 had brought havoc to the railroads and business of the nation, E. H. Harriman emerged as the strong man in the Union Pacific system. He supported Portland against James J. Hill and Seattle. Portland went steadily ahead, building solidly and retaining her New England flavor and conservatism.

The impact of World War II altered her greatly, though perhaps only temporarily. The mushrooming of her shipyards and their record-breaking production set a tempo and created an atmosphere that was foreign to pre-war Oregon. The great influx of shipyard employees, strikingly alien in the Northwest, inflated the population of Portland and made of nearby Vanport the second city of Oregon. But with the end of the conflict the fever was calmed and Portland began to reassert her former self.

Spokane. The falls of the Spokane River—a break in transportation and a water power site—marked the location for a city. But the land was long unoccupied and the waterfalls unharnessed. These falls halted the up-stream movement of the salmon and here the fish were easily caught by the Spokane Indians.

In 1871 the first white men settled at the site. They started a sawmill, using an overshot water wheel. James N. Glover set up a store for trade with the Indians and then laid out the town of Spokane. The place grew slowly until the Northern Pacific Railroad came in 1881, when things began to happen. Wheat fields spread over the surrounding plains; the livestock industry flourished. Then rich mines were discovered in the Coeur d'Alene panhandle of Idaho and soon entertainment houses and private mansions in Spokane were reflecting the wealth from the mines. The city became a transportation center as railroads radiated out from this junction point. Flour mills sprang up as the surrounding wheat acreage increased.

Surrounded by vast resources from agriculture, from forests and mines, Spokane is the proud capital of the "Inland Empire." The development that will follow complete utilization of the Grand Coulee Dam should add new laurels.

BIBLIOGRAPHY

Most of the numerous books on city life and municipal problems do not give the historical data wanted for our present discussion. Two volumes that will be found especially useful, supplying historical sketches of western cities, are: Glenn C. Quiett, *They Built the West; an Epic of Rails and Cities* (New York, 1934); and Lyman P. Powell, *Historic Towns of the Western States* (New York, 1901). For earlier accounts, see L. P. Brockett, *Our Western Empire* (San Francisco, 1881); and William M. Thayer, *Marvels of the New West* (Norwich, Conn., 1888).

Individual books are available upon most of the American cities. The number of such volumes is too large for listing here. For up-to-date treatments and interesting appraisals of various American cities see the series of articles that have recently appeared in the *Saturday Evening Post, Holiday, Fortune,* and other magazines.

35

UTILIZATION OF NATURAL RESOURCES

$\rm T$HE SETTLEMENT of the trans-Mississippi West was accompanied by that reckless exploitation of natural resources that has characterized the American people since they first set foot in the New World. The forests seemed boundless, rich soil limitless and inexhaustible. With ax and fire the settlers leveled the forests; with rifle and trap they slaughtered game and birds and fur-bearing animals. Nature was so bountiful that scarcity or depletion was unthinkable. Even immigrants, schooled in Old World frugality, cast restraint aside in this new land and became as prodigal as the native-born. Not until the latter years of the nineteenth century was there any apparent consciousness that nature's gifts were exhaustible, that future generations were justly entitled to a share in the natural heritage.

Thoughtful men called attention to the criminally wasteful policies being pursued, especially with respect to our forests. Memorials by the American Association for the Advancement of Science presented in 1873 and in 1890 materially assisted in bringing the creation of a forestry bureau in the Department of Agriculture. Major J. W. Powell and others pointed out the irrigation needs and opportunities in the arid West. A campaign of education was begun.

It remained for the administration of Theodore Roosevelt to launch an aggressive program for the conservation of natural resources. In this work, Gifford Pinchot, director of the Forestry Service, took a leading part. In March, 1907, Roosevelt appointed an Inland Waterways Commission, which in its first report emphasized the interrelation of conservation problems, pertaining to forests, waters, soils, and minerals, and suggested a conference of governors to consider these vital national questions. There followed the White House Conference of May, 1908, attended by governors of states, members of Congress, and other prominent officials. This conference drew up a Declaration of

Principles, which in a sense is the basic charter of the conservation movement in America. From it we quote:

We declare our firm conviction that this conservation of our natural resources is a subject of transcendent importance, which should engage unremittingly the attention of the Nation, the States, and the people in earnest co-operation. These natural resources include the land on which we live and which yields our food; the living waters which fertilize the soil, supply power, and form great avenues of commerce; the forests which yield the materials for our homes, prevent erosion of the soil and conserve the navigation and other uses of the streams; and the minerals which form the basis of our industrial life, and supply us with heat, light, and power.

We agree that the land should be so used that erosion and soil wash shall cease; and that there should be reclamation of arid and semiarid regions by means of irrigation, and of swamp and overflowed regions by means of drainage; that the waters should be so conserved and used as to promote navigation, to enable the arid regions to be reclaimed by irrigation, and to develop power in the interests of the people; that the forests which regulate our rivers, support our industries, and promote the fertility and productiveness of the soil should be preserved and perpetuated; that the minerals found so abundantly beneath the surface should be so used as to prolong their utility; that the beauty, healthfulness, and habitability of our country should be preserved and increased; that sources of national wealth exist for the benefit of the people, and that monopoly thereof should not be tolerated.

A National Conservation Commission, headed by Pinchot, was appointed by the President. In its first report in 1909, an inventory of the nation's natural resources was given. The Secretary of the Interior now withdrew from entry 148,000,000 acres of forest land, 80,000,000 acres of coal lands, 4,700,000 acres of phosphate lands, and 1,500,000 acres of water-power sites. The President recommended that title to all coal, oil, and gas lands remaining in possession of the government be retained for the nation and be exploited only under regulations and leases of the government. In 1920, this ideal was in part realized.

The aims of the conservation movement were and are to protect and to develop the fullest permanent usefulness of the government national resources—land, water, minerals, and forests. Natural resources vary greatly in permanence. Water supply, being continually replenished, is perpetual. The ideal is, therefore, to utilize it to the full. Quite different are mineral fuels, such as coal and natural gas. These can be used but once and are gone. Sound policy requires economy in their use and the development of substitutes. Between these extremes are forests and soils, resources that are slow in creation and that wise management can conserve and replenish. Most metals, once extracted from the ground, may be used over and over again. Reduction to the minimum of losses from wear and dissipation is, therefore, an object of conservation with respect to metals.

Our present purpose is to sketch briefly the utilization of these re-sources and to consider the conservation measures that have had most bearing on the history of the West.

THE LAND

Land is the basic natural resource. From it come man's food, cloth-ing, and fuel—his fundamental needs. The supplying of these through the acquisition and use of land has, indeed, been the force behind most individual actions and mass movements traced in previous chapters. We need mention here only some of the recent aspects of the land question. F. J. Turner and other historians have called attention to the disappearance, about 1890, of the American frontier. By that time practically all the good farming land of the nation, capable of utiliza-tion by ordinary methods, had been taken up by home-seekers. There-after marginal lands were tilled, frequently with dire results. Efforts to utilize such lands, especially in the arid region, constitute one of the unique and important phases of far western history.

Most of the western half of the United States receives insufficient rainfall for successful farming with the methods traditionally employed east of the hundredth meridian. The consequent recourse to irrigation, as practiced in this region, will be discussed in the following section. In other areas so-called "dry farming" is undertaken. By the devel-opment of drought-resisting crops and the devising of tillage methods for conserving moisture, scientific farming has made some progress in the production of crops in semi-arid regions. But possibilities in this direction are definitely limited.

Rainfall varies from year to year, with a tendency to come in cycles. A series of dry years is generally followed by a series of comparatively wet ones. During the favorable years farmers generally push out onto the marginal land; and in dry years the settlement frontier recedes. Land that receives too little precipitation for successful farming may be entirely satisfactory for grazing purposes. Large areas of the high plains east of the Rocky Mountains and of the inter-mountain country of the Far West fall in this category. Under natural primitive condi-tions this was good cattle and sheep country. Through centuries, native grasses had covered the surface with a protective carpet that prevented undue erosion and that utilized the moisture for plant growth. Under those conditions the plains provided food for millions of animals such as the buffalo, deer, antelope, and elk.

When white men slaughtered this native fauna and replaced it with domestic cattle and sheep, the stock industry thrived. But its very success invited undue exploitation. By over-stocking, much grass was tramped out; the range was over-grazed and ruined. Then came the nester, to plow the ground and complete the destruction of the protective sod. Now the winds could work their full havoc. Soil was whipped away, and there was nothing to stay the destructive erosion.

Soil is precious. Few realize its importance or the factors involved in its creation. It is something far different from mere surface earth. Soil is composed of pulverized rock and humus, the first being inorganic mineral matter, and the second partly decomposed organic material. Essential, also, are water, air, and bacteria; without these the soil is barren. Through the complex processes of nature—the forces of heat, light, and gravity; the agents of water, air, and ice; the operations of plants and animals—soil is gradually made. Agronomists estimate that the average rate of manufacture of soil is less than an inch in 500 years. Writes C. R. Van Hise: "The surface layer of soil, manufactured by the processes of nature through millions of years, is the most precious natural resource of the nation. Of all of our duties to our descendants that of maintaining the soil unimpaired in thickness and in richness is the most serious."

The tragedy of soil erosion is thus apparent. In the Far West the problem has become especially serious. Dust storms in the 1930's made the citizenry conscious of it, and the "dust bowl" area of northern Texas and the adjacent region was publicized. Federal and local governmental agencies have taken a hand to stay the destruction and to repair the damage, so far as may be. Cessation of plowing and removal of farmers were the first steps taken in certain marginal land areas. In such country the Indian's instinctive hatred of the plow has found justification. Now the white man is wooing and nurturing the native grasses, planting trees for wind breaks, and trying to aid nature in her work of restoration over part of the denuded areas.

In addition to destruction of soil through erosion, there is deterioration through loss of valuable elements. This problem is common to the whole nation and not peculiar to the West. Of the various elements used as plant food, the majority are practically illimitable in amount. Nitrogen, potassium, and phosphorus are the vital ones needed to feed the plants that feed man. By rotation of crops, growing of leguminous plants, utilizing manure, and extraction of nitrogen from the air by electric power, an adequate future supply of nitrogen is assured. Potassium exists in such quantities in concentrated deposits and in original rock that there is little danger of its exhaustion. But the situation with respect to phosphorus is more crucial. This element is an essential constituent of flesh and blood, bone and brain. Soils are being depleted of it as grains are grown, meat and milk produced, and these products shipped away from the farm. Leaching and sewage account for additional losses. Only by careful use of suitable fertilizers can this important element be maintained.

Land in the West, having been farmed for a shorter period than that of the eastern seaboard, has not as yet suffered such a loss of fertility. With less rainfall, western soils have lost less through leaching. Inasmuch as a portion of the total supply of phosphorus is constantly being dissipated, conservation of this element is of primary concern. The greatest remaining phosphate fields of America are in the West—in Idaho, Wyoming, and Utah. But even these comparatively large storehouses must be carefully safeguarded if the future welfare of man in America is to be assured.

WATER

Water is essential to life. Indeed, it is the major constituent of living organisms; plant tissue is from three-eighths to three-fourths water, and animals are about 80 per cent water. In humid regions water is so plentiful that its importance is hardly appreciated. In arid lands, it is the all-important concern; the extent of plant and of animal life is determined by the amount of water available. The mean annual rainfall in the United States is about 30 inches. The quantity of water that falls on the United States each year is, therefore, some 215,000,-000,000,000 cubic feet, or about 1,500 cubic miles. About half of this amount evaporates, one-third runs off to the sea, and one-sixth is consumed by plants or joins the body of underground water. These proportions are being altered slightly by irrigation and reclamation developments in the West.

The western two-fifths of the United States receives less than 20 inches of rainfall, which is the amount usually required for normal crop production without irrigation. More, however, is needed in the hot southern section than in the cooler northern area. The seasonal distribution of precipitation also affects the result, less water being required if it comes at suitable intervals during the growing season. The needs for crop production vary from 15 to 60 inches. The 20-inch rainfall line, which roughly follows the one-hundredth meridian, thus divides the United States into two quite different sections. Except for the high mountains and a strip along the northern Pacific Coast, the whole far western area is arid or semi-arid. In the more favored sections, dry farming meets with some success, but for the most part agriculture is dependent on irrigation. And the area capable of development under irrigation is very restricted because of limitations of water supply and topography. The western arid two-fifths of the United States embraces some 768,000,000 acres. About two-thirds of this area would be suitable for irrigation from the standpoint of altitude and topography. But less than ten per cent of this can actually be irrigated, even under the fullest possible development. So at best the arid western region can support but a relatively small population.

Farming by irrigation is older than recorded history. In ancient Egypt and Babylonia, land was artificially watered for the production of crops. In our own Southwest, the Pueblo Indians were irrigating small tracts of land before the white man came, and Spanish missionaries and early settlers adopted the practice. But it was the middle of the nineteenth century before extensive irrigation development began in the United States. We have already mentioned the beginnings in Utah and in other far western states.

There are several stages in the development of western irrigation. In the earliest years farmers settled on the bottomlands beside the streams, and dug small ditches to divert water over the adjoining land. Then larger canals were constructed through the co-operative efforts of interested persons, and water was carried onto the higher bench lands. Then corporate capital came, built larger and longer canals, and sold water rights to farmers. The processes of ditch building and water diversion continued into the 1890's, when the normal flow of many western streams was entirely diverted. Then began reservoir development, the high water of spring being stored and made available for release later in the summer when regular stream flow was low. This was especially prompted by the late summer needs of such crops as potatoes, sugar beets, and alfalfa. Finally came federally constructed reclamation projects that were too large and costly to be financed by private capital. Diverting water from the Pacific slope to the Atlantic through tunneled mountains is the latest phase.

In the West, irrigation water has become a commodity like hay or wheat, to be bought and sold, measured and delivered. The new conditions met with here have not only brought changes in farming practice and social organization, but have altered legal concepts as well. The English Common Law, which the United States inherited, contained the doctrine of "riparian rights"—that the landholder was entitled to an undiminished flow of water in the streams abutting his land. This principle did not fit conditions in an arid country. So there developed the practice of "appropriation," which meant that a person might divert and use water from a stream without reference to ownership of adjoining land, provided that his use did not interfere with an earlier similar use. Priority of appropriation thus became the recognized principle, with the courts determining the priority sequence and the amount of water of each appropriation. Later legal developments took into account "beneficial use." Under this principle, for ex-

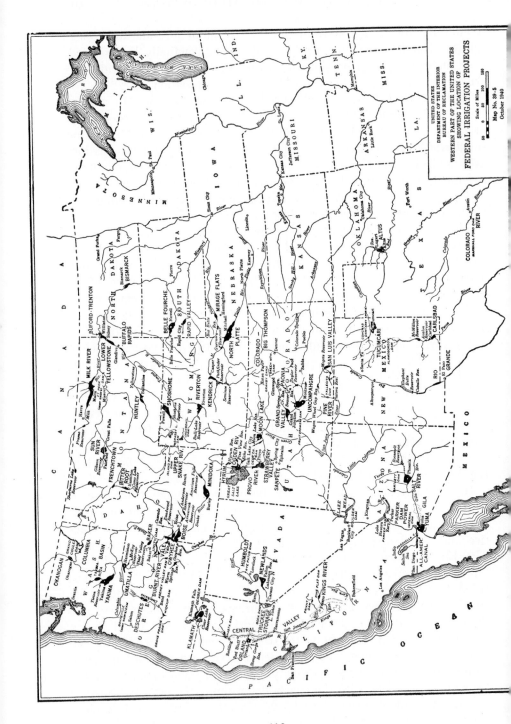

ample, needs for culinary supply take precedence over irrigation use.

Important federal participation in irrigation development began with the passage of the Reclamation Act of 1902. Back of its enactment, however, was a period of serious study and a campaign of education. Major J. W. Powell, the one-armed soldier who traversed the Grand Canyon of the Colorado in 1869, made a special study of the arid West, and in 1879 issued his report on irrigation possibilities there. Further surveys were made during the two following decades, and the problem was discussed in and out of Congress. The great drought of 1890 drew increased national attention to irrigation. In 1894 Congress passed the Carey Act, which provided for the cession of not over 1,000,000 acres of desert land to each of several western states on condition that they cause the land to be irrigated, reclaimed, and occupied. Achievement of the objective was left to the states or to private capital, with no federal funds provided. Under this arrangement but little was accomplished. When Theodore Roosevelt came to the White House in 1901, he gave vigorous support to a reclamation program. A bill introduced by Congressman F. G. Newlands of Nevada was finally passed as the Reclamation Act of 1902.

This law created the Reclamation Fund from the proceeds of public land sales in 16 western states. Use of this money was authorized for the survey, construction, and maintenance of irrigation works, and for the storage and diversion of water for the reclamation of arid lands. The costs of these projects were to be repaid by the settlers on the reclaimed land. The money would thus become a revolving fund for the building of additional projects. Subsequent legislation has added to the funds other revenue, such as the proceeds from oil and mineral royalties and from federal power licenses. The Warren Act of 1911 authorized the sale of surplus water from federal projects to provide supplemental supplies to land already irrigated but with insufficient water reserves. This has become a very important extension, vital to certain areas of the West.

With financing, planning, and construction work in federal hands, a fine objectivity has been achieved and a notable record made. The accompanying map shows the wide distribution of projects and the area served. In the last decade or so direct appropriations from the general treasury have been made to the Reclamation Bureau for specific projects, thus enabling it to undertake work on a far grander scale than its ordinary revenues would permit. The Boulder Dam on the Colorado and the Grand Coulee on the Columbia are perhaps the most impressive. On these and many lesser projects, the original objective of a regulated and assured water supply for irrigation has been supplemented by the generation of enormous heads of electric power. In addition, other purposes have been served, such as flood control, improvement of navigation, the providing of domestic water supplies for urban areas, and provision for recreation opportunities and wild life refuges.

The Boulder Dam project, built at a cost of about $132,000,000, has provided the largest reservoir and the largest power plant in the world. It has made possible the construction of the All-American Canal, leading from the Colorado River to the Imperial Valley of California. This canal, several times the size of the original Erie Canal in New York, is the largest irrigation ditch in the United States. It is 80 miles long and has an initial capacity of 15,000 cubic feet of water per second. The maximum section has a width of 232 feet at the water surface, a bottom width of 152 feet, and a water depth of 21 feet.

Regarding electric power produced in the West by the federal government, the Reclamation Bureau reported in 1939:

The ultimate capacity of plants already constructed on projects and of power developments on projects still under construction will approximate 5,590,000 horsepower.

Power revenues are expected to repay more than half a billion dollars of utimate construction cost of the reclamation projects now completed or under construction, including Boulder Dam. This is nearly half of the estimated total cost of these projects.

John C. Page, Commissioner of the Bureau of Reclamation, wrote in his Annual Report of 1939:

Work done during the year brought to a grand total of 156 the number of storage and diversion dams which have been completed by the Bureau since its origin in 1902. Of these, Shoshone, Arrowrock, Owyhee, and Boulder were each, at the time of completion, the highest in the world. Shasta, now under construction on the Central Valley project in California, will be 560 feet in height and rank next to Boulder, and Grand Coulee Dam, under construction on the Columbia Basin project in Washington, follows closely with a maximum height of 553 feet above foundation. . . .

In the 37 years the following construction has been completed by the Bureau of Reclamation: 156 storage and diversion dams; 48 powerhouses; 2,812 buildings; 20,101.4 miles of canals, ditches, and drains; 81.8 miles of tunnels; 4,661.6 miles of telephone lines; 285.4 miles of ditches; 6,337 flumes; 20,597 culverts; 13,738 bridges; 198,521 other irrigation structures. Reservoirs of the Bureau of Reclamation now have a combined capacity of 47,121,170 acre-feet of water. [This storage water would cover the state of Colorado about nine inches deep, or the whole United States about three-tenths of an inch.]

MINERALS AND METALS

Mineral productions of the United States, which have been important for many years, have assumed their largest proportions since

VIEW OF BOULDER DAM

On September 28, 1940, during an annual test of the needle valves in the canyon wall outlet below Boulder Dam, for the second time in the 5-year life of the dam, surging torrents of water shot from all but one of the 12 outlets. More than 20,000 visitors witnessed the spectacle, a record for one day. (Boulder City, Nevada.)

1900. In 1880, the value of metallic and nonmetallic mineral products totaled $367,463,000. Thereafter, for several decades, the rise was rather rapid, as the following figures for total annual production show:

1890	..............$ 615,000,000	1920 ....$6,981,000,000
1900	 1,109,000,000	1930 4,765,000,000
1910	 1,988,000,000	1940 5,613,900,000

Detailed tables show that the value of metallic minerals approximately equalled that of mineral fuels (coal, petroleum, and so forth) prior to 1917; and that thereafter fuels greatly exceeded the metals in value.

Coal production in the United States has shown a remarkable in-

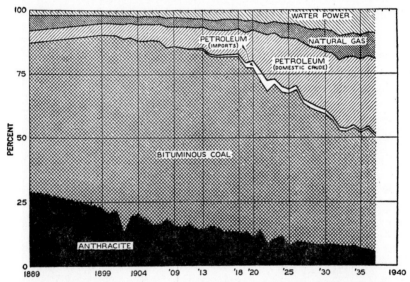

PER CENT OF TOTAL B. T. U. EQUIVALENT CONTRIBUTED BY THE SEVERAL SOURCES OF ENERGY, COUNTING WATER POWER AT CONSTANT FUEL EQUIVA-LENT, 1889–1937. If water power is counted at the prevailing fuel equiva-lent of central stations in each year, its proportion is 3.2 per cent in 1899 and 3.5 per cent in 1937, and the proportions of the other sources of energy are affected accordingly.

crease, with the annual output approximately doubling every decade from 1850 to 1910. In 1850 the annual output was 7,000,000 tons; in 1910 it was 502,000,000 tons. In the peak year of 1918 the production was 678,212,000 tons. Since then the general trend has been down-ward, with the production of 1932 being about half that of 1918, though there was some rise thereafter. Trans-Mississippi states have been comparatively small producers of coal. Their total combined production, from the date of earliest record to the end of 1937,

TOTAL PRODUCTION OF THE PRECIOUS METALS TO 1936

States (in order of rank)	Gold	Silver	Copper	Lead	Zinc	Total
Arizona	$ 188,407,368	$ 172,084,218	$2,335,053,026	$ 25,947,540	$ 12,811,927	$ 2,932,860,233
Montana	326,693,995	493,289,644	1,663,636,836	59,366,288	234,590,850	2,784,625,255
California	1,973,809,992	74,452,773	187,519,874	13,957,893	9,376,286	2,259,116,818
Utah	164,303,337	456,479,303	817,317,945	409,254,444	70,955,987	1,918,311,009
Colorado	769,492,739	530,645,687	51,988,055	219,317,201	157,411,318	1,728,854,000
Nevada	486,565,586	516,943,584	343,185,696	51,329,863	28,345,960	1,426,370,689
Idaho	149,218,313	258,742,345	27,218,601	536,217,070	81,817,111	1,053,213,440
New Mexico	42,065,913	46,489,018	254,402,065	20,886,807	56,724,799	420,569,602
South Dakota	378,547,304	6,075,699	34,598	34,820	—	384,692,421
Total for these nine western states	$4,479,105,547	$2,555,212,271	$5,568,056,696	$1,336,311,926	$652,034,138	$14,850,813,467
Total for United States	$5,129,381,478	$2,630,532,589	$7,686,127,000			

615

amounted to but slightly over two billion tons, which is less than 10 per cent of the total output of the nation.

For the story of petroleum discoveries, development, and production, see the following chapter.

It is interesting to note the changing contributions of coal, petroleum, and water power to the national energy supply. The accompanying drawing tells the story graphically.

To arrive at a common denominator for such different things as coal, oil, gas, and electricity is difficult. The government statisticians converted each into British thermal units; for example, they assumed "a constant fuel equivalent of 4.02 pounds of coal for each kilowatt-hour of water power produced."

In 1889 coal was supplying about 87 per cent of the total energy; by 1937 its contribution was reduced to about 50 per cent. Petroleum made the outstanding gain over coal, with natural gas and water power making notable replacements as well. If the situation in the trans-Mississippi region were charted separately, the picture would be entirely different. Coal would be shown as making the minor contribution, with petroleum far in the lead and water power making substantial gains in recent years.

In this volume we have already devoted considerable space to precious metals, especially in so far as their discovery and production have induced settlement and development in a number of the far western states. Now let us call attention to the amount and the sources of the so-called "precious metals" (gold, silver, copper, lead, and zinc). From the accompanying table, it will be noted that copper is the most valuable of our precious metals. The total amount produced in this country is worth nearly the combined values of gold and silver. It is primarily copper production that gives Arizona first rank among the metal mining states. The total value of her copper well exceeds that of California's gold. It is copper, also, that has put Montana in second place. The ranking positions of other western states, as to total metal production, are indicated in the accompanying table.

The four states that have produced the most gold are: California, Colorado, Nevada, and South Dakota. From 1850 to 1861 California produced gold valued at more than $40,000,000 annually, with a peak of over $81,294,700 in 1852. From 1862 to 1928 the production has been rather consistent, never dropping below $10,000,000 per year, and averaging approximately $15,000,000. Colorado's annual gold production was in excess of $10,000,000 from 1895 to 1918, with a peak of $28,762,036 in 1900. This large amount came primarily from the Cripple Creek District. Nevada's gold output exceeded $10,000,000 annually from 1872 to 1878 (from the Comstock Lode) and from 1906 to 1915 (primarily from the Goldfield and Tonopah districts). South Dakota has been a consistent gold producer since 1876. Rarely has production from the Black Hills District dropped below $6,000,000 per year since 1899.

In the production of silver, the honors are rather evenly divided between four states—Colorado, Montana, Utah, and Nevada. They rank in the order named as to amount produced, but from the standpoint of value, Nevada would rank second, inasmuch as the bulk of her silver was produced at an earlier time, when the price was much higher. Colorado's production exceeded 10,000,000 ounces per year from 1879 to 1907, with an output of 25,838,600 ounces in the peak year 1893. Her total yield to 1931 was approximately 690,000,000 ounces. In 1887 silver production in Montana exceeded 10,000,000 ounces and averaged above that amount through 1929. The total to 1931 amounted to about 632,000,000 ounces. Utah produced an average of over 10,000,000 ounces of silver per year from 1901 to 1930. Her entire production amounted to 585,000,000 ounces by 1931. Nevada produced in excess of 10,000,000 ounces annually from 1871 to 1878, and from 1909 to 1918. The peak was reached in 1875, with 21,913,153 ounces. By 1931 her total output amounted to 541,000,000 ounces.

The great copper-producing states are Arizona, Montana, and Utah. Important developments and big yields have come only in comparatively recent years. Arizona passed 100,000,000 pounds annual production for the first time in 1898. She showed a fairly steady increase, and reached a peak of over 830,000,000 pounds in 1929. The total yield to 1931 approximated 15 billion pounds. Montana passed 100,-000,000 pounds annual production in 1890, and has produced rather consistently since, reaching a total production by 1931 of over 10 billion pounds. Utah's annual copper output passed 100,000,000 pounds in 1909 and reached a total of almost 5 billion pounds by 1931.

The principal producers of lead are Idaho, Utah, and Colorado. The value of Idaho's lead is double that of her silver and more than three times that of her gold. Her annual production of lead passed the 100,000,000 pounds figure in 1897. Production continued on a large scale, to reach a combined total of over 9 billion pounds by 1931. In 1902 Utah reached an annual production of 100,000,000 pounds of lead. She continued a high output that brought the total to approximately 7 billion pounds by 1931. From 1882 to 1906, the average annual production of lead in Colorado was well above 100,000,000 pounds. Thereafter it fell off materially, the total amounting to 4.6 billion pounds.

Montana has been the principal zinc producer. From 1914 to 1929 her output was over 100,000,000 pounds annually. The total production amounted to about 2.7 billion pounds. Colorado ranks second as a zinc producer. Between the years 1912 and 1917 she averaged over 100,000,000 pounds annually. Her total production is about 2.2 billion pounds. Idaho and Utah have each produced about half as much zinc as Colorado.

Of all the metals, iron is most important; but because iron ores are rather plentiful, they are still fairly cheap in price. Of the total available iron ore in the United States, approximately three-fourths is in the Lake Superior region. Well over two billion tons had been produced in this area prior to 1946. The annual production of the United States, which was about 5,000,000 tons in 1875, showed a fairly steady increase to about 27,000,000 tons in 1900. The production mounted rapidly, to reach a level of some 75,000,000 tons annually during World War I. Thereafter the output was very irregular; for example, it was over 70,000,000 tons in 1929 and less than 10,000,000 in 1932. It rose to 91,000,000 tons in 1942, during World War II, and declined to less than 60,000,000 in 1946.

Space will not permit discussion of the numerous other mineral products. Some idea of their relative importance in the western states may be conveyed by the following list, taken from the *Minerals Yearbook, 1946.*

STATES AND THEIR PRINCIPAL MINERAL PRODUCTS IN 1946

Rank	State	Principal Mineral Products in Order of Value
14	Arizona	Copper, zinc, lead, gold
24	Arkansas	Petroleum, coal, bauxite, natural gas
3	California	Petroleum, natural gas, natural gasoline, cement
22	Colorado	Coal, petroleum, zinc, molybdenum
26	Idaho	Zinc, lead, silver, phosphate rock
29	Iowa	Cement, clay products, stone, coal
10	Kansas	Petroleum, natural gas, zinc, cement
6	Louisiana	Petroleum, natural gas, natural gasoline, sulphur
11	Minnesota	Iron ore, stone, sand and gravel, manganiferous ore
20	Missouri	Lead, cement, coal, stone
25	Montana	Copper, petroleum, natural gas, coal
43	Nebraska	Cement, sand and gravel, clay products, stone
27	Nevada	Copper, zinc, tungsten, concentrates, gold
13	New Mexico	Petroleum, potassium salts, natural gas, copper
44	North Dakota	Coal, sand and gravel, natural gas, clay products
7	Oklahoma	Petroleum, natural gas, zinc, natural gasoline
40	Oregon	Sand and gravel, cement, stone, clay products
37	South Dakota	Gold, stone, cement, sand and gravel
1	Texas	Petroleum, natural gas, natural gasoline, sulphur
18	Utah	Copper, coal, zinc, lead
31	Washington	Cement, coal, sand and gravel, stone
21	Wyoming	Petroleum, coal, natural gas, natural gasoline

Forests

A fourth great natural resource is our forests. Approximately one-half of the territory of the United States was once forest-covered. The eastern forest originally extended from the Atlantic seaboard to the Mississippi, and through and beyond the first tier of states west of the great river. West of this timber country lay the treeless plains, extending from Texas to Canada. Throughout the Rocky Mountain region much of the high-altitude country is covered with timber. A dense and magnificent forest covers the Pacific slope region of Washington, Oregon, and northern California.

Great inroads upon the primeval forest have been made in the United States, especially in the eastern and central sections. Here the first move toward the making of a home was to clear the land of trees. Early pioneers thus developed the attitude that since trees impeded the progress of settlement, it was praiseworthy to cut and destroy them. Here, as frequently occurs elsewhere, what was once a virtue became a vice. There came a time when the cutting and burning of forests was no longer a patriotic act.

The movement for the preservation of our forests, which began in the 1870's, resulted in the establishment of the division of forestry in the Department of Agriculture in 1886. In 1891 Congress authorized the president to set aside forest reserves in order to protect the remaining timber on the public domain from destruction and to insure the regular flow of streams. The first such designation was the Yellowstone Park Timberland Reserve, made the same year by President Harrison. Thereafter the movement gained momentum, with succeeding presidents making additions to the timber reserves. Theodore Roosevelt, during his administration, quadrupled the area of the reserves. By 1939 there were 217 national forests, experimental forests, and purchase units, with a total net area of about 175,000,000 acres in 43 states, Alaska, and Puerto Rico.

The original withdrawals of land from entry met with vigorous disapproval in the West, where most of these reserves were located. But as the federal government made provision for administering these forests, the opposition gradually disappeared. A system of scientific forestry was evolved, with long-term planning directed toward the greatest good for the whole people.

At the time when the national-forest movement began, practically all the public domain within states east of the Great Plains, except some inferior remnants, had passed to private or state ownership. Even in the Far West much of the forest land had gone into private hands.

Our principal virgin forest area today is in the Northwest. The states of Washington, Oregon, Idaho, and Montana contain about three-fifths of all our remaining old-growth timber. The "West Coast area," lying in the western half of Oregon and Washington, contains about one-third of all the remaining saw timber of the United States. Five-sixths of this area is forest land, of which 51 per cent is privately owned and 49 per cent publicly owned. About one-third of the "Interior region" of the Columbia River Basin is forest land, of which 68 per cent is public property and 32 per cent private.

In 1911 Congress authorized the purchase of lands valuable for protection of the headwaters of streams or for timber production and their reorganization as national forests. Subsequent acts have enlarged the scope of this work and have made possible reforestation on denuded areas. Most of this activity is in the eastern states, but there are 15 established purchase-areas in western states where this commendable work is being carried forward.

Ideal management is concerned with the development and perpetuation of the forests, that they may continue these many benefits to mankind: furnishing wood and other products for man's use; preventing erosion of soil and damage by floods; regulating stream flow and water supply for irrigation, domestic use, and power; harboring wild life; and providing opportunities for outdoor recreation.

The great dependence of our civilization on wood and wood products need not be emphasized here. The direct uses of wood for making buildings, furniture, and boxes, for firewood, mine timbers, and telephone poles, are apparent and important. Tar, turpentine, and dyestuffs are forest products, and an ever increasing list of commodities, such as paper, plastics, films, rayons, lacquers, and distillates, are manufactured wholly or in part from wood. The maintenance of an assured wood supply is obviously an important part of national conservation.

Fire is a grave and ever-present danger to the forests. Reducing this hazard to a minimum is, of course, a cardinal principle of conservation. Inasmuch as half of the forest fires are man-caused, campaigns of education, with techniques for fire detection and control, are fruitful of results.

In the semi-arid sections of the West the protection of watersheds is a primary concern in wise forestry policy. The forest, as a natural soil holder and water reservoir, exerts a powerful influence upon the regularity of stream flow. It therefore aids in flood control, in checking silting, in providing a steady stream head for electric-power plants, and helps conserve water for irrigation and domestic uses.

The forest areas afford grazing for domestic and wild animals. On the national forests over 12,000,000 domestic animals are grazed annually, special permits being issued that the number of stock may be controlled. The forests are becoming increasingly important in preserving and restoring wild life in America. In the West as a whole, about 75 per cent of the remaining big-game summer ranges are now within the national forests. Under governmental protection, big game has increased more than 100 per cent in the last two decades. Wild life in the forest area, including game, birds, and fish, constitutes a national economic resource valued at more than $1,000,000,000 annually.

Closely allied to the wild life phase of the forests are the opportunities afforded for recreation. This feature is gaining increasing importance, as national forests are being provided with roads, trails, campgrounds, and similar facilities. In the two decades preceding 1937 the number of annual visitors to the national forests increased from 3,000,000 to 33,000,000. Entirely primitive conditions are maintained in selected areas of the forests.

Despite widespread destruction in this country through 300 years, our timber resources are still great. The National Forest Service estimates that of the 820,000,000 acres of original forest in this country, 462,000,000 acres of commercial forest lands remain. Some 215,000,-000 acres of this is virgin forest, bearing trees of saw-timber size. The remainder is in part depleted and in need of silviculture.

This heartening note comes from the Chief of the United States Forest Service in his Report of 1938: "On an overall basis, with reasonable care, the forest lands we now have are capable of producing all the timber we need for domestic consumption plus a comfortable margin for export."

BIBLIOGRAPHY

On the general aspects of conservation, see: C. R. Van Hise, *The Conservation of Natural Resources in the United States* (New York, 1910); N. S. Shaler, *Man and the Earth* (New York, 1905); and *Report of the National Conservation Commission, Senate Document 676,* 60th Cong., 2nd sess. (Washington, 1909), and succeeding Reports of the Commission.

For discussions of irrigation and reclamation problems, consult: F. H. Newell, *Irrigation in the United States* (New York, 1902); R. P. Teele, *Irrigation in the United States* (New York, 1915); G. W. James, *Reclaiming the Arid West. The Story of the United States Reclamation Service* (New York, 1917); W. E. Smythe, *The Conquest of Arid America* (New York, 1911); J. W. Powell, *Report on the Lands of the Arid Region of the United States* (Washington, 1879); *National Irrigation Policy—Its Development and Significance (Senate Document 36,* 76th Cong., 1st sess.); the *Yearbook of the United States Department of Agriculture;* R. Tavernier and M. O. Leighton, "The Public Utility of Water Powers and their Governmental Regulation," *Water Supply Paper 238,* U. S. Geological Survey.

The following books are devoted to mineral production: T. A. Rickard, *A History of American Mining* (New York, 1932); J. F. Kemp, *The Ore*

Deposits of the United States and Canada (New York, 1900); H. C. Hoover, *Principles of Mining* (New York, 1909); *Ore Deposits of the Western States Lindgren Volume)* (New York, 1933); E. C. Jeffrey, *Coal and Civilization* (New York, 1925); James Macfarlane, *The Coal Regions of America* (New York, 1873); W. T. Thom, *Petroleum and Coal; the Keys to the Future* (Princeton, 1929); and United States Bureau of Mines, *The Minerals Year-book* (published annually since 1933).

For data on forests and forestry, see: C. L. Pack and Tom Gill, *Forests and Mankind* (New York, 1929); F. S. Baker, *Theory and Practice of Silviculture* (New York, 1934); B. E. Fernow, *Economics of Forestry* (New York, 1902); S. B. Green, *Principles of American Forestry* (New York, 1903); A. B. Recknagel, *Forestry; a Study of its Origin, Application and Significance in the United States* (New York, 1929); *Work of the United States Forest Service (Miscellaneous Publication No. 290*, of the U. S. Dept. of Agriculture); O. W. Price, R. S. Kellogg, and W. T. Cox, *The Forests of the United States; Their Use* (U. S. Dept. of Agriculture Forest Service, Circular 171); and Annual Reports of the Chief of the United States Forest Service.

36

IMPACT OF PETROLEUM

In an abstract sense immigrants saw many horizons of hope and opportunity in the West—the Great Plains sea of grass, ideal for cattle grazing; the rich wheat and corn lands of Kansas and Nebraska; the gold and silver bearing strata of the Sierra Nevadas and Rocky Mountains; and the cool, green slopes and deep canyons of the Sangre de Cristos, where for many decades Spanish-American *pastores* had driven their sheep to pasture. These and many more western areas had friendly horizons inviting thousands of pilgrims to fortune and new life. But other thousands found drouth, sickness, and disaster and returned to established communities farther east. Yet many of their abandoned claims, as in Kansas, New Mexico, and Texas, in later years brought fabulous returns to those who held their mineral rights, for hundreds and sometimes thousands of feet below plowed fields, wagon roads, and cattle trails were oil riches beyond their fondest dreams.

Lamp and Lubrication Period

Indians knew of the value of petroleum long before Europeans came to America. In Mexico, for example, mosaics of the Toltecs, who preceded the Aztecs, were finely set in bitumen; and in the Gulf Southwest were numerous "medicine springs" which the native tribesmen visited to heal their sick.

The Southwest may well claim the earliest record of the white man's use of a petroleum product in what is now the United States. While survivors of the De Soto expedition, in small hand-made ships, were sailing along the Texas coast en route to Mexico, a storm drove them on shore approximately 3½ miles west of Sabine Pass, on July 25, 1543. There, according to their journal published at Evora, Portugal, fourteen years later, they saw "a scum which the sea cast up, called

623

'copee,' . . . like pitch" then used in Europe. The Spaniards "payed the bottoms of their vessels with it." [1]

In the mouths of creeks emptying into Sabine Bay are yet found patches of asphalt, or "copee" scum as the Spaniards called it; and along the entire Gulf Coast are numerous salt domes that have helped to trap oil in rich strata, of which Spindletop, two miles south of Beaumont, is perhaps the best known.

Until 1855 outcrops of oil-bearing formations, causing "tar seeps" or "medicine springs," attracted little attention. Santa Fe traders had greased their wagon axles at one beside the trail. Samuel M. Kier, a Pennsylvania manufacturer, had drawn oil from a shallow well and bottled it as "Kier's Rock Oil," guaranteed to cure rheumatism when externally applied and almost anything if taken internally. But such a market was necessarily limited. In 1855 George H. Bissell, a Dartmouth College graduate, hastened the dawn of the "oil age" by his experiments with crude oil. Believing that he could supplant tallow candles and whale-oil lamps with a superior illuminant, he leased oil land in western Pennsylvania and sent for analysis a sample of its oil to Benjamin Silliman, Jr., professor of chemistry in Yale College. Soon Silliman reported that from the sample he had obtained an excellent illuminant and such other useful products as naphtha and paraffin.

Bissell now became an oil well promoter, securing sufficient capital from friends and neighbors for his venture and employing Edwin L. Drake to drill a well on his lease near Titusville, Pennsylvania. "Drake's folly," as local visitors called the well, became a producer on August 28, 1859, making twenty barrels of oil a day.

Meanwhile, other oil discoveries were made along the eastern border of the Gulf Southwest's Mid-Continent area. One of these, a well drilled by a Cherokee, Lewis Ross, is said to have antedated the Drake well by several weeks. This well was drilled near present-day Salina, Oklahoma. But Ross was drilling for salt; consequently, he did not regard oil as of commercial importance.

At Nacogdoches, in eastern Texas, oil springs had long been visited by local citizens seeking axle grease and medicine. Here Jack Graham, in 1860, had drilled a well by use of a spring pole (churning method) and found a small quantity of oil, but the Civil War's looming shadow caused all East Texans to forget local problems. Lynis T. Barret had leased the "Skillern tract" for another oil test, but it was not until after the war, on December 20, 1865, that he could drill it. At that time John F. Carll of Pennsylvania furnished him and his associates with approximately $5,000 worth of equipment, and after several small

---

[1] Edward Gaylord Bourne (ed.), *Narratives of the Career of Hernando de Soto* . . . (2 vols., New York, 1904), I, 290.

producing wells of little commercial importance had been drilled, Carll returned home.

Northward 650 miles, on the northeastern fringe of the Mid-Continent region, near Paola, Kansas, G. W. Brown organized a company to drill for oil. This company sank three wells during 1860–61 but only small quantities of oil were found. Here the outbreak of the Civil War, as at Nacogdoches, Texas, suspended further operations.

After the war, drilling was resumed in each of these areas. Near Chelsea, about 30 miles northwest of Ross' old well, in 1882, Edward Byrd discovered oil on the surface of Spring Creek. He leased a large tract of land contiguous to the creek, organized an oil company and sank his first oil well seven years later. Other wells were also drilled and for a time oil was sold to wagoners for axle-grease and to cowmen, as an ointment for their tick-afflicted cattle. But the Chelsea field had neither railroad nor pipe line outlet and soon declined in importance. Another small producer, drilled at Muskogee in 1894, attracted little attention. But three years later, at Bartlesville, Michael Cudahy drilled a gusher on the Caney River, the first oil well of great commercial importance in Oklahoma, for presently Bartlesville, Oklahoma's first oil boom town, had a railroad outlet. Caney oil could now be shipped to the Standard Oil refinery at Neodesha, Kansas.

As at Chelsea, a minor oil-producing area was found near Paola, Kansas, in June, 1888, a small refinery was built, and preparations were made to launch a boom. But before it could gain momentum, W. M. Mills brought in a gusher on the T. J. Norman lease near Neodesha and oil men were drawn there. The well known Pennsylvania firm of Guffey and Galey presently took over Mills's interests, leased additional land, and launched a widespread drilling campaign; but in 1895 they, in turn, sold their interests to the Forest Oil Company, a producing branch of the Standard Oil Company. This company built an extensive pipeline system to furnish a market for Kansas oil, erected a refinery at Neodesha, and continued the drilling campaign. Like Bartlesville, Neodesha boomed, becoming the center of a prosperous oil country.

Colorado, too, on the western edge of this oil zone, had its first oil boom prior to the Civil War. On November 10, 1860, the *Rocky Mountain News* (Denver) reported that a "Mr. Dunn has a quantity of petroleum or coal oil from the recently discovered springs on the headwaters of the Arkansas," six miles northwest of Canon City. Three years later, on January 2, the *News* gave further details. "Messrs. Roup, Cassaday and Pratt are pushing improvements upon their oil springs. . . . The spring discharges from the surface, but to get a larger supply they are boring. The hole is 4 inches in diameter, and at last accounts was down 23 feet. . . . The machinery for their refinery is on the ground and the boilers set up ready for work."

More than a decade elapsed before the *News* reported other important developments. "Oil Production—Fremont County Oil Company Organized," ran a headline. "This State annually sends out to the east for illuminating oil alone, nearly two thousand dollars, and yet it is a fact that in all reasonable possibilities, Oil Creek, in Fremont County, . . . possesses a basin of oil quite as favorable . . . as does Oil Creek or Pit Hole, in Pennsylvania." But despite this friendly promotion, Canon City never made headlines in the nation's press. Yet its *Times* reported that as early as 1862–63, Cassaday had processed and sold 300,000 gallons of oil for lubricating and illuminating purposes. By 1887 Colorado produced 75,000 barrels of crude oil annually, and five years later 824,000 barrels.

Wyoming's early recorded history of petroleum begins with Captain Benjamin Bonneville's report to the War Department, which states that in 1833 Indian guides led him to an oil seep at what was later called the Dallas Dome in the south central part of Fremont County. (Here, 53 years later, a hole was drilled, resulting in spasmodic flows of oil and gas.) In 1848 W. Clayton described in his *Mormon Guide Book* another spring "covering a surface of several rods of ground." This was known as the Brigham Young oil spring near Hilliard, in southern Uinta County. Mormons frequently visited this and two other springs in this general vicinity—Judge White's and the Carter spring—and dug pits near them, from which they skimmed oil to sell in Salt Lake City for lubrication and medicinal purposes.

For many years oil seeps had also been known in the Salt Creek field, Natrona County, approximately 45 miles north of Casper. Four wells were drilled here (1889–1891) and about 2,300 barrels of oil were hauled by 12- and 16-horse teams to Casper. Other wells were drilled in the Shannon pool during the next few years. A federal report of 1902 reveals that the only "regular production in Wyoming came from 10 wells in the northeastern part of Natrona County, fifty miles north of Casper"; and eight years later the Bureau of Mines reported a State yield of 100,000 barrels of oil from the Salt Creek, Shannon, Dallas, Garland, and Spring Valley fields.

California, too, had its early oil springs. In fact, archeologists have found the bones and implements of Indians in the famed La Brea asphalt pits near Los Angeles. Spaniards used asphalt from this spring in roofing their houses; and in 1856 Andreas Pico is reported to have distilled oil from a nearby spring to illuminate the San Fernando Mission.

The first oil well discovery in California was in 1860. Five years later a Mexican hunter found seepages in Los Angeles County, news of which was carried to a Dr. Gelsich, a former Pennsylvanian. In 1870 Gelsich organized a company, staked claims, and drilled a well that produced about 70 barrels a day. But development came slowly here as in other early-day fields of the West. In 1875 production was found in Pico Canyon, near Newhall. Except for another discovery at Puente, near Los Angeles, about 1880, the only oil activity reported for the next few years was in minor fields of the Ventura-Newhall region. The discovery at Coalinga, near Los Angeles, in 1892, started this state toward its first real oil boom, and by the end of the century it had a 15,000-barrel yield of crude oil daily.

In Texas, the Corsicana oil discovery was of great importance. In 1894 the town authorized the drilling of a deep water well, which, at 1,027 feet, reached oil. A boom followed and John H. Galey presently came with drilling equipment. His first well was completed south of the city's water well, on October 15, 1895, and by the end of the next year Corsicana's oil production had reached 1,450 barrels per day. Then J. S. Cullinan arrived from the East and agreed to build a pipeline system, erect storage tanks, a refinery, and develop a market. The refinery stills, built and operated under the supervision of E. R. Brown, were fired on Christmas day, 1898, thus launching Texas' extensive refining business. The first shipment of refined oil left Corsicana for an outside market in the next year when this field's crude oil yield reached 668,483 barrels.

But down to the close of the nineteenth century the crude oil market was limited, for the nation was still in its "Lamp and Lubrication Period," as E. L. DeGolyer has so aptly put it. Motor vehicles and gasoline were not yet in general use. Even oil men did not foresee the mighty role in world affairs that the American petroleum industry was to play. Significantly, too, all wells drilled up to this time were shallow; cable-tool and rotary drilling rigs had not been designed to reach deep horizons.

The Fuel Oil Period

Spindletop, two miles south of Beaumont, Texas, was the first western oil-field bonanza. On January 10, 1901, when the Hamill brothers' rotary rig drilled into its oil-bearing sand, at a little deeper than 1,000 feet, from 75,000 to 100,000 barrels of oil per day came roaring from the well. Small wonder that Anthony F. Lucas, the well's promoter and a skilled salt-dome operator, stood transfixed watching this mighty gusher, the roar of which was heard around the world! Its significance far outweighed James Marshall's discovery of gold at Sutter's Fort in California.

A few months later Robert T. Hill, a Texas geologist, wrote an interesting narrative about Spindletop (Franklin Institute *Journal,* August-October, 1902). At that time, Spindletop's 214 gushers attracted large crowds daily. Tank storage exceeded 5,000,000 barrels and several hundred thousand barrels more of crude oil were impounded in ground reservoirs, although 1,500 railroad tank-cars were transporting a part of the field's enormous output. Hill reported that Guffey and Galey were building five oil steamers, one of which had a capacity of 60,000 barrels. "The shipments for 1901," he said, "were 1,750,000 barrels; for the first three months of 1902 they exceeded that total, those for March alone being more than 800,000 barrels. The field will probably ship 20,000,000 barrels."

Spindletop had thus hastened the end of the "Lamp and Lubrication Period" and the dawn of the "Fuel Oil Era." Temporarily, the market was swamped. The Lucas gusher alone produced annually more oil than the coal oil market could consume! By the summer of 1901 crude oil sold at Spindletop for three cents a barrel and cold water for five cents a cup!

Many thousand adventurers, oil scouts, and investors came to this new *eldorado*—Pennsylvanians and West Virginians to lend their skill, training, and experience; merchants and professional men to open new enterprises; and promoters and investors to find new fields. Real estate was at a premium. Hill stated that "Thousands of acres of land 150 miles from Beaumont . . . sold for as much as $1,000 per acre." Land within the proved field [Spindletop] sold for nearly $1,000,000 an acre." Jefferson County "justly assessed" Spindletop at $100,000,000.

Texas crude oil yield jumped from 836,039 barrels annually in 1900 to 4,393,658 barrels in the next year. This caused a frantic search for other salt-domes (salt plugs that in past ages had pushed upward through other strata and had trapped oil). In 1901 W. Scott Heywood discovered the huge Jennings, Louisiana, oil field; in the next year another was found at Sour Lake, Texas; and within the next six years Batson, Matagorda, Humble, and Dayton, Texas, were added.

By 1905 Texas oil production had climbed to 28,136,189 barrels, running far ahead of transportation, storage, and refining—and market demand. Other discoveries at Petrolia, just south of the Red River, in Clay County, and at Glenn Pool, twelve miles south of the Arkansas River town of Tulsa, added still more oil to an already large surplus. The old adage, "Necessity is the mother of invention," was now given a severe test that proved successful. New railroads, each furnishing long trains of tank-cars for oil transportation, were built; many miles of pipe lines were laid; refineries at Beaumont, Port Arthur and Baton Rouge were enlarged and smaller ones built; and a new market was created.

Oil promoters and salesmen saw that the millions of barrels of crude oil output had swamped the kerosene and lubricant market, and that they must find other uses. After successful tests had been made they announced to an incredulous public that oil was not only an ideal lubricant and illuminant but a cheaper and superior fuel than any other. Commercial users verified this claim and by 1905 hotels, factories, railway and steamship lines had installed crude oil burners in boiler fireboxes. Thus, the oil market was immeasurably strengthened and the fuel oil era had gained momentum.

THE GASOLINE ERA

But this second oil period was brief; the rapid development of the motor car industry opened a vast market for another petroleum product—gasoline. For the year in which the first Corsicana oil well was drilled the National Automobile Chamber of Commerce lists the registration of only four motor cars; by 1910 there were 458,500 passenger cars and 10,000 trucks. This new mode of travel revolutionized American rural life; afforded people quick and inexpensive transportation; and eliminated distance as a factor in social and business relations. Obviously, too, the good roads movement, including many thousand miles of paved highways, followed.

In many parts of the West new major oil fields furnished an ever increasing supply of crude oil for a rapidly expanding market and an increasing number of refineries (with many small "skimming" plants in every producing area) supplied large quantities of petroleum products. In North and Central Texas, Electra, Burkburnett, Ranger, Mexia, Powell, Desdemona, and Ranger (1911–1921); in Oklahoma, Cushing, Healdton, Burbank, Tonkawa, Hewitt, Greater Seminole, and Oklahoma City (1912–1928); in Kansas, El Dorado and Augusta (1916–1917); in California, Lost Hills, East Coyote, South Belridge, North Belridge, and Elk Hills (in the San Joaquin Valley) and Ventura Avenue (1910–1916)—all added other millions of barrels of crude oil by 1930.

Meanwhile, science assumed a major role in the petroleum industry. Anthony F. Lucas was both a Gulf Coast engineer and geologist; and in 1903 geology was introduced to Oklahoma oil fields in the person of H. B. Goodrich, employed by the Santa Fe Railway Company to explore Carter County oil possibilities. A decade later major oil companies were setting up geology staffs. Western universities (Texas, Oklahoma, and others) offered courses in petroleum geology and states began to set up geological surveys. Petroleum engineering also came with the "Gasoline Era," providing stronger drilling rigs, an improved drilling technique, better pipe lines, and sundry other mechanical improvements. Then in the mid-1920's E. DeGolyer and Alexander Duessen brought geophysical instruments (the seismograph and torsion balance) to the Gulf Coast. These and other geophysical instruments were subsequently used with surface geology in finding deep oil zones.

The growing number of major oil companies during this era was also significant. The need for large-scale prospecting, drilling, pipe-line operations, oil field installations, and the employing of well-trained personnel called for investments far beyond the means of the early-day operator. Here and there independent operators of ability, enterprise, and means were able to meet the new challenge, but those of small capital and skill dwindled rapidly in number. The oil business was costly. Many wells drilled were dry and much of the land leased proved sterile. The new era brought competition on a large scale, involving a vast exploration coverage, drilling, the building of a network of pipe lines, oil storage, refineries, and providing a broad-scale marketing of petroleum products. Hence, by the 1920's, such oil company trade names as Standard Oil of New Jersey (with its subsidiaries and affiliates), Gulf, The Texas, Sun, Sinclair, Shell, Phillips, and Cities Service were familiar throughout the West.

As exploration and drilling were carried to undeveloped areas of the West, still other major oil fields sprang up like mushrooms, as in Colorado, central Kansas, Wyoming, and California. Dr. Charles Gould, a modest but alert geologist, discovered and helped to delineate the enormous Texas Panhandle dolomite oil and gas area (1905–1920); and other prospectors equally skilled mapped and began to drill the vast Permian Basin of Texas and New Mexico (at Big Lake, Hendricks, Yates, Hobbs, and numerous other major fields) during the 1920's. At Yates, near the Texas border of the Permian Basin, on the Pecos River, geologists estimated a potential yield of 40,000 barrels to the acre, or 640,000,000 barrels for the field. One Yates well, the No. 3 Bob Reid, owned by the Standard Oil Company of Texas, reached a potential output of 170,000 barrels a day. In October, 1930, "Dad" Joiner, a veteran wildcatter, drilled the first well in the huge East Texas field, the world's largest single oil field.

Production figures of the Panhandle and East Texas oil and gas fields were equally impressive. By 1926 the Panhandle had an annual output of 25,551,000 barrels of oil, and produced approximately 600,-000,000 cubic feet of gas per day. In 1930 the United States was the major oil-producing nation (67.5 per cent of the world total), Venezuela second, and Russia third. Texas and Oklahoma each produced twice as much oil as Russia. Texas oil production leaped to even greater volume when in 1933 East Texas' 17,000 wells (under severe proration) produced at the rate of 900,000 barrels of crude oil daily. In this vast field alone was enough oil to swamp the market.

OIL PRODUCTION IN WESTERN STATES, 1947[2]

(Thousands of Barrels)

State	Production for 1947	Cumulative Production
Arkansas	29,609	702,987
California	332,958	7,619,267
Colorado	15,766	82,466
Kansas	105,072	1,779,101
Louisiana	159,276	1,978,549
Montana	8,700	141,576
New Mexico	40,971	539,505
Oklahoma	141,325	5,790,759
Texas	817,987	11,242,720
Wyoming	43,980	749,780
Western States Total	1,695,644	30,626,710
United States Total	1,853,166	35,079,053
Western State Percentage of United States Production	91%	87%

[2] *World Oil* (July, 1948), CXXVIII, No. 3, Section 2, pp. 99, 101.

Fortunately, refining and pipelining kept stride with production. In 1927 the petroleum refining output, according to the Census of Manufactures, ranked fifth in the value of manufactured products. The wholesale value of oil products in that year was $2,142,648,503. These products were numerous. The refining process first yields hydrocarbon gases—fuel gas; "gas black" for making rubber tires, inks, and paints; a series of alcohols, used in hospitals and homes as solvents, and in industry for making lacquers, soaps, and essentials; liquefied gases, employed in metal cutting and as an illuminant; petroleum ether, for priming motors and for laboratory work; natural gasoline, which yields naphthas; pentane, for candle-power standardization; hexane, utilized in laboratories; and chemical solvents for drug extraction.

White distillates are next obtained, including naphthas and kerosene. From naphthas come aviation gasoline, motor gasoline, commercial solvents, blending naphtha and varnish-makers' and painters' naphtha. Refined oil, another yield, including kerosene, was used for "illuminating oil, stove oil, tractor oil, signal oil by railroads and lighthouses, and mineral seal oil for coach and ship illumination and for gas absorption." [3]

There are yet four other derivatives. Furnace oil, the next product, is a fuel for heating homes and office buildings. Intermediate distillates, the succeeding general fraction, yield gas oil and absorber oil, for use in manufacturing plants, in the carburation of water gas, as a metallurgical fuel, and in refinery "cracking." Absorber oils are used in gasoline and benzol recovery.

The next important derivative is heavy distillate, producing technical heavy oils, waxes, and lubricating oil, candles, chewing gums, candy, and many other things. Lubricating oils, refined from crude oil, grease machinery, with special oils or compounds being made for different types. And the heavy residuum furnishes various greases— gear grease, switch grease, and cup grease. By refining greases, petrolatum is made, which, when compounded with other products, becomes a base for salves, creams, ointments, and petroleum jelly. Residual fuel oil is burned under industrial plant boilers, on ships, and in railroad locomotives. . . . All these, and many other products, broadened the market demand enormously.

Still, the tempo of western oil production (and enormous waste) was increased. By 1940 the Kern River and Huntington Beach oil fields had added to California's prestige as a producing state and Salt Creek, Wyoming, had produced cumulatively 64 per cent of that state's oil and 46 per cent of its gas. Butler County, Kansas, also had an impressive record. In addition to oil production in those states, Texas' and Oklahoma's output was little less than sensational. State and interstate regulation and production agreements became necessary. Giant fields pouring out daily their floods of oil caused Governors W. H. ("Alfalfa Bill") Murray of Oklahoma and Ross Sterling of Texas to call out the national guard and temporarily close down state fields until the market could be stabilized and waste prevented. Unscientific drilling methods were commonly employed, often because of the operators' ignorance of petroleum engineering and geology or because of the intemperate operations of "get-rich-quick" companies, speculators, and stock gamblers. Waste was also caused by one leaseholder's drilling to prevent an adjacent leaseholder from draining the oil from a common pool. Often, gushers were allowed to gush to promote the sale of stock; and gas, an oil field's self-producing force, was vented to the air or burned at the well.

But state conservation laws and commissions, in Texas, Oklahoma, and elsewhere, imposed proration, proper well spacing, and oil reservoir

---

[3] *Petroleum Facts and Figures* (Second Edition. American Petroleum Institute, New York, 1929), 158–159.

maintenance by 1940. Federal departments and laws buttressed these state measures; and co-operative agreements negotiated by the Interstate Compact Commission added regional force. In addition, the findings of petroleum engineers and geologists, pointing the way to maximum oil field production, and trade journal and newspaper articles, explaining the need for conservation, kept alive the spirit of reform.

A rapidly growing demand and an increasing variety of uses made petroleum one of the world's most useful raw materials. Not dozens, but 1,000-plus new commodities were manufactured from it by 1940. Regional refineries—giant cities of steel—as at Port Arthur and Houston, Texas, and at Baton Rouge and Lake Charles, Louisiana, each with a daily capacity of 100,000 barrels or more of crude oil, new cracking processes, and other refinery techniques have made these products possible.

Gasoline, however, remained a prime refinery objective. The enormous growth of motor vehicles in the United States kept the demand for crude oil reasonably steady. In 1919 there were 7,565,000 motor vehicles registered in the United States, which consumed 88,648,000 barrels of motor fuel. In 1930 motor vehicles had increased to 26,523,779 and consumption had grown to 398,075,000 barrels.

MOTOR VEHICLE AND FUEL CONSUMPTION, 1946 [4]

	Motor Vehicle Registration	Motor-Fuel Consumption (Thousands of Barrels)
Trans-Mississippi States	12,790,866	12,404,333
United States Total	34,373,002	30,039,823
Trans-Mississippi States Percentage of United States	37%	41%

Oil's impacts have been important. Every oil-producing state of the West has benefited enormously. Giant oil companies employ many thousand day-laborers, and pay several hundred million dollars annualy in royalties, leases, and taxes to land-owners and states, thus providing enormous sums for schools, roads (in 1928 almost 200,000 miles of surface) and public improvements. Thus, western oil is a strong support for America's peacetime economy.

[4] *Petroleum Facts and Figures* (Eighth Edition, American Petroleum Institute, New York, 1947), 16, 20–21. States included in Trans-Mississippi group are: Arizona, Arkansas, California, Colorado, Idaho, Iowa, Kansas, Louisiana, Minnesota, Missouri, Montana, Nebraska, Nevada, New Mexico, North Dakota, Oklahoma, Oregon, South Dakota, Texas, Utah, Washington, and Wyoming.

In many oil fields (as at Caddo, Louisiana, and in the Panhandle of Texas) gas has been almost as rich a natural resource as oil. At Caddo, and in other fields, in earlier years it was regarded as of little worth and burned at the well or vented to the air. But by the late 1920's and the 1930's it was piped to mid-western cities as a fuel, and processed in carbon black and natural gasoline plants. Western states had also recognized its great value as a fuel and raw commodity and had brought it under state conservation laws. In the Panhandle alone, by 1938, were 1,498 gas wells that had produced approximately seven trillion cubic feet of gas. A part of this was being processed by 49 natural gasoline plants and 26 carbon black plants and much of it was piped to Upper Mississippi Valley cities as a fuel.

In war, western petroleum has been equally important. During the last half of World War I, when tanks and airplanes were becoming numerous and decisive weapons of war, oil from Cushing and Healdton, Oklahoma, from Ranger, Texas, and from other newly discovered western fields gave America a sufficient supply to seal the fate of the Central Powers. Indeed, Viscount Curzon of Great Britain well said that the Allies "floated to victory on a sea of oil."

And in World War II, armies had become highly mechanized and motorized, and merchant marines, navies, air-fleets, and industries required enormous supplies of oil products. Before the end of the war, the Axis Powers' lack of these grounded their air-armadas, stopped their motorized field units, and drastically curtailed their sea power. German cities and communication and transportation lines then became vulnerable to American and English aerial bombs; and General Douglas MacArthur's island-hopping strategy, when Japan's store of oil was exhausted, left Nipponese armies stranded.

Thus, the West's major war service, beyond its man-power contribution, was its production, refining, and distribution of oil. Many new oil and gas fields were discovered, developed, and exploited. The nation's petroleum output was sharply increased, its refineries (largely western) produced vital high-octane gasoline, rubber, and other products; and a network of pipe lines, railroad tank-cars, and tankers made oil available for its war needs. The federal government financed the building of the Big Inch pipe line to supply Eastern refineries with crude oil and the Little Big Inch to funnel gasoline to Atlantic cities. In this way, Allied needs were met. In 1945 American refineries produced an all-time high of 775,460,000 barrels of gasoline and ran to stills 1,720,000,000 barrels of crude oil!

So it is not surprising that western oil played a vital role in the Allied victory. On November 10, 1945, the United States Army-Navy Petroleum Board, composed of ranking officers, in a letter to Deputy Petro-

PUMPING DERRICKS IN THE BIG LAKE OILFIELD OF THE PERMIAN BASIN

OIL WELL ON THE SCHOOL YARD AT CEMENT, OKLAHOMA

leum Administrator Ralph K. Davies, praised the oil industry's war service as "a superb contribution . . . to the victory of the United States by providing in full and on time the vast flood of petroleum products required by the Armed Forces during World War II." "No Government agency," ran the citation, "and no branch of American industry achieved a prouder war record." The industry made an "outstanding . . . contribution to the victory of the United Nations."

The post-war western oil industry worked on just as vast a scale. As a result, intensive prospecting, drilling, field operations, and refining helped both the West and the nation to make economic re-adjustments. The world's deepest well, the Superior Oil Company's of Caddo County, Oklahoma, a dry hole at 17,832 feet, was drilled in 1947. In the next year 40,000 oil wells were completed and for the first time the nation's crude oil yield passed the two-billion-barrel mark. Several thousand oil fields, each with its forest of derricks; oil field and refinery installations, worth billions of dollars; a maze of 78,000 miles of crude and refined oil pipelines and numerous tank-cars, barges and tankers, carrying daily much of the nation's freight; manufacturing and supply-house centers; and upward of 250 refineries and almost that many more gasoline separating plants—all constitute the West's vast framework of an industrial tomorrow.

W. Jett Lauck estimates that all the gold and silver mined in the world from 1493 to 1875 was worth only $15,375,753,000. Not counting refined oil products, western crude oil has produced since 1859 more than three times that much wealth. At present, the petroleum industry makes an annual cash payment of $4,000,000,000 to the nation. Of this amount $200,000,000 is paid to landowners as royalties, bonuses, and lease rentals; $875,000,000 to industries for equipment, supplies, and services; $260,000,000 to railroads; $1,365,000,000 for equipment and minor purchases; and $1,300,000,000 in taxes to federal, state, and local governments.

Western cities, towns, and communities are conspicuously benefited by oil. Some—like Amarillo, in the Texas Panhandle; Tulsa, near the rich Osage oil lands; Wichita Falls, beside the Red River Uplift; and Odessa, Kermit, and Hobbs, of the sand-dune Permian Basin of West Texas and New Mexico—are largely oil-made. And others—Kansas City, Wichita, Oklahoma City, Fort Worth, Dallas, Houston, and Los Angeles—have oil wealth added to other sources of economic power to place them among the region's leading cities.

Among the smaller towns, El Dorado, Arkansas increased in population 322 per cent from 1920 to 1930; Monroe, Louisiana, 150 per cent; Wewoka, Oklahoma, 584 per cent; and Breckenridge, Texas, 310 per cent. Ranger, Desdemona, and Burkburnett, Texas; Rodessa,

Louisiana; and Augusta and El Dorado, Kansas are today better towns than before nearby oil fields were discovered.

Rural population has also increased because of oil discovery and development. In 1910 fifteen Oklahoma oil-producing counties had substantial increases in population in three years, while this state's non-oil counties had gained only slightly. Ten years later 25 oil-producing counties had increased 29.5 per cent as compared with 12.6 per cent for other counties in the state. And by the end of the next decade oil-producing counties had increased 30.7 per cent over 1920 as compared with a slight decline for the non-producing counties. In fact, in the 469 counties and parishes of Arkansas, Louisiana, Oklahoma, and Texas from 1920 to 1930, there was an increase in population amounting to 1,934,606, nearly 47.3 per cent of which was in the 88 oil-producing counties.

For the first seven years of the 1940's, with slight year-to-year fluctuations, oil production from the great Southwestern storehouse (of Arkansas, Louisiana, Oklahoma, Kansas, New Mexico, and Texas) increased from 884,000,000 to 1,334,196,000 barrels. Specialization and a wide use of scientific techniques made this possible. Deep oil zones have been carefully mapped by use of the seismograph and other geophysical instruments, powerful drilling rigs have been manufactured, a variety of muds for sealing off water formations or "heaving sand" were offered for sale, and deep oil production was reached.

Still, by the end of 1948 almost 60 per cent of American oil came from 130 major oil fields, 121 of which were in the West. Texas led with 51 major oil fields and was followed by California with 29 major fields, Oklahoma 18, Louisiana 9, the Rocky Mountain area 5, New Mexico 4, Kansas 3, and Arkansas 2. At present, the West produces more than 90 per cent of the nation's oil.

The modern petroleum industry is a conspicuous example of American free enterprise. Generally, its executives have been trained in the exacting school of experience, rising from day-laborers to positions of leadership. Daily, men like these, representing 34,000 companies, engage in a highly competitive enterprise. In fact, it is hardly possible for an industry with so many rival units, employing more than 1,500,-000 workers, to become monopolistic. At present, the industry is stream-lined, guided by alert men, employs many trained scientists, and uses a wide variety of technical equipment—all essential to meet the future challenge.

BIBLIOGRAPHY

For miscellaneous information on early petroleum production and refining, especially in Pennsylvania, West Virginia, Ohio, and Indiana, and occasional references to the West, *The Derrick's Hand Book of Petroleum* (2 vols., Oil City, Pennsylvania, 1898, 1900) is invaluable for its short sketches of oil men, statistics, and yearly oil field developments. Other volumes have sketches on the discovery and production of oil in various parts of the West: A. C. Veatch, *Geography and Geology of a Portion of Southwestern Wyoming* (*Professional Paper, No. 56,* United States Geological Survey, Washington, 1907), a history of development, 136–166; Matthews and McMahan, *Handbook, Kansas Oil Field* . . . (n.p., circa 1904); F. O. Williams, *In the Heart of the Oil Fields* (Neodesha, Kansas, 1904); T. O. Bosworth, *Geology of the Mid-Continent Oil Fields* . . . (New York, 1906), 7–27, 62–64, 103–127; *Texas Petroleum, Bulletin No. 5* (University of Texas, Mineral Survey *Bulletin, No. 1,* Austin, July, 1900); and Edwin Higgins, *California's Oil Industry* . . . (Los Angeles, 1928).

Only a few historical narratives of the western oil industry have been written, and then only in part. The following industry and area studies should be used for supplemental readings: Carl Coke Rister, *Oil! Titan of the Southwest* (Norman, 1949); Max Ball, *The Fascinating Oil Business* (New York, 1940); Paul H. Giddens, *Early Days of Oil* (Princeton, 1948) (in Pennsylvania); C. A. Warner, *Texas Oil and Gas Since 1543* (Houston, 1939); Gerald Forbes, *Flush Production* . . . (Norman, 1942); Samuel W. Tait, Jr., *The Wildcatters, An Informal History of Oil-Hunting in America* (Princeton, 1946); John J. Floherty, *Flowing Gold* (Philadelphia, New York, 1945); Isaac F. Marcosson, *The Black Golconda* (New York, 1924), a popular account; John W. Leonard *et al., Romance of American Petroleum and Gas* (2 vols., New York, n.d.); and *Structure of Typical American Oil Fields, A Symposium* (2 vols., American Association of Petroleum Geologists, London, 1929; reprinted Menasha, Wisconsin, 1947), with historical sketches of each field presented.

A wide variety of miscellaneous volumes on various phases of the petroleum industry—geology, prospecting, production, and refining—are also available. Among these are Charles B. Eliot, *Petroleum Industry of the Gulf Southwest* (United States Department of Commerce, Part II, The Commercial Survey, . . . Washington, 1931); and H. C. Miller and Ben E. Lindsly, "Report on Petroleum Production and Development," in *Hearings Before a Subcommittee of the Committee on Interstate and Foreign Commerce, House of Representatives, Seventy-Third Congress (Recess) on H. Res. 441 (Printed Herein), September 17, 18, 19, 20, 21, and 22, 1934* (Washington, 1934), Part II, 1087–1306. State-by-state production summaries, yearly data and tables are found in the annual *Mineral Resources of the United States, Part II, Nonmetals* (by United States Geological Survey, 1882–1924; and by Bureau of Mines, 1924–1931; and by Bureau of Mines, as *Minerals Yearbook and Statistical Appendix,* 1932–1945). Excellent articles about the various major oil and gas fields, state and regional production, and other oil industry subjects are carried in the bulletins of the United States Geological Survey. And state publications, too, of geological surveys and conservation commissions, are similarly helpful.

Annual and periodic trade publications present weekly, monthly, and yearly news of developments in the various states and oil fields. *Petroleum Facts and Figures* (American Petroleum Institute, Baltimore and New York, 1930–1947) reviews in general the major problems of the petroleum industry and also includes (as in the First Edition) "Production of Oil in the United States," "Transportation . . . ," and "Refineries." In addition, there are the numerous bulletins of the American Association of Petroleum Geologists; and the annual *Petroleum Development and Technology* (Petroleum Division, American Institute of Mining and Metallurgical Engineers); and such trade periodicals as the *National Petroleum News, Oil and Gas Journal, Texas Oil Journal,* and *Oil Weekly* (now *World Oil*).

37

WESTERN CULTURE

E<small>NVIRONMENT</small> WAS a large factor in shaping western culture. Immigrants brought to this frontier traditional ways, institutions, and techniques, some of which were later discarded and others changed by environmental influence into new customs and adaptations. Ordinarily, as environment changed, border culture was modified. West of the Mississippi, climatic and topographic conditions were strikingly different from those of the East. Here the homeseeker found the Great Plains, the silent deserts and semi-desert lands, the majestic and half-barren Rocky Mountains (with deep "parks" tucked between towering peaks and tortuous ranges), great rivers and mighty cataracts, and the Great Basin—all composing a *Young America*. Even its flora and fauna were regionally adapted—the mesquite, cactus, sagebrush, chaparral, greasewood, and yucca; and the jackrabbit, prairie-dog, Gila-monster, and horned-toad. The immigrants' daily toils and life patterns, after years of experience, were also modified. For example, hunting (as in hunting the mustang or buffalo), the range cattle industry, the settlers' perennial quest for wood and water, farming under the handicaps of drastic weather changes, and the destruction of crops by grasshopper invasions—all were problems requiring new solutions.

A NEW CULTURE'S BEGINNINGS

A history of western culture is interlaced with the pioneer's struggle with nature, his adaptations and new methods, and his triumphs over climatic and physical handicaps. On a treeless plain he housed his family in an adobe hut, a dugout, or a sodhouse, and inclosed his property with barbwire. Where water was found only in sub-surface formations, he bored a deep well (a hundred feet or more) and erected a windmill; or, where a well was not possible, he built a cistern and ground tank. To farm the semi-arid and arid wastes, he impounded a large body of water, turned the mountain stream into aqueducts and flumes, and to raise crops he employed a new dry-farming technique. Thus, his daily activity and thought helped to form a new culture, not superior perhaps to other regional patterns, but unquestionably resourceful, progressive, and colorful. Nowhere else in the nation could Bret Harte, Samuel Clemens, Owen Wister, and Andy Adams have found such promising literary subjects, for nowhere else had the extraordinary mining camp scenes, overland stage travel, and cowboy life added such heroic color and drama to border history. Here was a new land, new opportunities, new conditions, and the makings of new institutions, which Horace Greeley sensed when he urged adventurous youth to go West.

Although the trans-Mississippi West was strikingly unlike other North American regions, it, too, had its smaller topographic areas, each unlike the others—the Great Plains, the Rocky Mountains, the Sierra Nevada, the Great Basin, the California Basin, and the range and plateau country of southern Arizona and New Mexico. Each of these geographic provinces made its own contributions to a composite western life, yet there was a common denominator for all. Although the society of the mining camp, the cattle range, and the farm irrigation district felt the imprint of environment, those elements of the Salt Lake Basin, certain (German) Great Plains communities, and parts of California, New Mexico, and Texas were more reflective of non-Anglo-American cultures.

German and Spanish cultures predominated over other non-Anglo-American patterns. A lengthy discussion of each of these would serve little purpose here. A visitor at St. Louis and San Antonio during the late 1860's said that about one-third of St. Louis's 162,179 people were Germans, industrious and enterprising; and that in San Antonio, "The Germans settled in large numbers, bringing old-fashioned industry along with their lager beer. Their neat cottages and vegetable gardens are noticeable all about the suburbs." Others who traveled among the German settlements in Texas, Kansas, Nebraska, and elsewhere in the West were similarly impressed, but were uniformly critical of the average Spanish-American community. Josiah Gregg (in 1831), George F. Ruxton (1846), and James M. Steele (1872) each characterized the New Mexicans as indolent and contented.

An Eastern traveler, Frederick Law Olmsted, in 1857 found the San Antonio *peones* the same, as did another writer 10 years later. The latter said that their houses (many of them built of adobe, one story high, and thatched) swarmed with their mixed denizens, white, black, and copper-colored. And as to their even-tenored life, he added:

The free-and-easy style of life which is characteristic of the lower order of Mexicans is sure to surprise the stranger. He sees children of both sexes, from two to six years of age, strolling about in the economical and closely-fitting costume bestowed upon them by nature. Women, short and dumpy, with forms guiltless of artificial fixtures, and in the single article of attire denominated a petticoat, brief at both ends, are observed in-doors and out, manifesting not the slightest regard for the curious glances of the passers-by. Parties of men, women, and children bathe in the San Antonio River, just outside the corporate limits, without the annoyance of dresses. This comfortable fashion was formerly in vogue within the city, until the authorities concluded it might with propriety be dispensed with.

Moreover, he described their popular pastimes. "Cockfights and fandangoes help to elevate and refine the people of San Antonio, such as choose to participate." The fandangoes took place every evening. A large hall or square room, lighted by a few lamps hung from the walls or lanterns suspended from the ceiling, a pair of Negro fiddlers, and 20 or 30 couples in the full enjoyment of a *bolero* (Mexican polka), helped to make up the scene. In the corner of the room were refreshment tables, under the charge of women, where coffee, *frijoles,* *tortillas,* boiled rice, and other eatables might be obtained; and, from the brawls and free fights which often took place, the visitor believed that liquor was sold surreptitiously. Concerning the several types of revelers, he added:

At these fandangoes may be seen the muleteer, fresh from the coast or the Pass, with gay clothes and a dozen or so silver dollars; the United States soldiers just from the barracks, abounding in oaths and tobacco; the herdsman, with his blanket and long knife, which seems a portion of every Mexican; the disbanded ranger, rough, bearded and armed with his huge holster pistol and long bowie knife, dancing, eating, drinking, swearing, and carousing, like a party of Captain Kidd's men just in from a long voyage. Among the women may be seen all colors and ages from ten to forty; the Creole, the Poblana, the Mexican, and rarely the American or German—generally in such cases, the dissipated widow or discarded mistress of some soldier or follower of the army.

The description of the *peones* here—and, indeed, they constituted the large majority in every southwestern Spanish-American community —could just as well have been applied to those at Santa Fe, El Paso, Monterey, or Tucson. But it should be remembered that in each of these places, too, were the *ricos,* a small, wealthy landholding group— the merchants and traders who composed the more substantial and controlling class. These lived in well-built houses, with rooms of comfortable and, occasionally, elegant furnishings opening onto interior patios; and their manners and customs were yet reminiscent of those of the *conquistadores.* Also, Spanish-American culture influenced to a marked degree that of the incoming Anglo-Americans. But, in return, Mexican folkways were strongly counter-marked by American manners and customs. Here and there at the present time a visitor at Santa Fe, at San Antonio, or elsewhere in Texas, New Mexico, Arizona, southern Colorado, and California will observe an interesting fusion of the two cultures, by which Anglo-American enterprise seems to have declared a truce with peon indolence.

Yet all western cultures had much in common; everywhere boomtown optimism, hospitality, social democracy, ingenuity, and adaptability were apparent. The West, during its early stage of development, was primarily a man's country, requiring exacting toil and masculine strength to master its perversities and handicaps. The streets of St. Louis were thronged "only with men" in 1840, as was true in Omaha two decades later. In 1869 Samuel Bowles found that the Colorado settlements lacked two things—"appreciation at the East and women." Bancroft stated that two things remarkable about California were its "youthfulness and paucity of women." In 1850 females constituted only eight per cent of the state's population, but by 1880 this had been raised to one-third. And early visitors noticed the same conditions in other western communities.

In 1872 James W. Steele (in the *Kansas Magazine*) was impressed with the West's masculinity. But he also pointed out other characteristics, one of which was social democracy. "The Borderer is a man not born," he wrote, "but unconsciously to himself, made by his surroundings and necessities." Although he might have been born on the Chesapeake or the banks of the Juniata, although he might have hailed from Lincolnshire or Cork, yet western life had clothed him with a new individuality, made him forget the tastes and habits of early life, and transformed him into one of "that restless horde of cosmopolites who formed the advance guard of that slow wave of humanity which year by year crept toward the setting sun." The typical Westerner during this early period was described as "defiant in dress, manners and in general deportment. He hates 'aires,' cannot abide to be patronized, and is ugly to all who chance to disagree with him. His great fault is intolerance, but he is brave, sincere, and faithful when once enlisted in any cause."

But early uncouth adventurers—traders, trappers, outlaws, teamsters, and hunters—were presently joined or supplanted by tens of thousands of farmers, ranchers, and merchants, who brought women and children with them. The 1880's, therefore, ushered in a new social amalgam, softened by feminine influence and matured by long-established customs, yet to be strongly modified by the new ways of the earlier settlers.

Few of the first immigrants had desired to remain in the West. Charles Moreau Harger has stated that whether they sought to found homes or to serve as traders and storekeepers, they had come to make a fortune soon, then to retire in comfort to their old homes; and Bowles agreed that they had hoped to "strike it rich some day" and then go back to old Ohio, Pennsylvania, or New England to cheer the fading eyes of fathers and mothers, or to claim the patient-waiting, sad-hearted girls to whom they had pledged their youthful loves.

This tendency caused an ebb and flow of western people. More moved in than returned to the old country, but, nevertheless, those returning East were considerable. An 1872 observer noticed that border life was changing, "fast passing away." Another believed that indifferent crops—not failures—beginning in 1890 caused a quarter of a million people to move out of western Nebraska and Kansas. If this were equally true of other border states in this year, the eastward migration must have passed the million mark. But always some stayed and adapted themselves to the country. "The West is a land of milk and honey," said an immigrant after spending a hard year on a prairie farm, "providing one brings with him cows and bees." Throughout the pioneer period, a process of selection was going on; western society was emerging, nurtured by adversity, experiment, trial, and hardship. But its migratory aspect was to remain. Even at present it is seldom that more than one generation is reared under one roof.

Western agriculture had encountered much the same economic cycle as ranching: a lively farm-products market because of post-war shortages; a period of spectacular expansion; overproduction; and in the end, financial demoralization. In addition to a favorable market, four other developments stimulated agricultural expansion: (1) the Homestead Act and other friendly federal legislation, making possible land ownership; (2) the consequent influx of thousands of immigrants to acquire widely advertised homes in the West on easy terms; (3) the adequate marketing of western products because of railway and steamship transportation not available in the pre-war years; and (4) the rapidly spreading use of labor-saving machinery.

The expansion of the agricultural frontier was unprecedented. Between 1860 and 1880 the farming center had moved west hundreds of miles and farms had doubled, increasing lands under cultivation by 120,000,000 acres. A large per cent of this acreage increase was on the Great Plains. Here such staple crops as wheat, corn, oats, barley, and rye were produced in such quantities as to overstock the American market. This made necessary a large export trade, which quickly grew in volume. For example, the average annual agricultural exports during 1894–98 were valued at $963,000,000, of which agricultural exports were $663,500,000. Within the three decades after 1860 more land had been brought under cultivation than in all history. So rapid was this expansion that by 1890 immigrants were claiming (under terms of the Homestead Act) 160-acre farms on the High Plains where formerly only cattle-grazing was thought possible.

Clever, and at times lurid, real estate advertising had stimulated this land rush. Ponderous volumes, travel guides, state immigration booklets, and land-company publications lent momentum to western magazine and newspaper promotions. William M. Thayer and L. P. Brockett were authors of books describing the West and its possibilities in glowing terms. Thayer invited the land seeker to any part of the arable West. He stated that the Salinas Valley of California produced 102 bushels of wheat to the acre and that the New Orleans World's Fair exhibited a 165-pound California squash and a 168-pound Dakota pumpkin. Nor did he neglect the advantages of other western states and territories. "Who has not heard of the cornfields of Kansas and the wheatfields of Dakota?" he asked. He quoted from both federal and local reports to show that Colorado wheat made 25 bushels per acre and its corn 35 bushels per acre; and that by irrigation-farming in New Mexico, Idaho, and other western states abundant crops were harvested. Brockett was equally enthusiastic, using federal census figures of 1880 to support his claims for the West.

These and other writers told of the general use of new machines in farming. Although the reaper and thresher had been invented before the Civil War, it was not until the decade 1870–1880 that many inventions of labor-saving machines completely transformed western farming. Mechanical corn planters and huskers, and gang plows, seeders, and improved threshers were typical labor-saving inventions. These machines plowed the land, sowed it in wheat, and then threshed it, cleaned it, sacked it, and weighed it, without the touch of human hands.

In turn, labor-saving machines, when applied to cheap land, made possible bonanza farming, which was given a conspicuous tryout in the Red River Valley of Dakota. Here Oliver Dalrymple had a 75,000-acre farm, 30,000 acres of which were devoted to wheat. Dalrymple employed thirty-five steam-threshers and over one hundred self-binding reapers at harvest time, not counting the many gang plows, harrows, and seeders he used at other times. Within this general area in the 1880's over 200 farms contained 1,000 or more acres.

Federal enactments also supported this agricultural metamorphosis. In addition to friendly land laws, the Morrill Act of 1862 and a supplementary measure twenty-eight years later made possible land-grant agricultural colleges; and the Hatch Act of 1887 provided an experiment station in every state where there was a land-grant college. Then the Department of Agriculture, with its bureaus of animal husbandry, entomology, and plant industry, was created. The Bureau of Plant Industry was responsible for more than 30,000 new varieties of plants in the United States, among which were drought-resisting corn and wheat. These plants helped to make farming profitable in much of the semi-arid West.

Agrarian Unrest

The Westerner's spirit of ingenuity and experimentation in his initial pioneer experiences was equally apparent in his subsequent economic and social relations. Yet his buoyant optimism was chilled by reverses, beginning with the early seventies. On every hand tidal movements had early foreshadowed an inflow of a stable culture, for example, the relinquishment of Indian titles to large areas of tillable land; the rise of the range-cattle industry; the large-scale exploitation of mineral resources; the rapid occupation of the public lands; the building of railroads; and the amazing growth of towns. But by the mid-eighties each brought reactionary consequences. The cattle range was overstocked, the beef market collapsed, and financial ruin dragged down many a cattleman. Within the mining country hard times engendered by the low price of silver left more than one "ghost town" silent and deserted as ever-present reminders of misspent optimism.

With steadily mounting crop surpluses, because of a rapidly expanding acreage in cultivation and because of an increasing use of mechanical and scientific aids, the Western farmer had also been brought to a period of diminishing prices and profits. Indeed, for twenty years after the Panic of 1873 prices fell steadily. Wheat sold as low as 50 cents a bushel; cattle brought from 2 to 3 cents a pound; and corn was so cheap that farmers used it for fuel. In one year, wheat sold for 90 cents on a Western farm and $1.50 in New York. Farmers blamed the railroads for this price differential. The railroads had been their main dependence for the marketing of crops and now, they thought, they were selfishly operated by such financial buccaneers as Jay Gould and Jim Fisk. By excessive freight rates and discriminations, they had become the oppressors of isolated communities and individuals.

Under such circumstances it is little wonder that the Westerner was ready to listen to the "political spell-binder." Here were economic reverses, the causes of which he could not understand, problems that were puzzling, but for which he was told there were solutions. As a consequence, the Patrons of Husbandry, the Greenback Party, the free silver movement, and Populism, each in its day, had eager western recruits.

The Patrons of Husbandry, or the Grange, a secret ritualistic movement, organized in 1867 by O. H. Kelley and W. H. Saunders, offered panaceas for agrarian ills; and, after the Panic of 1873, midwestern and Great Plains farmers flocked to its standard. Upon joining the Grange, once or twice a month they could attend its impressive meetings, listen to or take part in its literary programs, and bring their wives and children to occasional socials. But the average program was shaped to voice farmer grievance. Banks were blamed for deflation and an inelastic credit system; tariff-protected monopolies controlled prices of the necessities of life; commission men and brokers conspired to reduce farm produce; rapacious railroad managers made secret agreements to fix high rates, bribed public officials, and evolved a system whereby discriminations were made against small shippers. Yet, occasionally, seed selection, crop rotation, soil rebuilding, and co-operative buying and selling were discussed.

In the Middle West the Grange membership leaped to 750,000 by 1875; and in the Great Plains states it was almost as large. In California the movement first appeared as the Farmer's Club of Sacramento; and by 1873, largely because of the efforts of W. H. Baxter, 91 Grange units were organized in protest against excessive railroad rates. Then the movement spread rapidly to the Oregon settlements. The first Kansas Grange appeared in December, 1872, and presently 12 locals were organized, concomitantly with others in Iowa and Nebraska. And in Texas, two years later, an organization was effected in Bell County. In this state the Grange membership grew to 45,000 by 1877.

Grange effort was primarily concerned with enlivening the farmer's sense of political responsibility and with the establishment of co-operative buying and selling. From the earliest organization, Grange leaders had attacked the monopolists and large-scale manufacturers, and had occasionally charged that local merchants were in a conspiracy with them to extort excessive prices. To correct these evils they urged the setting up of co-operatives. As a result, many such enterprises were launched. Through state organizations, western farmers operated harvester works, plow factories, grain elevators, packing plants, insurance companies, banks, and numerous retail stores; but in the end their experiments failed. The intricacies of business transactions—buying, jobbing, and selling—when coupled with the competition of private enterprise, brought disaster.

The agrarians met with more success in politics. During 1873–1874, farmer votes elected substantial blocs to the legislatures in 11 western states. Illinois promptly set up a rate-fixing commission. Iowa, Wisconsin, and Minnesota proceeded to control rates without a commission by enacting elaborate codes governing all railroads within the states;

and the new constitutions of Missouri, Nebraska, and California contained clauses on the pass evil, the short-haul practice, pooling, and other harmful railroad practices. By 1886 enthusiasm for state control had largely run its course, probably because the Grange movement had subsided; and by its Wabash decision (1886), the Supreme Court forbade states the right to regulate interstate commerce and had hinted that relief could come only by Congressional action, although 10 years earlier, in the Munn *vs.* Illinois case, it had declared that railroads were quasi-public in character and that a state might regulate a business of a public nature.

Yet the decline of the Grange by no means ended the agrarian revolt; presently two other similar organizations, one succeeding the other, had arisen. It made little difference to the distraught farmer under what banner he marched, so long as he fought in the agrarian cause. So the Patrons of Husbandry was presently supplanted by the Farmers' Alliance. During the summer of 1874 the farmers of Lampasas County, Texas, organized a protective association against marauding Indians and horse thieves and held occasional forums to discuss co-operative buying and selling. The movement quickly spread to other counties, and by 1880 it had blossomed into a Grand State Alliance, "a secret and benevolent association." By 1882 a similar movement, the Agricultural Wheel, had also been launched in Arkansas, which at the end of five years claimed a membership of 500,000. In 1885 also, a less powerful organization, the Farmers' Union, had arisen in Louisiana. In December, 1888, at Meridian, Mississippi, these agrarian organizations were consolidated as the Farmers' and Laborers' Union of America, soon attracting a membership of 3,000,000 persons.

Also, a Northern Alliance had sprung up in Cook County, Illinois, advocating much the same measures but with less stress on co-operatives, and remaining independent of the southern movement although generally in harmony with its efforts. At St. Louis in 1889 the Farmers' and Laborers' Union in annual assembly championed co-operatives and government financing of agricultural marketing; complained of monopolistic practices and railroad discriminations and asked for corrective laws, demanding "equal rights to all and special favors to none"; proposed to develop "a better state, mentally, morally, socially and financially"; and set forth other Utopian objectives. By 1902, however, its force was spent, and another movement, the Farmers' Educational and Co-operative Union of America, had taken its place. Twelve years later, it had been established in 20 states of the South and Middle West and in two states of the Pacific Northwest.

Each agrarian movement, although primarily non-political, exerted profound political influence on the West and the nation. There is little doubt that the Greenback Party in 1876 was western in composition. It promised its constituency the repeal of the Specie Resumption Act of 1875 and an adequate medium of exchange by advocating that the government should issue legal tender notes which could be converted on demand into bonds bearing a low rate of interest. Western farmers generally believed that the lack of a medium of exchange was the result of a conspiracy of the "gold East," and that "cheap money makes dear prices." But in the election of 1876 the Greenback candidate for the presidency, Peter Cooper, of New York, polled only 81,700 votes, a majority of which were from the States of Illinois, Indiana, Iowa, Kansas, Michigan, Missouri, and Arkansas. In 1888 the Union Labor Party, presenting once more the Greenback platform and representing much the same areas, launched its first national ticket and won 147,000 votes, 75 per cent of which were from Missouri, Arkansas, Texas, Nebraska, Iowa, and Kansas!

The Farmers' Alliance had equal influence with the Populists, or People's Party. The latter organization was a culmination of the agrarian and other discontented elements. In May, 1891, upward of 1,500 representatives of various agrarian and labor groups met in Cincinnati, Ohio, to form the People's Party (Populists); and on July 2 of the next year at Omaha, Nebraska, it launched its first national ticket. The platform charged both the Democrats and the Republicans with jeopardizing "our homes, lives, and children on the altar of Mammon." During the campaign which followed, farmers crowded community schoolhouses and meeting places to listen to such colorful crusaders as "Sockless Jerry" Simpson and Mary Elizabeth Lease of Kansas; "Bloody Bridles" Waite of Colorado; Reverend J. H. Kyle of South Dakota; and C. W. McCune of Texas. And in simple faith they accepted Miss Lease's admonition to "raise less corn and more hell," and Waite's warning that it was "better that blood should flow to the horses' bridles" than that their national liberties should be destroyed. In the election of 1890 Kansas agrarians talked much of railroad oppressions, trusts, national banks, mortgage companies, and loan sharks; and in Colorado they demanded, in addition, free silver. Indeed, Kansas was the first state in which a sweeping Populist victory was gained. Five Populist Congressmen and a majority in the lower house of the state legislature were their fruits of victory.

But this success was minor when compared with that of 1892. The enthusiastic Populists held their national convention at St. Louis on February 22, 860 delegates attending. Among the leaders present were Senator W. A. Peffer of Kansas, whose long, flowing beard made him a conspicuous figure; Senator Kyle of South Dakota; Jerry Simpson of Kansas; General W. B. Weaver of Iowa; C. W. McCune of

Texas; H. E. Taubeneck of Illinois; Ignatius Donnelly of Minnesota; and Robert Schilling of Wisconsin. The platform, as announced, included such demands as a safe, sound, and flexible currency; free and unlimited coinage of silver and gold at the ratio of 16 to 1; speedy increase of the circulating medium to not less than $50 per capita; a graduated income tax; postal saving banks; government ownership of railroads and telegraph and telephone systems; and a more restrictive public land policy, excluding alien ownership. In the election that followed, the Populists were astonishingly successful. They won a total of 10 Congressmen, 5 Senators, 50 state officials, and 1,500 county officers and state legislators. Among the western states they carried Colorado, Idaho, Kansas, and Nevada, and elected single electors in North Dakota and Oregon. Weaver, their presidential candidate, polled 1,041,600 popular votes and 22 electoral votes. But the Populists had reached the peak of success. Four years later, the Democrats, led by William Jennings Bryan of Nebraska, demoralized Populism by championing much of its platform and by winning many of its members. And in later years, Bryan was generally regarded as the political spokesman for the Farmer's Educational and Co-operative Union.

Yet western reforming zeal had not spent itself. Since the late sixties, untiring pressure had been felt in state and nation, from decade to decade, until success came. As early as 1897, Robert M. La Follette had urged the direct primary as a means of safeguarding government against political bosses and corrupt interests. Wisconsin passed its direct primary law in 1903, and other states presently followed her example. At the close of 1915, primaries for state elections were found in 37 states and territories, and were usually accompanied by corrupt practices acts.

In 1904 Oregon had created, in effect, the popular election of senators, by holding its legislators morally responsible for the naming of Senators chosen in elections by the people; and by 1912, 29 states were employing a similar system. And after May 31, 1913, as a result of the Seventeenth Amendment to the federal Constitution, Senators were elected by the people. Oregon was also the first state to adopt, in 1902, a thoroughgoing initiative and referendum, though South Dakota in 1897 and Utah in 1900 had accepted this form of direct legislation for ordinary measures. Before the progressive movement had spent itself, about 20 states (most of them west of the Mississippi) had adopted this device, whereby usually about five per cent of the electorate might initiate measures while a majority of those voting could enact them. Voters in some states exercised fully their law-making powers. In Oregon, in six biennial elections (1904–1916), they were asked to pass upon 41 constitutional amendments and 62 statutes.

The recall of elective officials was first adopted in Los Angeles in 1903 and in Seattle in 1906. Oregon, in 1908, extended the device to include all elective officials. In the next six years ten other states followed. The movement for the recall of judges prompted solemn warnings by judges, politicians, and laymen; and in 1911 Congress was thrown into great panic over this new "heresy" when Arizona, seeking admission to the Union, submitted a constitution including such a political device. President Taft would not approve statehood until Arizona expunged the undesirable provision from her constitution; but in an election during the next year, the voters restored it. Later, eight states permitted the recall of judges, and one, Colorado, in 1912, adopted a constitutional amendment also providing for the recall of judicial decisions.

Agrarians of the twentieth century were more politically minded than those of previous decades had been. Those of North Dakota, led by Arthur C. Townley, in 1916 were particularly incensed at the rapacity of the "middle men"—railroads, meat packers, terminal elevator companies, and grain merchants—through whose hands their products passed to the consumer. Their movement was first organized as the Farmers' Non-Partisan League, then changed to the Nonpartisan League, and finally (by 1917) to the National Nonpartisan League. In the state election of 1916 they took control of the lower house of the General Assembly and of the governorship, and secured three judges of the supreme court. But a hostile senate prevented the enactment of the League's program.

The movement also spread to South Dakota, Minnesota, and as far west as the Pacific Coast. In each state or territory its demands for state ownership of terminal elevators, flour mills, meat-packing houses, and stock-yards, security from taxation of farm improvements, and the establishment of state credit banks met with approval. In no other state, however, did it have such enthusiastic support as in North Dakota. In this state were many German-American Leaguers, and with the outbreak of World War I they were accused of using the Nonpartisan League as a propaganda medium. But the League overcame this handicap. It swept the elections of 1918, took control of the General Assembly, and enacted into law some of its demands. Candidates for office, Democratic or Republican, who had run on the League's platform, were elected. Then advertisers set in. The hard times of 1920 and 1921, bad management, and the loss of confidence of the people in agrarianism brought the movement to a period of decline. It sought to increase its strength, as had the Farmers' Alliance, by enlisting organized labor under its banner; and a number of western states launched Farmer-Labor tickets in 1920. Here and there local successes were announced, but generally the new alliance bore little fruit.

The panics of 1873 and 1893 and a steadily declining market by no means halted western farm expansion. From 1890 to 1910 a vast prairie empire was turned over by the plow—24,000,000 acres in Texas alone, and almost eighty-six and one-half million acres between the Mississippi River and the Rocky Mountains, or two and one-half times the area of England. This of course added to an already difficult surplus problem and accelerated the downward trend of the market. The price of wheat dropped from $2.14 per bushel in 1920 to 90 cents in 1922; cotton, from 38 cents to 20 cents; and corn, from $1.59 to about 62 cents. For thousands of farmers this spelled ruin. Of approximately 2,289,000 farmers in 1922, 600,000 went bankrupt and almost half of these lost their farms. These reverses drove many of them into the Socialist Party and agrarian organizations; but sweeping New Deal legislation during the 1930's and steadily rising prices in later years because of world shortages brought agriculture to better days.

THE CHURCH AND SCHOOL

It was not until toward the close of the nineteenth century that the West's population had become fairly well stabilized. Yet, decades before this time, western editors, observers, and promoters had proclaimed a regional culture, fresh and vigorous, which, they generally agreed, would compare favorably with that of the East. Every community of any great size was represented by one or more newspapers, and hence had one or more boosters. In 1880 the sparsely settled Territory of Idaho supported 20 newspapers, and two decades later Oregon had 202, of which 20 were dailies. And each editor harped on the glories of his home town and community. No western town was better publicized than Portland. In 1885 its *Oregonian* and *News* (morning dailies with weekly editions) and its evening *Standard, Telegram,* and *Freie Presse* praised Oregon in general and Portland in particular. The town also had from 15 to 20 other periodicals, among which was the *West Shore,* hardly inferior to such other contemporary western magazines as *The Pioneer,* or the *California Monthly Magazine,* or, during the seventies and eighties, to the *Kansas Magazine,* or the *Texas Pioneer Magazine; The American Sketch Book.*

Generally, western editors and writers gave the library, the school, and the church much attention. "St. Louis," said a local editor in 1860, "can boast of 40,000 books in its libraries, available to the reading public"; and an eastern visitor found this no idle claim, for the St.

Louis Mercantile Library alone had 14,000 volumes! He was also interested in two of this library's displays—an original model of John Fitch's steam engine, and a marble slab from the ruins of ancient Nineveh, covered with a figure in bas-relief and interesting cuneiform inscriptions. In the St. Louis University museum he inspected "a dagger of Cortez, fourteen inches long, the blade consisting of two divisions, with an apparatus and spring in the hilt for containing and conveying the poison." But St. Louis' claim of cultural leadership was sharply challenged by New Orleans, by San Francisco, and, two and one-half decades later, by younger western cities. Among the latter class was Denver, the culture of which was a perennial subject for the *Rocky Mountain News*. With a Chamber of Commerce and Board of Trade Library of 16,000 volumes (and six other smaller libraries), one of the largest of all western theaters, wide-awake civic and literary clubs, and well-developed churches and schools, Denver was regarded by the *News* as the Rocky Mountain cultural nerve center.

The average editor and writer stressed particularly the church and school. In this, as observed in previous chapters, he could show that teachers and preachers were generally found in the van of the settler movement. The work of the Protestant missionary was hardly less important than that of the early French and Spanish *padres*. For example, in 1819 Epaphras Chapman and Job Vinall, Presbyterian missionaries, did effective work among the Kansas Osages; and a decade later, within the same area, they were followed by William Johnson, a Methodist; while still farther south, within the Cherokee and Creek Oklahoma country, was an outstanding Baptist, Isaac McCoy. During the 1830's the Reverend Z. N. Morrell was an early Baptist preacher on the Texas frontier; and Reverend Daniel Baker, founder of the first Presbyterian college in Texas, also saw border service.

The work of Methodist and Presbyterian missionaries in Oregon has been discussed in a previous chapter, as has that of Father Pierre-Jean de Smet, a Jesuit, farther east in the northern Rockies. In 1846 the Oregon Protestant influence overflowed into California in the person of William Roberts, and encountered here as a rival the long-established Catholic mission system. By 1849 such men as W. Ingraham Kip, William A. Scott, T. Starr King, Joseph S. Alemany, Andrew L. Stone, Horatio Stebbins, and a long list of eloquent, scholarly, and zealous preachers had left their impress upon the thought of this territory. Indeed, soon after the appearance of the missionaries in the West, Protestant or Catholic, churches and schools were founded, and their leaders became conspicuous pioneers of higher education. Western editors were careful to notice this. Moreover, emphasis was generally laid on the elegance and beauty of church houses and on the substantial qualities of sectarian schools.

It was not until the last two decades of the nineteenth century that the West attempted material improvement in its public school system, although here and there were local exceptions. Early public education in Utah was much under the influence of the Mormon Church. Here, during pioneer days, as much attention was devoted to adults as to children. Indeed, Brigham Young was a pupil of Utah's early common school. Four decades after the first settlement had been planted in Oregon, only 21,464 of the territory's 53,462 children of school age (from 4 to 20) were in daily attendance. The progress of Texas was also slow. Hardly one-third of its children were in school in 1860, and twenty years later little improvement had been made. Although Kansas could report only 2,310 children enrolled in 1860, by 1879 it had made substantial improvement, with 188,884 enrolled out of 283,326 children of school age.

Farther west, in New Mexico and Arizona, conditions were even worse. During Mexican control, many things had conspired to discourage public education—the secular efforts of an ignorant priesthood, the poverty of Mexico, the family's struggle for existence in a semi-arid land, and the apathy of the average citizen. The eastern observer was amazed at the prevailing illiteracy and the lack of educational interest. Josiah Gregg thus presents the average impression: "There is no part of the civilized globe, perhaps, where the arts have been so much neglected, and the progress of Science so successfully impeded as in New Mexico. Reading and writing may fairly well be set down as the highest branches of education that are taught in the schools." In 1880 there were 87,966 people over 10 years of age in New Mexico, 57,156 of whom could neither read nor write. But by 1890, under a new dispensation, illiteracy had dropped to 45 per cent, and by 1910 to 20 per cent. In Arizona, progress has been even more marked during the last 50 years.

Pioneer parents were in part responsible for the lack of training of their children. Increased taxation for school purposes was often bitterly resented, and the establishment of teacher-training schools was viewed with indifference. Knowing nothing of science, art, music, and history themselves, many pioneers were only interested in having their children taught "'readin', 'ritin', and 'rithmetic." In these subjects it was hardly necessary for the teacher to know much more than the pupil; consequently, few could boast of more than a third- or second-grade teacher's certificate, the awarding of which had been a mere formality. But the scarcity of schoolhouses, the lack of books and equipment, and the short school terms were also retarding influences. State and territorial school funds were scant. Seldom could a state, during the sixties and seventies, pay $50 per month for a teacher, and seldom was the term longer than four and one-half or five months. And many a schoolhouse was a "soddy," a dugout, or a community assembly hall, poorly ventilated, lighted, and heated.

But in the chief western towns and cities there were schools of fair quality. San Francisco, as early as September 24, 1847, launched a program which became the basis of California's public school system, when a committee consisting of William Leidesdorff, William S. Clark, and William Glover was appointed to take measures for the establishment of schools. Here a schoolhouse, called the "Public Institute," was erected on Portsmouth Square, and Professor Thomas Douglas, a graduate of Yale University, was employed at a salary of $1,000 annually.

Thirteen years later the isolated mining town of Virginia City, Nevada, equally well known during the gold-rush days for its lawlessness, had churches of various denominations and schools crowded daily by nearly 1,000 children. The town's streets were macadamized, well lit with gas, and water was piped to consumers. Its three theaters were "devoted to dramatic entertainments." Its opera house seated 2,000 people and "Italian and other operas of the best composers were produced by artists equal to any who appeared before audiences of much older communities." Another mining town, Butte, Montana, was described as "neat," had attractive houses of worship, public schools with modern improvements, and teachers who were among the best.

In 1882 Denver was in the same relative stage of growth as San Francisco thirty-five years earlier when its schools were inspected by a former Boston, Massachusetts, superintendent, John D. Philbrick. He pronounced Denver's schools the equal of those he had known in the East. And at Omaha, Nebraska, in 1885, another qualified observer found the schools much the same. The high school building on Capitol Hill was imposing—176 feet long and 80 wide, with a spire rising 185 feet. This structure had been completed nine years earlier at an estimated cost of $250,000. Also in the 1880's Portland's seven school buildings were "large and elegant, . . . a credit to any city in the land."

Western settlers were also interested in higher education. State universities—Washington, Oregon, California, Colorado, Texas, Kansas, and Nebraska—competed with those of the Midwest or Upper Mississippi Valley, although most of them were little more than colleges. For example, on August 22, 1875, the Topeka *Commonwealth* advertised that the University of Kansas offered "six full collegiate courses; namely, Classical, General, Scientific, Modern Literature, Civil Engineering, Natural History, a special course in Chemistry, and a preparatory course of three years"; and that it had "an enthusiastic faculty, buildings, cabinets, apparatus, and libraries unsurpassed in the West." Five years later the University of California made similar claims. It was the rival of the independently endowed Leland Stanford University. State universities and colleges also encountered serious competition from sectarian schools, such as Baylor University in Texas, St. Louis University in Missouri, Denver Seminary in Colorado, and Willamette University and others in Oregon. Teachers' colleges, normals, and institutes also greatly improved instruction in the common schools and vied with other institutions of higher learning for public support.

There were still other cultural developments. Proud of their pioneer past, western states founded libraries and organized historical societies and published scholarly magazines. Debating societies, singing schools, dramatic clubs, literary clubs, and lyceums added variety to community life. Thus, by the end of the nineteenth century the West had emerged from its cultural swaddling clothes, ready to challenge the leadership of the effete East. By 1850 such famous actors and actresses as Junius Brutus Booth, Mlle. Celeste, Dan Marble, and Helen Tree had given performances in midwestern cities, and 20 years later far western towns were regularly visited by stage celebrities. Local talent found opportunity in Thespian clubs and musical organizations. Painting had not yet been given much encouragement, since frontiersmen regarded it as an effeminate pastime. Yet George Catlin by 1840 had gained wide recognition for his Indian paintings, and a short time later Carl G. Iwonski and Richard Petri, two German immigrants in Texas, were doing excellent work in Biblical pictures and landscapes.

LITERARY BEGINNINGS

For forty years prior to the Civil War western journalists and gazetteers promoted regionalism. As early as May 15, 1824, the Cincinnati *Literary Gazette* announced that it "would cherish a Western feeling" and with the passing of years this sentiment gained momentum. Dr. Daniel Drake, also of Cincinnati, in 1833 declared the West's independence by saying that "our enlightened and zealous teachers, professors, lawyers, physicians, divines, and men of letters" should "foster western genius, encourage western writers, patronize western publishers, augment the number of western readers, and create a western heart."

Jubilantly western gazettes, magazines and newspapers accepted the championship of the new movement. Among these "voices of the Western wilderness" monthlies were especially strident. "The very names of the magazines," point out David Donald and Frederick A. Palmer (in *Miss. Val. Hist. Rev.*, Dec., 1948), "indicate their sectional emphasis: William G. Hunt's *Western Review and Miscellaneous Magazine* (Lexington); William T. Coggeshall's *Genius of the West* (Cincinnati); Moore's *Western Lady's Book* (Cincinnati); George Brewster's *Western Literary Magazine* (Columbus); Zebina Eastman's *Chicago Magazine; The West As It Is;* Micajah Tarver and T. F. Risk's *Western Journal and Civilian* (St. Louis)—and dozens of others."

But the West was not yet ready for its declaration of independence. Newly established western publishers were inexperienced; local authors were few; and westerners were yet too busy winning a wilderness to spend much time in reading.

Distinctiveness in western topography, life, and institutions was a never-failing source of inspiration of gazetteers, government and scientific explorers, and visiting fiction writers and poets seeking themes for exploitation. Consequently, their diaries, journals, descriptive books, stories, and poems appeared concomitantly with the advance of the frontier. Timothy Flint and James Hall were two of the earliest western writers to gain recognition. Flint's *Recollections of the Last Ten Years* (1826), his *Condensed Geography and History of the Western States* (1828), and Hall's *Letters from the West* (1828) and *Sketches of the History, Life and Manners in the West* (1835) are excellent descriptive narratives. Both also essayed the roles of fiction writers. Flint's *Francis Berrien or the Mexican Patriot* and his *Shoshonee Valley* were disappointing in that neither reflected the life of the West with which the author was acquainted. Hall, too, ignored western realism, with which he was familiar. His *Harpe's Head; a Legend of Kentucky* was synthetic and highly melodramatic.

But trans-Mississippi literature was becoming more distinctive and significant. It was about this area that Washington Irving, Bret Harte, and Samuel Clemens (Mark Twain) were to write. They and other writers had been stimulated either by their own travels or by reading the numerous scientific and popular narratives coming from the press. By the end of the first decade of the nineteenth century, the official reports of government explorers (for example, Pike, Lewis, and Clark) were widely distributed and read. These revealed to the incredulous Easterner the West's vastness, its topographic and climatic features, its flora and fauna, and its wild Indian life. Here was portrayed a wonderland of beauty, of strange fascination, of romance and adventure—a dreamland for romancers and adventurers, who presently appeared on the trails of the first explorers.

Unofficial observers first visited the Great Plains and Rocky Moun-

tain regions of the West, some with government troops. Thomas Nuttall accompanied troops from Fort Smith, Arkansas, to the Kiamichi
River country in present southeastern Oklahoma in the spring of 1819,
and later journeyed along the Cimarron River. His subsequent *Travels
into Arkansas Territory during the Year 1819* is yet a valuable first
source on western flora and fauna. Another Englishman, Charles La-
trobe, came to the same region 13 years later, in company with the
more celebrated Washington Irving, and wrote an interesting narrative
of the journey through the Cross Timbers and the Buffalo Plains, as
well as of the wild life seen. Irving, too, in his *Tour of the Prairies*
(1835), wrote of this expedition in an entertaining, pleasing style. He
made his reader see the scrubby oaks of the Cross Timbers and their
impenetrable briars and brambles which tore his clothing and scratched
his face and hands, and experience the vicissitudes of travel in a semi-
arid land. Moreover, his *Astoria* and *Captain Bonneville* (in two
volumes), based on the northern Rockies and the Columbia River
Valley, were no less valuable as first-hand descriptive narratives of
trader and trapper life. Irving's associations with John Jacob Astor,
after his tour of the southern plains, and his possession of the unpub-
lished memoirs of a western trapper made possible these two volumes.

Spanish-American life in the Southwest was interestingly described
by more than one early observer. Josiah Gregg, a Santa Fe trader who
traveled much across the prairies of the Southwest, left an interesting
narrative in his *Commerce of the Prairies* (1844). His graphic account
of border caravans and traffic and the folkways of the New Mexicans
remains unrivaled. George Wilkins Kendall, editor of the New Orleans
Picayune, journeyed to New Mexico with Colonel Hugh McLeod's
expedition of 1841, and in his *Texan Santa Fe Expedition* (1844) told
of the many misfortunes of the Texans and also described with interest
the southern plains and their wild life.

But neither Gregg nor Kendall could surpass Captain George F.
Ruxton in graphic portrayal. In 1846, Ruxton, formerly of the British
Army, traveled from Mexico City to the Rocky Mountains country of
the United States *via* Chihuahua and El Paso. He encountered exciting
adventures on his journey, saw great devastation and chaos in the
north Mexican states wrought by Apache and Comanche raiders, was
unfavorably impressed with Mexicans, and became greatly interested
in border personalities whom he met in New Mexico and on the Santa
Fe Trail. But his contacts with bullwhackers, trappers, traders, and
adventurers gave him a false conception of the rank and file of American
frontiersmen. His *Adventures in Mexico and the Rocky Mountains*
(1847) and *Life in the Far West* (1848), both vivid adventure nar-

ratives, present realistically Spanish-American folkways and the turbulent characters whom the author met on his travels.

Just as England had taken centuries to advance from the simplest ballad to the modern Kipling, so in the early nineteenth century the West started on its literary road with slow, awkward strides. Theodore Roosevelt noticed a comparison between medieval England and the West, and wrote that it was so striking as to include "sympathy for the outlaw, Jesse James taking the place of Robin Hood." Like Roosevelt, William Allen White also observed amusing incongruities of early western literary expression, but he believed that they were the natural consequences of environment.

Early western fiction writers may be grouped into two classes: (1) the Westerners, who wrote with a flamboyant but crude style, employing regional slang and settings; and (2) the Easterners (and Europeans), who exhibited more skill and polish, but who often lacked experience in the region. Eastern critics were more prone to deal gently with the latter class. Few critics had visited the trans-Mississippi country; therefore, their own literary horizon was appreciably restricted. An Indian fight, an encounter with a rattlesnake, an escape from a wolf pack or stampeding bison herd, a grasshopper scourge, a blizzard, a mining camp scene—all seemed "overdrawn and unreal."

But it was exactly these "overdrawn and unreal" narratives and stories which were demanded by American readers and which were the nebulae of a virile regional literature. When polished and matured, they composed the foundation for a style truly western, alien to the more prosaic Easterner. Border life never repeats itself as it moves from one distinctive environment to another; so the West's literary expression was to remain lively and stimulating. Its boldness and reckless abandon were qualities stimulating general reader interest. The Westerner ignored the Puritanic *motif*, commonly employed by sophisticated writers, and featured the tobacco-chewing, "cussin' " miner, soldier, trapper, hunter, bullwhacker, or Indian fighter, yet ascribing generous impulses and unselfish deeds to each. Instead of contending with conscience, the hero became involved in a desperate struggle with an inhospitable environment and with nomadic Indians or outlaws, enduring super-human fatigue, suffering, and accomplishing amazing deeds. All this added richness of tone and color quite popular with readers.

In the literature of the Far West, Richard Henry Dana pointed the way for his more celebrated contemporaries, Bret Harte and Samuel Clemens. During the period when New England ships dealt extensively in trade with the *Californios,* Dana made a voyage on the *Pilgrim* to the West Coast *via* the Horn, and subsequently gave to the American readers his *Two Years before the Mast* (1840), a genuinely readable part-factual and part-fictitious narrative. But Bret Harte was to accomplish a more lasting fame. As a boy, he had been carefully schooled by his father, who was a professor of Greek in a New York college; but "scholasticism" made less impression on his fertile mind than reports of fabulous gold finds in California. The result was a journey to California. Here he met with failure as a miner, but finally found employment as a compositor in a printing office and afterwards undertook the editing of a local newspaper. In 1867 he published a collection of clever parodies on the leading American and English writers, entitled *Condensed Novels*. In the next year he became editor of the *Overland Monthly*, which he sought to raise to the literary level of the *Atlantic Monthly*. In this magazine some of his best-known western stories appeared. In 1870 he published his sketch of mining life entitled "The Luck of Roaring Camp," characterized by the eastern critic as unreal, but finally given a high rating for its vivid portrayal of mining camp life. His easy, flexible style, his vividness and animation in describing the Argonauts, seasoned with a delicious humor, demonstrated a rare literary talent. Harte's western successes brought him world-wide fame and a much-coveted offer from the *Atlantic Monthly* of $10,000 for anything which he cared to write.

Clemens (Mark Twain) was equally well known in his day. He not only wrote realistically of river valley folkways (in his *Life on the Mississippi* (1883), *Tom Sawyer* (1884), *Huckleberry Finn* (1885), and *Pudd'nhead Wilson* (1895)—all stories reflecting an inimitable humor and factual color) but earlier he had also qualified with his *Roughing It* (1872) as a far western writer. The basis for this story was an overland stage journey to the Nevada mining fields and adventures along the way and in Nevada, including his contacts with leading Mormons of Utah. Soon after *Roughing It* appeared, English critics proclaimed its author a writer of the first rank.

Generally, western poets were less widely known than western fiction writers. Cincinnatus Heine Miller (Joaquin Miller) was perhaps the only exception. Born in Wabash County, Indiana, in 1841 Joaquin moved with his family to Oregon. Here he began his restless, and somewhat turbulent, career. While yet a lad, he sought his fortune in the California mining fields; next, he joined Walker's adventurers on a Nicaragua filibustering expedition; and then returned to the West to practice law in Idaho, to serve as a judge, and to edit newspapers. His first volume of poems, published in 1871, was received with enthusiasm in London, where critics styled him "the American Byron." His word-pictures were drawn in fanciful colors but without great depth of meaning. Among his best-known books of poems are *Songs of the*

Sierras (1871); *Songs of the Sun Lands* (1873); *Songs of the Desert* (1875); and *First Families of the Sierras* (1875). Albert Pike, a less known poet, was a Bostonian who journeyed over the Santa Fe Trail to New Mexico in 1831. The settings of some of his poems were in his experiences here and his trips from Santa Fe to the mountains and prairies, as reflected in "Dirge Over a Companion Buried in the Prairie," "War Song of the Comanches," and "Song of the Nabajo"—poems, musical and winsome, but revealing strongly the influence of Byron and Shelley. His *Prose Sketches and Poems* (1834) is among his best-known literary remains. There were other poets of lesser note, among whom was Eliza R. Snow, sister of Apostle Lorenzo Snow, a Utah Mormon. Eliza, according to Bancroft, while a small girl, commenced writing for various publications, under an assumed name. Later in life her works were published in nine volumes, two of which were poetry of fair quality.

Early nineteenth-century descriptive narratives, fiction, and poems based on Indian and cowboy life were quite popular. As early as the California mission period, Father Boscana had well described the ways of the local Indian in his *Chinigchinick* (translated in 1846), a pattern which Joaquin Miller employed without marked success in his *Paquita* (1881). Helen Hunt Jackson, a conspicuous Indian rights advocate of the 1890's, wrote perhaps the best Indian novel in *Ramona* (1884), judged by A. W. Turger as the best written by an American woman, although it was influenced by the Cooper concept. It is doubtful, however, that it was far superior to Adolph F. Bandelier's *The Delight Makers* (1899), a story of the legendary Pueblos, whom the author environed with nineteenth-century customs. Poets romanticizing the Indians, such as Albert Pike and Joaquin Miller, are better-known today than they were by their contemporaries.

Only a few novels written about the cow country deserve particular notice. Andy Adams' *Log of the Cowboy* (1903) has little plot, but it is enlivened with range lingo and striking realism. Owen Wister's *The Virginian* (1911) makes the cowboy a popular literary figure. It is more polished than Adams' story, but not so accurate in historic setting. Equally well written, and perhaps even better known, are Emerson Hough's *The Story of the Cowboy* (1897) and *North of 36* (1923). His first novel, too, is without plot, but it pictures cowboy life graphically, and clothes its actors in lively range mannerisms. His second story carries an absorbing reader interest, a better plot, a romantic vein, and exciting adventure, but is not so authentic in detail. Eugene Manlove Rhodes, Zane Grey, Harold Bell Wright, and others wrote with some degree of success on ranch life, but followed the Adams, Wister, and Hough patterns.

A more popular way of presenting to the masses the glamorous West, its wild cowboys, Indians, and outlaws was the dime novel movement beginning during the 1860's. Edward Zane Carroll Judson, under the pen name of Ned Buntline, is generally credited with its inauguration. His career had been as varied as that of Joaquin Miller's in that he had early gone to sea, had fought in the Florida Seminole War, had explored the northern Rockies in company with trappers, and had again served as a soldier during the Civil War. Later, while on the staff of the *New York Mercury,* he gave vent to his restless genius by contributing racy, highly melodramatic stories of the West in which his heroes fought successfully vast enemy odds, performed prodigious tasks, and lived through numerous thrilling adventures. But it was Erastus Beadle and others who finally sensed the opportunity for commercial exploitation of these "thrillers." Beadle's dime novel series began with *Malaeska, the Indian Wife of the White Hunter* (1860), of which about 65,000 copies were sold; then W. F. Cody, Captain "Bruin" Adams, Major St. Vrain, and Captain Crawford entered the field. Presently, dime novels by the hundreds of thousands came from the press and were eagerly bought and read by all classes—miners, harvest hands, professional men, and school children (surreptitiously). These became the forerunners of the present western "pulps," and perhaps also hastened the appearance of the "Wild West" shows.

Until the closing decade of the nineteenth century, poets and fiction writers could glean little from western historical studies. Only John W. Monette and Samuel P. Hildreth had written dependable histories of the Mississippi and Ohio Valley settlements, and there was none of merit related to the trans-Mississippi region. Monette and Hildreth, therefore, pioneered for other midwestern historians of five decades later, such as Clarence E. Alvord, B. A. Hinsdale, Theodore Roosevelt, and Francis Parkman, whose enthusiastic endeavors by 1914 had not only made available authoritative accounts but had also launched the *Mississippi Valley Historical Review.* Not only did five decades elapse from the time of Monette and Hildreth until other historians of similar rank appeared, but there was also a transfer in interest from the Mississippi Valley to the West Coast. During the nineties, Spanish culture, the mining fields and society, the Oregon immigrant movement, and other colorful subjects were exploited by Francis Parkman, Theodore H. Hittell, Joseph Schafer, and Josiah Royce; and during this period Hubert Howe Bancroft assembled a large collection of early materials from which he published more than 30 volumes on the Pacific Coast and Rocky Mountain states and territories. This new trend toward the West stimulated George P. Garrison to write *Westward Extension* (1906) and Frederick Jackson Turner to emphasize the frontier as a shaping force in American life. Turner's interchange of the terms "West" and "Frontier," and some of his tenets, are not accepted by many present-day historians. In more recent years, Herbert Eugene Bolton, Frederic L. Paxson, Walter Prescott Webb, and Eugene C. Barker have done much toward creating a lively interest in the Far West and Southwest.

BIBLIOGRAPHY

H. H. Bancroft's *Works* are invaluable for a study of the several aspects of western culture. Three volumes which portray Great Plains life are W. P. Webb, *The Great Plains* (Boston, 1931); Everett Dick, *The Sod House Frontier, 1854–1890* (New York, 1937); and C. C. Rister, *Southern Plainsmen* (Norman, 1938). On life in the Rocky Mountains and along the Pacific Coast, see William M. Thayer, *Marvels of the New West* (Norwich, Conn., 1888); L. P. Brockett, *Our Western Empire; or the West Beyond the Mississippi* (San Francisco, 1881); William Taylor, *California Life Illustrated* (New York, 1860); Josiah Royce, *California, A Study of American Character* (Boston, 1886); John W. Barber and Henry Howe, *All the Western States and Territories* . . . (Cincinnati, 1867); Samuel Bowles, *Our New West* (Hartford, 1869); and A. D. Richardson, *Beyond the Mississippi* (Hartford, 1863).

Helpful articles in early periodicals are James W. Steele, "Among the New Mexicans," in the *Kansas Magazine*, II (February, 1872); ——, "The Sons of the Border," *ibid.*, II (July, 1872); ——, "Women Under Difficulties," *ibid.*, II (Sept., 1872); ——, "La Senorita," *ibid.*, II (November, 1872); George D. Clift, "The Kansas Settler," *ibid.*, III (February, 1873); Tom Monaghan, "Wyoming," *ibid.*, IV (August, 1873); T. C. Harby, "Texan Types and Contrasts," in *Harper's Magazine*, November, 1870; Ray Standard Baker, "The Great Southwest," in *Century Illustrated Magazine*, LXIV (May-October, 1902); Charles Moreau Harger, "The New Westerner," in *North American Review*, August, 1907; and E. E. Dale, "The Spirit of Soonerland," in *Chronicles of Oklahoma*, I (June, 1923).

The western agrarian movement is adequately treated in Solon J. Buck, *The Agrarian Crusade* (in *The Chronicles of America Series*, LXV, New Haven, 1920); ——, *The Granger Movement* (in *Harvard Historical Studies*, XIX, Cambridge, Mass., 1913); John Hicks, *The Populist Revolt* (Minneapolis, 1931); Nathan Fine, *Labor and Farmer Parties in the United States, 1828–1928* (New York, 1928); P. R. Fossum, *The Agrarian Movement in North Dakota* (in Johns Hopkins University *Studies*, XLIII, No. 1, Baltimore, 1925); and numerous articles in such contemporary periodicals as the *Forum, Cosmopolitan, North American Review, Review of Reviews*, and *Nation*.

For general works on education which deal in part with the West, consult C. F. Thwing, *Education in the United States Since the Civil War* (New York, 1906); Ellwood P. Cubberley, *Public Education in the United States* (Boston, 1919); and Donald D. Tewksbury, *The Founding of American Colleges and Universities Before the Civil War* (in Columbia University *Contributions to Education*, No. 543, New York, 1932). Clarence R. Aurner, *History of Education in Iowa* (5 vols., Iowa City, 1914–1918) is perhaps the most extensive study that has been done on a single state, although not equal in quality to Frederick Eby, *The Development of Education in Texas* (New York, 1925). For a federal survey on the West, see "The Development of the Common School in the Western States from 1830 to 1850," in United States Commissioner's *Report,* 1898–1899, I, 357–450. Out-of-print volumes on the West first listed in this bibliography, and particularly Bancroft's, should also be consulted. Detailed data are found in the reports of state and territorial superintendents, and in the Federal Census.

Volumes previously listed should also be consulted for religious data. For an excellent general survey, see Colin B. Goodykoontz, *Home Missions on the American Frontier* (Caldwell, Idaho, 1939). Then, for the activity of each sect or for the missionary's reminiscences, see Motier A. Bullock, *Congregational Nebraska* (Lincoln, 1905); J. M. Carroll, *A History of Texas Baptists* (Dallas, 1923); Richard Cordley, *Pioneer Days in Kansas* (Boston, 1903); Truman O. Douglass, *The Pilgrims of Iowa* (Boston and Chicago, 1911); Thomas C. Battey, *A Quaker Among the Indians* (Boston, 1875); Z. N. Morrell, *Flowers and Fruits in the Wilderness* (Dallas, 1886); Rev. William M. Baker, *The Life and Labours of the Rev. Daniel Baker* (Philadelphia, 1858); Thomas Harwood, *History of New Mexico Spanish and English Missions of the Methodist Episcopal Church from 1850 to 1910* (2 vols., Albuquerque, 1908–1910); James B. Finley, *Sketches of Western Methodism* (Cincinnati, 1857); Gustavus Hines, *A Voyage Round the World; with a History of the Oregon Mission* (Buffalo, 1850); James Woods, *Recollections of Pioneer Work in California* (San Francisco, 1878); P. J. De Smet, *Life, Letters and Travels* (4 vols., New York, 1905); and John Gilmary Shea, *History of the Catholic Missions Among the Indian Tribes of the United States* (New York, 1855).

Western literature is discussed in H. H. Bancroft, *Essays and Miscellany* (*Works,* XXXVIII, San Francisco, 1890); Levette Jay Davidson and Prudence Bostwick (eds.), *The Literature of the Rocky Mountain West, 1803–1903* (Caldwell, Idaho, 1939); Percy H. Boynton, *Literature and American Life* (New York, 1936); Squire Omar Barker, *Buckaroo Ballads* (Santa Fe, 1938); James Frank Dobie (ed.), *Texas and Southwestern Lore* (Austin, 1927); Rufus Coleman, *Western Prose and Poetry* (New York, 1932); Dixon Ryan Fox, *Sources of Culture in the West* (New York, 1934); Lucy Hazard, *Frontier in American Literature* (New York, 1927); Albert Keiser, *The Indian in American Literature* (New York, 1933); John Albert Macy (ed.), *American Writers on American Literature* (New York, 1929); Mabel Major, Rebecca W. Smith, and T. M. Pearce, *Southwest Heritage, A Literary History and Bibliography* (Albuquerque, 1938); Ralph Leslie Rusk, *The Literature of the Middle Western Frontier* (New York, 1925); and W. P. Webb, *The Great Plains* (Boston, 1931).

INDEX

A

665

O